SUPERVISION
CONCEPTS AND PRACTICES OF MANAGEMENT
11TH EDITION

EDWIN C. LEONARD, JR.

Professor Emeritus of Management and Marketing,

Richard T. Doermer School of Business and Management Sciences

Indiana University-Purdue University Fort Wayne

SOUTH-WESTERN
CENGAGE Learning™

Australia • Brazil • Japan • Korea • Mexico • Singapore • Spain • United Kingdom • United States

SOUTH-WESTERN
CENGAGE Learning™

Supervision: Concepts and Practices of Management, 11e
Edwin Leonard

Vice President of Editorial, Business: Jack W. Calhoun

Editor-in-Chief: Melissa Acuña

Executive Editor: Joe Sabatino

Acquisitions Editor: Michele Rhoades

Developmental Editor: Jennifer King

Editorial Assistant: Ruth Belanger

Marketing Manager: Nathan Anderson

Executive Marketing Manager: Kimberly Kanakes

Senior Marketing Coordinator: Sarah Rose

Senior Marketing Communications Manager: Jim Overly

Content Project Manager: Jared Sterzer

Technology Project Editor: Rob Ellington

Manufacturing Coordinator: Doug Wilke

Production Service: Pre-Press PMG

Copyeditor: Deborah Laws

Senior Art Director: Tippy McIntosh

Cover and Internal Designer: Craig Ramsdell, Ramsdell Design

Cover Image: Rob Colvin/Veer.com

Photo Researcher: Don Schlotman

For product information and technology assistance, contact us at
Cengage Learning Customer & Sales Support, 1-800-354-9706

For permission to use material from this text or product,
submit all requests online at **www.cengage.com/permissions**
Further permissions questions can be emailed to
permissionrequest@cengage.com

Exam*View*® is a registered trademark of eInstruction Corp. Windows is a registered trademark of the Microsoft Corporation used herein under license. Macintosh and Power Macintosh are registered trademarks of Apple Computer, Inc. used herein under license.

© 2008 Cengage Learning. All Rights Reserved.

Cengage Learning WebTutor™ is a trademark of Cengage Learning.

Library of Congress Control Number: 2008941609

ISBN 13: 978-0-324-59092-0

ISBN 10: 0-324-59092-X

South-Western Cengage Learning
5191 Natorp Boulevard
Mason, OH 45040
USA

Cengage Learning products are represented in Canada by Nelson Education, Ltd.

For your course and learning solutions, visit **www.cengage.com**

Purchase any of our products at your local college store or at our preferred online store **www.ichapters.com**

Printed in China by China Translation & Printing Services Limited
3 4 5 6 7 12 11 10

BRIEF CONTENTS

ROB COLVIN

To my family, friends, and students—past and present!

The 11th edition and previous editions of Supervision: Concepts and Practices of Management *have come about through the encouragement and support of many people. I am most grateful for my wife of almost 50 years, Ginger; our three children, Lori, Teo, and Lisa; their spouses Stacie and Gary; and our two wonderful grandchildren, Haley and Tyler Koss.*

Ginger, the English major, has been my # 1 encourager, supporter, and cheerleader ever since she picked me up on that cold winter day as I was walking back from class in West Lafayette, Indiana. On too many occasions, she leveled me—especially when I was ready to "blow a fuse." In spite of all my foibles, she remained calm and clearheaded. Throughout the years, she pushed the right buttons and provided constant support for all of us—unconditionally. I've lived a better life because of her inspiring me to do the right things at the right time and place. Her favorite notation is "DMS" as she read and reread this and other manuscripts. Her notation meant, "If it Doesn't Make Sense to me, it may not make sense to anyone else!"

I would like to thank my family, friends, and students who have truly enriched my life. Ideally, I would like to have my eulogy read that God, family, friends, students, and work were the most important things in Ed's life as he journeyed this earth. But, oftentimes my good intentions were dashed in reality by that thing called work. Over the years, I taught many evening and weekend classes or was out of town overnight on consulting, business, or professional trips. Many times, my schedule prevented me from attending the tap dance recital, the ball game, or the choir performance, but I was there in spirit. In thought and mind, my family members, friends, and many former students were always there for me as I was for them. A mentor once told me, "You, Ed Leonard, are the richest man in the world because you have family and friends who love you and will do anything for you."

I have been truly blessed! May you be blessed as you journey through life!

CONTENTS

ROB COLVIN

v

Part 2: Supervisory Essentials   83

Part 3: Planning and Organizing   219

Chapter 7: Supervisory Planning   220

Chapter 8: Supervisory Organizing at the Departmental Level   256

Part 3: Cases   289

Part 4: Staffing   303

Chapter 9: The Supervisor and Employee Recruitment, Selection, Orientation, and Training   304

Chapter 10: Performance Management   340

Part 4: Cases   376

Part 5: Leading   389

Chapter 11: Supervisory Leadership and the Management of Change   390

PREFACE

Now more than ever, there is a need for leaders to emerge. Recent developments and instability in the financial markets and other sectors of the world economy are causing me concern. The increased mortgage default rates, the failure of major financial institutions, the concerns whether long-time pillars of American industry—General Motors, Ford, Chrysler, amongst others—would merge, consolidate, or die, and the wild run of the Dow Jones Industrial Average has led to fear about what the future holds. People continually ask me, "Are we in a recession?"

My response has been to quote others. First, the Merriam-Webster Dictionary defines a recession as "a period of reduced economic activity." BusinessDictionary.com defines it as a "period of general economic decline, defined as contraction in Gross Domestic Product (GDP) for six months or longer." The National Bureau of Economic Research (NBER) says "A recession is a significant decline in economic activity spread across the economy, lasting more than a few months, normally visible in production, employment, real income, and other indicators. A recession begins when the economy reaches a peak of activity and ends when the economy reaches its trough. Between trough and peak, the economy is in an expansion." The recent period of declining growth in some sectors along with deteriorating credit conditions, slumping housing markets, weakening world-wide economies, and rising commodity prices has led to an era of uncertainty. But one thing is certain: The demand for good managers and supervisors will always be there.

I would be remiss if I did not share a little bit of history with you. On July 9, 1932, the Dow closed at 41.63, down 91% from its pre-crash level of October 1929. "Brother, Can You Spare a Dime" was the song of the time. The world was in the "great depression." Yet, even during those times, there were some businesses that were great places to work. Their leadership and the use of sound management principles separated those organizations from the rest.

In the past 20 years, there have also been 31 "bear markets," defined as a decline of 20% or more in market indexes, followed by 31 recoveries. I have reason to believe that better times will return. Today, we have a productive work force, great technology, and lots of "hope." Government leaders, corporate CEOs, managers, and supervisors must exercise sound judgment, create visions, and institute sound management practices that will enable their respective organizations to be the "very best they can be," regardless of the economic conditions.

Throughout the economic ups and downs, I have focused on doing one thing: seeking ways to do a better job of managing myself and guiding others. A quick history lesson is relevant at this point: Two inspirational works were published in 1776 that have helped guide my beliefs and actions. The *Declaration of Independence*, authored by Thomas Jefferson among others, and Adam Smith's *Wealth of Nations* should be required reading for all. In my opinion, both embrace common threads: *the advantages of individual liberty and the importance of personal responsibility.*

ROB COLVIN

Early in my management career, a mentor said, "Every employee is a manager!" That notion is perhaps more relevant today than at any time during my life. The skills, concepts, and principles of management presented in this text are relevant for everyone. Each and every person will be responsible for supervising someone or something at some time in his or her life. However, not every student can or should choose to pursue a supervisory position as a lifelong career. We can make sure, however, that each student is well-informed about the challenges of supervision and that we give every person a solid skill foundation so that he or she can make informed decisions when necessary.

While no advice is guaranteed to be foolproof, in the 11th edition, I have again tried to provide meaningful suggestions and tips for making supervision more exciting, fulfilling, and practical. In order to provide the most current and relevant information on issues that managers face, I have developed a Web site (www.SupervisionConcepts.com) on which I will post tips for dealing with current and relevant economic and organizational challenges.

In keeping with this textbook's previous editions, I have constantly tried to blend the practical and applied approach to supervisory management. Consistent with prior editions, I have tried to include the most current management and organizational theories, as well as emphasize the skills that supervisors need to cope in the rapidly changing world. *Supervision* has provided thousands of students and practitioners with a solid foundation of management and organizational theory while emphasizing the practical applications of supervisory management.

Supervision 11th edition has been thoroughly revised and updated from its predecessor while retaining its thrust as a comprehensive single source and leading textbook on supervisory management. First, this was designed as an introductory undergraduate academic text in that it offers materials that are organized to be taught in a one-semester or one-term introductory concepts and principles of management course. I have also used the text effectively in our 12-session non-credit continuing education supervisory and leadership course.

Organization of *Supervision*

Over the years, professors and reviewers have told me that their students need to "experience real-world" situations in order to gain awareness of and proficiency in analytical, communication, decision-making, and conflict resolution skills. Students have repeatedly reported that *Supervision: Concepts and Practices of Management* has made them more aware of the interrelatedness of the planning, organizing, staffing, leading, and controlling functions. Most importantly, they have confirmed that the skills applications, skill development modules, internet activities, and end-of-part cases have enabled them to "experience" supervision and to "think outside the box."

In keeping with prior editions, this edition of *Supervision: Concepts and Practices of Management* is divided into six parts.

- Part 1 introduces the fundamentals of management and the business operating environment. Briefly, we discuss social, demographic, economic, technological, and global challenges to modern day management, including the impact of labor unions. Students are also introduced to the managerial functions of planning, organizing, staffing, leading, and controlling.
- Part 2 deals with four key skills that are requisite for success: communication, motivation, decision making, and disciplining.

- Part 3 explores the principles of planning and organizing. Issues of crisis-management are presented, and there is also an expanded discussion of the necessity for developing metrics.
- Part 4 focuses on the human resource activity of staffing and performance appraisal. The notion of *onboarding*—the process of engaging new employees into the work team—is introduced in this edition.
- Part 5 covers leadership, managing change, building effective work teams, and diversity and inclusion issues.
- Part 6 addresses the controlling function and strategies for resolving conflict.

Applications-Oriented Text Features

I spend at least one day a week walking through organizations, talking to and working with first-line supervisors, soliciting their thoughts and ideas, listening to their problems, and providing suggestions to help them. As facilitator of Do it Best Corp.'s (one of the nation's largest member-owned hardware, home center and lumber cooperatives) Retail Management Course, I spend three or four weeks each year interacting with owners, store managers, and those who have been identified as potential department or store managers. The journey has been one of mutual benefit. The real benefit is that I have been able to incorporate many of these personal learning and supervisory development experiences into this edition of *Supervision*. Like the previous editions, the 11th edition of *Supervision* presents the concepts and practices of supervision from the diverse perspectives of practicing supervisors, employees, and organizational theorists. All of the resulting learning activities and concepts have been field-tested in classroom situations.

In the beginning, my co-author Professor Hilgert and I designed this to be a skills-based text, and to that end I have continued to provide the best set of Skills Applications, Skills Development Modules, cases, self-tests, and a variety of experiential exercises that provide students the opportunity to hone their supervisory skills. Some of the features that best facilitate student learning are:

- **An Integrated Teaching and Testing System.** The text and all supplements are organized around learning objectives that form a comprehensive teaching and learning system. Each chapter begins with a series of learning objectives covering key concepts. The objectives then appear in the text margins, identifying where each objective is fulfilled. The key concepts are reinforced at the end of the chapter, where they are summarized as related to their learning objectives. Organization based on learning objectives continues into the supplement package, including the integrated lecture outlines in the Instructor's Manual and the Test Bank.
- **Comprehensive Learning and Practice Activities.** When I served as Editor of the *Business Case Journal*, I developed a set of definitions that will, in part, clarify the learning experiences that we provide in this edition.
  - A *case* is a written account of a situation that individuals have actually confronted. It may include the facts of a complex situation and also the beliefs, attitudes, and prejudices of the individuals involved and how these influenced their actions. A case is a decision-based situation while a *case study* is a description of an aspect of an organization that does a specific management function.
  - An *incident*, on the other hand, is essentially a very short case for which there is a problem (or problems) and decisions must be made. Case-type incidents may represent complex issues to be analyzed and resolved, even

though the incidents are presented in a brief format with limited or no data and minimal information.

- *Experiential exercises* are often similar to cases and incidents, but they are written in a manner that places the student directly into the problem situation as if he or she were experiencing it. Experiential exercises may require some type of role-play, simulation, project assignment, or problem-solving in which the student personally becomes involved in analyzing and attempting to solve the issues at hand.

Our goal in the 11th edition is to provide a series of learning activities to intellectually involve students, and in some situations, to get them emotionally connected to their course work, our text, and the situations they are involved in. Thus, students will have a greater sense of responsibility for their learning.

- **"You Make the Call!"** Opening Vignettes. To stimulate student interest, we begin each chapter with a business scenario, "You Make the Call!" Each presents a real business supervisory situation that will challenge students to apply the concepts presented in the chapter. These case-like scenarios draw students into a problem situation and ask them to decide what to do.

At the conclusion of the chapter, in either the Questions for Discussion or a specific Skills Application, students can develop their own approach to the problems in the scenario by applying the concepts they just learned in the chapter. By applying chapter concepts to these opening problems and comparing their analysis and answers to questions we provided, students are more prepared to grapple with the challenging end-of-part cases.

- **Contemporary Issues.** To better comprehend today's business world, students must recognize and understand the complex issues that supervisors face. Throughout the text, I have integrated real people, real organizations, and real situations to help students gain practical knowledge about supervisory and management situations. On a regular basis, I will be posting contemporary issues and concerns at www.SupervisionConcepts.com.

- **Supervisory Tips.** Each chapter contains a "Supervisory Tips" box that draws from the author's personal experience, thorough reviews of research presented in various business and academic publications, and discussions with practicing supervisors. These tips, together with skill-building activities, give students guidelines for addressing complex issues.

- **Skills Applications.** Each chapter contains several Skills Applications, which allow students an opportunity to build their analytical and thinking skills, including those identified in the "Supervisory Tips" boxes. The Skills Applications include a variety of self-assessment and "thinking outside the box" activities. Many of these were developed to introduce students to some of those people who make life difficult for others. A supervisor or an employee relates how the person's behavior may create havoc in the organization. These mini-cases require students to assess and analyze the situation, learn strategies for dealing with these situations, and apply solutions. We have classroom tested all applications and have found that they help students develop the competencies needed in today's fast-paced society.

- **Cases.** Instructors throughout the country have told us that our case studies are excellent tools for teaching and learning supervisory skills. In response to this feedback, we have increased the number of cases and varied their lengths. The 48 cases in the text, many of which are new to this edition or substantially revised, address a wide range of supervisory management issues. Because the cases involve concepts from more than one chapter, they appear at the end of each part. Most cases are short—some less than a page each—and are challenging without being overwhelming. The cases are based on actual experiences of supervisors in numerous work environments. End-of-case discussion questions help students to focus their thinking.

As in previous editions, optional Internet assignments are attached to at least one case for each of the book's six parts. These optional assignments provide opportunities for students to search the Internet for information that may be associated with or included in the concepts of the case. These are identified by an icon in the margin. For ease of recognition, this is the same icon shown with skills applications that use the Internet. Students are urged to further apply their critical thinking and analysis of the case to broader aspects of current business information.

You can use the cases in several ways: as fuel for class or seminar discussion, as written homework assignments, for team analysis and presentation, or as examinations. Case assignments are an excellent way for students to practice their skills on real supervisory problems and to assess their abilities to apply what they have learned.

Role-Playing. With this edition, in response to reviewers' requests for more role-playing opportunities for students, several cases have been revised so they are readily adaptable to role-play. Based on my use of these in class, I have included guidance in the Instructor's Manual on how these can be incorporated into the students' learning experience.

Skills Development Modules Video. Because students like visual presentations, we now provide 15 Skills Development Video Modules, one video per chapter. A brief discussion is contained in the text—identified in the margin by the Skill Development Module icon—along with any updates regarding the various organizations presented in the video segments.

Among the organizations highlighted in the Skills Development Modules are:

- McDonald's
- Navistar International Corporation
- U.S. Music Corp—Washburn Guitars
- Second City
- Green Mountain Coffee Roasters
- Hard Rock International
- Zingerman's
- Whirlpool Corporation
- Honda
- Accenture
- American Flatbread
- Finagle a Bagel

It has been my experience that students like video cases and, as such, find that the challenging discussion questions listed in the text for each Skills Development Module reinforce the chapter concepts and help them think analytically.

New and Expanded Topics

- Throughout the text, we focus on Skills, Knowledge, and Abilities (SKAs). The appendix to Chapter 1, coupled with Skills Application 1–2: "Who Are You: What Do You Really Want to Be?" and Skills Application 1–4: "Assessing Your Toolbox—What Do I Need to Get Into Supervision?" provide students an opportunity to assess their SKAs and prior experience and to match them with supervisory career opportunities. Students are encouraged through the Skills Application to outline a career plan, to plan for securing a supervisory position, to develop a resumé, to develop a list of questions to ask the interviewer, and to outline a self-development plan to add to their own personal toolbox. Throughout the text, there are ample opportunities for students to identify the steps they need to take to reach their career goals.

- Throughout this edition, there is expanded coverage of how to work successfully with people who make life difficult.
- Recognizing the benefits of hiring "winners" or at least individuals who have the potential to be winners, many organizations are starting to adopt a process of "onboarding," a concept new to this edition. Onboarding means that from the moment a person is being considered for employment, the supervisor takes steps to foster that individual's growth, to get them off the bench and into the game, and to engage them in the process of learning and doing the tasks at hand. In short, onboarding means doing everything needed to help the employee be the best he or she can be.
- There is expanded coverage of discrimination, harassment, incivility, outsourcing, and the role of supervisors as "change agents."
- Chapter 5 discusses and illustrates various decision-making styles.
- Throughout the text there is expanded emphasis on issues related to crisis management.
- Many if not all of the chapters recognize how a key group of supervisory issues (personal responsibility, communication, problem solving, leadership, conflict resolution, trust, and loyalty) can be turned into a coherent treatment of supervisory responsibilities.
- Discussions of servant-leadership, appreciative inquiry, quality, customer service, metrics, and global issues have been added or received expanded coverage.
- Recognition of ethical behavior is interwoven throughout the text. Many of the skills applications, contemporary issues, and end-of-part cases help students appreciate the importance of ethical behavior in the workplace.
- Survey after survey reports the lack of trust that employees have in their immediate managers and, even less, in top management. Throughout the text, we offer tips and suggestions on how to create a "great workplace."
- A greater emphasis on motivating and engaging—giving employees opportunities for growth—has been added throughout the text so that students can use a variety of learning activities to reinforce those notions.

To the Instructor

First and foremost, this is a practitioner text. Using your personal career and life experiences along with the Skills Applications and other experiential exercises from the text, you can help the student identify problems and challenges by tapping into their life and business experiences. Coupling these past personal experiences with the concepts presented in the text, they are led to make recommendations for solution or organizational improvement.

I believe that the greatest gift a professor has to give is to prepare students, inspire them to excel in the classroom, enable them to reach their full potential, and encourage them to take risks. I am certain that your legacy will be that you invested wisely in your students, as they will be the ones who make our nation's future even brighter. The 11th edition of *Supervision: Concepts and Practices of Management* will help engage your students in the learning process and get them to recognize and understand the complex issues supervisors face.

Supplements to Ease the Teaching Load

Instructor's Manual by Edwin C. Leonard, Jr. Instructors always have more to do than there are hours in a day. To make class preparation easier, we have developed a comprehensive Instructor's Manual, designed to assist you—the instructor—in providing an exciting and innovative learning opportunity for your students. The Manual provides classroom-tested advice from the text author as well as several other instructors who have contributed to its development.

The Instructor's Manual includes suggestions for making the course "come alive" for your students. You will find that the integrated learning system found in the main text applies to the supplementary package as well. The Instructor's Manual is organized by learning objectives so you can easily customize your lectures and emphasize the concepts your students need the most. Specifically, the Instructor's Manual includes:

- Summaries of key concepts by learning objective
- Chapter lecture outlines covering all key concepts, correlated with Power-Point presentation slides
- Solution guidelines for all end-of-chapter discussion questions
- Commentaries on Skills Applications, including suggested solutions and follow-up approaches
- Evaluation tools for assessing student presentation and teamwork contributions
- Additional supplemental material of interest to instructors and students alike
- Support for Case Content (We have made supporting the Case Content a priority. We supply a grid to facilitate the selection of cases to correspond to text material and offer suggestions for integrating Case Content in your class. Full commentaries on all cases help guide your classroom discussions or evaluate student written analyses, and answers are supplied for the case discussion questions. In addition to the traditional cases found within the text, you will also find commentaries on the Skill Development Module video cases, including guidance for implementing them and evaluating students' answers to video case discussion questions.)

PowerPoint Slides. A complete set of lecture slides in PowerPoint format have already been created for you, minimizing your time spent preparing lectures. These slides are correlated with the lecture notes in the Instructor's Manual

Test Bank. Our comprehensive Test Bank contains true/false, multiple-choice, and essay questions. Questions are linked to chapter learning objectives so that you can tailor exams to complement your teaching emphasis. We supply an ample number of questions so that you can easily create several different versions of exams. The Test Bank has been thoroughly revised, updated, and certified for this edition.

ExamView® Testing Software. Computerized testing software contains all of the questions in the certified Test Bank. This program is an easy-to-use test creation software compatible with Microsoft Windows. Instructors can add or edit questions, instructions, and answers, and select questions by previewing them on the screen, selecting them randomly, or selecting them by number. Instructors can also create and administer quizzes online.

Instructor's Resource CD. The Instructor's Resource CD includes the Instructor's Manual, the complete PowerPoint slide presentation, the Test Bank in the ExamView® format, and the video modules as a one-stop resource for all your teaching and testing preparation.

Instructor's Support Web Site. We offer a product support Web site at www. cengage.com/management/leonard where instructors can download files for the

Instructor's Manual, Test Bank, PowerPoint®, and video modules. Interactive Pre-Tests and Post-Tests, as well as flashcards and additional cases, are also provided here so you can enhance your students' learning opportunities.

Premium Student Web Site (www.cengage.com/login). Give your students access to additional study aids for your Supervision course. With this optional package, students gain access to the Leonard Premium Web site. There your students will find interactive Pre- and Post-tests, flashcards, PowerPoint slides, and video clips to reinforce chapter concepts. Add Leonard *Supervision* 11e to your bookshelf at www.cengage.com/login and access the Leonard Premium Web site to learn more.

Student Companion Web Site. Visit www.cengage.com/management/leonard, where valuable learning resources including learning objectives, quizzes, and flashcards are available to enrich students' learning experience.

To the Student

Over the past twenty-some years, I have greeted each new class with the following questions: "Right now, what do you feel is the most important issue facing the United States?" and "Five years after graduation, what do you think will be the most important issue facing the United States?" Then, I asked the same two questions with a slight variance: "What is the greatest challenge you face today?" and "What is the most important challenge you will face five years after graduation?" Then I ask two other questions: "What do you want to be known for when your days on earth have ended? What strategy (plan) do you have for getting where you want to go or becoming what you want to be?" Reaction to those questions has been intense, extensive, and varied. Not surprisingly, most students could not grasp the challenges they might be facing in the future.

Historically, we have wanted this book to encourage *you*—the student—to think, communicate, and make decisions, unpleasant as they may be. We have found these to be the skills that make the difference in the "real world" of business.

The chapter objectives, listed at the beginning of each chapter, are what we expect our students to learn or be able to do after completing the assigned readings and associated activities. Our students have been encouraged to read the objectives, write them on a separate page in their notebook, make notes on that page that will serve as reminders, and then compare their notes with those we have provided at the conclusion of each chapter. Our students have also found it beneficial to make a list of all the key concepts and terms prior to reading the chapter.

In addition to the features previously described, *Supervision* 11e provides a number of other features to enhance your learning, including:

- **Marginal Definitions.** In an introductory Supervision course, students must learn business language. Therefore, we have placed concise definitions of all key terms in the margins of the text where they are first introduced. The key terms and their definitions are also compiled in a glossary at the end of the book for quick reference. It will be helpful if you develop a storage bank of these terms as they may be used repeatedly throughout the text.
- **Summary Points.** Major chapter concepts are summarized at the end of each chapter with reference to the learning objectives. By reviewing these summaries, students can quickly identify areas in which they need further review. Then, using the learning objective number in the text margins, students can easily locate the concepts they want to review.

- **Questions for Discussion.** The end-of-chapter discussion questions are designed to help students check their understanding of chapter material.
- **Key Terms.** All terms are listed at the end of the chapter with page numbers to make their explanations easy to find.
- **Appendices.** Relevant appendices are found in the end of chapter for easy referencing.
- **Index.** A combined name and subject index at the end of the book was designed to help students in finding key topics, companies, and individuals referenced throughout the book.
- **Chapter Endnotes and References.** I take great pride in the currency of our end-of-chapter references and chapter citations.
- **Premium Student Web Site (www.cengage.com/login).** Gain access to additional study aides for your Supervision course. With this optional package, you will receive interactive Pre- and Post-tests, flashcards, PowerPoint slides, and video clips to reinforce chapter concepts. Add Leonard *Supervision* 11e to your bookshelf at www.cengage.com/login and access the Leonard Premium Web site to learn more.
- **Student Companion Web site.** At www.cengage.com/management/leonard, valuable learning resources including learning objectives, quizzing, and flashcards are available to enrich your learning experience.
- **Supervision Web Site.** New to this edition as a supplement is the author's own Web site (www.SupervisionConcepts.com). On this site, I will be posting up-to-date information that impact supervisors. Since this is in the development and trial stages for the current edition, your suggestions and comments are appreciated. You can also e-mail me at Leonard@ipfw.edu.

I hope and pray that you will enjoy the journey as you travel through Supervision *11e.*

Acknowledgments

I could not have developed this edition without the help and encouragement of my family and friends. As most successful authors know, you begin planning the next edition while you are working on the current one. Questions, skills applications, contemporary issues, and cases come to light during the production of one edition too late to be included, but they are saved for the next one. Even though I am officially retired, I still teach noncredit continuing education courses and conduct supervisory development programs for various organizations. This gives me an opportunity to classroom-test the various Skills Applications, You Make the Calls!, and cases before they find their way into my text. I should note that I expect to be back teaching full-time in the fall semester 2009–2010.

Over the years, I came to believe the learning activities that I developed were really very, very well done. Collaboration with other faculty throughout the U.S. has allowed me an additional opportunity to have the cases, Skills Applications, and other learning devices field-tested by others who can provide candid feedback on how to make the learning experience better. From this approach, I learned that what I thought was the "best" student learning activities often had a few holes that I could not see since I was too close to the material. Thus, all of the cases, Skills Applications, and other learning activities have been tested in several different venues, and the feedback from those tests have enabled me to make adjustments to this edition. Thanks to all who have helped me on this journey.

I am eternally indebted to the administration of Indiana University – Purdue University Fort Wayne, who continue to allow me space, computer support services, secretarial assistance, and other resources essential to the production of this book. Of particular note are Chancellor Mike Wartell; John Wellington, former dean of the Richard T. Doermer School of Business and Management Sciences; and the secretarial support staff of Louise Misegades, Jayla Heller, Andra Burkhart, Jane Hirschbiel, and Bobbie Barnes. Thanks to all for your support and encouragement for this and previous editions. I would be remiss if I did not give thanks to Candi Pierson, studio manager at JCPenney Glenbrook, who again found a way to make this grumpy old man look better than he really felt at the time of the picture talking.

A long time ago, I became convinced that the author is but one spoke in the wheel that drives a successful text. Simply stated, the 11th edition of *Supervision* has come about through the support and encouragement of many people. I especially want to thank the Cengage/South-Western Learning team for its tremendous support and assistance during the preparation of the 11th edition of *Supervision*. I want to acknowledge Jennifer King, Developmental Editor, who kept me on a tight schedule and made significant suggestions to content. "Thank you! Thank you!! Thank you!!!" does not come close to how much I appreciated her contributions and suggestions. A bouquet of roses is much deserved as Jennifer has provided timely guidance and support.

I also thank Michele Rhoades, Acquisitions Editor, and Nathan Anderson, Marketing Manager, for their efforts on behalf of this text.

Most of the opening You Make the Calls and end-of-part cases resulted from my consulting activities. A few of them were contributed in earlier editions by Professor Hilgert. Several colleagues collaborated with me in the production and presentation of these, including Roy A. Cook of Fort Lewis College, Karen Moustafa-Leonard of IPFW, and Francine Segars of IPFW. Several Skills Applications and cases were adapted for inclusion in this edition of *Supervision* from Edwin C. Leonard, Jr., and Roy A. Cook, *Human Resource Management: 21st Century Challenges*. Their contributions and others who granted us permission to adapt, quote, or reprint their original works are appropriately recognized in the text.

As I put the final touches on this edition, I have tears in my eyes and difficulty seeing the computer screen. On August 23, 2003, my long-time friend and co-author, Ray Hilgert, went home to be with the Lord. Even though Ray was in failing health during the production of the eighth and ninth editions, we talked every day. Ray married his high-school sweetheart, Bernice. Never a day went by that Ray and I did not chat about our respective family, friends, and students who brought much joy to our hearts. We collaborated on so many research projects and other activities in the past thirty-some years. As my family and friends will testify, the journey through this edition was the toughest—I did not have Ray to bounce ideas, concepts, and thoughts off of. I am most grateful for his help and generous encouragement. He was a great strength to me throughout the previous editions of this text. Thanks, Ray!

This edition was enhanced because of the comments and suggestions of many reviewers. I am grateful for the contributions of the following professors who reviewed the previous edition and who offered timely, constructive feedback and numerous helpful suggestions and comments for this edition:

Melissa K. DeFrench, Esq.

Susan C. Greer, Horry-Georgetown Technical College

Zack McNeil, Longview Community College

Daniel Montez, South Texas College

Appreciation also goes to those who offered worthwhile suggestions and guidance on the previous editions:

Vondra Armstrong, Pulaski Technical College, North Little Rock, Arkansas

Jacquelyn Blakley, Tri-County, Technical College, Pendleton, SC

Charles O. Blalock, Kilgore College

Lynda Clark, Maple Woods Community College, Kansas City, MO

Bruce L. Connors, Kaskaskia College

Pam Jones DeLotell, Lindenwood University

Leroy Drew, Central Main Technical College, Auburn, ME

Timothy A. Elliott, San Jacinto College Central

Patrick G. Ellsberg, Lower Columbia College

Amy A. Enders, Northampton Community College

Richard W. Foltz, Roane State Community College

Janie R. Gregg, Mississippi University for Women

Helen T. Hebert, EAI-Remington College, Cleveland

James P. Hess, Ivy Tech State College

Karen Heuer, Des Moines Area Community College

Michael L. Hoots, Colorado State University-Pueblo

Charles R. Jones, Oregon Institute of Technology

George Kelley, Erie Community College—City Campus

T. Kevin McNamara, Suffolk Community College

James R. Mulvihill, South Central College, Mankato

Michael O'Toole, Purdue University, Calumet

Clare Pennino, Dominican College, New York

Scottie Putman, Lansing Community College

Kris Sperstad, Chippewa Valley Technical College

Jane George Surges, SPHR, Indiana Wesleyan University

Tony Urbaniak, Northern State University, Aberdeen, SD

Susan Verhulst, Des Moines Area Community College

John D. Watt, University of Central Arkansas

SUPERVISION: CONCEPTS AND PRACTICES OF MANAGEMENT, 11TH EDITION

Edwin C. Leonard, Jr.
January 2009

MEET THE AUTHOR

Dr. Edwin C. Leonard, Jr., is Emeritus Professor of Management and Marketing at Indiana University Purdue University Fort Wayne (IPFW). He received his bachelor, master, and doctor degrees from Purdue University. Since joining IPFW more than 40 years ago, Dr. Leonard has held various faculty and administrative positions, including chair of the Management and Marketing Department in the School of Business and Management Sciences.

Dr. Leonard has designed and conducted workshops and seminars for thousands of supervisors and managers. Since 1978, he has served as academic advisor and coordinator of Do it Best Corp.'s Retail Management Training Course. This comprehensive program is for store owners, managers, and those who have potential for management. A member-owned cooperative, Do it Best, Corp. is one of the nation's largest hardware and building materials retailers. From 1970 through 2001, Dr. Leonard was affiliated with a full-service management consulting firm. He continues to provide strategic visioning, leadership, and board member training for a variety of not-for-profit agencies.

His community service has included the Tax Adjustment Board, the Indiana Labor Wage and Hour Board, the March of Dimes/Birth Defects Foundation, and the League for the Blind and Disabled. He is a member of Rotary International, life member of the American Legion, and numerous other civic, professional, and philanthropic organizations.

Dr. Leonard's primary research interests are in the areas of management development, organizational climate and leadership, human resource management interventions, and case development. He has published in varied academic and professional journals, instructional supplement manuals, and proceedings. Dr. Leonard has received several "best paper" and "distinguished case" awards from various organizations.

He served as Editor of the *Business Case Journal* from 2001 through 2006. In addition to *Supervision 11e*, Dr. Leonard has authored or coauthored five books dealing with management, three of which are in their third, seventh, and eleventh editions. In addition to *Supervision*, they include:

Labor Agreement Negotiations, 7th ed. (2003) with Claire McCarty Kilian and Raymond L. Hilgert.

Cases, Incidents and Experiential Exercises in Human Resource Management, 3rd ed. (2000) with Hilgert and Cyril C. Ling.

Human Resource Management: 21st Century Challenges, 1st ed. (2005) with Roy A. Cook.

Assessment of Training Needs, (1973).

He has served as president of the Society for Case Research, the Midwest Society of Human Resources/Industrial Relations, and the Fort Wayne Area Chapter of the Society for Training and Development. He has served as a board member of numerous not-for-profits but since retirement in 2004 has taken a broader approach to community service. His professional memberships include the Society for Case Research, the Society for Human Resource Management, the Midwest Business Administration Association, and the North American Case Research Association.

Dr. Leonard received the National University Continuing Education Association's Service Award for Continuing Education for the Professions, and he received the Award of Teaching Excellence from the Indiana University School of Continuing Studies. Over the years, he has received special recognition from Services for Students with Disabilities (Dasel), the International Students Organization (ISO), and the Honors Program for his outstanding service to students.

In addition to election in various "Who's Who?" Dr. Leonard was elected into Ordo Honorium of the Kappa Delta Rho Fraternity for his outstanding service to the fraternity, his community, and his profession. This is the highest award the fraternity bestows on an alumnus. In 2004, Dr. Leonard received a Distinguished Alumnus Award from his alma mater Purdue University, and in 2005, he was inducted into his high school Hall of Fame.

The Leonard family has used textbook royalties and consulting income to create the Ed and Ginger Leonard Advised Fund, Community Foundation, to provide spiritual and educational opportunities for needy and deserving youth under 14 years of age in Allen County, Indiana; the Leonard Family Endowed Scholarship for Volleyball at IPFW; the Leonard Family Endowed Football Scholarship; the Leonard Family Endowed College of Education/Cheerleader-Spirit Squad Scholarship; and the Leonard Family Endowed College of Agriculture / Purdue Musical Organizations Scholarship. Upon his retirement in 2004, family, friends, former students, and business leaders created the Professor Ed Leonard Endowed Scholarship at IPFW.

He and his wife, Ginger, have three children, Lori, Teo (spouse Stacie), and Lisa (spouse Gary Koss); and two grandchildren (Haley and Tyler Koss).

He resides part of the year at their Jekyll Island, Georgia home, which provides a sanctuary for doing research and developing cases. While on the Island, he is an active member of the Jekyll Island United Methodist Church, the Jekyll Island Rotary Club, the Friends of Historic Jekyll Island, and other off-island causes.

Leonard

(Ed Leonard)

PART 1

CHAPTER 1

(Supervising in Uncertain Times)

After studying this chapter, you will be able to:

1 Explain the demands and rewards of being a supervisor.

2 Describe the contributions of four schools of management thought.

3 Identify and discuss the major demographic and societal trends that will affect supervisors.

4 Explain why supervisors must continually grow and develop as professionals.

YOU MAKE THE CALL!

Every chapter in this book begins with a short case section titled, "You Make the Call!" After reading each case, decide which decision(s) or course(s) of action the person described in the case should make or take. As you read each chapter, think about how the concepts apply to the opening problem.

I was one of the students in Professor Edwards's "Principles of Supervision" class. It was the second week of school and, as usual, I was behind. I had registered late for the class, missed the first class (the class met one night a week), and there I was—rushing in just as the professor began. Professor Edwards began the class by introducing Alisha McDonald, the manager of the new IHOP that had just opened two miles north of the campus. "¿Se habla Español?" she began. Like many of my classmates, I just sat there wondering what would come next. Would this be a lecture that I didn't understand, or would she have something important to share with us? "When I was twenty years old, I sat right there where you are sitting," said Alisha, pointing directly at me. She continued, "At the time, I was feeling intense pressure. My dad wanted me to go to one of the Ivy League schools like my older brother, but my high school years were so stressful from trying to be like my brother. There were so many constant comparisons to him that I had trouble sleeping. I would feel sick to my stomach and get painful headaches. I had gone to a major university in another state and failed miserably. After two years, I came home, got a job working at the local Dairy Queen, and a couple of friends convinced me to come to school here and explore the Transition Studies Program. My counselor, Julie, took me under her wing and guided me to the two-year associate degree option with a supervision concentration. The nice thing about that option was that most everything that I had taken at my other school could be used toward that degree, and everything in the associate degree program would count toward my bachelor's degree."

Pausing to look at Professor Edwards, Alisha continued, "My first week in this class brought forth my worst fears. The first day of class, you told us to take out a sheet of paper and print our names at the top, and asked us to answer the following questions." Looking again at Professor Edwards, she said, "Yes, I still have my book and notes from all your courses.

"'What is the worst thing that could happen to you? What do you want to be doing five, ten, fifteen years from now? Describe the ideal company that you would like to work for. What would you want to be doing for that organization? What S (skills), K (knowledge), and A (abilities) will you have to add to your toolbox so that you can make a contribution to your chosen organization?' He collected them, and we didn't get them back until the last day of the semester. At that time, he asked us the same questions. After we had answered the questions and turned them in, he gave us back our answers to the first quiz. Those questions are still ones that I wrestle with daily.

"Professor Edwards made the class come alive. I see that you are using a more recent version of the text that we used. He integrated skills applications, assigned cases, had us interview practicing managers, and brought in professional speakers. In fact, I now realize that I was responsible for my own learning. He was just the guide. He really didn't lecture—he coached! And as a coach, he made us do things that most of us had not done before. In many of my previous classes at Big State University, the professors or grad assistants had us read the text and then gave us the word. Not Professor Edwards. I can say these things and I want you to know they come from the heart. I don't need any 'brownie points.' He was high-energy. He worked in business and industry and had lots of professional contacts. He was and has been my cheerleader—and not just mine, but countless other students'. He was encouraging to me, and I took the initiative to take his help. One word of advice: If you have a problem, let him help. He won't solve it for you, but he will serve as your guide, just as he has been mine!" Turning to Professor Edwards, she asked if he still had the posters in his office, the ones that come into view as you walk in the door: "If you have a problem, let me help!" and "Let the words I speak today be soft and tender because tomorrow you may have to eat them." Professor Edwards nodded in the affirmative.

"Professor Edwards saw that I got an invitation to join Delta Sigma Pi—the professional business fraternity. I got off the bench and into the game. My job at Dairy Queen gave me some excellent customer service experience. Mostly, I learned what not to do. Our fraternity got involved in the building of a home for Habitat for Humanity. It was probably the most fun project of any I've ever been involved with. Marketing students worked on securing funds. For those of us without 'hammer' experience, Habitat for Humanity put on 'women build' classes to give us some knowledge, skills, and familiarity with working on the project. The area Habitat affiliate is expected to build fourteen homes this year and can always use volunteers. It was projects such as this that not only assured me I was a 'good' person, but also gave me a real appreciation of the teamwork needed to help those who are truly in need. I knew nothing about building a house, but I learned lots about working with a diverse group of people. Projects like this one and others allowed me to develop and demonstrate my personality traits and professional abilities to others. Working with professors, fellow students, and 'real' business people on those projects helped me build a solid support network. These networks have been very valuable during the past twelve years.

"Professor Edwards has been a mentor to me. He's a caring, listening, and understanding person, but still very assertive when it comes to prodding you to get into the game. I don't know if he still does it or not, but when I was in this class, he gave extra credit points for things like attending one of the sporting events, going to one of the Theatre Department plays, attending a Music Department recital, viewing an art exhibit, or attending a public meeting. For the latter, I attended a school board meeting, and now I still go to those meetings. The one thing that stuck out to me was that I enjoyed going to those things. In the beginning, I thought it was a waste of time. I had school, work, and a social life. I thought that attending those things would cause me to give up some other things that I liked, but I learned how to do a better job of managing my time. The hard part was writing the one-page paper describing what I did, when I did it, and what I learned. Surprising to me at the time was that Professor Edwards did not require a ticket or have a signup sheet at the various activities—he trusted us!"

After pausing to get something out of her purse and to take a sip of her Diet Coke, Alisha continued, "Of the many campus activities I participated in, the one that made the greatest impact was when General Colin Powell came as part of our campus Lecture Series and shared his view of leadership. I realize that I do not have his charisma or flair, but I want to paraphrase his presentation. He said, 'I've learned that leadership is leadership is leadership. In my military leadership training, they made it clear to us that leadership is all about follower-ship. You don't lead alone! You lead with follower-ship. You have to convey your vision for the organization's mission to each person on the team. And you have to do it in a way that becomes infectious. Good leaders are trusted by those who follow.' Wow! I thought at the time, *I'm going to put those thoughts on a card and carry them in my purse*. And to this day, that's where they are.

"I quit my job at Dairy Queen—imagine a McDonald working at Dairy Queen—and got a summer internship through the Cooperative Work Experience Office. Dianna and Lyman worked with me and, with Professor Edwards's recommendation and phone call to some executive he knew, I got a summer and fall internship at Disney World. What an experience! I learned enough about customer service and teamwork in those eight months to write a couple of books.

"After graduation, I found the job market to be tough, so I took a job at Applebee's. You think of a job that needed to be done—I did it. Ronald Schmidt, my manager there, was another of my mentors. I enjoyed learning the total business. I became a shift supervisor and later an assistant manager. He instilled in me the notion that you

constantly have to look at how to do it better, and how to be more effective, efficient, and provide 'positively outrageous customer service.' Then the unbelievable happened: IHOP acquired Applebee's. The regional investment group decided to open a couple of new IHOPs. I never really wanted to be 'the' manager, but I interviewed and was selected to manage the new facility just two miles north of the campus. I called Professor Edwards, and we had lunch at Applebee's—my treat!" She laughed. "When I told him what was going on in my life, he asked me what my plan was. We talked about my vision for where I wanted to go and what I would need to do to work toward that goal. As the leader, I was involved in all aspects of the construction and facility layout. So that Habitat for Humanity experience really was most beneficial. I had to assemble a team, create a training strategy, and quickly develop a 'facility culture.' I wandered from restaurant to restaurant within a hundred-mile radius to see what I could learn from their best practices. I asked for a listing of the top five IHOPs—in sales and customer satisfaction— and off I went. I met with managers and shift leaders, talked to customers, and took notes. I had my newly hired team members visit some of the better facilities within an hour's drive. Then we would sit down and share what we learned from our journeys. Then, in collaboration with the owners, we created a vision (our dream) and strategies to achieve that vision. While noted author Jim Collins talked about 'good to great,' we wanted to be the best of the great. That has been our purpose since we opened two years ago. We're close on all metrics. We need to do a better job of getting our team members engaged in the process. That has been our continual struggle. Our turnover rate is half the industry average, but in my opinion it is still too high. Most of my best ideas come from others. Professor Edwards recommended *Quiet Strength* by Indianapolis Colts coach Tony Dungy. He gave me a copy, and we meet every two weeks with a small group of his former students and discuss a chapter. We take turns being the facilitator and he, in his usual fashion, plays the 'devil's advocate.' Some of my best ideas come to me when I'm driving back from that meeting. Work and family—I am a big sis to two youngsters—and my church are part of the fun. All those things play into my sense of balance and help me to cope with life's adventures. I really enjoy being around positive people and my support groups help me to think about work problems and how to tackle them. I realize that I have rambled a bit and this may not have been exactly what Professor Edwards wanted me to share with you today. Now I will entertain questions."

What questions do you have for Alisha McDonald?
YOU MAKE THE CALL!

What Does It Mean to Be a Supervisor in Uncertain Times?

1 Explain the demands and rewards of being a supervisor.

"These are the times that try men's souls!" What happened yesterday is not relevant unless it can be used as a learning experience. Virtually every aspect of contemporary life has undergone major changes during the past few years. Think back to when you were in the fifth grade. What was your world like? No doubt it was a little different from your parents' world. Today, with the technology available, it is very easy to look up various employment, economic, and other demographic statistics to compare our lot in life with that of others and to see how we are progressing from one year to the next. But what else is new? Look at Figures 1.1 and 1.2 to get a glimpse of how things were in the past.

The early days of the twenty-first century will be noted in the future by those who experienced them as "another day of infamy"—except that the day turned into weeks, months, and years. Where were you on September 11, 2001? Do you remember what thoughts went through your mind as you heard the early reports of the planes crashing and the days of uncertainty that followed? What were you doing on April 14, 2007, when the murderer wreaked havoc on the Virginia Tech campus?

FIGURE 1.1 The Year 1910—What a Difference a Century Makes

- The average life expectancy in the United States was 48.4 (males) and 51.4 (female).
- Two out of every 10 adults couldn't read or write.
- Only 6 percent of Americans had graduated from high school.
- Standard Oil of Ohio and U.S. Steel were the largest employers and under Justice Department scrutiny for being monopolies.
- Eggs were fourteen cents a dozen. Milk was 32 cents a gallon. Coffee was 15 cents a pound.
- A bomb exploded in the *Los Angeles Times* building (the *Times* was a strong anti-union employer), killing 21 persons.
- Canada passed a law that prohibited poor people from entering into their country.
- Fewer than 10 percent of all Americans had graduated from high school.
- Only 14 percent of the homes in the U.S. had a bathtub. Only 8 percent of the homes had a telephone.
- Marijuana, heroin, and morphine were available over the counter at the local corner drugstore.
- Women did not have the right to vote.
- There were only 8,000 cars in the U.S.
- Alabama, Mississippi, Iowa, and Tennessee were each more heavily populated than California.
- California was the twenty-first most populous state in the U.S.
- There was no federal income tax, nor was there a federal minimum wage law.
- The average wage in the U.S. was 22 cents per hour.
- More than 95 percent of all births in the U.S. took place at home.
- Most women only washed their hair once a month and used borax or egg yolks for shampoo.
- The American flag had 45 stars.
- Theodore Roosevelt became the first president to ride in an airplane.

FIGURE 1.2 Where Were You in 1990?

- Microsoft introduces Windows 3.0.
- 5 million fax machines—but communication via the Internet is expected to grow.
- Average public university tuition less than $2,000 per year.
- East and West Germany reunited.
- 19.7 percent of those over age 5 speak a language other than English in the home.
- Women earn about 67 cents for each dollar a man makes doing comparable work.
- Americans with Disability Act (ADA) signed into law.
- Communist Party relinquishes sole power in Soviet government.
- Iraqi troops invade Kuwait, setting off Persian Gulf War.
- Oil prices soar. Gas rises to $1.33 per gallon. In France, gas prices are $4.37 per liter.
- Cost of first class stamp rises to 25 cents.
- A new immigration bill is signed that permits entry of more people who have no family ties to U.S. citizens. Slots for skilled workers are increased.

As you watched the newscasts in the summer of 2008, you had a hard time seeing the "good news" (see Figure 1.3). America was still debating the war in Iraq; government and social service agencies were still working to help people recover from 2005's Hurricane Katrina; and there were ill-fated rescue attempts, intended to provide support to those in remote parts of China and Myanmar who suffered tragic loss of life and home due to natural disasters. One poll reported that the top priorities for the president should be the economy, education, health care, jobs, and energy.[1]

Consumer confidence had fallen to its lowest level since 1973.[2] Oil was up and housing was down. Food prices were at an all-time high. Weak demand in the housing market had ripple effects on the construction and financial sectors. The delinquency rate on mortgages, coupled with a decline in household net worth and declining stock prices, led to a forecast that the U.S. economy was vulnerable.[3]

For many employees, it was a time of employers imposing work-rule concessions, wage freezes, or pay cuts, and asking them to pay for a larger percentage of their healthcare costs, if they even had healthcare insurance.[4]

The news is filled with the stories of middle-aged employees who expected to be in their peak earning years but now face the stark reality of looking for work—no doubt in a service industry that pays substantially less than what they made at their previous employment. Many workers are angry and disillusioned. A study by CareerJournal.com and the **Society for Human Resource Management (SHRM)**, the organization for Human Resource (HR) professionals, found that 79 percent

SHRM
The Society for Human Resource Management is a professional organization for HR professionals

FIGURE 1.3 How bad can things get?

of employee respondents were either actively or passively searching for a new job with a new employer. Employees age 55 and older were much less likely than other employees to begin a new job search. The potential loss of talent has many implications for an organization, most of them negative.[5]

Unfortunately, more than half of American workers believe that their bosses lack integrity and say that their managers do not treat them fairly. Across the American workforce, only 45 percent of workers say they are satisfied with their jobs.[6] The list of fallen CEOs grows longer and longer. Many have been in the financial services sector, but most leave with a "golden parachute." Did you wonder why there was no public outcry when it was reported that Comcast CEO Brian Roberts's estate will receive almost $300 million if he dies in office? Or when Philip Purcell stepped down as CEO of Morgan Stanley and walked away with a going-away gift of $62.3 million? Who can blame the rank-and-file employee for feeling abused? Corporate insiders seem to have made out like bandits. Not surprisingly, one poll reported that 81 percent of investors had little confidence in those running "Big Business." Americans want business to clean up its act—legally and ethically—and regulators to beef up policing.[7] There is little doubt that major changes will continue to take place in our society during the coming years, and continuing change will challenge every organization.

If they and their organizations are to survive, managers at all levels will be at the forefront of planning and coping with trends, factors, and problems requiring attention and more effective management. This book focuses primarily on the first tier of management, which is generally called the supervisory level, or supervisory management. **Supervisors** are first-level managers who are in charge of entry-level and other departmental employees. In *The Effective Executive*, noted management authority Peter F. Drucker defined an executive as "any member of the organization who makes decisions that materially affect the capacity of the organization to perform and obtain results." Drucker, revered as the father of modern management, died in 2005. Figure 1.4 is a tribute to Drucker and presents an overview of his thoughts and ideas.

Today's managers and supervisors, whether they are in factories, nursing care units, business offices, retail stores, or government agencies, realize that authoritarian direction and close control usually do not bring about the desired results. Managers everywhere will continue to expect supervisors to obtain better performance from their human resources and to do so in an environment that is constantly changing.

In many organizations, much of the supervisory work is performed by individuals who may not officially or legally be considered part of management. While these individuals perform many of the supervisory functions discussed in this book, they usually have limited authority and are typically **working supervisors**. Other designations for these individuals include foreman/forewoman, group/team leader, lead person, coach, or facilitator. For brevity, we use the term *supervisor* to identify all first-level individuals who carry out supervisory functions. The concepts and principles discussed in this text generally apply to such individuals, whom we consider to be "managers," even though officially or legally they are not part of the recognized management structure.

Most people obtain their first management experience in supervisory management positions. Supervisory work has become more complex, sophisticated, and demanding, and it requires professional and interpersonal skills.[8]

Supervisors
First-level managers in charge of entry-level and other departmental employees

Working supervisors
First-level individuals who perform supervisory functions but who may not legally or officially be part of management

Peter Drucker, considered "the father of modern management," contributed many important ideas about management theory and practices that are still relevant today

FIGURE 1.4 A Tribute to Peter F. Drucker, Father of Modern Management

Peter Drucker was a writer, teacher, and consultant specializing in strategy and policy for businesses and not-for-profit organizations. He wrote for most of the contemporary business publications and authored books that set the foundation for this and other texts.

Drucker was born in 1909 in Vienna and was educated there and in England. After working as an economist for an international bank, Drucker came to the United States in 1937. He began his teaching career at Bennington College, taught for more than twenty years at the Graduate Business School of New York University, and was Clarke Professor of Social Studies at Claremont Graduate University. Its Graduate Management School was named after him in 1984. To say that he revolutionized business by systematizing the study of management would be an understatement.

USA Today perhaps said it best: "Peter Drucker, who died Friday, 11 days short of his 96th birthday, was his own best advertisement for the concept of the knowledge worker, which he identified more than 40 years ago; those who work with their minds, and thus own their means of production."[1] In 1997, Drucker was featured on the cover of Forbes magazine under the headline "Still the Youngest Mind," and *BusinessWeek* called him "the most enduring management thinker of our time." In 2002, President Bush honored him with the Presidential Medal of Freedom.

In the early 1940s, General Motors invited Drucker to study its inner workings. That experience led to his 1946 book *Concept of the Corporation*. He went on to write more than 30 books. His books and thoughts are available at http://www.peter-drucker.com/. A few of Drucker's comments are included below:

- A manager is responsible for the application and performance of knowledge.
- Company cultures are like country cultures. Never try to change one. Try, instead, to work with what you've got.
- Efficiency is doing things right; effectiveness is doing the right things.
- In a period of upheaval, such as the one we are living in, change is the norm.
- Making good decisions is a crucial skill at every level.
- The most important thing in communication is hearing what isn't being said.
- The most efficient way to produce anything is to bring together under one management as many as possible of the activities needed to turn out the product.
- Most of what we call management consists of making it difficult for people to get their work done.
- There are an enormous number of managers who have retired on the job.
- Time is the scarcest resource, and unless it is managed, nothing else can be managed.
- We now accept the fact that learning is a lifelong process of keeping abreast of change. The most pressing task is to teach people how to learn.

Sources: (1) Bruce Rosenstein, "Visionary Writer Mined the Mine," *USA Today* (November 11, 2005), p. B3. Also see William Cohen, "A Class With Drucker—The Lost Lessons of the World's Greatest Management Teacher," AMACOM, 2007; http://www.peter-drucker.com; http://www.leadertoleader.org. It is hard to select from among Drucker's books, but I recommend the following: *The Practice of Management* (New York: Harper Collins Publishing, 1954); *The Effective Executive* (New York: Harper & Row, 1964, 1986); *Management Challenges for the 21st Century* (New York: Harper Collins, 1999); *The Daily Drucker: 366 Days of Insight & Motivation for Getting the Right Things Done* (New York: Harper Collins, 2004).

Although the systematic study of management has largely been a twentieth-century phenomenon thanks, in part, to the contributions of Drucker, some knowledge of the past is helpful when looking to the future. Further, a brief overview of the major schools, or approaches, to management theories and practices can provide some foundation and perspective for the supervisory concepts and practices presented in this book.

This book is intended for both practicing and potential supervisors, especially students who are studying the field of management as one of their career choices. At the end of this chapter is a "Supervisory Tips" section that helps those who are seeking supervisory or management positions to identify and discuss some important factors when job hunting. This section includes a number of career tips that are essential for those aspiring to be supervisors and that probably are vital to almost any type of career planning, regardless of one's choice of position or organization.

Schools of Management Thought

2 Describe the contributions of four schools of management thought.

Management practices can be traced throughout history. The Great Wall of China, the Pyramids of Egypt, the Roman Coliseum, the Eiffel Tower, and the Statue of Liberty all resulted from the application of management principles. Many early schools of thought still influence the way people approach the supervisory task. While there is no universally accepted theory of management, there is a common thread among the theories. Each theory attempts to answer the question, "What is the best way to manage the task at hand?" While there is little agreement on the number and nomenclature of the various management theories, four deserve mention: (1) the scientific management approach, (2) the functional approach, (3) the human relations/behavioral approach, and (4) the quantitative/systems approach.[9]

SCIENTIFIC MANAGEMENT APPROACH

One of the first approaches in the twentieth-century study of management was the **scientific management approach**, which focused on determining the most efficient ways to increase output and productivity. Frederick Winslow Taylor, the father of scientific management, believed that managers should plan what, when, where, and how employees should produce the product. He felt a manager's job was to perform mental tasks, such as determining the "one best way" to do a job. The employees' jobs, then, would be to perform the physical tasks of their jobs. To this end, Taylor developed certain principles to increase productivity.

Scientific management approach
School of management thought that focuses on determining the most efficient ways to increase output and productivity

Taylor believed that many workers did not put forth their best effort and that, as a result, production often suffered. While observing workers in a steel plant, Taylor was shocked at the lack of systematic procedures, output restrictions among groups of workers, and the fact that ill-equipped and poorly trained workers typically were left on their own to determine how to do their jobs. Taylor believed that engineering principles could be applied to make people perform somewhat like machines—efficiently, mindlessly, and repetitively. By eliminating choice, operations could be standardized. In brief, Taylor's principles of scientific management include:

1. Analyze the tasks associated with each job. Use the principles of science to find the one best way to perform the work.
2. Recruit the employee best suited to perform the job; that is, choose the person who has the skills, aptitude, and other attributes to do the job.
3. Instruct the worker in the one best way to perform the job.
4. Reward the accomplishment of the worker. Taylor believed that workers were economically motivated and would, therefore, do the job the way they were instructed if rewarded with money.
5. Cooperate with workers to ensure that the job matches plans and principles.
6. Ensure an equal division of work and responsibility between managers and workers.

Similarly, other leaders of the early twentieth-century scientific management movement focused on determining ways to improve productivity through the systematic study and application of engineering principles. Some of you have seen the classic movie or the 2003 version of *Cheaper by the Dozen*, an adaptation of the book of the same name about how the Gilbreths managed their home. Frank and Lillian Gilbreth pioneered the use of time and motion studies of job operations, through which efficient ways to perform a job could be determined and time standards could be developed. These standards would then be used to improve productivity and to compensate employees appropriately.[10]

FUNCTIONAL APPROACH

In the early 1900s, Henri Fayol, a French industrialist, identified fourteen principles of management that he believed could be applied universally. Some writers have referred to this concept as the universality of management, which suggests that basic functions, principles, and their applications in management are similar, regardless of an organization's nature. In general, Fayol believed that a manager's authority should equal that manager's responsibility, and that the direction and flow of authority through an organization should be unified.

Functional approach
School of management thought that asserts that all managers perform various functions in doing their jobs, such as planning, organizing, staffing, leading, and controlling

Fayol introduced the **functional approach** to the study of management. This approach defined the manager's role and proposed that managers do their jobs by performing various functions. Fayol identified five functions as critical to managerial effectiveness:

1. Planning: Setting down a course of action
2. Organizing: Designing a structure, with tasks and authority clearly defined
3. Commanding: Directing subordinates' actions
4. Coordinating: Pulling organizational elements toward common objectives
5. Controlling: Ensuring that plans are carried out

Other writers built on these ideas. This textbook is organized around the more current version of the functional approach to the study of management: planning, organizing, staffing, leading, and controlling.

HUMAN RELATIONS/BEHAVIORAL APPROACH

The contributions of Taylor and others gave rise to the notions that (1) if managers used the principles of scientific management, worker efficiency would increase and productivity increases would follow, and (2) if managers strove to improve working conditions, productivity would increase. The studies at the Hawthorne plant of Western Electric provided some of the most interesting and controversial results in the study of management.

Elton Mayo and Fritz Roethlisberger, leaders of a Harvard research team, conducted a series of illumination experiments from 1924 to 1932. In these experiments, Mayo and Roethlisberger hypothesized that if lighting improved, then productivity would increase. Contrary to expectations, productivity rose in both the control group (no change in working conditions) and the experimental group (working conditions varied). Numerous variations in working conditions were introduced, and no matter what change was introduced, productivity continued to rise until it stabilized at a relatively high level.

Hawthorne effect
The fact that personalized interest shown in people may cause them to behave differently

The researchers concluded that the workers performed differently than they normally did because the researchers were observing them. This reaction is known as the **Hawthorne effect**. Other phases of the Hawthorne studies emphasized the attitudes and behaviors of workers in small, informal groups and how those aspects can significantly influence performance and productivity in positive or negative directions.

The experiments at the Hawthorne plant gave rise to what was known as the **human relations movement**, and later as the **behavioral science approach**. This approach focuses on the behavior of people in organizations. Contributions from psychologists, sociologists, and other behavioral disciplines have provided numerous insights into individual and group behavior in work settings and the impact of supervisory practices and procedures on employee motivation and work performance. Chapter 4, which discusses employee motivation in relation to supervisory approaches, mentions various social and behavioral scientists and their contributions to understanding and managing human behavior in organizations.

Human relations movement/ behavioral science approach
Approach to management that focuses on the behavior of people in the work environment

QUANTITATIVE/SYSTEMS APPROACHES

While somewhat beyond the scope of this text, **quantitative/systems approaches** to management rely heavily on mathematical modeling. Through such models, which attempt to quantitatively describe the interrelationships of variables through data, data can be manipulated and outcomes predicted. Quantitative approaches are often closely connected with systems approaches, in which mathematical models are developed as series or collections of interrelated variables or parts that can be analyzed and used in decision making.

Quantitative/systems approaches
Field of management study that uses mathematical modeling as a foundation

Quantitative/systems approaches are frequently found in large organizations where sales, costs, and production data are analyzed using computer technology. Mathematical modeling typically is used to build "what-if" situations (e.g., what would be the effect on sales if the price rose 10 percent? 20 percent?). A number of planning concepts introduced in Chapter 7 rely on these types of approaches.

Factors and Trends Affecting the Role of the Supervisor

3 Identify and discuss the major demographic and societal trends that will affect supervisors.

In the foreseeable future, supervisors will have to understand and address many complex environmental factors and trends. Therefore, we examine here some major demographic and societal factors and trends that are likely to affect the supervisory management position. Figure 1.5 illustrates many of the challenges a supervisor faces. While every supervisor is responsible for managing numerous resources, unquestionably the most important, overriding aspect of supervision is the management of people. Therefore, the nature of the workforce should be of vital concern to the supervisor who plans for the future. Finding and developing qualified people have always been among the most important supervisory responsibilities. The *SHRM 2004–2005 Workplace Forecast* projects the top ten overall trends that human resource professionals believe will have the biggest impact on the workplace (see Figure 1.6).

However, the traditional challenges of attracting and retaining the most qualified employees may be superseded by the more acute challenge of leading and motivating an increasingly changing workforce. The most significant characteristic of this changing workforce will be its **diversity**. Work groups will be composed of employees with different cultural, ethnic, gender, age, educational level, racial, and lifestyle characteristics. The supervisor will need to get people from many different cultures to work together.

Diversity
The cultural, ethnic, gender, age, educational level, racial, and lifestyle differences of employees

POPULATION AND WORKFORCE GROWTH

Despite the rather low birthrate in recent decades, both the population and the workforce will continue to grow. Figure 1.7 provides employment projections

FIGURE 1.5 Effective supervisors must be adaptable and be able to maintain their perspective in the face of rapidly changing conditions

FIGURE 1.6 Workplace Trends 2008–2009

1. Continuing high cost of health care in the United States.
2. Large number of baby boomers (1945–1964) retiring at around the same time.
3. Threat of increased health care/medical costs on economic competitiveness of the United States.
4. Aging population.
5. Growing need to develop retention strategies for current and future workforce.
6. Federal health care legislation.
7. Preparing organizations for an older workforce and the next wave of retirement.
8. Threat of recession in the United States or globally.
9. Labor shortage at all skill levels.
10. Demographic shifts leading to a shortage of high-skilled workers.

Sources: Adapted from "The Top Workplace Trends: 2008–2009," *SHRM Workplace Forecast*, June 2008.

FIGURE 1.7 Workforce Projections 2006–2016

- Employment: Total employment is expected to increase by 10 percent–down substantially from earlier periods.
- The service-producing sector will generate almost all of the employment gain during this time period. Three out of every four persons will be employed in this sector.
- Professional, business services, health care, and social assistance are also expected to grow substantially.
- Those employed in management, scientific, and technical consulting services; employment services; and general medical and surgical hospitals have projected growth.
- There will be a substantial decline in the manufacturing sector, including printing and motor vehicle parts manufacturing.
- Office and administrative support occupations are projected to grow more slowly than in the past, reflecting trends in office automation.
- Labor Force: The civilian labor force is projected to reach 164.2 million by 2016.
- The number of workers over 55 is projected to grow more than five times the projected overall labor force growth rate.
- The Hispanic labor force is expected to grow by 30 percent, while the non-Hispanic labor force is projected to grow by only 5.1 percent.
- Whites will remain the largest component (79.6 percent), despite a relatively slow growth rate of 5.5 percent.
- Blacks (the U.S. Department of Labor uses this term rather than African-American) will constitute 12.3 percent of the labor force.
- Asians are expected to be the fastest growing group.
- The labor force participation rates for women in nearly all age groups are projected to increase.

Source: Adapted from "Employment Projections: 2006–16 Summary," Bureau of Labor Statistics, December 4, 2007; Occupational Handbook and Career Guide to Industries, December 2007; (go to http://www.bls.gov/oco and http://www.bls.gov.oco/cg to access the handbook and guide). More detailed information is available in five articles in the November 2007 issue of the Monthly Labor Review (go to http://www.bls.gov/opub/mlr/welcome.htm to view the articles and more current employment and labor data).

for the next few years. A word of caution: These projections, which are updated every two years, can be wrong.

Immigration has accounted for, and will continue to account for, a considerable share of the nation's population and workforce growth. Some employment analysts advocate granting an increased number of immigration visas to meet the growing demand for Information Technology (IT) workers, professionals, and other highly skilled workers.[11] The growth in the number of new immigrants (refugees, legal, or illegal) may expand certain interracial and intercultural problems that have faced supervisors managing diverse workforces.

While managing a diverse workforce presents some difficulties, it also presents numerous opportunities for supervisors to build on the strengths of individuals and groups of individuals. In the following sections, we intend not only to create an awareness of the expected differences but also to "raise consciousness." Supervisors must understand the rights of both their employees and their employers, regardless of workforce differences. Supervisors must recognize the value of a diverse workforce and their own need to become more adaptable to change. Perhaps more than ever, supervisors will have to be scrupulously fair in supervising diverse groups of employees through nondiscriminatory and progressive actions.

CHANGING AGE PATTERNS

Both the population and the labor force are getting older. The percentage of older Americans (55 and older) in the workforce is increasing dramatically—at nearly 5.5 times the projected growth rate of the labor force overall. The number of women over age 60 in the workforce has also risen dramatically. By 2016, workers between 16 and 24 will decline in numbers and those "prime age" workers between 25 and 54 are expected to increase slightly.[12]

The growth in the number of people in these mature age categories will provide an ample supply of experienced individuals who are promotable to supervisory and other management positions. Yet it is interesting that almost half of these workers over age 55 are not with the same employer that they were with when they were 40. Apparently, job mobility is not exclusive to any one age group. At the same time, because there are so many older workers, there may be a "glut" of younger employees waiting for opportunities. This possible "mismatch" in many firms between the number of employees desiring advancement and the number of opportunities available may lead to dissatisfaction, causing younger workers to leave and seek positions elsewhere. However, many factors will determine when the "Boomers" retire and, if some projections are accurate, there will be many opportunities for those seeking supervisory positions.

Various descriptions of worker categories have been provided by placing workers in several major groups. Ann Clurman and J. Walker Smith define the population in three major categories: (1) "generation Xers," those born between 1964 and 1981; (2) "Boomers," those born between 1946 and 1963; and (3) "matures," those born before 1945. Members of generation X will be replacing matures, but generation Xers have fundamentally different ideas about work, loyalty, and commitment. In general, generation Xers have far less concern about staying with companies for long periods. They tend to want more personal and leisure time and have considerable skepticism about management's values and

Aging baby boomers are living and working longer, dramatically increasing the overall labor force

© JOSE LUIS PELAEZ INC/BLEND IMAGES RF/JUPITERIMAGES

management's concerns for employees.[13] Your author falls into the last category and is often described by his grandchildren as being "nostalgic"—one of those who long for the "good old days," want to feel prepared for the unexpected, and resist the frivolous. I, personally, have found that health, safety, and security are increasingly important to those in my group. Other prognosticators have drawn their inferences about the characteristics of each group. We strongly urge you not to "judge a book by its cover" but to look at each individual as an individual and to view him or her from the "inside out."

What about those born since 1982? Neil Howe and William Strauss, authors of the book *Millennials Rising*, state that these young people prefer group activities and want clear rules set for them—a combination that is distinctly different from their mostly Boomer parents. Howe and Strauss believe that this group of new entrants to the workforce, called by some "Gen Y" or "millennials," are more spiritual and less individualistic than their parents.[14]

Some have described this group as having a short attention span—"flippers" on the remote control. Supervisors should be aware of a noticeable cultural phenomenon: Each generation of young people goes through a period in which it questions and even rejects the beliefs and values of its parent generation. There is little question that the success of supervisors will depend to a considerable extent on those supervisors' abilities to tap into the interests and motivations of all members of the workforce.

WOMEN IN THE WORKFORCE AND RELATED ISSUES

Perhaps the most dramatic change in the last several decades has been the increase in both the number and percentage of women in the U.S. workforce. Currently, some 60 percent of adult women are employed, and women constitute almost half the U.S. labor force. In recent years, women have assumed many jobs formerly dominated by men. Women now hold 48 percent of the nation's managerial positions. Regardless of perceptions that women are stealing jobs formerly held by men, the reality is that as of 2007 women held only 15.4 percent of corporate officer positions in Fortune 500 companies. Women earn half of the nation's law degrees, but account for only 16 percent of equity partners at the top firms.[15] If college degrees are a prerequisite for managerial positions, we wonder why there is not a smooth path for women?

While the Equal Pay Act was designed to lessen the gap between pay rates of males and females, studies show that women's earnings on average are 77% of men's. Some account for the disparity by pointing out that fewer women than men major in engineering, business, and other fields leading to high-paying jobs.[16] The movement of women into the workforce has affected employers with respect to women's roles as both employees and mothers. Nearly 60 percent of employed women are married, and many are raising children. Further, the number of families headed by women has steadily increased to the point that almost 20 percent of U.S. families are headed by women. Substantially higher percentages of African-American and Hispanic families are headed by women, and many of them are single working mothers.[17]

Employees may bring their family problems to work. Supervisors must understand that their employees' work performance may be impeded by conflicts between job and family obligations. To attract and retain qualified employees, more employers will be providing quality child-care facilities or helping employees make suitable child-care arrangements. Employees will continue to experiment with different types of workdays and work weeks, such

Flextime
Policy that allows employees
to choose their work hours
within stated limits

Job sharing
Policy that allows two or more
employees to perform a job
normally done by one full-time
employee

Telecommuting
Receiving work from and
sending work to the office
from home via a computer
and modem

as **flextime**, in which employees choose their work schedules within certain limits; **job sharing**, in which two or more employees share a job; **telecommuting**, in which the employee works at home and is linked to the office by computer and modem; and 4-day, 10-hour-a-day work weeks.

A recent study indicates that working mothers go to great lengths to keep family matters out of the workplace, but it is more likely that work-related issues will intrude on their home lives. A demanding job leaves almost half of parents too tired to do things with their children. Sixty percent of working mothers say they have to put work ahead of family at least some of the time and feel less successful in their relationships with spouses, children, and friends. Efforts to help employees balance the responsibilities of home and job will require better supervisory coordination, planning skills, and training to help managers handle work/life issues.[18]

Another major challenge for supervisors will be to ensure that sexual harassment does not occur in the work environment. Sexual harassment has been perpetrated against both men and women, but more attention has focused on the latter. Recent court decisions have reiterated the implications for supervisors, who are obligated to take action to prevent harassment and to take steps to remedy reported incidents of harassment. Recently, over one-third of women reported hearing sexual innuendo, wisecracks, or taunts in the workplace.[19]

Even though most corporate executives tell shareholders and other stakeholders that they ascribe to equal opportunity, the litigation awards say otherwise. A jury awarded $175 million to Wal-Mart employees in California in a case involving breaks and meal times. Boeing Company, while admitting no wrongdoing, agreed to pay thousands of female employees $72.5 million and to change its hiring, pay, promotion, and complaint-investigation procedures.[20] The topics of sexual harassment and other discriminatory actions are explored in greater detail in Chapter 13.

MINORITIES IN THE WORKFORCE

To what extent racial minorities will enter the workforce is a guess at best. Figure 1.7 provides projections for the major racial classes of the U.S. population. One issue is very real. Many people believe that illegal immigrants and businesses that hire them are lawbreakers. The current debate about what to do with the 12 million or more illegal and undocumented workers who have entered the labor force in recent years is not expected to be resolved quickly. Should they be identified, rounded up and prosecuted, deported, or given a chance to keep their jobs and apply for legal status? One thing we do know for certain is that often they are working in jobs that many Americans would consider too difficult or too low paying to accept.

Census data reveal that almost 20 percent of U.S. residents speak a language other than English at home. Just one-third of Latino immigrants in the country for less than a decade speak English well. But 75 percent of those who have been here for 30 years or more speak English very well. It takes time to assimilate to the culture and workplace.[21]

Supervisors know that many of their employees are natives of different countries and that English may not be the workplace language. The challenge for supervisors will be to learn cultural, racial, and language differences and to develop strategies for promoting cooperation among racially and ethnically diverse groups. English is the dominant language of technology, although there will be many different languages and dialects spoken in the workplace. A report published by the U.S. Defense Department recommends "immediate . . . engagement by public, private, and government agencies to improve the nation's foreign language and cultural competency." Many U.S. citizens are not proficient in another language because they haven't had to be—the rest of the world is learning English.[22]

BARRIERS FOR WOMEN AND MINORITIES

Progress in upgrading the status of women and minorities has been mixed. Some firms still seem to relegate women and minorities to lower-skilled and lower-paying jobs and have not fully realized the contributions many have to offer. While strides have been made, women and minorities remain concentrated in lower-level jobs. There appears to be an invisible barrier—a "**glass ceiling**"—that limits advancement. To compound the problem, many organizations have placed women and minority employees in certain specialized occupations, such as human resources and accounting. These **glass walls** that segment employees can deny them the opportunity to develop the variety of skills needed to advance.

Glass ceiling
Invisible barrier that limits the advancement of women and minorities

Glass walls
Invisible barriers that compartmentalize women and minorities into certain occupational classes

A recent study reported what most males have long suspected: that women employ a different leadership style than men. Even though women make up less than 15 percent of the senior executives at Fortune 1000 corporations, their leadership style might actually be more effective than men's. The study purports that women executives "demonstrate more empathy, better listening skills, and a more inclusive style of leadership. And successful female leaders tend to be more assertive, more persuasive, and more willing to take risks than their male counterparts."[23] If women are actually better at leadership, why are so few women in key executive positions? Is it that women and minorities are unwilling to fight to shatter the glass ceiling? Or is it that the "old boys' network" still controls the path to the top? You can draw your own conclusions.

Two studies found that minority professionals left their jobs at rates two to three times higher than did Caucasian men and women. The primary reason cited for high turnover rates among minority professionals is that they did not feel recognized as valuable resources. According to these studies, many minority professionals asserted that their organizations were publicly claiming support for promoting diversity, but in reality the minority professionals were excluded from many relationships, mentoring assignments, and other situations, which impeded their progress. Minority professionals usually resent the notion that they were hired because of affirmative action and that many of their companies do not really concern themselves with enhancing a minority employee's career. Interestingly, a number of minority professionals candidly acknowledged that they moved from their current positions to other positions because companies looking for qualified minorities were willing to pay higher salaries to obtain their services.[24]

Minority and women employees will continue to need an effective combination of educational and job-related experiences to provide them with opportunities to develop their talents. Organizations will be expected to design programs to attract and develop women and minority employees and to provide these employees with the full range of opportunities open to everyone else.

EDUCATIONAL PREPARATION

Accompanying the changes in the racial and ethnic composition of the workforce are educational-preparation factors that also will challenge supervisors in the future. The ability to read and use documents is essential in today's global economy. Yet one-third of the U.S. population has below-basic or basic document literacy, causing communication problems.[25]

Some forecasters believe that we may soon encounter problems with an overeducated workforce. That is, more and more college-trained employees will compete for jobs that do not necessarily require a college education. For example, according to government data, about 70 percent of the occupations expected to have the most job openings in the first decade of the twenty-first century will involve skills that do not require a college education.[26] Nevertheless, every study shows the value of a college education. Clearly, college graduates' pay has increased (in constant dollars) substantially in the last 25 years, while wages for less-educated workers have remained stagnant.[27]

Underemployment
Situations in which people are in jobs that do not use their SKAs

SKAs
A person's skills, knowledge, and abilities

The competition for jobs and the increase in low-level service-industry jobs will probably create underemployment. **Underemployment** occurs when employees bring a certain amount of skills, knowledge, and abilities (**SKAs**) to the workplace and find that their jobs lack meaning and/or the opportunities to fully use their SKAs. A challenge for many supervisors will be to enhance workplace environments to satisfy the underemployed. The current abundance of college graduates gives corporate recruiters a distinct challenge to select the best candidates available.

We must keep in mind the other side of the picture, namely that millions of workers in the workforce will not have completed a secondary school education. In 2007, of people 25 years and older, only 84.1 percent have graduated from high school and only 27 percent have a bachelor's degree or higher. The bad news is that the nation's dropout rate, as estimated by the percentage of public school freshman who graduate on time, is high—almost 25 percent.[28] Of those who complete high school, many will receive an inferior education because their schools do not offer the variety or quality of classes that other schools offer. In addition, many individuals entering the workforce will have had considerable formal education, but this education will not have prepared them with the specific skills that apply directly to the job market.

Competitive advantage
The ability to outperform competitors by increasing efficiency, quality, creativity, and responsiveness to customers and effectively using employee talents

An organization seeking to obtain a **competitive advantage** can do so by hiring qualified and adaptable people, training those people thoroughly, and then appropriately using those people's skills. Unfortunately, many job applicants lack proper workplace attitudes and skills. To this end, companies will be required to spend more time and effort training employees, particularly those who are unprepared and unskilled and who need to have their latent talents developed if they are to be successful and motivated to work. Supervisors will be required to allocate more time for on-the-job employee training and to ensure that employees are encouraged to capitalize on all opportunities for continuing education.

OCCUPATIONAL AND INDUSTRY TRENDS

Imagine reading this newspaper headline as you prepare to finish your college work and embark on a new career search: "Employment expectations down substantially in manufacturing, up in service sector. New-hire compensation growth slows in both manufacturing and service sectors." Unfortunately, in May 2008, that was the headline. Cheer up, because at the same time the U.S. Bureau of Labor Statistics (BLS) was projecting that there will continue to be a steady need for people in professional occupations and service occupations. Those opportunities are expected to account for more than 60 percent of new jobs created between now and 2016. These are at opposite ends of the educational and earning ranges.[29] For many of those occupations expected to be the fastest-growing, on-the-job training will be the most significant post secondary education and in only half of those fast-growing occupations will a bachelor's or higher degree be required.[30] We have found that employees with technological backgrounds who can manage and supervise products, relationships, and people will find themselves of particular value to their organizations. At the same time, low-paying jobs will be on the rise. Millions of new service workers, such as cashiers at campus bookstores, servers and washers at local restaurants, and home healthcare workers, will be needed. Unfortunately, many of these service workers will find themselves in low-paying jobs.

Déjà vu—a sense that you have previously seen, heard, or experienced something that is, in fact, new to you—is presented in the next few paragraphs. The BLS projects that the labor force will grow more slowly because of economic conditions and that employment growth will be concentrated in the service sector. They estimate that service-providing industries will generate almost all of the employment gain from 2006 to 2016. It should not be a surprise, but manufacturing jobs are expected to decline substantially. However, the need for construction workers is expected to grow.[31] When was the last time you heard someone encourage someone to explore an apprentice program, such as carpentry, plumbing, or electrical? These are well-paying skilled jobs, but fewer and fewer people want to be "Bob the Builder."

At the same time, many of the nation's largest industrial corporations have eliminated thousands of jobs, a trend that probably will continue. More and more companies are outsourcing certain functions or major departments to trim their budgets. Departments or services such as call centers, data processing, human resources, public relations, and accounting are especially vulnerable to outsourcing or downsizing.

While the media and popular press tend to focus on large-scale businesses such as General Motors, small and midsize firms are expected to create most of the job growth in the coming decade. Currently, only about 15 percent of the workforce is employed in firms that have 1,000 or more employees, and more than half the workforce is employed in enterprises with fewer than 100 employees. U.S. Bureau of Labor Statistics projections suggest that the largest growth in supervisory and management positions—and jobs in general—will be in small and rapidly growing organizations, especially service- and technology-based companies. Many small businesses can provide unique opportunities for new college graduates, and many supervisors have found that they can gain broader and more diverse experiences in smaller firms than in large companies where they may be assigned to specialized areas.

CHANGING TECHNOLOGY AND BUSINESS CONDITIONS

Consider the events that have occurred since the turn of the century: a volatile stock market, 9/11, war in Iraq, gasoline prices rising to over $4.00 per gallon in most of the country, cheap and easy credit creating a housing and financial institution crisis, the decline of the dollar against world currencies, banks and other financial institutions looking for bailouts, airlines merging and raising fares, food prices soaring, auto companies cutting productions and shutting down plants, natural calamities such as Hurricane Katrina, the cyclone in Myanmar, an earthquake in China, and even terrorism on college campuses, just to name a few.

© JEFF GREENBERG/PHOTO EDIT

Collectively, these events, along with technological advances, changing markets, and other competitive influences, have forced businesses to adjust their way of doing business. Most consumers have felt the pain in their wallets as organizations have passed higher energy and raw material costs on to consumers in the form of higher prices for goods and services.

As implied in the previous section, computer skills are a must for those seeking careers in management. Computers now give managers access to a tremendous amount of information that is necessary for making effective decisions. IT allows people to be no more than a few seconds away from anybody else in communication terms. The meteoric rise in Facebook, MySpace, and other social networking sites has altered the traditional mode of face-to-face communication and the way things are done. The "IT revolution" will continue to be apparent throughout most organizations.

A major problem that is likely to worsen is that of too much information. With the growth of communication capabilities, including e-mail, text messaging, voice mail, fax, telephone, and other devices, supervisors are being inundated by hundreds of messages sent and received every day. Many individuals have difficulty with the extra work generated by these messages, many of which waste time. The ability to properly manage information will be another of the many demanding responsibilities of supervisors, both now and in the future.

Because it is difficult to forecast specifically when and how technological change will impact a supervisor's position, every supervisor will have to be broadly educated. Supervisors will have to prepare themselves and their employees, both technologically and psychologically, for changes. Supervisors who keep up to date with changes unquestionably will be more valuable to their organizations.

GLOBAL CHALLENGES

Global challenges will continue to impact the supervisor. The Saudis, Chinese, British, Germans, Swiss, Canadians, Japanese, and others have substantially invested in U.S. firms. In 2008, InBev NV, the Belgium brewer of Stella Artois, acquired Anheuser-Busch Company. Carlos Brito, CEO of InBev, said in a statement that the deal "will create a stronger, more competitive, sustainable global company which will benefit all stakeholders." Miller, the "tastes great—less filling" beer is already part of London's SAB-Miller PLC.[32] Identifying the cultural/value systems and work-ethic differences of these phenomenon is beyond the scope of this text. However, the supervisor must recognize that management practices differ culturally and structurally in these firms as compared to U.S.-owned and -operated firms.

The production facilities of U.S. firms are being drawn to China, India, South Korea, Eastern Europe, South America, Africa, Mexico, and other locations by low wages and other factors that help create a competitive advantage. South Korea, which until the 1960s ranked among the poorest countries in the world, now has the world's eleventh-largest economy.[33] One corporate executive, when asked why his company had outsourced work to the low-wage countries, responded: "The customers we supply have plants in those countries. Even though we have a high turnover rate among employees, we still enjoy a tremendous cost advantage."

Then throw in the China Factor. While many of us view China's economy as backward, we should think about the Great Wall, which stretches farther than the distance from New York to Los Angles, as the potential China has. The People's Republic of China with more than 1.4 billion people has become the world's second largest economy after the U.S. While China has a checkered human rights past, a history of clamping down on dissent, and a toxic haze that causes breathing difficulties, they have a seemingly unlimited number of workers, modern production facilities, and untapped mineral resources. Look at the clothes you are wearing or the light bulbs overhead. Where were they made? Not in the USA. Electronics, heavy-equipment, furniture, and other manufacturers have migrated to China and other Asian countries. Even with world-wide economic problems and increased transportation costs, China's exports are expected to continue to grow.[34]

In *The Pursuit of WOW!*, management consultant Tom Peters wrote that the "it's not important unless it happens here [in the United States]" attitude has become a problem. To be successful in foreign countries, U.S. firms must make a strong effort to understand the cultural customs in these environments. Over half the world's population lives in Asia, and a majority of that population is under the age of 25, which is dramatically different from the rest of the world. As new entrants to the Asian labor force become more literate, everything will change.[35] International opportunities for technically competent U.S. supervisors will increase. However, transplanted U.S. supervisors will need to learn about cultural differences and find ways to adapt to nontraditional management styles, particularly telecommuting techniques.

Outsourcing of high-end manufacturing and information technology jobs to low-cost countries is expected to continue. Outsourcing is not new, as companies have long sought to reduce operating costs and capital expenditures.[36] The next time you have to call to complain about a product not working properly or to inquire about a warranty, ask where the employee you are talking to is located. Chances are that the call center is located in India or the Philippines—not in the United States.

WORK SCHEDULING AND EMPLOYMENT CONDITIONS

General working conditions have changed and will continue to evolve. Only about one-third of employed Americans over age 18 still work a traditional Monday-through-Friday work week. In the future, even fewer Americans will be working a standard 9-to-5 day shift because of the projected growth in jobs with evening, night, and weekend requirements.

Contingent workforce
Part-time, temporary, or contract employees who work schedules dependent primarily on employer needs

Another phenomenon that is likely to continue is the **contingent workforce**. The contingent workforce primarily consists of part-time and temporary or contract employees. These employees are roughly 25 percent of the total employment base in the United States. This is a type of "interim" workforce consisting of people who can be called in and sent home depending on the employer's needs. Employers have used these types of workers in an effort to reduce the wages and benefits that usually are paid to full-time employees. Temporary or contract employees often are supplied to employers by temporary agencies. It is likely that temporary and contract employment will continue because of the economic advantages to employers who use such services. Recruitment, training, and other associated costs are minimal, even though the per-hour cost of contract labor may be higher than that for regular employees. When a project is finished or business necessity dictates, contract or temporary employees can easily be dismissed.[37] Supervisors often encounter difficult situations when trying to motivate temporary employees who consider themselves transient. These employees work at firms only until something better comes along. Further, a number of studies have indicated that lower productivity and increased accidents can occur when employees are not fully committed to their jobs, which, of course, is complicated by the contingent workforce situation.

Other employment factors are likely to complicate the supervisor's job in the future. Retail sales reports from 2007–2008, and forecasts through 2010, indicate a substantial cutback in consumer spending. Couple that with the rise in food and energy costs, along with the decline in quality job opportunities, and more and more employees are being pushed to work multiple part-time jobs to try to make ends meet. Imagine the plight, for example, of the single parent with several school-aged children who is trying to balance work/life responsibilities. How can he or she devote full attention to the job requirements when worried about stretching a household budget? We are all aware of the turnover rate in the fast food industry. It is not unusual for a shop with 40 employees to experience a 100 percent or higher turnover rate. Turnover of employees is statistically documented by the fact that, on average, employees stay at their jobs only about 3.6 years.[38] Figure 1.8 shows the dilemma faced by one employee who left his job prematurely.

Work scheduling problems, caused by employees demanding greater flexibility to attend to family needs, are likely to accelerate during the foreseeable future.[39] Still another thorny issue is the growing disparity in executive compensation as compared to the income of most employees. What impact does it have on morale and dedication to work when the worker reads that his/her CEO is making mega-millions while he/she is struggling to make ends meet? Clearly, the disparity of income between executives and employees in companies can erode morale and, consequently, performance.

CORPORATE CULTURE AND ETHICAL CONDUCT
Social Responsibility, Corporate Culture, and Ethical Conduct

Corporate social responsibility (CSR)
A notion that organizations consider the interests of all stakeholders

Corporate social responsibility (CSR) is a concept whereby organizations consider the interests of society by taking responsibility for the impact of its actions on employees, customers, suppliers, shareholders, and other stakeholders as well as the environment and communities in which they operate. Author Archie Carroll

FIGURE 1.8 It is easier to find a job when you have one

"I'M BETWEEN JOBS ... THE ONE I DIDN'T WANT AND THE
ONE I COULDN'T GET."

developed a four-part definition of CSR that provides a medium for analyzing a company's responsibilities.

- Legal responsibilities. To comply with statutory obligations, i.e., to play by the rules of the game.
- Economic responsibilities. To be profitable, i.e., to make money for the shareholders.
- Ethical responsibilities. To do what is right, just, fair.
- Philanthropic responsibilities. To contribute resources to improve the community and society at large.[40]

According to the *2008 Corporate Sustainability Employee Study*, "one-third of businesses are taking on CSR by attempting to assess their environmental footprints, collaborating with nongovernmental organizations to institute social programs, and developing approaches to positively impact society or reduce harmful impacts."[41] Supervisors such as Alisha McDonald in this chapter's opening *You Make the Call* is involved in Habitat for Humanity projects and encourages others to become involved. Numerous organizations will raise funds to build a Habitat home and encourage employees to volunteer their talents to construct a home. This is but one example of corporate CSR.

Corporate culture is the set of shared purposes, values, and beliefs that employees have about their organization. Top-level management creates the overall vision and philosophy for the firm. To provide a foundation for the type of corporate culture that is desired, many companies develop mission statements and ethical conduct statements.

Figure 1.9 is an example of a values-and-beliefs statement that was developed by the top management of Community Medical Center (CMC). Throughout the text, there are several CMC "You Make the Calls" and end-of-part cases that will feature situations arising at CMC. You can use this statement as a reference point for many of the decisions that will confront you. Supervisors are major influencers in determining the direction of the corporate culture in

Corporate culture
Set of shared purposes, values, and beliefs that employees hold about their organization

FIGURE 1.9 A Sample Values and Belief Statement

Every Pine Village Community Medical Center (CMC) employee is important. With mutual respect, trust, and open communication, we will work together to create an organization that consistently meets or exceeds the expectations of patients, visitors, physicians, employees, and other stakeholders. We believe that when employees are actively engaged in their work, they will work with passion because they know that they can positively impact the quality of patient care.

CMC is dedicated to providing consistently superior services to all our customers. We believe in fostering an environment that encourages superior service and performance.

We believe that superior service and performance result from:

- A clear understanding of goals and clear job expectations.
- Knowing that every job is important and doing the job right the first time.
- Effective communication.
- Proper application of skills, knowledge, and abilities.
- Wise use of resources.
- High standards of conduct that embody 'trust' and 'integrity.'
- A safe and aesthetically pleasing work environment.
- Shared involvement in attaining goals.
- Opportunities for personal and professional growth.

their departments. Supervisors play significant roles in informing, educating, and setting examples for ethical behavior. Although ethical behavior and fair dealing have always been foundations for good management, it is clear that ethical conduct has become one of the most challenging issues confronting U.S. business. The daily news is filled with information regarding the misuse of business power and the contention that corrupt business practices are the primary way to make profits. Ethics and morality are back on the front page as a result of illegal and unscrupulous behavior. The public consistently gives business managers low marks for honesty. Author Archie Carroll said it well:

> If management is actively opposed to what is regarded as ethical (substitute the word legal), the clear implication is that management knows right from wrong and chooses to do wrong. Thus, it is motivated by greed. Its goals are profitability and organizational success (substitute the words ego enhancement and personal success here) at almost any price. Immoral management does not care about others' claims to be treated fairly or justly.[42]

The Society of Human Resources Management's (SHRM) core principle of Professional Responsibility should apply for all those in supervisory positions. We are responsible for adding value to the organization we serve and contributing to the ethical success of those organizations. As supervisors, we must accept professional responsibility for our individual decisions and actions.[43] In the future, as never before, it will be important that ethical behavior and fair dealing are at the forefront of good management practices, beginning at the supervisory level. A supervisor's personal ethics also are an important guide for making decisions when facing ethical problems in the workplace. Chapter 5 further discusses the importance of the ethical standards that can serve as guides for decision making.

GOVERNMENTAL AND SOCIETAL ISSUES

Other emerging governmental and societal issues will continue to complicate the supervisory management position. For example, numerous environmental concerns remain serious long-term problems for business, government, and the general public. Energy availability and costs may be determined by international and domestic political and economic changes. These types of issues and societal pressures often become part of business planning and operations.

Figure 1.10 reviews the federal legislation affecting the supervisor's job. State and local governments also have laws and regulations that impact businesses.

FIGURE 1.10 Overview of Federal Employment Legislation Affecting Supervisors

Family and Medical Leave Act (FMLA) (1992). Provides for up to 12 weeks of unpaid leave for certain personal and family health-related circumstances. http://www.dol.gov/esa/whd/fmla/.

Americans with Disabilities Act (ADA) (1990). Prohibits discrimination based on physical and mental disabilities in places of employment and public accommodation. http://www.usdoj.gov/crt/ada/adahom1.htm.

Worker Adjustment and Retraining Act (WARN) (1988). Requires firms employing 100 or more workers to provide 60 days' advance notice to employees before shutting down or conducting substantial layoffs. http://www.doleta.gov/layoff/warn.cfm.

Pregnancy Discrimination Act (1978). Requires employers to treat pregnancy, childbirth, or related medical conditions the same as any other medical disability if the employers have medical/hospitalization benefit programs for employees. http://www.eeoc.gov/facts/fs-preg.html.

Occupational Safety and Health Act (OSHA) (1970). Designed to protect the safety and health of employees; holds employers responsible for providing workplaces free of safety and health hazards. Created the Occupational Safety and Health Administration to carry out the Act's provisions. http://www.osha.gov/.

Title VII of the Civil Rights Act, as amended (1964). Prohibits discrimination in hiring, promotion, discharge, pay, benefits, and other aspects of employment on the basis of race, color, religion, gender, or national origin. The Equal Employment Opportunity Commission (EEOC) has the authority to bring lawsuits against employers in federal courts. http://www.eeoc.gov/policy/vii.html.

Labor Management Relations Act (Taft-Hartley) (1947). Amended the Wagner Act; specified unfair labor practices for unions, provided for Federal Mediation and Conciliation Service (FMCS) to assist in resolving labor-management disputes, and more clearly identified requirements for bargaining in good faith. (On the NLRB home page, http://www.nlrb.gov, click on *What is the National Labor Relations Act; Employee Rights;* and *Read the NLRA.*)

Fair Labor Standards Act (FLSA) (1938). Established that employers covered by the Act must pay an employee (1) at least a minimum wage and (2) time and a half for all hours worked in excess of 40 in a given week. Classified a person working in a job that is not subject to the provisions of the Act as "exempt" from the overtime pay provisions. The change effective August 2004 set forth new criteria for determining overtime. http://www.dol.gov/elaws/flsa.htm.

National Labor Relations Act (Wagner Act) (1935). Gave workers the right to unionize and bargain collectively over hours, wages, and other terms and conditions of employment. Specified five unfair labor practices for employers. Created the National Labor Relations Board (NLRB) to (1) certify labor unions as the sole bargaining representatives of employees and (2) investigate unfair labor practices. (Go to http://www.nlrb.gov to review the National Labor Relations Act, court decisions, employee rights, and employer responsibilities.)

NOTES: See the following U.S. Department of Labor Web sites for additional information on employment laws and applications: www.dol.gov.osbp (for those relate to small businesses); www.dol.gov (click on summary of major laws); and www.dol.gov/elaws. (Students have found that this site provides easy-to-understand information on federal employment law.)

"Going green" means that individuals and organizations voluntarily take steps to conserve energy and behave in environmentally friendly ways

The effects of such legislation can be quite costly, and organizations may be required to change their methods of operation to comply.

Supervisors are influenced both directly and indirectly by such governmental requirements, and they must continue to stay abreast of any legislation that may influence their operations. Furthermore, supervisors must be sensitive to pressures exerted by special-interest groups. Consumer groups, in particular, have demanded better products and services from business, labor, and government. Environmentalists seek to influence business decisions that may adversely impact the environment. "**Going Green**" could become a more important issue as more organizations are volunteering to operate in a more environmentally responsible way. Some local governments are providing incentives to encourage businesses to become greener. Students, faculty, and alumni from Indiana University Purdue University Fort Wayne (IPFW) recently designed and constructed a Habitat for Humanity home intended to be environmentally sustainable in Fort Wayne, Indiana.[44]

Questions need to be asked: "Are you willing to make double-sided copies? Power down your computer when not using it for a few minutes? Use energy-efficient/more expensive bulbs in your light fixtures? Share rides to and from campus?" In part, that is what it will take for us to become "green."

Some employees, especially the parents of young children or employees who have elderly parents, will expect their employers to provide daycare facilities so that they can better combine their family and job responsibilities. It seems likely that numerous other permanent and temporary special-interest groups will continue to place community and political demands on firms in ways that will affect how supervisors will operate in the future.

All indications are that these pressures will remain intense. A utility company supervisor said recently, "I have to be more of a lawyer, cop, teacher, accountant, political scientist, and psychologist these days than a manager!" Although a bit overstated, this supervisor's comment reflects a realistic aspect of every supervisor's contemporary role.

WORKPLACE INCIVILITY AND PEOPLE WHO MAKE LIFE DIFFICULT

The typical employee will spend most of his or her waking hours going to, at, or coming home from work. It is logical to expect that whenever people convene in one place for so long, their different personalities, expectations, values, and needs may clash from time to time. Many students can relate to the playground bullies of their childhoods. In some instances, the playground bully has grown up and now works alongside us. The dilemma for many employees is, "How can you expect me to get along with that troublemaker?" A number of studies report that "rude behavior is on the rise in the workplace and can undermine an organization's effectiveness."[45]

Almost everyone has been on the receiving end of a rude person's temper or a bully's wrath. Whether crude or impolite behavior takes place behind closed doors or out in the open, it directly affects the recipients and lowers group morale. Who are these people? In his book *Coping with Difficult People*, Robert M. Bramson writes:

> *They are the hostile customers or coworkers, the indecisive, vacillating bosses, and the overagreeable subordinates of the world who are constant headaches to work with. Although their numbers are small, their impact is large. They are responsible for absenteeism, significant losses in productivity, and lost customers or clients. They frustrate and demoralize those unlucky enough to have to work with them, and they are difficult to understand. Worst of all, they appear immune to all the usual methods of communication and persuasion designed to convince them or help them to change their ways.*[46]

Throughout this text, we have identified some people who might make life difficult for you. Typically, employees arrive in an organization with little or no foundation for how to handle these types of people. Because we believe that it is crucial that you understand how to deal with incivility and difficult people, this topic is discussed in greater detail in Chapters 4 and 12. So that you may better understand strategies for dealing with people who make life difficult, beginning with Skills Application 3–1 in Chapter 3, we introduce you to some of these coworkers, associates, or supervisors. Unfortunately, you may find one or two whom you know fairly well.

The Three E's—Engagement, Empowerment, and Employee Participation in Decision Making

How do you get people off the bench and into the game? How do you get diverse groups of people to work together? Those questions have been with us since the beginning of time. Some employees will demand a greater voice in workplace decision making, while others will adopt the 'what-how-when' attitude: "Just tell me what you want done, how you want it done, and when you want it done." Many employees will want more from their jobs and will demand a voice in decisions concerning their employment. This does not have to be objectionable to a supervisor. In fact, once supervisors realize that their employees have something to contribute, they will welcome employee participation in decisions rather than fear it.

What kind of employee would you like to work with and have work for you? A supervisor who prefers a "telling style" would want the employee with the "what-how-when" attitude. It is my contention that most employees want more than that—they want to be engaged in the place where they spend most of their waking hours. In his book, *Getting Engaged: The New Workplace Loyalty*, author Tim Rutledge explains that the "truly engaged employees are attracted to, and inspired by, their work ('I want to do this'), committed ('I am dedicated to the success of what I am doing'), and fascinated ('I love what I am doing').[47]

The 2006 Conference Board review of employee engagement research identified certain factors that need to be present for employees to act in ways that further both their own self-interests and the interests of their organization. These are:

- Do I believe that my job is important?
- Do managers communicate expectations, provide regular feedback, and lead by example?
- Is the job mentally stimulating?
- Is there a direct connection between what I do and the organization's performance—quality, service, bottom-line?
- Are there opportunities for personal and professional growth?
- Am I willing to work with a passion because I am connected to what the organization stands for?
- Is there a climate of open and honest communication between the manager, team members, and myself?
- Have I been empowered to make decisions that impact what I do and how I do it?[48]

As you review the bulleted points, it should become clear that an **engaged employee** is one who is enthused about what they do, where they do it, and who they do it with. They are fully involved because they have been engaged.

Empowerment means giving employees the authority and responsibility to achieve objectives. Opportunities to make suggestions and participate in decisions affecting their jobs can and should be supported. However, some supervisors become worried when workers challenge what have traditionally been management rights, thinking that certain areas should be beyond employee challenge. Many quality circles and other participatory management approaches of the last decade failed, in part, because managers failed to listen to the suggestions of employees, did not act on those suggestions in a timely fashion,

Engaged employee
One who has a strong emotional bond to his/her organization and is committed to its objectives

Empowerment
Giving employees the authority and responsibility to accomplish their individual and the organization's objectives

An employee is engaged when he or she feels totally connected, needed, appreciated, committed, and thus, willing to put forth his or her best effort for the good of the organization

© ANDY SACKS/GETTY IMAGES

or felt threatened by those suggestions. Nevertheless, there will continue to be pressure from employees, labor unions, minorities, and other groups for more influence in decisions pertaining to the workplace.

Many supervisors have become accustomed to the practice of **participative management**, which essentially means a willingness to permit employees to influence or share in managerial decisions. If supervisors learn to react to this practice in a positive way, it should improve their own and their company's performance.[49] Although forecasts are, at best, precarious, experienced supervisors will recognize that these trends have already begun. Supervisors must understand and plan for them. Empowerment and participative management are discussed further in Chapters 4, 5, 7, 8, and 11.

Participative management
Allowing employees to influence and share in organizational decision making

Supervision: A Professional Perspective

4 Explain why supervisors must continually grow and develop as professionals.

The primary responsibility of most supervisors is to manage their firms' most important resources—human resources. It is human resources on which any organization ultimately depends. Managing people starts with selecting and training individuals to fill job openings, and it continues with ongoing development, motivation, leadership, and preparation of employees for promotion.

Thus, supervisors will have to become true professionals with a growing professional perspective, and they will have to develop as innovators and idea people. They must look to the future with a professional awareness of the trends influencing human behavior and observe how those trends impact the management of people in a complex society.

In all of this, it is an imperative to take the professional perspective, which recognizes the need for constant self-improvement and self-renewal. No amount of formal or informal education can ever be enough to fulfill a supervisor's personal program of self-improvement. Supervisors must recognize that they, too, can become obsolete unless they constantly take measures to update their own skills and knowledge through a program of continuous self-development.

Students, as well as practicing managers, need to understand that "As long as you live, keep learning to live," should be a guide for all of us to live by.[50] Peter Senge, author of *The Fifth Discipline*, provides further insight:

> *Real learning gets to the heart of what it means to be human. Through learning we re-create ourselves. Through learning we become able to do something we never were able to do. Through learning we extend our capacity to create, to be part of the generative process of life. There is within each of us a deep hunger for this type of learning.*[51]

Stephen Covey, author of *The Seven Habits of Highly Effective People*, presented the following illustration:

> *Suppose you were to come upon someone in the woods working feverishly to saw down a tree.*
>   *"What are you doing?" you ask.*
>   *"Can't you see?" comes the impatient reply. "I'm sawing down the tree."*
>   *"You look exhausted!" you exclaim. "How long have you been at it?"*
>   *"Over five hours," he returns, "and I'm beat! This is hard work."*
>   *"Well, why don't you take a break for a few minutes and sharpen the saw?" you inquire. "I'm sure it would go a lot faster."*
>   *"I don't have time to sharpen the saw," the man said emphatically. "I'm too busy sawing."*[52]

Both newly appointed and experienced supervisors should begin each day by asking, "What can I do to sharpen my saw?" Throughout the text and on the Student Support Web site, through skills applications, experiential exercises, case studies, skill development modules, Internet activities, and other learning opportunities, we will provide you with opportunities to sharpen your saw.

Covey suggests renewing the four dimensions of your nature—(1) spiritual (value clarification and commitment, study and meditation); (2) mental (reading, visualizing, planning, writing); (3) social/emotional (service, empathy, synergy, intrinsic security); and (4) physical (exercise, nutrition, stress management)—to improve your personal effectiveness.[53] Supervisors who master the managerial concepts and skills discussed in this textbook should make considerable progress in terms of personal development, but just knowing concepts and approaches is not enough. Supervisors must constantly seek new ways to apply this knowledge in the challenging, complex, and dynamic situations they will encounter.

No one is certain what the future will bring, but we see reasons to be optimistic. When the time comes, will you—our students of today—be prepared so that you can achieve your dreams? At the beginning of each term, I ask students to look back, to take time to reflect on the past and learn from the mistakes that others have made; to look up, to contemplate what meaning they want from life; and to look ahead, to develop strategies for getting to where they want to be. I issue the same challenge to you!

SUMMARY

1 Supervisors are the first tier of management. They manage entry-level and other departmental employees. In the face of a rapidly changing environment, successful supervisors will find ways to balance the requirements for high work performance with the diverse needs of the workforce.

Supervisory management focuses primarily on the management of people. For many people, being a supervisor provides a variety of satisfying experiences. Among these are the challenge of getting diverse people to work together, the increased responsibility that comes with climbing the management hierarchy, the unpredictable nature of the job, and the sense of accomplishment from doing a job well. Conversely, there are reasons people avoid supervisory responsibility. Being a supervisor is a demanding position that often places the supervisor in the middle of organizational pressures and conflict. A supervisor must endeavor to reconcile the needs of the organization and the needs of employees, which often is an elusive target.

In addition, major environmental factors impact everything the organization does. These factors are not static. The whole world is changing rapidly, and some people do not want to deal with change.

2 There is no one universal school of management thought. The scientific management approach attempts to find the most efficient or "one best way." In this approach, the manager's primary function is to plan the work. Time and motion study and other industrial-engineering principles are used to analyze the work to be done. The functional approach assumes that there are essential functions that all managers should perform. The human

relations movement/behavioral science approach emphasizes that managers must understand what causes employees to behave the ways they do. This approach began with the Hawthorne studies at Western Electric Company. The quantitative/systems approach applies mathematical models to help solve organizational problems. An understanding of the various schools of management thought gives supervisors a foundation on which to build their own supervisory philosophies.

3 Many factors and trends in the workforce will impact how most organizations operate. The workforce is expected to become more racially and ethnically diverse. Starting around 2012, the Baby Boomers are expected to be leaving the labor market in droves. Even though some of the Boomers will continue to work beyond retirement age, the overall age composition of the workforce will change drastically. Women and minorities will continue to enter the workforce in increasing numbers, and they will be used more fully than they have been in the past, including in supervisory and management positions. Substantial numbers of part-time and contract employees will be found in the workplace. The more diverse workforce will create numerous problems (e.g., multicultural and multilingual problems, family obligations versus job obligations). The workforce generally will consist of more college graduates, but millions of people will not be prepared educationally to qualify for many employment opportunities. The growth of the Latino population and other immigrants will have a profound effect on organizations in which they work and the culture and traditions in communities where they reside. We fully expect that immigration issues will be debated and debated and, perhaps eventually, a solution will be found for the millions of illegal immigrants.

Most manufacturers have or are in the process of downsizing, outsourcing, or off-shoring their production activities. While many jobs are becoming more complex because of the technology involved, the fastest growth will take place in the service sector. Occupational and industry trends, changing technology and business conditions, and the competition from the global marketplace will be significant influences on supervisory management. Governmental laws and regulations will continue to have a major impact on the policies and activities of most organizations.

China, China, China! What does the future hold as China becomes an even more formidable force in the world's economy? China's gross domestic product ranks it second in the world only behind the U.S. Many U.S. and European manufacturers have found China an attractive place because of an abundance of willing workers and few environmental restrictions. One only had to look at the massive investment and construction effort put forth to host the 2008 Olympic Games to see the potential in China.

Corporate social responsibility (CSR) implies that organizations must be both profitable and responsible to their various stakeholder groups. Supervisors need to look at each decision in two ways: (1) who will be impacted by the decision, and (2) is it "fair to all concerned?"

Because of increased incivility, workplace violence, and the threat of terrorism, firms will establish programs and procedures to help supervisors recognize the symptoms of troubled employees.

Supervisors will have to be sensitive to existing and expected employee trends. For example, more employees will expect their jobs to have greater personal meaning to them as individuals. Many will want to be engaged or at least more involved via participation in their organizations. Employees will continue to expect a greater voice in workplace decision making, and they will expect to be empowered. It is likely that supervisors will have to be somewhat flexible in their approaches to managing.

4 The habits of highly effective people can be developed. Supervisors who want to be more effective will put themselves in situations in which they can practice new techniques. Finally, supervisors who aspire to become more effective leaders need a professional outlook and must recognize the need for a personal program of continuous self-development.

KEY TERMS

Behavioral science approach (p. 11)
Competitive advantage (p. 18)
Contingent workforce (p. 22)
Corporate culture (p. 23)
Corporate Social Responsibility (CSR) (p. 22)
Diversity (p. 11)
Empowerment (p. 28)
Engaged employee (p. 28)

Flextime (p. 16)
Functional approach (p. 10)
Glass ceiling (p. 17)
Glass walls (p. 17)
Going Green (p. 26)
Hawthorne effect (p. 10)
Human relations movement (p. 11)
Job sharing (p. 16)
Participative management (p. 29)

Quantitative/systems approaches (p. 11)
Scientific management approach (p. 9)
SKAs (p. 18)
Society for Human Resource Management (SHRM) (p. 6)
Supervisors (p. 7)
Telecommuting (p. 16)
Underemployment (p. 18)
Working supervisors (p. 7)

QUESTIONS FOR DISCUSSION

1. What are some advantages to being a supervisor? What are some disadvantages?

2. From the standpoint of the prospective supervisor, what is the significance of the following?
   - Taylor's scientific management
   - Fayol's functions of management
   - The Hawthorne studies
   - Behavioral science
   - The quantitative/systems approaches

3. Of those factors or trends projected to reshape the workplace, how might the changes over the next five years affect you, your lifestyle, and the work of your organization? Which will create the greatest challenge for supervisors? Why?

4. Peter Drucker said, "Making decisions is a critical skill at every level."
   a. Do you agree with Drucker? Why or why not?
   b. Review Figure 1.4 or *The Daily Drucker* or *http://www. peter-drucker.com* to see some more of Drucker's practical wisdoms. Select one that is important to you and explain how it might be useful to your personal and professional growth.

5. At the end of the day, how do you measure whether you have been successful?

SKILLS APPLICATIONS

Skills Application 1-1: What Call Did You Make?

1. Refer to the opening "You Make the Call!" Make a list of the questions that you have for Alisha McDonald. Now put yourself in Alisha's shoes and write a brief answer to each of the questions you have posed.

2. Arrange to interview two supervisors, preferably from different organizations and industries. Ask each practicing supervisor the following questions:
   a. What was your first job with your current organization?
   b. How did you find your way into a supervisory position? (For example, were you promoted from a non-supervisory position, or did you come to the position directly after your academic preparation?)
   c. What do you see as the primary satisfactions/rewards of being a supervisor or manager?
   d. How has supervising people changed since you began as a supervisor?
   e. What do you see as the downside (negative aspects) of being a supervisor or manager?
   f. What's one piece of advice you would offer to someone who wants to be a supervisor?
   g. If you were retiring, what would be next for you? (I encourage you to use probing kinds of questions to clarify their responses and to secure additional information as necessary.)

3. After completing your interviews, compare the responses you receive with the concepts in this chapter. To what degree were the interviewee's responses similar/different? How do you account for any differences?

4. As a result of completing this skills application project, do you feel more or less inclined to become a supervisor/manager? Explain.

Skills Application 1-2: Experiential Exercise—Who Are You? Who Do You Really Want to Be?

1	2	3	4	5
Courageous	Thoughtful	Smart	Honest	Resourceful
Intriguing	Daring	Fearless	Impulsive	Ordinary
Curious	Bold	Consistent	Humorous	Boring
Comforting	Intense	Dependable	Informed	Supportive
Visionary	Fun	Strong	Intelligent	Contemporary
Credible	Authentic	Informative	Romantic	Forgiving
Confident	Mature	Interesting	Innovative	Trailblazer
Influential	Genuine	Relevant	Unpredictable	Trustworthy
Surprising	Provocative	Exciting	Committed	Independent
Informed	Predictable	Timely	Brave	Unique
Dynamic	Undaunted	Focused	Solid	Results-oriented

a) From the list of adjectives, select two from each column (1, 2, 3, 4, 5) that you think best describe you.

b) Make six copies of the list above, give one copy each to six people, and ask them to circle the two adjectives in each column that best describe you and check the two items in each column that describe you least. (In our classroom experience, I have found it to be most effective if you give them the list and suggest they ponder the list for a day or two before completing the exercise. Include a variety of people in your survey, e.g., a family member, a friend, a co-worker or two, someone from a non-work group that you belong to, etc.)

c) After the survey is returned, compile the data to determine how you are viewed by others. Are the perceptions of others consistent with how you perceive yourself? Why or why not?

d) Think of the most effective (successful) supervisor whom you have ever known. Which ten traits from the list would you use to describe him or her? (Note: You are not restricted to two from each column. Just select the ten traits regardless of which column they are in.) How does your self-analysis (a) and how others perceive you (b) compare with those attributes you identified for the most effective supervisor?

e) Now identify those ten attributes that you would like to add to your toolbox or improve upon. Then develop a self-development action plan for enhancing your skills, knowledge, and abilities (SKAs). As we will emphasize throughout this text, visualize (see what it is you want to achieve), develop an action plan, and do it. Write down your self-improvement plan and refer to it on a regular basis—Plan the work! Work the plan! Make adjustments as necessary!

(NOTE: This Skills Application was developed by Professor Ed Leonard and Professor Karen Moustafa Leonard of Indiana University Purdue University Fort Wayne (IPFW) and is reproduced here with permission. © 2008.)

Skills Application 1-3: Thinking Outside the Box—How Is That Possible?

Consider the following situation: Two women apply for jobs at Community Medical Center (CMC). They look exactly alike. On their applications, they list the same last name, address, and phone number. They were born to the same parents, on the same day, same month, and same year. They attended the same schools, and listed the same people as personal references. Everything is identical. The receptionist says, "You must be twins." They say, "No."

1. How is it possible that the two women are not twins? Explain your rationale.

2. Peter Drucker said, "Making decisions is a crucial skill at every level." Do you agree with Drucker? Why or why not?

3.  Review either *The Daily Drucker* or http://www.peter-drucker.com/ to find another one or two of Drucker's practical wisdoms that relate to this skills application. Then write a one-page paper detailing what you learned from this skills application.

Skills Application 1-4: Assessing Your Toolbox—What Do I Need to Get into Supervision?

You are encouraged to carefully read the Appendix to Chapter 1—Getting Into Supervision before you begin this Skills Application.

Each employee brings a "toolbox" to work each day. The toolbox consists of skills, knowledge, abilities, and experiences. Below, we have listed eight supervisory jobs. Carefully read each one and then pick the two you are most interested in. Then:

1. Make a list of the requirements (skills, knowledge, abilities experiences) needed for those jobs.

2. Make a list of your strengths (SKAs) and compare them with the requirements for each job.

3. Determine what you need to do to add to your "toolbox" (i.e., sharpen your saw) in order to improve your chances of getting the job.

4. Outline a plan for adding those essential ingredients to your "toolbox."

5. Explain how you will put the plan into action.

6. Refer to your plan once a week to assess your progress, and make changes as required.

Opening #1: Supervisor Wanted
A manufacturer of plastic containers for the food industry has a third-shift Production Supervisor position to fill. This position will direct the daily activities of hourly production personnel to accomplish production, safety, and quality goals. The successful candidate will possess strong people skills and good communication skills and will demonstrate leadership and problem-solving techniques. An associate degree with a minimum of two years' experience in a manufacturing environment is required for this position. Experience in the plastics industry would be a plus. We

offer a competitive wage and benefits package. Interested candidates should send their resumes and salary histories to ABC.

Opening # 2: Restaurant—Management Trainee Position
A rapidly growing restaurant chain with operations in ten southeastern states is looking for motivated people to join our management training program. Previous customer service experience is required. Our extensive training program is one of the best in the nation. We are seeking dynamic, motivated, detail-oriented persons who have the potential to lead their own teams in our facilities. Must be well-organized, have the ability to multi-task, and be able to work without supervision.

We offer a competitive salary, vacation incentives, weekly bonuses, and promotion opportunity after 90 days. Send cover letter, resume, and three references to DEF.

Opening #3: Call Center Supervisor—Second Shift
A financial services company has an immediate need for a second-shift Call Center Supervisor to supervise and coordinate all second-shift collections and call center activities. This position will supervise department staff and ensure that workflow deadlines are met. Qualifications include a minimum of two years' management experience, call center experience, strong communication and decision-making skills, and the ability to effectively train and motivate staff. Must be willing to work 2 P.M. to 11 P.M. and some Saturdays. This company offers an excellent benefits package that includes medical, dental, vision, and 401(k). Qualified candidates may apply by sending a resume to GHI.

Opening #4: Inventory Control Supervisor
Responsibilities include coordinating cycle counts, analyzing and validating results, preparing and entering inventory adjustments, reviewing inventory obsolescence, ensuring accuracy of procedures manual, maintaining necessary records for regulatory

compliance, and supervising, counseling, and leading approximately five hourly associates on two shifts. Intermediate Microsoft Word and Excel knowledge, AS400 experience, excellent written communication and organizational skills, and deductive reasoning required. Associate degree or equivalent work experience required as well as at least two years of inventory and supervisory experience. Previous experience in document control and procedures writing desired. The company offers an excellent compensation and benefits package. Please forward resume and salary requirements to JKL.

Opening #5: Store Management Opportunity

We are a leader in the arts and crafts industry with eight stores in the tri-state area. Candidates must have previous retail store management experience in one of the following: supermarket chain, craft chain, mass merchant, drug chain, or building supply chain. Must be willing to relocate. Benefits include competitive salary, paid vacation, 401(k) plan, medical/dental/life insurance, merchandise discount, flexible spending plan. Qualified candidates who are self-motivated and top performers must apply online at http://www.MNO.com.

Opening #6: Manufacturing Team Leader

Area automotive supplier currently has openings for first- and second-shift Manufacturing Team Leaders. The Team Leader is responsible for planning, leading, organizing, and controlling the various production processes. The Team Leader will work closely with the Production Supervisor to coordinate job assignments, motivate employees, schedule daily production, encourage health and safety activities, and complete daily reports and data entry. High school diploma or GED, 3–6 months related experience and Workkeys scores consisting of Reading for Information (3), Locating Information (4), Teamwork (4), and Observation (4) required. Workkeys testing will be required for selected candidates without prior Workkeys scores. Pay range: $12.41 to $13.66 per hour plus overtime. For consideration, please register with the Department of Workforce Development.

Opening #7: Management

AAA large property development/management company searching for candidates who are professional and possess excellent communication and leadership skills. Qualified individuals will enter a formal training program leading to management of large apartment communities. College degree and experience helpful, but willing to train the right individual. Competitive compensation package and housing provided. If you are qualified and willing to relocate, mail or fax your resume and cover letter to: PQR.

Opening #8: Patient Financial Services Manager

Come and see why we have high physician, employee, and patient satisfaction. CMC has an opening for a full-time Patient Financial Services Manager. This position supervises, directs, and coordinates all billing and collection follow-up activities and is responsible for all PFS staff. The ideal candidate will possess a bachelor's degree and a minimum of two years' experience in a management position within an insurance company or healthcare-related environment working with accounts receivable. We offer a competitive wage and benefits package. Apply online at http://www.STU.com.

7.   These were actual advertisements appearing as recent want ads. For the sake of this exercise, we have used letters rather than the actual organization contact. Select the one that you are most interested in, and write a cover letter expressing your interest in the position. Your instructor may want to see your cover letter as a graded assignment or have you share it with a classmate—you critique his or her cover letter while he or she critiques yours. In the latter case, make constructive and cogent suggestions.

8.   If you have not done so, develop a resume. See the Appendix to this chapter for suggestions on resume development.

9.   Develop a list of questions you would ask if you were selected for a job interview.

10. Visit your college placement office now to see what services it provides students. Start your journey now—work to develop the skills and expertise desired by employers.

SKILLS DEVELOPMENT

Skill Development Module 1-1:

This is the first in a series of Skills Development Modules. Before you view the Skills Development Module video for Chapter 1, please review the discussion of the schools of management thought provided in this chapter.

1.   Most of the concepts contained in our discussion of the schools of management thought is based primarily on writing fifty or more years ago; what is the purpose of studying it today?

2.   Most organizations strive to be 'the best of the best.' Yet, those same organizations all have the two resources available, super-

visors and the people they supervise. How might you in a position of supervisory responsibility, use the ideas presented in the video to help your organization be 'the best of the best?'

3.   Supervisors must continually strive to develop new skills that enable them manager in a rapidly changing environment. How did reviewing this Skills Development Module help you to understand that how the manager applies the various theories, techniques, tools, and treats employees is the key to success?

APPENDIX: GETTING INTO SUPERVISION

Job hunting is not usually easy. The spring of 2008 was one of the worst for new graduates as many employers were cutting back their hiring plans. Some graduates expecting to get multiple offers only got one. Many college graduates modified their expectations and job search criteria due to the rocky job market. For some people, opportunities appear when they least expect them. For others, the road appears to be steep.

Many individuals are promoted to their first supervisory positions from non-supervisory jobs in the same organization. It may be in the same department or in another area. They may have formally applied for the position or had a manager recommend them. In either case, the organization made a conscious effort to promote from within. The author is familiar with many middle-aged managers who did not continually find ways to sharpen their saws. Often, they felt they had "paid their dues" by being loyal to a particular firm for a long period of time.

If you are employed while going to school, it can be tough to find the time to do an effective job search for a position outside your current firm. In addition, you will have the added burden of being discreet. Many employers take a dim view of employees who are seeking employment elsewhere; their loyalty and commitment are questioned. Do not make or receive job-search-related calls at work. Advise prospective employers to contact you at home or through the college placement office. Schedule interviews before or after work or on your days off. In today's difficult economy, do not leave your job until you have a new one and then give, if possible, two weeks' notice. We don't want you to burn any bridges; leave on good terms.

Consider the situation of one former student who stated that she had sent her resume to a blind advertisement—neither the firm nor its address was listed. Her immediate supervisor informed her that he had received her resume and was wondering why she was unhappy with her current position. She had applied for a job similar to the one she currently had, but the advertisement listed broader responsibilities and sounded challenging. She was at a loss for words. She later left the organization, not for a better job but because she felt the supervisor never gave her a chance after that.

Where to Look for Information

Students in need of more detailed information, additional career opportunities, and salary information can refer to the latest *Occupational Outlook Handbook* or the *Career Guide to Industries* published by the U.S. Department of Labor (the *Handbook* and the *Career Guide* are available online at http://www.bls.gov/ovo and http://www.bls.gov/coc/cg). *Planning Job Choices: A Guide to Career Planning, the Job Search, Graduate School, and Work-Related Education*, published by the College Placement Council, contains information on successful job search strategies, how to research companies, what employers really want from applicants, interviewing techniques, networking, and finding additional employer information. Check with your college placement office and review these publications before beginning your job search.

Many students find that networking is a useful strategy. One study found that employee referrals were the single largest source—30 to 40 percent—of new hires. That is at least double the number of people hired through job listings.[54] This means meeting and talking with personal and professional colleagues and friends to help you identify potential opportunities. Talk to people you know through school, church, family, or other associations to gather information and referrals. "I'm finishing my degree in June and am thinking about making a change," you might say. "Your company has a reputation for being a good place to work. Do you know of any opportunities there?" Such an approach could be a good networking start.

A visit to the library or the Internet will turn up many sources of information about an organization, such as annual reports, trade magazines, and newspaper articles. This information will give you a good picture of the company's financial position, management style, and future. Increasingly, employers list jobs online and describe their products and services on company Web sites. Figure 1.11 contains a partial listing of online services. You can submit your resume to databases that feed search engines used by employers to find candidates. My students enjoy looking at the *Business Week* listing of the best employers for entry-level workers. (For the complete rankings go to businessweek.com/go/07/ranking.)

FIGURE 1.11 Sources for Online Job Searches

This list of online sources is far from complete. There are always new bulletin boards, databases, and job search information on the Internet. Once you become familiar with the Internet job search process, you can access information quickly. If you need help with your Internet search, speak with the staff at the college or local public library. Enjoy the journey!

AARP (http://www.aarp.org/money/careers) offers tips to assist with career transitions. This site includes information on starting your own business, charting a career change, reentering the job market, and coping with work-life issues. Click on the link "How to Find a Career Counselor or Coach" for tips on choosing an advisor to help you find that new career or job.

About.com (http://careerplanning.about.com) has a variety of self-assessments, career tests, and other valuable information to help you to determine whether you have the skills, interests, personality, and values necessary for your intended career.

America's Job Bank (http://www.ajb.dni.us) provides job-market information for employers and job seekers and enables employers to register job openings.

Bureau of Labor Statistics (http://stats.bls.gov) offers data and economic information, including wage/salary surveys for various job classifications.

CareerBuilder.com (http://www.careerbuilder.com) allows you to search for jobs or careers using thirteen different criteria, or lets you post resumes so that employers with job openings can find you. It also provides salary information and tips on job hunting and resume writing.

CareerJournal.com (http://www.careerjournal.com) is maintained by the *Wall Street Journal*, and you can browse sections on salary and hiring information, job hiring advice, and managing your career.

Monster.Com (http://www.monster.com) is one of the largest online recruiting sites.

Salary.com (http://www.salary.com) allows you to research job titles, descriptions, and salaries in your area.

SnagAJob (http://www.SnagAJob.com) is another online source for information.

While many job opportunities can be found in the classifieds and on Web sites, the vast majority of positions never get advertised. We suggest that you make a list of organizations for which you would like to work. Most firms with Web sites prefer e-recruiting. Complete their online application and e-mail your cover letter and resume. Make sure you have correctly spelled the name and title of the person who is to receive your letter. Most recruiters and corporate HR professionals tell us that a well-written cover letter saves them time. The cover letter gives the reader a quick overview of you, your history, and your expectations. Usually it is the only factor that determines whether the resume gets read or not.

Many colleges have an Office of Career Services to assist students and alumni in the job-search process. Some colleges coach students in resume writing, the art of interviewing (particularly telephone interviewing), and anything else their students need to know to pass the recruiting process. You need a professional resume. Today's word-processing programs have made it easier to develop a resume by offering fill-in-the-blank templates. Check out the Microsoft Office Template Gallery at http://officeupdate.microsoft.com/templategallery. At our last check, there were more than 90 templates to choose from. A word of caution: E-mail is now the preferred format for receiving resumes and cover letters. Send your resume and cover letter as a Microsoft Word document. Practically everyone uses Word. Check the organization's requirements carefully because some companies will not accept resumes submitted as attachments. Our students have found it effective to copy the resume and cover letter from Word and paste it to Notepad. Save and copy it from Notepad to your e-mail program. Before you send it, e-mail it to yourself so you can double-check the formatting and appearance.

Make Yourself More Valuable

In general, we believe the best way to get a supervisory position and/or to prosper in your current position is to find ways to make yourself more valuable. Always try to improve yourself. For example, if you are a student, make yourself available for internships and co-ops, or perhaps volunteer for some type of meaningful activity. Volunteer experiences in community groups can increase your networking opportunities, give you ideas and practical experiences, and help you become more comfortable working with and leading groups of diverse people. Get involved in one or more student organizations on your campus. The benefits of applying your expertise and using opportunities to enhance your communication and leadership skills are invaluable. We want you to be successful.

Remember, too, that continuing your educational preparation is an ongoing challenge. Finishing an academic degree is only a start; consider going further by enrolling in graduate study degree and non-degree programs that may enhance your technical/managerial/supervisory knowledge. Increasingly, colleges and universities are offering distance learning or online programs that can be taken at a remote location via computer.

Look in the mirror. What are your SKAs that you have in your toolbox? What experiences do you have that can add value to the organization? How might the SKAs and experiences be matched to a particular job opportunity? Remember that when applying for any position, particularly a supervisory position, you must discover the specific needs of the hiring organization and show how you can add value to the firm. Our message to you: "Be assertive enough, bold enough, and knock on enough doors (see the accompanying 'Supervisory Tips box')."[55]

SUPERVISORY TIPS
Career Tips: Keep on Knocking!

1. Look for a job in the right places.
   - Network
   - College placement office
   - Bulletin boards or Web sites
   - Newspaper classifieds
   - Job fairs
   - Recruiting firms
   - Temporary-help agencies
   - Individual employers
2. Think like an employer.
   Ask yourself the following question: "If you were the one hiring for a position, what would you want to see in a resume?"
   - Who are you?
   - What do you know?
   - What have you done?
   - What have you accomplished?
   - What can you do to add value to this organization?
   - Who can give you a good recommendation?
3. Prepare for the interview.
   - Research the company.
   - What business is this company really in?
   - What does the company's past, present, and future look like?
   - What can you learn by reading its annual report?
   - Who are the company's major competitors, and how do they compare?
   - What is the companys reputation?
   - Is the company a leader in the field?
   - Is the company regarded as a good place to work? Why or why not?
   - Find the gatekeepers, those people who may be in touch with those doing the hiring.
4. Be proactive.
   - Clean up your social networking Web pages if you have some (some companies check).
   - Prepare your resume with the job you are applying for in mind.
   - Prepare short statements on how your experience and training match the job. Rehearse prior to the interview. Prepare mentally for what the interviewer may ask.
   - Ask questions about the job or the company (e.g., Which qualifications are most important for this position? What are the expectations of the ideal person for this job?)
   - Listen carefully during the interview. Watch the interviewer's body language and make sure your own conveys interest and enthusiasm.
   - Sell yourself—demonstrate how you can use your SKAs to help the organization achieve its goals.
   - Use each minute of the interview to sell yourself: Listen! Ask questions! Answer the questions that are asked!
5. Follow up.
   - Write a thank-you note to the interviewer(s).
6. Continuously seek ways to "sharpen your saw." I suggest that students do a couple of practice interviews to gain experience.

ENDNOTES

1. "Economic Advantage," the *Wall Street Journal* (June 9, 2008), p. A4. Report of data from the Pew Research Center survey conducted May 21–25, 2008.

2. "Economic Body Blows," *BusinessWeek* (June 9, 2008), p. 2, and James C. Cooper, "Housing: The Recovery Wrecker," p. 8.

3. Whether the economy is in a recession or a depression is subject to debate. I have provided the following to help you understand some of the terms that are commonly used in the popular press and in the classroom. A recession indicates a slowdown in economic activity. By one definition, it is six straight months of declining GDP. A longer recession is known as a depression. GDP (Gross Domestic Product) is the market value of all the goods and services produced in the U.S. Consumer confidence is the measure of optimism consumers have about the performance of the economy. Several groups publish results of their surveys. Inflation is an increase in the price of a representative basket of goods and services. Deflation is when prices are declining over time. Stagflation is a condition where slow economic growth and relatively high unemployment—a period of stagflation—accompanied by a rise in prices or inflation. At the time of this writing, I would concur that we are experiencing stagflation and on the verge of a recession. Jobless recovery is when the economy grows steadily but job creation is flat. Economic headwinds are economic forces that make it difficult for an organization or individual to succeed. For additional information see Joseph E. Stiglitz, "StagflationRedux," *Inc. Magazine* (June 2008), pp. 75–75; and Economics.About.com, www.investopedia.com, and other economic databases.

4. Health insurance premiums have outpaced inflation for the past ten years. In 2006, only 61 percent of the workforce had employer-provided health insurance. The average expense to employers for a health savings account plan was $5,679 and $7,352 for a preferred provided plan. See "Numbers," *BusinessWeek* (December 10, 2007), p. 13 and data from the U.S. Bureau of Census.

5. Steve Bates, "Many Employees Itching to Leave," *SHRM Home* (September 16, 2005). The survey report released November 16, 2005, by the SHRM and CareerJournal.com showed that 44 percent of respondents were actively searching for a job—going for interviews and prepared to leave their current employer if offered a position elsewhere. Thirty-five percent said they were passive job seekers—taking steps to see what opportunities were available by posting their resumes online and browsing classified ads but not yet certain whether they wanted to leave.

6. "Majority of Workers Believe Their Bosses Lack Integrity, Fairness," AccountingWeb (http://www.accountingweb.com) (January 25, 2005). The representative nationwide survey conducted by Harris Interactive, Inc. for Age Wave found that only 36 percent of workers said they believed top managers acted with honesty and integrity. Twenty-nine percent believe that management cares about advancing employee skills, while one-third of all workers feel they have reached a dead end with their jobs.

7. For detailed findings from the IPSOS-Reid Poll, see *BusinessWeek* (February 25, 2002), p. 108. Median pay for the CEOs of the nation's 100 largest companies was $17.9 million in 2005. See "Special Report: Executive Compensation," *USA Today* (April 10, 2006), pp. 1B–3B.

8. See "Special Report: The Best & Worst Managers of the Year," *BusinessWeek* (January 10, 2005), pp. 55–86. Also see Timothy D. Schellhardt, "Off the Ladder: Want to Be a Manager? Many People Say No, Calling Job Miserable," the *Wall Street Journal* (April 4, 1997), p. A1; Joe B. Hill, "Strategies of Successful Managers," *Supervision* (February 2005), pp. 10–13; Joseph Cottringer, "Being the Kind of Supervisor Every Employer Loves," *Supervision* (June 2005), pp. 8–10; Patricia M. Buhler, "Managing in the New Millennium," *Supervision* (July 2005), pp. 20–22. For a discussion of the problems of developing universal agreement on management approaches, see the classic article by Harold Koontz, "The Management Theory Jungle Revisited," *Academy of Management Review* (Volume 5, 1980), pp. 175–88.

9. An overview of the evolution of management thought is provided in J. Baughman, *The History of American Management* (Englewood Cliffs, NJ: Prentice-Hall, 1969); C. George, *The History of Management Thought* (Englewood Cliffs, NJ: Prentice-Hall, 1972); and Allen C. Bluedorn, ed., "A Special Book Review Section on the Classics of Management," *Academy of Management Review* (Volume 11, April 1986). The principles of scientific management are described in Frederick W. Taylor, *Shop Management* (New York: Harper & Brothers, 1911); Frank G. Gilbreth and Lillian M. Gilbreth, *Applied Motion Study* (New York: Sturgis & Walton, 1917); and Edwin A. Locke, "The Ideas of Frederick W. Taylor: An Evaluation," *Academy of Management Review* (Volume 7, January 1982), pp. 22–23. See Henri Fayol, *General and Industrial Management*, trans. Constance Storrs (London: Pitman Publishing Corp. 1949), for the functional approach to describing and analyzing management principles. Additional information on the human relations/behavioral science school of thought can be found in E. Mayo, *The Human Problems of Industrial Civilization* (New York: Macmillan, 1933); Fritz J. Roethlisberger and W. J. Dickson, *Management and the Worker* (Boston: Harvard University Press, 1939); A. Maslow, "A Theory of Human Motivation," *Psychological Review* (Volume 50, July 1943), pp. 370–96; D. McGregor, *The Human Side of Enterprise* (New York: McGraw-Hill, 1960); and J. A. Sonnenfeld, "Shedding Light on the Hawthorne Studies," *Journal of Occupational Behavior* (Volume 6, 1985), pp. 111–30. For an overview of the quantitative/systems approaches to management, see Andrew J. DuBrin, *Essentials of Management*, 8th Ed. (Mason, OH: Southwestern/Thomson 2006), chapter 6.

10. For a most interesting insight into the principles of scientific management, see *Cheaper by the Dozen*. Either of the versions will provide you with many laughs as the family puts the principles of scientific management into practice. The movies were based on the lives of Professors Lillian and Frank Gilbreths who were disciples of Taylor.

11. Miriam Jordan, "Factories Turn to Refugee Workers," the *Wall Street Journal* (May 6, 2008), p. A1; Dave Montgomery, "Illegal Immigration in U.S. Bringing out 'Deep-Seated' Anger." *The Jacksonville, FL Times-Union* (August 19, 2007), pp. A1, A6; Alan Fram, "Hispanics Feel Fallout of Immigration Debate," *The Fort Wayne, Indiana Journal Gazette* (December 15, 2007), p. 8C; Edward Iwata, "Immigrant Business Can Have Wide Economic Impact," *USA Today* (November 16, 2005), p. 1B. Iwata's article reports on the study by noted Harvard Business School Professor Michael Porter.

12. Statistics and projections included in this and other sections are drawn from James C. Franklin, "An Overview of BLS Projections to

2016," *Monthly Labor Review Online*, (November 2007), Vol. 130, No. 11. (Also see "Employment Projections: 2006–2016 Summary," Bureau of Labor Statistics (December 4, 2007). For more current projections, see http://www.bls.gov/emp/emppub01.htm. The 2008–2009 data will be available after May 2009 at http://www.bls.gov/emp/optd/home.htm. To access the Census Bureau's population estimates go to http://factfinder.census.gov.

13. See Anne Houlihan, "When Gen-X is In Charge," *Supervision* (April 2008), pp.11–13; and Houlihan, "The New Melting Pot: How to Effectively Lead Different Generations in the Workplace," *Supervision* (September 2007), pp. 10–12; and James A. Johnson and John Lopes, "The Intergenerational Workforce, Revisited," *Organizational Development Journal* (Spring 2008, 26,1). Much of the information on the various generators was adapted from Andrea Healey, "Figuring Out Generation X," *ACA News* (February 1998), pp. 10–15. Workforce classifications described in this article were from Ann S. Clurman and J. Walker Smith, *Rocking the Ages: The Yankelovich Report on Generational Marketing* (New York: HarperBusiness, 1997). See also Bruce Tulgan, "Managing Generation X," *HR Focus* (November 1995), pp. 22–23; and Julius Steiner, "Six Steps to Guaranteeing Generation Y Productivity," *Supervision* (July 2007), pp. 6–7. See our student support Web site for a more comprehensive generational listing.

14. Neil Howe and William Strauss, *Millennials Rising: The Next Generation* (New York: Vintage Books, 2000), p. 45. See Sommer Kehrli and Trudy Sopp, "Managing Generation Y: Stop Resisting and Start Embracing the Challenges Generation Y Brings to the Workplace," *HR Magazine* (May 2006), pp. 113–119.

15. Julie Bennett, "Women Get a Boost Up That Tall Leadership Ladder," the *Wall Street Journal* (June 10, 2008), p. D6. Also see Alice Eagly and Linda Carli, "Women and the Labyrinth of Leadership," *The Harvard Business Review* (September 2007).

16. Carol Hymowitz, "On Diversity, America Isn't Putting Its Money Where Its Mouth Is," the *Wall Street Journal* (February 25, 2008), p. B1.

17. Over ten million single mothers living with children under 18 years old and 55 percent of women with infant children are in the labor force. See http://www.census.gov/population/socdemo/hh-fam/tabFM-2.pdf for additional workforce data. Also review the Census Bureau Facts and Figures that were prepared to commemorate Mother's Day (May 11, 2008). The authors believe that it is imperative that employers adopt family-friendly policies and procedures to accommodate these worker needs.

18. From the Families and Work Institute as reported by Alison Ashton, "When It's Work vs. Family, Work Usually Wins," *Working Mother* (December 2001/January 2002), p. 10. Also see Sue Shellenbarger, "How Stay-at-Home Moms Are Filling an Executive Niche," the *Wall Street Journal* (April 30, 2008), p. D1. Also see U.S. Bureau of Labor Statistics Report (March 2007); Sharon Jayson, "New Moms Taking Less Time Off with Babies," *USA Today* (November 14, 2005), p. 5D; Stacey Hirsh, "Flex-Time 'No-Brainer' for Firms," *Baltimore Sun* as reported in the *Fort Wayne, Indiana Journal Gazette* (November 2, 2004), p. 7B; Joanne Gordon, "Family Champion," *Working Mother* (October 2001), pp. 84–87; and the "100 Best Companies for Working Mothers." See www.WorkingMother.com for information on the strategies and programs companies use to help employees balance work and life.

19. Christopher Farrell, "Is the Workplace Getting Raunchier?" *BusinessWeek* (March 17, 2008), p. 19.

20. See "Legal Report," *SRHM*, April 2008, p.1 for a list of recent class-action litigations against employers. Also see "Boeing to Pay $72.5 Million to Women in Sex Bias Suit," *The Jacksonville, FL Times-Union* (November 11, 2005), p. A14.

21. See 2006 American Community Survey Date Profile Highlights (http://factfinder.census,gov) and Jason L. Riley, "Keep the Immigrants: Deport the Multiculturalists," the *Wall Street Journal*, May 15, 2008, p. D1.

22. See "Review & Outlook: Tongue Tied," the *Wall Street Journal* (July 29, 2005), p. W13; and Maureen Minehan, "Future Focus," *HR Magazine* (1998 50th Anniversary Edition), pp. 86–87.

23. Herb Greenberg, CEO of Caliper Corp., a Princeton, NJ–based consulting firm, has undertaken a multi-year global study of leadership qualities in men and women. Preliminary results were reported by Ann Pomeroy, "Executive Briefing: Female Executives Lead Differently From Men," *HR Magazine* (June 2005), p. 24. Also see Steve Bates, "Women vs. Men: Which Make Better Leaders?" *SHRM Home* (November 11, 2005), and Del Jones, "What Glass Ceiling?" *USA Today* (July 20, 1999), p. 18.

24. See the Bureau of Labor Statistics (www.bls.gov) to access the specific data regarding job loss, unemployment, turnover, and other employment and career outlook information.

25. "Numbers," *BusinessWeek* (March 24, 2008), p. 15. Also see the National Center for Educational Statistics and the Bureau of Labor Statistics for additional data on educational attainment of the workforce.

26. See Bob Fernandez, "Underemployment Stems Economic Growth," as reported in the *Fort Wayne, Indiana News-Sentinel* (September 6, 2004), p. 12.

27. U.S. Census Bureau information reported by Bill Leonard, "College Education Pays Off Big Time for Workers," *SHRM Home* (March 31, 2005).

28. As reported by Mike Klesius, "Power of 50," *AARP Bulletin* (September 2007), p. 35.

29. "Employment Projections: 2006–2016 Summary," Bureau of Labor Statistics (December 4, 2007). Also see SHRM/Rutgers Line®: Leading Indicator of National Employment for their monthly report of employment, new-hire, and recruiting issues.

30. Ibid.

31. Ibid.

32. See "Anheuser Discloses Early-Retirement Plans," the *Wall Street Journal* (August 13, 2008), p. B6; Heidi N. Moore, "Will Dollar Rise Hurt Mergers?" the *Wall Street Journal* (August 12, 2008), p. C3; David Kesmodel and Matthew Karnitschnig, "InBev UnCorks Anheuser Takeover Bid," the *Wall Street Journal* (June 12, 2008), pp. A1, A14.

33. See William Nobrega, "Why India Will Beat China," *BuinessWeek on line Politics & Economics* (July 22, 2008); Dexter Roberts, "China's Brands: Damaged Goods," *BusinessWeek* (September 24, 2007), p. 47; Richard J. Newman, "Can America Keep Up? A Special Report on What America Must Do To Keep Up with Roaring Economies Like Those of China, India, and South Korea," *U.S. News & World Report* (March 27, 2006), pp. 48–56; Ted Fishman, "Made in Asia," *USA Today* (November 15, 2005), p. 13A; "China Changes Everything," *Inc. Magazine* (March 2005), pp. 70–84; and *China, Inc: How the Rise of the Next Superpower Challenges America and the World* (New York: Scribner/Simon & Schuster, 2005). Also see Dianne Nilsen, "Managing Globally," *HR Magazine* (August 2005), pp. 111–115.

34. See Bill Powell, "Suburbia Comes to China," *Fortune* (August 18, 2008), pp. 120–128; Reena Jana, Frederick Balfour, and Oriana Schwindt, "Learning From the Olympics," *BusinessWeek* (August 18, 2008), pp. 036–049; Andrew Batson and Shai Oster, "China's Power Woes

Undermine Growth," the *Wall Street Journal* (August 12, 2008), p. A17; Austin Ramzy, "Postcard: Beijing," *Time* (August 11, 2008), p. 9; Pete Engardio, "Can the U.S. Bring Jobs Back From China," BusinessWeek (June 30, 2008), pp. 039–043;

35. Adapted from "Conversations with Tom Peters," *Quality Digest* (November 1996), pp. 37–38. Peters's books *In Search of Excellence, Passion for Excellence, Thriving on Chaos,* and *Liberation Management* ranked at or near the top of *The New York Times* bestseller list.

36. For information on outsourcing, see the *BusinessWeek* cover story "The Real Cost of Offshoring," (June 18, 2007), pp. 28–31; and C.K. Prahalad, "The Art of Outsourcing," the *Wall Street Journal* (June 8, 2005), p. A14; and Prahalad, *The Fortune at the Bottom of the Pyramid: Eradicating Poverty Through Profits* (Philadelphia: Wharton, 2004). Also see John Graham, "Outsourcing a Company's Marketing: A Better Way to Meet Competitive Challenges," *Supervision* (May 2007), pp. 15–17; H. James Harrington, "Rightsizing, Not Downsizing: Layoffs are Costlier Than You Think," *Quality Digest* (July 2005), p. 12; and "Exploring the Future of the Workplace: Offshoring," *SHRM Research*, no. 2 (2004).

37. See Merrill Goozner, "Longtime Temporary Employees Are Rebelling," reprint of article in *St. Louis Post-Dispatch* that originally was published in the *Chicago Tribune* (July 1, 1999), p. C7. Also see Aaron Bernstein, "A Leg Up for the Lowly Temp," *BusinessWeek* (June 21, 1999), pp. 102–3.

38. From "Workweek," the *Wall Street Journal* (June 8, 1999), p. A1.

39. See Stacey Hirsh, op.cit.; and Bill Leonard, "Employees Want More Quality Time with Families," *HR Magazine* (June 1999), p. 28.

40. Adapted from Archie B. Carroll and Ann K. Buchholtz, *Business & Society: Ethics and Stakeholder Management,* 7th Edition (Cengage/South-Western, 2009), chapter 2. Also see, Carroll, "The Pyramid of Corporate Social Responsibility,: *Business Horizons* (July-August 1991), p. 39–48.

    Also see, Adrienne Fox, "Corporate Social Responsibility Pays Off," *HR Magazine* (August 2007), pp. 42–47; and Fox, "Be An Insider On Social Responsibility," *HR Magazine* (February 2008), pp. 49–51.

    After a hiatus, *Business Ethics* returned as an online magazine (http://www.business-ethics.com). View the magazine to keep abreast of the critical issues in CSR. Also review the listing of the 100 Best Corporate Citizens.

41. See Aliah D. Wright, "Creating Sustainable Environs at Work," *SHRM Home* (August 4, 2008). Wright quotes from the following studies: *2008 Corporate Sustainability Employee Study* conducted by Fresh Marketing; *2008 MetLife Foundation/Civic Ventures Encore Career Survey* conducted by Peter D. Hart Research Associates Inc.

42. Archie B. Carroll, "In Search of the Moral Manager," *Business Horizons* (March/April 1987), pp. 7–15. Also see Archie B. Carroll and Ann K. Buchholtz, *Business and Society—Ethics and Stakeholder Management, 7th Ed.* (Mason, OH: Southwestern/Thomson 2006), chapter 7. Also see Reni Trudel and June Cotte, "Does Being Ethical Pay?" *The Wall Street Journal* (May 12, 2008), p.R1; Kunal Basu and Guido Palazzo, "Corporate Social Responsibility: A Process Model of Sensemaking," *Academy of Management Review* (Vol. 33, Is. 1, January 2008), pp. 122–136; Frank C. Bucaro, "If Good Ethics is Good Business, What's the Problem?" *Supervision* (June 2007), pp. 6–7; Kathryn Taylor, "Do the Right Thing," *HR Magazine* (February 2005), pp. 99–102; Linda Wasmer Andrews, "The Nexus of Ethics," *HR Magazine* (August 2005), pp. 53–57; Sue Shellenbarger, "How and Why We Lie at the Office," the *Wall Street Journal* (March 24, 2005), p. D1; and Roderick M. Kramer

and Karen S. Cook, eds, *Trust and Distrust in Organizations* (New York: RSF Publications, 2004).See Becky Manley, "IPFW Helps Local Habitat Build 1st Green Home," *The Fort Wayne, Indiana Journal Gazette* (June 1, 2008), p. 3c. For more information, contact Don Cross, executive director of Habitat for Humanity.

43. Go to www.shrm.org to see a listing of the expectations, responsibilities and professional code of conduct for Human Resource (HR) professionals.

44. See Becky Manley, "IPFW Helps Local Habitat Build 1st Green Home," *The Fort Wayne, Indiana Journal Gazette* (June 1, 2008), p. 3c. For more information, contact Don Cross, executive director of Habitat for Humanity.

45. See Kathy Gurchiek, "Workplace Violence on the Upswing," *HR Magazine* (July 2005), pp. 27–32; Christine M. Pearson, Lynn M. Andersson, and Christine L. Porath, "Assessing and Attacking Workplace Incivility," *Organizational Dynamics*, 29, 2 (2000), pp. 123–37; Jenny McCune, "Civility Counts," *Management Review* (March 2000), pp. 6–8; and Michael A. Verespej, "A Call for Civility," *Industry Week* (February 12, 2001), p. 17.

46. Robert M. Bramson, *Coping with Difficult People* (New York: Dell Publishing Company, 1989).

47. Tim Rutledge, *Getting Engaged: The New Workplace Loyalty*, Mattanie Press (October 2005). Also see Kay Greasley, et al., "Understanding Empowerment from an Employee Perspective: What Does It Mean and Do They Want It?" *Team Performance Management* (Vol. 14, Is.1/2, 2008); Nancy R. Lockwood, "Leveraging Employee Engagement for Competitive Advantage," *HR Magazine* (March 2007), p. 11; John Gibbons, "Employee Engagement: A Review of Current Research and Its Implications," *The Conference Board of New York* (November 2006), pp. 1–18; Gerald H. Seijts and Dan Crin, "The Ten C's of Employee Engagement," *Ivey Business Journal* (Vol. 70, No. 4, March/April 2006), pp. 1–5; and Alison M. Konrad, "Engaging Employees through High-Involvement Work Practices," *Ivey Business Journal* (Vol. 70, No. 4, March/April 2006), pp. 6–11.

48. See *Employee Engagement: A Review of Current Research and Its Implications* (New York: The Conference Board, November 2006), pp.1–18. Also see, *2008 Employee Engagement Report* (New York: Blessing White Research, April 2008); and Patricia Soldati, "Employee Engagement: What Exactly Is It?" *Management-Issues on line* (March 8, 2007).

49. A 1994 survey indicated that 75 percent of employers had incorporated some means of employee involvement to empower employees. For another twist on the employee involvement issue, see Mary E. Pivec and Howard Z. Robbins, "Employee Involvement Remains Controversial," *HR Magazine* (November 1996), pp. 145–50.

50. The statement "As long as you live, keep learning to live" is from Seneca as quoted in Burton E. Stevenson, *The Home Book of Quotations, Classical and Modern* (10th ed.; New York: Dodd, Mead, 1967), p. 1131.

51. See Peter Senge, *The Fifth Discipline: The Art and Practice of the Learning Organization* (New York: Doubleday, 1990), p. 14. Also see Senge et al., *The Fifth Discipline Fieldbook: Strategies and Tools for Building a Learning Organization* (New York: Doubleday, 1994).

52. Stephen R. Covey, *The Seven Habits of Highly Effective People: Restoring the Character Ethic* (New York: Simon & Schuster, 1989), p. 287. Also see Covey's *Principle-Centered Leadership: Strategies for Personal and Professional Effectiveness* (Bellevue: Simon & Schuster, 1992) and *First Things First: To Live, to Love, to Learn, to Leave a Legacy,* (New York: Simon & Schuster, 1994).

53. Ibid., p. 288.

54. As reported in Ann Harrington, "Make That Switch," *Fortune* (February 4, 2002), p. 162. Also see Marcus Buckingham, "The Strong Shall Inherit the Earth," *Fast Company* (August 2005), p. 89. Gallup Leadership poll asked "What internal strengths will help you achieve success?" Only 41 percent of the people believed that focusing on strengths was the key to success.

55. See Robert D. Ramsey, "The Seven Critical Choices that Shape Your Career," *Supervision* (August 2007), pp. 10–12; and Ramsey, "Should You Go Back to School," *Supervision* (July 2005), pp. 3–4; and "Ten Career-Boosting Additions for your Professional Bookshelf," *Supervision* (August 2005), pp. 8–9. For a discussion of what some laid-off workers have done to increase their chances of success, see Kris Maher, "Laid-Off Workers Turn to Web For Job Search Advice, Support," the *Wall Street Journal* (November 5, 2002), p. B8.

CHAPTER 2

(The Managerial Functions)

After studying this chapter, you will be able to:

1 Summarize the difficulties supervisors face in fulfilling managerial roles.

2 Explain why effective supervisors should have a variety of skills.

3 Define management and discuss how the primary managerial functions are interrelated.

4 Discuss the important characteristics of the supervisor as team leader.

5 Explain the difference between management and leadership.

6 Discuss the concept of authority as a requirement of any managerial position.

7 Describe the types of power potentially available to the supervisor.

8 Explain the need for coordination and cooperation and how they depend on the proper performance of the managerial functions.

9 Explain how labor unions affect the management functions.

YOU MAKE THE CALL!

Charlotte Kelly is the evening shift admitting service team leader for Pine Village Community Medical Center (CMC). Pine Village is a 180-bed facility located in a small southern city approximately 70 miles from its nearest competitor. (Review Figure 1.8 in Chapter one prior to reading about Charlotte's journey.)

When Charlotte graduated from nursing school 30 years ago, nursing jobs were plentiful, and she did not need a B.S. degree to become certified as a Registered Nurse (R.N.) Charlotte began as a cardiac care nurse at a hospital in Greenville, South Carolina, where she met her future husband and began a family. Shortly after her youngest child graduated from high school, Charlotte's husband was tragically killed in an automobile accident. She moved to Pine Village to be near her sister and her family. At that time, nursing jobs were scarce, but CMC was looking for someone to be the admitting department's evening shift team leader, and Charlotte accepted the position. As her children were growing up, Charlotte served in various volunteer-type positions, which gave her a chance to hone her clerical and record-keeping skills. As a shift team leader, she assumed some supervisory responsibilities, but she had limited authority and was not part of the medical center's management team. The admitting department's supervisor was Patricia Graham.

Shortly after arriving at CMC, Charlotte began attending classes at the local community college. She received a certificate in medical records technology and decided to pursue an associate's degree in supervision and organizational leadership. With work requirements, she was able to attend only on a part-time basis. The supervision classes were taught by instructors with relevant work experience. Charlotte's favorite instructor was Fred Stinson, a middle-aged supervisor at a local company who incorporated many personal "real-world" stories into his classes. Mr. Stinson usually started each class with a current problem or issue that required students to interact and develop their own supervisory perspectives. He was not afraid to tell them stories of how he made some mistakes along the way and how he used each as a learning opportunity. As he said many times, "I learned what not to do and overcame adversity through creativity." Charlotte liked this "team" or "collaborative" approach to learning because her fellow classmates brought a variety of experiences to the class and they learned from each other.

Late Wednesday afternoon, her boss, Patricia Graham, summoned Charlotte to her office. To her surprise, Bob Murphy, vice president of administration, was also present. Murphy began the conversation. "Charlotte, we are very pleased with the job you've done as a team leader on the evening shift," he said. "You are an excellent role model and a good listener. You have a reputation as someone who expects the best out of people and does the things necessary to enable them to be the best they can be. Effective Monday morning, we want you to become the ER (emergency room) supervisor. You've earned a promotion to management, and this is a big step, but we know that you will be able to handle this assignment, even though you haven't worked in ER previously. This position reports to me, and I'll be available to help if any problems arise." Graham added, "Charlotte, you've done such a good job of cross-training your people and delegating, we'd like you to recommend your replacement."

When Charlotte returned to her department, she was both exhilarated and a bit sobered by this event. "Wow!" she thought to herself. "This is the culmination of a six-year odyssey. It's been hard, but I knew after taking Mr. Stinson's class that I wanted to be a supervisor someday. Professor Stinson is still my coach. He invites small groups of us in for coffee and Danish. We get a chance to network, tell our 'war stories,' and stretch our minds on management-related issues. We all work in different organizations and get to see that everyone has problems, i.e., opportunities. He continually encourages us and shows us how to help each other. Patricia Graham has been a great mentor, too. She helped me to navigate the organization, introduced me to others, provided guidance and support, and encouraged me to be creative —'Think outside the box.' She shows interest in each employee and in increasing their skills, knowledge, and abilities. Both of them will still be there for me!"

On Friday afternoon, Charlotte reflected on the events of the past two days. She had learned that Amy Talmadge had been fired as ER supervisor. The ER department had become the butt of many employee jokes, and turnover had been extremely high. She also learned that Amy Talmadge had the reputation of being an autocratic, demanding, and insensitive supervisor. She expected her employees to do as she demanded and, at times, she was known to have criticized and embarrassed people in public. The ER department consists of a very diverse group of employees, which apparently added to Amy's difficulties.

Sitting at her desk, Charlotte contemplated the situation. "I know that my past successes as team leader are irrelevant. Relying on yesterday's skill set will not work on Monday morning. I know that I will need to be proactive and cautious. I've learned a lot from Patricia Graham and my instructors, but I wonder if I've got the right stuff to be in this position. Do I really want all of the headaches, responsibilities, and pressures that a supervisor has to deal with? I know some things not to do, but I'm not certain that I can make the move from team leader to supervisor. What should I do and where should I begin?"

YOU MAKE THE CALL!

AMIR BAHADORI

1 **Summarize the difficulties supervisors face in fulfilling managerial roles.**

The Person in the Middle

The supervisory position is a difficult and demanding role. Supervisors are "people in the middle"—the principal links between higher-level managers and employees. See Figure 1.5 in Chapter 1 for an overview of the difficult challenges faced by supervisors. A supervisor is a first-level manager, that is, a manager in charge of entry-level and other departmental employees. Every organization, whether a retail store, fast-food restaurant, manufacturing firm, hospital, or government agency, has someone who fills this role.[1]

Throughout this textbook, we use the terms *worker*, *employee*, *associate*, *team member*, and *subordinate* interchangeably to refer to individuals who report to supervisors or managers. Regardless of the term used, employees may view their supervisors as the management of the organization, since the supervisor is their primary contact with management. Employees expect a supervisor to be technically competent and to be a good leader who can show them how to get the job done.

The supervisor must also be a competent subordinate to higher-level managers. In this role, the supervisor must be a good follower. Moreover, the supervisor is expected to maintain satisfactory relationships with supervisors in other departments. Therefore, a supervisor's relationship to other supervisors is that of a colleague who must cooperate and must coordinate his or her department's efforts with those of others in order to reach the overall goals of the organization.

In general, the position of any supervisor has two main requirements. First, the supervisor must have a good working knowledge of the jobs to be performed. Second, and more significant, the supervisor must be able to manage the department. It is the supervisor's managerial competence that usually determines the effectiveness of his or her performance.

2 **Explain why effective supervisors should have a variety of skills.**

Managerial Skills Make the Difference

Most organizations have some supervisors who appear to be under constant pressure and continuously do the same work as their subordinates. They are getting by, although they feel overburdened. These supervisors endure long hours, may be devoted to their jobs, and are willing to do everything themselves. They want to be effective, but they seldom have enough time to supervise. Other supervisors appear to be on top of their jobs, and their departments run smoothly and in an orderly fashion. These supervisors find time to sit at their desks at least part of the day, and they keep their paperwork up to date. What is the difference?

Of course, some supervisors are more capable than others, just as some mechanics are better than others. If we compare two maintenance supervisors who are equally good mechanics, have similar equipment under their care, and operate under approximately the same conditions, why might one be more effective than the other? The answer is that effective supervisors manage their departments in a manner that gets the job done through their people instead of doing the work themselves. The difference between a good supervisor and a poor one, assuming that their technical skills are similar, is the difference in their managerial skills and how they apply them.

The managerial aspects of the supervisor's position too often have been neglected in the selection and development of supervisors. Typically, people are selected for supervisory positions based on their technical competence, their seniority or past performance, and their willingness to work hard. Charlotte Kelly, the newly promoted supervisor in this chapter's "You Make the Call!", was expected to jump right into her new management position. Fortunately, she had a chance to develop some of the skills that would be necessary in her new assignment. When Charlotte was a team leader, her boss, Patricia Graham, provided opportunities for her to grow and develop and hone certain skills. She had done a good job of cross-training and delegating. These are two activities that many experienced supervisors have problems with. Patricia Graham saw mentoring as part of her job. It should be obvious that Graham had confidence in Charlotte and vice versa. While the "You Make the Call!" does not provide all the details, Patricia Graham provided—not only to Charlotte, but to all of her direct reports—opportunities for growth by coaching and delegating tasks, which allowed them to add skills to their personal toolboxes.

Unfortunately, many organizations do not adequately prepare prospective supervisors for these responsibilities or equip them with the necessary skills. While new supervisors begin their new assignment with great enthusiasm, they often become disenchanted when the first sign of trouble appears or when they mismanage a situation. Figure 2.1 will help you take some smart first steps down the supervisory path.

Employees wanting to move into supervisory or upper-level management positions must make a conscious effort to develop their managerial skills by learning from their own managers, by completing company training programs, and by taking other avenues available to them. Fortunately, Charlotte Kelly took

FIGURE 2.1 Making Your Mark as a New Supervisor

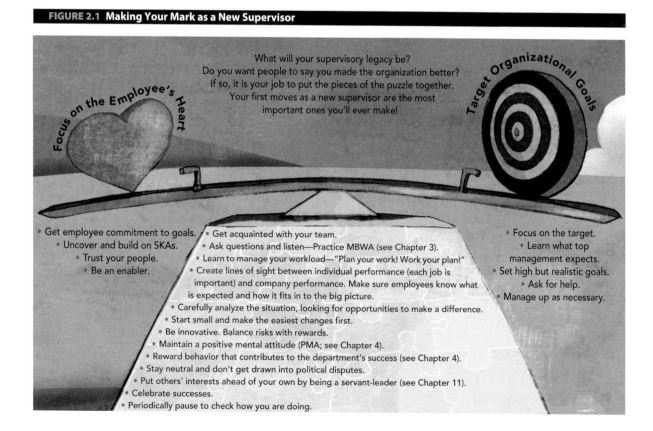

the initiative to learn. She took college courses that would help her explore various leadership styles and gain an understanding of group dynamics and motivational techniques. She also observed the strategies employed by the more successful managers at CMC. Not only did she learn some things that effective supervisors need to do, but she also observed some things that should not be done.

To this end, we have grouped the managerial skills supervisors need into the following eight major classifications:

1. **Technical skills:** The ability to perform the jobs in the supervisor's area of responsibility.
2. **Human relations skills:** The ability to work with and through people; these skills include open-mindedness and the ability to motivate team members.
3. **Communication skills:** The ability to give—and get—information.
4. **Administrative skills:** The ability to plan, organize, and coordinate the activities of a work group.
5. **Conceptual skills:** The ability to obtain, interpret, and apply the information needed to make sound decisions.
6. **Leadership skills:** The development of a leadership style that emphasizes collaboration, trust, and empathy; engages followers in all aspects of the organization; and helps followers to better themselves—i.e., **servant leadership.**[2]
7. **Political skills:** The savvy to ascertain the hidden rules of the organizational game and to recognize the roles various people play in getting things done outside of formal organizational channels.
8. **Emotional intelligence skills:** The "intelligent use of your emotions to help guide your behavior and thinking in ways that enhance your results. You can maximize your emotional intelligence by developing good communication skills, interpersonal relationships, and mentoring relationships."[3]

Your challenge is presented in Figure 2.2. People no longer grant automatic deference to those in positions of authority. The only way to earn their respect and trust is by appropriately using these skills. The notion of knowing oneself is not new, nor is it the only thing that supervisors need to master. Supervisors such as Charlotte Kelly must strive to understand and manage the moods and

Technical skills
The ability to do the job

Human relations skills
The ability to work with and through people

Communication skills
The ability to give—and get—information

Administrative skills
The ability to plan, organize, and coordinate activities

Conceptual skills
The ability to obtain, interpret, and apply information

Leadership skills
The ability to engage followers in all aspects of the organization

Servant leadership
The notion that the needs of followers are looked after so they can be the best they can be

Political skills
The ability to understand how things get done outside of formal channels

Emotional intelligence skills
The ability to intelligently use your emotions

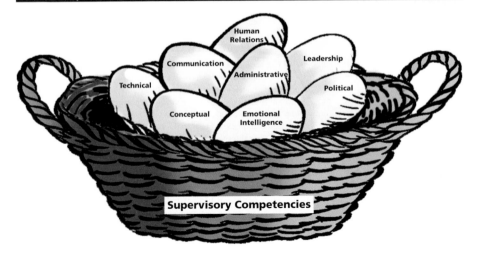

FIGURE 2.2 Your goals are to put all of your skills in one basket and be able to use them effectively

emotions of others.[4] Chess master Bruce Pandolfini stresses that there are two basic forms of intelligence: (1) the ability to read other people and (2) the ability to understand one's self.[5]

Unfortunately, it was not too many years ago that corporate America believed you could take "the best mechanics" or "the best salespeople" and give them the title of "supervisor" or "manager," and success would automatically follow. You may have heard horror stories about the supervisors who did their homework, did everything aboveboard, and called on the aforementioned skills, but somehow something went wrong. These supervisors made judgment errors; others would say they lacked common sense.

MANAGERIAL SKILLS CAN BE LEARNED AND DEVELOPED

Many people believe that good managers, like good athletes, are born, not made. Much research has indicated that this belief is generally incorrect, even though it is true that people are born with different potentials and that, to some degree, heredity plays a role in intelligence. An athlete who is not endowed with natural physical advantages is not likely to run 100 yards in ten seconds flat. On the other hand, many individuals who are so-called natural athletes also have not come close to that goal.

Most superior athletes have developed their natural endowments into mature skills with practice, training, effort, and experience. The same holds true for a good manager. The skills involved in managing are as learnable as the skills used in playing tennis or golf, for example. It takes time, effort, and determination for a supervisor to develop managerial skills. Supervisors will make mistakes, but people learn from mistakes as well as from successes. By applying the principles discussed in this textbook, the supervisor can develop the skills that make the supervisory job a challenging and satisfying career.

Tiger Woods is noted for his relentless preparation, practice routine, and daily physical training. He says, "Even the best continually seek ways to sharpen their skills."[7]

Simply talking about supervisory management is somewhat like Mark Twain's comment about the weather: "Everybody talks about it, but no one does anything about it." Therefore, throughout this textbook are tips, suggestions, and activities that are designed to reinforce concepts. However, these tools alone do not guarantee supervisory success. For example, if you wanted to learn to play golf or play the game better, you might strive to emulate the games of Annika Sorenstam, Lorena Ochoa, or Tiger Woods. Golf Hall of Famer and golf analyst Johnny Miller said, "Tiger, unfortunately for other pro golfers, has more intelligence than any golfer ever. He's probably more fit than any golfer, and the 'choke factor' (the ability to play under pressure) is better than any golfer ever."[6] Hopefully, for you, supervision will not be a spectator sport. Once you gain a supervisory position, if that is your dream, it will require your total commitment to be successful. I encourage you to take your talents to new heights.

However, if you really want to learn to play golf, you should take lessons from the coaches who provided "the best" with the solid fundamentals of the game. The great golfers—like great supervisors—have used multiple coaches during their careers. Unfortunately, their teachers might not have the time and you might not have the money to pay what they might charge for the lessons. Then you would take another course of action—find someone who has knowledge of the fundamentals and the ability and willingness to instruct. Select a coach or mentor who will help you uncover your desires and help you chart a course of action to achieve them.

Think again to the game of golf. The #1 goal of most golfers, whether they are in a competitive event, a friendly match, or just trying to beat their personal best, is to shoot lower scores.[8] The novice golfer, like newly appointed supervisor Charlotte Kelly, would want to have multiple coaches because no one is best in teaching all facets of the game. Ideally, the beginner who aspires to lofty goals would want a fitness coach; a driving coach; a short-game coach; a putting coach; and mental attitude coach. They would want a coach who would help them stretch beyond "just being good enough" to being the "best they can possibly be." It is doubtful that one could do it on their own. We all know of some individuals who would prefer to go it alone, i.e., the "I can do it myself" mentality. They might use self-teaching techniques such as viewing videos, trying to emulate the more successful players, reading an article, or reviewing a series of *Golf Digest* instructional tips. To be great golfer, like being a great supervisor, takes a lot of hard work. One has to master all aspects of the game. It does one no good to be able to hit the ball 300 yards straight down the middle of fairway if they have the "yips"—the tendency to miss short putts on a regular basis. All of the skills and functions have to work in combination. In the supervisory position—like the game of golf—there are "no do-overs."

You would also need the proper tools (e.g., the right clubs) and the time to practice, learn from your mistakes, and make corrections. There is one major difference between the beginning golfer and the newly appointed supervisor. Unlike beginning golfers, who can go to the driving range or the practice green to work on their games, newly appointed supervisors are on the job. Supervisors go through a learning curve that offers very little room for trial and error. The supervisor cannot hit it out of bounds and tee it up again for another chance. To get the job done the right way, the supervisor must avoid some common mistakes. Consider our supervisory tips and remember that the challenge for any professional is to stay on the path of continuous improvement.

Even the best continually seek ways to sharpen their skills. Tiger says, "My creative mind is my greatest weapon. It is a kind of inner vision that enables me to see things that others might not—like a certain way to play a shot. The psychology of golf can be complicated as it does entail mental toughness, self-confidence, the conquering of mental demons, instant recall of past successes, and being able to purge failures. It is a game within the game. I developed mine early. I cannot overemphasize the importance of developing yours now."[9]

Management
Getting objectives accomplished with and through people

3 Define management and discuss how the primary managerial functions are interrelated.

Functions of Management

The term *management* has been defined in many ways. In general, **management** is the process of getting things accomplished with and through people by guiding and motivating their efforts toward common objectives.

Successful managers will assure you that their employees are their most important asset. Most successful managers recognize that they are only as good as the people they supervise. In most endeavors, one person can accomplish relatively little. Therefore, individuals join forces with others to attain mutual goals. In all organizations, top-level managers or administrators are responsible for achieving the goals of the organization, but this requires the efforts of all subordinate managers and employees. Those who hold supervisory positions significantly influence the effectiveness with which people work together and use resources to attain goals. In short, the managerial role of a supervisor is to make sure that assigned tasks are accomplished with and through the help of employees.

With this in mind, we believe the term **enabler** more closely defines the new role of the manager.[10] Clearly, the foundation for success is built when the manager clarifies what is expected in the way of performance and specifies the behaviors that are acceptable in the work group. Then the role of the supervisor is to do all those things that enable employees to be the best they can be (i.e., effectively and efficiently achieve organizational objectives). Figure 2.3 illustrates the notion of the supervisor as an enabler. The better the supervisor manages,

Enabler
The person who does the things necessary to enable employees to do the best possible job

FIGURE 2.3 The Supervisor's Multiple Roles as Enabler

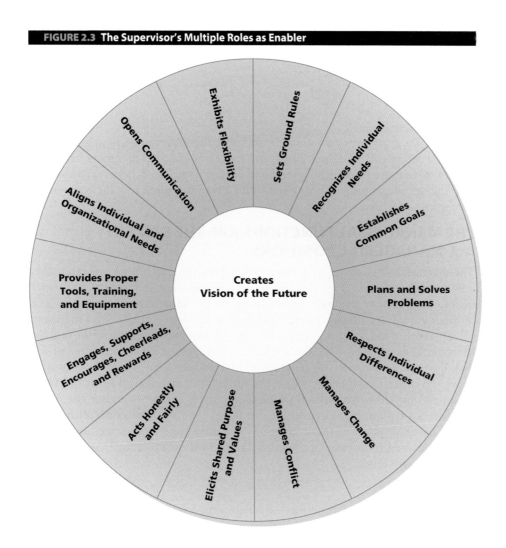

SUPERVISORY TIPS
The E-Z Route for Supervisory Success

- Above all, supervisors should do all of the things necessary to **Enable** employees to be the best they can be at their assigned tasks.
- Supervisors must foster and sustain a commitment to **Excellence**.
- Employees need to know what is **Expected** in the way of performance.
- Supervisors should **Establish** common goals and purpose.
- Employees must be **Educated**, that is, they must acquire the requisite job skills through coaching and/or training.
- Employees must be **Equipped** with the necessary tools, supplies, and equipment to do the job.
- Employees need to be **Encouraged** to see things that need to be done and to do them.
- Employees should be **Empowered** so that they have the authority and responsibility to achieve objectives.

- Supervisors should nurture an **Exciting** workplace where employees can find meaning and fulfillment of their individual needs.
- Employees should **Experience** a variety of tasks and thus become experienced in many areas that use a variety of skills.
- Supervisor should attempt to create a climate that fully **Engages** their employees in the organization. Open, honest, two-way communication is essential.
- Supervisors should understand and manage their **Emotions**.
- Supervisors should possess **Empathy**, that is, they should understand their employees' feelings, needs, and concerns.
- Supervisors should **Enthusiastically Exalt** employees when the job is well done.

the better the departmental results. In addition, the supervisor who manages well becomes capable of handling larger and more complicated assignments, which could lead to more responsibility and higher-paying positions in the organization. (See the accompanying "Supervisory Tips" box for some tips on becoming a successful supervisor.)

THE MANAGERIAL FUNCTIONS ARE THE SAME IN ALL MANAGERIAL POSITIONS

The managerial functions of a supervisory position are similar, whether they involve supervision of a production line, a sales force, a laboratory, or a small office. The primary managerial functions are the same regardless of the level in the hierarchy of management: first-level supervisor, middle-level manager, or top-level manager. Similarly, the type of organization does not matter. Managerial functions are the same whether the supervisor is working in a profit-making firm, a nonprofit organization, or a government office. Supervisors, as well as other managers, perform the same basic managerial functions in all organizations. In this textbook, we classify these functions under the major categories of planning, organizing, staffing, leading, and controlling. The following description of these functions is general and brief since most of the book is devoted to discussing the applications of these concepts, particularly at the supervisory level.

PLANNING

Planning
Determining what should be done

The initial managerial function—determining what should be done in the future—is called **planning**. It consists of setting goals, objectives, policies, procedures, and other plans needed to achieve the purposes of the organization. In planning, the manager chooses a course of action from various alternatives. Planning is primarily conceptual. It means thinking before acting, looking ahead and preparing for the future, laying out in advance the road to be followed, and thinking about how the job should be done. It includes collecting and sorting information from numerous sources and using that information to make decisions. Planning not only includes deciding what, how, when, and by whom work is to be done, but also includes developing "what-if" scenarios. A word of caution: Regardless of how well a supervisor like Charlotte Kelly ("You Make the Call!") plans, crises will happen, and supervisors must anticipate them, considering what they will do if this or that happens. (We will discuss crisis management and contingency planning more fully in Chapter 7.)

Many supervisors find that they are constantly confronted with crises. The probable reason for this is that these supervisors neglect to plan; they do not look much beyond the day's events. It is every supervisor's responsibility to plan; this task cannot be delegated to someone else. Certain specialists, such as accountants, production schedulers, or engineers, may help the supervisor plan, but it is up to each supervisor, as the manager of the department, to make specific departmental plans that coincide with the general objectives established by higher-level management.

Planning is the management function that precedes all others. New supervisors should establish the team's purpose and inspire people to do their best

Planning is the managerial function that comes first. As the supervisor proceeds with other managerial functions, planning continues, plans are revised, and alternatives are chosen as needed. This is particularly true as a supervisor evaluates the results of previous plans and adjusts future plans accordingly.

ORGANIZING

Once plans have been made, the organizing function primarily answers the question, "How will the work be divided and accomplished?" The supervisor defines various job duties and groups these duties into distinct areas, sections, units, or teams. The supervisor must specify the duties, assign them, and, at the same time, give subordinates the authority they need to carry out their tasks. **Organizing** means arranging and distributing work to accomplish the organization's goals.

Organizing
Arranging and distributing work among members of the work group to accomplish the organization's goals

STAFFING

The managerial tasks of recruiting, selecting, orienting, and training employees may be grouped in the function called **staffing**. This function includes appraising the performances of employees, promoting employees as appropriate, and giving employees opportunities to develop. In addition, staffing includes devising an equitable compensation system and rates of pay. In many companies, some activities involved in staffing are handled by the human resources (HR) or personnel department. For example, if the HR department and top-level managers establish the compensation system, then supervisors do not perform this task. However, day-to-day responsibility for the essential aspects of staffing remains with the supervisor.

Staffing
The tasks of recruiting, selecting, orienting, training, appraising, promoting, and compensating employees

LEADING

Leading means guiding the activities of employees toward accomplishing objectives. The leading function of management involves guiding, teaching, and supervising subordinates. This includes developing employees to their potential by directing and coaching those employees effectively. It is insufficient for a supervisor just to plan, organize, and have enough employees available. The supervisor must attempt to motivate employees as they go about their work. Leading is the day-to-day process around which all supervisory performance revolves. Leading is also known as directing, motivating, or influencing because it plays a major role in employee morale, job satisfaction, productivity, and communication. It is through this function that the supervisor seeks to create a climate that is conducive to employee satisfaction and, at the same time, achieves the objectives of the department. Finding ways to satisfy the needs of a diverse employee workforce is a significant challenge.

Few employees are willing to blindly obey. They no longer grant automatic deference to the person in charge. We all know about the top-down hierarchical, autocratic style of leader. But as you will see in subsequent chapters, we have a strong preference for the servant-leader style.[11] In fact, most of a supervisor's time normally is spent on leading. It is the function around which departmental performance revolves.

CONTROLLING

The managerial function of **controlling** involves ensuring that actual performance is in line with intended performance and taking corrective action as needed. Here, too, the importance of planning as the first function of management is obvious. It would be impossible for a supervisor to determine whether work was proceeding properly if there were no plans against which to check. If plans or standards are superficial or poorly conceived, the controlling function is limited. Therefore, controlling means not only making sure that objectives are achieved, but also taking corrective action in case of failure to achieve planned objectives. It also means revising plans as circumstances require.

THE CONTINUOUS FLOW OF MANAGERIAL FUNCTIONS

The five managerial functions can be viewed as a circular, continuous movement. If we view the managerial process as a circular flow consisting of the five functions (Figure 2.4), we can see that the functions flow into each other and that each affects the others. At times, there is no clear line to mark where one function ends and the other begins. Also, it is impossible for a supervisor to set aside a certain amount of time for one or another function because the effort spent in each function varies as conditions and circumstances change. Undoubtedly, planning must come first. Without plans, the supervisor cannot organize, staff, lead, or control.

Remember: All managers perform essentially the same managerial functions, regardless of the nature of their organizations or their levels in the hierarchy. The time and effort involved in each of these functions varies depending on which rung of the management ladder the manager occupies, the type of tasks subordinates perform, and the scope and urgency of the situation.

FIGURE 2.4 The circular concept illustrates the close and continuous relationship between the five management functions

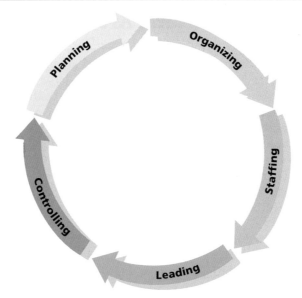

The Supervisor as Team Leader

4 Discuss the important characteristics of the supervisor as team leader.

Many organizations have implemented a team-based organizational structure focused on customer satisfaction, productivity, profitability, and continuous improvement. In Chapter 13, we will discuss the impact of teams in greater detail. Teams are a means to an end, and that end is superior performance to what team members would achieve working as individuals.[12] Author, trainer, and consultant Fran Rees identified several reasons for the increasing use of teams:

- Given the complexity of jobs and information, it is nearly impossible for managers to make all the decisions. In many cases, the person closest to the job is the one who should decide.
- The focus on quality and customer satisfaction has increased attention on the importance of each employee's work.
- The shift from a homogeneous workforce to a diverse one requires managers to work effectively with multiple employee perspectives.
- There is a growing realization that an autocratic, coercive management style does not necessarily result in productive, loyal employees. The fact that people support what they help create is behind the team approach.
- People are demanding strong voices in their work lives, as well as meaningful work, respect, and dignity.[13]

One example of how well teams perform is illustrated in the movie *Apollo 13*. The five little words "Houston, we have a problem" caused a diverse group of ground-crew specialists at Mission Control—working against the clock, borrowing and fabricating resources, and working against the odds—to figure out a way to bring the astronauts home.

5 Explain the difference between management and leadership.

Managers and Leaders: Are They Different?

In the years since the classic *Harvard Business Review* article "Managers and Leaders: Are They Different?" appeared, debate has abounded among scholars regarding the differences between managers and leaders.[14] Not surprisingly, hundreds of articles and books have tried to clear up the confusion. While some have contended that only labels or semantics separate managers and leaders, others have identified more substantive differences. For example, author Stephen Covey wrote, "Leadership is not management. Leadership deals with the top line—what are the things."[15] Covey also proclaimed, "Management is efficiency in climbing the ladder of success; leadership determines whether the ladder is leaning against the right wall."[16] Another noted writer on leadership, Warren Bennis, has pointed out other differences between managers and leaders (see Figure 2.5).

Harvard professor John P. Kotter also draws a similar distinction between leadership and management. He contends that management involves keeping the current system operating through planning, budgeting, staffing, controlling, and problem-solving, while leadership is the development of vision and strategies, the alignment of relevant people behind those strategies, and the empowerment of people to make the vision happen. Kotter states:

> The point here is not that leadership is good and management is bad. They are simply different and serve different purposes. Strong management with no leadership tends to entrench an organization in a deadly bureaucracy. Strong leadership with no management risks chaos; the organization might walk off a cliff.[17]

When people have the title of "manager," does it necessarily follow that they will be leaders? Clearly, the answer is no—title alone does not guarantee success. On the other hand, when people have the title of "team leader," does it mean they will display the SKAs to excel in that position? Again, the answer is no. What does it take for an individual to be both a good manager and a good leader? Is it possible for individuals to learn to be both good managers and good leaders? In subsequent chapters, we clearly identify the necessary ingredients—the managerial skills necessary for success—and devote the bulk of Chapter 11 to further discussion of leadership and change.

FIGURE 2.5 Who does what?

- The manager does things right; the leader does the right thing.
- The manager relies on control; the leader inspires trust.
- The manager focuses on systems and structures; the leader focuses on people.
- The manager administers; the leader innovates.
- The manager asks how and when; the leader asks what and why.
- The manager accepts the status quo; the leader challenges it.

Source: Adapted from Warren Bennis, *On Becoming a Leader* (Reading, MA: Addison-Wesley Publishing Company, paperback edition 1994), pp. 44–45.

Managerial Authority

Does the individual have the authority to perform managerial functions? If the answer is no, the individual cannot perform well as a manager (see Figure 2.6). **Authority** is the legitimate or rightful power to lead others, the right to order and to act.[18] It is the formal, positional right by which a manager can require subordinates to do or not to do a thing the manager deems necessary to achieve organizational objectives. Managerial authority is not granted to an individual, but rather to the position the individual holds at the time. When individuals leave their jobs or are replaced, they cease to have that authority. When a successor assumes the position, that person then has the authority.

6 Discuss the concept of authority as a requirement of any managerial position.

Authority
The legitimate right to direct and lead others

FIGURE 2.6 **To be effective, a manager must be able to use the managerial functions and possess requisite SKAs, power, and authority**

Included in positional managerial authority are the right and duty to delegate authority. The delegation of authority is the process by which the supervisor receives authority from a higher-level manager and, in turn, makes job assignments and entrusts related authority to subordinates. Having managerial authority means the supervisor has the power and the right to issue directives in order to accomplish the tasks assigned to the department. This authority includes the power and right to reward and discipline, if necessary. When a subordinate performs well, the supervisor has the power to give that subordinate a raise or another reward, within company guidelines. If a worker refuses to carry out a directive, the supervisor's authority includes the power and right to take disciplinary action, even to the extent of discharging the subordinate. Of course, this power, like all authority, is limited.

The **acceptance theory of authority** states that a manager does not possess real authority until and unless the subordinate accepts it. For example, a supervisor may instruct an employee to carry out a certain work assignment. The employee has several alternatives from which to choose. Although such a response is not likely, the employee can refuse to obey, thereby rejecting the supervisor's authority. Alternatively, the employee may grudgingly accept the supervisor's direction and carry out the assignment in a mediocre fashion. Supervisor Charlotte Kelly (see this chapter's "You Make the Call!" segment) can expect to experience this type of resistance from some of her employees. When some employees reject Charlotte's authority, she will have no choice but to impose disciplinary action on those employees. At the time that Charlotte is introduced as the ER supervisor, Bob Murphy should lay the foundation for her acceptance. Every manager requires the support of his or her boss, and Charlotte Kelly is no exception.

Numerous limitations to authority exist—union contract provisions, government or regulatory agency restrictions, company policies, and ethical considerations. Generally, supervisors find there are limits to their authority to use resources and to make certain managerial decisions.

AVOIDING RELIANCE ON MANAGERIAL AUTHORITY

Most successful supervisors know that to motivate workers to perform their duties, it is usually best not to rely on formal managerial authority but to employ other approaches. Generally, it is better for a supervisor not to display power and formal authority. In practice, many supervisors prefer to avoid even speaking about their authority. They prefer to speak instead of their responsibilities, tasks, or duties. Some supervisors consider it better to say that they have responsibility for certain activities instead of saying that they have authority in that area. Using the words *responsibility*, *tasks*, and *duties* in this sense—although these certainly are not the same as *authority*—helps the supervisor to avoid showing the "club" of authority. We contend that employees are likely to perform better if they understand why the task needs to be done and have a voice in how to do it.[19] Regardless of how a supervisor applies authority, the point to remember is that the supervisory position must have managerial authority. Without it, a supervisor cannot perform well as a manager.

DELEGATING AUTHORITY

As mentioned previously, the **delegation** of authority is the process by which the supervisor receives authority from a higher-level manager and, in turn, makes job assignments and entrusts related authority to subordinates. Just as the possession of authority is a required component of any managerial position, the process of delegating authority to lower levels in the hierarchy is required for an organization to have effective managers, supervisors, and employees. Chapter 11 discusses in detail the concepts of authority, responsibility, and the delegation of authority.

Power—The Ability to Influence Others

7 Describe the types of power potentially available to the supervisor.

Among the most confused terms in management are *authority* and *power*. The effective supervisor understands the difference between the two. Some behavioral scientists contend that a manager's power comes from two sources: position power and personal power.[20] **Position power** comes from a person's organizational position. For example, a division manager has more position power than a first-line supervisor. **Personal power,** on the other hand, emanates from the relationship a supervisor has with other people. A supervisor's personal power depends to a greater extent on the followers' perceptions of that supervisor's knowledge, skill, and expertise.

Position power
Power derived from the formal rank a person holds in the chain of command

Personal power
Power derived from a person's SKAs and how others perceive that person

Other theorists, such as French and Raven, assert that power arises from the following five sources:

1. Reward power: Supervisors have reward power if they can grant rewards.
2. Coercive power: Supervisors who threaten punishment and discipline use coercive power.
3. Legitimate power: Some supervisors gain compliance by relying on their position or rank (e.g., "I'm the boss—do it my way").
4. Expert power: Knowledge or valuable information gives a person expert power over those who need that information.
5. Referent or charismatic power: People are often influenced by another person because of some tangible or intangible aspect of another's personality.[21]

Effective supervisors understand the effect their power has on others. Research indicates that reward power, coercive power, and legitimate power often force employees to comply with directives but do not get those employees' commitment to organizational objectives. Accordingly, supervisors who use expert power and referent power effectively have the greatest potential for achieving organizational goals.[22]

The acceptance theory of authority is also relevant to the application of power. For example, you can be an expert in computer applications, but if others do not need that knowledge, you will have very little influence over them. Therefore, two supervisors can hold the same title, occupy the same level in the hierarchy, and have equal authority, yet have different degrees of power, depending on their abilities and how others perceive them.

Coordination

8 Explain the need for coordination and cooperation and how they depend on the proper performance of the managerial functions.

Management has generally been defined as a process of getting things done through and with the help of people by directing their efforts toward common objectives. In a sense, all levels of management could be broadly visualized as involving the coordination of efforts of all the members and resources of an organization toward overall objectives. Some writers, therefore, have included the concept of coordination as a separate managerial function.

Coordination
The synchronization of employees' efforts and the organization's resources toward achieving goals

Coordination is the orderly synchronization (or putting together) of efforts of the members and resources of an organization to accomplish the organization's objectives. Coordination is not a separate managerial function; it is an implicit, interrelated aspect of the five major managerial functions previously cited. That is, coordination is fostered whenever a manager performs any of the managerial functions of planning, organizing, staffing, leading, and controlling. In a sense, coordination can best be understood as being a direct result of good management rather than as a managerial function in and of itself. The ability to communicate clearly and concisely is essential for coordination.

Achieving coordination typically is more difficult at the executive level than at the supervisory level. The CEO has to synchronize the use of resources and human efforts throughout numerous departments and levels of the organization. A supervisor of one department has the responsibility to achieve coordination primarily within the department. However, this too can be difficult to achieve, especially during periods of rapid change.

COOPERATION AS RELATED TO COORDINATION

Cooperation
The willingness of individuals to work with and help one another

Cooperation is individuals' willingness to work with and help each other. It primarily involves the attitudes of a group of people. Coordination is more than the mere desire and willingness of participants. For example, consider a group of workers attempting to move a heavy object. They are sufficient in number, willing and eager to cooperate with each other, and trying their best to move the object. They are also fully aware of their common purpose. However, in all likelihood their efforts will be of little avail until one of them—the supervisor—gives the proper orders to apply the right amount of effort at the right place at the right time. Then the group members can move the object. It is possible that by sheer coincidence some cooperation could have brought about the desired result in this example, but no supervisor can afford to rely on such a coincidental occurrence.

While cooperation is helpful and the lack of it could impede progress, its presence alone will not necessarily get the job done. Efforts must be coordinated toward the common goal.

Cooperation, coordination, and communication lead to success

ATTAINING COORDINATION

Coordination is not easily attained, and the task of achieving coordination is becoming more complex. As an organization grows, coordinating the many activities of various departments becomes an increasingly complicated problem for high-level managers. At the supervisory level, as the number and types of positions in a department increase, the need for coordination to obtain desired results similarly increases. On the other hand, organizational downsizing may force supervisors to be even more effective in coordination.

The complexities of human nature present added coordination problems. For example, every employee comes to the workplace with a baggage cart. Loaded on that baggage cart are all of his or her off-the-job issues. We remind employees to leave their personal problems at the door when they come to work and to leave their work-related issues at the door when they leave. While it sounds good, in reality it doesn't happen. Many employees understandably are preoccupied with their own work and their personal baggage. In the final analysis, they are evaluated primarily on how they do their individual jobs. Therefore, employees tend not to willingly become involved in other areas and often are indifferent to the fact that their activities may affect other departments.

Supervisors can achieve coordination by building networks focused on attaining common objectives. According to *Merriam Webster's Collegiate Dictionary*, a network is "a fabric or structure of cords or wires that cross at regular intervals and are knotted or secured at the crossings." Think of it this way. A person's relationships are the knots, and the strength of the relationships equals the strength of the network.

Refer back to the chapter's opening "You Make the Call!" and think of all the individuals who have a stake in what the department does and how well it performs. Charlotte Kelly is the proverbial person in the middle. There are patients, their families, physicians, insurers who may pay for the care, government and other regulatory agencies, and a myriad of departments within the medical center. Networking will be very useful to Charlotte as she carries out her supervisory responsibilities. She should develop networks with others, both inside and outside the organization. Also, she must understand that network members must give as well as receive. When Charlotte has a need, she contacts another person in her network who might be a resource, and vice versa. Networking allows Charlotte to balance autonomy on one hand and dependence on the other. **Networking** facilitates the flow of ideas across organizational barriers and thereby eases the coordination effort.

Networking
Individuals or groups linked by a commitment to shared purpose

COORDINATION AS PART OF THE MANAGERIAL FUNCTIONS

While performing the managerial functions, the supervisor should recognize that coordination is a desired result of effective management. Proper attention to coordination within each of the five managerial functions contributes to overall coordination.

Initially, the supervisor must ensure that the various plans are aligned with the right people. For example, a supervisor may wish to discuss departmental job assignments with the employees who are to carry them out. In this way, the employees can express their opinions or objections, which need to be reconciled in advance. Furthermore, employees may be encouraged to make suggestions and to discuss the merits of proposed plans and alternatives. When employees are involved in initial departmental planning, the supervisor's chances of achieving coordination usually improve. The purpose of establishing who is to do what, when, where, and how is to achieve coordination. For example, whenever a new job is to be done, a supervisor assigns that job to the unit with the employees best suited to the work. Therefore, whenever a supervisor groups activities and assigns subordinates to those groups, coordination should be uppermost in the supervisor's mind. Achieving coordination also should be of concern as a supervisor establishes authority relationships within the department and among employees. Clear statements as to specific duties and reporting relationships in the department foster coordination and prevent duplicate efforts and confusion.

When leading, the supervisor is significantly involved in coordination. The essence of giving instructions is to coordinate the activities of employees in such a manner that the overall objectives are reached in the most efficient way possible. In addition, a supervisor must assess and reward the performance of employees to maintain a harmonious work group.

The supervisor is also concerned with coordination when performing the controlling function. By checking, monitoring, and observing, the supervisor makes certain that activities conform to established plans. If there are any discrepancies, the supervisor should take immediate action to reprioritize or reassign tasks. In so doing, the supervisor may achieve coordination at least from then on. The very nature of the controlling process contributes to coordination and keeps the organization moving toward its objectives.

COORDINATION WITH OTHER DEPARTMENTS

Not only must supervisors coordinate activities within their own departments, but they also must coordinate the efforts of their departments with those of others. For example, a production department supervisor must meet with supervisors of scheduling, quality control, maintenance, and shipping to coordinate various activities. Similarly, an accounting supervisor typically meets with supervisors from production, sales, and shipping to coordinate cost accounting, inventory records, and billing. Achieving coordination is an essential component of the supervisory management position.

Cooperation and Coordination—Easier Said than Done

A group of employees becomes a team when its members share values and a purpose. How well the objectives are achieved depends on the supervisor's coordination and team-building skills. The move toward increased employee participation, broader spans of control, and fewer managerial levels causes a greater need for coordination skills. Meanwhile, many supervisors have higher aspirations; they eventually want to be promoted to positions of increased responsibility. In reality, competition among supervisors may impede cooperation.

9 Explain why and how labor unions affect the managerial functions.

Labor Unions are Part of Supervisory Concerns

Unions remain an important element of the workforce that supervisors should know about and be prepared to deal with appropriately. Most employees in the private sector of the U.S. workforce have legal rights to join or not to join labor unions under the National Labor Relations Act as amended. Federal government workers have their collective bargaining rights established under the Civil Service Reform Act. Rights of other public-sector workers generally are covered by various state and local government legislation. (See http://www.flra.gov/statue; click on *Read the National Labor Relations Act* or *What is the NLRA?* to gain some tips for dealing with a unionized workforce.) Although the strength and influence of labor unions have declined considerably in recent years, labor unions nevertheless continue to be a major influence on the manager's right to manage.[23]

We use the terms **labor union** and **labor organization** interchangeably to describe any legally recognized organization that exists for the purpose of representing a group or "bargaining unit" of employees. The union negotiates and administers a labor agreement with the employer. A **labor agreement**, also called a union contract, is the negotiated document between the union and the employer that covers terms and conditions of employment for represented employees.

The labor agreement that has been agreed on by management and union representatives becomes the document under which both parties operate during the life of the agreement. Although no two labor agreements are exactly alike, most agreements cover wages, benefits, working conditions, hours of work, overtime, holidays, vacations, leave of absence rules, seniority, grievance procedures, and numerous other matters. The labor agreement outlines union/management relationships. In essence, it is a policy manual that provides rules, procedures, and guidelines—as well as limitations—for management and the union. To make it an instrument for fostering constructive relationships, the agreement must be applied with appropriate and intelligent supervisory decisions. The best labor agreement is of little value if it is poorly applied by the supervisor.

COMPLYING WITH THE LABOR AGREEMENT

Wherever the labor agreement applies, supervisors are obliged to manage their departments within its framework. Therefore, supervisors should know the provisions of the agreement and how to interpret those provisions. One way to do this is for higher-level managers or the human resources department to hold meetings with supervisors to brief them on the contents of the agreement and to answer questions about any provisions. Copies of the contract and clarifications of various provisions should be given to supervisors so that the supervisors know what they can and cannot do while managing their departments (see Figure 2.7).

Supervisors should recognize that a labor agreement has been negotiated, agreed upon, and signed by both management and union representatives. Even if a provision in the agreement causes problems for a supervisor, the supervisor should not try to circumvent the contract in the hope of doing the firm a favor. For example, assume that a provision specifies that work assignments must be made primarily on the basis of seniority. While this provision may limit the supervisor in assigning the most qualified workers to certain jobs, the supervisor should comply with it or be prepared to face probable conflict with the union. If a labor agreement provision is clear and specific, the supervisor should not attempt to ignore it. When supervisors do not understand certain provisions, they should ask someone in higher-level management or the human resources department for help before trying to apply the provisions in question.

ADJUSTING FOR THE UNION

A labor agreement does not fundamentally change a supervisor's position as a manager. Supervisors still must accomplish their objectives by planning, organizing, staffing, leading, and controlling. Supervisors retain the right to require employees to comply with instructions and to get their jobs done. The major adjustment required when a union is present is that supervisors must perform their managerial duties within the framework of the labor agreement. For example, a labor agreement may spell out some limitations to the supervisor's authority, especially in areas of disciplinary actions, job transfers,

Labor union/labor organization
Legally recognized organization that represents employees and negotiates and administers a labor agreement with an employer

Labor agreement
Negotiated document between union and employer that covers the terms and conditions of employment for represented employees

FIGURE 2.7 The supervisor must know the provisions of labor agreements, how to interpret them, and how to apply them fairly and consistently

and assignments, or the labor agreement may specify procedures concerning the seniority rights of employees with regard to shift assignments, holidays, and vacations. Supervisors may not like these provisions. However, they must manage within them and learn to minimize the effects of contractually imposed requirements or restrictions by making sound decisions and relying on their own managerial abilities.

As members of management, supervisors have the right and duty to make decisions. A labor agreement does not take away that right. However, it does give the union a right to challenge a supervisor's decision that the union believes to be a violation of the labor agreement. For example, virtually all labor agreements specify that management has the right to discipline and discharge for "just" (or "proper") cause. The supervisor who follows **just cause** ensures that the disciplinary action meets certain tests of fairness and elements of normal due process, such as proper notification, investigation, sufficient evidence, and a penalty commensurate with the nature of the infraction. Therefore, disciplinary action remains a managerial responsibility and right, but it must meet the just-cause standard. Because a challenge from the union may occur, the supervisor should have a sound case before taking disciplinary action. If a supervisor believes that disciplinary action is called for when an employee breaks a rule, the supervisor should examine thoroughly all aspects of the problem, take the required preliminary steps, and think through the appropriateness of any action. In other words, unless there is a contractual requirement to the contrary, the supervisor normally will carry out the disciplinary action independent of union involvement. However, some labor agreements require that a supervisor notify a union representative before imposing discipline or that a union representative be present when the disciplinary action is administered. In Chapter 6, we will discuss in detail the handling of disciplinary matters in both union and nonunion work environments.

Just or proper cause
Standard for disciplinary action requiring tests of fairness and elements of normal due process, such as proper notification, investigation, sufficient evidence, and a penalty commensurate with the nature of the infraction

RELATING SUPERVISORY DECISION MAKING TO THE LABOR AGREEMENT

In practice, the supervisor may amplify provisions of the labor agreement by decisions that interpret and apply those provisions to specific situations. In so doing, the supervisor might establish precedents that arbitrators consider when deciding grievances.

A **grievance** is a complaint that has been formally presented by the union to management and that alleges a violation of the labor agreement. Most labor agreements specify several steps as part of a grievance procedure before a grievance goes to arbitration. An **arbitrator** is someone who is selected by the union and management to render a final and binding decision concerning a grievance when the union and management cannot settle the grievance themselves. Procedures for arbitrating grievances are included in most labor agreements. Figure 15.3, in Chapter 15, is a typical grievance-arbitration provision in a labor agreement.

Grievance
Formal complaint presented by the union to management that alleges violation of the labor agreement

Arbitrator
Person selected by the union and management to render a final and binding decision concerning a grievance

MAINTAINING EMPLOYEES' COMPLIANCE WITH THE LABOR AGREEMENT

Grievances can be filed over any workplace issue that is subject to the collective bargaining agreement, or they can be filed over the interpretation and administration of the agreement itself. It is the supervisor's duty to act whenever employees do not comply with provisions of the labor agreement. Employees may interpret lack of action to mean that the provisions are unimportant or are not to be enforced. Supervisors should ensure that employees observe the labor agreement, just as supervisors must operate within the agreement. The supervisor's inaction could set a precedent or could be interpreted to mean that the provision has been set aside.

A few words of wisdom at this point:

- The management functions and their application are the same regardless of whether the organization is unionized or not.
- All employees need to have a clear vision of what is expected in the way of performance.
- Honest, sincere, authentic, daily feedback and dialogue between the supervisor and employees is a must.
- Cooperation, coordination, and consistency may be more critical in a unionized environment.
- Supervisors must convey a clear description of what is going on and how "we are doing."
- All employees want praise and recognition for a "job well done."

The supervisor's daily relationships with employees and union representatives make the labor agreement a living document for better or worse. For the most part, the supervisor's involvement in union/management relations has two phases: learning what the labor agreement contains and applying it fairly and consistently on a daily basis.

A supervisor must understand that unionized employees have divided or dual loyalties concerning their unions and their employers

© JIM WEST/ALAMY

SUMMARY

1 Supervisors are the "people in the middle." Employees see their supervisors as being management, but supervisors are subordinates to their own managers at higher levels. To supervisors of other departments, supervisors are colleagues who must cooperate with each other. Supervisors must have both good working knowledge of the jobs being performed in their departments and the ability to manage.

2 Effective supervisors must have technical, human relations, administrative, conceptual, and political skills. It is most critical that supervisors be able to intelligently use their emotions. Supervisors must understand the technical aspects of the work being performed. When attempting to manage job performance, understanding employee needs is essential. "People skills" help supervisors accomplish objectives with and through people. It is equally important for supervisors to understand the dynamics of the organization and to recognize organizational politics.

These skills are important to all levels of management. Most supervisors come to the job equipped with some of these skills. Supervisors have daily opportunities to apply managerial skills and must continually strive to develop them. Blending these skills with a dose of common sense and applying them with maturity help accomplish organizational objectives and allow supervisors to stay on top of the job. Supervisors who effectively apply these skills can contribute suggestions to higher-level managers and can work in harmony with their colleagues. In short, skilled supervisors are candidates for advancement and additional job responsibilities.

3 While there are numerous definitions of management, we define it as the process of getting things accomplished through people by guiding and motivating those people's efforts toward common objectives. Supervisors should look at themselves as enablers, that is, by clarifying expectations for employees and giving employees the right tools, training, and opportunities to succeed. In short, supervisors should do all those things that enable their employees to be the best they can be while achieving organizational objectives.

The five major managerial functions are planning, organizing, staffing, leading, and controlling. These functions are viewed as a continuous flow—the functions flow into each other, and each affects the others.

Planning is the first function of management. The performance of all other managerial functions depends on it. The five managerial functions are universal regardless of the job environment, the activity involved, or a person's position in the management hierarchy. Typically, supervisors spend most of their time leading and controlling. A supervisor's planning covers a shorter time and narrower focus than that of a top-level executive.

4 Some companies have redefined the role of the supervisor as team leader. While team leaders must possess certain skills as identified earlier in the chapter, it is important to remember that teams are usually formed for such purposes as improving customer service, productivity, or quality. As such, developing a work environment in which team members share a purpose

and goals is essential. Regardless of the term used, the first-line supervisor or team leader must be an enabler—helping others to be the best they can become in the continuous pursuit of organizational objectives. Information giving and information gathering allow team members to function most effectively.

5 Leadership and management go hand in hand. As one of the management functions identified in this text, leadership is concerned with establishing a vision, aligning people behind that vision, and empowering those people to accomplish the intended results (doing the right thing) while management is getting things done. The distinction is more than a semantic one.

6 A supervisor must have authority to perform well as a manager. Authority is the legitimate or rightful power to lead others. Authority is delegated from top-level managers through middle-level managers to supervisors who, in turn, delegate to their employees. All supervisors must be delegated appropriate authority to manage their departments.

The acceptance theory of authority suggests that supervisors have authority only if and when their subordinates accept it. In reality, an employee's choice between accepting or not accepting a supervisor's authority may be the choice between staying in the job or quitting. Most supervisors prefer not to primarily rely on formal managerial authority but to use other approaches for enhancing employee performance.

7 Supervisors have power because of the positions they occupy. Position power increases as a person advances up the organizational hierarchy. Supervisors derive personal power from their relationships with others. Subordinates' perceptions of the supervisor's SKAs play an integral role in the supervisor's ability to influence those subordinates.

Theorists French and Raven identify five sources of power: reward, coercive, legitimate, expert, and referent or charismatic. Research indicates that supervisors who use expert power and referent power effectively have the greatest potential for achieving organizational goals. The power a supervisor has is based, for the most part, on the willingness of the employee to accept it.

8 Coordination is the orderly synchronization of efforts of the members and resources of an organization toward the attainment of stated objectives. Cooperation—as distinguished from coordination—is the willingness of individuals to work with and help each other. While cooperation is helpful, it alone will not get the job done. Efforts must also be coordinated. Both coordination and cooperation are attainable through good management practices.

9 Supervisors need to know how to apply the managerial functions when departmental employees are represented by a union. The supervisors are the key to good union/management relations because they apply the labor agreement from day to day. The presence of a labor union gives a formal mechanism for challenging a supervisor's actions.

KEY TERMS

Acceptance theory of authority (p. 56)
Administrative skills (p. 46)
Arbitrator (p. 63)
Authority (p. 55)
Communication skills (p. 46)
Conceptual skills (p. 46)
Controlling (p. 52)
Cooperation (p. 58)
Coordination (p. 58)
Delegation (p. 56)

Emotional intelligence skills (p. 46)
Enabler (p. 49)
Grievance (p. 63)
Human relations skills (p. 46)
Just or proper cause (p. 62)
Labor agreement (p. 61)
Labor union/labor organization (p. 61)
Leadership skills (p. 46)
Leading (p. 52)
Management (p. 48)

Networking (p. 59)
Organizing (p. 51)
Personal power (p. 57)
Planning (p. 50)
Political skills (p. 46)
Position power (p. 57)
Servant leadership (p. 46)
Staffing (p. 51)
Technical skills (p. 46)

QUESTIONS FOR DISCUSSION

1. Identify the major managerial skills every supervisor needs. Why are these skills important?

2. It is often said that planning is the most important managerial function. Do you agree? Why or why not?

3. Stephen Covey observed that "Effective leadership is putting first things first. Effective management is discipline, carrying it out."[24] Do you agree? Why or why not? What distinction have you observed between management and leadership? Why is the distinction important for one who desires to be a supervisor or team leader?

4. We suggest that supervisors should view themselves as enablers. The logical extension of this notion would be that the supervisor clarify the objectives that must be obtained, provide the training and tools needed to complete the tasks, and get out of the way. Should "management by getting out of the way" be an appropriate philosophy of management? Why or why not?

5. What are the obstacles that the supervisor may encounter when trying to gain cooperation by coordinating the department's various activities? What could a mentor or coach do to help a supervisor understand how cooperation, coordination, and communication have to work together to attain a satisfactory end result?

6. Discuss why the supervisor should not attempt to ignore or circumvent the labor agreement, even if it seems like the right thing to do.

SKILLS APPLICATIONS

Skills Application 2-1: Great CEOs Put Themselves Last, or Do They?

When I first began teaching, a colleague said that "the ultimate criterion of organizational worth is whether or not the organization survives." Today, I contend that survival is not the objective. I want to work and be affiliated with an organization that thrives and is thought of as being "Great!" A 2003 *Fortune* magazine article stated, "Great CEOs build organizations that thrive long after their tenure. In addition to legacy, great CEOs also preside over innovation, lead through major transformations or crises, and improve financial performance. The one trait that distinguishes this group of CEOs is their deep sense of connectedness to the organizations they ran, the employees they inspired, and the customers they served."

1. See "The 10 Greatest CEOs of All Time," *Fortune* (July 21, 2003), pp. 54–68. Choose any one of the CEOs from the list of ten. Conduct an Internet search to learn more about that person's reign as CEO. Write a one-page paper detailing what you learned about the person's leadership, the success

of the organization, and the person's legacy. In your concluding paragraph, briefly describe the strategies and style of your chosen CEO.

2. Compare the organizations that these 10 CEOs represented to *Fortune* magazine's most recent listing of the Most Admired Corporations in America (this usually appears in the March issue). You might also want to review "America's Best Leaders" in *U.S. News & World Report* (November 19, 2007) to get a glimpse of those who "motivate people to work collaboratively to accomplish great things." Answer the following:

   a. What were the ingredients that led to the organization's ranking in *Fortune's* list?

   b. How did the CEO lay the foundation for his or her organization to remain as one of America's most admired corporations?

   c. How successful has the company been since the CEO stepped aside?

d. To what extent do you believe the culture developed by the great CEO and the CEO's ability to select a successor who would follow down that path contributed to where that organization is today?

e. Write a one-page summary detailing what you learned from this exercise.

Skills Application 2-2: Attributes of a Successful Manager

Think of the most successful manager you have ever known or heard about. Write a paragraph describing what that manager does to be described as successful. Compare your paragraph with that of a classmate. Are there SKAs common to both? Why do you think there are common items?

Skills Application 2-3: Role-play Application

1.  Review this chapter's opening "You Make the Call!" Your instructor will determine who will play each role. You might be selected to play the role of Charlotte Kelly or you might be Patricia Graham, Bob Murphy, Professor Stinson, or an observer.

2. Charlotte Kelly decided to share the following scenarios with either Graham, Murphy, or Professor Stinson:

   a. "On Monday morning, Gloria Bellio, a new front-end receptionist who had completed her orientation the previous Thursday and Friday, didn't show up on time for work. It was her first day and my first day. I didn't even know she was supposed to be here or that we had a personnel shortage on the reception desk until Diane Harms informed me that they were overloaded and that the new employee hadn't shown up. About thirty minutes later (an hour and a half after the beginning of her shift), Gloria Bellio strolled in. I told her I needed to speak with her when she had a few minutes. I met with her in private and reinforced our expectations regarding attendance. She explained that she had car problems and got here as soon as she could. She then told me that I wasn't being fair since Amy Talmadge had hired her, and she was disappointed to know that I was the new boss. Then I took out CMC's policy manual and informed her that I had no choice under our 'no fault' attendance policy but to write her up. I tried to reaffirm my expectations regarding her ability to be a very good employee. But it appeared that the more I tried, the more disgruntled she became."

   b. "Tomas Bingi, one of the ER physicians, is sort of a nuisance. He has asked me for a date four times this week. When we have work to do, I find it unprofessional to see him rushing around to get a chance to talk with me again about going out with him. A couple of the staff have made comments such as 'Dr. Bingi appears to really like you. When are you going out with him?'"

   c. "Bev Miller, CMC's compliance officer, just walked in and dropped a compliance report on my desk. It was for the previous quarter, and she wanted it before the end of the day. I inquired and found that Jane Levy, who usually does the report, is on maternity leave for another two weeks. I'm clueless as to the report requirements, and Bev said it was my job!"

   d. "I've become increasingly aware that many employees and certain physicians are working with cell phones and PDAs, and appear to be conducting personal business on hospital time. This is not unique to any one category of ER employee, but it seems to be all too common to see people standing, walking, or doing a task while talking on a cell phone. I am not able to distinguish a personal call from a business call, but it looks to be unprofessional. Unfortunately, I can find nothing in CMC's policy manual to guide my actions."

   e. "After the first week, it has become very apparent that one employee is mismatched for the position she is in. I reviewed her prior performance appraisals, and even Amy had written her up and given her below-average ratings. Several employees have complained that she should have been fired but that top management frowns on termination. I wonder what options I have?"

3. In your role as one of those assigned above in #2, what suggestions do you have for Charlotte?

4. Write a one-page summary of what you learned from this skills application.

Skills Application 2-4: Attitudes about Labor Unions

1. The following statements are about labor unions. Respond to each, applying the following rating scale:

   Strongly Agree = 4   Agree = 3
   Disagree = 2   Strongly Disagree = 1

   _____ 1. Unions are necessary to protect employees from job favoritism and discrimination.

   _____ 2. Job seniority is the fairest way to reward employees for their services.

   _____ 3. Unions are needed to ensure that workers are paid good wages and receive adequate benefits.

   _____ 4. Without a labor union, employees have little chance to have their complaints handled fairly.

   _____ 5. Every employee who benefits from the union should be required to join and support the union (i.e., a union shop).

_____ 6. Most employees join a labor union because they want to join and they agree with the union's objectives.

_____ 7. The best form of employee job participation occurs when a union can negotiate a labor agreement with an employer to cover the terms and conditions of employment.

_____ 8. Stronger unions and wider representation of employees by unions are needed to counter corporate greed and management's indifference toward workers.

_____ TOTAL (add your scores)

2. Compare your total with the following:
   8–15 You generally do not agree with or approve of labor unions.

16–23 You have mixed attitudes about labor unions.

24–32 You generally support unions and their objectives.

3. Do you agree with the results? Why or why not?

4. Make four copies of this survey, and ask four other people to respond to the statements. At least two of them should be active members of a labor organization. Compare their perceptions with yours. Is there a difference in perceptions? If so, write a one-page paper accounting for the difference in perceptions.

5. Compare your scores with those of another student (or students). Can you explain any differences in perceptions?

Skills Application 2-5: Think Outside the Box

1. Using nine matches, arrange them into three triangles as shown.

2. Your challenge is to try to make five triangles by moving only three matches.

3. Your instructor has been provided with the correct response on the instructor support web site.

Source: Reprinted with permission from QCI International's *Timely Tips for Teams,* a monthly Internet newsletter (July 2005), QCI International, PO Box 438, Red Bluff, CA 96080.

SKILLS DEVELOPMENT VIDEO

Skills Development Module 2-1: McDonald's

This is the second in a series of Skills Development Modules. After viewing the Skills Development Module 2-1 video clip, answer the following questions.

The Golden Arches of McDonald's are known throughout the world. With four global business units—North American, Latin America, Asia/Pacific/Middle East, and Europe and with more than 14,000 locations in the United States McDonald's has a presence unlike others in the food-service business. Millions of customers visit McDonald's each day.

Health conscious customers and economic factors eroded profits in the early years of this century. In January 2003, McDonald's announced its first quarterly loss since going public in 1965. Under the "Plan to Win" program announced in 2003, the company consolidated operating divisions and focused on service and selection at existing locations rather than developing new locations. Menu strategies in the U.S. switched to chicken, breakfast, beverages, and convenience.

At the time of this writing, McDonald's was testing modifications to its popular $1 double cheeseburger and other dollar menu items. Adding espresso drinks, smoothies, ice-blended coffee, and other beverages is expected to add dollars to the bottom-line. The menu changes are expected to be complete by 2009.

Don Thompson, President of McDonald's USA has responsibility for strategic direction and overall business results of 14,000 restaurants in the U.S. He has played a crucial role in the reorganization of the U.S. business which has had four years of unprecedented positive sales growth (2003–2007).[25]

In 2008, high gas prices, the weak housing market, and inflation led to lower consumer spending. At the same time, restaurants have seen rapidly rising ingredient prices. Bennigans, Steak & Ale, Village Inn, Bakers Square, Roadhouse Grill, and other competitors either closed company stores or liquidated. Ruby Tuesday Inc. and other mid-priced, family restaurants saw their sales and profits slide. For some families a night out meant dining off the dollar menu at McDonald's. The competitive environment has intensified and McDonald's must continue innovative management practices to retain customers and be profitable.

1. If you have visited a McDonald's in the past thirty days, evaluate your experience as a customer. How did it compare to that of other restaurants you also visited during that time period?

2. If you have not visited a McDonald's in the past thirty days, why not?

3. Building a customer-oriented workforce is the goal of every tourism, hospitality, and food-service business. After viewing the video and your own experience with McDonald's, what does McDonald's do to differentiate its service from its direct competitors? What else could it do?

4. If you could ask Don Thompson, president of McDonald's USA, LLC, a question, what would it be?

5. After reviewing the skills development video, what do you think his answer would be?

ENDNOTES

1. At the time of this writing, the Supreme Court is wrestling with the definition of what is a supervisor. The issue revolves around "working supervisors," primarily in unionized work environments, and during what percentage of the work day one has to conduct "managerial-type" activities to be considered a "worker" for representation purposes or a "supervisor."

2. Robert Greenleaf coined the phrase "servant-leader." In their essay, "Servant-Leadership and Philanthropic Institutions," Larry Spears and John Burkhart list the ten characteristics central to the development of servant-leaders: listening, empathy, healing, persuasion, awareness, foresight, conceptualization, commitment to the growth of people, stewardship, and building community. See "Leading By Serving," *Philanthropy Matters* (Spring 2008), pp. 8–10, and visit the Greenleaf Center for Servant Leadership (http://www.greenleaf.org) for additional thoughts and research on servant leadership.

3. You can take a free Emotional Intelligence (E.I.) test. Go to http://www.queendom.com/test/access-page/index.htm. This will give you a free "snapshot" report. For a current review of the E.I. research, go to http://www.uh.edu/emotionalintelligence/ or the *Annual Review of Psychology* (2008). Students may also want to review *Emotional Intelligence: Special Issue of The Journal of Organizational Behavior*, Volume 26, Issue 4 (June 2005) for additional insights. Following on the works of others, Hendrie Weisinger identified four building blocks that help to develop skills and abilities, which are to: (1) accurately perceive, appraise, and express emotion; (2) access the ability or generate feelings on demand when they can facilitate understanding of yourself or another person; (3) understand emotions and the knowledge that derives from them; (4) regulate emotions to promote emotional and intellectual growth. See Weisinger, *Emotional Intelligence at Work* (San Francisco: Jossey-Bass, 1998). Also see Daniel Goleman, *Emotional Intelligence* (New York: Bantam Books, 1995); Benedict Carey, "Measuring Emotions: Employee Tests Quantify Degree of Introspection," *Los Angeles Times* (April 20, 2004), p. 8B; Mayer, Salovey, and Caruso, *Emotional IQ Test: CD-ROM Version* (Needham, MA: Virtual Entertainment, 1997); and Steve Bates, "Your Emotional Skills Can Make or Break You," *Nation's Business* (April 1999), p. 17.

4. See Jennifer George, "Emotions and Leadership: The Role of Emotional Intelligence," *Human Relations*, Vol. 53, No. 8 (2000), pp. 1027–1055.

5. For additional information on Pandolfini's principles for making the right decision under pressure, see "All the Right Moves," *Fast Company* (May 1999), p. 34. Also see Dave Kahle, "Characteristics of a Professional . . . Are You Serious About Your Job?" *Supervision* (May 2007), pp. 12–14.

6. As quoted in Steve DiMeglio, "How No. 1 Keeps Getting Better," *USA Today* (March 21–23, 2008), pp. 1A–2A. Woods has won 64 tournaments and is America's highest-paid athlete, earning more than $100 million a year. Between January 2006 and June 2008, Lorena Ochoa won 17 LPGA events. "I'm going to try to just keep getting better and hopefully win a lot of tournaments. I took my five years to get to the top and really feel comfortable with the position. But it's definitely tough," Ochoa was quoted in Steve DiMeglio, "Ochoa Takes Major Dip," *USA Today* (April 17, 2008), p. 14c.

   Annika Sorenstam at the age of 18 became attracted to the concept called "Vision 54"—the idea that she could make birdie on every hole in a round of golf. She didn't get there having to settle for being the only player in LPGA history to shoot a 59. On May 13, 2008, at the time she announced her retirement, Sorenstam had won 72 events including ten majors. "It's all or nothing for me. I know what it's like to play good golf. If I can't play good golf, I don't want to play. I give 100%. There has never been an alternative. I'm leaving the game on my terms." (As adapted from Doug Ferguson, "Sorenstam Ends Run at Perfection," *The Fort Wayne, Indiana Journal Gazette* (May 14, 2008), p. 2B.

   There are many similarities between these great golfers and truly great supervisors.

7. Eldrick (Tiger) Woods became the first person to hold all four major golf championships at the same time. For information on his career and his tips for improvement, see http://www.tigerwoods.com. Quote from Tiger Woods used with permission of Tiger Woods via IMG, Cleveland, OH 44114-1782 (August 17, 2005). One has to go no further than to revisit Tiger's performance in the 2008 U.S. Open Golf Tournament at Torrey Pines to be reminded of his tenacity in the face of adversity (out of action for eight weeks following his knee surgery)—you could see the pain with every shot. Yet he won another Major Championship.

8. Adapted from the Titleist ad, "Which Ball is Best for Your Game?" *Golf Digest* (September 8, 2008), pp. 5–6. Also see, "Tiger Woods' Lesson Tee," *Golf Digest* (September 8, 2008), p. 29.

9. Ibid; The back cover of *Golf Digest Tips* (July 2008) finds an action shot of Tiger and an advertisement for Accenture: "We know what it is like to be a Tiger. To see insights from our research and experience including our study of 500 high performers, visit accenture.com/research."

10. We first heard the term *enabler* used in the video The Performance Appraisal, produced and distributed by Business Advantage, Inc., of West Des Moines, Iowa.

11. op,cit. Servant-Leader (see end note # 2 above).

12. Glenn M. Parker, *Cross-Functional Teams: Working with Allies, Enemies, and Other Strangers* (San Francisco: Jossey-Bass, 1998). Support for the team concept comes from testimonials like those cited in Paulette Thomas, "Teams Rule According to U.S. Manufacturers," the *Wall Street Journal* (May 28, 1996), p. 1. Students have found the Center for the Study of Work Teams (http://www.workteams.unt.edu) to be a valuable source for learning about work team implementation.

13. Fran Rees, *How to Lead Work Teams: Facilitation Skills* (San Diego: Pfeiffer & Company, 1991), pp. 1–2. Also see Wolfgang Jenewein and Felicitas Morhart, "Navigating Toward Team Success," *Team Performance Management*, Vol. 13, Iss.1/2 (2008), pp. 102+; Maria Isabel Delgado Pina, Ana Maria Romero-Martinez and Luis Gomez Martinez, "Teams in Organization: A Review on Team Effectiveness," *Team Performance Management*, Vol. 13, Iss.1/2 (2008), pp. 7–21; and Casimer DeCusatis, "Creating, Growing and Sustaining Efficient Innovation Teams," *Creativity and Innovation Management*, Vol. 17, Iss.2 (June 2008), pp. 155–164.

14. See Abraham Zaleznik, "Managers and Leaders: Are They Different?" *Harvard Business Review* (May–June 1977), pp. 126–35 and "Letting Leaders Replace Corporate Managers," *The Washington Post* (September 27, 1992), pp. 1–5. For a definitive description of managerial roles, see Henry Mintzberg, *The Nature of Managerial Work* (New York: Harper & Row, 1973), and Peter F. Drucker, *Management Challenges for the 21st Century* (New York, HarperBusiness, 1999). Also see Joan Magretta and Nan Stone, "The Original Management Guru," the *Wall Street Journal* (November 11, 1999), p. A20 for Drucker's insights regarding "knowledge work."

15. Stephen R. Covey, The Seven Habits of Highly Effective People (New York: Simon & Schuster, 1989), p. 101; The Speed of Trust (New York: Free Press, 2007); Principle-Centered Leadership: Strategies for Personal & Professional Effectiveness (Bellevue: S&S Trade, 1992); and The 8th Habit (New York: Simon & Schuster, 2003).

16. See Noel Tichy and Warren Bennis, *Judgment: How Winning Leaders Make Great Calls* (New York: Portfolio-Penguin Group, 2007) and as discussed in *BusinessWeek* (November 18, 2007), pp. 68–72; Scott M. Patton, "It's About Leadership, Stupid," *Quality Digest* (March 2008), p. 56. A 2007 study by The Forum Corp. found that most leaders weren't equipped with the skills necessary to execute their companies' growth strategies. (As reported in Pamela Babcock, "Survey: Many Leadership Development Programs Too Tactical," *SHRM News* (May 2008). Also see Warren Bennis, *On Becoming a Leader* (Reading, MA: Addison-Wesley Publishing Co., 1994) and Peter Drucker, *Management Challenges for the 21st Century* (New York: Harper Collins, 1999) for insights into the differences between managers and leaders. Also, see what is going on at the Center for Creative Leadership (www.ccl.org).

17. Adapted from John P. Kotter, *John P. Kotter on What Leaders Really Do* (Boston: Harvard Business School Press, 1999). Also see M. Avesson and S. Sveningsson, "Managers Doing Leadership: The Extra-Ordinarization of the Mundane," *Human Relations*, 56, 12 (December 1, 2003), pp. 1435–59.

18. One of Fayol's fourteen principles of management defined formal authority as the "right to give orders." Henri Fayol, *General and Industrial Management*, trans. Constance Storrs (London: Sir Isaac Pitman & Sons, 1949), pp. 19–43.

19. See W. H. Weiss, "The Art & Science of Managing," *Supervision* (October 2007), pp. 16–20; and David Sirota, Louis A. Mischkind, and Michael Irwin Meltzer, "Stop Demoting Your Employees!" *Harvard Management Update*, 11, 1 (January 2006). In about 85 percent of companies, employee morale sharply declines after only six months on the job. Sirota, Mischkind, and Meltzer's research shows how an individual manager's style of supervision contributes to the problem.

20. Much has been written about power. For additional information on position power and personal power, see Amitai Etzioni, *A Comparative Analysis of Complex Organizations* (New York: The Free Press, 1961), pp. 4–6; and John P. Kotter, "Power, Dependence, and Effective Management," *Harvard Business Review* (July–August 1977), pp. 131–36.

21. John R. P. French and Bertram Raven, "The Bases of Social Power," in *Studies in Social Power*, ed. Dorwin Cartwright (Ann Arbor: University of Michigan Press, 1959), pp. 150–67. Also see A. J. Stanhelski, D. E. Frost, and M. E. Patch, "Uses of Socially Dependent Bases of Power: French and Raven's Theory Applied to Working Group Leadership," *Journal of Applied Social Psychology* (March 1989), pp. 283–97.

22. See Timothy R. Hinkin and Chester A. Schriesheim, "Relationships Between Subordinate Perceptions and Supervisor Influence Tactics and Attributed Bases of Supervisory Power," *Human Relations* (March 1990), pp. 221–37. Also see K. S. Cameron, D. Bright, and A. Carza, "Exploring the Relationships between Organizational Virtuousness and Performance," *American Behavior Scientist*, 47, 6 (February 1, 2004), pp. 766–790; and Office Team, "Survey Highlights Traits Employees Want Most in Managers," as reported by AccountingWeb.com (September 13, 2004).

23. See Merriam-Webster's Website (HYPERLINK "http://www.merriam-webster.com/dictionary/network" www.merriam-webster.com/dictionary/network). As of June 2008, 12.1 percent of the total workforce was unionized, mostly in the public sector. I suggest that you secure a copy of a *Guide to Basic Law and Procedures Under the National Labor Relations Act* (Washington, D.C.; U.S. Government Printing Office, NLRB; or visit the National Labor Relations Board Web site (http://www.nlrb.gov/nlrb/legal/manuals/rules/act.asp) for an overview of labor law. For comprehensive information concerning U.S. labor relations laws, processes, and issues, the following are recommended: Susan Jackson, Randall S. Schuler, and Steve Werner, *Managing Human Resources*, 10th Edition (Mason, OH; South-Western/Cengage Learning, 2009); Darlene Y. Motley and Jeffrey Guiler, "Betwixt and Between—How to Assist Union Supervisors with the Changing Roles of Responsibilities," (January 2008), pp. 3–5; Robert L. Mathis and John H. Jackson, *Human Resource Management*, 12th Edition (Mason, OH: Thomson/South-Western, 2008); George Bohlander and Scott Snell, *Managing Human Resources*, 14th Edition (Mason, OH: South-Western/Cengage Learning, 2007); Edwin C. Leonard, Jr. and Roy A. Cook, *Human Resource Management: 21st Century Challenges* (Mason, OH: Thomson Custom Publishing, 2005); Edwin C. Leonard, Jr., Claire M. Killian, and Raymond L. Hilgert, *Labor Agreement Negotiations*, 7th Edition (Mason, OH: Thomson Custom Publishing, 2004).

24. Stephen R. Covey as quoted at http://quotations.about.com/od/stillmorefamouspeople/a/StephenCovey1/.htm (accessed July 8, 2005).

25. Information gleaned from personal interviews with McDonald's USA executives, annual reports and internal information provided by McDonald's USA (August 2008). For information on what the casual restaurants were doing to attract customers, see Jacob Stokes, "Honey, Let's Eat at Home Tonight," *BusinessWeek* (August 25–September 1, 2008). P. 073.

CASE 1-1
The Opportunity of a Lifetime?

Randy Harber, a 36-year-old construction crew chief, is employed by one of the largest mechanical contractors in the country. His employer operates in 44 states and 14 foreign countries. Randy and his spouse, Eileen, have two children, seven-year-old Kelly and three-year-old Jason. Eileen is a registered nurse and works part-time in a family-practice office. Randy began his career in the construction field by entering the apprenticeship program immediately upon completing high school. He served as an officer in the local union and became a crew chief three years ago. His technical skills rank among the best. During the past two years, he has taken evening courses at the local community college to enhance his supervisory skills and to improve his chances of becoming a field superintendent. However, the construction industry has experienced no real growth, and opportunities for advancement are slim. During the past winter, Randy and others suffered reduced work weeks and had their use of the company truck severely restricted.

Randy Harber had been called to meet with Kevin Cook, vice president of field operations, in Cook's office. The following conversation took place:

KEVIN: Randy, you know that our revenues are down about 25 percent from last year.

RANDY: Yes. (Thinking to himself, "Here it comes: I'm going to get laid off.")

KEVIN: We've been trying to expand our base of operations and have bid on contracts all over the world. I think we have the opportunity of a lifetime, and you figure to be one of our key players. The United Methodist Church is collaborating in a joint venture in Liberia to build a hospital on the outskirts of Monrovia, the capital city. They have a medical missionary program there, and this hospital is a $23-million project. The general contractor will be out of Milan, Italy, and we have received the mechanical portion of the contract.

RANDY: That's great! We can use the work.

KEVIN: This project will give us a strategic advantage in the European-African corridor. Top management has talked it over, and we would like for you to be our field superintendent on this project. Not only is this a great opportunity for us, but it will give you invaluable experience. In addition, your salary will almost double. All the people on this project will be our very best. You'll be leaving in three weeks, and we'd expect you to be on-site for fourteen months. What do you think?

RANDY: Geez, that sounds fascinating. How soon do you need an answer?

KEVIN: Go home, think it over, talk to Eileen, and let's get back together tomorrow afternoon at about 3:00.

Questions for Discussion

1. Evaluate the offer made to Randy Harber. Do you agree that this is the opportunity of a lifetime? Why or why not?

2. What factors should Harber consider, and how should Harber evaluate his career options?

3. (**INTERNET ACTIVITY**) If you were Randy Harber, what would you do and why? (Before you answer these questions, you may want to check some Web sites to get information on the country's history, economy, business and governmental practices, policies, culture, language, and living conditions.)

CASE 1-2
The Socializing Supervisor

Terry Miles was promoted to a supervisory position in the Glendale street department's repair (chip and seal with new asphalt) section. He was chosen for the position by the manager of utility operations, Ronnie Callahan, who felt that Miles was the "ideal" candidate for the position. Miles had been hired five years earlier as a general-purpose employee. Utility operations cross-trained all new employees so they were capable in a variety of functions. Although two other employees had been in the division for at least twelve years, they had constantly expressed their dislike for supervisory responsibilities. In addition, Miles's job performance ratings had been very good, his attendance was near-perfect, and he seemed to be well liked by his colleagues and others who knew him well.

When Callahan told Miles that he was to become supervisor of the repair section, Miles expressed apprehension about leaving the security that his union position afforded and worried that his fellow employees would see him as a "turncoat." He asked Callahan how he should handle the problem that his fellow employees now would be his "subordinates." Callahan told Miles not to be concerned about this and assured him that his former associates would soon accept the transition. Callahan also told Miles that the company would send him to a supervisory management training program sponsored by a local college just as soon as time became available.

After several months, however, Jerry Mitchell, general superintendent of the street department who reported to Callahan and who was Miles's immediate manager, was getting the impression that Miles was not adjusting to his new position. Although Mitchell had not been directly involved in Miles's selection, he felt Miles was an excellent worker who was not progressing in the supervisory position. Mitchell was particularly concerned because he had observed Miles socializing with his employees during lunch periods and coffee breaks. Callahan had received reports that Miles often socialized with several of his employees after work, including going on double dates and to ballgames and parties arranged by these employees. Despite Miles's assurances, Mitchell had received a number of reports directly from City Council members and the mayor's office that the work of the repair section was not being performed as efficiently as it should be. Another utilities department manager even told Callahan, "Since Miles became supervisor, there is little discipline in the department, and it's just a big social group that reluctantly does a little work."

After reviewing various productivity reports, Mitchell realized that Miles had not made a good adjustment to supervising employees in his department. Overtime had been substantially higher when compared with the preceding two years. Rework had increased, and it appeared that the crews were not doing the job right the first time. The previous evening, one of the local television stations had announced a "pothole of the week" contest. He wondered how much of this was attributable to Miles's lack of experience as a team leader, and he worried that Miles's former colleagues might be taking advantage of him. At the same time, Mitchell was concerned that Miles perhaps did not have the desire to disassociate himself from socializing and being a "buddy" to his employees. Mitchell wondered what his next step should be.

Questions for Discussion

1. Evaluate the decision to promote Terry Miles to supervisor. Discuss the problems in promoting anyone to team leader or supervisor over his or her former fellow employees.

2. Besides sending Miles to a supervisory training program, what other actions could Callahan and Mitchell have taken to prepare Miles for the transition to the supervisor role? On a sheet of paper, outline a training evaluation strategy that Jerry Mitchell and Ronnie Callahan could use to evaluate Miles's progress as a newly elevated supervisor.

3. Why is it dangerous for a team leader or supervisor to socialize with direct-report employees? Why does this leave a team leader or supervisor open to criticism as exemplified in this case?

4. At the end of the case, what should Jerry Mitchell do? Consider alternatives that may be open.

5. (**INTERNET ACTIVITY**) Surf the Web to find information that supports the hiring decision of Terry Miles by Ronnie Callahan. Is it a good practice for the immediate manager not to be directly involved in the hiring process? Why or why not?

6. What are the consequences if the decision is made to demote or terminate Miles? If the position becomes vacant, what criteria should be used to determine who will get the job? Did your criteria dovetail with the list of eight management skills presented in Chapter 2?

CASE 1-3

Where Should Glen Go from Here?

Glen Rogers is a production supervisor at Crandall Automotive, a Midwestern piston manufacturer. Thirty years ago, he joined the tool-and-die apprentice program at Crandall immediately upon graduation from high school. He was a better-than-average athlete and played on the company's softball team. Almost immediately after becoming a journeyman tool-and-die maker, Roger's became active in the union. During the good time of the late 1980s and 1990s, he was a member of the union's bargaining team.

About twelve years ago, company president Fred Crandall asked him to consider joining the company's supervisory team. However, Rogers found the transition to supervision problematic. Things changed constantly, and he spent increasingly more time explaining why things had to be done differently. Top management expected him to identify problems and to solve those problems as quickly as possible. Rogers found himself in the proverbial position of being between a "rock and a hard place." His former colleagues wanted to only "work to the rules of the contract," but top management was constantly pushing to find efficiencies and improve production processes.

When the plant opened in 1942, it had 900 employees and the average wage was much higher than that of the larger community, making jobs at Crandall Automotive attractive. In 2008, the average wage of hourly workers, including benefits and overtime, was about $44 an hour.

In early October, the union rejected a three-year proposed contract that called for an estimated twelve percent across-the-board wage cut and other concessions, including a requirement for employees and retirees to contribute a larger percentage for their healthcare coverage. New bookings for orders had fallen substantially in the preceding quarter, and the forecast for the next six months was bleak at best. Ford, one of Crandall's largest customers, said it would slash 35,000 jobs, shut five plants, and drop four models. At that time, all employees received a registered letter informing them of the company's intention to eliminate a substantial portion of the workforce.

The week before Thanksgiving, the Crandall family announced plans to relocate its corporate staff and to lease its entire headquarters building to a local hospital. The real shock came when a local reporter broke the story that the Crandall family had tentatively accepted an offer from a Chinese firm for the purchase of its physical assets, as well as its intellectual properties. Media coverage indicated that the sale was subject to approval from various government agencies. According to the writer, "Chery's Chairman and CEO Yin Tongyao explained how he sees the energy crisis as an opportunity for Chery—China's leading car exporter—to sell Chery's small and midmarket cars in European and U.S. markets." The article also pointed out that other U.S. firms were contemplating offers from Chinese conglomerates.

U.S. automakers were in dire straits. General Motors, Ford, and Chrysler offered customers opportunities to purchase their autos at the same price that employees would pay. GM announced that several plants would be shuttered and that 20,000 or so employees were accepting "buy-outs" to leave the company. Analysts estimated that on-lot inventory was a half-year supply. With gasoline prices between $4 and $5 per gallon, gas-guzzling SUVs and pickups were begging for buyers. Deep incentive discounts offered to customers, coupled with other incentives, were not having much of an impact on consumers. Headline writers were predicting a grim future for the industry. As Christmas approached, Crandall laid off another 160 workers, shrinking its workforce to about 260, including salaried employees, from more than 1,200 in 2001. Some Crandall employees had been idle for a long time and did not expect to return. Rogers wondered if this restructuring would return Crandall to profitability. Good or bad, the company and union were unable to find common points of agreement. The current contract would expire on June 30.

On December 26, Jon Crandall, vice-president of finance and grandson of the founder, announced that Crandall would be shutting down the entire facility. A few highly skilled maintenance employees and several members of management would have an opportunity to relocate on a temporary basis to the new Chinese facility. Even though the sale to the Chinese company was not expected to be completed for some time, the company had developed a production site in China that would be fully operational no later than June. The union was expected to file unfair labor practice charges against the company. While the current contract had specific prohibitions regarding subcontracting, the contract was mute on closing the entire plant. Like many automotive suppliers, Crandall Automotive was looking for a way to survive, and management contended that the only way to survive was to lower total manufacturing costs. Glen Rogers's job would be eliminated no later than April 15. He knew that he would get one week of severance pay for each year of service with the company and that medical benefits could be extended under COBRA regulations. He worried about his prospects for a new job. Who would need a 50-year-old former-tool-and-die-maker-turned-supervisor? Rogers wondered whether the company would have sufficient finances to cover all the severance payments. Whether the U.S. economy was or was not in a recession was debatable. Rogers remembered the adage, "It's a recession when your friends are unemployed, but it's a depression when you're unemployed." No one could remember worse economic conditions.

It was the Friday afternoon after Christmas as Rogers reflected on the events of the past two days. Christmas Day had been a time of celebration. Today, it felt like the end of the world. Rogers was sitting in the car thinking about how he would tell Nancy, his wife of 28 years, and their three children, Samantha, age 27, Andrew, age 23, and Hope, age 18. Andrew would be graduating from college in the spring, and Hope, a high school senior, was expecting to go to college in the fall. Nancy worked full-time as a retail clerk for the first several years of their marriage, but had been a full-time homemaker for many years. When Hope entered high school, Nancy had contemplated getting a part-time job, but since Glen's yearly income was approximately $75,000 per year, she had decided to wait.

Like many of their friends, Glen and Nancy Rogers had not saved for a rainy day—they had lived from paycheck to paycheck with the belief that Glen's job at Crandall Automotive would always be there. Unfortunately, the recent low interest rates had enticed them into the new home market two years ago. Their monthly mortgage payments were in excess of $1,100 a month on the 20-year mortgage. Glen Rogers had invested 30 years at Crandall Automotive, and, in three months, it would be over. He knew that he could probably get a job as a greeter at the new Wal-Mart Super Store opening in June or work the counter at Taco Bell, but the reality was that it might be very difficult to get a good job at his age. Rogers knew that whatever job he might find would not provide him the standard of living to which he had grown accustomed. And few companies offered medical benefits nearly as good as those offered by Crandall. Crandall's human resources director said the company would provide some outplacement counseling to assist the displaced workers.

Questions for Discussion

1. Should Glen Rogers have anticipated that his job at Crandall might not come with a "lifetime guarantee"? What could he have done to prepare for a second career?
2. List the strengths and weaknesses Glen Rogers might have as he begins a new job search. Make a list of his SKAs.
3. If you were Glen Rogers, what would you do? What steps would you take to find gainful and meaningful employment?
4. What should Glen and Nancy Rogers do to survive?
5. Look carefully at Skills Application 1-4 on pages 33 and 34. Which of those jobs, if any, should Glen Rogers consider? Assume that you are Glen Rogers. Write a cover letter expressing an interest in one of the jobs.
6. What important life lessons did you learn from this case?

CASE 1-4
Who Should Be Promoted to Team Leader?

Henry Hardware and Home Center is owned by the Henry family. Great-grandpa Samuel Henry (now deceased) opened his first store in 1927. Sons Bob, Joe, and Tom followed him into the hardware business. The family now owns eight hardware/home centers in central Ohio. Competition from the "big box" stores—Lowe's, Home Depot, and Menard's—has not severely impacted Henry. At the time of this case, housing-starts were spiraling downward, foreclosures were on the rise, mortgage rates were rising, and food and gasoline prices were at record highs. These issues, coupled with a weak job market, caused management to take a more proactive approach. They increased advertising and promotion expenses; began actively cultivating the industrial- and government-sector market; and encouraged employees to be engaged in a process of continuous improvement. Historically, Henry had taken pride in their "positively outrageous customer service" and use of variable pricing techniques to effectively compete with the big boxes. All employees have been cross-trained in the various product lines and services that Henry provided, including the rental and garden centers.

Amanda Frazier is the store manager for Henry Hardware Mansfield store. Early one morning, Yah Say, a stock clerk, approached her.

YAH SAY: Amanda, I hear that Tim Stapleton was promoted to team leader. Why didn't I get a chance at the promotion? I've been working here eight years, and he's only been here six. Doesn't seniority count as long as two people are equally qualified?

Before she could answer, Yah continued, "I came to this country when I was ten. I started working here when I was sixteen as a sophomore in high school. I've done a good job for you, haven't I?"

FRAZIER: Yah, you were one of those considered for the job, but I didn't feel you were qualified to handle the job. So you were passed over.

YAH SAY: What do you mean, I'm not qualified? I've done the job several times in the past while filling in for other team leaders when they were on vacation or an emergency came up. You've never told me before that I couldn't handle it. It was my understanding that I'd get the next team leader slot on the basis of my seniority. Now you are telling me that I don't have the ability to do what I've already done before.

FRAZIER: Nevertheless, that's our decision.

YAH SAY: That may be your decision now, but you'll think differently when Sue Henry contacts you [Sue Henry is the company's Human Resources (HR) manager.]

With that, Yah Say walked away.

Frazier started to think about what Yah Say had said and remembered certain facts that she would bring out if HR did get involved. She considered Yah a satisfactory stock clerk but certainly not above-average. She believed Yah lacked the ability and dependability to handle the job of team leader. On several occasions, when Yah had relieved or filled in for the other team leaders, the store had experienced out-of-stocks as a result of his poor ordering. Twice Frazier had received telephone calls from the police on the nights that Yah had closed up the store and had accidentally set off the burglar alarm. She further noted that Yah was frequently absent from work. During the previous year, Yah been absent eighteen days, offering illness as the reason for his absences.

Several days later, Frazier was confronted by her boss, Joe Henry III (referred to as "III") and Sue Henry, grandchildren of the founder. As district manager, III was responsible for four of the Henry stores. The following dialogue took place:

SUSAN HENRY: Amanda, Yah Say came to see me yesterday and he has a gripe about the promotion decision. He wanted to know more about our grievance procedure. [Henry Hardware and Home Center uses a conflict-mediation technique to resolve employee grievances, complaints, and concerns.] Yah is claiming that we should have let him have a chance to prove he can handle the job. How well has he done when he's filled in as a temporary team leader?

FRAZIER: Terrible, Susan. The police called me twice because Yah bungled the burglar alarm, and we had numerous out-of-stocks from his ordering.

III: Why didn't you tell me about this before? Did you talk to Yah about these things?

FRAZIER: I thought I did tell you, Susan, didn't I? But I think I did talk to Yah about it and discussed what he needed to do prevent it from happening again but I never took time to write it down. Yah has caused me a lot of headaches – more than all the other employees put together.

SUSAN: Well, according to his personnel file, he has never been written up. And as far as I can see, by seniority he was in line for a promotion. In response to his complaint, I told him that I would talk to you about the situation and get back with him. Before we go much further with this discussion, I want to refer to a statement in our Employee Handbook: "Henry Hardware and Home Center believes in providing employees with opportunities for growth. As the organization prospers and grows, so shall our employees . . . When an opening occurs, employees within that store will be the first ones considered . . . All else being equal, seniority with Henry Hardware will be the primary criterion for advancement."

FRAZIER: That's a big mistake, Susan, because Yah cannot handle it. Besides all that, he is absent too often.

III: What do you mean, "absent too often"?

FRAZIER: Over the past year he has been "sick" 18 days.

SUSAN: There's no mention of any sick pay granted in his file. Was he paid for sick leave?

FRAZIER: Darned if I know. I don't have time to pay attention to all these paperwork details. You know our store is one of the busiest and most profitable of all the stores and if I spent all my time on paperwork, important things wouldn't get done.

III: Okay, Amanda. I guess we've got a real problem. When we leave here, I want you to close your office door and carefully read the employee handbook. Take a look at this provision on promotions. It has been our policy to give preference to the most senior employee, provided merit and ability are equal. Think about what we should do and let's get back together this evening.

SUSAN: I have to be honest with both of you. This situation scares me. Yah Say is a refugee from Burma (Myanmar) and, thus, is a member of a protected class. I know that this refugee group has a strong support network, and if Yah Say is disgruntled it could have both legal and financial implications.

FRAZIER: I think we should take a stand and stick with our original decision. Yah just doesn't deserve the promotion, and I'll have nothing but trouble if he becomes a head stock clerk.

Questions for Discussion

1. Discuss the relative effectiveness of Amanda Frazier's performance as store manager. (In framing your answer, be sure to touch upon each of the management skills discussed in Chapter 2.)
2. Did Amanda Frazier handle the situation with Yah Say appropriately? Why or why not?
3. What advice would you give to Amanda Frazier on how to be a more effective leader at the Mansfield store?
4. What are some arguments for and against Yah Say being promoted to the team leader position? How does Yah Say being a refugee affect your answer?
5. Using the Internet, answer the following:
   a. How pervasive is the absenteeism problem in the U.S.?
   b. What costs are associated with absenteeism?
   c.  What strategies might Amanda use to get employees such as Yah Say to be punctual and at work when scheduled?

Malcolm Peters could not believe his ears. He was sitting in a classroom at Old Ivy University for his morning class with Professor Cary Raymond. On this day, an invited guest and young alumnus, Donnie Sanchez, was speaking to the class.

Sanchez was stating that his experiences as a student had prepared him for the "real world." Sanchez first recalled that about a year earlier, he had been sitting where the students were sitting and wondering what the future would hold. As Malcolm Peters listened intently, he heard echoes of some of Professor Raymond's recent lectures. Peters thought to himself, "Can it be that my professor actually knows what he is talking about?"

Donnie Sanchez continued: "Each term, Professor Raymond posed the question to our class, 'Where do you want to go tomorrow?' Every semester, he preached that we needed career self-reliance or at least career self-direction. It was the question facing each of us as we planned our sprint into the full-time job market. Throughout the '90s, the U.S. economy had surged but then peaked with the dawn of the millennium. Jobs were in plentiful supply for the 'techies' and those willing to work for basic entry-level wages. I played on the college baseball team and in summer leagues, so a co-op program or internship was out of the question. I felt I had pretty good interpersonal skills, persistence, and a high energy level, but no experience. The college placement officer told me that I would probably have trouble finding meaningful work. After posting my resume on the Web and reviewing many Internet databases, I found that restaurants, computer companies, and engineering firms were hiring at a brisk pace. Even though I love to eat, the restaurant field was not appealing, and I lacked technical and computer courses and experience to apply for a computer or engineering firm job. As a native of Puerto Rico, I had braved the cold Midwest winters to play college sports and pursue a basic liberal arts degree.

"Midway through my sophomore year, I heard some of my teammates extolling the virtues of Professor Cary Raymond. After enrolling in his Principles of Management class, I changed my major to general management. I don't want to embarrass Professor Raymond in front of his students, but I can honestly say that he was my best teacher. He played the role of brain surgeon; he asked thought-provoking questions and demanded a lot from us. He extracted my best efforts and output, even after a strenuous day of practice. Professor Raymond required us to read *What Color Is Your Parachute? A Practical Manual for Job-Hunters and Career-Changers*. I decided to follow the advice offered by the author, Richard Boles, so I contacted Tom Mercer, a supervisor at a local electronics firm. Luxor employs about 280 people and manufactures and assembles electronic components for the telecommunications industry. I had the opportunity to shadow Tom Mercer as part of my senior class project in Professor Raymond's Management of Technological Change course. Mercer's project team was changing some of Luxor's methods and processes. I learned a lot about the process of change and gained a mentor and friend in the experience. Toward the end of my last semester, I really just wanted to touch base with Tom Mercer and ask him one simple question: 'Do you know of any jobs in general management?' I got the surprise of my life when he told me to come to Luxor that afternoon and meet with him and Philip Lynn, the plant manager. I was hired on the spot. I guess having a recommendation from Professor Raymond didn't hurt!

"Even though the work is somewhat technical, I was hired. They put me through a series of tests to prove that I was a self-starter and a team player. Mr. Lynn says he hires for attitude over aptitude. He claims that technical stuff is teachable but initiative and ethics aren't. The plant is organized on a self-directed work-team approach. Teams elect their own leaders to oversee quality, training, scheduling, and communication with other teams. The goals are created by Mr. Lynn and his staff after in-depth consultation with all teams. The plant follows simple ground rules, such as *commit yourself to respect all team members*, *communicate openly and honestly*, *continually look for ways to improve on what we do well*, and *do the right job the right way the first time*.

"The sales staff, customers, engineers, and assemblers constantly 'noodle ideas around,' and there are no status symbols or an attitude of 'us' versus 'them.' There are no sacred cows in the company. Many procedures are written down, but any employee can propose changes to any procedure, subject to approval by those whose work it affects. When we change processes or methods, an employee logs onto the network to make it a part of the record—the law of the plant. There is plenty of feedback on performance. Team leaders share the good and the bad. Each day begins with a recap of the previous day's performance. Every employee knows the destination of every product they touch. Each employee puts his or her signature on the part.

"In conclusion, let me say that I have been in an intensive apprenticeship with experienced employees as my guides. Tom Mercer serves as my mentor, and we meet each day to discuss my progress. I have visited customers to understand how they use our products. The company has a bonus system based on individual performance, team performance, and ideas generated. Last year the bonus averaged in excess of twenty percent of regular pay. Even though I have only limited authority, I'm getting an education for a lifetime and getting paid to learn. It doesn't get any better!"

Malcolm Peters reflected on Donnie Sanchez's remarks: "Is he making this up, or are there really companies like Luxor, and how in the world could I be as lucky as this guy in finding a great job?"

Questions for Discussion

1. Do you think Donnie Sanchez really has a great job? Or was he exaggerating his experiences? Why or why not?
2. Evaluate why Sanchez is excited about his job and future.
3. Evaluate the "techniques" Donnie Sanchez used to obtain the job at Luxor. Do you think Malcolm Peters could use the same techniques to find a great job? Discuss.
4. Would you like to work at Luxor? Why or why not? What would be your concept of a "great job to launch a great career"?

CASE 1-6
Fear of Being Passed on the Corporate Ladder

Mark Wells is the evening shift warehouse supervisor for Sanders Supermarkets, a large grocery-store chain. Over the past 12 years, with only a high-school education, Mark has worked his way up from being a laborer to a supervisor. The 35-year-old Wells is married with two school-aged children, and wants to move to the day shift so that he can spend more time with his family.

Two days ago, Mark's boss, John Swanson, told him that the current day-shift supervisor was retiring at the end of the month and Mark was first in line for the job. This would be a lateral move; there would be no change in title and no pay increase. Actually, Mark would take a $20-per-week reduction because the evening shift salary included a premium shift differential. Nevertheless, Mark Wells was very interested because he saw it as his only near-term opportunity to move to the day shift.

PART 1 CASES

Mark's assistant, or leadman, on the evening shift was Sam Melton, an energetic and intelligent young man in his mid-twenties who had been with the company for three years. Sam had been attending a local community college, and he recently completed a two-year management certification program. Mark felt somewhat intimidated by Sam's credentials, his easygoing personality, his exceptional communications skills, and his ability to get work crews to go the "extra mile." On several occasions, Sam was able to get work crews to complete difficult projects that Mark could not accomplish. Mark knew that if he took the day-shift position, Sam likely would be promoted to evening-shift supervisor. Then Sam would be able to demonstrate to upper management his superior supervisory skills. Because opportunities for advancement beyond the supervisory position were limited, Mark was concerned that Sam would soon pass him by on the corporate ladder. Thus, Mark would be forever trapped in a first-tier supervisory position with little hope for advancement.

Questions for Discussion

1. What factors account for Mark Wells's apprehensions in this situation?
2. What should Mark do if the day-shift supervisory position is offered to him? Why?
3. Is it realistic for supervisors like Mark Wells to expect that younger former subordinates will not pass them on the corporate ladder? Why?
4. What specifically could Mark Wells do to increase the value of his services and potential (e.g., increase the SKAs he brings to work each day)?

CASE 1-7
Coping with the New Manager

Cindy Smith is a supervisory training facilitator at the Barry Automotive Albion plant. The plant makes composite plastic components for the automotive industry. Plastic components are more durable and resist dents and scratches better than components made of steel. The non-unionized facility employs about 450 personnel. Eight years ago, Smith began as a second-shift entry-level worker in the modeling section. After a series of advancements, she was promoted to production supervisor and then to training facilitator, and she had been performing this function for about sixteen months. New employees were assigned to Smith's section for orientation and training, usually lasting a week or more. Depending on the company's needs, employees then were reassigned to a specific production department. In recent months, however, the high turnover rate—25 percent of new hires quit within six weeks of hire—coupled with requirements to produce a variety of high-quality products for individual customer specifications have led to a deterioration of morale.

Traditionally, the average car buyer waited 26 to 35 days from the time a custom order was placed at a dealership until the customer could drive the vehicle off the lot. However, during the past decade, some manufacturers had cut the time to build a car—from the moment the customer places an order at the dealership to the time the vehicle rolls off the assembly line—to five days. No more than five days for travel was allotted from the plant to the dealership. Reducing the time to build a car to customer specifications, including color, engine type, and other options, had been an ongoing effort. As a supplier to the automotive industry, additional quality and production pressures were placed on the plant management team.

About one year earlier, Operations Manager George Patterson was replaced by Don May. Even though the plant often had missed delivery deadlines and labor costs as a percentage of product costs were escalating, Patterson had been content with the status of the plant. Patterson had the reputation of expecting department managers to correct problems after they occurred, and "crisis management" was the prevalent style. Don May, a former military officer, was expected to turn the place around. Under May's direction, the culture of the plant seemed to change overnight. May immediately announced to all supervisors that he was not willing to accept the high rate of product rejects. May practiced management by wandering around (MBWA), and he met and talked with supervisors, group leaders, and facilitators one-on-one. Further, he met with small groups of employees and listened to their concerns. Initially, May was positively received, but the situation soon deteriorated.

Shortly after assuming the position of operations manager, Don May informed all managers and supervisors that they were being placed on a salary-and-bonus system. He told them that their hard work was appreciated and would be rewarded. Yet because of costly rework production delays and overtime for hourly employees, the bonus system did not yield any tangible benefits. Among the supervisory complaints: "You told us the new system would result in greater compensation, and it hasn't. We're making less than before. We'd be better off financially if we were hourly production workers!"

Most supervisors now were working six days a week, ten to twelve hours a day. Employees and machinery were being stretched to the limit. Several supervisors had quit during the past month, and some took less-demanding plant jobs. Surviving supervisors often worked "double duty" in overseeing several production departments. On any given day, ten to twenty percent of employee production positions could be vacant. Cindy Smith and her only remaining employee (five were assigned to fill in for vacant supervisory positions and one was placed in the quality department) were directed by Don May to cut the normal one-week training time to a half day. The most recent customer quality audit was a disaster. There were rumors that some work would be transferred to other Barry plants or even to competitors.

To Cindy Smith, it was like someone had flipped a switch. Any supervisor who spoke out and didn't agree with Don May "fell from grace," and May put pressure on all who questioned what he was doing. Most supervisors were afraid to speak up. To Smith, supervisors appeared to be "mindless robots going through the motions." Smith's crowning blow came at a choir rehearsal in her church Wednesday night. Amy Richardson, a fellow choir member and a front-office secretary to Don May, told Smith, "Mr. May told me that when he was meeting with and interviewing our supervisors he was actually getting the scoop on everyone. He took names and tucked them away. I even heard him tell Bill Arnold, Barry's president, that he'd get rid of all malcontents." Cindy Smith felt betrayed.

Questions for Discussion

1. How would you evaluate Cindy Smith's situation in terms of job satisfaction?
2. Compare and contrast the management styles of George Patterson and Don May.
3. What should Cindy Smith do? Why?
4. Have you ever experienced a situation like the one described in this case? If so, how did you handle those problems?
   If not, how would you have handled the situation?
5. $\left(\begin{array}{c}\textit{INTERNET}\\\textit{ACTIVITY}\end{array}\right)$ Using the Internet, find at least two sources that provide examples of how employees view managers who use their authority to an extreme. To help you, I would suggest that

you begin by entering "bad bosses" and view several of the sites that appear. Students have found the following to be interesting: http://www.badbossology. com; http://www.abcnews.go.com/gma/takecontrolofyourlife/story. Write a one-page paper explaining what you learned from this experience.

CASE 1-8
Help Me Get Off to A Good Start!

Eddie Hollander had just begun his first official day on the job as manager of the International Division of Allison Travel, Midvale branch. Allison Travel was a large travel agency with about 15 branches in a tri-state area. The Midvale Branch was one of the largest and was known for its high volume. Eight years ago, Eddie had started as a travel agent for another firm in another mid-Atlantic state. Eventually, through hard work, study, and determination, he worked his way up to a team leader position in that organization. When he heard about the opening at the Midvale branch, he updated his resume, confident that he could handle any challenge that might come his way.

Eddie reported directly to the branch manager, Jan Wilhelm. The Midvale Branch had two divisions—international and domestic. He considered the manager position at Allison as an ideal professional advancement. He and the manager of domestic travel reported directly to the branch manager, who in turn, reported to the Director of Branch Operations, Bob Wendling. Wendling was in the home office two hundred miles away and had responsibility for all phases of branch operations, including personnel policies and practices, products, services, advertisement, and promotion. He was charged with ensuring the branches cooperated with each other when appropriate and coordinating all functions within and between the branches. Wendling, along with branch manager, Jan Wilhelm, conducted Eddie's initial and subsequent interviews.

The first day on the job had not begun the way he envisioned. Branch manager Jan Wilhelm only spent about five minutes with him. With the exception of Wilhelm's private office, the branch employed an open-office concept. Upon leaving her office, Wilhelm said, "If you have any questions, come see me. My door is always open." After meeting briefly with the associates responsible for international travel, Eddie spent two hours reviewing company policies and procedures. Putting the policy manual aside, he wandered back to the break room. Jean Bryan, one of the employees in the domestic division, sat down across the table from him. Bryan asked Eddie how his morning was going. "Okay," Eddie responded before taking another sip of coffee.

"Let me give you some motherly advice," Jean began. "I've been working here for eleven years and have learned to go with the flow—if you get what I mean? It took me a while to learn how to play the game. No one told me—I had to learn without anyone to guide me. Remember, when you're dealing with Jan, you must be willing to say anything to her as long as it's what she wants to hear." Pausing to add some more sugar to her coffer, Jean continued, "Saying what Jan wants to hear is more important than the truth. Remember, it's the only way to survive here at Allison. Jan wants staff members who always take their cue from her. You need to listen carefully to what she says and watch her closely—take her ideas and make them work. If there is ever any doubt about what you should do, take your cue from her. Without question, accept her decisions and if you have an idea of your own, figure out a way to make her think it's her idea. Let her take the credit. You'll be the puppet and she'll be the puppeteer. You make her look good and she will take care of you. Gosh, I've got to run, see you later."

Eddie was startled by Jean's comments. He wondered how reliable the advice was. On his way back to his desk, he paused to consider where he should begin.

Questions for Discussion

1. In your opinion, what is the single most important thing that Eddie must do to get off to a good start? Why?

2. Outline a process by which Eddie could get to know the members of the international division team. Make a list of the things that Eddie should know about each employee.

3. What should Eddie do regarding Jean's comments? Why?

4. Before class, individually rank the following items from 1 to 10 in order of importance to you, with 10 as most important and 1 the least important.

___ Ability to think critically and creatively

___ Understand how to get diverse groups to work together as a team

___ Aligning individual and organizational needs

___ Getting information

___ Work ethic

___ Information technology application

___ Giving Information

___ Setting ground rules

___ Ensuring a balance of coordination and cooperation

___ Giving credit when credit is due

During class, your instructor may chose to divide you into small groups and have you reach a group consensus on which items are most or least important.

a. Try to reach consensus.

b. Avoid changing your mind simply to reach agreement.

c. Do not use "conflict-reducing" techniques, such as majority vote, averaging, or trading, in order to reach a group decision.

d. Your goal is to use a variety of the eight managerial skills listed on page 46.

5. Two days after Eddie's discussion with Jean Bryan, branch manager Jan Wilhelm told Eddie that she had scheduled a meeting in two hours to get his input into cross-training certain people within the two divisions. If you were Eddie:

a. What would you do to prepare for the meeting?

b. What might be other alternatives to the cross-training proposal?

c. When Jan Wilhelm asks you how you feel about cross-training and how people should be chosen, what will you say?

d. How will you say it?

e. What do you see as a 'downside' of this meeting?

Supervisory Essentials

PART 2

CHAPTER 3

(Communication: The Vital Link in Supervisory Management)

© GETTY IMAGES

After studying this chapter, you will be able to:

1 Define communication and discuss its implications for effective supervisory management.

2 Discuss the major channels of communication available to the supervisor.

3 Explain the benefits of the various methods of communication.

4 Identify and discuss barriers to effective communication.

5 Describe ways to overcome communication barriers.

6 Describe how supervisors can better manage meetings with their own managers.

YOU MAKE THE CALL!

James Mathews is the department supervisor of the water maintenance department for the city of Middletown. Middletown is a medium-sized Midwestern city that revitalized itself in the past two decades by aggressively pursuing new business and industry and providing economic incentives to support expansion of existing firms. However, the amounts that residents pay for city services are generally higher than comparable cities in the Midwest. The current mayor, David Graham, maintains that fee and tax increases were necessary to pay for utility and road improvements, bolster police and fire protection, and pay bond debt for improvements to the existing water and sewage systems. Some of the water and sewer lines are antiquated. The city has increased local income tax rates and garbage collection fees. In July, the city council approved additional separate storm water charges and dramatically increased water and sewage fees to help fund the $90-million bond issue for infrastructure water and sewer lines. These changes were not popular with the public. Taxpayers can see direct results when streets and sidewalks are replaced, but the water and sewer line upgrades are belowground and improvements are not readily visible.

Six months ago, James was promoted from day-shift supervisor. His management style is characterized as "managing by wandering around" (MBWA). He can be expected to show up during any of the four shifts—days (7 A.M. to 3 P.M.), evenings (3 P.M. to 11 P.M.), mornings (11 P.M. to 7 A.M.), or weekends (7 A.M. to 7 P.M. or 7 P.M. to 7 A.M.). Two-thirds of the workforce is on the day shift with the remainder divided among the skeletal crews of the evening, morning, and weekend shifts. Back-up crews supplement these skeletal crews as needed. James believes that he is familiar with all employees and knows their strengths and weaknesses. His employees know that he is willing to help out when needed even though he prefers to let employees work through problems on their own. One of his first actions was to promote George Harris to the position of evening shift leader.

About a month ago, James heard through the grapevine that Thomas Smith, an employee on the evening crew, had threatened Harris during a verbal confrontation witnessed by several employees. When James discussed the incident with Harris, he apologized and said that he had resolved the disagreement. Harris further explained that Smith appeared to be having some personal problems that were negatively affecting his work performance, and in the discussion about performance, Smith became angry and raised his voice. Harris assured James that the problem had been resolved. Harris explained that he was extremely busy with his new supervisory responsibilities and the increased workload of the evening shift and, therefore, had not bothered James about the incident.

Late yesterday (Wednesday), James again heard through the grapevine that Smith had been overheard to say, "I'm going to shoot Harris!" Another visit to Harris revealed that he thought the grapevine had blown the situation out of proportion. James was concerned and made an appointment for Friday to see Deb Barnes, the director of human resources, to discuss the matter. He pondered what future actions he should take.

Shortly before midnight on Thursday, the ringing of the telephone woke James from a sound sleep. The call from the on-duty emergency room policeman informed him that George Harris had been shot in the water maintenance parking lot and was pronounced dead at the scene.

A subsequent call from the desk sergeant informed James that Thomas Smith had strolled into the jail, admitted the shooting, and turned himself in. Smith, a 25-year city employee, had allegedly waited in the parking lot with a .22-caliber handgun. Police reported that Smith shot Harris three times, twice at close range and once—the final shot—when standing over Harris, who had fallen to the ground. Smith told police that Harris "was ruining his life and giving him a hard time."

Later, as James interviewed several employees, he realized that he didn't know the workers as well as he thought. Not only were both Smith and Harris separated from their wives, but most employees knew more about the situation than he did. They knew that Smith and Harris had argued over a woman.

The local newspapers were filled with additional details. Smith's attorney announced that a set of mitigating circumstances should weigh in his client's favor when the case went to trial. Smith had turned himself in almost immediately and had no past criminal record. Even though Smith and Harris had been friends for many years, Smith had accused Harris of having a relationship with his wife and being hostile toward him since becoming a supervisor. Smith claimed that Harris was "obsessed" with his wife and had sent her flowers on the day of the murder.

Now James is having trouble sleeping at night and wonders what he could have done to prevent this tragedy. **YOU MAKE THE CALL!**

Communication
The process of transmitting information and understanding

Need for Effective Communication

Communication is the process of transmitting information and understanding from one person to another. Effective communication means a successful transfer of information, meaning, and understanding from a sender to a receiver. In other words, communication is the process of imparting ideas and making oneself understood to others. While it is not necessary to have agreement, there must be mutual understanding for the exchange of ideas to be successful. Simply stated, there is no managerial function a supervisor can fulfill without effectively using their giving- and getting-information skills. The ability to communicate effectively is key to supervisory success.

Most supervisory activities involve interacting with others, and each interaction requires skillful handling of the information process. Communication links all managerial functions. Supervisors must explain the nature of work, instruct employees, describe what is expected of those employees, and counsel those employees. Supervisors also must report to their managers, both orally and in writing, and discuss their plans with other supervisors. All these activities require communication.

Noted author Peter Senge believes that people who develop and exchange information are not merely talking about the learning organization; they use the information as a springboard for experiments and initiatives. With each effort people make, they create a new facet of the overall image of what the learning organization can be.[1] Senge feels that:

> *If there is one single thing a learning organization does well, it is helping people embrace change. People in learning organizations react more quickly when their environment changes because they know how to anticipate changes that are going to occur (which is different than trying to predict the future) and how to create the kinds of changes they want.*[2]

Sharing information takes effort on everyone's part, and the organization's effectiveness depends on good communication. Think of your own experiences. Who do you trust? Why? Does your answer, in part, revolve around the person's ability to communicate effectively? I suspect so! Due to the various business implosions—Bear Stearns, Enron, Arthur Andersen, and others—people have little faith in CEOs.[3] Their credibility is suspect. I suspect that your trustworthy person is one who has the ability to communicate honestly, openly, candidly, and in a timely fashion—and leave the door open for questions you might have. Remember: As the *Titanic* was rapidly sinking, the captain of the ship was telling everyone not to panic, to believe there was no problem, and to implicitly trust the ship's staff. Now, more than ever, mutual respect and trust is at the heart of effective communication. Yet, in an era where more messages are being sent and received, the primary objective in every organization is "doing a better job of communicating."

EFFECTIVE COMMUNICATION REQUIRES TWO-WAY EXCHANGE

Communication was defined as the process of transmitting information and understanding from one person to another. The significant point is that communication always involves at least two people: a sender and a receiver. For example, a supervisor who is alone in a room and states a set of instructions does not communicate because there are no receivers. While the lack of communication

FIGURE 3.1 Communications does not take place unless information is transferred successfully

is obvious in this case, it may not be so obvious to a supervisor who sends an e-mail message. Once he or she hits the "send" button, the supervisor may believe that communication has taken place. However, this supervisor has not really communicated until and unless the e-mail has been received and the information and understanding have been transferred successfully to the receiver (see Figure 3.1).

It cannot be emphasized too strongly that effective communication includes both sending and receiving information. Understanding is a personal matter between people. If an idea received has the same meaning as the one intended, then we can say that effective communication has taken place. If, however, the idea received by a listener or reader is not the one intended, then communication has not been effective. The sender has merely transmitted spoken or written words. This does not mean that the sender and receiver must agree on a message or an issue; it is possible to communicate and yet not agree. Author and Professor Chip Heath developed key principles for making an idea "stick." Heath says, "A sticky idea is one that people understand when they hear it, that they remember later on, and that changes something about the way they think or act."[4]

EFFECTIVE COMMUNICATION MEANS BETTER SUPERVISION

An analysis of supervisory activities would likely find that more than half the workday involves giving and receiving information. Unfortunately, formal communication training is often limited to basic writing and speaking courses in school.[5] Many people assume they know how to communicate, and they do not work at developing their communication skills. A recent study of HR professionals concluded that "senior management has problems communicating with millennials—those twenty-something employees."[6] A supervisor's effectiveness depends on the ability to create an environment that fosters communication. Employees must understand their supervisor's instructions to achieve their objectives. Similarly, the supervisor must know how to receive information and understand the messages sent by employees, other supervisors, and high-level managers. Fortunately, the skills of effective communication can be developed. By using some of the techniques and suggestions in this chapter, we hope you will become a more effective communicator and, ultimately, a more effective manager.

2 Discuss the major channels of communication available to the supervisor.

Channels of the Communication Network

In every organization, the communication network has two primary and equally important channels: (1) the formal, or official, channel of communication and (2) the informal channel, usually called the "grapevine." Both channels carry messages from one person or group to another in organizations—downward, upward, and horizontally.

FORMAL CHANNELS

Formal communication channels are established primarily by an organization's structure. Vertical formal channels can be visualized by following the lines of authority from the top-level executive down through the organization to supervisors and employees.

Downward Communication

The concept of a downward formal channel of communication suggests that upper-level management issues instructions or disseminates information that managers or supervisors at the next level receive and pass to their subordinates, and so on down the line. The downward channel is most often used by high-level managers to communicate. Downward communication, which helps to tie levels together, is important for coordination. Managers use it to start action by subordinates and to communicate instructions, objectives, policies, procedures, and other information. Generally, downward communication is informative and directive and requires subordinates to act. Downward communication from a supervisor involves giving instructions, explaining information and procedures, training employees, and engaging in other types of activities designed to guide employees in performing their work.

Unfortunately, in practice downward communication leaves much to be desired. When asked to describe the communication in their organization, only 22.2 percent of respondents in a survey reported that it was "open and honest." Surprisingly, 22.6 percent responded by asking, "Communication? What communication?" Another study reported that 87 percent of CEOs failed the candor test. If top managers are not perceived to provide "open, honest, sincere, and genuine" communication, what impact does that have on the rest of the organization?[7] We have found that employees want to be told what they need to know when they need to know it.

UPWARD COMMUNICATION

Upward communication is equally important to the official network. Supervisors who have managerial authority accept an obligation to keep their superiors informed and to contribute their own ideas to management. Similarly, employees should feel free to convey their ideas to their supervisors and to report on activities related to their work. Managers and supervisors should encourage a free flow of upward communication.

Upward communication usually involves informing and reporting, including asking questions, making suggestions, and lodging complaints. This is a vital means by which managers can determine whether proper actions are taking place and can obtain valuable employee insight into problems facing a unit. For example, employees may report production results and also present ideas for increasing production.

Frequently, no one knows the problems and possible solutions to those problems better than the employees who are doing the work

Supervisors should encourage upward communication from employees and give ample attention to the information being transmitted. Supervisors must show that they want employee suggestions as well as the facts, and then those supervisors must evaluate information promptly. It has become clear that often no one knows problems—and possible solutions—better than the employees doing the work.[8] To tap into this important source of information, supervisors must convey a genuine desire to obtain and use the ideas suggested by employees. (See the accompanying "Supervisory Tips" box.) The key word is "probe." Ask questions such as, "How can we improve . . . ?" "What can we do better?" "What if . . . ?" and "What will make it work?" Effective supervisors develop rapport with their employees and other stakeholders, really listening to ideas and suggestions and acting on suggestions. A supervisor with effective information-getting skills usually wins the respect and admiration of colleagues and employees.

Most supervisors acknowledge that it is often easier to converse with their subordinates than with their managers. This is particularly true when supervisors must tell their managers they failed to meet schedules or they made mistakes.

Nevertheless, it is a supervisor's duty to advise the upper management whenever there are significant developments and to do so as soon as possible, before or after such events occur. It is quite embarrassing to a manager to learn important news elsewhere; this can be interpreted to mean supervisors are not abreast of their responsibilities.

High-level managers need complete information, because they retain overall responsibility for organizational performance. Of course, this does not mean that supervisors need to pass upward every bit of trivial information. Rather, it means that supervisors should mentally place themselves in their managers' positions and consider what information their managers need to perform their own jobs properly.

A supervisor's upward communication should be sent on time and in a form that enables the manager to take necessary action. The supervisor should assemble

SUPERVISORY TIPS
Management By Wandering Around (MBWA) Improves Communication

The most effective leaders have always led from the front line, where the action is.[1] Today, any leader, at any level, who hopes for even limited success must likewise lead from the trenches. Getting out and about (commonly known as "management by wandering around," or MBWA) deals with gathering the information necessary for decision making, making a vision concrete, engendering commitment and risk taking, and caring about people.[2] But I do not know how to wander. How do I begin?

1. Get away from your workstation, your desk; get out of your cubicle and start talking with employees. Meet on their turf and try to learn something about them: Why did they decide to work here? What are their interests? Where do they want to be three years from now? What can you do to enable them to be the best they can be? In short, to get the job done the right way the first time, you need to know where they are coming from and be able to link that knowledge to get buy-in to the goals of the organization.[3]
2. Learn about their problems and concerns. Ask for their ideas and suggestions on how to fix their problems.
3. Developing a climate of mutual trust and respect is critical to getting everyone committed to the common purpose.
4. MBWA means more than wandering to where your employees are. It is not enough to advertise an open-door policy. It means being available to answer any questions that might arise. Accessibility is a crucial part of developing an effective corporate culture. It is important for you to stay in touch with everyone.
5. Tell people that you want feedback and be prepared to receive it. The technique of probing—asking the right

questions and encouraging everyone to ask questions, listening to those affected by problems, learning all the facts, "walking the talk"—and acting on and incorporating suggestions as part of the process can lead to a more productive organization.

6. As you wander, catch people doing something right. Tell them how good you feel about what they have done and encourage them to do more of the same. Make sure you link good performance to rewards people value.
7. Remember:
   - Be available to provide guidance and direction. Set aside a certain time when everyone knows you are accessible and able to listen to their ideas/suggestions/concerns.
   - Do not wander just for the sake of wandering. Have a purpose.
   - Wander at different times and in different ways.
   - Look for opportunities chat in informal settings, over coffee or at lunch.
   - Your work group is made up of individuals. Tailor the message to each person.
   - Tell people you want feedback and go out of your way to get it.
   - To be a good wanderer, you have to be a good listener. Stop what you are doing and listen.
   - When you can't answer a worker's question on the spot, get back to them with an answer within a specified period of time. Tell them when you will get back to them and do it! This is one way to build credibility, trust, and loyalty.
   - Effective communication is the key to your success.

Sources: The author's list would include (1) What are characteristics of a Great Leader? Most major business publications have developed their own methods of determining who fits that description. My list would include Mohandas Gandhi, Alfred Sloan, Sam Walton, Jack Welch, General Colin Powell, and Colleen Barrett. Business publications such as *Fortune, BusinessWeek, Time, Fast Company,* and others publish their lists. (2) MBWA was developed by executives of Hewlett-Packard in the 1970s. Noted author Tom Peters popularized the concept in the book *In Search of Excellence: Lessons Learned from America's Best Run Companies* (New York: Harper & Row, 1982). In a subsequent book, Peters strongly advised that managers need to become highly visible and do a better job of listening to subordinates: *Thriving on Chaos* (New York: Alfred A. Knopf, 1988), pp. 423–440. (3) D. Michael Abrashoff, Commander of the *USS Benfold,* sits down with his new crew members and tries to learn something from them. As reported in Polly LaBarre, "The Agenda—Grassroots Leadership," *Fast Company* (April 1999), pp. 114+. For a twenty-first century perspective on MBWA, see Harry K. Jones, "Does MBWA (Management by Wandering Around) Still Work?" http://www.achievemax.com/newsletter/01issue/management-by-wandering-around.htm (accessed April 2006).

and check facts before passing them on, though this may be quite difficult at times. A natural inclination is to "soften" information a bit so that things do not look quite as bad in the manager's eyes as they actually are. When difficulties arise, it is best to tell the manager what is really going on, even if it means admitting mistakes. High-level managers depend on supervisors for reliable upward communication, just as supervisors depend on their employees for the accurate, upward flow of information.

HORIZONTAL COMMUNICATION

A third direction of formal communication is essential for efficient organizational functioning. This is lateral, or horizontal, communication, which is concerned mainly with communication between departments or people at the same levels but in charge of different functions. Horizontal communication must be open and freely flowing to coordinate functions among departments.

Horizontal communication typically involves discussions and meetings to accomplish tasks that cross departmental lines. For example, a production manager may have to contact managers of the marketing and shipping departments to ascertain progress on a delivery schedule for a product, or someone from the human resources department may meet with a number of supervisors to discuss how a new medical leave policy is to be implemented at the departmental level. Still another example is the cashier who pages the stock clerk to inquire when a particular item will be available. Without an open communication environment—upward, downward, and sideways—it would be virtually impossible to coordinate specialized departmental efforts toward a common purpose.

INFORMAL CHANNELS—THE GRAPEVINE

Informal communication channels, commonly referred to as the **grapevine**, are a normal outgrowth of informal and casual groupings of people on the job, of their social interactions, and of their understandable desire to communicate with one another. Every organization has its grapevine. This is a perfectly natural element because it fulfills employees' desire to know the latest information and to socialize. The grapevine offers members of an organization an outlet for imagining, as well as an opportunity to express apprehensions in the form of rumors.

Grapevine
The informal, unofficial communication channel

UNDERSTANDING THE GRAPEVINE

The grapevine can offer considerable insight into employees' thoughts and feelings. An alert supervisor acknowledges the grapevine and tries to take advantage of it whenever possible. The grapevine often carries factual information, but sometimes it carries half-truths, rumors, private interpretations, suspicions, and other bits of distorted or inaccurate information. Research indicates that many employees have more faith and confidence in the grapevine than in what their supervisors tell them.[9] In part, this reflects a natural human tendency to trust one's peers to a greater degree than people in authority, such as supervisors or parents.

The grapevine cannot be predicted because its path today is not necessarily the same as its path yesterday. Most employees hear information through the grapevine, but some do not pass it along. Any person in an organization may become active in the grapevine on occasion; some individuals are more active than others. Some people feel that their prestige is enhanced if they can pass along the latest news, and they do not hesitate to spread and embellish upon that news. Rumors serve, in part, as a release for emotions, providing an opportunity to remain anonymous and say whatever is wanted without being held accountable. Many people know of allegations, rumors, gossip, and old wives' tales that have found their way into homes and offices via the Internet. Not surprisingly, most of these pieces of information are passed along as "fact," even though they lack truth and scientific accuracy. How often have you heard, "It must be true, I found it on the Web"?

According to author Nigel Nicholson, we have all seen the two sides of rumors. One side is positive, the result of spending time with a friend and sharing stories about mutual acquaintances. The other side is negative, the erosion of self-esteem, frustration, and anger arising when someone spreads bad news about you.[10]

The grapevine sometimes helps clarify and supplement formal communication, and it often spreads information that could not be disseminated as well or as rapidly through official channels.

THE SUPERVISOR AND THE GRAPEVINE

The supervisor should realize that it is impossible to eliminate the grapevine. It is unrealistic to expect that all rumors can be stamped out, and the grapevine is certain to flourish in every organization. To cope with the grapevine, supervisors should tune in to the grapevine and learn what it is saying. Supervisors should also determine who leads the grapevine and who is likely to spread its information.

Many rumors begin in the wishful-thinking stage of employee anticipation. If employees want something badly enough, they may start passing the word to other employees. For example, if secretaries want a raise, they may start the rumor that management will offer an across-the-board raise. Nobody knows for certain where or how the rumor started, but the story spreads rapidly because everyone wants to believe it. Of course, morale suffers when hopes are built up in anticipation of something that does not happen. If such a story is spreading and the supervisor realizes it will lead to disappointment, the supervisor should move quickly to refute the story with facts. The best cure for rumors is to expose the facts to all employees and to give straight answers to all questions.

Especially during periods of economic uncertainty, the grapevine carries bits of distorted information that flow quickly through the organization

Other frequent causes of rumors are uncertainty and fear. If business is slack and management is forced to lay off some employees, stories multiply quickly. During periods of insecurity and anxiety, the grapevine becomes more active than at other times. St. Patrick's Day is often a time of celebration, especially in New York City. Look back to March 17, 2008, when 14,000-plus Bear Stearns employees were reading e-mails or news releases on their computers about the likely merger with J.P. Morgan and the collapse of their employer. Bear Stearns would be no more. The mortgage and sub-prime crisis, in part, had done them in. Can you see the picture: employees—none of whom had full and complete information about what was really happening—frantically using their Blackberries to gain information from the "street" or from co-workers? Imagine their frustration. No one could or would tell them what was going on. For many, the grapevine was their primary source of information, much of it rumor. For many, they went home or to the bars, suspecting the good job they had enjoyed was gone.

Often, rumors are far worse than reality. If a supervisor does not disclose facts to employees, those employees will make up their own "facts," which may be worse than reality. Thus, much of the fear caused by uncertainty can be eliminated or reduced if the truth of what will happen is disclosed. Continuing rumors and uncertainty may be more demoralizing than even the saddest facts presented openly.

Rumors also arise from dislike, anger, and distrust. Rumors spread through the grapevine can be about such topics as the company, working conditions, or the private or work-life happenings of its members. The Web has accelerated the access to the "truth" and "untruth." Think about some of the e-mails that have been forwarded to you. At first glance, they may even seem to be credible. Just take a trip to www.snopes.com to see some of the rumors that are spreading rapidly. Rumors, like gossip and storytelling, ease the boredom of organizational life and, in extreme cases, harm people. Occasionally, an employee grows to hate a company, supervisor, or fellow employee. This employee could fabricate a sensational story about the target of animosity.[11]

Rumors often start small but are spread quickly by a few who embellish those rumors. Others may be shocked to hear such rumors, and their trust and respect for the people in the rumors may erode. Unfortunately, there is no one best way for repudiating rumors and rebuilding credibility. If you mention a rumor without refuting it, some people may speculate that the rumor is at least partly true. Again, the best prescription is to state the facts openly and honestly. When supervisors lack all the information, they should admit it, try to assess the real situation, and report the situation to employees. One of the best ways to stop a rumor is to expose its untruthfulness. Supervisors should remember that the receptiveness of a group of employees to rumors is directly related to the quality of the supervisor's communication and leadership. When employees believe their supervisors are concerned about them and make every effort to keep employees informed, employees tend to disregard rumors and to look to their supervisors for answers.

The supervisor should listen to the grapevine and develop skills to address it. For example, an alert supervisor knows that certain events cause undue anxiety. In this case, the supervisor should explain immediately why such events have occurred. When emergencies occur, changes are introduced, or policies are modified, the supervisor should explain why and answer all employee questions as openly as possible. Otherwise, employees will make up their own explanations, and often these explanations will be incorrect. In some situations, supervisors do not have the facts. In these cases, supervisors should seek appropriate high-level managers to explain what is bothering employees and to ask for specific instructions as to what information may be given, how much may be told, and when. Also, when something happens that might cause rumors, it is helpful for supervisors to meet with their most influential employees to give them the real story. Then, those employees can spread the facts before anyone else can spread the rumors.[12]

---

3 **Explain the benefits of the various methods of communication.**

Methods of Communication

The preceding sections described various communication flows or channels of communication. The effective supervisor is concerned with not only the content of communication but also the context of communication. The following sections explore various methods for delivering a message. Especially during periods of economic uncertainty, the grapevine carries bits of distorted information that flow quickly through the organization.

BEHAVIOR IS COMMUNICATION

Body language
All observable actions of the sender or receiver

Supervisors should realize that their behavior as managers on the job is an important form of communicating with their subordinates. **Body language** is the observable actions of the sender or the receiver. The supervisor's body language communicates something to employees, whether it is intended or not. Gestures, a handshake, a shrug of the shoulder, a smile, or even silence—all have meaning and may be interpreted differently by different people. For example, a supervisor's warm smile and posture slightly bent toward employees can send positive signals to employees. Particularly in an uncertain and sometimes chaotic world, smiling may be somewhat difficult, but it is definitely more effective than scowling. Conversely, a scowl on a supervisor's face may communicate more than ten minutes of oral discussion or a printed page of information. Many of us have seen news clips of President John F. Kennedy's 1961 inauguration address in which his gestures changed from a clenched fist to a wagging finger as he delivered those famous words: "Ask not what your country can do for you, ask what you can do for your country." Clearly, President Kennedy used body language to reinforce the important points of his message.

Body language is not universal. The messages sent by different expressions or postures vary from situation to situation and particularly from culture to culture. Touching, like the "pat on the back," may be perceived differently by different people. Studies report that women distinguish between touching for the purpose of conveying warmth and friendship and touching to convey sexual attraction, while men may not.[13] Male supervisors must recognize that touching female employees may cause resentment or even charges of sexual harassment.

A supervisor's unexplained action may create a meaning that is not intended. For example, a supervisor arranged to have some equipment removed from the production floor without telling the employees that the equipment was removed because it needed mechanical modifications. To the employees, who feared a shutdown, this unexplained action communicated a message that the supervisor had no intention of sending.

ORAL AND WRITTEN COMMUNICATION

Spoken and written words are the most widely used forms of communication in an organization. They also challenge every supervisor who wishes to communicate effectively. Words can be tricky. Instructions that mean one thing to one employee may have a different meaning to someone else. A collection-agency supervisor told a new employee, "Get tough with Mr. Stump. His account is two months overdue." Upon checking an hour later, the supervisor found that the new employee had started foreclosure proceedings against Mr. Stump. Obviously, instructions like "get tough" can be interpreted in several different ways.

Supervisors have fewer occasions to use the written medium because most supervisory communication takes place orally. Oral communication generally is superior to written communication because it facilitates understanding and takes less time. This is true both with telephone and face-to-face communication. Face-to-face discussion between a supervisor and employees is the principal method of two-way communication. Employees like to see and hear their supervisors in person, and no written communication can be as effective as an interpersonal discussion. In a face-to-face discussion, both employees and supervisors can draw meaning from body language as well as the oral message. Another reason oral communication is more effective is that most people can express themselves more easily and completely by voice than by letter or memo.

Probably the greatest advantage of oral communication is that it can provide an immediate opportunity for determining whether communication between the sender and receiver has been effective. Although the response may only be an expression on the receiver's face, the sender can judge how the receiver is reacting to what is being said. Oral communication enables the sender to find out immediately what the receiver hears and does not hear. Oral communication enables the receiver to ask questions immediately if the meaning is not clear, and the sender can clarify. The human voice can impart a message with meaning and clarity that pages of written words cannot convey. Body language and tone of voice help convey the message.

The principal problem with oral communication is that usually there is no permanent record of it and, over time, speakers' and listeners' memories blur the meaning of what was conveyed. This is why many supervisors follow up certain meetings and discussions with some type of memoranda or documents to have written bases for recalling what was discussed.

To reiterate, a supervisor must always remember that effective communication takes place only when the meaning received by the listener is the same as that which the sender intended to send. Supervisors who are effective communicators know how to speak clearly and to be aware of the listener. They are sensitive to the many barriers to effective communication, which can distort communication. They also know how to overcome these barriers. Such supervisors recognize that a speaker and a listener are unique individuals who live in different worlds and that many factors impact the messages passing between them.

A PICTURE IS WORTH A THOUSAND WORDS

The power of visual media in conveying meaning should never be underestimated. Pictures, charts, cartoons, and symbols can be effective visual aids, and the supervisor should employ them as appropriate. These tools are particularly effective when used with well-chosen words that complete the message. Businesses use such visual aids as blueprints, charts, drafts, models, and posters extensively to communicate information. Movies, videos, and comic strips demonstrate the power of visual media in communicating.

Pictures, charts, cartoons, and symbols can be effective visual aids

© DANIEL BOSLER/GETTY IMAGES

Noise
Obstacles that distort messages between people

Barriers to Effective Communication

Human differences and organizational conditions can create obstacles that distort messages between people. These obstacles can be called **noise**. Misunderstandings, confusion, and conflicts can develop when communication breaks down. These breakdowns not only are costly in terms of money but also create dilemmas that hurt teamwork and morale. Many supervisory human-relations problems are traceable to faulty communication. The ways supervisors communicate with their subordinates constitute the essence of their relationships.

Speak to any group of employees about the communication in their workplace and their first response is usually, "There's so much noise. Can you get someone to turn down the volume?" This problem has increased substantially as an increasing number of organizations have moved to "open offices" in which employees are separated only by cubicle panels. Imagine being on an important call with a client and having the background noise reach such a level that it is impossible to carry on a conversation. According to some reports, the open-office concept, which was intended to foster creativity, collaboration, and teamwork, and to facilitate communication, has given rise to numerous complaints of having to work in a stereophonic environment. "Acoustical privacy remains the biggest concern of workstation employees," according to commercial architect Richard Pollock. "It's that everything is too noisy."[14]

LOCATION, LOCATION, LOCATION

Managing workers in remote locations is increasingly becoming a challenge. Some organizations are making huge investments in "telepresence" systems, which simulate the sensation of two groups of people at identical tables facing each other through windows.[15] IBM team members, for example, use voice over Internet protocol (VOIP), video streaming, and instant messaging to communicate around the globe.[16] Regardless of the medium used to communicate with remote workers, listening carefully to what the other person is saying and asking questions to seek clarification is essential.

LANGUAGE AND VOCABULARY DIFFERENCES

People differ greatly in their abilities to convey meanings. Words can be confusing, even though language is the principal method used to communicate. Not long ago, the author needed to change his mailing address for his Chase Visa card. He tried to do it using their Web site, but found it too complicated to navigate. He called the toll-free number and got a person in India. Both were speaking English but with the dialect and other pronunciation differences, he was not able to complete the task. In frustration, he asked to speak to a supervisor, was put on hold, and waited patiently until a supervisor came to the phone. The supervisor was in Memphis, Tennessee. The author can converse in several languages but the difficulty communicating with someone who spoke English—a distinctly different version from his Midwestern U.S. dialect—was a challenging task.

In regions of the world with common languages, differences in cultures, accents, dialects, and word meanings can be profound.[17] Within the organization, an accounting department supervisor, for example, may use specialized words that may be meaningless when conversing with a computer technician. Similarly, if an information technologist uses technical terms when interfacing with the accounting department supervisor, the latter could be confused. This communication problem stems from the inappropriate use of what is known as **jargon**, or the use of words that are specific to a person's background or specialty.

Jargon
Words that are specific to an occupation or a specialty

Another consideration relates to the number of languages that may be spoken in a work environment. Some Hispanic-Americans and native Mexicans may speak Spanish fluently but have difficulty with English. A native of Southeast Asia may speak Vietnamese but very little English. Some organizations have launched Spanish-language Web sites to more effectively communicate with those who speak primarily Spanish (see Figure 3.2). Motor vehicle license branches in Indiana will provide interpreters for those needing assistance. The increasing number of immigrants from Asian, Eastern European, Central American, and Latin American countries has led some to clamor that only English be spoken in the workplace.[18] Others support a bilingual working environment.

Another communication problem lies in the multiple meanings of words, known as **semantics**. Words can mean different things to different people, particularly in English, which is one of the most difficult languages in the world. The ways some words are used in sentences can cause people to interpret messages in manners

Semantics
The multiple meanings of words

FIGURE 3.2 Please explain this to me!

YOU UNDERSTAND, DON'T YOU?

"No importa cuál sea tu idioma o descendencia, tecnología e involucramiento con la comunidad, solamente, no son capaces de ganar el corazón del Cliente. Una sonrisa vale mil palabras en cualquier idioma, y nuestros Empleados son expertos en compartir sus corazones con todos nuestros Clientes. Southwest está muy agradecido a todos los Clientes que nos honran con su elección, y a la hora de escoger una aerolínea, espero que lo que digas sea: 'Vámonos con Southwest Airlines.'"

—*Colleen Barrett*
—Presidenta, Southwest Airlines

Source: Reprinted with permission from "Hablemos de Servicio," *Southwest Airlines Spirit* (July 2005), p. 16. In each issue of *Spirit*, SWA's president sends the message in both English and Spanish.

other than the ways they were intended. *Roget's Thesaurus*, a book of synonyms, identifies words with the same or similar meanings. When a word has multiple meanings, the desired meaning must be clarified because receivers tend to interpret words based on their perceptions, experiences, and cultural backgrounds.

The question is not whether employees *should* understand words; it is whether employees *do* understand. Supervisors should use plain, direct words in brief, simple statements. When needed, supervisors should restate messages to clarify the intended meaning or context.

DIFFERENCES IN LISTENING STYLES AND ATTENTION SPANS

According to Edward E. Scannell, past president of the National Speakers Association, "Today's audiences are far different from their counterparts of even a few years ago. The majority of audiences are younger, better educated, and more sophisticated, and they don't want to be 'talked at' by a speaker. They want to be part of the process. People want to contribute their own experiences. Maybe it's the MTV effect—a generation with shortened attention spans who demand constant visual stimuli—or maybe it's just that people today, in all areas of life, are bombarded by ever-more-provocative messages."[19]

TOO MUCH INFORMATION—TMI[20]

In today's business world, employees and supervisors are inundated with hundreds of bits of information every day. Many messages are long and wordy, which can cause misunderstanding and lost productivity. The typical written message is loaded with words that have little or no bearing on the message's purpose. Giving employees too much information results in "information overload" and causes employees to complain of being overwhelmed with irrelevant and redundant messages. How long does it take before employees consider all messages to be "junk mail" and discard them? Regardless of the medium used, you should use the "**KISS**" technique—keeping it short and simple means using as few words and sentences as possible.

KISS technique
An acronym that stand for keep it short and simple

THE INTERNET AND TMI

With the advent of electronic forms of communication, it seems that employees should have all the information they need to do their jobs. On the one hand, companies want employees to have access to the best and latest information and resources to do a better job. On the other hand, Internet use can become time-consuming for some employees, and, if left unchecked, can impede productivity.

How much are employees using the Internet for personal use? One recent study reported that U.S. workers are wasting at least two hours a day at work. Not surprisingly, surfing the Web for personal enjoyment was at the top of the nonwork activity list.[21] Another study found that 68 percent of companies have detected employees surfing sexually explicit Web sites.[22]

Some small-business owners cite this lost productivity as their major reason for forbidding employees to use the Internet. Another survey conducted by the American Management Association and the ePolicy Institute reported that electronic monitoring of employee Internet use and e-mail has become standard operating procedure (SOP) for most organizations. More than three-quarters of employers monitor Internet surfing by their employees, and 55 percent retain and review e-mail messages.[23]

Clearly, employees must be able to gather information. The key is that the information is pertinent and timely and helps employees do their jobs. Supervisors should begin by asking, "What information do my employees need to do their jobs?" The answer should be the foundation for gathering and giving information. Employees must know what is expected and what is and is not allowed. In short, effective supervisors do the following:

- Provide employees with timely and complete information.
- Keep messages short and simple—"manageable pieces for maximum impact."
- Understand how your behavior and body language influences others.
- Encourage everyone to ask questions.
- Strive to be understood and to understand—feedback is vital to success.

STATUS AND POSITION

An organization's structure, with its multilevel managerial hierarchy, creates a number of status levels among members of the organization. **Status** refers to the attitudes the members of an organization hold toward a position and its occupant. The statuses of executive-level positions and supervisory-level positions, supervisors and employees, differ. Differences in status and position become apparent as one level tries to communicate with another. For example, a supervisor who tries to convey enthusiasm to an employee about higher production and profits for the company may find the employee indifferent. The employee may instead be concerned with achieving a higher personal wage and security. By virtue of their positions in the company, the supervisor and the employee represent different points of view, and these views may be obstacles to understanding.

When employees listen to a supervisor's message, several factors come into play. First, employees evaluate the supervisor's words in light of their own backgrounds and experiences. Second, they also consider the supervisor's personality and position. It is difficult for employees to separate a supervisor's message from the feelings they have about the supervisor. As a result, employees may infer nonexistent motives in a message. For example, union members may be inclined to interpret a management statement in very uncomplimentary terms if they are convinced management is trying to weaken their union.

Obstacles due to status and position also can distort the upward flow of communication when subordinates are eager to impress management. Employees may screen information passed up the line; they may tell their supervisor only what they think the latter likes to hear and omit or soften unpleasant details. This problem is known as **filtering**. By the same token, supervisors are eager to impress managers in higher positions. They may fail to pass on important information to their managers because they believe the information portrays their supervisory abilities unfavorably.

Status
Attitudes toward a person based on the person's position

Filtering
The process of omitting or softening unpleasant details

RESISTANCE TO CHANGE OR NEW IDEAS

Some people prefer things as they are; they do not welcome change in their work situations. It is normal for people to prefer their environments to remain unchanged. If a message is intended to convey a change or a new idea—something that will upset work assignments, positions, or the daily routine—employees are inclined to resist the message. A message promising to change the equilibrium may be greeted with suspicion. Employees' receiving apparatuses work like screens, causing employees to reject new ideas if those ideas conflict with a currently comfortable situation.

Most listeners receive that portion of a message that confirms their beliefs and ignore the portion that conflicts with those beliefs. Sometimes beliefs are so fixed that listeners hear nothing. Even when they hear a statement, listeners reject that statement as false or find a convenient way of twisting its meaning to fit their perceptions.

Receivers usually hear what they wish to hear. When receivers are insecure or fearful, these barriers become even more difficult to overcome. Employees become so preoccupied with their own thoughts that they attend only to those ideas they want to hear, selecting only parts of the message they can accept. Employees brush aside, fail to hear, or explain away bits of information they do not like or that are irreconcilable with their biases. Supervisors must be aware of these possibilities, particularly when a message is intended to convey some change that may interfere with the normal routine or customary working environment.

PERCEPTUAL BARRIERS

Deborah Tannen's book *That's Not What I Meant!* explains that people have different conversational styles. When people from different parts of the country or the world, or from different ethnic or class backgrounds, communicate, their words are unlikely to be understood exactly as intended.[24] Messages can be misunderstood because people perceive the situation or circumstances (i.e., the world) differently.

Stereotyping
The perception that all people in a group share attitudes, values, and beliefs

Other barriers arise from deep-rooted personal feelings, prejudices, and physical conditions. The perception that all people in a group share attitudes, values, and beliefs is called **stereotyping**. Stereotyping influences how people respond to others. It becomes a barrier to effective communication as people are categorized into groups because of their gender, age, or race instead of being treated as unique individuals. Managers must be aware of stereotyping because it can impede communication.

In her book *You Just Don't Understand*, Tannen illustrates a common problem: In the workplace, if women's and men's conversational styles differ, women— not men—are usually told to change. Consider the following conversation from Tannen's book, which occurred between a couple in their car.

The woman had asked, "Would you like to stop for a drink?" Her husband had answered truthfully, "No," and they hadn't stopped. He was later frustrated to learn that his wife was annoyed because she had wanted to stop for a drink. He wondered, "Why didn't she just say what she wanted? Why did she play games with me?" The wife was annoyed, not because she had not gotten her way but because her preference had not been considered. From her point of view, she had shown concern for her husband's wishes, but he had no concern for hers.[25]

Tannen adds, "Both parties have different but equally valid points. In understanding what went wrong, the man must realize that when she asks what he would like, she is not asking an information question but rather starting a negotiation about what both would like. The woman must realize that when he answers 'yes' or 'no' he is not making a nonnegotiable demand. Men and women must both make adjustments."[26] It is sad that neither party worked toward what was really important and targeted that goal with specific inquiries. Imagine how the conversation could have gone from the man's perspective: "No, I'm not really thirsty. But if you'd like to do that, it would be okay with me." Being considerate of other people and keeping an open mind go a long way toward improving understanding. Tannen's example clearly illustrates the importance of "saying what you mean and meaning what you say."

INSENSITIVE WORDS AND POOR TIMING

Sometimes, one party in a conversation uses so-called "killer phrases." Comments like, "That's the stupidest idea I've ever heard!" "You do understand, don't you?" or "Do you really know what you're talking about?" can kill conversation.

Often, the receiver of the killer phrase becomes silent and indifferent to the sender. Sometimes, the receiver takes offense and directs anger back to the sender. Insensitive, offensive language or impetuous responses can make understanding difficult. These exchanges happen in many workplaces. Often, the conflict that results impedes organizational goals.

Another barrier to effective communication is timing. Employees come to the workplace with "baggage"—events that happened off the job. It can be difficult to pay attention to a sender while anticipating a test, for example. An employee can pretend to listen politely but receive little to nothing. When other issues demand attention, attentiveness and responsiveness to work information will fail to meet the other party's expectations.

Differences in perception can lead to misunderstanding

Many companies have installed "impersonal media"—e-mail, fax, Internet, PC-based video conferencing, and voicemail systems. Such systems enable employees to have almost immediate contact with many more people. However, there is a downside. Rambling is an oft-cited complaint by those receiving voicemail messages. Some callers forget to leave their phone numbers or reasons for calling, inadvertently wasting other people's time. To avoid this, communicate messages slowly. Remember to identify yourself clearly and concisely. Susan Bixler, who counsels business executives on social graces, emphasizes the basics of voicemail: "I have to tell them to be articulate, never to eat, drink, chew gum, or suck on candy while they're leaving their messages."[27] When used properly, electronic communication systems can help provide information in a timely manner.

INABILITY TO CREATE MEANING

Communication begins when the sender encodes an idea or a thought. For example, when managers set out to draft responses to issues, they address several questions, including:

- What conclusion have I formed about this issue?
- What claim do I want to make?
- What evidence or reasons can I offer in support of my claim?
- What data can I provide to back up my claim?[28]

Decoding is the receiver's version of encoding. During decoding, receivers put messages into forms they can interpret. To analyze a manager's position on an issue, an employee must find and weigh management's claim, evidence, and data, but the employee can ask more: "Does the writer's choice of words influence how I feel about this issue?" "Do I agree with management's basic premise or with the assumptions underlying management's position?" Often, the receiver's interpretation of a message differs from what the sender intended.

The author recently saw a promotional piece on laundry detergent. The label read "New and Improved." I wondered what it really meant. I pondered the following: (1) If it's new, how can it be improved? (2) If it's improved, how can it be new? Have you ever wished that other people would say what they mean and mean what they say? I have!

5 Describe ways to overcome communication barriers.

Overcoming Barriers to Effective Communication

Most techniques for overcoming communication barriers are relatively easy and straightforward. Supervisors will recognize them as techniques they use sometimes but not as frequently as they should. A supervisor once remarked, "Most of these are just common sense." The reply to this comment is simply, "Yes, but have you ever observed how uncommon common sense sometimes is?" The lesson is, "If you do not know, find out—then follow up." In short, supervisors must proactively ensure that communication is effective.

PREPARATION AND PLANNING

A first major step toward becoming a better communicator is to avoid speaking or writing until the message to be communicated has been thought through to the point that it is clear in the sender's mind. Only when supervisors can express their ideas in an organized fashion can they hope for others to understand. Therefore, before communicating, supervisors should know what they want and should plan the steps needed to attain their objectives (see Figure 3.3). Regardless of the method

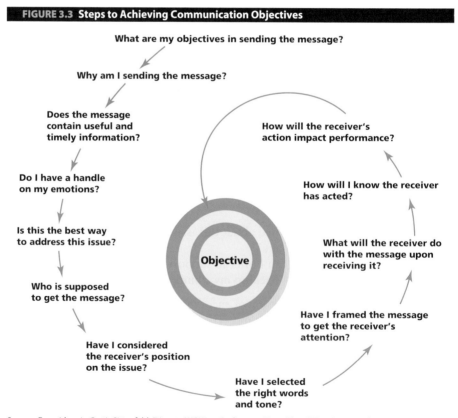

FIGURE 3.3 Steps to Achieving Communication Objectives

What are my objectives in sending the message?

Why am I sending the message?

Does the message contain useful and timely information?

Do I have a handle on my emotions?

Is this the best way to address this issue?

Who is supposed to get the message?

Have I considered the receiver's position on the issue?

Have I selected the right words and tone?

Have I framed the message to get the receiver's attention?

What will the receiver do with the message upon receiving it?

How will I know the receiver has acted?

How will the receiver's action impact performance?

Objective

Sources: From ideas in Curtis Sittenfeld, "How to WOW an Audience—Every Time," *Fast Company* (August 1999), pp. 86+; Carol Leonetti Dannhauser, "Shut Up and Listen," *Working Women* (May 1999), p. 41; Sean Morrison, "Keep It Simple," *Training* (January 1999), p. 152; Douglas Stone, Bruce Patten, and Sheila Heen, *Difficult Conversations: How to Discuss What Matters Most* (New York: Viking, 1999); Paul A. Argenti, "Should Business Schools Teach Aristotle?" *Strategy & Business* (Third Quarter, 1998), pp. 4–6; and A. Blanton Godfrey, "Quality Management: Getting the Word Out," *Quality Digest* (June 1996), p. 7.

of communication—face-to-face; written; signs, posters, graphs, or charts; fax; or e-mail—supervisors must consider many elements before sending messages.

For example, when supervisors want to assign jobs, they should first analyze those jobs thoroughly so they can describe them properly. An employee's ability to do a job depends on determining what information is important. Therefore, the supervisor needs to plan the method of communication—visual (body language), vocal (tone of voice), verbal (words), and emotional (feelings). When supervisors must give their bosses bad news, those supervisors should study the problems until they can explain the problems easily. Supervisors may even want to try to see the problems from their bosses' points of view. Supervisors should write down all important points to ensure they are covered.

A point of caution: Supervisors should only raise problems with their bosses after having formulated suggestions on how to solve or prevent those problems.[29] When communication is to involve disciplinary action, supervisors should investigate the cases sufficiently and compile all relevant information before issuing penalties. Clearly, communication should not begin until supervisors know what they should say to achieve their goals.

USING FEEDBACK

Among the methods for improving communication, feedback is by far the most important. In communication, **feedback** is the receiver's verbal or nonverbal response to a message. Feedback can be used to determine whether the receiver understood the message and to get the receiver's reaction to that message. The sender can initiate feedback by using questions, discussion, signals, and clues. Merely asking the receiver, "Do you understand?" and receiving "Yes" as an answer may not suffice. More information is usually required to ensure that a message was received as intended.

Feedback
The receiver's verbal or nonverbal response to a message

A simple way to obtain feedback is to observe the receiver and to judge that person's responses based on such nonverbal clues as expressions of bewilderment or understanding, raised eyebrows, frowns, and eye movement. Of course, this kind of feedback is possible only in face-to-face communication, which is one of the major advantages of this form of communication.

Perhaps the best feedback technique for ensuring that the sender's message is understood is for the sender to ask the receiver to "paraphrase" or "play back" the information just received. This is much more satisfactory than merely asking whether the instructions are clear. The process of restating all or part of the person's basic idea in the receiver's own words, rather than "parroting back verbatim" the sender's message, shows that communication has taken place. For example, the receiver might say, "Let me see if I understand correctly. Your understanding of the _____ is thus and so." When the receiver states the content of the message, the sender knows the receiver has heard and understood the message. The receiver may then ask additional questions and request comments that the speaker can provide immediately. Do not ask questions that can be answered "yes" or "no." Phrase questions that force the other person to clarify and elaborate their position(s).

The feedback technique also applies when a supervisor receives a message from an employee or a higher-level manager. To clear up possible misunderstandings, a supervisor can say, "Just to make sure I understand what you want, let me repeat in my own words the message you just gave me." An employee or a manager will appreciate this effort to improve communication. A similar technique to paraphrasing is reflective feedback. This is used when the supervisor reflects the feelings (emotions) expressed by the sender. To illustrate, the supervisor might say, "You feel _____ because _____."

FIGURE 3.4 Why didn't you understand my instructions the first time?

Feedback can also help when written communication, e-mail, or texting is involved. Before sending a written message, the supervisor can have someone else—perhaps a colleague—read the message for comprehension. Most writing can be improved. It may be necessary to develop several drafts of a written message and have various people provide feedback as to which draft is the most clearly stated and readily interpreted.

Similarly, after sending a memo, a fax, a letter, an e-mail, or a text message, it often is desirable to discuss the message over the telephone or face-to-face to ensure that the receiver understands the message. When a supervisor receives a written message and doubts any part of its meaning, that supervisor should contact the sender to discuss and clarify the message. In an amusing way, Figure 3.4 indicates that the teacher's original message was not received as intended. In a clear and direct way, the expectations are clarified.

DIRECT AND CLEAR LANGUAGE

Another sound approach to effective communication is to use words that are understandable and as clear as possible. Supervisors should avoid long, technical, complicated words. They should use language receivers can understand easily. Jargon, or "shop talk," should be used only when receivers are comfortable with it.

A CALM ATMOSPHERE

As mentioned earlier, tension and anxiety are serious barriers to effective communication. When supervisors try to communicate with employees who are visibly upset, the chance for mutual understanding is minimal. It is much better to communicate when both parties are calm and unburdened by unusual tension or stress. One of the best ways for supervisors to create the proper atmosphere for communicating with employees is to set times to meet in quiet rooms. This usually enables both parties to prepare to discuss problems calmly and unhurriedly.

Similarly, if supervisors want to discuss something with their managers, they should make appointments for times and places that allow calm, uninterrupted discussion. How (the tone), when (the time), and where (the place) are as important as the message.

TAKING TIME TO LISTEN

Another approach to overcoming communication barriers is for both senders and receivers to take more time to listen, that is, to give the other parties full opportunity to express their feelings. The supervisor who listens to employees learns more about employees' values and attitudes toward the working environment. Supervisors should provide feedback by restating employees' messages from time to time and by asking, "Is this what you mean?" A supervisor should always listen patiently to what the employee has to say. Intensive listening helps reduce misunderstanding and, by listening, the supervisor can respond in ways that are appropriate to the concerns of the employee.

One of the worst things supervisors can do is to appear to be listening while their minds are elsewhere. Supervisors can avoid this situation by politely stating, "Right now is not a convenient time for us to have this discussion. It needs my full attention, and if we can reschedule this meeting for ten in the morning, you will have my undivided attention." Attentiveness to the speaker goes a long way toward building trust. Figure 3.5 lists some practical do's and don'ts of effective listening.

Listening is a very important part of the supervisor's job, whether in one-on-one conversations or in meetings. The ability to listen is critical to success as a supervisor. Therefore, supervisors should work to develop their listening skills every chance they get. To ensure that they have understood the message, supervisors must confirm it by restating in their own words what they have heard. In this way, they get confirmation of the accuracy of the message, and both sender and receiver are on the same page of the playbook.

FIGURE 3.5 The Do's and Don'ts of Effective Listening

DO'S OF LISTENING

- Do adopt the attitude that you will always have something to learn.
- Do take time to listen, give the speaker your full attention, and hear the speaker out.
- Do withhold judgment until the speaker is finished. Strive to locate the main ideas of the message.
- Do try to determine the work meanings in the context of the speaker's background. Listen for what is being implied as well as what is being said.
- Do establish eye contact with the speaker. Read body language. Smile, nod, and give an encouraging sign when the speaker hesitates.
- Do ask questions at appropriate times to be sure you understand the speaker's message.
- Do restate the speaker's idea at appropriate moments to make sure you have received it correctly.

DON'TS OF LISTENING

- Don't listen with only half an ear by "tuning out" the speaker and pretending you are listening.
- Don't unnecessarily interrupt the speaker or finish the speaker's statement because of impatience or wanting to respond immediately.
- Don't fidget or doodle while listening. Don't let other distractions bother you and the speaker.
- Don't confuse facts with opinions.
- Don't show disapproval or insensitivity to the speaker's feelings.
- Don't respond until the speaker has said what he or she wants to say.
- Don't become defensive.

FIGURE 3.6 A supervisor communicates by actions as much as by words

OFFICE OPEN 9:00 to 5:00

SUPERVISOR

REPETITION OF MESSAGES

It often helps to repeat a message several times, preferably using different words and different methods. For example, a new medical insurance claim process might be mentioned in a staff meeting, discussed in an article in the company newsletter, posted on the bulletin board, and maintained in a policy file for employee use. The degree of repetition depends largely on the content of the message and the experience and background of the employees or other people involved in the communication. However, the message should not be repeated so much that it gets ignored because it sounds too familiar or boring. When in doubt, some repetition probably is safer than none.

REINFORCING WORDS WITH ACTION

To succeed as communicators, supervisors must complement their words with appropriate and consistent actions. Supervisors communicate a great deal through their actions; actions do speak louder than words (see Figure 3.6). Therefore, one of the best ways to give meaning to messages is to act accordingly. When verbal announcements are backed by action, the supervisor is more credible. However, when a supervisor says one thing but does another, employees will eventually behave similarly.

6 Describe how supervisors can better manage meetings with their own managers.

Managing Meetings With the Boss

Still another supervisory responsibility is communicating "up the organization."[30] For example, supervisors may want to report the most recent department/team meetings at their manager staff meetings. Supervisors should communicate not only the issues and items impacting their departments but also the positive contributions of their team members and other members of the organization.

As discussed earlier in this chapter, all managers should develop a climate that encourages a free flow of upward communication. However, in reality, the responsibility for upward communication typically falls to the supervisor. Increasingly, in an era of intense competition replete with organizational mergers, restructurings, and facility closings, supervisors must take the responsibility for keeping upper management informed and for managing the relationships with their own bosses. Supervisors also must be prepared to contribute suggestions, ideas, and opinions on a timely basis.

How many times have you heard someone say, "Treat others the way you want to be treated"? The same holds true for the supervisor's relationship with upper management. Most upward communication occurs in meetings between supervisors and their managers. Supervisors should try to build bonds with their bosses. Supervisors must clearly understand what their bosses expect of them, and the bosses must know what their subordinates need from them to achieve the organization's objectives. Each interaction that the supervisor has impacts the boss's perception of the supervisor, and vice versa. Obviously, how supervisors manage upward is vital to their careers. The following list provides insight on how the supervisor can more effectively manage meetings with the boss:

1. Respect the boss's time. Remember that "every boss has a boss" and, as such, has time demands of which you are not aware. Many bosses advocate an open-door policy, so be careful not to burden your boss with trivial issues or issues you can handle yourself. Choose a time when the boss is not busy and can give you and the issue undivided attention. A good approach might be, "I need about five minutes of your time to discuss _____. What would be a convenient time?" If the boss says, "two o'clock," be a few minutes early. It may sound basic, but think of the impression you make when you are late.

2. Check your motives. Is a meeting the best way to address the issue or problem and achieve your purposes? If the answer is "no," the meeting may not be worth having. Don't barge in on the boss when you are angry and upset.

3. Analyze the boss's listening style. Some bosses are analytical listeners who like to hear the facts and draw their own conclusions. Others may be emotional listeners who want you to start with how you feel about the message, then present the factual information, and close with your suggestion or conclusion.[31] Turn yourself 180 degrees, put yourself in the boss's shoes, and try to see the situation from his or her perspective. This will help you outline a plan.

4. Plan your agenda. To ensure you cover what you want in the meeting with the boss, have in front of you a few notes on the important points or issues. Be prepared by always carrying a notepad to list in advance the most important things you want to discuss. Managing upward successfully begins with preparation and planning. When planning the agenda, remember the KISS technique.

5. Do not go to the boss "naked." An effective manager encourages subordinates to develop alternatives, solutions, or suggestions to problems. No one wants a problem or an issue simply given to them to solve. You should start with a review of the situation and end with your suggestions. Bring suggestions on how to resolve the problem or prevent the situation from happening again. One manager the author knows only wants you to bring a problem to her after you have discussed it with others who have a stake in the outcome

and have developed at least two viable options for solving it. You want to leave the boss with the feeling that you are on top of things, and this is one way to do it.

6. Commit to the truth. In *The Fifth Discipline*, noted author Peter Senge calls honesty a commitment to the truth, which he argues is necessary for the discipline of personal mastery.[32] We could not agree more. A meaningful relationship is built on mutual trust and respect. Explain your position on the issues objectively using facts, figures, and examples.

7. Advertise success. Make certain that upper management knows the successes of your work group and others you rely on to succeed. The supervisor who, in a meeting, tries to claim all credit loses respect.

8. Learn to say no. Upper managers can impose unrealistic workloads or deadlines. There may be tremendous pressure from above to "buy in." Do not over-commit your team. The supervisor who does not learn to say "no" loses the respect of subordinates and ends up looking bad to the boss.

9. Do not keep information from your boss. Do not tell bosses only what they want to hear. Supervisors sometimes fail to pass along information because it might reflect unfavorably on them.

10. Anticipate problems. When you need the boss's help, ask for it in a timely fashion. The best time to get the help you need is at the beginning. A common error supervisors make is to wait until they are overwhelmed by a project or job assignment or when failure is imminent.

11. Meet periodically to clarify expectations. In our fast-paced world, job requirements change rapidly. You must take responsibility for knowing what is expected from you. You may have to ask your boss to help you understand. Conversely, you need to analyze your job expectations and take the initiative to ensure that your boss knows what you need from him or her in order to succeed.

12. Do not be a complainer. As mentioned above, it is essential to apprise the boss of problems, but do not complain constantly. The supervisor who only approaches the boss to complain becomes part of the problem, not part of the solution.

13. Do not put the boss on the defensive. Supervisors can become upset or angry. They can attack the boss by demanding, pointing fingers, or venting their anger. These behaviors and words are an aggressive attack on the boss. Many people lack the ability to cope with attacks on them, and they attack back with vigor. The encounter then becomes antagonistic rather than favorable. In a favorable environment, colleagues focus on understanding the issues from the viewpoint of the other person and strive to reach agreement and to develop follow-up steps. Attack the problem, not the person.

14. Leave on a positive note. Get an agreement on a course of actions. Summarize the meeting in writing so that you have documentation that on a specific date, at a specific place, with specific individuals present, a specific issue was discussed and, from your perspective, the outcome was as you have stated. What is said and done day-to-day on the job is an important part of communication.

15. Make a resolution. Treat the boss as though you are a dedicated and competent employee, ready to make a difference. Resolve to manage upward effectively.

SUMMARY

1 Effective communication means that information transfers successfully and understanding takes place between a sender and a receiver. The ability to communicate effectively is one of the most important qualities of supervisory success.

Communication is a two-way process—getting and giving information. Communication succeeds only when the receiver understands the message. The receiver doesn't have to agree with the message, just understand it as the sender intended.

2 Formal channels of communication operate downward, upward, and horizontally. These communication channels primarily serve to link people and departments to accomplish organizational objectives. Supervisors communicate downward to their employees, but equally important is the supervisor's ability to communicate upward to management and horizontally with supervisors in other departments. In addition to formal channels, every company has an informal channel, called the grapevine. The grapevine can carry rumors as well as facts. MBWA is one technique for getting information and staying in touch with the employees. Supervisors should stay in touch with the grapevine and counteract rumors with facts, where necessary.

3 Communication methods range from oral, written, and visual to body language. Spoken and written words are the most important means of communication. However, body language—a person's actions, gestures, posture, and so forth—also communicates, often more powerfully than words. Oral communication is generally superior because it enables face-to-face interaction. Feedback is instantaneous. Written words and visuals often are preferred because of their permanency. Visual aids, such as pictures, charts, and videos, can be powerful tools for conveying meaning.

4 Human differences and organizational conditions can create obstacles, called noise, which distort messages between people. The use of jargon that receivers do not understand can impede communication. Also, words have different meanings, so the sender must ensure the receiver understands the intended meaning. However, TMI is just as bad as too little information. Information overload has become a major problem in today's society.

People at different status or position levels in an organization bring different points of view to interactions, which can distort meaning. People may filter out unpleasant information when communicating with their managers. Also, people's natural resistance to change can cause them to avoid hearing messages that upset the status quo or conflict with their beliefs.

Individuals perceive the world from the context of their backgrounds and prejudices. Perceptual barriers between sender and receiver, such as biases and stereotyping, can impede communication, as can conversation-killing phrases and poor timing.

Both sender and receiver share responsibility to ensure that information is successfully transferred. The inability of the receiver to properly analyze the content of a message causes misunderstanding. Misunderstanding may lead to suspicion and a lack of trust.

5 To overcome communication barriers, supervisors should adequately prepare what they wish to communicate. During face-to-face communication, the receiver's verbal and nonverbal responses, called feedback, can help the supervisor determine whether the receiver understood the message. Asking the receiver to restate the message is one feedback technique that helps verify understanding. For written communication, the supervisor can obtain feedback by asking a colleague to comment on the message before it is sent and by discussing the message with receivers after it is sent.

Clear, direct language the receiver can understand facilitates communication. Also, both parties should agree on a time to talk when they are not overly stressed and have time to really listen to each other. Repeating the message in various words and formats can improve understanding if not done to excess. Also, to be effective, words must be reinforced with consistent actions.

6 Most people are not comfortable managing up. In today's fast-paced world, it is essential that supervisors keep higher management abreast of the developments and problems in their work areas. The tips for managing upward in this chapter blend practical applications with common sense. Supervisors who effectively manage meetings with higher management gain credibility and likely accomplish organizational goals.

KEY TERMS

Body language (p. 94)
Communication (p. 86)
Feedback (p. 103)
Filtering (p. 99)

Grapevine (p. 91)
Jargon (p. 97)
"KISS" technique (p. 98)
Noise (p. 96)

Semantics (p. 97)
Status (p. 99)
Stereotyping (p. 100)

QUESTIONS FOR DISCUSSION

1. What is meant by effective communication? Why is mutual understanding at the heart of any definition of effective communication?

2. If you were arrested and accused of being a "good communicator," would there be enough evidence to convict you? Why or why not?

3. Refer to this chapter's opening *You Make the Call!*
   a. What were the barriers to effective communication?
   b. Discuss techniques by which supervisor James Mathews can cope more effectively with the grapevine.
   c. What should James Mathews have done to improve communication within his department?

4. I am choking on all the e-mails I get every day. On most days, there are over 150. My grandkids say, "It is the information age. Learn to cope with it." What is the best way to manage my e-mails? Give me some ideas. (Note: This question may require you to "go outside the box" to get some creative ideas for coping with e-mail overload.)

5. The president and the two top managers of a 44-employee organization in northeastern Indiana meet quarterly with every employee on an individual basis. Employees can talk directly about any issue that concerns them, ask any question, and make suggestions for improvements. The president feels this session not only gives employees a chance to gripe, it also helps management understand things from the employees' viewpoints. According to the president, "One of our biggest concerns was that our employees were not being heard. While we espoused an 'open-door' policy, few employees came to the door. So we go to the employees. I assumed I knew what my employees' problems were instead of talking to them. Now I talk with them instead of assuming that I know what is going on. We weren't picking up the signs from disgruntled employees."

   a. In your opinion, what are the advantages of this practice?
   b. What are the difficulties in adopting such an approach for communicating with employees?
   c. Suppose you could ask the employees in this organization the following questions. What do you think their response(s) would be? Why?
      (1) "If you disagreed with one of the company's policies, would it be the end of your career here?"
      (2) "If you told the president everything you felt about the department/organization, would you get into trouble?"
   d. What about you? In your present or most recent work experience, what would be your answers to those two questions? Why?

SKILLS APPLICATIONS

Skills Application 3-1: Test Your Reading Skill

1. Read the following carefully:
   - The bandage was wound around the wound.
   - James could lead if he would get the lead out.
   - Since there is no time like the present, I thought it would be a good time to present you with your birthday present.
   a. What is the problem with these three sentences?
   b. How do these three examples illustrate a communication problem?

2. A professor friend said that sometimes only one letter in a word makes a big difference.
   a. Look at the word "here." What does the word mean to you?
   b. Now add a "t" and the word becomes "there." What does that word mean to you?
   c. What is the difference between the two words?
   d. Write a paragraph of less than 40 words illustrating what you learned from this skills application. Moral of the application: While one little letter in a word may not seem like much to you, in this case, it does make a big difference.

3. Count every F in the following text:
   FINISHED FILES ARE THE RESULT OF YEARS OF SCIENTIFIC STUDY COMBINED WITH THE EXPERIENCE OF YEARS.
   a. How many Fs did you count? Did you find three Fs?
   b. Your instructor will provide you with the correct answer so you can compare your answer with your analysis.
   c. Write one paragraph summarizing what you learned from this skills application.

Skills Application 3-2: Time to Tell Your Story

The purpose of this skills application is to give you an opportunity to tell your story by sharing information with others.

1. Round 1: Each student has 30 seconds to tell about the company/organization where they work or most recently worked.

2. At the conclusion of all presentations, in turn, each student should ask one question for something they would like to have clarified in the presentation.

3. Round 2: Each student will have one minute to tell his or her story on the topic you assigned.

4. At the conclusion of each presentation, each student shall prepare a report for each of the other presenters in their group.

a. Identify one thing you learned from the presentation.
b. What one question would you ask to seek clarification?
c. What one tip would you give to the presenter for improving his or her presentation?
d. If you were giving a speech on that topic, what would you have done differently?

Skills Application 3-3: Unpleasant Situations

1. Consider the following situations:
   a. An employee is performing a task improperly, and you show him how you want it done. The employee says, "I was doing this before you were born, and I don't need your advice."
   b. An employee has suddenly developed a tardiness problem. When you confront her, she says, "My spouse is an alcoholic; I am worried about him. I have to get the kids' breakfast and send them off to school before I can get here."
   c. One of your better employees has been caught in the organization's downsizing. As you hand him a pink slip, he says, "I don't know what I'm going to do. I guess my kids will have to drop out of college and go to work."

For each situation, do the following:

2. List all the questions you will ask to determine the meaning of the employee's message.

3. Decide on an appropriate response.

4. Pair with a classmate. Decide which of you will play the supervisor and which will be the employee. Alternate roles for each situation so that both of you get to play the supervisory role. Pick up the action where the situation leaves off.

5. (**ROLE PLAY**) Evaluate the interaction. Are you pleased with your follow-up to the situation? What did you do well? What could you have done more effectively?

Skills Application 3-4: English Only Spoken Here!

The increased diversity of the workplace has created the need for better communication skills. Consider the following:

More than two-thirds of the employees of Maple Grove Farms, a Midwestern food-processing facility, are Hispanic, Asian, or refugees from the former Soviet Bloc states. Most of them have limited proficiency in the English language. The company has provided ESL (English as a second language) training courses at no cost to the employees. Maple Grove Farms pays the full tuition for the ESL program (including up to four of each employee's dependents). For the first six weeks of employment, all new non-native-English-speaking hires are given one hour a day off with pay to take the in-plant ESL course. Supervisors have constantly complained about this practice as it wreaks havoc with their production scheduling.

Many of the employees are accustomed to switching back and forth between English and their native tongue while at work and take pride in using their new-found skills. During break time, however, the employees tend to group together with only those who speak the same native language. Rarely is English spoken during break or lunch periods. It also appears that few employees practice their newly acquired English-language skills while off the job.

At Monday's management meeting, the discussion focused on the fact that production expectations were not being met and waste and spoilage were at all-time highs. Several supervisors complained that having employees with so many different languages was a major part of the problem. Quality manager Jorge Rodriquez countered that he had problems communicating with the Bosnians. "When I ask if they understand, they nod their heads and then do the job the same way they have been doing it. Some of them do it the same wrong way every time. I've even tried showing them. Just this morning, I got Rolf to act as an interpreter and that seemed to help—temporarily." Supervisor Lori Whitten added, "Some Caucasian employees have complained that they feel excluded. The break room is like the United Nations with segregated areas for those who speak a common tongue—and that tongue is not English."

The general manager, Barth Davis, questioned whether the company needed a written policy that gave employees permission to speak their native languages during breaks but required them to speak only English on the job.

1. (**INTERNET ACTIVITY**) Using the Internet, see if there are any prohibitions that limit Maple Grove Farms from implementing an "English only" policy in the workplace.

2. What are the advantages of such a policy?

3. Do you think such a policy will improve communications at Maple Grove Farms?

4. You are supervisor Lori Whitten. General manager Barth Davis has asked you to develop a couple of suggestions for getting the employees to work more effectively as a team. You, personally, believe that diversity can be a source of strength for the organization. But in practice, you have seen how the language and cultural differences have created barriers to teamwork. What suggestions will you offer? What obstacles might prevent their successful implementation?

Skills Application 3-5: Dealing with Employees that Make Life Difficult—"Stretch"

All one has to do is to read a newspaper or magazine, listen to the radio, or watch television, and it becomes apparent that some people in the world are angry, hostile, uncaring, uncivil, or vociferous malcontents who are ready to battle for any or no reason. There are always one or two of these people at work—you know them. They are the people who make your life difficult, and you must work with them. What do you do?

This is the first in a series of Skills Applications to introduce you to some people who will make your life difficult. In the workplace, these characters share certain characteristics. First, they show up regularly in our lives. Second, there is no one "best" way to deal with them.

1. Consider the following statement from Alice, a project engineer at Supreme Electronics:

   I work for a boss who has the uncanny ability to stretch the truth. He selectively remembers things and uses his selective memory to nullify agreements or change things. On a proposal we submitted to a customer, we spelled out that a particular key team member would be leaving the project after two weeks, and my boss altered it to make it look like he would be running the whole thing. Another time, he cited his ability to develop people as the reason there was a high turnover rate in the department. In fact, most employees jump at a chance to transfer to other departments or to leave the organization. Not long ago, during a department meeting, my boss was talking about the importance of mental toughness. To illustrate the point, he told us about how he had played football at Cornell against Mike Ditka, among others. A coworker got a copy of the Cornell media guide, and nowhere in the All-Time Roster List was our boss's name. When the coworker confronted him, he said we had misunderstood. The guy is a compulsive liar. I'm locked into this job and can't afford to leave. I've repeatedly tried to transfer out of the department, but while my boss tells me to my face that "he'll support my efforts for advancement," I've found out that he continually stonewalls my requests.

2.  Using the Internet, find at least three sources of information for dealing with people who stretch the truth. Carefully review each of these for suggestions on how to deal with "stretch."

3. Based on your findings, what suggestions would you make to Alice on how to deal with her boss?

4. Write a one-page paper explaining how this Skills Application increased your working knowledge of coping with the behaviors of this type of person.

SKILLS DEVELOPMENT

Skills Development Module 3-1: Navistar International Corporation

 After viewing the Skills Development Module video clip, answer the following questions. Hopefully, these will stimulate your analytical and thinking skills.

The merger of the McCormick Harvesting Machine Company and Deering Harvester Company in 1902 resulted in the formation of the International Harvester Company (IH). The company evolved to become a diversified manufacturer of farming equipment, construction equipment, gas turbines, buses, and trucks. Mismanagement, rising gasoline prices, and a poor agricultural economy caused IH to fall on hard times. Shedding most of its operating divisions, the company changed its name to Navistar International Corporation (NAV). The truck and engine divisions were all that remained.

In January 2006, Navistar fell on hard times and the New York Stock Exchange (NYSE) de-listed it from the exchange. It was re-listed on the NYSE on July 1, 2008. Go to the firm's Web site (www.navistar.com) for more information on the history and current events.

A documentary, "Drive and Deliver," for and about truckers showcased a rig designed and engineered at International Truck and Engine Corp. in Fort Wayne, Indiana. The International Lone-Star, a long-haul truck debuted in October 2008 with a sticker price of $120,000 to $140,000. To see video, photos, and other information about "Drive and Deliver," go to the film's Web site www.internationaltrucks.com/film.

QUESTIONS OF DISCUSSION

1. Few of the CEOs running the largest U.S. corporations are fluent in any language other than English. The author contends that the United States' competitiveness in future years will be hampered by managers' lack of foreign language skills and global awareness. Do you agree with this contention? Why or why not?

2. Discuss how communication between the innovative, technological, production, and sales components of Navistar are the key ingredient to production of quality products.

3. How is Navistar International Corporation working to improve the communication process between various stakeholders?

ENDNOTES

1. Peter M. Senge, Art Kleiner, Charlotte Roberts, Richard B. Ross, and Bryan J. Smith, *The Fifth Discipline Handbook: Strategies and Tools for Building a Learning Organization* (New York: Doubleday, 1994), p. 6. A Korn/Ferry International Survey found that at least 70 percent of the surveyed workers "are reinventing the wheel daily at their jobs." For more information, see Leah Miller, "Wanted: Improved Communication," *The Internal Auditor* (October 2000), p. 13.

2. Ibid., p. 11. Senge's latest field book, *The Dance of Change: The Challenges of Sustaining Momentum in Learning Organizations* (New York: Doubleday, 1999), uses theory, case studies, and exercises to illustrate the importance of "open, honest, sincere, and genuine" communication to create change in an organization, foster real learning environments, and sustain a positive culture. A study reported in the *Academy of Management Journal* concluded that providing relevant information appears to be a *sine qua non* for a communication climate and, thus, for improving employee identification with the organization. See Briarcliff Manor et al., "The Impact of Employee Communication and Perceived External Prestige on Organizational Identification," (October 2001), pp. 1051+.

3. Much has been written about the high-profile corporate scandal cases. Bernie Ebbers, former WorldCom chief executive, received the stiffest sentence to date—25 years in prison (July 14, 2005). Also, see Donna Fenn, "Sometimes Even CEOs Have to Say They're Sorry," *Inc.* (October 2007), pp. 37–38; and "Survey Shows 87 Percent of CEOs Fail Candor Test," The Rittenhouse Rankings as reported on AccountingWeb.com (http://www.accountingweb.com/news) (June 9, 2004). The bottom-line question is: "If you cannot believe the CEO or the CFO, who in the organization is trustworthy?"

4. Ted Pollock, "9 Ways to Improve Communications," *Supervision*, 69, 4 (April 2008), p. 26, reports that the average manager spends at least 80 percent of his or her time communicating. Also see, Lenny T. Mendonca and Matt Miller, "Crafting a Message That Sticks: An Interview with Chip Heath," *The McKinsey Quarterly—The Online Journal of McKinsey & Co.* (December 2007). Also see, Chip Heath and Dan Heath, *Made to Stick: Why Some Ideas Survive and Others Die* (New York: Random House, 2007) for ideas and tips on how to sell your ideas and be a more effective presenter.

5. There has been discussion regarding the inability of school systems to adequately prepare students for the business world. An SHRM survey identified the knowledge and skills employers expect to increase in importance over the next few years. Would it surprise you to know that oral communications and written communications were at the top of the list? See "Workplace Visions," *Society for Human Resource Management* #2 (2008). Also see Kathy Gurchiek, "Shoddy Writing Can Trip Up Employees, Organization," *SHRM Home* (April 27, 2006), and "Writing: A Ticket to Work . . . Or a Ticket Out: Survey of Business Leaders," National Commission on Writing for America's Families, Schools, and Colleges, as reported by AccountingWeb.com (September 17, 2004); "Communication in Management," *Harvard Management Communication Letter* (September 2000), p. 12; Research by Business Intelligence reported that the three most important competencies for managers and directors responsible for internal communication are strategic thinking, internal communication practice, and change management. Unfortunately, the study found that fewer than half the people occupying these positions have relevant professional qualifications. See Alyssa Danigelis, "Like, Um, You Know; Verbal Tics May Be Holding You Back: How to Identify Them and Overcome Them," *Fast Company* (May 2006), p. 99; Ron McMillan, Kerry Patterson, Joseph Grenny, and Al Switzer, *Crucial Conversations: Tools for Talking When Stakes are High* (2004); or David Cottrell and Eric Harvey, *The Manager's Communication Handbook: A Practical Guide to Build Understanding, Support, and Acceptance* (Dallas, TX: The Walk The Talk Company, Performance System Corporation, and Cornerstone Leadership Institute, 2003).

6. Kathy Gurchiek, "HR Struggles To Communicate with Generation Y." *SHRM Home* (March 31, 2008). The advice offered is to "take part in two-way discussion and don't try to wow them with a fancy presentation. The millennials have been 'weaned on electronic communication that is quick, to the point and perfunctory and their communication is very informal.'"

7. See, among others, Ed Frauenheim, "Is Your Boss Monitoring Your E-mail?" CNET News.com (May 18, 2005) and Mike Verespej, "Who Should Be Monitoring Your Employees' Messages," *SHRM Home* (July 14, 2005).

8. See Keith H. Griffin, "Metaphor, Language, and Organizational Transformation," *Organizational Development Journal*, 26, 1 (Spring 2008), pp. 89–93; and "An Operating Manual for Business: Hands on Managing—Lost in Translation," *Inc.* (September 2005), pp. 38–39. Noted author Tom Peters has strongly advised managers to become highly visible and to do better jobs of listening to subordinates. We agree. For additional information on "management by wandering around (MBWA)," see Tom Peters, *Thriving on Chaos* (New York: Alfred A. Knopf, 1988), pp. 423–40. For an example of MBWA in practice, see Polly LaBarre, "The Agenda—Grassroots Leadership," *Fast Company* (April 1999), pp. 114+.

9. The grapevine cuts across the formal channels of communications. See Stanley J. Modic, "Grapevine Rated Most Believable," *Industry-Week* (May 15, 1989), pp. 11 and 14, and Walter Kiechel III, "In Praise of Office Gossip," *Fortune* (August 19, 1985), pp. 253–256. The classic article on this subject is Keith Davis's "Management Communication and the Grapevine," *Harvard Business Review* (September–October 1953), pp. 43–49.

10. Nigel Nicholson, "The New Word On Gossip," *Psychology Today* (May/June 2001), pp. 40–45.

11. There were two 2007 court cases that dealt with free speech. In both cases, a student had written in his/her notebook or personal Web page threatening a "Columbine-style attack" or recalling "having a dream of shooting a teacher." The courts held that the students' free speech rights were not violated when the school system disciplined them. See *Ronce v. Socorro Independent School District* and *Boim v. Fulton County School District*.

12. For further discussion of informal channels of communication and the grapevine, see Rudolph F. Verderber and Kathleen S. Verderber, *Inter-Act: Using Interpersonal Communication Skills* (Belmont, CA: Wadsworth Publishing Company, 1995); William W. Hull, "Beating the Grapevine to the Punch," *Supervision* (August 1994), pp. 17–19; "Stopping Those Nasty Rumors," *HR Focus* (November 1990), p. 22; J. Mishra, "Managing the Grapevine," *Public Personnel Management* (Summer 1990), pp. 21–28; Keith Davis and Curtis Sittenfield, "Good Ways to Deliver Bad News," *Fast Company* (April 1999), pp. 58+.

13. Brenda Major, "Gender Patterns in Touching Behavior," in Nancy M. Henley, ed., *Gender and Non-Verbal Behavior* (New York: Springer-Verlag, 1981). Also see Rich McGuigan, "Communication: Your Most Valuable Tool," *Supervision* (November 2001), pp. 3–5, for tips on how managers can interpret body language; and K. Van Nostram, "Top-Down: Building a Better Organization Through Effective Communication," *Communication World*, 21, 2 (2004), p. 10.

14. As reported in Motoko Rich, "Shut Up So We Can Do Our Jobs!" the *Wall Street Journal* (August 29, 2001), pp. B1, B8.

15. Justin Scheck and Bobby White, "'Telepresence' is Taking Hold," the *Wall Street Journal* (May 6, 2008), p. B8.

16. Elizabeth Garone, "Managers Learn to Bond with Remote Workers," the *Wall Street Journal* (May 6, 2008), p. D5; and N. Lamar Reinsch, Jr., Jeanine Warisse Turner, and Catherine H. Tinsley, "Multi-Communicating: A Practice Whose Time Has Come," *Academy of Management Review*, 33, 2 (April 2008), pp. 391–403.

17. Quality guru Joseph Juran used the simple explanation that managers needed to be bilingual—that is, they had to speak the language of both upper management and of the workforce. See A. Blanton Godfrey, "Speak the Right Language," *Quality Digest* (July 1998), p. 18. The English language is estimated to contain some 750,000 words, but the vocabulary of the average person is only 20,000 to 40,000 words. While English is generally recognized as the world's primary business language, not all employees will understand the common tongue. In one section of their book, Rodin and Hartman observe that IT staff use technical terms because at most companies "they're herded into one, isolated department." The authors argue that "the best IT professionals live with the business units." Rob Rodin and Curtis Hartman, *Free, Perfect, and Now: Connecting to the Three Insatiable Customer Demands* (New York: Simon & Schuster, 1999), pp. 49, 56.

18. Carrie Mason-Draffen, "English-only Policy Tricky for Companies," *Newsday* as reported in the *Fort Wayne, Indiana News-Sentinel* (November 11, 2007), p. 3B.

19. "Not Your Father's Audience: How to Speak to Today's Listeners," *Southwest Airlines Spirit* (September 2004), p. 115. Also, Barry Wellman contends that people tend to be less inhibited and more prone to conflict on the e-mail network. See Barry Wellman (http://www.chass.utoronto.ca/~wellman) for information on his Internet research.

20. The term "TMI" was first brought to our attention in Rebecca Ganzel, "Editor's Notebook: Too Much Information," *Training* (February 1999), p. 6. Also, Michael J. Shaw, ed., *E-commerce and the Digital Economy*, (Armonk, NY: M.E. Sharpe, 2005); Michael Schrage, "Working in the Data Mines: Sixteen Tons of Information Overload," *Fortune* (August 2, 1999), p. 244, and "Data, Data," *Inc. Magazine* (January 1999), p. 70, provided impetus for this discussion.

21. "Workers Say They Waste 2 Hours a Day," San Antonio, TX WOAI News (July 12, 2005).

22. See Vara Vauhini, "New Sites Make It Easier to Spy on Your Friends," the *Wall Street Journal* (May 13, 2008), pp. D1, D3; and Richard Y. Wang, Elizabeth M. Pierce, Stuart E. Madnick, and Craig C. Fisher, *Information Quality* (Armonk, NY: M. E. Sharpe, 2005). "You've Got Junk," *Training* (June 1999), p. 18, reported that nearly one-third of all Internet e-mail threatens corporate assets and worker productivity.

23. In December 2007, the U.S. Equal Employment Opportunity Commission (EEOC) gave notice of a 'phishing' e-mail circulating to companies that purports to be from the EEOC regarding a harassment claim. The bogus e-mail contained a Trojan horse virus that had the potential to harm the recipient's computer if the user clicked on the references Web link and/or downloaded the attached file. This is but one example of attempts by hackers to cause harm. Also, see Kevin J. Delaney, "Web Start-Ups Vie to Detect 'Click Fraud,'" the *Wall Street Journal* (June 9, 2005), p. B1; Mike Verespej, "Who Should Be Monitoring Your Employees' Messages?" *SHRM Home* (July 14, 2005). Also see "Many Corporations Employ Staff to Monitor, Read Outbound E-mail," AccountingWeb.com (July 13, 2004), which reported the findings from a survey conducted by Proofpoint. Another study conducted by Forrester Consulting found that more than 43 percent of large corporations have staff members specifically charged with monitoring and reading outbound e-mail.

24. See Deborah Tannen, *You Just Don't Understand: Women and Men in Conversation* (New York: William Morrow, 1990), pp. 13–15. Also see Tannen, *That's Not What I Meant! How Conversation Style Makes or Breaks Your Relations with Others* (New York: Morrow, 1986); Tannen, *Talking from 9 to 5: Women and Men at Work* (New York: Quill, 2001); and Stephanie Clifford, "Young, Female, and Demanding," *Inc.* (January 2006), p. 27. "Women today aren't just multitasking—they are multi-minding, constantly thinking about and preparing for the myriad dimensions in their complex lives," *Fast Company* (January/February 2006), p. 37.

25. Ibid. Also see Michael S. Mitchell and Clifford M. Koen, Jr., "Write and Wrong: Improving Employee Communication," *Supervision*, 68, 12 (December 2007), pp. 5–11; Holly Weeks, "Taking the Stress Out of Stressful Conversations," *Harvard Business Review* (July/August 2001), pp. 112–19.

26. Ibid.

27. Nancy Keates, "After the Beep, Please Mind Your Manners," the *Wall Street Journal* (May 29, 1996), pp. B1, B5. Also see, Christopher Farrell, "Is the Workplace Getting Raunchier?" *BusinessWeek* (March 17, 2008), p. 019. Farrell reports that 38 percent of women have heard "sexually inappropriate" comments at work.

28. Kathleen H. Jamieson as quoted in *Critical Thinking About Critical Issues* (Williamsburg, VA: Learning Enrichment, Inc., 1995), p. 9; and Jamieson, *Dirty Politics: Deception, Distraction & Democracy* (Oxford, England: Oxford University Press, 1993), p. 38.

29. "When the author started his business career in the early 1960s, his style of management was such that when employees went to him with a problem, his job was to solve it for them. One day the author realized that he was spending all his time solving their problems. One of his coaches suggested that he try another approach: The next time an employee comes to you with a problem, pause, think about it for a second, and if it is not a crisis, then tell the employee

to go back and think about the problem, identify who is affected by the problem and talk with them, and then come back with at least two recommendations on how to solve the problem. Then explore their options and help them make a decision. Then, if possible, give them permission to implement the solution, making sure they understand the need to get those others who have to live with the decision involved in the implementation. His coach stressed the notion of 'ownership.'" Also see, Daisy Sanders, "Create an Open Climate for Communication," *Supervision*, 60, 1 (January 2008), pp. 6–8; and Rick Mathes, "Building Bridges Through Effective Communication," *Supervision*, 68, 10 (October 2007), pp. 3–4.

30. The author cannot remember when he heard the term "Managing Up!" but the article by John J. Gabarro and John P. Kotter, "Managing Your Boss," *Harvard Business Review* (January–February 1980), pp. 92–100 still has relevance today as every boss has a boss. The ideas and suggestions in this list were derived from material on Meryl Natchez's Web site, "Managing Up: The Overlooked Element in Successful Management" (http://www.techprose.com/managing_up.html); Mike Lynch and Harvey Lifton's *Training Clips: 150 Reproducible Handouts, Discussion Starters, and Job Aids* (HRD Press, 1998), p. 16; and Douglas Stone, Bruce Patton, and Sheila Heen's *Difficult Conversations: How to Discuss What Matters Most* (New York: Viking, 1999). Also see Stanley Bing, "Zen and the Art of Managing Up," *Fortune* (March 18, 2002), pp. 115–16, and Bing's *Throwing the Elephant* (HarperCollins Publishers, 2002). Also see Andrew Park, "Taming the Alpha Exec (AKA: 'How to Tame the Boss from Hell')," *Fast Company* (May 2006), pp. 86–90. For interesting approaches to managing the relationship with one's boss, see Sue Shellenbarger, "The Care and Feeding (and the Avoiding) of Horrible Bosses," the *Wall Street Journal* (October 20, 1999), p. B1, and Thomas J. Zuber and Erika H. James, "Managing Your Boss," *Family Practice Management* (June 2001), pp. 33–36.

31. See Andrew Sikula, Sr. and John Sikula, "Management by Interruptions (MBI)," *Supervision*, 68, 12 (December 2007), pp. 3–4; and Mike Lynch and Harvey Lifton, "Delivering Bad News," *Training Clips: 150 Reproducible Handouts, Discussion Starters, and Job Aids* (HRD Press, 1998), p. 16.

32. Peter M. Senge, *The Fifth Discipline* (New York, NY: Currency/Doubleday, 1980), pp. 159–161.

CHAPTER 4

(**Principles of Motivation**)

After studying this chapter, you will be able to:

1 Discuss the reasons people behave in the ways they do.

2 Compare various motivational theories and explain their importance for understanding employee behavior.

3 Cope with people who make your life difficult.

4 Explain the ABCs for shaping behavior.

5 Compare the assumptions and applications of Theory X and Theory Y in supervision.

6 Discuss supervisory approaches for stimulating employee motivation, especially job redesign, broadened job tasks (multi-tasking), and participative management.

YOU MAKE THE CALL!

Don Davis is the director of reloading operations for Economy Moving and Storage, a large international shipping company. Due to a corporate reorganization, Don was recently transferred and promoted to the Dublin center, where he is in charge of four team leaders who supervise 100 employees. Two of the teams operate on the first shift (7 a.m. – 3:30 p.m.) with one team on each of the other two shifts. The second shift works from 3:00 p.m. – 11:30 p.m., and the graveyard shift 11:00 p.m. – 7:30 a.m. The latter is a skeleton crew comprised of team leader Ryan and eight or so employees. Don was looking forward to the challenge and responsibility of his new position.

In Don's first week on the job, it became obvious that the Dublin center had some serious problems that had to be corrected quickly. Recently, customers had begun to complain that packages shipped from the Dublin center arrived at their destinations late and in poor condition. For a company that prides itself on quality customer service and timely delivery, these conditions are unacceptable, and it is Don's responsibility to correct the situation.

The first thing Don did was gather information regarding the customer complaints. Then he checked with Holly Henderson, the human resources supervisor, to gather information on the employment characteristics at the Dublin center. Don discovered that his center had the company's highest employee turnover and lost-time injury rates. Absenteeism and tardiness were running rampant, and the number of employee grievances had been increasing over the past six months. Realizing that unhappy employees equal poor customer service, Don decided to meet with the four team leaders to understand why the employees were performing below expectations.

As Don was taking one last sip of coffee, he took a look at his e-mails. One caught his eye: "For Management Eyes Only: Sensitive Information." It was from the President and Chief Operating Officer of the company. In short, the message read:

Most shareholders and members of management are aware of our last quarter's financial performance. I won't dwell on it. We understand that it was completely unsatisfactory. We continue to struggle with a weak economy and soaring fuel costs. Low retail spending continues to restrain demand for shipment of manufactured goods.... Another issue is CEO and top management compensation. All senior-level management personnel will immediately take a ten percent reduction in total compensation. We do not expect our compensation to increase until Economy's performance improves.... During the last quarter, our volume dropped 8 percent and our operating costs rose 14 percent in part because of fuel costs. We will offset the deteriorating situation by putting off capital projects, parking some aircraft and fuel-inefficient vehicles, and shaving employee work hours . . . I'd like to thank each of you for your patience and support during these very challenging times. Finally, I, along with other members of top management, will be visiting each of the facilities during the next three weeks. During that time we will meet with all managers, individually and in small groups, to apprise you of the bleak situation we face, and to get suggestions and ideas we might be able to implement. I encourage you to think about ways to (1) increase revenues and (2) reduce costs.

"Ouch," Don thought, "I wonder what that really means? I wonder if my team leaders got the e-mail? I'd better not mention it until I find out what is really going on."

During the meeting, Don illustrated with charts and graphs the most recent month's performance results to Amy, Steve, Joe, and Ryan and asked for their input. Amy, the senior team leader, pointed out that the conditions in which the employees worked were terrible. "We had record temperatures every day last week," she said. "Two days, it was over 100 degrees in here. How can you expect people to perform in extreme heat?"

Joe, the newest of the supervisors, added, "Most workers are part-time and combine their part-time work here with another part-time job or two to make ends meet. Some are college students and are only working here until they complete school. They come in here tired and with other things on their minds. Most of the injuries I see are related to a lack of concentration. They are just stupid mistakes. Even during our safety meetings, workers seem bored and do not seem to pay attention." Steve claimed, "The job the employees perform is very repetitive. They seem bored and lack enthusiasm. In fact, on several occasions employees have pointed out that their work is mindless and never changes. If you ask me, boredom is the main problem with employee performance."

Ryan continued, "I think the performance of our employees is affected by a few 'bad apples.' Overall, most of our people are good workers. They want to do a good job. I've seen them get frustrated because of a poorly performing coworker who should be reprimanded. I can't do anything about it; we're short-staffed, and if I discipline someone, he or she will probably quit. That's what happened a week ago when I leaned on Reuben to improve his performance. He quit. They know what to do, but sometimes they just don't or won't do it. Even when I plead with them to improve or threaten to write them up, it doesn't work. If I could only get the poor performers motivated, I think the rest would fall in line and overall performance would improve."

AMIR BAHADORI

Last, Amy chimed in, "I'm having trouble motivating my workers. Just yesterday, one of my best workers left with a back injury and the rest failed to pick up the slack. If we don't find a way to motivate these people, none of us will have a job."

The real question is: How can Don motivate employees to perform better? He cannot tempt them with pay increases because that is outside his authority. He knows he will have to do something quickly. What should he do? **YOU MAKE THE CALL!**

1 Discuss the reasons people behave the way they do.

Determinants of Human Behavior

In Chapter 2, we defined management as getting things accomplished with and through people by guiding and motivating their efforts toward common objectives. To manage effectively, as this definition suggests, supervisors must understand employee motivation and develop approaches that encourage employees to work to their full capabilities.

People are the most important resource that a supervisor is asked to manage. Human beings have values, attitudes, needs, and expectations that significantly influence their behaviors on the job. The feelings people have toward their supervisors, their job environments, their personal problems, and numerous other factors are often difficult to ascertain.[1] However, they have a tremendous impact on employee motivation and work performance.

What causes employees to behave in the ways they do? This question is difficult to answer because each individual is unique. The behavior of people is often rational, consistent, and predictable. However, people's behaviors at other times may seem irrational, inconsistent, and unpredictable. People tend to associate with others who are like themselves—"birds of a like feather flock together." This may lead to distrust and misunderstanding of those who are not of their "flock." Have you ever behaved differently because of the group you were in? Of course you have. Was that behavior inconsistent with your family's or organization's expectations? If so, then problems arose for your parents, your supervisor, and eventually you. Remember: Behavior is influenced by many forces, making it difficult for the supervisor to formulate simple principles that apply to every situation.

The forces that stimulate human behavior come from within individuals and from their environments. To illustrate, think about why parents' behavior changes when they become grandparents. One answer might be that the grandparents are older and perhaps more mature or experienced. They have received feedback on their earlier parenting efforts and have taken corrective action. Many grandparents have extra income to spend or more time to devote to grandparenting. As grandparents, duties and responsibilities change. Also, grandparents can always send their grandchildren home to their parents. All these factors together may lead to behavioral change.

Every day, employees confront issues that were unheard of a decade or two ago. The typical employee today spends more waking hours "going to, being at, and coming home from work." With the current economic conditions, an increasing number of workers are seeking to work multiple jobs to try to make ends meet. Some Boomers, for example, are caring for grandchildren and looking after their aging parents, and have less time to spend on leisure-time activities or go on vacations. Often, employees find themselves in intolerable or soured personal relationships. Many experienced managers speak about the people who were their star performers but who lost their luster. Understanding the "baggage" that affects employee performance is critical to the supervisor's success in dealing with people.

DETERMINANTS OF PERSONALITY[2]

Every individual is the product of many factors, and it is the unique combination of these factors that results in an individual human personality. **Personality** is the complex mix of knowledge, attitudes, and attributes that distinguishes one person from all others.

Many people use the word personality to describe what they observe in another person. However, the real substance of human personality goes far beyond external behavior. The essence of an individual's personality includes his or her attitudes, values, and ways of interpreting the environment, as well as many internal and external influences that contribute to behavioral patterns. Several major schools of personality study can help explain the complexity of human behavior. First, we will discuss the primary determinants of personality, and then describe how some major theories relate these factors to employee motivation.

> **Personality**
> The knowledge, attitudes, and attributes that make up the unique human being

PHYSIOLOGICAL (BIOLOGICAL) FACTORS

One major influence on human personality is physiological (or biological) makeup. Such factors as gender, age, race, height, weight, and physique can affect how a person sees the world. Intelligence, which is at least partially inherited, is another. Most biological characteristics are apparent to others, and they may affect the way in which a person is perceived. For example, a person who is tall is sometimes considered to have more leadership ability than a shorter person. While physiological characteristics should not be the basis for evaluating an employee's capabilities, they do exert considerable influence on an individual's personality as well as defining certain physical abilities and limitations.

EARLY CHILDHOOD INFLUENCES

Many psychologists feel that the very early years of a person's life are crucial to an individual's development. The manner in which a child is trained, shown affection, and disciplined has a lifelong influence. Parents who encourage autonomy, independence, exploration, and the ability to deal with risk while instilling a willingness to work with others give the child valuable lessons. Author and consultant Sandra A. Crowe says, "Our history creates our present. So, people's backgrounds affect the way they are—and the way they act at work. Problems with a critical parent in younger years, for instance, may lead to insecurity in adult life. Such folks often end up humiliating others, blaming them for their shortcomings, and taking credit for others' work."[3] Various biographies illustrate that an individual's ability to cope with problems and work with others may be determined in part through the influences on that individual in childhood.

ENVIRONMENTAL (SITUATIONAL) FACTORS

Sociologists and social psychologists emphasize the immediate situation or environment as being the most important determinant of adult personality. Such factors as education, income, employment, home, and many other experiences that confront an individual throughout life influence who that person is and eventually becomes. Have you ever talked about "the good old days"? Where you lived during your formative years and what you experienced during that time has, in part, shaped who and what you are today.

Each day's experiences contribute to an individual's makeup. This is particularly true in terms of the immediate working environment. For example, the personality of the blue-collar worker performing routine, manual labor on an assembly line is affected by work differently than the personality of a white-collar worker who performs primarily mental work involving thought and judgment. Stated another way, what a supervisor does in a work situation affects the personalities of the people being supervised.

CULTURAL (SOCIETAL) VALUES

Culture also influences personality. In the United States, such values as competition, rewards for accomplishment, equal opportunities, and similar concepts are part of a democratic society. Individuals are educated, trained, and encouraged to think for themselves and to strive to achieve worthwhile goals. However, some cultural values are changing. For example, for many years the workforce in the United States was relatively homogeneous, and the cultural values of most workers tended to be similar. In recent decades, however, the workforce has become increasingly diversified, reflecting many different subcultures and subgroups. The number of Asians and Hispanics in the workforce has increased dramatically. As the diversity of the workforce has increased, so has the effect of different cultural norms and values on the workplace. In particular, the values of certain ethnic, age, and other minority groups may be quite different among employees. By recognizing and respecting different cultural values, supervisors should become more adept in dealing effectively with people unlike themselves.

EVERY EMPLOYEE HAS A "'TUDE"[4]

Not long ago, a manager expressed to the text's author that her biggest challenge was an employee with an attitude ('tude) problem. The employee constantly complained. The manager was upset with herself because she had taken the path of least resistance and avoided the employee. Supervisors must recognize that the positive or negative behavior of one person spills over—someone else now has either a positive or negative attitude. We have all seen situations where one employee with a bad attitude is like cancer and can affect the entire system if left unchecked. You and I don't have a bad attitude; it's all those other people!

Positive Mental Attitude (PMA)
A person with a PMA usually responds favorably to the job, other people, and most situations

How do others see you? Think about a person you know who has a **positive mental attitude (PMA)**. Is this person fun to be around (i.e., work with)? Is this person's attitude infectious? Does an employee with a PMA perform better in the workplace? How about you? Are you known for having a PMA? Do others see you as having a negative attitude? Skills Application 4-4 at the end of this chapter gives you an opportunity to develop strategies for coping with this type of behavior.

Not surprisingly, there is a rule of reciprocity that suggests that humans react and respond in like manner to the attitude and action of others. Consider these two scenarios:

- As we drive down the highway, we can see this rule in effect. Suppose someone is driving much slower than the speed limit and another person is in a hurry. What happens? The second driver may blast the horn, yell obscenities, and gesture until there is an opportunity to pass the slower driver. Who has the bad attitude? Now they both do!
- On the other hand, if a driver lets someone cut into a traffic flow, what happens? A wave of the hand, a mouthed "thanks," and perhaps a little later that person lets someone else into the traffic flow. The notion of "one good deed warrants another" comes into play.

Often our 'tudes are caused by what others do and say. Remember an axiom of supervision: Focus on what the person does or does not do.

RECOGNIZING HUMAN DIFFERENCES AND SIMILARITIES

The many complexities of human personality have been discussed here only briefly because there are any number of factors that cause a person's personality and attitude to change. Realistically, it is impossible to understand all the unique characteristics of a person's personality. Fortunately, behavioral studies have demonstrated that people tend to be more alike than different in their basic motivational needs and their reasons for behaving in the ways they do. Supervisors can implement managerial techniques that emphasize the similarities, rather than the differences, of people. This does not mean that unique differences in people should be overlooked. Supervisors can understand the unique needs and personality makeup of individual employees enough to adapt general approaches to individuals to some extent. However, a consistent supervisory approach based on similarities rather than differences is a practical way to lead a group of employees toward achieving company goals.

Understanding Motivation and Human Behavior

2 Compare various motivational theories and explain their importance for understanding employee behavior.

Too often, motivation is viewed as something one person can give to, or do, for another. Supervisors sometimes talk in terms of giving a worker a "shot" of motivation or of having to "motivate employees." However, motivating employees is not that easy, because human motivation really refers to an inner drive or impulse. Motivation cannot be given to another. In the final analysis, motivation comes from within a person. **Motivation** is a willingness to exert effort toward achieving a goal, stimulated by the effort's ability to fulfill an individual need. In other words, employees are more willing to do what the organization wants if they believe that doing so will result in a meaningful reward. The supervisor's challenge is to stimulate that willingness and ensure that the rewards are commensurate with the results. The rewards need not always be money; they can be anything employees value. For example, praise and recognition can be powerful motivators.

Motivation
A willingness to exert effort toward achieving a goal, stimulated by the effort's ability to fulfill an individual need

Because employee motivation is crucial to organizational success, it is a subject about which there has been much debate. The theories in this chapter are fundamental and emphasize the similarities, rather than differences, in human needs.

THE HIERARCHY OF NEEDS (MASLOW)

Most psychologists who study human behavior and personality are convinced that all behavior is caused, goal-oriented, and motivated. Stated another way, there is a reason for everything a person does, assuming the person is rational, sane, and in control (i.e., not under the influence of drugs or alcohol). People constantly strive to attain something that has meaning to them in terms of their needs and in relation to how those people see themselves and the environments in which they live. Often, we may be unaware of why we behave in a certain manner, but we all have subconscious motives that govern the ways we behave in different situations.

One of the most widely accepted theories of human behavior is that people are motivated to satisfy certain well-defined and more or less predictable needs. Psychologist Abraham H. Maslow formulated the concept of a **hierarchy** (or priority) **of needs**.[5] He maintained that these needs range from low-level needs to high-level needs, in an ascending priority (see Figure 4.1). These needs

Hierarchy of needs
Maslow's theory of motivation, which suggests that employee needs are arranged in priority order such that lower-order needs must be satisfied before higher-order needs become motivating

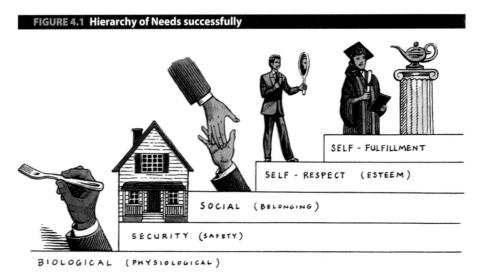

FIGURE 4.1 Hierarchy of Needs successfully

actually overlap and are interrelated, and it may be preferable to consider them as existing along a continuum rather than as being separate and distinct from one another.

Maslow's theory of a hierarchy of human needs implies that people try to satisfy these needs in the order in which they are arranged in the hierarchy. Until the lowest, or most basic, needs are reasonably satisfied, a person will not be motivated strongly by the other levels. As one level of need is satisfied to some extent, the individual focuses on the next level, which then becomes the stronger motivator of behavior. Maslow even suggested that once a low level of need was reasonably satisfied, it would no longer motivate behavior, at least in the short term.

BIOLOGICAL (PHYSIOLOGICAL) NEEDS

Physiological needs
Basic physical needs (e.g., food, rest, shelter, and recreation)

On the first level of Maslow's hierarchy are **physiological** (or biological) **needs**. These are the needs everyone has for food, shelter, rest, recreation, and other physical necessities. Virtually every employee views work as a means of caring for these fundamental needs. A paycheck enables a person to buy the necessities vital to survival, as well as some of the comforts of life.

SECURITY (SAFETY) NEEDS

Security needs
Desire for protection against danger and life's uncertainties

Once a person's physiological needs are reasonably satisfied, other needs become important. The **security** (or safety) **needs** include the need to protect ourselves against danger and to guard against the uncertainties of life.[6] Most employees want some sense of security or control over their future. To satisfy such expectations, many employers offer various supplementary benefits. For example, medical, retirement, hospitalization, disability, and life insurance plans are designed to protect employees against various uncertainties and their possible serious consequences. Wage and benefit packages are designed to satisfy employees' physiological and safety needs. By fulfilling these basic needs, organizations hope to attract and retain competent personnel. Imagine what goes through a person's mind when he or she reads that 16,000 GM jobs will be eliminated or thousands of Bear Stearns employees will lose their jobs. In today's economic environment, job security may not be as important as having enough income to provide the basic needs. See how the needs are intertwined?

SOCIAL (BELONGING) NEEDS

Some supervisors believe that good wages and ample benefits suffice to motivate employees. These supervisors do not understand the importance of the higher-level needs of human beings, beginning with social (or belonging) needs. **Social needs** are needs people have for attention, for being part of a group, for being accepted by their peers, and for love. Many studies have shown that group motivation can be a powerful influence on employee behavior at work, either negatively or positively. For example, some employees may deliberately perform contrary to organizational goals to feel that they are accepted in an informal group. On the other hand, if informal group goals are in line with organizational goals, the group can influence individuals toward exceptional performance. Some employers provide off-the-job social and athletic opportunities for their employees as a means of helping those employees satisfy their social needs and to build loyalty to the organization as a whole.

Social needs
Desire for love and affection and affiliation with something worthwhile

Think about these questions: Do you have friends? Or, do you have a group of acquaintances? Do you have a group you can sit around with to enjoy a cup of coffee or tell a few jokes, but then go your own way? Or, do you have someone you can call at 3 A.M. to discuss a personal problem and who will listen critically without passing judgment? Think back to when you were ten years old. Who was your very best friend? Where is that person today? Or ask someone who has been married for more than 25 years these questions: "Who was the best man or maid/matron of honor at your wedding? Where are they today? Are they still there for you? Have they stood alongside you (unconditionally, without strings attached)?" In some cases, the answer is "yes." In many instances, these are illustrations of the "here today–gone tomorrow" phenomenon.

Sadly, the following illustration hits close to home for the author. Not long ago, I attended the funeral of a colleague. His grieving widow was overheard to say, "Jim knew a lot of people. I had no trouble getting pallbearers, but no one visited us after he got sick and went into the nursing home. I thought we had a lot of friends." Human connectedness is at the top of the list for some people.

We all know many people who like their jobs but not the people they work with and, as such, seek fulfillment of their social needs through off-the-job interactions.

SELF-RESPECT (ESTEEM) NEEDS

Closely related to social needs are **self-respect** (or esteem or ego) **needs**. These are needs everyone has for recognition, achievement, status, and a sense of accomplishment. Self-respect needs are very powerful because they relate to personal feelings of self-worth and importance. Supervisors should look for ways to satisfy these internal needs, such as providing varied and challenging work tasks and recognizing good performance. Something as simple as saying "good job" to someone can keep that person doing good work.

Self-respect needs
Desire for recognition, achievement, status, and a sense of accomplishment

SELF-FULFILLMENT NEEDS

At the highest level of human needs are **self-fulfillment** (self-realization or self-actualization) **needs**—the desires to use one's capabilities to their fullest. People want to be creative and to achieve within their capacities. Presumably, these highest-level needs are not satisfied until people reach their full potential. As such, these needs persist throughout a person's life and can go unsatisfied. Many jobs frustrate rather than fulfill this level of human needs. For example, many factory and office jobs are routine and monotonous, and workers must seek self-fulfillment in pursuits off the job and in family relationships. However, supervisors can provide opportunities for self-fulfillment on the job by assigning tasks that challenge employees to use their abilities more fully.

Self-fulfillment needs
Desire to use one's abilities to the fullest extent

Some employers provide off-the-job social and athletic opportunities for their employees to help those employees satisfy their social needs and to build loyalty to the organization

© MICHAEL NEWMAN/PHOTOEDIT

APPLYING THE NEEDS THEORIES TO SUPERVISORY MANAGEMENT

Supervisors can use the hierarchy of human needs as a framework for visualizing the kinds of needs people have and for assessing those needs' relative importance in motivating individuals in the workplace. The supervisor's challenge is to make individual fulfillment the result of doing a good job. For example, if the supervisor senses that an employee's most influential motivator is social needs, the employee is most likely to do a good job when assigned to work with a group and the whole group is rewarded for doing the job well. If an employee seems to be seeking self-respect, the supervisor might provide visible signs of recognition to influence this employee toward good performance, such as awarding a bonus or praise in front of the employee's peers at a departmental meeting. The key for the supervisor is to recognize where each employee is in the hierarchy so that the supervisor can determine which needs are driving the employee. Withholding praise and not recognizing employee accomplishment is a common pitfall (see Figure 4.2).

Ultimately, all motivation is self-motivation. Therefore, a good supervisor structures the work situation and reward systems such that employees are motivated to perform well because good work performance leads to satisfaction of their needs.

We all know someone for whom work appears to be the only focus of their life. Others have found work to be a source of comfort, security, and meaning. Their values combine Edison's "There is no substitute for hard work . . ." and Emerson's "We put our love where we put our labor."[7] However, we challenge you to find someone who, when on his or her deathbed, says, "As I look back over my life, I wish I had spent more time at work."[8]

It is normal for team members like those in this chapter's "You Make the Call!" to expect good wages, generous benefit plans, pleasant working conditions, and job security. You likely have heard stories of older family members who spent 40-some years working for the same company. Today,

FIGURE 4.2 Learn from the Mistakes of Others

As mentioned in earlier chapters, each organization has its own culture—that set of shared values, beliefs, and behaviors formed by members of the organization over time. The leadership style of top management helps to shape the culture. Words alone do not produce culture or commitment to the organization's purpose; rather, the actions of managers do. When asked, "What is the biggest mistake you have ever made as a boss?," executives representing some of the largest corporations in the United States reported:

- I didn't give recognition to someone who turned out to be one of my best employees, and I soon lost her.
- I didn't give credit when it was due to individuals who made major contributions.
- I failed to acknowledge someone who needed to be rewarded.
- I wish I had provided more opportunities for subordinates to engage in projects they enjoyed.
- I didn't recognize my associates' birthdays or anniversaries.
- I didn't understand that my staff had reached a limit on their ability to produce.
- I was overly harsh in my criticism, and that brought about insecurities in my employees.

Not surprisingly, withholding of praise was a mistake admitted by many of the respondents. Others regretted not being more supportive of staff. Will you repeat the same mistakes?

Source: Survey conducted by Accountemps as reported in "Executives Surveyed Reveal Biggest Mistakes They've Made as Supervisors," AccountingWeb.com (June 28, 2004). Also see, Max Messmer, chairman of Accountemps, and author of *Motivating Employees for Dummies* (New York: John Wiley & Sons, Inc., 2003).

business closings and downsizings have become facts of life. As the downsizing trend continues, company loyalty may lessen. Surprisingly, in a 2008 survey it was reported that only 44 percent of male workers between 58 and 62 still work for the firm that employed them at 50.[9] Managers who are asked to develop effective work teams may find it increasingly difficult as employees become less enthusiastic about "winning one for the firm!" Further, the lack of trust and low job security may create a strong individual orientation that one must take charge of one's own future. Realistically, there is no guarantee a job will be there tomorrow.

Is money everything? For some employees, it is the only thing! A recent study found compensation including benefits was very important to nearly 60 percent of U.S. workers. The top five most important aspects of employee job satisfaction were compensation, benefits, job security, work/life balance, and communication between the employee and his/her supervisor.[10] At a management seminar the author conducts, a retail store manager said, "We have employees for whom time is just as important as money. Many working mothers need time off to spend with kids. They also have a psychological need to be healthy and not worn out. Time becomes more valuable than money." The slogan "Different strokes for different folks" should be part of every supervisor's management practice.

In some organizations, there is a phenomenon called employee entitlement. **Employee entitlement** is a belief held by some individuals that the organization owes them something regardless of the effort they put forth. This attitude manifests itself in the workplace in many ways: the poor performer who asks for a severance package after being fired, employees who fail to meet sales goals but demand bonuses anyway ("we got one last year"), or college professors who expect a substantial pay raise because they survived another year.[11]

Employee entitlement
The belief that the organization "owes" them

MOTIVATION-HYGIENE THEORY

Another theory of motivation is the **motivation-hygiene theory**, sometimes called the "two-factor theory" or the "dual-factor theory," developed by Frederick Herzberg.[12] Herzberg's research has demonstrated that some factors in the work environment that were traditionally believed to motivate people actually serve primarily to reduce their dissatisfaction rather than motivate them.

Herzberg and others have conducted numerous studies in which people were asked to describe events that made them feel particularly good or bad about their jobs. Other questions were designed to determine the depth of feelings, the duration for which those feelings persisted, and the types of situations that made employees feel motivated or frustrated. These studies were conducted with employees in varied organizations and industries, including personnel at all levels and from different technical and job specialties. Interestingly, the general pattern of results was fairly consistent. It revealed a clear distinction between factors that tend to motivate employees (motivation factors) and those that, while expected by workers, are not likely to motivate them (hygiene factors).

MOTIVATION FACTORS

Herzberg identified **motivation factors** as elements intrinsic in the job that promote job performance. Among the most frequently identified motivation factors were the following:

- Opportunity for growth and advancement
- Achievement or accomplishment
- Recognition for accomplishments
- Challenging or interesting work
- Responsibility for work

Stated another way, job factors that tend to motivate people are primarily related to higher-level needs and aspirations. These factors all related to outcomes associated with the content of the job being performed. Opportunity for advancement, greater responsibility, recognition, growth, achievement, and interesting work are consistently identified as the major factors making work motivating and meaningful. The absence of these factors can be frustrating and nonmotivating. These motivation factors are not easily measured, and they may be difficult to find in certain types of jobs.

HYGIENE FACTORS

Also called "dissatisfiers," **hygiene factors** are elements in the work environment that, if positive, reduce dissatisfaction, but do not tend to motivate. Herzberg identified the following hygiene factors:

- Working conditions
- Money, status, and security
- Interpersonal relationships
- Supervision
- Company policies and administration

The factors that employees complained about most were the following conditions in the work environment:

- Poor company policies and administrative practices
- Lack of good supervision in both a technical and a human-relations sense

- Poor working conditions
- Inadequate wages and benefits

Herzberg concluded that these job-context factors tend to dissatisfy rather than motivate. In recent years, the conflict between work demands and personal life has been identified as another hygiene factor. When these factors are negative or inadequate, employees are unhappy. When these factors are adequate or even excellent, they do not, by themselves, promote better job performance. This does not mean that hygiene factors are unimportant. They are very important, but they serve primarily to maintain a reasonable level of job motivation, not to increase it.

APPLYING HERZBERG'S THEORY TO SUPERVISORY MANAGEMENT

To improve performance, Herzberg's theory suggests that the supervisor should implement strategies that target the motivation factors—that is, those that contribute to the satisfaction of employees' social, self-respect, and self-fulfillment needs. One of the supervisor's strategies should be to "catch people doing something right" and "give them credit when credit is due." A note of caution: Praise and other forms of recognition must be highly individualized and genuinely deserved to be effective. A key element in effective supervision is to give employees an opportunity to fulfill their needs as a result of good job performance.

The supervisor should not conclude from Herzberg's work that hygiene factors such as money, benefits, good working conditions, and the like are unimportant. These factors are extremely important, and organizations must strive continuously to be competitive in these areas. However, employees often take such factors for granted, especially when job opportunities are plentiful. Employee motivation is related more to their higher-level needs.

Some employees find meaning outside work

EXPECTANCY THEORY

Expectancy theory
Theory of motivation that holds that employees perform better when they believe such efforts lead to desired rewards

Another interesting and practical way of looking at employee motivation is provided by expectancy theory.[13] **Expectancy theory** is based on the worker's perception of the relationships among effort, performance, and reward. According to expectancy theory, workers will be motivated to work harder when they believe their enhanced efforts will improve performance and that such improved performance will lead to desired rewards. Figure 4.3 illustrates the expectancy theory model.

Expectancy theory is based on worker perceptions and on relationships called linkages. Employee motivation depends on workers being able to perceive an effort/performance linkage, as well as a performance/reward linkage. When employees cannot clearly recognize that such linkages exist, they will not be highly motivated.

For example, when an employee at Economy (this Chapter's You Make the Call) does not receive adequate training, they will probably be unable to perceive a relationship between their effort and their performance. Instead, they will conclude that no matter how much effort they expend, there will be no significant improvement in their job performance. Similarly, when nurses' aides perceive that their high-performing coworkers are not being rewarded any more than average or even substandard performers, they will not believe that a performance/reward relationship exists, so they will not be motivated to perform well.

Supervisors may believe that their organizations reward high-quality work. However, such a belief may be based on management's perception of the reward system. Supervisors should try to verify whether workers perceive linkages. Supervisors and employees often do not view reward systems in the same way.

FIGURE 4.3 Expectancy Theory

For example, when Don Davis and the HR assistant conducted a belated exit interview with Reuben, they asked him why he quit. Reuben stated that he came to work every day knowing that no matter how hard he worked, his extra efforts would not be visible on the goods shipped chart. He expressed anger when he never received any praise from Ryan.

In reality, expectancy theory is really a simple notion: People will do what is in their best interest. Employees will be motivated to put forth more effort if they believe the additional effort will result in something of value. For example, if a student believes that more work (study time) will not lead to a better performance on the forthcoming test, then he or she will not study more. We have all known a few students who are content to "just pass" a course. A grade of A or B is not sufficient enough reward for them to put forth additional effort. Therefore, the motivational effort is low when perception of improved performance is low and the anticipated reward is low.

It does not matter how clearly supervisors view the linkages among effort, performance, and rewards. If the workers cannot see them, the linkages might as well be absent. Supervisors should strive to show employees that increased effort will improve work performance, which in turn will increase rewards. Rewards may be extrinsic, in the form of additional pay, or intrinsic, such as a sense of accomplishment or some type of praise or recognition. Probably the most important characteristic of a reward is that it is something the recipient desires and values.

EQUITY THEORY

How many times have you heard the following: Ed, an employee, complains to anyone who will listen, "It's not fair! I've been here as long as Carl. We do the same job, but he gets paid more than I do." Ed's belief of inequity rests on the notion that his outcome/input ratio is lower than Carl's (see Figure 4.4). Inputs include such things as seniority, experience, age, skill, ability, job knowledge, and effort. Ed's exasperated statement suggests that Ed and Carl have similar inputs: They have both held the same job for the same time. Inequity exists because Carl evidently receives more outcomes (he is paid more than Ed). Outcomes can include salary, working conditions, degree of employee involvement and decision making, opportunity for advancement and promotion, challenging assignments, pay and benefits, and assorted forms of recognition.

Based on the works of J. Stacy Adams, **equity theory** is a theory of motivation that explains how people strive for fairness in the workplace. Since the beginning of time, people have compared themselves to others. They compare their own input/outcome ratios to those of others. When the ratios are unequal, there is inequity. This inequity will be followed by a motivation to achieve equity, or fairness, by making the outcome/input ratios equal.

Equity theory
Explains how people strive for fairness in the workplace

Adams also stressed that what is important in determining motivation is the relative, rather than the absolute, level of outcomes a person receives and the inputs a person contributes.[14] In Figure 4.4, Ed compares himself to Carl, a person performing similar work in the same organization. It is important to realize that while Ed believes Carl is paid more, this may not be the case. However, inequity still exists because of what Ed believes, and Ed will still be motivated to achieve equity.

People can make a number of different kinds of comparisons with others in order to draw conclusions about fairness. We have seen that Ed compares himself to Carl, someone who has the same job. Ed might also be inclined to compare himself to individuals or groups of people in other departments in his

FIGURE 4.4 It's Not Fair!—Equity Theory at Work

$$\frac{\text{Ed's Outcomes}}{\text{Ed's Inputs}} \quad < \quad \frac{\text{Carl's Outcomes}}{\text{Carl's Inputs}}$$

Ed's inputs are the same as Carl's; they both have the same job. Carl has higher outcomes than Ed, because he gets paid more. This makes Carl's outcome/input ratio greater than Ed's, which creates a feeling of unfairness. Equity theory holds that Ed will be motivated to change the situation so that his and Carl's ratios are equal.

organization, even if those people do different work than Ed. Ed might compare himself to his own expectations, such as where he expected to be at this stage of his career. Ed could even compare himself to an individual or a group in another organization. To illustrate, consider the following scenario, in which Ed uses a referent from another company:

Ed's next door neighbor, Carolyn, works at Magna Donnelly, the Holland, Michigan, manufacturer of mirrors, windshields, and other precision-glass products for the auto industry. Part of Carolyn's work satisfaction comes from the way employees work together. Her factory is organized into small teams. These teams set their own goals and have broad discretion in how they do their work. A cooperative decision-making process is used that includes all team members. Each team chooses a representative to serve on the equity committee, which is a forum for the entire building. The equity committee deals with pay structure, benefits, and grievances. One person from the equity committee is chosen as the representative to the Donnelly Committee, whose members also include senior management. The Donnelly Committee's power is limited to matters that concern employees directly. It solicits ideas from employees, studies solutions, debates issues, and develops plans for running the business in a way that is fair. Carolyn continually provokes Ed by talking about how great she has it there. She says that her satisfactions come from what she does, how she does it, and who she does it with. "Top management trusts us, we trust them, and we trust each other."[15]

To an interested audience of coworkers, Ed laments, "You should see how Donnelly listens to its employees and the input they have. No one listens to us.

FIGURE 4.5 A Disgruntled Employee's Response

It's not fair!" In this case, Ed is comparing his work situation to his perceptions of the work environment of another organization. Ed's frustration with his situation inspires him to prepare a poster like that in Figure 4.5. Some employees express their displeasure in other ways. It is not uncommon to find expressions of "hate" on personal blogs or on personal Web pages (e.g., MySpace).

TYPES OF INEQUITY

There are two types of inequity in the work environment. The first is negative or underpayment inequity. Ed perceives that he and Carl have relatively equal inputs and perform the same work. Because Carl's outcomes are greater—he is paid more—Ed's outcome/input ratio is lower than Carl's. Ed believes this to be unfair. Equity theory purports that when there is a substantial perceived inequity, people will be motivated to correct the situation. Ed might attempt to maximize the amount of positive outcomes he receives. In this case, Ed will be motivated to correct the perceived inequity by contacting his boss and building a case for a pay raise, or he may search for other positive outcomes. If Ed cannot increase his outcomes, he may resort to lowering his inputs by putting forth less effort on the job, by staying away at critical times, or by being at work physically but tuned out psychologically (inattentive) to the goals of the department. While Ed could increase his inputs by coming to work earlier, staying later, or taking classes to add to his knowledge base, research shows that most employees resist increasing their inputs when doing so requires substantial effort or when there is a belief the outcomes will be disproportionate to the effort expended.

The second type of inequity is positive or overpayment inequity. Carl, for example, experiences positive inequity because his outcome/input ratio is higher than Ed's. To say that he enjoys the situation may be incorrect, however. It is doubtful that Carl will be motivated to correct the situation. Rarely does an employee admit to being overpaid, but that employee may sense the situation is unfair and realize that a similar situation could impact him or her later. These feelings of discomfort may impede performance. However, some individuals may be motivated (willing to put forth the effort) to maintain the overpayment inequity.

SUPERVISORS AND EQUITY THEORY

What are the implications of equity theory for the supervisor? First, it provides another explanation for how perceptions and beliefs about what is fair influence job performance. Second, it acquaints managers with the disasters that can occur when rewards are misaligned with performance. Ed's constant complaints about the unfair situation could negatively affect other employees. While some people like to distance themselves from negativists, others find solace in continuing claims of unfairness and jump on the bandwagon. The situation can get out of hand; factions can develop to threaten organizational effectiveness. Effective supervisors must be vigilant for signs of unfairness and immediately address employee concerns. Questions like, "What is not fair?" "Why is it not fair?" and "What would it take to make it fair?" must be asked. Additionally, the supervisor may give Ed information that will help him to better assess his and Carl's outcomes/inputs. However, research indicates that rather than change perceptions about himself, Ed is more likely to change his perceptions of Carl's outcomes/inputs or to change to another referent.

Often, employees like Ed feel they must go somewhere else because their organizations do not appreciate their contributions. How many times have you heard someone say, "I'm not happy with the way I was treated—it's not fair!" Supervisors need to use information-getting, probing-type questions to find out what the person sees as unfair and why they consider it unfair. Supervisors must find out what employees want, need, and perceive as just and equitable rewards for their contributions. Only then can they address the problem.

---

3 Cope with people who make your life difficult.

Coping With People Who Make Your Life Difficult[16]

Everyone has a bad day once in a while. People get too little sleep, receive bad news, or carry family or personal problems. Some people blame others for their problems. Often, these blamers and complainers are referred to as "difficult people." A note of caution is warranted at this point: Do not tag a label on people; instead, focus on what they do that makes our lives difficult. We want to change their behavior.

We introduced "stretch" in Chapter 3. See this chapter's Skills Application 4-4 for another member of the cast of characters who make your life difficult. Throughout the rest of this text, you will see that these people come in all sizes and shapes. Students always want to know, "What am I supposed to do when confronted by the person who makes my life difficult?" My response has always been the same: "Tell me what you mean." "Describe this person to me." "Tell me how the person makes your life difficult." These and other questions can be used to focus attention on what the person does and how it impacts others. Because

FIGURE 4.6 Suggestions for Coping with People Who Make Your Life Difficult

- Do not label people as difficult, no matter how difficult they make your life.
- Think in terms of difficult behaviors, not difficult people.
- The easiest way to cope with some people is to avoid them, but the easiest answer isn't always the best answer. Change your mindset and focus on what they do well.
- Accentuate the positive—build on their strengths.
- Take control of the situation. Get their attention by calling them by name.
- Talk with them in private; give them your undivided attention.
- Avoid accusations, ask open-ended questions, and listen to their side of the story.
- Factually provide one specific situation that illustrates the problem behavior.
- Clearly state that you expect the behavior to improve.
- Focus on changing what they do, not who they are.
- Establish deadlines and timetables for the behavior to cease.
- If the behavior does not change, consider asking upper management or Human Resources to step in.

Remember: There is no recipe for dealing with people that make your life difficult. Search the Internet, review the literature, continually learn about what people want and need, and develop strategies for getting the best out of people.

there are many different variants of the people who make our lives difficult, and there is no prescription to cure all, we refer students to books and programs that are designed to guide people in successfully dealing with difficult people. There is also a great deal of information on the Internet. Consult Figure 4.6 for some generic suggestions for dealing with people who make your life difficult.

Often, the author is asked, "Why are some people so easy to get along with while others are so difficult?" After a brief pause, I ask them to describe their "best friend." What is it that he/she does that solidified that friendship? Then I ask them to tell me about the other person. Generally, it is what the person does and how they do it, or what they do not do. What causes some people to be frustrated, angry, and not easy to get along with? Often, conditions that do not bring about the fulfillment of a person's needs ultimately result in dissatisfaction and frustration. When their needs are not satisfied on the job, employees may resort to behavior patterns that are detrimental to their job performances and to the organization. A typical approach for frustrated employees is to resign themselves to just "getting by" on the job. They simply go through the motions and put in time without trying to perform in other than an average or marginal manner. Some employees involve themselves in off-the-job activities to fulfill their need for personal satisfaction. Others have been known to drown their sorrows by abusing alcohol or illegal substances. They may seek immediate, short-term pleasure outside of work.

Some employees constantly find things that distract them from doing the job, and, at times, they even try to beat the system. They often are absent or tardy, or they break rules as a way of trying to get back at situations they find frustrating. Increasingly, employees resort to searching the Web or engaging in "fantasy" computer games.[17] Still other employees who are dissatisfied adopt aggressive behavior, which ultimately may cause these employees to leave the job. Examples of aggressive behavior are vandalism, theft, fighting, and temper outbursts. When the situation becomes intolerable, these employees quit or almost force their supervisors to fire them.

These types of reactions to job situations are undesirable and should be prevented. Employee turnover, absenteeism, tardiness, poor performance, and other unsatisfactory conduct on the job can cost an organization a great deal. The supervisor is responsible for dealing with these behaviors. Rather than just accepting an employee's behavior, a supervisor should endeavor to relieve frustration by providing more opportunities for need fulfillment.

4 Explain the ABCs for shaping behavior.

Using The ABCs to Shape Employee Behavior

Organizational behavior researchers have long debated the influence of job satisfaction on performance. We believe that employees who experience high levels of job satisfaction are more likely to engage in positive behaviors that influence organizational efficiency and productivity. Performance management expert Aubrey Daniels developed a practical guide for shaping employee behavior.[18] According to Daniels, "behavior (the B) cannot be separated from the antecedents (the A) that come before it and the consequences (the C) after it."[19] See Figure 4.7 for suggestions on how to use the ABCs.

Common sense dictates that if supervisors expect good performance, they must set the stage so that the expected performance occurs. First, supervisors

---

FIGURE 4.7 Steps in ABC Analysis

- Regularly monitor employee performance to uncover areas of low productivity and to identify the behavior leading to undesirable performance.
- Describe the performance you don't want and who is doing it.
- Record the specific behavior that needs to be changed.
- Determine all possible links between the antecedents, the undesirable behavior, and its consequences.
- Tell the employee what is expected in the way of performance (i.e., set specific goals).
- Set the stage for good performance (i.e., arrange antecedents so that the employee can achieve the desired behavior).
- Eliminate any consequence that is irrelevant to the employee.
- Ensure an appropriate linkage between desired behavior and consequences the employee values.
- Monitor performance.
- Provide support and feedback on performance.
- Reinforce the positive aspects of the employee's performance with consequences the employee values.
- Ensure that consequences are positive, immediate, and certain.
- Evaluate results and continue to reinforce desired behavior with desirable consequences.
- Experiment to find the most effective forms of reinforcement and rate of reinforcement.

Remember:

1. You cannot change people; you can change only their behaviors.
2. You will get the behaviors you consistently expect and reinforce. Therefore, only expect the best from your employees.
3. Employees need to know exactly what behaviors will be reinforced and precisely what they are doing that is right or wrong.

Sources: Based, in part, on the book by Aubrey C. Daniels, Ph.D., *Performance Management* (Atlanta, GA: Performance Management Publications, Inc., 1989, 3rd ed.), with permission.

should clearly identify what they want the employee to do. Then, the employee must know what the job entails and what is expected in the way of performance. Ask someone you know to think back to his or her first day on the job. How did the person know what was expected? Many respondents will say it was a process of "trial and error"—that the supervisor never clearly explained what was expected. This has been particularly true in the current era of downsizings and outsourcings. The supervisor either does not sense the importance of expectations or is too busy to explain them. In Chapter 2, we discussed the supervisor's role as enabler. The enabler ensures that employees have all they need to do their jobs correctly the first time, including the appropriate instruction, training, tools, and materials. Unfortunately, this is often not the way it works. If the supervisor does not set the stage (provide the proper antecedents), employee performance is likely to be unsatisfactory. Consequences can affect behavior in one of two ways. Thorndike's **law of effect** postulates that "behavior with favorable consequences tends to be repeated while behavior with unfavorable consequences tends to disappear."[20] Unfortunately, some supervisors assume that what would be a favorable consequence for them would also be a desirable consequence for others. Consider the following:

> Question 1: When you do your job exceptionally well and your immediate supervisor knows you do your job exceptionally well, what happens?
>
> Answer 1: "Nothing—absolutely nothing. My supervisor takes good performance for granted."
>
> Implication 1: When good performance is ignored or goes unrecognized, what happens? Clearly, the lack of feedback and recognition for good performance can cause employee discontent. Also, the good performance is weakened because it is not reinforced. This process is called **extinction**.
>
> Question 2: When you do your job exceptionally well and your immediate supervisor knows you do your job exceptionally well, what happens?
>
> Answer 2: "He gives me more work to do."
>
> Implication 2: If the employee perceives that the additional work will require a variety of skills or fulfill higher-order needs, then the consequence is desirable. This is called **positive reinforcement**. Linking something the employee values or sees as pleasing to good performance strengthens behavior. As a result, good performance is likely to repeat itself. On the other hand, if the employee perceives the extra work to be boring, monotonous, or mundane, then the consequence of good performance is perceived to be **punishment**. The employee got something unwanted—an unfavorable consequence. The result is that the employee's good performance will decrease. Chapter 6 discusses punishment and discipline in greater detail.
>
> Question 3: When you do your job exceptionally well and your immediate supervisor knows you do your job exceptionally well, what happens?
>
> Answer 3: "We really appreciate the good job you did. I've recommended moving you from the six-person cubicle into your own office."
>
> Implication 3: This response gets back to the perceptual problem previously identified. Sincere and genuine praise for a job well done is positive reinforcement. For many employees, the move from a six-person shared cubicle to a private office would be **negative reinforcement**. By removing a consequence that is unpleasant or undesirable, the employee's good performance is reinforced. The employee will continue to do a good job.

Law of effect
Behavior with favorable consequences is repeated; behavior with unfavorable consequences tends to disappear

Extinction
Good behavior occurs less frequently or disappears because it is not recognized

Positive reinforcement
Making behavior occur more frequently because it is linked to a positive consequence

Punishment
Making behavior occur less frequently because it is linked to an undesirable consequence

Negative reinforcement
Making behavior occur more frequently by removing an undesirable consequence

Suppose the employee really enjoyed the close interaction with the other five employees of the cubicle. In this case, the relocation would be viewed as something the employee did not want (i.e., punishment).

Question 4: What happens when a coworker, Charlie, fails to show up on time for work regularly?

Answer 4: "Nothing happens."

Implication 4: The chronically tardy employee continues to be tardy regularly. Ignoring bad performance tends to strengthen the behavior. Unintentionally, management sends a message to the employee that "it's okay to show up late for work." When management ignores "poor performance" in one employee, that employee usually has a cancerous impact throughout the entire work group. Others might assume, and rightfully so, that management has sanctioned showing up for work late (a desirable behavior).

Question 5: What happens when a coworker, Charlie, fails to show up on time for work regularly?

Answer 5: "The employee was given an unpleasant task or made to stay late and complete necessary work."

Implication 5: The tardy employee perceives staying late as an undesirable consequence. Because of the punishment, the employee may make special efforts to get to work on time. Other employees also will see the linkage between performance and punishment. Remember: The process of removing undesirable consequences when an employee's behavior improves is called negative reinforcement.

Supervisors must continually be alert for what their employees perceive to be important, and, like so many things in life, timing is critical. Aubrey Daniels contends "that an intelligently timed consequence has much more influence than a random one."[21] Immediate feedback on performance and positive reinforcement are essential if the supervisor wants to shape employee behavior positively. Figure 4.8 presents an interesting picture of how workers' perceptions of consequences influence their behavior.

Comparing Theory X and Theory Y

5 Compare the assumptions and applications of Theory X and Theory Y in supervision.

A continuous (and unresolved) question that confronts supervisors is what general approach, or style, best contributes to positive employee motivation. This age-old dilemma typically focuses on the degree to which supervisory approaches should be based on satisfying employees' lower-level and higher-level needs. This often becomes an issue of the degree to which supervisors should rely on their authority and position instead of trying to use human-relations practices to provide more opportunities for employee motivation. In the following paragraphs and in Chapter 11, we will analyze approaches associated with various supervisory management styles. First, we shall look at the contributions of Douglas McGregor.

MCGREGOR'S THEORY X AND THEORY Y

In his book *The Human Side of Enterprise*, Douglas McGregor noted that individual supervisory approaches usually relate to each supervisor's perceptions about what people are all about. That is, each supervisor manages employees according to his or her own attitudes and ideas about people's needs and motivations. For comparison, McGregor stated that extremes in attitudes among managers could be classified as Theory X and Theory Y. Following are the basic assumptions of McGregor's Theory X and Theory Y.[22]

FIGURE 4.8 Antecedents and consequences influence behavior

Reprinted with special permission of King Features Syndicate.

Theory X: *The assumption that most employees dislike work, avoid responsibility, and must be coerced to work hard.*

Theory Y: *The assumption that most employees enjoy work, seek responsibility, and can self-direct.*

Supervisors who are Theory X–oriented have a limited view of employees' abilities and motivations. These supervisors feel that employees must be strictly controlled; closely supervised; and motivated based on money, discipline, and authority. Theory X supervisors believe that the key to motivation is in the proper implementation of approaches designed to satisfy employees' lower-level needs. Theory Y supervisors have a much higher opinion of employees' abilities. These supervisors feel that if the proper approaches and conditions can be implemented, employees will exercise self-direction and self-control toward the accomplishment of worthwhile objectives. According to this view, management's objectives should fit into the scheme of each employee's set of needs. Therefore, Theory Y managers believe that the higher-level needs of employees are more important in terms of each employee's personality and self-development.

The two approaches McGregor describes represent extremes in supervisory styles (see Figure 4.9). Realistically, most supervisors are somewhere between Theory X and Theory Y. Neither approach is right or wrong because the appropriateness of a given approach depends on the needs of the individuals involved and the demands of the situation. In practice, supervisors may sometimes take an approach that is contrary to their preferred approach. For example, even the strongest Theory Y

Theory X
Assumption that most employees dislike work, avoid responsibility, and must be coerced to do their jobs

Theory Y
Assumption that most employees enjoy work, seek responsibility, and can self-direct. The belief that well-designed jobs lead to increased motivation

FIGURE 4.9 The two extremes of managerial approach are typified by Theory X and Theory Y

supervisor may revert to Theory X in a time of crisis, such as when the department is shorthanded, when there is an equipment failure, when a serious disciplinary problem has occurred, or when a few employees need firm direction.

ADVANTAGES AND LIMITATIONS OF THEORY X

Supervisors who adopt Theory X typically find that, in the short term, a job is done faster. Because the questioning of orders is not encouraged, it may appear that workers are competent and knowledgeable and that work groups are well organized, efficient, and disciplined.

A major disadvantage of Theory X is that there is little opportunity for employees' personal growth. Because supervision is close and constant, employees are unlikely to develop initiative and independence. Moreover, most workers resent Theory X supervision, and thus may be unmotivated to do the required work. In the long term, they may exit the job—physically or emotionally. Traditionally, supervisors who advocated the Theory X approach could get employees to do what they wanted by using the "carrot-and-stick" approach ("Do what I want you to do and you will be rewarded").[23] Punishments were applied when the job was not done. This approach is still used by many. However, employees may rebel when confronted with the stick, and supervisors may not have sufficient rewards to motivate employees to subject themselves to this tight control.

ADVANTAGES AND LIMITATIONS OF THEORY Y

An overriding advantage of Theory Y supervision is that it promotes individual growth. Because workers are given opportunities to assume some responsibility on their own and are encouraged to contribute their ideas in accomplishing their tasks, it is possible for these employees to partially satisfy their higher-level needs on the job.

While the Theory Y approach is often viewed as more desirable than Theory X, it is not without disadvantages. Theory Y can be time-consuming, especially in the short term. Because personal development is emphasized, supervisors must become instructors and coaches if they are to help their employees move toward the simultaneous attainment of organizational and personal goals. Some supervisors find the extreme application of Theory Y to be more idealistic than practical because some employees expect firm direction from their supervisors.

Job redesign
The belief that well-designed jobs lead to increased motivation

---

Supervisory Approaches for Attaining Positive Employee Motivation

6 Discuss supervisory approaches for stimulating employee motivation, especially job design, broadened job tasks (multi-tasking), and participative management.

Having reviewed several prominent theories of employee motivation, the next question is, How can these theories be applied in the most meaningful ways? There is no simple set of guidelines a supervisor can implement to achieve high motivation and excellent performance. Human beings are much too complex for that. However, some generic tips apply (see this chapter's "Supervisory Tips" box). Supervisory skills can be learned and developed, but they often need to be modified to fit individuals and situations.

JOB REDESIGN

It is generally believed that well-designed jobs lead to increased motivation, higher-quality performance, higher satisfaction, and lower absenteeism and turnover. These desirable outcomes occur when employees experience three critical psychological states:

1. They believe they are doing something meaningful because their work is important to other people.
2. They feel responsible for how the work turns out.
3. They learn how well they performed their jobs.

Many **job redesign** programs are based on the model developed by Professors Hackman and Oldham (see Figure 4.10). Their model says that the greater the experienced meaningfulness of work, responsibility for the work performed, and knowledge of the results, the more positive the work-related benefits. According to this model, any job can be described in terms of the following five core job dimensions:

1. Skill variety: The degree to which an employee has an opportunity to do various tasks and to use a number of different skills and abilities.
2. Task identity: The completion of a whole, identifiable piece of work.
3. Task significance: The degree to which the job impacts the lives or work of others.
4. Autonomy: The amount of independence, freedom, and discretion an employee has in making decisions about the work to be done.
5. Feedback: The amount of information an employee receives on job performance.[24]

The instrument in Skills Application 4-1 can be used to evaluate your own job and to determine the

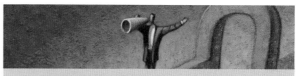

SUPERVISORY TIPS
Motivating Employees

- People need to know what is expected in the way of performance. Therefore, be sure to tell employees what they must do (the expectations you have for them) in order to receive reinforcement.
- People want to know how they are doing. Therefore, provide immediate feedback on performance.
- People want recognition for a job well done. Therefore, when employees do their jobs well, reinforce their behavior with the consequences they desire and value.
- Don't reward all people the same—different strokes for different folks.
- Make the consequences equal to the behavior.
- Remember that failure to respond has reinforcing consequences.
- People need to know that it is okay to make mistakes. Therefore, create a learning organization that says to all employees, "We'll learn what not to do from the mistakes we make." The supervisor can say, "Everything I've learned, I learned from either the mistakes I've made or the mistakes of others."
- Don't punish people in front of others.
- Employees will do their best work for people they trust and respect. Therefore, treat your employees as you want to be treated.

Remember: Be an **enabler**. Therefore, do the things that enable others to be the best they can be.

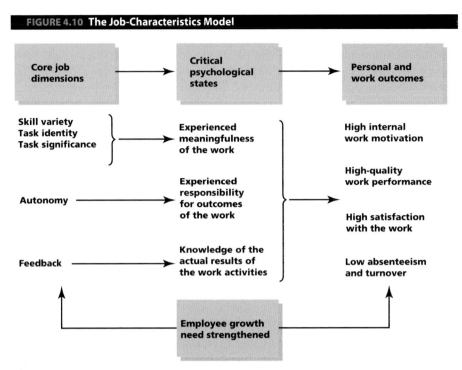

FIGURE 4.10 The Job-Characteristics Model

Source: J. Richard Hackman and Greg R. Oldham, *Work Redesign* (adapted from Figure 4–6), © 1980 by Addison-Wesley Publishing Company, Inc. Reprinted by permission of Addison-Wesley Longman, Inc.

extent to which each of these characteristics is present. With this instrument, it is possible to calculate a "motivating potential score" (MPS) for the specific job. Low scores indicate that the individual will experience low internal motivation from the job. Such a job is a prime candidate for job redesign. Suppose that close examination reveals that the task significance score is relatively low. The supervisor could, for example, assign workers in a word-processing pool to specific departments as opposed to letting the word-processing pool serve the company as a whole. This approach could increase both skill variety and task significance scores, thereby increasing the job's motivating potential.[25]

On the other hand, high scores indicate that the job is stimulating high internal motivation. According to Hackman and Oldham's theory, internal motivation occurs because the employee is "turned on to [his or her] work because of the positive internal feelings generated by doing well, rather than being dependent on external factors (such as incentive pay, job security, or praise from the supervisor) for the motivation to work effectively."[26]

BROADENING THE SCOPE AND IMPORTANCE OF EACH JOB

There are ways to give employees new tasks and new work experiences by which the basic nature of the job can be broadened in scope and importance. Variety and challenge can keep jobs from becoming monotonous and can fulfill employee needs. The following job-redesign strategies are similar in the sense that each attempts to increase employee performance by improving job satisfaction.

JOB ROTATION

Switching job tasks among employees in the work group on a scheduled basis is known as **job rotation**. Most supervisors can implement this process, which often is accompanied by higher levels of job performance and increased employee interest. Job rotation not only helps to relieve employees' boredom but also enhances employees' job knowledge. Although the different tasks may require the same skill level, learning different jobs prepares employees for promotion. A major side benefit to the supervisor is that job rotation results in a more flexible workforce, which can be advantageous during periods of employee absence. Moreover, job rotation should mean that employees share both pleasant and unpleasant tasks so work assignments are perceived as fair.

Job rotation
The process of switching job tasks among employees in a work group

MULTITASKING

When a person is able to perform more than one task at the same time, we say that he or she is **multitasking**.[27] Most students are familiar with this concept since they have learned to drive the car while talking on the cell phone, doing their laundry while reading this textbook or washing dishes while listening to their favorite CD.

In the organizational setting, another motivational strategy is when supervisors expand an employee's job with a greater variety of tasks. This notion of multitasking can be a powerful motivational tool if the employee can see that the tasks give them a chance to use previously acquired SKAs or develop new one. For example, tasks that were handled by several employees may be combined or consolidated into one or two enlarged jobs. Some employees respond positively to multitasking, and this positive attitude is reflected in their performance and in increased job satisfaction. In one furniture factory, for example, a number of routine jobs were changed so that each job required five or six operations rather than just one repetitive operation. Employees supported the change. Such comments as "My job seems more important now" and "My work is less monotonous now" were common.

There can be problems in implementing multitasking. Organizational policies and union work rules lines may limit the supervisor's authority to change job assignments. Attitudes toward taking on additional tasks without an increase in compensation also may present significant difficulties. Some employees, for example, object to expanded duties because they are content with their jobs and pay. Usually, these employees will not object if at least a small increase in pay comes with the enlarged job. Unfortunately, many employees (e.g., the survivors of organizational downsizing) have been asked to do more and more. Some have found themselves stretched too thin, and, as a result, frustration and discontent have crept into the workplace.

Multitasking
When an employee performs several tasks simultaneously

JOB ENRICHMENT

A variant of multitasking is **job enrichment**, which means assigning more challenging tasks and giving employees more decision-making responsibility for their jobs. Job enrichment goes beyond job rotation and job enlargement in an effort to appeal to the higher-level needs of employees. To enrich jobs, the supervisor should assign everyone in a department a fair share of challenging and routine jobs and give employees more autonomy in accomplishing their tasks. Unfortunately, many supervisors prefer to assign the difficult or more challenging jobs only to their best employees and the dull jobs to the weaker employees. However, this practice can be defeating in the long term. The supervisor should give all employees opportunities to find challenging and interesting work experiences

Job enrichment
Job design that helps fulfill employees' higher-level needs by giving those employees more challenging tasks and more decision-making responsibility for their jobs

within the framework of the department's operations. Sometimes, job enrichment can be accomplished by committee assignments, special problem-solving tasks, and other unusual job experiences that go beyond the routine of day-to-day work. For example, one supervisor enriched the jobs of machine operators by giving them a greater role in scheduling work and devising their own work rules for the group. The result was a schedule that better met employee needs and rules the employees were willing to follow because they helped create them. In its most developed form, job enrichment may involve restructuring jobs in such a way that employees are given direct control and responsibility for what they do.

Supervisors may be uncomfortable with job enrichment at first. It may require them to relinquish some control and to delegate some planning and decision making. However, job enrichment is not a cure-all for other organization problems that create dissatisfaction. In mid-2008, almost 19,000 GM employees opted for early retirement or a "buy out." They will be replaced, in part, by employees who will earn substantially less. Imagine two employees working side by side, doing similar work with one earning $70 per hour (total compensation) and the replacement worker earning $25 per hour in total compensation. What obstacles will the supervisor have to overcome in attempting to "enrich" their jobs? Overall, if job enrichment is practiced sincerely, however, subordinates usually assume an active role in making or participating in decisions about their jobs. The result can be better decisions and a more satisfied and motivated workforce.

In a sense, job enrichment involves the employees' assumption of some of the supervisor's everyday responsibilities. The supervisor remains accountable, however, for the satisfactory fulfillment of these obligations. Therein lies a major risk inherent in job enrichment. Despite the risk, many supervisors endorse job enrichment because it works.

PARTICIPATIVE MANAGEMENT

In his bestselling book *A Great Place to Work*, Robert Levering postulates that the high morale of great workplaces consists of pride in what you do (the job itself), enjoying the people you're working with (the work group), and trusting the people you work for (management practices and economic rewards).[28] Levering and others have been tracking the "best places to work." Historically,

Job enrichment can help reduce boredom and increase interest and knowledge for employees by giving employees more decision-making responsibility

© RF DIGITAL VISION/GETTY IMAGES

Dallas-headquartered Southwest Airlines has ranked among everyone's Top 10. Why Southwest? It is the largest airline in the world by number of passengers carried. In January 2008, the low-fare, highly unionized airline posted a profit for the 35th consecutive year. It leads the industry in customer satisfaction. How is that done—by magic? According to comments from enthusiastic employees: "Working here is truly an unbelievable experience. They treat you with respect, pay you well, and empower you. They use your ideas to solve problems. They encourage you to be yourself. I love going to work!"[29] Do the comments from Southwest Airlines employees translate to better company performance? Let me reaffirm my belief that "happy cows give more milk."

As mentioned in Chapter 1 of this text, empowerment refers to giving employees the authority and responsibility to accomplish organizational objectives. Providing opportunities to make suggestions and participate in decisions affecting their jobs is one of the most effective ways to build a sense of employee pride, teamwork, and motivation. To paraphrase author John MacDonald: In China, for example, management's use of the words "employee empowerment" can inspire fear. The workers' expectations are that they are going to have to take the responsibility—and the punishment—for everything that goes wrong. Empowerment simply means granting workers permission to give the customer priority over other issues in the operation. In practical terms, it relates resources, skill, time, and support to become leaders rather than mindless robots. The concept lies at the heart of managing with "common sense."[30]

This supervisory approach, in which employees have an active role in decision making, has historically been called participative management. Delegation, discussed in greater detail in Chapter 11, is important to motivating employees. Delegation does not mean turning all decisions over to employees, nor does it mean just making employees believe they are participating in decisions. Rather, it means the supervisor should earnestly seek employees' opinions whenever possible and be willing to be influenced by employee suggestions and criticisms. When employees feel that they are part of a team and that they can influence the decisions that affect them, they are more likely to accept the decisions and seek new solutions to problems.

The major advantages of participative management are that decisions tend to be of higher quality and that employees are more willing to accept those decisions. One disadvantage is that this approach can be time-consuming. Also, participation makes it easier for employees to criticize, which some supervisors find threatening. On balance, however, participative management is widely recognized as an effective motivational strategy. Its advantages far outweigh its disadvantages.

Supervisors who practice participative management properly are aware of the importance of their information-giving and information-getting skills. They also know that it is vital to respond fully to subordinates' suggestions as soon as those supervisors have had sufficient time to consider them.

EMPLOYEE SUGGESTION PROGRAMS

Many organizations actively solicit employee input via formal suggestion programs.[31] Other organizations have an open work environment where employees can share their ideas and suggestions without fear of retribution. While some suggestion systems provide monetary rewards for suggestions that are received and accepted, the monetary rewards are only part of the employee's overall compensation. Employees like to have their suggestions heard and answered. To some employees, the fact that a suggestion has been implemented may mean more than the monetary reward.

© CORBIS PREMIUM RF/ALAMY

EMPLOYEE INVOLVEMENT PROGRAMS

During the past two decades, most organizations have adopted various forms of participatory management programs. These types of programs often are known by other labels, such as employee-involvement programs, problem-solving teams, quality circles, or semiautonomous or self-directed work teams. Regardless of what they are called, these programs are based on the beliefs that employees want to contribute to the long-term success of the organization and that managers have a strong commitment to participatory management as a way of organizational life.

SUMMARY

1 Every human being is unique. Behavior is influenced by many factors in both the individual and the environment. Personality is the complex mix of knowledge, attitudes, and attributes that distinguishes one person from another.

Prominent factors that interact to form the personality of each individual include physiological makeup, early childhood experiences, the immediate and continuing environment through life, and cultural values. The working environment is one of the almost unlimited number of influences that become part of an employee's personality. A person's attitude impacts everyone that person contacts, and often negatively or positively impacts the organization's performance.

Supervisors need to be sensitive to individual differences and similarities. A consistent supervisory approach based on similarities is a practical way to lead employees.

2 Motivation is a willingness to exert effort toward achieving a goal, stimulated by the effort's ability to fulfill an individual need. According to Maslow, needs in ascending order of importance are biological, security, social, self-respect, and self-fulfillment. When a lower-level need is fulfilled, higher-level needs emerge that influence one's motivation.

It is important for supervisors to recognize the different need levels. Supervisors can influence employee motivation positively if they rely on supervisory approaches that promote higher-level need fulfillment. When employee needs are not satisfied on the job, job performance usually suffers. Some employees express their dissatisfaction through absenteeism. Others may display aggressive and disruptive behavior; still others may quit. The result is that the organization suffers from a decrease in production and a loss of quality.

Herzberg's motivation-hygiene research studies indicate that hygiene factors such as money, management policies, working conditions, and certain aspects of supervision must be adequate to maintain a reasonable level of motivation. Forces that stimulate good performance, called motivation factors, are intrinsic to the job. These motivation factors include the employees' needs for achievement, opportunity for advancement, challenging work, promotion, growth, and recognition. Effective supervisors implement strategies that target motivation factors to promote good job performance.

Expectancy theory suggests that employees will be motivated if they perceive links between their efforts and performance and between their performance and rewards. Supervisors must clarify such relationships for the workers or strive to develop them.

Equity theory of motivation explains how people strive for fairness based on an outcome/input ratio. Employees can compare themselves with many other people, even ones who do not work in their organizations, to determine if perceived equity or inequity exists. Supervisors need to watch for perceived inequity, know the possible effects, and address employee concerns.

3 Working conditions that do not fulfill employee needs ultimately cause dissatisfaction and frustration. Other factors may cause some people to do things that make other people's lives difficult. Incivility and other inappropriate behavior must be dealt with in a proper and timely manner.

4 The ABC model of behavior modification is built on the notion that antecedents (those things that precede behavior) and consequences (the results of behavior) can be used by the supervisor to condition desirable behavior or to extinguish undesirable behavior. The use of extinction, positive reinforcement, punishment, and negative reinforcement can make specific behavior occur more or less often. Feedback and positive reinforcement should be used regularly to shape employee behavior in the desired direction.

5 The Theory X supervisor believes primarily in authoritarian techniques, which relate to the lower-level human needs. The Theory Y supervisor prefers to build motivation by appealing to employees' higher-level needs.

6 The job characteristics model has been used to guide job redesign efforts. The major approaches to job design include job rotation, multitasking, and job enrichment.

The advantages of participative management are that decisions tend to be of higher quality and employees are more willing to accept decisions. Employee-participation programs are widely used and varied in application. Delegation strategies, suggestion programs, quality circles, and self-directed work teams are approaches that emphasize employee involvement. Getting people at all levels of the organization involved in objective setting and problem solving, rearranging duties and responsibilities, and creating ways to reward people for their accomplishments is the essence of the approaches to motivating employees to perform. The supervisor must learn to implement different supervisory approaches that are appropriate for different people and settings.

KEY TERMS

Employee entitlement (p. 125)
Equity theory (p. 129)
Expectancy theory (p. 128)
Extinction (p. 135)
Hierarchy of needs (p. 121)
Hygiene factors (p. 126)
Job enrichment (p. 141)
Job redesign (p. 139)
Job rotation (p. 141)

Law of effect (p. 135)
Motivation (p. 121)
Motivation factors (p. 126)
Motivation-hygiene theory (p. 126)
Multitasking (p. 141)
Negative reinforcement (p. 135)
Personality (p. 119)
Physiological needs (p. 122)
Positive mental attitude (PMA) (p. 120)

Positive reinforcement (p. 135)
Punishment (p. 135)
Security needs (p. 122)
Self-fulfillment needs (p. 123)
Self-respect needs (p. 123)
Social needs (p. 123)
Theory X (p. 137)
Theory Y (p. 137)

QUESTIONS FOR DISCUSSION

1. (a) Think of a time that you accomplished something that made you very proud. What caused you to behave that way?
    (b) Think of a time that you did something that made you ashamed. What caused you to behave that way?
    (c) How do you explain why people behave the way they do?

2. Compare and contrast each of the motivational theories discussed in this chapter. From the aspect of practical application, what are the benefits of each of the motivational theories discussed in this chapter?

3. What are the basic elements of Theory X and Theory Y? Can you think of any reasons Theory Y would be inappropriate for all supervisors?

4. With respect to the management problem of motivating subordinates to accomplish organizational goals, what conclusions can you draw from reading the material in this chapter?

SKILLS APPLICATIONS

Skills Application 4-1: What Motivates Employees?

1. Rank the following twenty items in order of their importance to you. In the left-hand column, place the number 1 next to the most important item, the number 2 next to the second most important item, and so on through to the least important item (number 20).

2. Option: If this skills application is used as an in-class exercise, to save time, we suggest that you use the following scale rather than the rank order: Select the four items that are most important to you and place the number one (1) in the blanks to the left of those items. Select the four items that

are least important to you and place the number four (4) in the blanks. From the remaining items, select the four that are most important to you and place the number two (2) in the blanks. Then place a three (3) in the blanks remaining.

3. When everyone has completed the task, your instructor will aggregate the rankings of all individuals.

4. Compare your individual rankings with those of other class members. How do you explain the differences?
___ Freedom to do my job
___ Supervisors who care about me as a person
___ One-on-one team meetings so I can keep up to date
___ Opportunity to learn and use new skills
___ A work environment where others listen and act on my ideas and suggestions
___ Job security
___ A manager who lets me know what is expected—one who springs no surprises
___ Interesting and challenging work
___ Material, equipment, and resources to do the job right the first time
___ Daily feedback on performance
___ Good compensation and benefits
___ Working for a company that is ethical, honest, and fair-dealing

___ Praise and recognition for accomplishments
___ Working for a company that is profitable
___ Coworkers dedicated to achieving company goals
___ Opportunity to make work-related decisions
___ Opportunity to use a variety of skills
___ Knowing what the future holds for me and the company
___ Support and encouragement when I make a mistake
___ A boss who allows me freedom to play to my strengths

5. Optional Internet Activity: Use the Internet to search for at least three research articles or reports that present findings on "what employees want from their jobs" or the "current state of employee morale." Write a one-page report summarizing your findings. Then write another one-page report answering the following questions:
a. Why do the perceptions of employees vary?
b. How different are the perceptions of members of your class?
c. Briefly identify the factors that account for the differences.

This instrument was developed by Edwin C. Leonard, Jr. and Roy A. Cook, *Human Resource Management: 21st Century Challenges*, 1st ed. (Mason, OH: Thomson Custom Publishing © 2005), p. 237. Reproduced here with permission.

Skills Application 4-2: Does One Size Fit All?

Motivating employees is central to the challenge facing Don Davis in this chapter's "You Make the Call!" There are probably times when he feels like screaming "shape up or ship out." The members of his supervisory team see the problem in different ways. But the bottom line is that if quality does not improve substantially, Economy Moving and Storage may lose customers, and many employees may lose their jobs.

1. Is Maslow's needs hierarchy relevant for the reloading operations' employees? Explain the rationale for your answer.

2. Do the younger, relatively inexperienced team members expect the same things from the job as do the more

experienced and more senior team members? Why or why not?

3. If you were Don Davis, how would you use Herzberg's dual-factor theory of motivation to increase morale in this department?

4. What steps must Don Davis and his direct reports take to develop trust between the workers?

5. Outline a strategy that Don Davis can use to do a better job of making the reloading operation more productive.

Skills Application 4-3: What Do You Want to Be When You Grow Up?

1. What are your objectives for this course?

2. What do you want to get out of this course?

3. Review the "Supervisory Tips" box for this chapter. Which of the tips do you want to learn more about? List no more than three.

4. What can the instructor or a particular classmate do to help you learn more about those tips?

5. What would be the best way for you to demonstrate that you have mastered those tips?

6. Now write a Personal Commitment Statement (the "Goal") regarding your journey to master those tips: "I, _____ (insert your name), will during the next month . . ."

7. What will be your personal reward for achieving the goal?

Skills Application 4-4: Dealing with People Who Make Your Life Difficult—"The Whiner"

This is the second in a series of Skills Applications that introduces you to people who might make your life difficult.

1. Read the following statement from Ed Wright, a shipping department employee at Sanders Supermarket's Ashton Distribution Center:

Nancy seemed really pleasant and nice when she interviewed for the job. She knew what was expected and that the job was physical and demanding at times. Most of the time, she gets her work done, but it's the baggage that comes with her that annoys me. Nancy brings her personal life to work. I see that in her daily conversations with me. Every day, I hear about her out-of-work husband, her lazy kids, and how she has to be a superwoman at home and at work. On top of that, every time the supervisor asks her to do something, she comes to me to tell me what a hard, nasty, hot job has been assigned to her. Every day is another poor, miserable, "everything-bad-always-happens-to-me" story. Nothing good ever happens to her. She never has a good day at work. Every day is the worst day of her life—much worse than yesterday.

Nancy's whining is like cancer in the department. No one in the group wants to work with her on any quality or methods-improvement projects. When she's in a really bad mood, everyone avoids her. If she's miserable, everyone's supposed to be miserable. I've learned to deal with her by developing a positive mental attitude and smiling. I suspect this probably aggravates her more, but she just leaves my work area and looks for another shoulder to whine on.

Nancy exhibits a negative attitude with a tendency to feel sorry for herself. Because she cannot set aside her personal agenda during the day, she impedes everyone's performance. I don't think people are born unhappy, and I'm running out of sympathy for her. What should I do?

2.  Using the Internet, find at least three sources of information on how to deal with people who complain all the time. Carefully review each site for suggestions on how to deal with these people.

3. Based on your findings, what suggestions would you make to Ed on how to cope with Nancy?

4. Have you ever acted like a "whiner" yourself? If so, what were the antecedents that caused you to behave that way? What were the consequences of your behavior? What made you change your behavior?

5. Write a one-page paper explaining how this skills application increased your knowledge of how to cope with the behaviors of this type of difficult person.

Skills Application 4-5: Reward and Punishment

 Often, supervisors are given assignments without much warning. This skills application gives you an opportunity to make an impression and practice your communication skills.

1. The instructor will randomly select two students and ask them to leave the room.
    a. The first student will be instructed to take a few minutes to plan and when called upon to come back and give a three-to-five-minute impromptu speech on "If I only had one year to live, I would . . ."
    b. The other student's topic will be "If I had just won the $50 million Mega Lottery jackpot, I would . . ."

    c. The other students are to be observers and will get their specific assignments while the two students are out of the room momentarily gathering their thoughts.

2. The students should be called back to the room one at a time to give their prepared talk.

3. At the conclusion of the presentations, the observers will be asked to critique the presentations.

4. Your instructor may wish to ask you to write a short paper addressing additional questions.

Skills Development Module 4-1: U.S. Music Corp.—Washburn Guitars

For the past hundred years, people have delighted in the rich, bold sounds that jumped from the strings of Washburn guitars. Washburn Electric Guitars have been featured in all of the *Wayne's World* sketches and movies. Before you view this chapter's video clip, you might want to go to http://www.washburn.com to learn a little more about the company, its product line or see product videos or podcasts. U.S., Music Corp. is the parent company of Washburn guitars, Parker guitars, Randall amplifiers and other music-oriented products (http://www.usmusiccorp.com).

After you have viewed the Skills Development Module video for this chapter, answer the following questions below.

This should help you to integrate many of the concepts introduced in this chapter.

1. Most of the employees that work at U.S. Music (Washburn) play an instrument. Discuss how playing a musical instrument might be the motivating factor for 'making the highest quality instrument.'

2. In your opinion, why is it important that an employee understands how a product functions and how the end-user will use it? Does this knowledge make it easier for supervisors to motivate employees? Why?

3. Consider the following statement from the video clip: "Employees were enthused to step it up a notch and take responsibility and pride in the new level of quality." Do you believe it? Why? Why not?

4. The author contends that "U.S. Music Corp. must provide an abundant quality of work life for their employees in order for them to produce the highest quality guitars." If you worked at Washburn, what would an "abundant quality of work life" mean to you? Would other students have a different response? Why or why not?

ENDNOTES

1. What is trust? What are the effects of trustworthy behavior? How do you react when a supervisor or manager unconditionally exhibited trust in their relationship with you? In part, does that cause you, in turn, to trust them? If so, this reflects what I call the "Rule of reciprocity." *Inside Training Online* (June 11, 2008) reported that a survey by BlessingWhite found that 75 percent of employees "trust" their immediate supervisor, but "trust" wanes the higher up the chain one goes (Only 53 percent of employees trust their senior management.) Also see Eric Krell, "Do They Trust You?" *HR Magazine*, 51, 6 (June 2006), cover story; J. Scott Colquitt and J. LePine, "Trust, Trustworthiness, and Trust Propensity: A Meta-analytic Test of Their Unique Relationships with Risk Taking and Job Performance," *Journal of Applied Psychology*, 92, 4 (2007), pp. 909–927; R.C. Mayer and M.B. Gavin, "Trust in Management and Performance: Who Minds the Shop While Employees Watch the Boss," *Academy of Management Journal*, 48, 5 (2005), pp. 874–888; and S. Albrecht and A. Travaglione, "Trust in Public-Sector Management," *International Journal of Human Resource Management*, 14, 1 (2003), pp. 76–92.

2. Many companies rely, in part, on personality assessment programs to evaluate employees. One of the more widely recognized approaches to the identification of individual differences is the Myers-Briggs Type Indicators. If your college has the Myers-Briggs test, use it to identify your basic personality type. You can also use it to identify personality types that do not complement yours. For additional information on personality development, see J. M. George, "The Role of Personality in Organizational Life: Issues and Evidence," *Journal of Management* (Volume 18, 1992), pp. 185–213; and R. C. Carson, "Personality," *Annual Review of Psychology* (Volume 40, 1989), pp. 227–248.

3. As quoted in Rebecca Meany, "What a Pain?" *Successful Meetings* (February 2001), p. 72. See Sandra A. Crowe, *Since Strangling Isn't An Option . . . Dealing with Difficult People: Common Problems and Uncommon Solutions* (New York: Perigee, 1999). Also see the classic by Margaret Henning and Anne Jardim, *The Managerial Woman* (New York: Anchor Press/Doubleday, 1977), p. 82. The social grouping of children at an early age can have lifelong psychological consequences. Congresswoman Carolyn Maloney's book makes interesting reading. See *Rumors of Our Progress Have Been Greatly Exaggerated: Why Women's Lives Aren't Getting Any Easier—And How We Can Make Real Progress for Ourselves and Our Daughters* (New York: Rodale, Inc., distributed by MacMillan, 2008). Additional research supports the contention that early influence is important in leadership development. Also see, Nan Mooney, *(Not) Keeping Up With Our Parents* (New York: Beacon Press, 2008).

4. See Paul Falcone, "When Employees Have a 'tude," *HR Magazine* (June 2001), pp. 189–94. See Kathy Gurchiek, "Bad Bosses—More than Bad Salaries—Drive Worker's Away," *SHRM Home* (January 11, 2007) for illustrations of how the supervisor's bad 'tude impacts the organization.

5. See Abraham H. Maslow, *Motivation and Personality* (2nd ed.; New York: Harper & Row, 1970), Chapter 4. Also see Ron Zemke, "Maslow for a New Millennium," *Training* (December 1998), pp. 54–58. Also see, T.J. Stanley, "A Motivated Workforce is a Marvelous Sight," *Supervision*, 69, 3 (March 2008), pp. 5–7 and Bryan Schaffer, "Leadership and Motivation," *Supervision*, 69, 2 (February 2008), pp. 6–9.

6. Feeling safe at work was ranked as a very important factor in job satisfaction by 62 percent of employees in a 2004 survey. It was the most important factor for women. See Jennifer Schramm, "Feeling Safe," *HR Magazine* (May 2004), p. 152.

7. The quotes attributed to Thomas Alva Edison and Ralph Waldo Emerson were cited in Steve Vogel, "She Just Keeps Rolling Along," *The Washington Post* (June 4, 1998), p. D-1. Also see the *Oxford Dictionary of Quotations* (Oxford: Oxford University Press, 1980), pp. 199, 206–8 for other quotes attributed to these two distinguished persons.

8. This quote is a variation of Lee Iacocca's "No one says on their deathbed, 'I wish I had spent more time with my business.'" See Daisy Sanders, "Appreciate Your Employees Today & Everyday," *Supervision*, 68, 8 (August 2007), pp. 6–7.

9. "Older Staffer Get Uneasy Balance," the *Wall Street Journal* (May 15, 2008), p. A2. Also see Jack and Suzy Welch, "What's Age Got to Do With It?" *BusinessWeek* (June 2, 2008, p. 128).

10. Stephen Miller, "Job Satisfaction: Workers, HR Pros Have Varying Views," *SHRM Online* (June 25, 2007). HR professionals predicted that the relationship with immediate supervisor, compensation, management recognition of employee job performance, benefits, and communication between employees and senior management would be what the employee wanted. Also see Pamela Babcock, "Find What Workers Want," *HR Magazine* (April 2005), pp. 50–56. Also see Kenneth Kovach, "What Motivates Employees? Workers and Supervisors Give Different Answers," *Business Horizons* (September/October 1987), pp. 58–65. See Stephen C. Lundin, Harry Paul, and John Christensen, Fish! (New York: Hyperion, 2000) for a description of how people working in a smelly, dirty, rough place (Pike Place Fish Market in Seattle) found ways to make their jobs productive and fun. Also see Spencer Johnson, *Who Moved My Cheese?* (New York: Putnam, 1988). The cheese represents what one wants out of life. Leave a piece of cheese on the counter for a week or so, and you will see it change before your eyes. Even if you don't see it change, you can tell it is changing. How? Smell it. Johnson says that one should savor new cheese, but not too much because inevitably it will move again. He also says it is easy to gag on too much cheese.

11. For a discussion of the factors that contribute to a culture of job entitlement, see Alison Stein Wellner, "Spoiled Brats," *HR Magazine* (November 2004), pp. 61–65. Also see, Brian Fitzgerald, "What's the Best Way to Manage and Motivate Young Workers Who Have an Inflated Sense of Entitlement?" *Inc.* (September 2007, pp. 60–61).

12. The complete dual-factor theory is well explained in Frederick Herzberg, Bernard Mausner, and Barbara Bloch Snyderman, *The Motivation to Work*, 2nd ed, (New York: John Wiley & Sons, 1967), and in Herzberg's classic article, "One More Time: How Do You Motivate Your Employees?" *Harvard Business Review* (Volume 46, January/February 1968), pp. 53–62. Also, see the BEST of HBR 1968, a reprint of Herzberg's 1968 article in *Harvard Business Review*, 81, 1 (January 2003).

13. For a discussion of expectancy theory, see Victor H. Vroom, *Work and Motivation* (New York: John Wiley & Sons, 1964), and Terrence R. Mitchell, "Expectancy Models of Job Satisfaction, Occupational

Preference, and Effort: A Theoretical, Methodological, and Empirical Appraisal," *Psychological Bulletin* (Volume 81, 1974), pp. 1053–77.

14. J. Stacy Adams, "Toward an Understanding of Inequity," *Journal of Abnormal and Social Psychology* (No. 67, 1963), pp. 422–36. Also see Jerald Greenberg and Claire L. McCarty, "Comparable Worth: A Matter of Justice," in Gerald R. Farris and Kendrith M. Rowland, eds., *Research in Personnel and Human Resource Management* (Greenwich: CT: JAI Press, 1990), pp. 265–303; Greenberg, "Cognitive Reevaluation of Outcomes in Response to Underpayment Inequity," Academy *of Management Journal* (March 1989), pp. 174–84; R. T. Mowday, "Equity Theory Predictions of Behavior in Organizations," in R. M. Steers and L. W. Porter, eds., *Motivation and Work Behavior* (New York: McGraw-Hill, 1987), pp. 89–110; and Robert P. Vecchio, "Predicting Worker Performance in Inequitable Setting," *Academy of Management Review* (January 1982), pp. 103–10.

15. Magna Donnelly's longstanding innovative approach to management has resulted in numerous awards and has been listed among the "Ten Best Companies to Work for in America." John F. Donnelly, a former seminarian and former president of the company, believed in sharing profits with employees. This approach evolved into a participatory management-style with work teams being involved in every aspect of the decision-making process. For more information on the Donnelly style of management visit their Web site (http://www.donnelly.com).

16. Robert M. Bramson, *Coping with Difficult People* (New York: Doubleday, 1988). Also see Maurice A. Ramirez, "Outrage or Enthusiasm: The Choice is Yours," *Supervision*, 69, 4 (April 2008), pp. 17–19; Cherie Carter-Scott, *Negaholics No More* (Shawnee Mission, KS: National Press Publications, 1999); Rick Brinkman and Rick Kirschner, *Dealing with People You Can't Stand* (New York: McGraw-Hill, 1994); and Muriel Solomon, *Working with Difficult People* (Englewood Cliffs, NJ: Prentice Hall, 1990).

17. Estimates vary on the amount of time employees are spending surfing the Web, playing fantasy football, or viewing pornographic Web sites. Most surveys set a minimum of two hours a day on non-work-related activities. Whatever it is today, it will increase tomorrow unless organizations establish guidelines and monitoring controls. Students find it interesting to read that "The University of Chicago Law School Dean sent an email to all students and faculty saying Web access would be blocked in classrooms because Web-surfing law students weren't paying attention to lectures and were distracting classmates," ("How Well Do You Know . . . the Digital World?" the *Wall Street Journal* (June 9, 2008), p. R14. Also see Vara Vauhini, "New Sites Make it Easier to Spy on Your Friends," the *Wall Street Journal* (May 13, 2008), pp. D1, D3.

18. The thoughts and ideas for the section on the ABCs were adapted from Aubrey C. Daniels, Ph.D., *Performance Management: Improving Quality and Productivity through Positive Reinforcement* (Atlanta: Performance Management Publications, Inc., 1989, 3rd ed.).

19. Ibid., pp. 14, 75+.

20. E. L. Thorndike, *Educational Psychology: The Psychology of Learning*, Vol. II (New York: Teachers College Columbia University, 1913). B. F. Skinner built on the works of Thorndike and identified S-R and R-S behaviors. The latter is known as operant conditioning and implies that individuals behave, in large part, to receive desired consequences. See Skinner, *The Behavior of Organisms* (New York: Appleton-Century Crofts, 1938).

21. Op. cit., Daniels, p. 45.

22. Douglas McGregor, *The Human Side of Enterprise* (New York: McGraw-Hill, 1960), pp. 45–57.

23. See Nathan W. Harter, "The Shop Floor Schopenhauer: Hope for a Theory-X Supervisor," *Journal of Management Education* (February 1997), pp. 87+. Among other notions, Harter acknowledges that even McGregor conceded that coercion works reasonably well under certain circumstances.

24. J. Richard Hackman, Greg R. Oldham, Robert Janson, and Kenneth Purdy, "A New Strategy for Job Enrichment," *California Management Review* (Summer 1975), pp. 51–71; J. R. Hackman and G. R. Oldham, *Work Redesign* (Reading, MA: Addison-Wesley, 1980); and Carol T. Kulik, Greg R. Oldham, and Paul H. Langner, "Measurement of Job Characteristics: Comparison of the Original and the Revised Job Diagnostic Survey," *Journal of Applied Psychology* (August 1988), pp. 462–66.

25. Hackman, Oldham, Jenson, and Purdy, p. 58.

26. Ibid.

27. Multitasking is the ability of a person to perform more than one task at the same time. The research by Rubinstein, Meyer and Evans that people lose time when they have to switch from one task to another, and time costs increased with the complexity of the tasks. David Meyer said that "For every aspect of human performance—perceiving, thinking, and acting—people have specific mental resources whose effective use requires supervision." See Joshua Rubinstein, David Meyer, and Jeffrey Evans, "Executive Control of Cognitive Processes in Task Switching," *Journal of Experiential Psychology: Human Perception and Performance*, 27, 4 (August 2001), pp. 763–797.

28. Robert Levering, *A Great Place to Work* (New York: Random House, 1988). See Patrick Lencioni, *The Three Signs of a Miserable Job* (New York: Wiley, 2007).

29. See Holman W. Jenkins, Jr., "The Second Death of the U.S. Airlines," the *Wall Street Journal* (June 18, 2008), p. A13. Also see "Airlines Face Grips About Service," the *Wall Street Journal* (May 20, 2008, p. D6); Hal Lancaster, "Herb Kelleher Has One Main Strategy: Treat Employees Well." the *Wall Street Journal* (August 31, 1999), p. B1; Kevin Frieberg and Jackie Frieberg, *Nuts! Southwest Airlines' Crazy Recipe for Business and Personal Success* (Austin, TX: Bard Press, 1996); and Colleen Barrett, "Corner on Customer Service: the Voices of Southwest Airlines," Southwest Airlines Spirit (April 2005), p. A11. Southwest has been a fixture on *Fortune's* list of "The 100 Best Companies to Work for in America." (See the most recent listing, usually in March.) In July 2008, President Colleen Barrett, who had been with the company since day one, stepped aside. SWA's management practices, particularly its use of hedging fuel, has helped the bottom line.

Also see Jeffrey Pfeffer, *The Human Equation: Building Profits by Putting People First* (Boston: Harvard Business School Press, 1998); Marcus Buckingham and Curt Coffman, *First, Break All the Rules: What the World's Greatest Managers Do Differently* (New York: Simon & Schuster, 1999). For a different viewpoint, see Glenn Bassett, "The Case Against Job Satisfaction," *Business Horizons* (May/June 1994), pp. 61–68.

30. Paraphrased and adapted from John MacDonald, *Calling a Halt to Mindless Change* (New York: AMACOM, 1998). MacDonald's example sheds light on what empowerment really is: "To allow the counter person at a burger bar to distribute additional packets of sauce if the customer wants them is not empowerment. If the same person working at the counter were allowed to close the burger bar for an hour because he believed the french fries were below standard, that would be empowerment." Also see Anne Houlihan, "Empower Your Employees to Make Smart Decisions," *Supervision*, 68, 7 (July 2007), pp. 3–6.

31. The oldest documented system of formal employee involvement is Eastman Kodak's employee-suggestion program, established in 1898. The Employee Involvement Association (EIA) annually reports suggestion system information. Visit EIA's Web site (http://www.eianet.org.). A monthly publication, "Ideas and Inspirations," is distributed via e-mail to all members. Numerous suggestions for getting employees involved in improvement activities can be found in Norman Bodek and Bunji Tozawa, *The Idea Generator: Quick and Easy Kaizen* (Vancouver, WA: PCS Press, 2001).

CHAPTER 5

(Solving Problems: Decision Making and the Supervisor)

After studying this chapter, you will be able to:

1 Explain the importance of problem-solving and decision-making skills.

2 Describe the types of decisions made in organizations.

3 Describe and apply the basic steps of the decision-making process.

4 Identify and describe various decision-making styles.

5 Explain why a supervisor should not make hasty decisions.

YOU MAKE THE CALL!

Shannon O'Neill is the transportation supervisor for the Fairfield County School Corporation. Her basic responsibilities include hiring, training, and evaluating all employees in the department; scheduling bus utilization; purchasing all fuels and maintenance supplies; coordinating extracurricular activities; activity transportation; arranging for transportation of special-needs children; and safely transporting 9,200 children to and from school each day. The school district covers approximately 50 square miles, and fewer than 20 percent of the students walk or drive to their respective schools.

Shannon developed a computerized planning system to schedule transportation requirements and preventive maintenance. The Fairfield School Corporation had substantially lower per-pupil transportation costs than other school corporations and was able to use the savings to provide enrichment experiences for the district's children. Shannon is frequently called upon to explain the workings and benefits of her system to other school districts, and last year she was invited to present her system at the American Association of School Administrators' annual meeting.

Shannon is highly regarded as an administrator. Employee turnover is minimal, and the list of people wanting to drive a bus for her is long. The employees meet quarterly to review progress, identify potential problem areas, and make recommendations for improvement. Shannon's department gets together socially twice a year to celebrate accomplishments.

The foundation of Shannon's supervisory style was inherited from her father, whose favorite saying was "Plan your work, and then work your plan." She has a weekly meeting with her key direct reports to recap the results of the previous week, develop expectations for the coming week, and discuss problems and issues affecting the department.

A new superintendent of schools arrived this summer amidst great turmoil and conflict within the community and among the board members. Fairfield, not unlike other school corporations and government agencies, had been running budget deficits for several years. State law prevented the school corporation from raising property tax rates beyond a fixed level, and state appropriations for education had declined. A major spike in costs for cafeteria food, heating oil, and diesel fuel for the yellow buses added to the budget woes. Falling real estate values and rising housing foreclosures are expected to translate into lower property-tax receipts. Upon arrival, the new superintendent with board approval (a 4-to-3 vote) announced the first phase of a cost-cutting program. A number of the enrichment programs were cut, along with tennis, golf, and other after-school programs. The new superintendent said these programs could continue but that participants would have to generate the money necessary for their continuation. School lunch costs were raised a dollar a day for all students. Even with the increase, the district's cafeteria program was projecting a $750,000 loss for the coming year. The district will skip a planned new elementary school and some of the renovations previously planned.

This morning when Shannon filled up her gas tank she paid over $4.50 a gallon. Just a few years ago, the district was paying $1.87 for diesel fuel. Four months ago, Shannon convinced the purchasing director, the then-superintendent, and the board to gamble and lock in half of this year's forecasted fuel needs at a fixed $4.33 a gallon. She had budgeted for increases in fuel costs, but the school corporation will be unable to fully cover the cost without eliminating additional extracurricular activities or running a larger deficit.

At an early afternoon meeting, the superintendent encouraged all supervisors, building principals, and other administrators to question their current supervisory practices and find ways to improve them. Each supervisor was asked to develop a list of three cost-cutting strategies for his or her areas of responsibility and submit them by week's end. Then the superintendent dropped the bombshell. An overall reduction in state funds means that there will be no new textbooks and that certain jobs won't be filled. If fuel and food prices continue to rise there will be more pressure on the district's budget. Each person was to develop a strategy for each of the following scenarios: (1) reduce department costs by 10 percent without eliminating positions, (2) reduce department costs 10 percent by eliminating or combining existing positions, and (3) reduce department costs by 20 percent.

Shannon believes that her supervisory style has served her well and that her system for continuously improving the transportation department is well in place. On the way home, she felt betrayed: "It's not fair! I've consistently run the most efficient operation in the school corporation. Some of the others have gotten fat! Now I've got to figure out ways to comply with the superintendent's request." **YOU MAKE THE CALL!**

<table>
<tr><td>

1 **Explain the importance of problem-solving and decision-making skills.**

</td></tr>
</table>

The Importance of Decision-Making Skills

All human activities involve decision making. Each of us faces problems at home, at work, at school, and in social groups for which decisions must be made. Problems can be large or small, simple or complex, life-threatening or trivial. Some problems can be dealt with almost automatically. Consider the following illustration:

> *Lori, a college student, has been juggling school work with her clerking job at Wal-Mart. As soon as her 7:00 A.M.-to-3:30 P.M. shift is completed, she runs to her car so she can get to class a few minutes early to review for her midterm exam that evening. The car won't start. She needs to get to campus quickly. She grabs her backpack out of the trunk and begs a coworker to give her a lift. "It shouldn't be too much out of your way, and I'm really in trouble if I miss this exam," she pleads. The coworker obliges and drops Lori off at the circle drive. Whew! Lori has solved one problem. It's almost 4:30 P.M., and she has just a few minutes to quickly review one last time before the exam. But now Lori is faced with another problem—answering the questions posed by the instructor. There are thirty multiple-choice questions, each one of which forces Lori to choose between four possible answers. The two essay problems require her to make additional choices. As the instructor collects the exam booklet, Lori heaves a sigh of relief. She really feels good about her performance on this test. As she walks out to the parking lot, she suddenly remembers that her car is back at the Wal-Mart parking lot. Even though Lori has solved several problems in the last few hours, there is another one waiting for her.*

All of us have encountered similar situations. Look at the events you experience each day. You constantly have to make choices. Some choices may be easier to make than others. Others seem to be insurmountable. Shannon O'Neill, in this chapter's "You Make the Call!", may find it easier to figure out strategies to reduce costs by 10 percent than to cut employee costs by 10 percent. Shannon has tough times ahead as her recommendations will affect a variety of stakeholders. Some will be impacted in negative ways. Often, a supervisor would like to know in which direction to go but has given little thought to the result (see Figure 5.1).

How many decisions have you made today? Each of us has to make choices, and sometimes, we do not make the "right" ones. Think back to a couple of your more recent decisions. Did you just "wing it?" Or did you use a systematic problem-solving approach? Decision making is an essential part of life and an integral part of all managerial functions. While it is particularly at the core of the planning function of management, we have placed this chapter on decision making in Part 2 of this text because the principles discussed here apply when supervisors carry out all their managerial functions and duties.

In work settings, when asked to define their major responsibilities, many supervisors respond that "solving problems" and "making decisions" are the most important components of what they do daily and throughout their ongoing supervisory management tasks. **Decision making** is the process of defining problems and choosing a course of action from among alternatives. The term *decision making* often is used with the term *problem solving* because many

Decision making
Defining problems and choosing a course of action from among alternatives

FIGURE 5.1 To make a decision, you must first know what you want to accomplish

supervisory decisions focus on solving problems that have occurred or are anticipated. However, the term *problem solving* should not be construed as limited to decisions about problem areas. Problem solving also includes decisions about realistic opportunities that are present or available if planned for appropriately. Therefore, throughout this chapter, we use these terms interchangeably.

Many of the problems that confront supervisors in their daily activities recur and are familiar; for these problems, most supervisors have developed routine answers. When supervisors are confronted with new and unfamiliar problems, however, many find it difficult to choose courses of action.

Managers and supervisors at all levels are constantly required to solve problems that result from changing situations and unusual circumstances. Regardless of their managerial levels, supervisors should use a similar, logical, and systematic process of decision making. While decisions at the executive level are usually wider in scope and magnitude than decisions at the supervisory level, the decision-making process should be fundamentally the same throughout the management hierarchy.

Of course, once a decision is made, effective action is necessary. A good decision that no one implements is of little value. In this chapter, we are unconcerned with the problem of getting effective action. Instead, we discuss the process before action is taken that should lead to the "best" decision or solution.

A decision maker is often depicted as an executive bent over some papers with pen in hand, contemplating whether to sign on the dotted line, or as a manager in a meeting who is raising an arm to vote a certain way. These images share one thing: They portray decision makers as people at the moment of choice, ready to choose an alternative. Supervisors must understand that information gathering, analysis, and other processes precede the moment of selecting one alternative over others.

Decision making is an important skill that can be developed just as golf skills are developed—by learning the steps, practicing, and exerting effort. By doing these things, supervisors can learn to make more thoughtful decisions and can improve the quality of their decisions.

At the same time, supervisors should ensure that their employees learn to make their own decisions more effectively. A supervisor cannot make all the decisions necessary to run a department. Many daily decisions in a department are made by the employees who do the work. For example, employees often have to decide, without their supervisors, what materials to use, how a job is to be done, when a job is to be done, and how to coordinate with other departments.

Appreciative Inquiry (AI)
The cooperative search for the best in people, organizations, and the world around them

This forward thinking is embodied in the notion of **appreciative inquiry (AI)**. Case Western Reserve Professor David Cooperrider explained that "AI is the cooperative search for the best in people, their organizations, and the world around them.... AI involves the art and practice of asking questions that strengthen a system's capacity to heightened positive potential."[1] Numerous organizations have embraced the concept in order to push performance to higher levels. What is appreciative inquiry? Read the definitions below to gain some insight.

- **Appreciate:** (1) To recognize the quality, significance, or magnitude of; (2) to be fully aware of; (3) to be thankful for; (4) to admire greatly; (5) to raise in value, especially over time.
- **Synonyms:** value, prize, esteem, treasure, cherish. These verbs mean to have a favorable opinion of someone or something.
- **Inquire:** (1) To seek information by asking a question, (2) to make an inquiry or investigation. Synonyms: discovery, search, study, systematic exploration.
- **Inquiry:** (1) The act of inquiring, (2) a question, (3) a close examination of a matter in the search for information or truth.[2]

According to Professor Cooperrider, "AI involves the art and practice of asking questions that strengthen an organization's capacity to apprehend, anticipate, and heighten positive potential. The excitement of discovering, dreaming, and designing can turn empowered employees into a revolutionary force for positive organizational change." Instead of relying on traditional managerial decision-making processes, AI assumes that every living system has many untapped resources and unexplored potentials and, as such, managers must believe that their employees want to be involved and will ultimately make decisions that are in the best interests of their organization.[3] In previous chapters we discussed the importance of engaging, empowering, and encouraging employees. In practice, those companies that are the "best companies to work for" are giving employees more active roles in charting the future of their organizations.[4]

---

2 Describe the type of decisions made in organizations.

Types of Decisions

Training subordinates to make decisions should be a high priority for all supervisors. Management decision-making theorists often classify managerial decisions as *programmed* or *nonprogrammed*, with many decisions falling somewhere between these two extremes.[5]

Programmed decisions
Solutions to repetitive and routine problems provided by policies, procedures, or rules

Programmed decisions are solutions to problems that are repetitive, well-structured, and routine. The term *programmed* is used in the same sense that it is used in computer programming; there is a specific procedure, or program, that applies to the problem at hand. Many problems that confront supervisors daily are easy to solve because relatively rote answers to those problems are available. These problems are usually routine or repetitive, and fixed answers, methods, procedures, or rules exist. Supervisors can delegate these kinds of decisions to subordinates and be confident that the decisions will be made in an acceptable and timely manner.

Nonprogrammed decisions occur when supervisors confront new or unusual problems for which they must use their intelligent, adaptive problem-solving behavior. Such problems may be rare, unstructured, or unique, and they are typically one-time occurrences. There are no pat answers or guidelines for decision making in these situations. Nonprogrammed decisions tend to be more important, demanding, and strategic than programmed decisions. In nonprogrammed decision making, supervisors are called on to use good judgment, intuition, and creativity in attempting to solve problems. In these situations, supervisors should apply a decision-making process by which they can approach problems consistently and logically, yet adaptively.[6] The remainder of this chapter refers primarily to nonprogrammed decision making.

Nonprogrammed decisions
Solutions to unique problems that require judgment, intuition, and creativity

The Decision-Making Process

When making nonprogrammed managerial decisions, supervisors should follow the steps of the **decision-making process** (see Figure 5.2). First, supervisors must define the problem. Second, they must analyze the problem using available information. Third, they must establish decision criteria—factors that will be used to evaluate the alternatives. Fourth, after thorough analysis, supervisors should develop alternate solutions. After these steps, the supervisor should carefully evaluate the alternatives and select the solution that appears to be the "best" or most feasible under the circumstances. The concluding step in this process is follow-up and appraisal of the consequences of the decision.

3 Describe and apply the basic steps of the decision-making process.

Decision-making process
A systematic, step-by-step process to aid in choosing the best alternative

STEP 1: DEFINE THE PROBLEM

Before seeking answers, the supervisor first should identify the real problem. Nothing is as useless as the right answer to the wrong question. Defining a

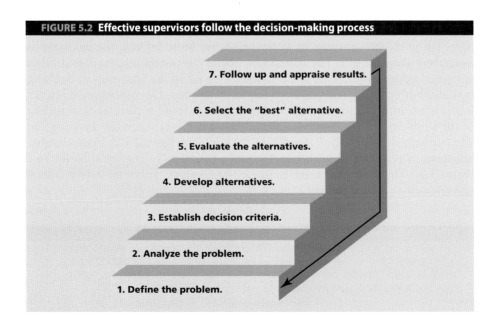

FIGURE 5.2 Effective supervisors follow the decision-making process

7. Follow up and appraise results.

6. Select the "best" alternative.

5. Evaluate the alternatives.

4. Develop alternatives.

3. Establish decision criteria.

2. Analyze the problem.

1. Define the problem.

problem is not easy. What appears to be the problem might merely be a symptom that shows on the surface. It is usually necessary to delve deeper to locate the real problem and define it.

Consider the following scenario. Tom Engle, an office supervisor, believes that a problem of conflicting personalities exists in his department. Two employees, Diana and Stuart, are continually bickering and cannot work together. Because of this lack of cooperation, the job is not being done in a timely manner. Engle must develop a clear, accurate problem statement. The problem statement should be brief, specific, and easily understood by others. A good problem statement addresses the following key questions:

- What is the problem?
- How do you know there is a problem?
- Where has the problem occurred?
- When has the problem occurred?
- Who is involved in, or affected by, the problem?

Expressing a problem through a problem statement can help the supervisor understand it. A careful review of the answers to key questions can lead to a problem statement, as shown in Figure 5.3, which reveals that the major problem is that the work is not getting done in a timely manner. When checking into this situation, the supervisor should focus on why the work is not getting done.

While defining a problem often can be time-consuming, it is time well spent. A supervisor should go no further in the decision-making process until the problem relevant to the situation has been specifically determined. Remember, a problem exists when there is a difference between the way things are and the way they should be. Effective supervisors use problem solving not only to take corrective action but also to improve the organization.

Unfortunately, many managers and supervisors do not spend the time necessary to properly frame the problems before them. Often, they resort to making snap decisions and taking quick actions that do not solve the problems at hand.

STEP 2: ANALYZE THE PROBLEM: GATHER FACTS AND INFORMATION

After the problem—not just its symptoms—has been defined, the next step is to analyze the problem. The supervisor begins by assembling facts and other pertinent information. This is sometimes viewed as the first step in decision making, but until the real problem has been defined, the supervisor does not know what information is needed. Only after gaining a clear understanding of the problem can the supervisor decide how important certain data are and what additional information to seek. In the computer age there is so much more information available, but is it relevant to the problems or current situation (see Figure 5.4)? The supervisor needs to pause and ponder whether the data is factual and relevant to the problem.

FIGURE 5.3 Sample Problem Statement

Bickering between the employees detracts from the completion of work assignments. Last Monday and Tuesday, customer callbacks were not completed. Customers, other department employees, and the shipping department all are affected.

FIGURE 5.4 The supervisor needs alternative sources of information

Tom Engle, the office supervisor in the Step 1 scenario, must find out why the work is not getting done. When he gathers information, he finds out that he never clearly outlined the expectations for his employees—where their duties begin and where they end. What appeared on the surface to be a problem of personality conflict was actually a problem caused by the supervisor. The chances are good that once the activities and responsibilities of the two employees are clarified, the friction will end. Engle must monitor the situation closely to ensure that the work is completed on time.

Being human, a supervisor may find that personal opinion impacts decision making. This is particularly true when employees are involved in the problem. For example, if a problem involves an employee who performs well, the supervisor may be inclined to show that employee greater consideration than a poor performer. The supervisor should try to be as objective as possible in gathering and examining information.

Sometimes the supervisor does not know how far to go in searching for additional facts. A good practice is to observe reasonable time and cost limitations. This means gathering all information without undue delay and

FIGURE 5.5 Sample Fishbone (Cause-and-Effect) Diagram

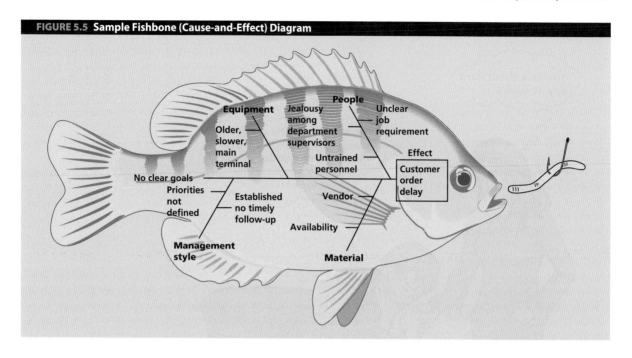

Fishbone technique (cause-and-effect diagram)
Cause-and-effect approach to consider the potential interrelatedness of problem causes in decision making

Decision criteria
Standards or measures to use in evaluating alternatives

without excessive costs. In the process of analysis, the supervisor should try to think of intangible factors that play a significant role. Some intangible factors are reputation, morale, discipline, and personal biases. It is difficult to be specific about these factors, but they should be considered when analyzing a problem. As a general rule, written and objective information is more reliable than opinions and hearsay. Another way to depict Step 1 and Step 2 of the decision-making process is the **fishbone technique (cause-and-effect diagram)** (Figure 5.5). This approach has the problem solver not only identify the various factors that have brought about the problem but also consider the potential interrelatedness of the causes of the problem. For a set of guidelines and a depiction of this process, see the appendix to this chapter.

STEP 3: ESTABLISH DECISION CRITERIA

Decision criteria are standards or measures for evaluating alternatives; they are typically statements of what the supervisor wants to accomplish with the decision. Such criteria also can be used to determine how well the implementation phase of the process is going—that is, whether the decision is doing what it was intended to do. To illustrate, suppose that Tom Engle's initial actions do not remedy the situation. It will be appropriate to establish decision criteria. Figure 5.6 provides examples of the decision criteria that can be used to evaluate other courses of action.

Once the decision criteria are established, the supervisor must determine which criteria are necessary and must establish their order of priority. Because no solution alternative is likely to meet all the criteria, the supervisor must know which criteria are most important so alternatives can be judged by how many of those criteria alternatives meet. The supervisor may want to consult with upper-level managers, peers, or employees when prioritizing criteria.

STEP 4: DEVELOP ALTERNATIVES

After the supervisor has defined and analyzed the problem and established decision criteria, the next step is to develop alternative solutions. The supervisor

---

FIGURE 5.6 Sample Decision Criteria

THE SOLUTION TO A PROBLEM

- Should result in the work assignments being completed on time.
- Should incur no financial cost.
- Must not impede quality of service to the customer.
- Should put no employee's job in jeopardy.
- Should allow differentiation of product or service in the marketplace.
- Should have no negative impact on employees.
- Must alleviate the problem within one week.

---

should consider as many solutions as can reasonably be developed. By formulating many alternatives, the supervisor is less apt to overlook the best course of action. A decision is only as good as the best alternative.

Almost all problems have a number of alternatives. The choices may not always be obvious, so supervisors must search for them. When supervisors do not do this, they are likely to fall into "either/or" kind of thinking. It is not enough for supervisors just to decide from among alternatives that employees have suggested, because there may be other alternatives to consider. Therefore, supervisors must stretch their minds to develop additional alternatives, even in the most discouraging situations. None of the alternatives may be desirable, but at least the supervisor can choose the one that is least undesirable.

Suppose an office supervisor has been directed to reduce employment by 20 percent because the firm is experiencing financial problems. After careful study, the supervisor develops the following feasible alternatives:

1. Lay off employees with the least seniority, regardless of job or performance, until the 20 percent reduction is reached.
2. Lay off employees with the lowest performance ratings until the 20 percent reduction is reached.
3. Analyze department duties and decide which jobs are essential. Keep the employees who are best qualified to perform those jobs.
4. Lay off no one and reduce work hours for all employees to achieve a 20 percent reduction.
5. Develop ways to increase the organization's revenues so that no employees must be laid off.

While Alternative 5 is most attractive, it may not be realistic given the current economic situation. While no other alternative may be the ideal solution to this unpleasant problem, at least the office supervisor has considered several alternatives before making a decision.

BRAINSTORMING AND CREATIVE PROBLEM SOLVING

When enough time is available, a supervisor should meet with a group of other supervisors or employees to brainstorm alternatives to a perplexing problem. **Brainstorming** is the free flow of ideas in a group, with judgment suspended, to identify as many alternatives as possible. Using this technique, the supervisor presents the problem, and the participants offer as many alternative solutions as they can in the time available. Any idea is acceptable—even one that may at first appear to be wild or unusual. Evaluation of ideas is suspended so that participants can give free rein to their creativity.

Brainstorming
A free flow of ideas in a group, while suspending judgment, aimed at developing many alternative solutions to a problem

Of course, brainstorming requires an atmosphere that encourages creativity. When supervisors are unwilling to devote sufficient time to brainstorming, or when supervisors try to dominate the process with their own opinions and solutions, the brainstorming effort is likely to fail.[7]

Alex Osborn, an authority on creativity and brainstorming, suggests the following four guidelines for effective brainstorming:

1. Defer all judgment of ideas. During brainstorming, allow no criticism by the group. People suppress ideas consciously and subconsciously, and this tendency must be avoided. Even if an idea seems impractical and useless, it should not be rejected because rejection could inhibit the free flow of more ideas.
2. Seek many ideas. Idea fluency is the key to creative problem solving, and fluency means quantity. The more ideas that are generated, the more likely some ideas will be viable.
3. Encourage "freewheeling." Being creative calls for a free-flowing mental process in which all ideas, no matter how extreme, are welcome. Even the wildest idea may, on further analysis, have some usefulness.
4. "Hitchhike" on existing ideas. Combining, adding to, and rearranging ideas often produce new approaches that are superior to the original ones. When creative thought processes slow or stop, review some of the existing ideas and try to hitchhike on them with additions or revisions.[8]

The preceding guidelines apply to both individual and group brainstorming. When it involves a large group, unstructured brainstorming can become long, tedious, and unproductive because many ideas are simply not feasible and because conflicts may develop. For this reason, the **nominal group technique (NGT)**, which provides a means of enabling group members to generate ideas more efficiently, is advocated. Typically, NGT involves having group members first write down their ideas and alternatives to the problem. Then, group members share, discuss, evaluate, and refine their ideas. The group's final choice(s) may be made by a

Nominal group technique (NGT)
A group brainstorming and decision-making process by which individual members first identify alternative solutions privately and then share, evaluate, and decide on an approach as a group

Using brainstorming, the supervisor presents the problem and the participants offer as many solutions as they can in the time available

series of confidential votes in which a list of ideas is narrowed until consensus is attained.[9]

Creative approaches and brainstorming meetings are particularly adaptable to nonprogrammed decisions, especially if the problem is new, important, or strategic. Even the supervisor who takes time to brainstorm a problem alone is likely to develop more alternatives for solving the problem than one who does not brainstorm.[10]

ETHICAL CONSIDERATIONS

Both when developing and evaluating alternatives, a supervisor should consider only those alternatives that are lawful and acceptable within the organization's ethical guidelines. In recent years, many firms have become concerned that their managers, supervisors, and employees make ethical decisions because they recognize that, in the long term, good ethics is good business.[11] Professor William Sauser of Auburn University says that "no organization can afford even a suspicion of unethical behavior and must take proactive steps to ensure that no suspicions arise."[12] Consequently, many firms have developed handbooks, policies, and official statements that specify their ethical standards and practices.[13]

The following list of guidelines or **ethical "tests"** for decision making is not comprehensive, but these considerations are relevant when addressing the ethical aspects of most problem situations.

Ethical "tests"
Considerations or guidelines to be addressed in developing and evaluating ethical aspects of decision alternatives

- **Legal/compliance test:** Laws, regulations, and policies are to be followed, not broken or ignored. The rationale and explanation that "everybody's doing it" and "everybody's getting away with it" are poor excuses if you get caught violating a law, policy, or regulation. If in doubt, ask for guidance from someone who knows the law or regulation. However, compliance should be only a starting point in most ethical decision making.
- **Public-knowledge test:** What would be the consequences if the outcome of an alternative decision became known to the public, one's family, the media, or a government agency?
- **Long-term-consequences test:** What would be the long-term versus short-term outcomes? Weigh these outcomes against each other.
- **Examine-your-motives test:** Do the motives for a proposed decision benefit the company and others, or are they primarily selfish and designed to harm or destroy other people and their interests?
- **Inner-voice test:** This is the test of conscience and moral values that has been instilled. If something inside you says the choice is or may be wrong, it usually is. It is then prudent to look for a different and better alternative.
- **Fairness test:** Are the decision and corresponding actions fair to all concerned such as the various stakeholders? Will it be beneficial to all concerned? When in doubt about the impact of the decision on various stakeholder groups, check and re-check the process used to arrive at the decision.

It cannot be stressed enough that when supervisors believe an alternative is questionable or might be unacceptable within the firm's ethical policies, they should consult their managers, the human resources department, or other staff specialists who can provide guidance in how to proceed. Many firms have an ethics "hotline" where individuals can call to seek assistance when confronted with ethical dilemmas. We believe that employees should have access to safe and confidential channels to raise concerns about possible ethics violations. It is not enough to just have an "ethics policy." Supervisors are responsible for ensuring that the company's ethical policies aren't just nice words posted in the company handbook; they must be words to "live by."

STEP 5: EVALUATE THE ALTERNATIVES

The ultimate purpose of decision making is to choose the course of action that will provide the greatest number of wanted and the smallest number of unwanted consequences. After developing alternatives, supervisors can mentally test each of them by imagining that each has already been put into effect. Supervisors should try to foresee the probable desirable and undesirable consequences of each alternative. By thinking alternatives through and appraising their consequences, supervisors can compare the desirability of choices.

The usual way to begin is to eliminate alternatives that do not meet the supervisor's decision criteria and ethical standards. The supervisor should evaluate how many of the most important criteria each alternative meets. The successful alternative is the one that satisfies or meets the most criteria at the highest priority levels. Often, there is no clear choice.

Nonprogrammed decisions usually require the decision maker to choose a course of action without complete information about the situation. Because of this uncertainty, the chosen alternative may not yield the intended results, and, as a result, there is risk involved. Some supervisors consider the risk and uncertainty of each course of action. There is no such thing as a risk-free decision; one alternative may simply involve less risk than others.[14]

Time may make one alternative preferable, particularly if there is a difference between how much time is available and how much time is required to carry out an alternative. The supervisor should consider the available facilities, tools, and other resources. It is also critical to judge alternatives in terms of economy of effort and resources. In other words, which action will give the greatest benefits and results for the least cost and effort?

When one alternative clearly appears to provide a greater number of desirable consequences and fewer unwanted consequences than any other alternatives, the

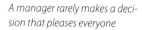

A manager rarely makes a decision that pleases everyone

decision is fairly easy. However, the "best" alternative is not always so obvious. At times, two or more alternatives may seem equally desirable. Here, the choice may become a matter of personal preference. It is also possible that the supervisor may feel that no single alternative is significantly stronger than any other. In this case, it might be possible to combine the positive aspects of the better alternatives into one composite solution.

Sometimes, no alternatives are satisfactory; all have too many undesirable effects, or none will bring about the desired results. In such a case, the supervisor should begin to think of new alternative solutions or perhaps even start all over again by attempting to redefine the problem.

A situation might arise in which the undesirable consequences of all alternatives appear to be so overwhelmingly unfavorable that the supervisor feels the best solution is to take no action. However, this may be deceiving because taking no action does not solve the problem. Taking no action is as much a decision as is taking another action, even though the supervisor may believe an unpleasant choice has been avoided. The supervisor should visualize the consequences that are likely to result from taking no action. Only if the consequences of taking no action are the most desirable should it be selected as the appropriate course.

STEP 6: SELECT THE BEST ALTERNATIVE

Selecting the alternative that seems best is known as **optimizing.** However, the supervisor sometimes makes a **satisficing** decision—selects an alternative that meets the minimal decision criteria. A famous management theorist, Herbert Simon, once likened the difference to finding a needle in a haystack (satisficing) and finding the biggest, sharpest needle in the haystack (optimizing).[15] Nevertheless, after developing and evaluating alternatives, the supervisor must make a choice.

Among the most prominent bases for choosing the best alternative are experience, intuition, advice, experimentation, and statistical and quantitative decision making. Regardless of the process, a supervisor rarely makes a decision that pleases everyone equally.

Optimizing
Selecting the best alternative

Satisficing
Selecting the alternative that meets the minimal decision criteria

EXPERIENCE

When selecting from alternatives, the supervisor should rely on experience. Certain situations will recur, and the adage, "Experience is the best teacher," applies to a certain extent. A supervisor can often decide wisely based on personal experience or the experience of some other manager. Knowledge gained from experience is a helpful guide, and its importance should not be underestimated. On the other hand, it is dangerous to follow experience blindly.

When looking to experience as a basis for choosing among alternatives, the supervisor should examine the situation and the conditions that prevailed at the time of the earlier decision. It may be that conditions are nearly identical to those that prevailed on the previous occasion and that the decision should be similar to the one made then. More often than not, however, conditions change considerably, and the underlying assumptions change. Therefore, the new decision probably should not be identical to the earlier one.

Experience can be helpful when supervisors are called on to substantiate their reasons for making certain decisions. In part, this may be a defense, but there is no excuse for following experience in and of itself. Experience must always be viewed with the future in mind. The circumstances of the past, the present, and the future must be considered realistically if experience is to help supervisors select from alternatives.

INTUITION

At times, supervisors base their decisions on intuition. Some supervisors even appear able to solve problems by subjective means.[16] However, a deeper search usually reveals that the so-called intuition on which the supervisor appeared to have based a decision was really experience or knowledge stored in the supervisor's memory. By recalling similar situations that occurred in the past, supervisors may be better able to reach decisions, even though they label doing so as "having hunches."

Intuition may be particularly helpful when other alternatives have been tried with poor results. If the risks are not too great, a supervisor may choose a new alternative because of an intuitive feeling that a fresh approach might bring positive results. Even if the hunch does not work out well, the supervisor has tried something different. Supervisors will remember doing so and can draw upon those experiences in future decisions.

ADVICE FROM OTHERS

Although a supervisor cannot shift personal responsibility for making decisions in the department, the burden of decision making often can be eased by seeking the advice of others. The ideas and suggestions of employees, other supervisors, staff experts, technical authorities, and the supervisor's own manager can be of great help in weighing facts and information. Seeking advice does not mean avoiding a decision because the supervisor still must decide whether to accept the advice of others.

Many believe that two heads are better than one and that input from others improves the decision process.[17] The following four guidelines can help the supervisor decide whether groups should be included in the decision-making process:

1. If additional information would increase the quality of the decision, involve those who can provide that information.
2. If acceptance of the decision is critical, involve those whose acceptance is important.

In decision making, two heads can be better than one

3. If people's skills can be developed through participation, involve those who need the development opportunity.
4. If the situation is not life-threatening and does not require immediate action, involve others in the process.[18]

Generally, the varied perspectives and experiences of others add to the decision-making process.

EXPERIMENTATION

In the scientific world, where many conclusions are based on tests in laboratories, experimentation is essential and accepted. In supervision, however, experimentation is often too costly in terms of people, time, and materials. Nevertheless, there are some instances in which a limited amount of testing and experimenting is advisable. For example, a supervisor may find it worthwhile to try several different locations for a new copy machine in the department to see which location employees prefer and which location is most convenient for the workflow. There also are instances in which a certain amount of testing is advisable to allow employees to try new ideas or approaches, perhaps of their own design. While experimentation may be valid from a motivational standpoint, it can be a slow and relatively expensive method of reaching a decision.

QUANTITATIVE DECISION MAKING

Numerous techniques and models of quantitative decision making have received much attention in management literature and practice. Among these techniques are linear programming, operations research, and probability and simulation models. These tend to be sophisticated statistical and mathematical approaches often used with computers.[19] They require the decision maker to quantify most of the information that is relevant to a decision. For many supervisors, these quantitative decision-making techniques are rather remote, yet many large firms have management-decision-support systems that help supervisors

Quantitative decision making techniques are sophisticated statistical and mathematical approaches usually involving computers

make nonprogrammed decisions. One desirable feature of quantitative decision making is the ability of the user to perform "what if" scenarios—the simulations of business situations over and over using different data for select decision areas.

With the increasing use of laptops and desktop computers and networks, many firms can develop programs and information-storage-and-retrieval systems that supervisors can use relatively easily for certain types of decisions, especially when historical and statistical databases are involved. For some types of problems, supervisors may be able to seek the help of mathematicians, engineers, statisticians, systems analysts, and computer specialists, all of whom can bring their tools to bear on relevant problems.

This procedure can be involved and costly, however, and decisions like those facing Shannon O'Neill in the "You Make the Call!" section of this chapter usually cannot be made from statistical or quantitative models.

STEP 7: FOLLOW UP AND APPRAISE THE RESULTS

After a decision has been made, specific actions are necessary to carry that decision out. Follow-up and appraisal of a decision's outcome are part of decision making.

Follow-up and appraisal of a decision can take many forms, depending on the decision, timing, costs, standards, personnel, and other factors. For example, a minor production-scheduling decision could be evaluated easily based on a short written report or perhaps even by the supervisor's observation or a discussion with employees. A major decision involving the installation of complex new equipment, in contrast, requires close and time-consuming follow-up by the supervisor, technical employees, and high-level managers. This type of decision usually requires the supervisor to prepare numerous detailed, written reports of equipment performance under varying conditions that are compared closely with plans or expected standards for the equipment.

The important point to recognize is that the task of decision making is incomplete without some form of follow-up and action appraisal. When the supervisor establishes decision criteria or objectives the decision should accomplish, it is easier to evaluate the decision's effects. When the consequences are good, the supervisor can feel reasonably confident that the decision was sound.

When the follow-up and appraisal indicate that something has gone wrong or that the results have not been as anticipated, the supervisor's decision-making process must begin all over again. This may even mean going back over each of the steps of the decision-making process in detail. The supervisor's definition and analysis of the problem and the development of alternatives may have to be completely revised in view of new circumstances surrounding the problem. In other words, when follow-up and appraisal indicate that the problem has not been solved, the supervisor should treat

SUPERVISORY TIPS

Some Thoughts and Suggestions for Improving Problem Solving and Decision Making

1. Take enough time to state the problem accurately and concisely and to identify the objectives you want to accomplish with your decision.
2. Whenever appropriate, seek opinions and suggestions from others who can contribute their ideas toward solving the problem.
3. Before deciding what to do, gather ample facts and information that will help define/clarify the problem and suggest solutions.
4. Stretch your mind to develop numerous alternative solutions; brainstorm with others when practicable.
5. Make your decision based on objective criteria; avoid letting personal biases and organizational political considerations direct your choice.
6. When implementing and following up your decision, do not hesitate to admit and rectify errors in the decision, even if doing so causes some personal embarrassment. (Admitting mistakes early is prudent and builds your integrity with others.)

the situation as a completely new problem and go through the decision-making process from a completely fresh perspective. See the accompanying "Supervisory Tips" box for some specific suggestions for improving your decision-making process.

Decision-Making Styles

4 Identify and describe various decision-making styles.

Decision making is influenced by many forces, making it difficult to formulate a simple "to do checklist" that applies to every situation in the same way. Earlier in this chapter, we stressed that when supervisors are faced with complex, unusual, or new problems, they must use good judgment, intuition, and creativity in the decision-making process. What processes do managers actually use when making decisions? We know from observing others and our own experiences that people make decisions differently. We have observed the two extremes: some people are like the "Waffler" (Skills Application 5-4) who takes forever to study the problem and never makes a decision, while others like the "Gunner" pull the trigger (Fire-Aim-Ready) quickly, and if things don't go the intended way, they fire again, again, and again until they hit the target (achieve the intended results).

We feel it is important for supervisors to know that different types of decisions require different decision-making styles. Supervisors are continually being asked to make decisions, and how they make those decisions is under constant scrutiny. Supervisors have many people looking over their shoulders, not necessarily to get their cues on how to make decisions but to criticize the decisions made. What can we learn from the decisions that we made earlier in our careers? How many times have you heard someone say, "If I had been in that situation, I would have done . . ." Our current "scientific" method focuses almost exclusively on identifying what worked best or what went wrong. Few have studied the process of decision making. When asked to think of words that describe one's decision-making process, what comes to mind?

Relying heavily on the Social Styles Model, Mike Lynch and Harvey Lifton developed the Decision-Making Styles Model to describe how people make decisions. Think of the most recent major purchase that you or someone in your family made. What process did you or they go through to make the final decision? To help you analyze your decision-making style, see Figure 5.7.

To assist you in understanding how you make decisions, look back at your recent decisions. Analyze them from the following perspective:

- What worked?
- What actually happened as a result of the decision?
- What kind of feedback did you receive about the success of a decision?
- What style did you use to make the successful decision?
- What didn't work?
- Why didn't it work?
- How much "tweaking" did you have to do to make it work?
- What caused the differences between the intended outcome and what actually occurred?
- What kind of feedback did you receive about a "failed" decision?
- What decision-making style did you use to make the "failed" decision?

The better you understand the answers to these questions, the better your decision-making skills will become. Learning may not be so much what we learn to do but what we learn not to do in the future.

FIGURE 5.7 What is your decision-making style?

FIGURE 5.7 What is your decision-making style?

Analytic

DEEP THINKER

Decisions are made based on the facts and evidence researched.
- Avoids risks
- Uses solid, tangible, realistic evidence to support decisions
- Makes decisions valid for the present and the future
- Is cautious and deliberate
- Has great need to be "right"
- Is very concerned with details
- Uses an organized process
- Stands behind decisions after they are made

Controls Emotion

Driver

GROUP COMMANDER

Decisions are made using the available information without help from others.
- Makes own decisions
- Uses power to influence
- Seeks control
- Overcomes obstacles with force
- Expresses conclusions quickly
- Bases decisions on facts and data
- Takes risks
- Prefers to be presented with options from which to choose

Abdicator

CONVENIENCE SEEKER

Decisions are made based on the easiest method readily available.
- Makes fast decisions
- Results in many errors
- Will assign decisions to anyone
- Doesn't care about results
- Has "Not my problem" attitude
- Gives no direction
- Wishes it would all go away
- Doesn't want to be involved

Asks

Tells

CONSENSUS BUILDER

Decisions are made that are acceptable to the group from shared Information and ideas.
- Likes the comfortable and known
- Uses own and others' personal opinions
- Wants guarantees of results
- Wants minimal risk
- Needs buy-in from others
- Avoids interpersonal confrontation
- Is reluctant to change beliefs
- Checks frequently for group agreement

Emotes

FREE SPIRIT

Decisions are made based on personal feelings and the feelings of others.
- Incorporates feelings of "important people"
- Sidelines facts and logic
- May be creative
- Takes risks
- Makes frequent mistakes
- Makes rapid decisions
- Looks for rewards that are social recognition and prestige
- Uses drama and/or humor to make a point

Amiable

Expressive

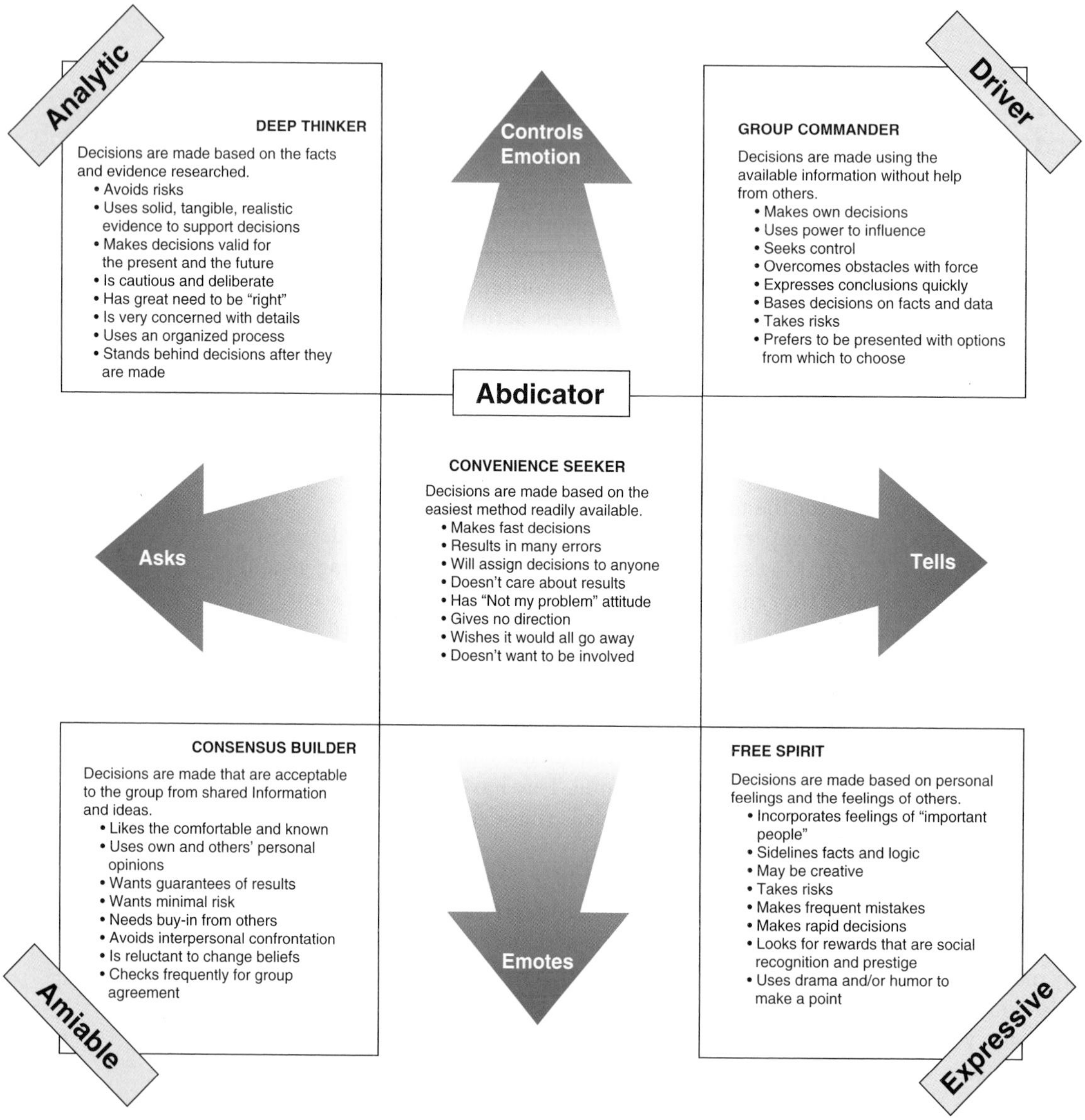

Source: Reprinted from *Training Clips: 150 Reproducible Handouts, Discussion Starters, and Job Aids*, by Mike Lynch and Harvey Lifton, copyright © 1998. Reprinted by permission of the publisher: HRD Press, Amherst, MA (800-822-2801), http://www.hrdpress.com.

5 Explain why a supervisor should not make hasty decisions.

Time Impacts The Decision-Making Process

In some situations, supervisors may feel they lack the time to go through the decision-making process outlined here. Frequently, a manager, a coworker, or an employee approaches the supervisor and says, "Here's the problem," and looks to the supervisor for an immediate answer. However, supervisors cannot afford to make decisions without considering the steps outlined here. Most problems do not require immediate answers.

Often, when an employee brings up a problem, the supervisor should ask questions like the following:

- How extensive is the problem?
- Does the situation need an immediate response?
- Who else (the stakeholders) is affected by the problem?
- Should they (the stakeholders) be involved in this discussion?
- Have you (the employee) thought through the problem, and do you have an idea of what the end result should be?
- What do you recommend? Why?

This approach is a form of participative supervision and can help to develop the employee's analytical skills. The supervisor then can better think through the problem, apply the decision-making steps, and make a decision.

Many supervisors get themselves into trouble by making hasty decisions without following all the steps in the decision-making process. During any stage of the process, if supervisors tell other people they "will get back to them," the supervisors should state a specific time and act within that time. When supervisors fail to make decisions or to give feedback to other people by the specified time, they may sacrifice trust.

Remember back to your early school years when the teacher called on you for the answer to the question: "What is two plus two?" Everyone looked to you for an answer. You didn't have time to consult with others. And the teacher expected you to provide the "one and only right answer." The pressure was on! In all likelihood, you paused, gathered your wits, thought of the alternatives, drew a deep breath, and answered "Four!" How did you feel? The joy that comes from doing the right thing at the right time is priceless. Even if you had given the incorrect answer, you would have learned "what not to do in the future."

SUMMARY

1 All supervisory activities involve problem solving and decision making. Supervisors must find solutions for problems that result from changing situations and unusual circumstances. Decision making based on careful study of information and analysis of various courses of action is still the most generally approved avenue of selecting from among alternatives. Decision making is a choice between two or more alternatives, and the decisions made by supervisors significantly affect departmental results.

Appreciative Inquiry (AI) is a cooperative search for the best in people, their organizations, and the environment around them. At the heart of AI is asking questions.

Decision making is a skill that can be learned. Organizations are giving employees a more active role in decision making today. A decision made today often sets a precedent for decisions made tomorrow.

2 Supervisors confront many decision situations that vary from the programmed type at one extreme to the nonprogrammed type at the other. Decisions for routine, repetitive-type problems are usually made according to policies, procedures, and standard practices. However, nonprogrammed decisions are usually one-time, unusual, or unique problems that require sound judgment and systematic thinking.

3 Better decisions are more likely to occur when supervisors follow these steps of the decision-making process:
1. Define the problem.
2. Gather facts and information and analyze the problem.
3. Establish decision criteria.
4. Develop a sufficient number of alternatives.
5. Evaluate alternatives by using the decision criteria or by thinking of the alternatives as if they had already been placed into action and considering their consequences.
6. Select the alternative that has the greatest number of wanted consequences and the least number of unwanted consequences.
7. Implement, follow up, and appraise the results.

Corrective action may be necessary if the decision is not achieving the desired objective.

The supervisor should develop a problem statement that answers the questions of what, how, where, when, and who. Proper problem definition clarifies the difference between the way things are and the way they should be.

After defining the problem, the supervisor must gather information. Decision criteria, which are measures or standards of what the supervisor wants to accomplish with the decision, should be specified. In developing alternatives, supervisors can use brainstorming and creative-thinking techniques.

Only alternatives that are lawful and ethical within the organization's guidelines should be considered. In the process of evaluation and choice, a supervisor can be aided by ethical guidelines, personal experience, intuition, advice, experimentation, and quantitative methods.

Once the decision has been made, specific actions are necessary to carry it out. Follow-up and appraisal are essential.

4 Supervisors constantly make decisions that vary in scope, complexity and impact on stakeholders. Figure 5.7 is used to illustrate five decision-making styles: *abdicator, free spirit, amiable, analytic,* and *driver.* Most supervisors will use all of the styles depending on the complexity of the problem, who is involved, and how much time the supervisor has. The key to effectiveness is matching the appropriate style to the situation.

5 Supervisors risk getting themselves into trouble unless they follow the steps of the decision-making process, which is time-consuming. Most problems do not require immediate answers. It is often valuable to allow subordinates to help make decisions. They may see the problem from a different perspective, and they may have information that bears on the problem.

KEY TERMS

Appreciative Inquiry (AI) (p. 154)
Brainstorming (p. 159)
Decision criteria (p. 158)
Decision making (p. 152)
Decision-making process (p. 155)

Ethical "tests" (p. 161)
Fishbone technique (cause-and-effect diagram) (p. 158)
Nominal group technique (NGT) (p. 160)
Nonprogrammed decisions (p. 155)

Optimizing (p. 163)
Programmed decisions (p. 154)
Satisficing (p. 163)

QUESTIONS FOR DISCUSSION

1. Define *decision making.* Does the decision-making process vary depending on where a manager or supervisor is located in the managerial hierarchy? Discuss.

2. Review the steps of the decision-making process in their proper sequence. Why should supervisors write problem statements when defining problems? What pitfalls should the supervisor avoid at each step?

3. "None of us is as smart as all of us." Theorists contend that groups generally make better decisions than an individual would.
   a. What are the advantages to involving an employee group in the decision-making process? The disadvantages?
   b. Identify the major elements of brainstorming, and explain how a supervisor can tap into the knowledge of the individual group members.

4. Define and discuss the factors a supervisor should consider when developing and evaluating alternatives in the decision-making process. To what degree should ethical issues be considered?

5. Your company has a rule prohibiting the use of the company computer for personal business.
   a. Is it realistic for your boss to expect you to abstain from conducting personal business on the company computer?
   b. During a slow period in the work day, you consider using the computer to surf for information on the fantasy football league. Discuss the five ethical "tests" that might come into play in your decision whether to surf or not to surf.

SKILLS APPLICATIONS

Skills Application 5-1: What Call Would You Make?

Refer back to the chapter's opening "You Make the Call!" Shannon O'Neill the transportation supervisor of Fairfield County School Corporation faces a difficult situation. She is under strict orders from the new superintendent to develop strategies for reducing the department's cost of operation. Put yourself in the position of Shannon O'Neill and answer the following questions:

1. List the major problems facing Shannon O'Neill.

2. Develop a strategy for determining the transportation priorities of Fairfield County Schools.

3. What comparative data from other school corporations would be useful in determining alternative strategies.

4. Describe what you would do to comply with the superintendent's request for cost-cutting measures.

5. Did you carefully consider all outcomes including possible downsides of your proposal?

6. What would be the most difficult challenges facing implementation of your recommendations?

Skills Application 5-2: Thinking Outside the Box

Taxicabs in Fairfield County can charge whatever they wish. One taxi company charges 75 cents for the first quarter-mile and 15 cents for each additional quarter-mile. The competing taxi company charges $1.00 for the first quarter-mile and 10 cents for each additional quarter mile.

1. What distances would produce the same fare for the two taxi companies?

2. How did you arrive at your answer?

3. Review the five decision-making styles presented in Figure 5.7.
   a. Which of the five styles best describes you?
   b. Draw a line down the center of a piece of notebook paper. On the right-hand side, list those attributes from the decision making style that best describes you. On the left-hand side, list those attributes from the style that least describes you.
   c. Think of your most recent major decision. Circle those characteristics which closely correspond with the process you used to arrive at that decision.
   d. Are most of the items you circled in your left-hand column or in the right-hand column?
   e. Ask someone who knows you really well to review the decision making styles and pick the one that best describes you. Is it the same as the one you selected? If there are differences, how do you account for those differences?
   f. What did you learn from this self-assessment?

Source: The taxicab exercise reproduced with permission from QCI International's *Timely Tips for Teams*, a monthly Internet newsletter. © 2007 QCI.

Skills Application 5-3: Self-Awareness of Problem-Solving Skills

This skills application is designed to help you identify key areas where your problem-solving skills could be improved.

1. Directions: Beside each statement, indicate the number that best describes your agreement or disagreement.
   Key:
   4 = Strongly Agree   3 = Agree   2 = Disagree Somewhat
   1 = Strongly Disagree
   1. I always ask, "Is this problem worth solving?" before beginning to solve it.
   2. I try to break big problems into manageable pieces instead of trying to solve the whole problem at once.
   3. To determine the cause of a problem, I gather enough data to know exactly where, when, and under what circumstances the problem occurs.
   4. I have a network of contacts within my company and elsewhere with whom I discuss the problems in my area.
   5. I usually use problem-solving tools, like pareto charts or cause-and-effect diagrams, to help me solve problems.
   6. I involve others in problem solving when I need their help to implement a major decision.
   7. During "crunch" times, when time is of the essence, I solve problems with little input from others.
   8. It's impossible for me to have all the information about a problem before taking action.
   9. I involve others when they know more about a situation than I do, even though it usually takes longer to get the problem solved.
   10. I usually use brainstorming techniques to generate ideas for solving problems.
   11. When I have a big problem to solve, I talk to everyone who has knowledge of the problem, those affected by the problem, and those who will have to implement the problem, before I come up with a solution.
   12. Once a solution is implemented, I have a follow-up plan to ensure that the solution fixes the problem.
   Total (add your scores)

2. Interpretation:
   12–23: Your present problem-solving skills thwart your attempt to reach a solution. Improve your problem-solving approach by following the suggestions in this chapter.
   24–35: Your problem-solving skills are satisfactory but could be improved.
   36–48: Your problem-solving skills are good. With a little improvement, they could be outstanding.

3. Carefully review the five decision making styles in Figure 5-7. Based on your responses to questions 1-12 above, which style would most appropriately describe your approach to decision making? Why?

4. Write a one-page paper detailing how you will continually look for ways to improve your problem-solving skills.

Source: Adapted with permission from The Mescon Group, Inc., *Techniques for Problem Solving: Leader's Guide* (Cincinnati, Ohio: Thomson Executive Press, 1995), pp. 11–12.

Skills Application 5-4: Dealing with People that Make Your Life Difficult—The "Indecisive" Waffler

This is the third in a series of skills applications that introduce you to the people who might make your life difficult as you journey through life.

1. Read the following statement from Kelly Klemm, a student at Southwest Tech:

    I had a friend, Henry, who wanted everyone to like him. I really liked him and thought we might have a future together. Most of the time he would say, "That is a great idea. Let me think about it and get back to you." When pressured, he would say, "I really don't know. Life seems so complicated. There are too many choices; I'll just go with the flow." That drove me up the wall. He felt that he needed to please everyone by acting as if each person's latest idea was the best he'd ever heard. Whether it was going to a movie or out to eat, he never had an opinion of where he wanted to go or what he wanted to see, but every alternative I came up with sounded like the best idea he had ever heard. When forced to make a decision, he took forever, and sometimes it seemed like it was torturing him inside as he was debating the options.

    One time, a bunch of us decided to go on a camping trip. Henry really acted like he wanted to go. He listened to all the details and acted excited about it. The day we all met to go, he never showed up and left a message saying he couldn't make it. This was not the first time he had done something like this.

    Henry was always "on the fence." He could not make a decision to save his life. He never wanted to take any action or make a choice that might hurt someone or make someone else uncomfortable.

I recall another time when we needed to decide where to spend New Year's Eve. Some of our friends wanted to go to Holly Hall for dinner and dancing while others wanted to go to the Savoy for dinner and then to the Rave for a movie. I told Henry that we needed to make a decision so that reservations could be made. One person could persuade him that one idea was the right way, then I could come along, and he would just "climb to the other side of the fence" and agree with me. One minute we were going to Holly Hall, and the next minute, we were going to the Savoy. Two hours later, it would be Holly Hall again.

Guess what? We ended up at his apartment, munching on some popcorn and watching an old movie. That was the last straw. Even though Henry was one of the kindest, gentlest people I'd ever met, I knew that Henry would never make a decision. So I made one. I decided I didn't have a future with him. I couldn't cope with him always sitting on the fence.

2. **(INTERNET ACTIVITY)** Using the Internet, find at least three sources of information for coping with a "waffler." Carefully review each site for suggestions.

3. Based on your findings, what suggestions would you have given to Kelly for coping with Henry?

4. Write a one-page paper explaining how this skills application increased your working knowledge of coping with the behaviors of the "waffler."

Skills Application 5-5: An Exercise in Brainstorming

A long-term customer tells you that your competitor can provide the same service you offer at a significantly lower price. The customer wants to know whether you can meet or beat that price. You have the authority to reduce prices, but not to the extent the customer implies. The competitor's price is less than your breakeven point. You promise to give the matter some thought, check with others, and get back with an answer tomorrow afternoon.

1. Working alone, take a few minutes to list at least three reasons the customer may have for wanting a price reduction.

2. Meet with three other students and brainstorm as many options as you can other than cutting the price that might meet the customer's needs.

3. Analyze the brainstorming activity. Did the process take more time than working alone? Did the process enable you to see a variety of options? Did the group generate several options you would not have thought of on your own?

4. What did you conclude from this exercise about the benefits and limitations of brainstorming?

SKILLS DEVELOPMENT

Skills Development Module 5-1: Crucial Decisions Need to Be Made at McDonald's

 Please refer back to the Skills Development Module 2-1 in Chapter 2, read the write up and review your notes before viewing this video clip (http://academic.cengage.com/management/leonard).

At the time of this video clip, chains had been increasing locations, updating menus, and attempting to attract customers with discount coupons, 'buy one – get one free,' and other promotions. As competition was heating up, McDonald's profitability fell to

record lows. McDonald's sales were declining and competition was heating up.

Confronted with its first quarterly loss since its founding, McDonald's management team needed to pause, survey the situation, and make crucial decisions.

In 2008, regional and national restaurant companies were being squeezed by falling sales and rising food costs. Many diners were either cutting back on eating outside the home, going out less often, or spending less on each visit. Competition in the hospitality industry was fierce.

1. The video clip makes reference to its six step decision process. How does the approach used by McDonald's management team differ from that process identified in Figure 5-2?

2. Identify the symptoms of problems McDonald's faced?
   a. For each symptom, describe what you think might be the underlying causes?
   b. For each of the symptoms, suggest an alternative or two to minimize or correct the problem.
   c. What would be a major difficulty in implementing each of the possible solutions?

3. What are the potential strengths and drawbacks of the approach used by McDonald's management team to address the problems?

4. In your opinion, what are the major problems McDonald's USA faces today?

APPENDIX: THE FISHBONE PROCESS

The fishbone technique, or cause-and-effect diagram (see Figure 5.5, on page 158), is a process primarily associated with Step 1 and Step 2 of the decision-making model. It facilitates analytical understanding by visually depicting a problem and its probable causes. One advantage of this approach is that it helps individuals see problems on single sheets of paper and perceive significant relationships between major causes of the problem.

Guidelines for Using the Fishbone Process

1. Once the problem is defined, print the problem on the head of the fish. Starting the diagram with the problem reminds all involved that the goal is to solve the problem.

2. The supervisor, independently or with a problem-solving team, should identify the causes of the problem. This can be done by asking, "What are the factors that cause the problem?" The diagram should be limited to a number of major causes, usually classified as people, machines or equipment, materials, methods and procedures, company policies, and management style. Alternatively, the latter three causes might be classified broadly as working conditions. The causes are attached to the fins of the fish.

3. Because the supervisor or problem-solving team will usually want additional information, contributors to the problem's various causes must be identified. Asking the right questions to uncover the contributing causes is a requirement of the process. Once these contributors are identified, print them on the diagram's horizontal lines to connect them to the appropriate causes. A person's brain works by association; grouping contributors to causes reflects the associative nature of the information. The diagram does not have to be perfect as long as everyone understands what it represents.

4. After the information has been entered on the diagram, the major causes of the problem can be isolated and circled on the diagram.

The fishbone technique has gained acceptance as many organizations have encouraged teams of employees to become more involved in the problem-solving process. The fishbone diagram helps employees understand how problem causes relate to each other.

Harold R. McAlindon, a leader in innovative management and author of *A Pocket Course in Creative Thinking* (Emeryville, CA: Parlay International, 1993), has stated that the art of drawing or sketching "can stimulate your thinking and may lead to other ideas." Also see The Mescon Group, Inc., *Techniques for Problem Solving: Participant's Guide* (Cincinnati: Thomson Executive Press, 1995), pp. 28–30, and C. Carl Pegels, *Total Quality Management: A Survey of Its Important Aspects* (Cincinnati: Boyd & Fraser Publishing Company/ITP, 1995), pp. 97–106.

The '3" x 5"' Technique

After the problem has been defined, contributors to the causes have been investigated and verified, and decision criteria have been established, alternative solutions can be developed. Instead of, or in addition to, brainstorming, the supervisor may use the '3" x 5"' technique.

Assume an employee survey has revealed a substantial number of employee complaints regarding inadequate maintenance assistance. The 3" x 5" process involves the following steps:

1. The supervisor writes the goal on the board for all to see (e.g., "How can we reduce the number

of employee complaints regarding maintenance without adversely affecting quality or costs?")

2. The supervisor gives each team member a stack of 3" x 5" cards. Each person writes down as many alternatives as possible in the next five minutes. Only one idea per person may be written anonymously on a 3" x 5" card.

3. The team is divided into subgroups of three to five people. The 3" x 5" cards are randomly distributed to the subgroups.

4. Each subgroup identifies preferred alternatives and then expands them.

5. The subgroup presents its recommendations to the overall group or team.

6. The overall group evaluates which alternatives are most relevant to solving the problem and how to implement those alternatives. As alternatives are implemented, contributors to the causes should be substantially reduced or eliminated.

ENDNOTES

I would encourage you to review the (a) *Journal of Behavioral Decision Making* (New York: Wiley); and (b) *Organizational Behavior and Human Decision Processes Journal* (Elsevier, Inc.). For recent perspectives on OB and decision process research, see (http://www.sciencedirect.com/science/journal/07495978) for a shortcut to their home page.

1. Much has been written about Appreciative Inquiry (AI) since David Cooperrider, under the guidance of his Ph.D. advisor, Suresh Srivastva, laid out the framework for AI. See David L. Cooperrider and Diana Whitney, *Appreciative Inquiry* (San Francisco, CA: Berrett-Koehler Publishers, 1999), p. 10. Also see this chapter's Contemporary Issue box.

2. Definitions from *The American Heritage Dictionary of the English Language*, 3rd ed. (Boston: Houghton Mifflin Co., 1992). The idea for including the definitions came from Appreciative Inquiry Commons http://appreciativeinquiry.cwru.edu/intro/whatisai.cfm.

3. David L. Cooperrider and Diana Whitney quote on Appreciative Inquiry Commons, "What is Appreciative Inquiry?" Also see David L. Cooperrider and Diana Whitney, *A Positive Revolution in Change: Appreciate Inquiry* (Berrett-Koehler, 2000). Also see the following: Whitney and Amanda Trosten-Bloom, *Power of Appreciative Inquiry* (Berrett-Koehler Publishers, Inc., 2002); Cooperrider, Whitney and Jacqueline Stavros, *Appreciative Inquiry Handbook* (Lakeshore Publishers, Inc., 2003); James D. Ludema, Whitney, Bernard J. Mohr, and Thomas J. Griffin, *Appreciative Inquiry Summit* (Berrett-Koehler Publishers, Inc., 2003); Cooperrider, Peter F. Sorenson, Therese Yaeger, and Whitney, *Appreciative Inquiry: An Emerging Direction for Organizational Development* (Stripes Publishing, 2001).

4. Review *Fortune's* yearly listing of the 100 Best Companies in America; or for a listing of the Best Small and Medium-sized Businesses to Work For go to www.greatplacetowork.com (Great Place to Work Institute, Inc.). Generally, the companies are selected, in part, on the basis of trust that exists between management and employees, perceptions of fairness, availability of employee empowerment, and a management style that engages employees.

5. See Harold Koontz and Heinz Weirich, *Management*, 11th ed. (New York: McGraw-Hill Irwin, 2004), p. 143.

6. John R. Schermerhorn, Jr., *Management*, 8th ed. (New York: John Wiley & Sons, 2004), pp. 59–64. Also see, Tilmann Betsch and Susanne Haberstroh, *The Routines of Decision Making* (Mahwah, N.J.: Lawrence Erlban Associates, 2004). For a detailed study on the effectiveness of decision making, see James W. Dean, Jr. and Mark P. Sharfman, "Does Decision Process Matter? A Study of Strategic Decision-Making Effectiveness," *Academy of Management Journal* (April 1996), pp. 368–96.

7. See Anne Houlihan, "Empower Your Employees to Make Smart Decision," *Supervision*, 68, 7 (July 2007), pp. 3–5; and "Harnessing Employee Creativity," *The Worklife Report* (2001), p. 14; Rita R. Culross, "Individual and Contextual Variable Among Creative Scientists: The New York Paradigm," *Roeper Review*, 26, 3 (Spring 2004), pp. 126–27; and Jennifer G. Brown, "Creativity and Problem-Solving," 87 *Marquette Law Review* 697 (2004), pp. 697–709.

8. For more information on brainstorming and creative problem solving, see Alex F. Osborn (with Alex Faickney), *Applied Imagination*, 3rd rev. ed. (Buffalo: Creative Education Foundation, 1993). Also see Alan G. Robinson and Sam Stern, *Corporate Creativity: How Innovation and Improvement Actually Happen* (San Francisco: Berrett-Koehler Publishers, 1997). For a list of ways to disrupt a brainstorming session, see Tom Kelley, "Six Ways to Kill a Brainstormer," *Across-the-Board* (March/April 2002), p. 12.

   Also see the following for ideas on how to "think outside the box:" Micahle Michalko, *Cracking Creativity: Secrets of a Creative Genius* (Berkeley, CA: Ten Speed Press, 2001); and James C. Adams, *Conceptual Blockbusting: A Guide to Better Ideas* (Cambridge, MA: Perseus Publishing, 2001).

9. Our students have found that an Internet search for Nominal Group Technique (NGT) provides a more expanded discussion than any of the contemporary management texts. A web page provided by University of Wisconsin Professor Randall Durham (http://instruction.bus.wisc.edu/obdemo/readings/ngt.html) identifies the circumstances under which NGT works best and presents the strengths and weaknesses of the approach. Other sites present similar information.

   Still another type of group brainstorming approach that has gained some acceptance in recent years is called storyboarding. Originally attributed to Walt Disney and his organization for developing animated cartoons, storyboarding can be especially helpful in generating alternatives and choosing among them. Depending on the nature of the problem, it may be appropriate to use a neutral party to manage the team process when alternatives, ideas, and other information are listed on index cards and arranged on "storyboards." For information on storyboarding, see James M. Higgins, "Story Board Your Way to Success," *Training and Development* (June 1995), pp. 13–17, or "Putting the Bang Back in Your TQM Program," *Journal for Quality and Participation* (October/November 1995), pp. 40–45.

   One study reported that the leader's (supervisor's) access to information and leader (supervisor) selection processes influence group discussion and decision quality. See David D. Henningsen, Mary Lynn Miller Henningsen, and Ian Bolton, "It's Good to Be Leader: The Influence of Randomly and Systematically Selected Leaders on Decision-Making Groups," *Group Dynamics: Theory, Research, and Practice*, 8, 1 (2004), pp. 96–111. Also see Michael Roberto, *Why Great Leaders*

Don't Take Yes for an Answer (Philadelphia, PA: Wharton School Publishing, 2005).

10. For guides to creating a more efficient and productive workforce, see T. L. Stanley, "The Best Management Ideas are Timeless," *Supervision*, 65, 6 (June 2004), pp. 9–11. Also see Charles W. Prather and Lisa K. Gundry, *Blueprints for Innovation: How Creative Processes Can Make You and Your Company More Competitive* (New York: American Management Association, 1995); Oren Harari, "Turn Your Organization into a Hotbed of Ideas," *Management Review* (December 1995), pp. 37–39; Ralph D. Stacey, *Complexity and Creativity in Organizations* (San Francisco: Berrett-Koehler Publishers, 1996).

11. In the wake of numerous business scandals, many job seekers and recent hires are now more concerned about whether their employers have high ethical standards and practices. See David T. Ozar, "The Gold Standard for Ethical Education and Effective Decision Making in Healthcare Organizations," *Organizational Ethics: Healthcare, Business, and Policy*, 1, 1 (Spring 2004), pp. 58–63.

    See also Kris Maher, "Wanted: Ethical Employer," *The Wall Street Journal* (July 9, 2002), pp. B1, B8. For a study of various socio-demographic, personal, and other factors influencing ethical decision making, see Irene Roozen, Patrick DePelsmacker, and Frank Bostyn, "The Ethical Dimensions of Decision Processes of Employees," *Journal of Business Ethics* (September, 2001), pp. 87–99.

12. See William I. Sauser, Jr., "Business Ethics: Back to the Basics," *SAM Advanced Management Journal*, 2, (2005), pp. 1–4.

13. For excellent discussions on both the theory and practice of sound business ethics, see T. J. Stanley, "Ethics in Action," *Supervision*, 69, 4 (April 2008), pp. 14–16; Archie B. Carroll and Ann L. Buchholtz, *Business and Society: Ethics and Stakeholder Management,* 7th ed. (Mason, OH: South-Western, 2009); Joseph W. Weiss, *Business Ethics: Stakeholder & Issues Management*, 4th ed. (Mason, OH: South-Western, 2006); David Mayer, et al., "How Low Does Ethical Leadership Flow?—Test of a Trickle-Down Model," (Matwah, N.J.: *O.B. and Human Decision Process*, online 17 June 2008. www.elsevier.com); and Lisa H. Harter and David P. Schmidt, *Wake Up Call—Classic Cases in Business Ethics*, 2nd ed. (Mason, OH: South-Western, 2004).

14. Some management theorists distinguish between the terms *risk* and *uncertainty* in decision making. According to Stephen Robbins, risk involves conditions in which the decision maker can estimate the likelihood of certain alternatives occurring, usually based on historical data or other information that enables the decision maker to assign probabilities to each proposed alternative. Uncertainty involves a condition in which the decision maker has no reasonable probability estimates available and can only "guesstimate" the likelihood of various alternatives or outcomes. See Stephen P. Robbins, *Managing Today*, 2nd ed. (Upper Saddle River, NJ: Prentice-Hall, 2000), pp. 64–65.

15. See J. G. March and H. A. Simon, *Organizations* (New York: John Wiley & Sons, 1958), pp. 10–12. Herbert Simon developed the normative model of decision making to identify the process that managers actually use in making decisions. As opposed to the rational decision model illustrated in Figure 5.2, Simon's normative model is characterized by limited information processing, the use of rules of thumb (intuition) or shortcuts, and satisficing.

16. See Jones Loflin and Todd Musig, *Juggling Elephants – An Easier Way to Get Your Most Important Things Done Now!* (New York: Portfolio, 2008). Life is a three ring circus: work, relationships, and self. You need to be a ringmaster and you can only be in one ring at a time. Also see Russ Holloman, "The Light and Dark Sides of Decision Making," *Supervisory Management* (December 1989), pp. 33–34. For a recap of the problem-solving approach, see William W. Hull, "What's the Problem?" *Supervision*, 65, 5 (May 2004), pp. 5–7.

17. See Jim Perrone, "Moving from Telling to Empowering," *Healthcare Executive* (September/October 2001), pp. 60–61.

18. The guidelines were adapted from Robert Kreitner and Angelo Kinicki, *Organizational Behavior*, 3rd ed. (Homewood, IL: Richard D. Irwin, 1995), pp. 312–13. Also see their 8th edition (New York: McGraw-Hill, 2008); and Kreitner, *Management* 11th edition (Mason, OH: Cengage Learning), Chapter 8.

19. For a general overview of several quantitative approaches to decision making, see Ricky W. Griffin, *Management* (Boston: Houghton-Mifflin, 2006), pp. 702–21. For a comprehensive discussion of problem solving and decision making that includes a number of applied quantitative models and examples, see William J. Altier, *The Thinking Manager's Toolbox: Effective Processes for Problem Solving and Decision Making* (New York: Oxford University Press, 1999); and G. Strasser, "Computer Simulation as a Research Tool: The DISCUSS Model of Group Decision Making," *Journal of Social Psychology*, 24 (1988), pp. 393–422.

CHAPTER 6

(**Positive Discipline**)

After studying this chapter, you will be able to:

1 Discuss the basis and importance of positive discipline in an organization.

2 Identify disciplinary situations that violate standards of conduct and discuss the need to confront those situations appropriately.

3 Discuss the disciplinary process and approaches that ensure disciplinary action for just (proper) cause.

4 Define and discuss the application of progressive discipline.

5 Explain the "hot stove rule" approach to discipline.

6 Discuss the need to document disciplinary actions and to provide the right of appeal.

7 Explain the "discipline without punishment" approach as an alternative to progressive discipline.

8 Describe the importance of "fairness" in the disciplinary process.

YOU MAKE THE CALL!

Bernie Collins was director of marketing for Software-n-Mor. Software-n-Mor was a major computer software, supplies, and services firm. The company had recently experienced tough financial times. As a result, there had been layoffs of employees, and several software development projects had been outsourced to India. Several supervisory positions were consolidated and the surviving supervisors were assigned additional duties and a broadened span of control. Virtually everyone felt stressed from seeing colleagues depart and having to do more in the same amount of time.

Don Williams, supervisor of customer service, was articulate and had a dry sense of humor. He could be counted on for occasional practical jokes, and he was non-discriminating in his targets. Williams decided he would create a humorous blog to try and boost morale. He expected that other employees would use Twitter (a free social networking and micro-blogging service to add updates) to vent their frustrations. He developed "The Chopping Block—Software-no-more." A few of the quotes posted from his office computer follow:

Question: Rich, what is your reaction to the loss of your beloved supervisor, Karen Kates?

Response: Ding dong, the witch is gone!

Question: Jackie, how do you like taking on the responsibilities of the parts department while continuing to supervise the testing lab?

Response: My boss, Dave Kohenski, gave me a half-hour pep talk, and I was up to speed and on top of things at the end of the morning.

Question: Ahmed in India, how you feel about our fearless leader's new motto, "Do more work for less money?"

Response: We feel that our president, Bob Swan, can teach us the true meaning of the motto, since he has lived it since birth.

Williams also printed copies of the blog (with instructions on how to add to it or use Twitter) and posted them as an email attachment sent to selected employees. By mid-morning, several employees had added their comments and updates were posted in the break room. It was the talk of the company, and everyone was laughing—that is, everyone but the company president, Bob Swan,

Swan contacted Jean Mane, director of human resources, and asked her to arrange a meeting with Don Williams and his immediate supervisor, Bernie Collins. Swan told Mane he was deeply concerned about the offensive remarks on the blog. He stressed that this type of so-called humor was unacceptable. If carried to extremes, it could result in lawsuits by individuals who felt they were being ridiculed or defamed.

Later that day, Don Williams was summoned to Jean Mane's office. Collins was present when Williams arrived. Mane said, "Don, this serious. You didn't exercise good supervisory judgment. Other supervisors and employees have been fired for less than this." Collins told Jean Mane that the increased workload had everyone feeling stressed out—that everyone needed a good laugh! If Williams was disciplined, it would alienate all the other employees. "Yes, his humor was a bit sarcastic, but compared to what other employees were saying in private and on the blog, what Don said was mild!"

Williams added, "People have a right to speak their mind—the first amendment gives us that right." Jean Mane asked Don to leave so that she and Collins could discuss the matter further. As Don left the room, Collins pondered what action, if any, should be taken. **YOU MAKE THE CALL!**

The Basis and Importance of Positive Discipline

The term *discipline* is used in several different ways. Many supervisors associate discipline with the use of authority, force, or punishment. In this text, however, we consider **discipline** as a condition of orderliness, that is, the degree to which members of an organization act properly and observe the expected standards of behavior. **Positive discipline** exists when employees generally follow the rules and meet the standards of the organization. Discipline is negative, or bad, when employees follow organizational rules reluctantly or when they disobey regulations and violate prescribed standards of acceptable behavior.

As Chapter 12 discusses, **morale** is a composite of the attitudes and feelings that people have toward their work, whereas discipline is primarily a state of mind. However, there is some relationship between morale and discipline.

Discipline
State of orderliness; the degree to which employees act according to expected standards of behavior

Positive discipline
Condition that exists when employees generally follow the organization's rules and meet the organization's standards

Morale
A composite of feelings and attitudes that individuals and groups of workers have toward their work environment

Positive self-discipline
Employees regulating their behavior out of self-interest and their normal desire to meet reasonable standards

Normally, there are fewer disciplinary problems when morale is high; conversely, low morale is usually accompanied by a higher number of disciplinary problems. However, a high degree of positive discipline could be present despite low morale; this could result from insecurity, fear, or sheer force. It is unlikely, however, that a high degree of positive employee discipline will be maintained indefinitely unless there is an acceptable level of employee morale.

The best type of discipline is **positive self-discipline**, in which employees essentially regulate themselves out of self-interest. This type of discipline is based on the normal human tendency to do what needs to be done, to do one's share, and to follow reasonable standards of acceptable behavior. Even before they start to work, most people accept the idea that following instructions and fair rules of conduct are normal responsibilities of any job.

Positive self-discipline relies on the premise that most employees want to do the right thing and can be counted on to exercise self-control. They believe in performing their work properly; coming to work on time; following the supervisor's instructions; and refraining from fighting, using drugs, drinking liquor, or stealing. They know it is natural to subordinate some of their personal interests to the needs of the organization. As long as company rules are communicated and are perceived as reasonable, most employees will observe those rules.

POSITIVE EMPLOYEE DISCIPLINE REQUIRES SUPERVISORY EXAMPLE

Unfortunately, there are always some employees who, for one reason or another, fail to observe established rules and standards, even after they have been informed of them. Employee theft from employers nationwide amounts to billions of dollars of loss annually.[1] When added to other forms of employee dishonesty, including habitual misuse or "stealing" of company time by unwarranted absenteeism and tardiness, doing personal business, and socializing on company time, the cost of employee theft, fraud, and abuse in U.S. businesses was estimated to be in the range of $650 billion in 2006. The Association of Certified Fraud Examiners (AFCE) reported that owners, executives, and managers committed 60.5 percent of reported fraud.[2]

Do employees care if the boss sees what's on their computer screens? It is estimated that employees spend at least two hour a day or more on non-work-related Internet abuse and misuse.[3] All of us know coworkers who use e-mail and the Internet at work for personal reasons. Look at the person sitting next to you in class—are they concentrating on the lecture, playing games or text messaging their friends? Do you know of anyone who receives inappropriate transmissions, such as pornography and sexist and racist materials, at work or at school?

Today, it is legal for an employer to use electronic devices to monitor employees. Not all companies that monitor their employees let them in on the secret during training or orientation. Most employers are monitoring employees' emails. Further, an estimated 64 percent of companies surveyed have adopted policies to monitor or restrict employees' personal usage of the Internet.[4] Many of us believe that the employer should notify employees that surveillance devices may be used, how they are being used, and the purpose they are intended to serve. Employees also should be assured that any information learned from such surveillance will be kept confidential.

Stellar Internet Monitoring LLC, among others, sells a web-based application that tracks employee Internet use to the tenth of a second. Via the Internet, your boss can log on from anywhere, and pull up graphs detailing the time you dedicated to business-related tasks, eBay, eTrade, Facebook, MySpace, or porn

FIGURE 6.1 Self-discipline must exist at the supervisory level before it exists at the employee level

sites. Not surprisingly, employees can purchase a StealthSurfer that allows them to cloak their surfing and e-mail activities from workplace monitoring systems such as Stellar's.[5]

Despite such unfortunate statistics, supervisors should maintain a balanced perspective since employees at the departmental level will take most of their cues for self-discipline from their supervisors and managers (see Figure 6.1). Ideally, positive self-discipline should exist throughout the management team, beginning at the top and extending through all supervisors. Supervisors should not expect their employees to practice positive self-discipline if they themselves do not set good examples. As we have stated several times previously, a supervisor's actions and behavior are easy targets for employees to either emulate or reject. Further, if the supervisor can encourage the vast majority of employees in the department to show a strong sense of self-discipline, those employees usually will exert group pressure on the dissenters. For example, if a no-smoking rule is posted for a building, usually someone in the work group will enforce this rule by reminding smokers to leave the premises before lighting a cigarette. As a result, the need for corrective action by the supervisor is reduced when most employees practice positive self-discipline. Oren Harari, a professor and management consultant, has commented that good employee discipline mostly depends on the supervisor's daily behavior and on decisions being aligned in the same positive direction and with consistency of actions. He states, "Discipline is the daily grind that makes things happen and lets people know that you're worthy of your word. In short, it's about honor and integrity."[6]

Identifying and Confronting Disciplinary Situations

Because individuals do not always agree on what are acceptable standards of conduct, top-level managers must define the standards for supervisors and employees. In many companies, standards are defined in statements of ethical codes and rules of conduct.

2 Identify disciplinary situations that violate standards of conduct and discuss the need to confront those situations appropriately.

ETHICAL CODES AND POLICIES

In Chapter 1, we discussed ethical considerations, and in the preceding chapter, we introduced ethical tests and guidelines for decision making. We mentioned that many organizations have developed statements of ethical standards or ethical codes. Such codes usually outline in broad, value-oriented terms the norms and ideals that are supposed to guide everyone in the organization. Figure 6.2 is an example of a statement of values and code of ethics. The seven principles of this code are expanded on in a policy manual that guides employees concerning the meaning of those principles and the importance of complying with them.

A code of ethics alone does not ensure ethical conduct. Some codes are documents that primarily outline legal requirements and restrictions, and they provide only limited guidance for solving moral and ethical dilemmas at work. Have you ever observed workplace conduct that was unlawful or that violated

---

FIGURE 6.2 A corporate values and code of ethics statement

OUR CORE VALUES

While Darden benefits from an industry that has strong long-term prospects and we employ terrific people, operate outstanding restaurant companies, follow a clear strategy, and enjoy excellent financial strength, we know we cannot be successful without an unmistakable sense of who we are. That's why we understand and appreciate our Core Values that have been forged over our more than 60-year history stated by our founder, Bill Darden. As we continue the journey to become the best casual dining company, we will look to these values for guidance and know they will be especially critical when we're faced with unexpected opportunities or challenges.

As an organization, we value:

- **Integrity and fairness**. It all starts with integrity. We trust in the integrity and fairness of each other to always do the right thing, to be open, honest, and forthright with ourselves and others, to demonstrate courage, to solve without blame and to follow through on all our commitments.

- **Respect and caring**. We reach out with respect and caring. We have a genuine interest in the well-being of others. We know the importance of listening, the power of understanding, and the immeasurable value of support.

- **Diversity**. Even though we have a common vision, we embrace and celebrate our individual differences. We are strengthened by a diversity of cultures, perspectives, attitudes, and ideas. We honor each other's heritage and uniqueness. Our power of diversity makes a world of difference.

- **Always learning—always teaching**. We learn from others as they learn from us. We learn. We teach. We grow.

- **Being "of service."** Being of service is our pleasure. We treat people as special and appreciated by giving of ourselves, doing more than expected, anticipating needs, and making a difference.

- **Teamwork**. Teamwork works. By trusting one another, we bring together the best in all of us and go beyond the boundaries of ordinary success.

- **Excellence**. We have a passion to set and to pursue, with innovation, courage, and humility, ever higher standards.

- *Our Core Values communicate the behaviors and attitudes we cherish as we strive to deliver on Darden's Core Purpose. That's what motivates us to be the best.*

Darden's Core Purpose: "To nourish and delight everyone we serve." Used here with permission of Darden Restaurants, Orlando, Florida (July 2008).

the employer's standards of ethical business conduct? If so, you are not alone. Have you or do you know of someone who has been pressured at times by other employees or managers to compromise their organization's business ethics standards to achieve business objectives? What did you do about it? If you observed a manger or another top-level employee turn their eyes and ears away from "what is right," what message did they send to all the other employees?

Because ethical standards and ethical behavior can be interpreted in varying ways, some firms have developed their ethical codes and policies with major input from teams of employees and supervisors. Further, some major firms have established hotlines or ethics-reporting systems by which employees are encouraged to report questionable situations or individuals who they believe are acting unethically, improperly, or illegally. These firms may have a "corporate ombudsman" who investigates the allegations and takes appropriate action. The person who reported the alleged wrongdoing, usually called a "whistleblower," should be afforded anonymity. There is supposed to be no retaliation, regardless of whether the report is substantiated by facts and evidence.[7] In this regard, it is generally recognized that a hotline or an ethics-reporting system requires top-level management's commitment to make the system credible, that is, both to deal firmly with wrongdoing when it is reported and, further, to prevent retaliation against a messenger who delivers an unwelcome message.[8] Of course, an unfounded or a false report with malice may require a disciplinary response by management.

In addition to the preceding tools, some firms have developed statements and policies for addressing conflicts of interest; these statements may be part of, or in addition to, ethical codes. Conflict-of-interest statements usually define situations and employee behaviors that are inconsistent with an individual's primary obligations to the employer. Figure 6.3 is an excerpt from one firm's statement on conflicts of interest. In the final analysis, a firm's commitment to high standards of ethical behavior must go far beyond just codes and policy statements. An ethical commitment requires everyone in the organization, especially those in management and supervision, to show daily, by word and deed, that behaving

---

FIGURE 6.3 Excerpt From a Conflict-of-Interest Policy Statement

CONFLICTS OF INTEREST

- Employees are duty bound and obligated to act—at all times—in the best lawful and ethical interests of the company.

- Employees are specifically prohibited from using their positions with the company for personal gain, favor, or advantage. For example, this specifically prohibits any unauthorized or personal use of official stationery; news-release masthead; logo; or any other forms, labels, envelopes, and so on bearing the name or logo of the company or any of its subsidiaries.

- Employees are expected to avoid relationships that might interfere with the proper and efficient discharge of their duties or that might be inconsistent with their obligations of loyalty to the company. For example, if an employee, a close relative, or any other person with whom the employee has a close personal relationship has a financial interest in an organization that does business or competes with the company, a conflict of interest may exist. Also, there may be a conflict if an employee or a close relative or any other person with whom the employee has a close personal relationship engages in certain transactions with; renders services to; or accepts payments, loans, or gifts from the company, vendors, contractors, or competitors.

ethically at work is not optional. There is ample evidence that good ethics means good business, which was stated eloquently by Nicholas Moore, retired Global Chair of PricewaterhouseCoopers (PwC), as follows:

> *When companies stand up for what's right, day in and day out, it has a positive impact. Positive in terms of whom it attracts, because good people want to work in ethical environments. It simplifies decision making. We know what we won't even think about doing. And, in the process, we earn the respect of our competitors, our clients, and our people. In the long term, that's very, very important. So ethical behavior is at the core of the way we do business, and it's the only way we're going to do business.*[9]

RULES OF CONDUCT

Not every organization has a published code of ethics or conflict-of-interest statement. However, virtually every large firm, and probably most other firms and organizations, have some formal statements or lists of rules of behavior to which employees are expected to conform.

In Chapter 7, we discuss the need for policies, procedures, methods, and rules to cover many aspects of ongoing operations. These tools are vital in informing employees which standards of behavior are expected and which behaviors are unacceptable.

Most organizations give their employees written lists of rules or codes of conduct. These lists are sometimes included in employee handbooks; sometimes they are provided as separate booklets or as memoranda posted in departments. Supervisors must ensure that employees read and understand general and departmental rules, which may include safety and technical regulations, depending on a department's activity.

Written rules and regulations provide a common basis and standards that should help the supervisor encourage employee self-discipline. Some organizations provide very detailed lists of rules and infractions; these lists may include classifications of the likely penalties for violations. Other organizations, probably most, prefer to list their major rules and regulations but not the consequences of rule violations. Such a list appears in Figure 6.4. Regardless of what type of list is used, the supervisor is the person most responsible for the consistent application and enforcement of company and departmental rules. In fact, the degree to which employees follow corporate rules in a positive, self-disciplined way is usually more attributable to the supervisor's role and example than to any other factor.

Rules of conduct and policy statements in employee handbooks and manuals are often subject to review and change because of legal problems and interpretations. While the review and revision of employee handbooks are usually the responsibility of human resources staff, supervisors should be very familiar with the content of employee handbooks. Supervisors should not hesitate to suggest revisions when those revisions appear justified.[10]

Confronting Disciplinary Situations

Despite their best efforts to prevent infractions, supervisors will at times confront situations requiring some type of disciplinary action. The following require immediate action by the supervisor:

- Infractions of rules regarding time schedules, rest periods, procedures, safety, and so forth.
- Excessive absenteeism or tardiness.

FIGURE 6.4 Partial List of One Company's Rules and Regulations

COMPANY RULES AND REGULATIONS

The efficient operation of our plants and the general welfare of our employees require certain uniform standards of behavior. Accordingly, the following offenses are considered violations of these standards. Employees who refuse to accept this guidance subject themselves to appropriate disciplinary action.

- Habitual tardiness and absenteeism
- Theft or attempted theft of company or another employee's property
- Fighting or attempting bodily injury upon another employee
- Horseplay, malicious mischief, or any other conduct affecting the rights of other employees
- Intoxication or drinking on the job or being in a condition that makes it impossible to perform work satisfactorily
- Refusal or failure to perform assigned work or refusal or failure to comply with supervisory instructions
- Inattention to duties; carelessness in performance of duties; loafing on the job, sleeping, or reading non-work-related material during working hours
- Violation of published safety or health rules
- Possessing, consuming, selling, or being under the influence of illegal drugs on the premises
- Unauthorized possession of weapons, firearms, or explosives on the premises
- Requests for sexual favors, sexual advances, and physical conduct of a sexual nature toward another employee on the premises

- Defective or inadequate work performance.
- Poor attitudes that influence the work of others or damage the firm's public image.

A supervisor may at times experience open insubordination, such as an employee's refusal to carry out a legitimate work assignment. A supervisor may even confront disciplinary problems stemming from employee behavior off the job. For example, an employee may have a drinking problem or may be taking illegal drugs. Whenever an employee's off-the-job conduct affects on-the-job performance, the supervisor must be prepared to respond to the problem appropriately. In Chapter 12, we discuss a number of ways to help employees with personal and work-related problems.

Situations that require disciplinary action are unpleasant, but the supervisor must have the courage to deal with those situations. If the supervisor does not take action when required, borderline employees might be encouraged to try similar violations.

A supervisor should be unafraid to draw on some of the authority inherent in the supervisory position, even though it might be easier to overlook the matter or to pass the matter to higher-level managers or the human resources department. Supervisors who ask the human resources department to assume all departmental disciplinary problems shirk their responsibility and undermine their own authority.

Normally, good supervisors will have to take disciplinary action infrequently. When such action is necessary, however, the supervisor should be ready to act, no matter how unpleasant the task may be.

Every supervisor will confront situations that require some type of disciplinary action

The Disciplinary Process and Just Cause

Supervisors must initiate any disciplinary action with sensitivity and sound judgment. The purpose of disciplinary action should not be to punish or to seek revenge but to improve employees' behavior. In other words, the primary purpose of disciplinary action is to prevent similar infractions. In this text, we do not consider directly those situations in which union contracts may restrict the supervisor's ability to take disciplinary action. The ideas discussed here apply generally to most unionized and non-unionized organizations.

DISCIPLINARY ACTION SHOULD HAVE JUST CAUSE

As discussed in Chapter 2, most employers accept the general premise that disciplinary action taken against an employee should be based on "just cause." Generally, to be viewed as "just," the disciplinary action must consider all the facts in the individual case and be consistent with past practice. Figure 6.5 lists eight questions arbitrators ask in union/management disciplinary-type grievance matters. A "no" answer to one or more of these questions means that the just cause standard was not fully met. As a result, the arbitrator or court might set aside or modify management's disciplinary action.

The preponderance of labor-union contracts specify a just-cause or proper cause standard for discipline and discharge. Similarly, many cases decided by government agencies and by the courts have required employers to prove that disciplinary actions taken against legally protected employees (discussed in Chapter 13) were not discriminatory but were for just cause. Even under various forms of alternative dispute resolution (ADR) (discussed in Chapter 15), a just-cause standard, or something approximating it, typically is applied in resolving disciplinary case matters.[11] For a number of years, some U.S. government offices

---

FIGURE 6.5 Eight Tests for Just Cause

EIGHT TESTS FOR JUST CAUSE

1. Did the company give the employee forewarning of the possible or probable disciplinary consequences of the employee's behavior? (Give Advance Warning)

2. Was the company's rule or managerial order reasonably related to (a) the orderly, efficient, and safe operation of the company's business and (b) the performance the company might properly expect of the employee? (Clarify Expectations—Everyone Needs to Know the Rules of the Game)

3. Did the company, before administering discipline to an employee, make an effort to discover whether the employee did, in fact, violate or disobey a rule or an order of management? (Investigate Immediately)

4. Was the company's investigation conducted fairly and objectively? (Be Objective)

5. After investigation, was there substantial evidence or proof that the employee was guilty as charged? (Analyze the Evidence)

6. Has the company applied its rules, orders, and penalties evenhandedly and without discrimination? (Be Consistent, Uniform, and Impersonal)

7. Was the degree of discipline administered by the company in a particular case reasonably related to (a) the seriousness of the employee's proven offense and (b) the record of the employee's service with the company? (Punishment in Relation to the Offense)

8. Has the company kept records of the offense committed, the evidence, and the decision made, including the reasoning involved in the decision? *(Cover Your Rear—Be Sure to Document Specifically the Who, What, Where, When, Why and How)*

Source: Presented here with permission from Edwin C. Leonard, Jr., and Roy A. Cook, *Human Resource Management: 21st Century Challenges* (Thomson, 2005), p. 133. Seven tests were originally adapted from a list suggested by arbitrator Carroll R. Daugherty. They are included in many texts and arbitral citations.

---

have used a mandatory alternative dispute-resolution system, and there have been legislative proposals to extend mandatory ADR for certain types of disputes in both the public and private sectors.[12] If this should take place, it would seem almost certain that a just-cause standard would prevail throughout most firms and organizations. Although the ramifications of a just-cause standard for disciplinary action can be rather complicated, the guidelines presented in this chapter are consistent with the principles and requirements needed to justify any disciplinary or discharge action. The supervisor who follows these guidelines conscientiously should be able to meet a just-cause standard, regardless of whether the case involves a unionized firm, a nonunionized organization, or a potential area of legal discrimination.[13]

PRECAUTIONARY QUESTIONS AND MEASURES

As a first consideration in any disciplinary situation, a supervisor should guard against undue haste or unwarranted action based on emotional response. A supervisor should answer and follow a number of precautionary questions and measures before deciding on any disciplinary action in response to an employee's alleged offense.

INVESTIGATE THE SITUATION

Before doing anything else, the supervisor should investigate what happened and why. The questions in the accompanying "Supervisory Tips" box can serve as a checklist as supervisors consider what to do.

SUPERVISORY TIPS

Checklist of Questions to Ask During a Disciplinary Investigation

1. Are all or most of the facts available, and are they reported accurately? That is, can the alleged offense be proved by direct or circumstantial evidence, or is the allegation based merely on suspicion?

2. How serious is the offense (minor, major, or intolerable)? Were others involved in or affected by the offense? Were company funds or equipment involved?

3. Did the employee know the rule or standard? Does the employee have a reasonable excuse, and are there any extenuating circumstances?

4. What is the employee's disciplinary record, length of service, and performance level? Does the offense indicate carelessness, absentmindedness, or loss of temper? How does this employee react to criticism?

5. Should the employee receive the same treatment others have had for the same offense? If not, is it possible to establish a basis for differentiating the present alleged offense from past offenses of a similar nature?

6. Is all the necessary documentation available in case the matter leads to outside review?

For certain gross violations, such as stealing, illegal substance use, and violence, an organization may call in law-enforcement authorities to investigate and take appropriate action. Some firms employ consultants to administer polygraph tests in an effort to determine who committed the violations, particularly in matters involving theft. Polygraph use, however, has been restricted by a 1988 federal law. This statute prohibits random polygraph testing but permits an employer with "reasonable suspicion" of employee wrongdoing to use a polygraph if certain safeguards are met. Supervisors, for the most part, do not decide to use a polygraph; such a decision is made by someone in higher-level management or on the human resources staff after consultation with legal counsel. There may even be situations in which it is decided that investigation of possible wrongdoing requires some form of personnel surveillance. An outside private investigator may be hired to conduct electronic surveillance or perhaps become part of the workplace as an undercover "employee." The supervisor may or may not be informed that such surveillance is taking place.[14] However, federal regulations require employees to notify workers if the company intends to have an outside party investigate or probe alleged workplace or other wrongdoings. Such disclosure is required if an inquiry could lead to an adverse decision against an employee, such as discipline, termination, or job movement.[15]

When an employee is injured on the job, many firms require the employee to take a drug-and-alcohol screening test. Such tests usually are given by a qualified person in the firm's first-aid room or by someone at an occupational-health clinic where the employee is treated. Safeguards concerning employee privacy and test result validation usually are followed although the results may be used as part of management's investigation and decision-making process.[16]

INVESTIGATORY INTERVIEWS

As part of the supervisor's investigation of an alleged infraction, it may be necessary to question the employee involved as well as other employees who may have relevant information. In general, such interviews should be conducted privately and individually, perhaps with a guarantee of confidentiality. These situations are usually less threatening to employees who may otherwise be reluctant to tell what they know. Such situations also help prevent employees from being unduly influenced by another's version or interpretation.

If a union employee is to be interviewed concerning a disciplinary matter, that employee may ask that a union representative or coworker be present during the interview. Normally, the supervisor should grant such a request. Under federal labor law (the Weingarten rights), a union employee has the right to have a union representative present during an investigatory interview if the employee reasonably believes the investigation may lead to disciplinary action.[17] However, a union representative or coworker cannot disrupt an investigatory interview or answer questions for the employee under investigation. Of course, if the employee is to have a witness present, the supervisor is well advised to have a fellow supervisor present to serve as a supervisory witness to the interview.

Occasionally, a nonunion employee will ask that a fellow worker or another supervisory witness be present during an investigatory interview. Recent court decisions have generally extended to nonunionized employees the right to have coworkers present in investigatory interviews that may lead to discipline. When faced with such a request, the supervisor should probably consult with the human resources department or a higher-level manager for guidance. Normally, such a request should be granted, but there may be reasons such a request should be denied and/or the interview voided.[18]

Most of the principles of interviewing and effective communication discussed throughout this text apply to investigatory interviewing. The supervisor should ask both directive and nondirective questions that are designed to elicit specific answers about what happened and why. Above all, the supervisor should avoid making final judgments until all interviews have been conducted and other relevant information assembled.

MAINTAINING SELF-CONTROL

Regardless of the severity of an employee's violation, a supervisor must maintain self-control. This does not mean a supervisor should face a disciplinary situation halfheartedly or indifferently, but if supervisors feel in danger of losing control of their tempers or emotions, those supervisors should delay the investigatory interviews and take no action until they regain control. A supervisor's loss of self-control or display of anger could compromise fair and objective judgment.

Generally, a supervisor should never lay a hand on an employee in any way. Except for emergencies, when an employee has been injured or becomes ill, or when employees who are fighting must be separated, any physical gesture could easily be misunderstood. A supervisor who engages in physical violence, except in self-defense, normally is subject to disciplinary action by higher-level management.

PRIVACY IN DISCIPLINING

When supervisors decide on disciplinary actions, they should communicate those actions to the offending employees in private. A public reprimand not only can humiliate the employee in the eyes of coworkers but also can erode department morale or inspire a grievance. If, in the opinion of other employees, a public disciplinary action is too severe for the violation, the disciplined employee might emerge as a martyr.

Unionized employees who believe that a meeting might result in disciplinary action have the right to union representation. If the employee's Weingarten rights are violated and he or she is fired, they will usually be reinstated with back pay and allowances. At the present time, these rights have not been extended to non-unionized employees. However, I have learned through experience that it is always desirable to have another management person present (e.g., the supervisor, the supervisor's superior, and perhaps the human resources director) to witness any discussion that might require corrective action. It is also essential that the witness confirm the discussion and actions that took place. In a litigious society it is most important to "cover your rear" (CYR).

Only under extreme circumstances should disciplinary action be taken in public. For example, a supervisor's authority may be challenged directly and openly by an employee who repeatedly refuses to carry out a reasonable work request, or an employee may be drunk or fighting on the job. In these cases, the supervisor must reach a disciplinary decision quickly (e.g., send the offending employee home on suspension pending further investigation). Supervisors may have to act in the presence of other employees to regain control of situations and to maintain their respect.

DISCIPLINARY TIME ELEMENT

When a supervisor decides to impose discipline, the question arises as to how long the violation should be held against the offending employee. Generally, minor or intermediate offenses should be disregarded after a year or so has elapsed since those offenses were committed. Therefore, an employee with a record of defective work might be given a "clean bill of health" by subsequently compiling a good record for six months or one year. Some companies have adopted "point systems" to cover certain infractions, especially absenteeism and tardiness. Employees can have points removed from their records if they have perfect or acceptable attendance during later periods.

In some situations, time is of no importance. For example, if an employee is caught brandishing a knife in a heated argument at work, the supervisor need not worry about the punishment period or previous offenses. Such an act is serious enough to warrant immediate discharge.

---

4 **Define and discuss the application of progressive discipline.**

Progressive discipline
System of disciplinary action that increases the severity of the penalty with each offense

Practicing Progressive Discipline

Unless a serious violation, such as stealing, physical violence, or gross insubordination, has been committed, rarely is the offending employee discharged for a first offense. Although the type of disciplinary action varies according to the situation, many organizations practice **progressive discipline**, which increases the severity of the penalty with each offense. The following stages compose a system of progressive disciplinary action:

- Informal discussion with the employee. (At this stage and subsequent stages, place documentation of discussion in the employee's file, including the reason for discussion; the date and time of discussion and who was present; and how the employee was strongly encouraged to modify his or her behavior.)
- Oral warning including counseling.
- Written warning.
- Disciplinary layoff. (Suspension without pay, usually for one to three days. The more serious the infraction, the longer the suspension.)
- Transfer or demotion.
- Discharge. (Very serious infractions may warrant termination in the first and only step.)
- Figure 6.6 details a company's progressive discipline policy and Figure 6.7 illustrates its use.

EARLY STAGES IN PROGRESSIVE DISCIPLINE

Many disciplinary situations can be handled solely or primarily by the supervisor without escalating those situations to difficult confrontations. In the early stages of progressive discipline, the supervisor communicates with the employee about the problem and how to correct it.

INFORMAL DISCUSSION

If the offense is relatively minor and the employee has no disciplinary record, a friendly and informal talk will clear up the problem in many cases. During this talk, the supervisor should try to determine the underlying reasons for

FIGURE 6.6 A Hospital's Progressive Disciplinary Policy

CORRECTIVE ACTION POLICY

Corrective action shall progress from verbal counseling to written reprimand, suspension, and termination. All actions shall reference the policy or procedure that has been violated, the adverse consequence resulting from the violation, the type of behavior expected in the future, and the corrective action that will be taken if further violations occur. A copy of the completed corrective action form shall be given to the employee.

Following are guidelines for the corrective action procedure:

- **Verbal counseling**—Verbal counseling shall be given for all minor violations of hospital rules and policies. More than two verbal counseling sessions in the past 12-month period regarding violations of any rules or policies warrants a written reprimand.

- **Written reprimand**—Written reprimands shall be given for repeated minor infractions or for first-time occurrences of more serious offenses. Written reprimands shall be documented on the "Notice of Corrective Action" form, which is signed by the department head or supervisor and the employee.

- **Suspension**—An employee shall be suspended without pay for one to four scheduled working days for a critical or major offense or for repeated minor or serious offenses.

- **Termination**—An employee may be terminated for repeated violations of hospital rules and regulations or for first offenses of a critical nature.

the employee's unacceptable conduct. At the same time, the supervisor should reaffirm the employee's sense of responsibility and acknowledge previous good behavior. Regardless of the offense, the supervisor should record the "date, place, time and nature" of the incident. If others witnessed the incident, their names also should be noted. See Figure 6.8 for an illustration of the type of information the supervisor should record.

FIGURE 6.7 A disciplinary-action program often begins with informal talk. With repeated offenses, penalties become more severe

FIGURE 6.8 Supervisors should record information on a regular basis. We suggest you begin with a blank sheet of paper and answer the following questions

Employee's Name _____ Time _____ Location _____
Date_____
Who else was present and witnessed the behavior?
_____
Specific policy violation_____
Behavior that needs correcting _____
Mitigating circumstances, if any? _____
Has this happened before? _____
Corrective action to be taken by employee _____
Deadline for corrective behavior _____
Follow-up meeting to be held on _____
Consequences if behavior is not corrected _____

ORAL WARNING

If a friendly talk does not take care of the situation, the next step is to give the employee an oral warning (sometimes known as verbal counseling). Here the supervisor emphasizes in a straightforward manner the undesirability of the employee's repeated violation. While the supervisor should stress the preventive purpose of discipline, the supervisor also should emphasize that unless the employee improves, more serious disciplinary action will be taken. In some organizations, a record of this oral warning is made in the employee's file. Alternatively, the supervisor may simply write a brief note in a supervisory logbook to document that an oral warning was given on a particular date. This can be important evidence if the employee commits another infraction.

At times, a supervisor may believe that the substance of verbal counseling should be put in writing so that the message is documented and, more likely, is impressed on the employee. In such a situation, the supervisor may resort to what is called a letter of clarification. Such a letter should clearly state that it is not a formal disciplinary document and that its primary purpose is to reiterate to the employee what was communicated verbally by the supervisor. In general, letters of clarification tend to apply most often when dealing with minor employee infractions in the early stages of progressive discipline.[19] If oral warnings and letters of clarification are carried out skillfully, many employees will respond and improve at this stage. The employee must understand that improvement is expected and that the supervisor believes the employee can improve and is ready to help the employee do so.

WRITTEN WARNING

A written warning contains a statement of the violation and the potential consequences of future violations. It is a formal document that becomes a permanent part of the employee's record. The supervisor should review with the employee the nature of this written warning and should once again stress the need for improvement. The employee should be placed on notice that future infractions or unacceptable conduct will lead to more serious discipline, such as suspension or discharge.

Written warnings are particularly necessary in unionized organizations because they can serve as evidence in grievance procedures. Such documentation also is important if the employee is a member of a legally protected group. The employee usually receives a duplicate copy of the written warning, and another copy is sent to the human resources department. Figure 6.9 is a written warning used by a supermarket chain. This form even provides space for the supervisor to note if the employee refuses to sign it.

Even at this stage in the disciplinary process, the supervisor should continue to express to the employee a belief in the employee's ability to improve and the supervisor's willingness to help in whatever way possible. The primary goal of disciplinary action up until discharge should be to help the employee improve and add value.

FIGURE 6.9 Written Warning Used By a Supermarket Chain

EMPLOYEE CORRECTIVE ACTION NOTICE

Employee's name _____ Date of notice _____

JobStore Address _____ Store # _____ Dept. _____ Classification _____

This notice is a: First warning   Second warning   Third warning   Final warning
                           ☐   ☐   ☐   ☐

Reason for corrective action: (Check below)

☐ Cooperation/interest   ☐ Cash register discrepancy   ☐ Insubordination

☐ Quality/quantity of work   ☐ Dress code   ☐ Time-card
                                                                    violation

☐ Tardiness/absenteeism   ☐ Disregard for safety   ☐ Other cause(s)
                                                                    (Explain)

Explanation must accompany reason checked above:

_____

_____

_____

I HEREBY SIGNIFY THAT I HAVE RECEIVED A FULL EXPLANATION OF MY FAILURE TO PERFORM AS EXPECTED. THE COMPANY AND I UNDERSTAND THAT FURTHER FAILURE ON MY PART WILL BE DUE CAUSE FOR DISCIPLINARY ACTION UP TO, AND INCLUDING, DISCHARGE.

_____   _____   _____   _____
Employee's signature   Date   Supervisor's signature   Date

                                             _____   _____
                                             Store manager's signature   Date

REFUSAL OF EMPLOYEE TO SIGN THIS NOTICE SHOULD BE SO NOTED HEREON.

Note: Prepare original and four copies. Send original and one copy to the human resources director. Send one copy to the store manager and one copy to the employee. Retain one copy.

DISCIPLINARY LAYOFF (SUSPENSION)

Unfortunately, not every employee responds to the supervisor's counseling and warnings to improve job behavior. In progressive discipline, more serious disciplinary actions may be administered for repeated violations, with discharge being the final step.

If an employee has offended repeatedly and previous warnings were of no avail, a disciplinary layoff would probably constitute the next disciplinary step. Disciplinary layoffs involve a loss of pay and usually extend from one day to several days or weeks. Because a disciplinary layoff involves loss of pay, most organizations limit a supervisor's authority at this stage. Most supervisors can only initiate or recommend a disciplinary layoff. The layoff must then be approved by higher-level managers after consulting with the human resources department.

Employees who do not respond to oral or written warnings usually find a disciplinary layoff to be a rude awakening. The layoff may restore in them the need to comply with the organization's rules and regulations. However, managers in some organizations seldom apply layoffs as disciplinary measures. They believe that laying off trained employees will hurt their production, especially in times of labor shortages. Further, these managers reason that the laid-off employees may return in an even more unpleasant frame of mind. Despite this possibility, in many employee situations, disciplinary layoffs are an effective disciplinary measure.

TRANSFER

Transferring an employee to a job in another department typically involves no loss of pay. This disciplinary action is usually taken when an offending employee seems to be experiencing difficulty working for a particular supervisor, working in a current job, or associating with certain employees. The transfer may markedly improve the employee if the employee adjusts to the new department and the new supervisor. When transfers are made primarily to give employees a final chance to retain their jobs with the company, those employees should be told that they must improve in the new job or be subject to discharge. Of course, the supervisor who accepts the transferred employee should be informed of the circumstances surrounding the transfer. This information helps the supervisor facilitate a successful transition for the transferred employee.

DEMOTION

Another disciplinary measure, the value of which is questionable, is demotion (downgrading) to a lower-paying job. This course of action is likely to bring about dissatisfaction and discouragement because losing pay and status over an extended period is a form of ongoing punishment. The dissatisfaction of the demoted employee also can spread to other employees. Therefore, most organizations avoid demotion as a disciplinary action.

Demotion should be used only in unusual situations in which disciplinary layoff or discharge is not a better alternative. For example, when a long-service employee is not maintaining the standards of work performance required in a certain job, this employee may accept a demotion as an alternative to discharge to retain seniority and other accrued benefits.

DISCHARGE (TERMINATION)

The most drastic form of disciplinary action is discharge or termination. The discharged employee loses all seniority and may have difficulty obtaining employment elsewhere. Discharge should be reserved only for the most serious offenses and as a last resort.

A discharge involves loss and waste. It means having to train a new employee and disrupting the makeup of the work group, which may affect the morale of other employees. Moreover, in unionized companies, management becomes concerned about possible prolonged grievance and arbitration proceedings. Management knows that labor arbitrators are unwilling to sustain discharge except for severe offenses or for a series of violations that cumulatively justify the discharge. If the discharge involves an employee who is a member of a legally protected group, management will have to be concerned about meeting appropriate standards for nondiscrimination.

In this regard, slightly more than one-half of human resources professionals who responded to a survey said their firms had been named in one or more employment-related lawsuits. Overwhelmingly, these lawsuits had been filed by former employees who alleged they were terminated or discriminated against unlawfully, which led to their exit or removal from employment.[20] Because of the serious implications and consequences of discharge, many organizations have removed the discharge decision from supervisors and have reserved it for higher-level managers. Other organizations require that any discharge recommended by a supervisor must be reviewed and approved by higher-level managers or the human resources department, often with the advice of legal counsel.[21]

Because of legal and other concerns, the final termination interview with the discharged employee may be conducted by a member of the human resources department. When supervisors conduct the termination interview, however, they should be careful to focus on the reasons for the termination and to respond to the questions of the employee being terminated. The supervisor should not lose emotional control or engage in a heated debate about the fairness of the termination decision. With luck, the supervisor will be able to close the termination interview by suggesting avenues or options the discharged employee should consider for possible employment elsewhere.[22]

Generally, all of the preceding considerations should be observed, even by employers who traditionally have had the freedom to dismiss employees at will, at any time, and for any reasons, except for unlawful discrimination, union activity, or where contracts, policy manuals, or some form of employment agreements impose restrictions. This has been called **employment-at-will**, and it still is generally considered applicable from a legal point of view.[23] Figure 6.10 is an employment-at-will policy statement from a bank's employee handbook.

Employers who primarily rely on the employment-at-will principle to terminate employees may find themselves facing legal difficulties.[24] State and federal courts have found various exceptions to employment-at-will, and a number of states have passed laws or are considering legislation that would restrict the at-will relationship in employment. As stated before, most employers recognize that a discharge action should have a rational basis, such as economic necessity, or should be for just cause or

Employment-at-will
Legal concept that employers can dismiss employees at any time and for any reasons, except unlawful discrimination and contractual or other restrictions

---

FIGURE 6.10 Sample Employment-at-Will Policy From a Bank

EMPLOYMENT-AT-WILL POLICY

Citizens Bank is an at-will employer. This means that employees may resign from the bank if they choose to do so. Similarly, the bank may discharge an employee at any time, for any reason, with or without notice. Nothing in this handbook or any other policy adopted by Citizens Bank in any way alters the at-will nature of Citizens Bank employment.

The separation decision is not to be made without serious consideration by either the employer or employee. Generally, an employee choosing to leave will give appropriate notice, and discharges are not likely to occur precipitously.

at least for good cause, as it has been sometimes called.[25] When employers follow the principles of progressive disciplinary action and couple them with good supervisory practices, those employers usually do not have to resort to employment-at-will to decide whether to terminate an employee who has not performed acceptably.

5 **Explain the "hot stove rule" approach to discipline.**

Hot stove rule
Guideline for applying discipline analogous to touching a hot stove; advance warning and consequences that are immediate, consistent, and applied with impersonality

Applying the Hot Stove Rule

Taking disciplinary action may place the supervisor in a strained or difficult position. Disciplinary action is an unpleasant experience that tends to generate employee resentment. To help the supervisor apply the disciplinary measure so that it will be least resented and most likely to withstand challenges from various sources, some authorities have advocated the use of the **hot stove rule**. This rule equates touching a hot stove with experiencing discipline. Both contain the following four elements:

1. Advance warning
2. Immediacy
3. Consistency
4. Impersonality

Everyone knows what happens if they touch a red-hot stove (advance warning). Someone who touches a hot stove gets burned right away, with no questions of cause and effect (immediacy). Every time a person touches a hot stove, that person gets burned (consistency). Whoever touches a hot stove is burned because the stove treats all people the same (impersonality). The supervisor can apply these four elements of the hot stove rule when maintaining employee discipline.

ADVANCE WARNING

For employees to accept disciplinary action as fair, they must know in advance their expectations as well as rules and regulations. Employees must be informed clearly that certain acts will lead to disciplinary action. Many organizations use orientation sessions, employee handbooks, and bulletin-board announcements to tell employees about rules and how those rules are to be enforced. In addition, supervisors are responsible for clarifying any questions that arise concerning rules and their enforcement.

It is important that employees be clearly informed that certain acts will lead to disciplinary actions

Some firms print their rules in employee handbooks that all new employees receive. As part of orientation, the supervisor should explain to each new employee the departmental rules and the rules that are part of the employee handbook. We believe strongly that organizations should require employees to sign documents stating that they have (a) received, (b) read, and (c) understood the company handbook and that they are willing to comply with the rules and regulations contained therein. For example, because of the numerous legal and performance problems associated with substance abuse, many firms give their employees detailed information about the firm's policies and procedures for dealing with employees who are found to have alcohol or drugs in their systems. Such policies and procedures may specify information and warnings that spell out the firm's intentions regarding testing, treatment, and disciplinary responses, including possible termination.[26] The basic premise requires that you have written documentation to prove that the employees have been forewarned.[27] When an employee violates a company policy or when his or her behavior does not meet expectations, you note information rather than rely on your memory. Review Figures 6.8 and 6.9 for the information that you should detail in these preliminary discussions.

Unfortunately, in some organizations rules are not enforced. For example, there may be a rule prohibiting smoking in a certain area that the supervisor has not enforced. Of course, it is improper for the supervisor to suddenly decide it is time to enforce this rule strictly and to try to make an example of an employee found smoking in an unauthorized area by taking disciplinary action against that employee. That a certain rule has not been enforced does not mean it can never be enforced. To enforce such a rule, the supervisor must warn the employees that the rule will be strictly enforced from a certain point onward. It is not enough just to post a notice on a bulletin board because not all employees look at the board every day. The supervisor must issue a clear, written notice and supplement that notice with oral communication.

IMMEDIACY

After noticing an offense, the supervisor should take disciplinary action as promptly as possible. At the same time, the supervisor should avoid haste, which might lead to unwarranted reactions. The sooner the discipline is imposed, the more closely it will be connected with the offensive act.

There will be instances when it appears that an employee is guilty of a violation, but the supervisor may doubt to what degree a penalty should be imposed. For example, incidents such as fighting, intoxication, and insubordination often require immediate responses from the supervisor. In these cases, the supervisor may place the employee on temporary suspension, which means being suspended pending a final decision. Temporarily suspended employees are advised that they will be told about the disciplinary decision as soon as possible or on a specific date.

Temporary suspension in itself is not a punishment. It protects both management and the employee. It gives the supervisor time to investigate and to regain control. When an ensuing investigation indicates that no disciplinary action is warranted, the employee is recalled and suffers no loss of pay. When a disciplinary layoff is applied, the time during which the employee was temporarily suspended constitutes part of the disciplinary-layoff period. The advantage of temporary suspension is that the supervisor can act promptly, but this action should not be used indiscriminately.

CONSISTENCY

Appropriate disciplinary action should be taken each time an infraction occurs. The supervisor who feels inclined to be lenient every now and then is, in reality, doing employees no favor. Inconsistent discipline leads to employee anxiety and creates doubts as to what employees can and cannot do. This type of situation can be compared to the relations between a motorist and a traffic police officer in an area where the speed limit is enforced only occasionally. Whenever the motorist exceeds the speed limit, the motorist experiences anxiety knowing the police officer can enforce the law at any time. Most motorists would agree that it is easier to operate in areas where the police force is consistent in enforcing or not enforcing speed limits. Employees, too, find it easier to work in environments in which their supervisors apply disciplinary action consistently.

Because of the numerous difficulties associated with inconsistently enforced absenteeism and tardiness policies, many firms have adopted no-fault attendance policies, especially for blue-collar employees. A **no-fault attendance policy** counts any unscheduled absence or tardiness as an "occurrence," and the accumulation of occurrences or assessed points during designated timeframes is used to invoke progressive discipline ranging from warnings to suspension and finally

No-fault attendance policy
Policy under which unscheduled absences and tardiness are counted as occurrences and their accumulation is used in progressive discipline

---

FIGURE 6.11 Excerpt from a Manufacturing Plant's No-Fault Attendance Policy

ABSENTEEISM AND TARDINESS POLICY

1. All employees are expected to report to work in sufficient time to receive job assignments as scheduled and to work their scheduled hours and necessary overtime. Employees will be charged with "absence occurrences" when they fail to report for scheduled work hours. Employees will be considered tardy and charged with "partial absence occurrences" when they report to work past their scheduled starting times. Similarly, workers who leave early will be charged with partial absence occurrences.

2. Partial absence occurrences will be combined so that for every three partial absence occurrences an employee will be charged with one absence occurrence.

3. Each employee will be allowed two nonchargeable absence occurrences supported by reasonable excuses in a 12-month period. To activate these allowances, the employee must notify the human resources department in advance.

4. Absences for which employees will be charged with occurrences consist of failure to work a scheduled shift, except for the following exclusions:

   • Jury or military duty

   • Work-related injuries or illnesses

   • Scheduled time off for vacations and holidays

   • Disciplinary suspension

   • Temporary layoff

   • Approved union business

   • Court-ordered appearances

   • Authorized bereavement leave

   Absences lasting several consecutive days due to non-work-related illness and injury of the employee will be treated as one occurrence. Nonconsecutive partial occurrences related to the same medical or dental condition also will be treated as one partial occurrence with pre-notification to the company. The employer has the right to require a worker to submit a doctor's note or to undergo a physical examination to verify a claim of illness or injury.

5. Accumulation of four occurrences in a 12-month period (not a calendar year) will result in an oral warning. The fifth occurrence will elicit a written warning; the seventh, a 1-day suspension; the eighth, a 3-day suspension; and the ninth, a 10-day suspension. Employees who are charged with ten occurrences in a 12-month period will be subject to discharge. The human resources department will provide counseling at each step of this progressive procedure and will refer employees for outside counseling and assistance in dealing with medical, physical, or personal difficulties related to their attendance problems, if necessary. For an employee to offset absence and partial absence occurrences, each 4-week attendance period in which that employee has no occurrences will entitle the employee to removal from the attendance file of the oldest occurrence, whether a full occurrence or a maximum of three partial occurrences, sustained in one attendance period during the prior 12 months.

termination. Supervisors often prefer a no-fault approach because they do not have to assess or determine the legitimacy of an employee's unscheduled absence. A firm's no-fault attendance policy may provide for rewarding good attendance and may designate certain absence exceptions. These provisions are spelled out so that employees and supervisors have a well-understood and consistent framework by which absences and tardiness are evaluated and handled.[28] Figure 6.11 is an excerpt from a manufacturing firm's "Absenteeism and Tardiness Policy," which is a no-fault system that applies to this firm's unionized plant employees.

Applying disciplinary action consistently does not necessarily mean treating everyone in the same manner in all situations. Special considerations surrounding an offense may need to be considered, such as the circumstances, the employee's productivity, job attitudes, and length of service. The extent to which a supervisor can be consistent and yet consider the individual's situation can be illustrated with the following example. Assume that three employees become involved in some kind of horseplay. Employee A just started work a few days ago. Employee B has been warned once before about this type of behavior, and Employee C has been involved in numerous cases of horseplay. In taking disciplinary action, the supervisor could decide to have a friendly, informal talk with Employee A, give Employee B a written warning, and impose a two-day disciplinary layoff on Employee C. Thus, each case is considered on its own merits, with the employees judged according to their work histories. Of course, if two of these employees had the same number of previous warnings, their penalties should be identical.

Imposing discipline consistently is one way a supervisor demonstrates a sense of fair play, but it may be easier said than done. There are times when the department is particularly rushed and the supervisor may be inclined to overlook infractions. Perhaps the supervisor does not wish to upset the workforce or does not wish to lose the output of a valuable employee at a critical time. This type of consideration is paramount, especially when it is difficult to obtain employees with the skills the offending employee possesses. Most employees, however, accept exceptions as fair if they know why the exception was made and if they consider the exception justified. However, employees must feel that any other employee in the same situation would receive similar treatment.

When a supervisor is imposing discipline, impersonality can help reduce the employee's resentment

IMPERSONALITY

All employees who commit the same or a similar offense should be treated the same way. Penalties should be connected with the offense, not with the offending employee. It should make no difference whether the employee is white or black, male or female, young or old, or a member of any other group. The same standards of disciplinary expectations and actions should apply uniformly.

When a supervisor is imposing discipline, impersonality can help reduce the amount of resentment that is likely to be felt by an employee. At the same time, supervisors should understand that employee reactions to discipline will vary, just as individuals who get burned touching a hot stove react differently. One person may shout, another may cry, another may reflexively inhale, and one may "push away" from the point of stimulus of pain with the opposite hand. Regardless of the individual, there will always be a reaction to being burned.

The optimal reaction to discipline is acceptance of responsibility for the wrongdoing and a change in behavior by the employee to the desired standards with no severe side effects, such as loss of morale, disruption of other employees, or a negative portrayal of the company to customers or external business associates.

Making a disciplinary action impersonal may reduce the level of resentment felt by the employee, but it is difficult to predict an employee's reaction. Personality, acceptance of authority, the job situation, and circumstances of the offense all factor into an employee's reactions. A supervisor may have to deal with an employee's reactions if they are detrimental. However, assuming the employee's reactions are not severe, the supervisor should treat the employee the same before and after the infraction and disciplinary action, without apologizing for what had to be done.

6 **Discuss the need to document disciplinary actions and to provide the right of appeal.**

Documentation and the Right to Appeal

Documentation
Records of memoranda, documents, and meetings that relate to a disciplinary action

Whenever a disciplinary action is taken, the supervisor must record the offense and the decision, including the reasoning involved in the decision. This is called **documentation**, and it may include keeping files of the memoranda, minutes of meetings, and other documents that were part of the case handling. Documentation is necessary because the supervisor may be asked to justify the action, and the burden of proof is usually on the supervisor. It is not prudent for the supervisor to depend on memory alone. This is particularly true in unionized firms where grievance-arbitration procedures often result in challenges to the disciplinary actions imposed on employees.

Right to appeal
Procedures by which an employee may request higher-level management to review a supervisor's disciplinary action

The **right to appeal** means it should be possible for an employee to request a review of a supervisor's disciplinary action from higher-level management. If the employee belongs to a labor union, this right is part of a grievance procedure. In most firms, the appeal is first directed to the supervisor's boss, thereby following the chain of command. Many large firms have hierarchies of several levels of management through which appeals may be taken. The human resources department may become involved in an appeal procedure. Complaint procedures in nonunion firms and grievance procedures in unionized organizations are discussed in Chapter 15.

The right to appeal must be recognized as a real privilege and not merely a formality. Some supervisors tell their employees they can appeal to higher-level management but that doing so will be held against them. This attitude reflects the supervisors' insecurity. Supervisors should encourage their employees to appeal to higher-level management if the employees feel they have been treated unfairly. Supervisors should not feel that appeals threaten or weaken their positions as department managers. For the most part, a supervisor's manager will be inclined to support the supervisor's action. If supervisors do not foster an open appeal procedure, employees may enlist outside aid, such as a union would provide. Management's failure to provide a realistic appeal procedure is one reason some employees resort to unionization.

During an appeal, the disciplinary penalty imposed or recommended by a supervisor may be reduced or reversed by the higher-level manager. The supervisor's decision might be reversed because the supervisor imposed disciplinary action inconsistently or failed to consider all the facts. Under these circumstances, supervisors may become discouraged and feel their managers failed to back them up. Although this situation is unfortunate, it is better for the supervisor to be disheartened than for an employee to be penalized unjustly. This is not too high a price to pay to provide every employee the right to appeal. Situations like these can be avoided when supervisors adhere closely to the principles and steps discussed in this chapter before taking disciplinary action.

Discipline Without Punishment

A growing number of companies have adopted disciplinary procedures called **discipline without punishment**. The major thrust of this approach is to stress extensive coaching, counseling, and problem solving and to avoid confrontation. A significant (and controversial) feature is the paid "decision-making leave," in which employees are sent home for a day or more with pay to decide whether they are willing to commit to meeting performance standards previously not met. If an employee commits to improving but fails to do so, the employee is terminated.

In general, this approach replaces warnings and suspensions with coaching sessions and reminders by supervisors of expected standards. The decision-making leave with pay is posed as a decision to be made by the employee, namely, to improve and stay or to quit.

Organizations that have implemented this approach successfully have reported various benefits, particularly reduced complaints and grievances and improved employee morale. It is questionable whether discipline-without-punishment programs will be adopted extensively because it is unclear that these programs are all that different in concept and outcome from progressive disciplinary action as discussed in this chapter. What is clear is that a discipline-without-punishment approach requires commitment from all management levels—especially from supervisors—if it is to be carried out successfully.[29]

7 Explain the "discipline without punishment" approach as an alternative to progressive discipline.

Discipline without punishment
Disciplinary approach that uses coaching and counseling as preliminary steps and a paid decision-making leave that allows employees to decide whether to improve and stay or to quit

It's Not Fair!

Every individual brings certain expectations to work. The values, beliefs, and perceptions are unique to that person. However, each work group has a set of norms. **Norms** are the organized and shared ideas regarding what members should do and feel, how this behavior should be regulated, and what sanctions should be applied when behavior does not coincide with organization or group expectations.[30] When an employee encounters a situation, whether new or old, his or her behavior is guided by past experiences and expectations. He or she may react in several different ways depending on how he or she perceives the situation and is impacted by it.

What is fair? What is just? What is not fair? Just the use of these questions conjures up memories. Some of these memories go back to our early childhood days and revolve around getting into or out of trouble. Trouble may have led to discipline and discipline usually meant punishment. To begin, imagine the following scenario:

8 Describe the importance of "fair treatment" in the disciplinary process.

Norms
Standards shared by most employees for how one should act and be treated in the organization

> *You and a group of friends were playing in the street. Someone threw your ball, someone else hit the ball, and the batted ball went further than anyone could imagine. Like the Energizer battery, it just kept going and going until it shattered Charlie's window. Unfortunately, you all knew Charlie—the "geezer," also known as the "old curmudgeon." What bad luck! Of all the windows in the neighborhood, it had to be that of "ill-tempered" Charlie.*

What would you have done in that situation? I suspect that you might have been the one to calmly and politely ring Charlie's doorbell, apologize for the damage done, and offer to make amends. Perhaps one of the hardest things you ever had to do was to offer a sincere, heartfelt apology while bearing the brunt of Charlie's rage. In reality, you and all the others involved fled the scene of the "crime."

What happened in your home when the angry Charlie arrived to tell your parents that he saw you running from the scene and you had broken his window? Holding the ball in hand—and it was your ball, though you did not throw it or hit it—he demanded restitution. What would your parents have done in this situation? We know that actions taken by parents will vary greatly, but for the sake of this illustration we will assume that your parents presumed you guilty—it was your ball and you were playing in the street. They may have presumed that Charlie's assessment of the situation was correct and did not bother to get your side of the story. You expected the worst and you got it. You were assigned extra chores including mowing Charlie's yard for the rest of the summer. You were grounded for a couple of weeks. Thus, you were going to miss a couple of forthcoming fun activities. Your friends got off without even a reprimand.

How did you feel? "It's not fair" was probably foremost in your mind. But what did you learn from this experience? Was the discipline effective? How did you feel about your parents who meted out the punishment? What about your friends who got off scot-free? Because the parents (the supervisors) did not listen to your view, or attempt to reach a mutual understanding of the severity of the group's actions, you had great difficulty accepting responsibility for what happened. No one likes negative outcomes, particularly when they are not warranted. In this scenario, the punishment was not fair! While your parents did not follow the proper protocol in applying discipline, it is to be hoped that they followed up by clearly communicating future behavioral expectations.

How did you respond? Were you angry? If so, toward whom was your anger directed? Your playmates? Charlie? Yourself? Your parents? Various writers purport that one's sense of **fair treatment** is contingent upon the following: the interactions that one has with one's supervisors (parents), the procedures used to arrive at the action taken (punishment or other supervisory actions), and outcomes (the punishment or reward). In retrospect, you may conclude that your parents' actions were appropriate in light of the offense, but when you compared your punishment (outcomes) with that of your playmates who got off "scot-free," fair treatment did not prevail.[31] Some of you are thinking about how a brother or sister might have been treated differently in the same or similar situation. The lack of consistency in disciplinary action or the inconsistency in meting out rewards may have led you to conclude that "life is not fair." Dissatisfaction is a potential source of trouble for parents (supervisors). All too often instances occur like this in organizations but the employee has an outlet—a grievance or appeal procedure. With a grievance procedure, supervisors are able to respond to employee concerns in a timely fashion. Without an appeal procedure, the dissatisfaction festers and can lead to bigger problems.

A couple of more thoughts on our parent–child illustration. Did your parents take the time to let you know how they determined the appropriate punishment? Did they treat you politely and courteously to help you understand that there may have been other options than fleeing the scene? Did they pause and ask you what might have been a "fair" solution to the problem? Were your parents always clear as to how they arrived at the degree and severity of your punishment? What could they have done to be more sensitive to the situation and your role in what happened? When you were treated unfairly in the disciplinary process, how did

Fair treatment
Impartial and appropriate actions taken that are free of favoritism and bias

Some employees will perceive discipline as "unfair" treatment. That's why it's important to deal with an employee's poor performance immediately and fairly by focusing on the behavior, not the person

you respond? Before succumbing to the temptation to place all the blame on the parents, remember you were playing the game when things went awry.

Have you ever been treated unfairly? How did you respond? Perhaps you recognized the errors of your behavior. We call this the "I really screwed up" syndrome. Feelings of embarrassment and shame may have led you to shed a few tears of remorse. Another response is to argue that you have been wronged; it was all those other people who were at fault. (This is a very common employee response.) Feelings of anger and being misunderstood (unfairly treated) are very common. Would you have stepped back, looked at the situation objectively, and bit your tongue to keep from saying some things that might have made the situation worse?

In a most basic sense, people react to unfair treatment in three ways:

- Fight
- Flight
- Go with the Flow

Most employees have company handbooks that provide grievance procedures. It is also easy to use the Web to access a variety of federal and state laws that provide mechanisms to deal with perceptions of workplace unfairness. It is common for employees to use the grievance procedure to see adjudication of situations deemed "not fair." There are numerous situations where the punished child will run away from home. The flight response is one used by "wronged" employees. The "I'll show them—they can take this job and shove it!" response is still prevalent in today's society.

With today's tight job market, it may not be practical for an employee to quit. This is where understanding the ABCs (see Chapter 4) becomes most important. The feeling of unfairness causes a person to stay with the organization and Go with the Flow.[32] They simply accept the situation and stay with the organization. If the feelings of unfairness are great, the employee may talk with others about how badly they were treated. This may bring up visions of personal situations which at the time might not have been important but, coupled with other illustrations of unfairness, may fester and escalate. Clearly, supervisors must be vigilant for feelings of employee dissatisfaction.

All too often, when a sense of "it's not fair" arises in the workplace, a worker will combine these responses. Recently, an employee who thought that he had been treated "unfairly" stayed with the organization, complained to any person—both inside and outside the organization—who would listen, and then brought a firearm to work. The end result—the supervisor, three other employees, and the disgruntled employee were dead.

Remember: People need to know what is expected in the way of performance. Dealing with employees who are not performing to expected standards requires taking corrective actions. Focus on performance. Not everyone will accept the fact that they must change their behavior. When problems occur, deal with them immediately and fairly.

SUMMARY

1 Employee discipline can be thought of as the degree to which employees act according to expected standards of behavior. If employee morale is high, discipline will likely be positive and there will likely be less need for the supervisor to take disciplinary action. Supervisors should recognize that most employees want to do the right thing. Positive self-discipline means that employees essentially regulate their own behaviors out of self-interest and their normal desires to meet reasonable standards. Supervisors should set positive examples for their employees to emulate.

2 Many employers have codes of ethics that describe in broad terms their enterprise values and ethical requirements. Ethical codes and conflict-of-interest policies usually include procedures for reporting possible violations.

3 Most organizations have written rules and regulations with definitions of infractions and possible penalties for infractions. Rules of conduct typically address areas of attendance, work scheduling, job performance, safety, improper behavior, and other matters. When infractions occur, supervisors must take appropriate disciplinary action. When ignored, problems do not go away.

Supervisors should take disciplinary action with the objective of improving employees' behavior. Before disciplining, the supervisor must first investigate the situation thoroughly. Disciplinary actions should be for just (proper) cause. Emotional and physical responses should be avoided. The supervisor should determine whether there is sufficient evidence to conclude that the employee knew about the rule or standard and, in fact, violated it. The supervisor should consider the severity of the violation, the employee's service record, and other relevant factors. If disciplinary action is necessary, normally it should be administered in private.

4 A number of progressively severe disciplinary actions, ranging from an informal talk to a warning, a suspension, and

discharge, are open to a supervisor as choices, depending on the circumstances and nature of the infraction. The supervisor's purpose in taking disciplinary action should be to improve the employee's behavior and to maintain proper discipline throughout the department. Progressive discipline is also desirable and applicable, though not required, for at-will employees.

5 Taking disciplinary action can be unpleasant for both the employee and the supervisor. To reduce the distasteful aspects, disciplinary action should fulfill as much as possible the requirements of the hot stove rule. These requirements are advance warning, immediacy, consistency, and impersonality.

6 Documentation of a supervisor's disciplinary action is important to substantiate the reasons for the action. This is especially important if there is appeal of the disciplinary decision to higher-level management through a grievance or complaint procedure. In the interest of fairness, an appeal procedure gives the employee a review process through which the supervisor's disciplinary decision may be sustained, modified, or set aside.

7 The discipline-without-punishment approach uses extensive coaching and counseling as preliminary steps. If there is no improvement in the employee's performance, a paid decision-making leave may be imposed on the employee to force the employee to decide whether to commit to improving or to be terminated.

8 Another challenge for supervisor's is to treat people fairly in the workplace. Finding answers to the question, "What is fair?" is not an easy task. Supervisors need to use good communication skills to understand what employees perceive as "fair." Supervisors need to understand how employees might react when they are treated unfairly. Disciplining employees is not one of the supervisor's favorite tasks. Remember applying the concepts of progressive discipline require consistent application of practical and sound supervisory skills.

KEY TERMS

Discipline (p. 177)
Discipline without punishment (p. 199)
Documentation (p. 198)
Employment-at-will (p. 193)
Fair treatment (p. 200)

Hot stove rule (p. 194)
Morale (p. 178)
No-fault attendance policy (p. 196)
Norms (p. 199)
Positive discipline (p. 177)

Positive self-discipline (p. 178)
Progressive discipline (p. 188)
Right to appeal (p. 198)

QUESTIONS FOR DISCUSSION

1. During a major exam, you notice that the student sitting across the aisle from you is apparently cheating. It appears that he (your school's star athlete) is using his cell phone to get information to answer the questions. What would you do, if anything? Why? If he is caught and confessed to the "crime," what should the discipline be?

2. Discuss the relationship between discipline and morale. Evaluate the following statement: "The best type of discipline is positive self-discipline."

3. What are the differences between a code of ethics, a conflict-of-interest policy, and written rules and regulations? What are their respective purposes?

4. Who do you trust? "Blessing White's *2008 Employee Engagement Report* found that 75 percent of employees trust their immediate managers, while only 44 percent of disengaged employees actually trust their immediate supervisors. Four years earlier, Watson Wyatt's *Work USA Survey* found that 51 percent of workers said they have trust and confidence in their bosses. The Wyatt survey also reported that the percentage of workers who believe what management tells them had jumped from 37 percent in 2002 to 50 percent in 2004."[33]
   a. How would you account for the increase?
   b. In your opinion, are bosses really doing a better job of communicating with workers or are there other factors at work? Why or why not?

   c. What is the relationship between high perceptions of trust and "fair treatment" and the disciplinary process? Explain.

5. Why should supervisors be unafraid to confront disciplinary situations when they occur? What is meant by "Disciplinary action should have just cause"?

6. Define and evaluate each of the following elements of the hot stove rule:
   a. Advance warning
   b. Immediacy
   c. Consistency
   d. Impersonality

7. Why is fair treatment important to people? How might thoughts of "It's not fair!" affect an employee's behavior? Look at Question 1 above; the student who is apparently cheating does not get caught. He gets an "A" and you get a "C."
   a. On the next exam, it appears that he is cheating. What would you do? Why?
   b. Thorndike's Law of Effect (discussed in Chapter 4) states that "behavior with favorable consequences tends to be repeated." Assume that is question 1 above, that you reported your suspicions to the instructor and nothing happened. Assume that the student appears to continually cheat, goes unpunished and get better grades than you. What are the consequences of cheater's actions?

SKILLS APPLICATION

Skills Application 6-1: Software-n-More Role-Play Exercise

This chapter's "You Make the Call!" can be used as a role-play exercise. There are many variants that instructors may use to introduce this role play. We have suggested one that we have found to be effective. Procedure for the role-play exercise could include the following:

1. ACT I: The instructor should assign three students the following roles: Bernie Collins (director of marketing), Jean Mane (director of human resources), and Don Williams

(supervisor of customer services). Other class members should act as observers of the role play.

2. The three students should be given adequate notice so that they can individually contemplate their positions, what they might say, and how they might say it.

3. ACT II: After Don Williams leaves the meeting, Jean Mane and Bernie Collins are to decide upon a course of action.

4. ACT III: Jean Mane (or Mane and Collins) shall make the recommendation to President Bob Swan. At this time, the

rationale for the recommendation should be conveyed as well as how the recommendation was arrived at. President Swan must then make the final decision regarding the action, if any, to be taken.

5. The observers should identify things that the group did well, things that should have been done that weren't, and things that should not have been done.

6. ACT IV: After you have covered Chapter 15 (Resolving Conflicts), you may wish to return to this Skills Application. For this ACT only, assume that Don Williams is 47 years of age and member of a protected class. In Software-n-Mor's handbook the president has the final say in all personnel actions. Don Williams does not think that he was treated fairly in the

situation. He files a complaint with the local Human Rights Commission which in turns refers it to the State Equal Employment Opportunity Commission (EEOC).

a. Each student should individually write a one-page paper outlining the key points that illustrate the alleged violations, the challenges to the company's actions, and the redress sought for Williams.

b. Divide students into groups of three or four. The assigned roles include Bob Swan, Jean Mane, Loren (an attorney specializing in equal employment law), and Trish (an EEOC-specialist with the law firm). This group is to assist Bob Swan in preparing a rebuttal to the allegations.

c. Select one group to present their findings to a panel of three EEOC commissioners.

Skills Application 6-2: Employee Dress and Appearance Standards

Among major supervisory concerns are issues associated with informal dress and appearance standards in the workplace. Employee dress and appearance have been problems for supervisors for many years, but they have become one of the most difficult areas for disciplinary policies. This concern is especially important when employees deal directly with the public, such as in banks, retail stores, and restaurants. There also is concern about individual rights because racial, gender, ethnic, and other differences can cause problems or potential issues of favoritism or discrimination.

1. The Law School at the University of Chicago, among others, has recently identified standards and expectations for classroom behavior.

    Let's assume that your college or university decides to add an "appropriate attire" policy to your student handbook. You have been selected to be a member of the faculty/student committee charged with developing draft guidelines.

    a. If possible, obtain employee handbooks from two different organizations. If they both have dress/appearance

codes, identify the similarities and differences between their policies and procedures. How do the firms handle violations of the policy? Can you explain the reasons for these differences?

b. Which of the policies would be appropriate for your college or university? Why?

c. Give at least two examples of attire and appearance for which some disagreements about acceptability could arise, and propose how you would handle such disagreements.

2.  Using the Internet, search for examples of problems that organizations have been having regarding appearance standards in the workplace. Write a one-page paper in which you either (a) present a persuasive argument for a rigorous dress code or (b) present an argument for why organizations should not adopt dress codes.

Skills Application 6-3: Thinking Outside the Box—What's Your Answer?

1. Without using your calculator or paper/pen answer the following question: Which is bigger: 18 percent of 87, or 87 percent of 18?

2. How easy was it to make the calculations in your head?

3. Why is it important for supervisors to document discussions related to employee performance?

    This Skills Application was adapted with permission from QCI International's *Timely Tips for Teams* (© 2008 QCI), a monthly Internet newsletter.

Skills Application 6-4: Rules of Conduct and Codes of Ethics

 Many organizations today publish their own code of ethics. Some, like Texas Instruments, Inc. (TI), have even established ethics offices. Visit TI's Web site (http://www.ti.com/csr) to learn more about the company's values and ethics. You also might want to read the online version of the article by Kathryn Taylor, "Do the Right Thing," *HR Magazine* (February 2005), pp. 99–102, at http://www.shrm.org/hrmagazine/05February for her analysis on how TI handles its ethics training.

1. "As a global leader in technologies that are driving profound social change, Texas Instruments takes responsibility for carefully defining the scope, direction and pace of that change." Carefully read the following sections from their Web site: Corporate Citizenship at TI; Employee Well-Being; The TI Commitment; The Values and Ethics of TI; Conflicts of Interest; and Ethical Inquiries and Issues.
   a. How does the company work with employees to promote ethical conduct?
   b. What is TI's policy regarding positive discipline?

2. What is the company's "Ethics Quick Test"?

3. Search for other companies' codes of ethics on the Web. You will find links to several at the Centre for Applied Ethics (http://www.ethics.ubcca/resources/business). Then, write your own code of ethics that will govern your own behavior in the workplace.

SKILLS DEVELOPMENT

Skills Devlopment Module 6-1: Who Should Blow the Whistle?

Someone who exposes a violation of organizational policy, professional standards, ethics, or the law is known as whistleblower. Several issues developed in this chapter are presented in this skills development module.

Andrew, a relatively new accountant for FACN (Feed African Children Now) is faced with an ethical dilemma involving a very successful fund raiser. Andrew believes that Cameron is misusing the non-profit agency's travel funds. Cameron brings in lots of money through his ability to schmooze with potential donors. (Note: While the video clip is mute on whether or not Andrew is a CPA, we shall assume that he is. Go to www.aicpa.org to see a full text of that profession's code of conduct.)

The video clip shows Andrew as he tries to work within the organization to get guidance regarding his concerns that funds are being improperly used for personal gain. You will see Andrew's frustration grow as he discusses his allegations with a more senior employee, Nathan; HR director Diane Magnasco; and his pregnant wife, Patty. In a way, Andrew is 'blowing the whistle' by bringing his concerns to others.

After viewing the Skills Development Module 6-1 video clip, answer the following questions:

1. It appears that Andrew places a high value on his professional code of ethical behavior. FACN's culture, ethical values, and the actions of top-management will shape the attitudes and actions of others who work there.
   a. Do you believe that Andrew is right in voicing his concerns, i.e., blowing the whistle? Why or why not?
   b. Were you able to empathize with Andrew as he tried professional, organizational, and personal issues?
2. Prior to viewing the Epilogue to this video clip, evaluate HR manager Diane Magnasco's handling of the discussion with Andrew. What could she have done to leave Andrew feeling better about his allegations?

3. In the Epilogue, Diane says that she will investigate the allegations and if she believes Cameron's actions are unethical, illegal, or outside the bounds of FACN's polices and procedures then she will take it to the board of directors.
   a. Using the concepts presented in this and previous chapters, outline an approach that Diane could use to determine whether Andrew's allegations are true.
   b. If the allegations are true, do they, in your opinion, violate standards of conduct and warrant disciplinary action. Why?
   c. If FACN does not have a specific policy regarding Cameron's actions, should a "reasonable person" know that using the organization's funds for personal benefit is "wrong."
   d. After presenting her findings to the board, the board agrees that Cameron's conduct warrants disciplinary action. They ask Diane to make recommendations regarding the appropriate discipline. If you were Diane, what would you recommend? Why that rather than some alternative?

4. What if Diane investigates and finds that Andrew's allegations are unfounded. What should be done to Andrew— "the whistle blower who blew the wrong whistle?"

5. If Andrew had witnessed Nathan or another employee taking home office supplies to stock their children's school backpack, do you think that Andrew would have had the same concerns? Explain your rationale.

6. What else should Diane Magnasco do to help employees fully understand the consequences of their actions?

ENDNOTES

For a general overview of the disciplinary process including the grievance procedures used in unionized work environments, see the following: Thomas Salvo, "Practical Tips for Successful Progressive Discipline," *SHRM White Paper* (July 2004); "Was this Employer Consistent in Its Discipline?" *SHRM Business and Legal Reports* (February 2006); Susan E. Jackson, Randall S. Schuler and Steve Werner, *Managing Human Resources*, 10th ed. (Mason, OH: South-Western/Cengage Learning, 2009), Chapter 4; Richard M. Hodgetts and Kathryn W. Hegar, *Modern Human Relations at Work*, 10th ed. (Mason, OH: Thomson/South-Western, 2008), Chapter 10; Robert L. Mathis and John H. Jackson, *Human Resource Management*, 12th ed. (Mason, OH: Thomson/South-Western, 2008), pp. 511–514, 546–548; and George Bohlander and Scott Snell, *Managing Human Resources*, 14th ed. (Mason, OH: South-Western/Cengage Learning, 2007), Chapter 13.

1. Estimates of employee theft in the U.S. vary and are hard to verify since some employers don't want other employees, customers, or shareholders to know that controls were not in place. One commonly used figure is $652 billion. The Fort Wayne, Indiana Tower Bank acknowledged losses of over $720,000 from the embezzlement by a vice-president. Another northeastern Indiana bank executive is alleged to have made off with millions. See Sherry Slater, "Catching On," *The Fort Wayne, Indiana Journal Gazette* (July 7, 2008), pp. 1C–4C.

2. The Association of Certified Fraud Examiners (ACFE) Report to the Nation on Occupational Fraud and Abuse (www.acfe.com, 2006) reported that more than 60 percent of the crimes were committed by managers, executives, or owners. It is not surprising that anonymous tips prompted the company to take action in more than a third of the incidents. Also, see "Hard Core Offenders," *HR Magazine* (December 2004) for a discussion regarding employees who continue to stretch the rules.

3. Numerous studies have reported that the typical employee spends 20 to 25 percent of his or her workday on non-work-related computer activities. The following provide insight into the e-mail problems: B. Roberts, "Avoiding the Perils of Electronic Data," *HR Magazine* (January 2007), pp. 72–77; A. Smith, "Federal Rules Define Duty to Preserve Work E-Mails," *HR Magazine* (January 2007), pp. 27+.

4. See Mimi Hall, "Surveillance System Raises Privacy Concerns," *USA Today* (February 29, 2008), p. 3A; and Vara Vauhini, "New Sites Make it Easier to Spy on Your Friends," *The Wall Street Journal* (May 13, 2008), pp. D1, D3.

5. See Stephen Baker and Brian Grow, "Scandals—A Painful Lesson: E-Mail is Forever," *BusinessWeek* (March 21, 2005), p. 36; and Bill Leonard, "New Business E-Mail Rules Proposed," *HR Magazine* (July 2005), pp. 34–35. Lucas Conley, "The Privacy Arms Race," *Fast Company* (July 2004), pp. 27–28; and Michael Stroh, "Workers Beware: Big Browser May Be Watching You," *St. Louis Post Dispatch* (August 18, 1999), pp. E1, E4. Also see Dana Hawkins, "Lawsuits Spur Rise in Employee Monitoring," *U.S. News and World Report* (August 13, 2001), p. 53; and Stephen H. Wildstrom, "Stamp Out Smutty Spammers," *BusinessWeek* (February 25, 2002), p. 25.

6. From Oren Harari, "U2D2: The Rx for Leadership Blues," *Management Review* (August 1995), pp. 34–36.

7. All supervisors should know that it is unlawful to retaliate against an employee for engaging in activity protected by civil rights laws. The question of what constitutes "retaliation" will be for the courts to decide. In 2007, the Supreme Court provided guidance in the case of Burlington Northern and Santa Fe Railway Co. *v.* White.

8. Though dated see, Kate Walter, "Ethics Hot Lines Tap into More Than Wrongdoing," *HR Magazine* (November 1995), pp. 79–85; Debra R. Meyer, "More on Whistleblowing," *Management Accounting* (June 1993), p. 26; and Marcy Mason, "The Curse of Whistleblowing," *The Wall Street Journal* (March 14, 1994), p. A14.

9. From Nicholas G. Moore, *Ethics: The Way to Do Business*, published pamphlet of his Sears Lectureship in Business Ethics at Bentley College (February 9, 1998), p. 9. In light of the Enron and other scandals during the first part of this century, worker trust in top management waned. See Ann Pomeroy, "Senior Management Begins Regaining Employee Trust," *HR Magazine* (February 2005), p. 16 for some ideas on "how to walk the talk."

10. See "Review Employee Handbooks," *News-You-Can-Use Letter* (St. Louis, MO: AAIM Management Association (February 1996), pp. 4, 6, or go to the SHRM Web site (www.shrm.org) to ideas as to what should be included in employee handbooks.

11. See Milton Bordwin, "Do-It-Yourself Justice," *Management Review* (January 1999), pp. 56–57.

12. See "Accountability Board Urges Greater Use of Dispute Resolution," *HR News* (April 1999), p. 14.

13. For expanded information on grievance-arbitration procedures, particularly as related to discipline/discharge cases, see Susan E. Jackson, Randall S. Schuler and Steve Werner, *Managing Human Resources*, 10th ed. (Mason, OH: South-Western/Cengage Learning, 2009), pp. 534–538; and George Bohlander and Scott Snell, *Managing Human Resources*, 14th ed. (Mason, OH: South-Western/Cengage Learning, 2007), pp. 621–626.

14. See James G. Vigneau, "To Catch a Thief . . . and Other Workplace Investigations," *HR Magazine* (January 1995), pp. 90–95.

15. See Albert R. Karr, "Some Employers Are Alarmed About Disclosing Employee Investigations," *The Wall Street Journal* (June 1, 1999), p. A1.

16. Many companies also conduct random and other drug tests on their employees, especially federal government contractors and employers as mandated by the Drug-Free Workplace Act of 1988. Companies usually have policies and procedures that outline how tests will be taken, safeguards, and possible penalties for violations.

17. This is called a unionized employee's Weingarten rights, based on a U.S. Supreme Court decision. See Raymond L. Hilgert and David A. Dilts, *Cases in Collective Bargaining and Industrial Relations*, 10th ed. (Boston: Irwin/McGraw Hill, 2002), pp. 113–5; Martha B. Pedrick, "Weingarten Rights in Non-Union Settings," *Labor Law Journal* (Winter 2001), pp. 195–201.

18. See C. R. Deitsch, D. A. Dilts, and Francine Guice, "Weingarten Rights in the Non-Union Workplace," *Dispute Resolution Journal* (May/July 2006), p. 46; Victoria Roberts, "Court Upholds Extending Weingarten Rights to Nonunion Workers," *HR News* (December 2001), p. 13; Margaret M. Clark, "Nonunion Employers Face Charges in Investigating Misconduct," *HR News* (January 2002), p. 9; and Margaret M. Clark, "High Court Rebuffs Appeal in Nonunion Weingarten Case," *HR News* (July 2002), p. 8.

19. For an expanded discussion of the technique and applications of letters of clarification, see Paul Falcone, "Letters of Clarification: A Disciplinary Alternative," *HR Magazine* (August 1999), pp. 134–40.

20. See "Survey Reveals More Than Half of Employers Have Been Sued," *HR News* (August 1999), p. 13.

21. See Francis T. Coleman, *Conducting Lawful Terminations* (Alexandria, VA: SHRM Foundation, 1995).

22. See Dennis L. Johnson, Christie A. King, and John G. Kurutz, "A Safe Termination Model for Supervisors," *HR Magazine* (May 1996),

pp. 73–78; and Gary Bielous, "How to Fire" *Supervision* (November 1996), pp. 8–10.

23. See Michael J. Phillips, "Toward a Middle Way in the Polarized Debate Over Employment at Will," *American Business Law Journal* (November 1992), pp. 441–83, or Kenneth Gilberg, "Employers Must Protect Against Employee Lawsuits," *Supervision* (November 1992), pp. 12–13.

24. See "Loss of At-Will Job is Compensable," *HR News* (February 1999), p. 8.

25. See Matt Siegel, "Yes, They Can Fire You," *Fortune* (October 26, 1998), p. 301.

26. See Diane Cadrain, "Helping Workers Fool Drug Tests Is a Big Business," *HR Magazine* (August 2005), pp. 29, 32. This article purports that Quest runs over seven million drug tests annually. Federal agencies spent $16.1 million in 2004 under the Federal Drug-Free Workplace Program. The U.S. Department of Labor says that alcohol and drug abuse costs American businesses roughly $81 billion in lost productivity. Employers also shouldered hidden costs related to tardiness, absenteeism, healthcare benefits, and turnover. The newest cost: As new drug-masking products enter the market, test labs have to develop new detection technologies, and they pass the costs along to employers.

    The American Council on Drug Education said that drug abusers are 10 times more likely to miss work, 3.6 times more likely to be involved in on-the-job accidents, and 5 times more likely to file a workers' compensation claim. They also are two-thirds as productive and are responsible for healthcare costs that are 3 times as high.

27. The author first heard the term *CYR (cover your rear)* while an ROTC student in 1958. For a recent discussion on the advantage of CYR, see Jared Sandberg, "Covering Yourself is Counterproductive But May Save Your Job," *The Wall Street Journal* (June 8, 2005), p. B1.

28. For an expanded discussion of no-fault and other employee attendance policies, see M. Michael Markowich, "When Is Excessive Absenteeism Grounds for Disciplinary Action?" *ACA News* (July/August 1998), pp. 36–39.

29. For a thorough discussion of the pros and cons and applications of discipline-without-punishment approaches, see Dick Grote, *Discipline without Punishment* (New York: American Management Association,

1995). See also Dick Grote, "Discipline without Punishment," *Across-the-Board* (September/October 2001) pp. 52–57; and Jathan Janove, *Managing to Stay out of Court* (Berrett-Kohler, 2005). Janove reaffirms that the following will likely land you in court: acting inconsistently, treating one employee differently from another; treating employees differently from what documented policies require; letting documents conflict with one another; or treating one person in different ways over time.

30. Definition of norms adapted from discussion by Don Harvey and Robert Bruce Bowin, *Human Resource Management; An Experiential Approach* (Upper Saddle River, NJ: Prentice Hall, 1996), pp. 15–21.

31. For a discussion of what fairness means to employees, see Susan E. Jackson, Randall S. Schuler and Steve Werner, *Managing Human Resources,* 10th ed. (Mason, OH: South-Western/Cengage Learning, 2009), pp. 116–120. Also See Maurice A. Ramirez, "Outrage of Enthusiasm: The Choice is Yours," *Supervision*, 69, 4 (April 2008), pp. 17–19; Bill Catlette and Richard Hadden, "Consistency Does Not Equal Fairness," *Supervision*, 69, 2 (February 2008), pp. 19–21; T. Simons and Q. Roberson, "Why Managers Should Care about Fairness: The Effects of Aggregate Justice Perceptions on Organizational Outcomes," *Journal of Applied Psychology*, 88, 3 (2006), pp. 432–443; and M. L. Williams, M. A. McDonald and N.T. Nguyen, "A Meta-Analysis of the Antecedents and Consequences of Pay Level Satisfaction," *Journal of Applied Psychology*, 91 (2006), pp. 392–413.

32. Many psychology and biology texts discuss the psychological and biological aspects of stressful situations. For an expanded discussion of the fight/flight responses see Bronston T. Mayes and Daniel C. Ganster, "Exit and Voice: A test hypotheses based on the fight/flight response to job stress," *Journal of Organizational Behavior*, 9, 3 (July 1998), pp. 199–216 (published online November 20, 2006). Also see, S. E. Taylor, et.al., "Biobehavioral responses to stress in females: Tend-and-befriend, not fight-or-flight," *Psychological Review*, 107 (2000), pp. 411–429; or H.S. Friedman and R.C. Silver, *Foundations of Health Psychology* (New York: Oxford University Press, 2007).

33. See "Employee Engagement Report 2008 (BlessingWhite, http://www.blessingwhit.com/EEE, April/May 2008). Also see Ann Pomeroy, "Senior Management Begins Regaining Employee Trust," *HR Magazine* (February 2005), p. 14.

CASE 2-1
The Picnic Conversation

Barry Automotive's Glendale Plant's annual picnic was well attended, as usual. It was a well-planned, daylong family affair for all employees of the firm, giving them an opportunity to get together informally. At the picnic, Charlene Knox, one of the supervisors, had a long chat with her boss, Jim Cross, the general manager. They spoke about many things, including some work problems. Cross greatly emphasized the need to cut costs and generally tighten company finances. He told Knox that he had already received a number of written suggestions and plans from some other supervisors. He highly praised their efforts as appropriate and helpful.

Three weeks after the picnic, Charlene Knox received a memo from her boss asking her why her "report in reference to cost cutting" had not yet arrived. At first, she wondered what Jim Cross was referring to, and then she remembered their talk at the picnic. She realized that was the only time Cross had discussed with her the need to cut costs. Knox pondered what her response should be.

Questions for Discussion
1. Is it appropriate for a supervisor to give a directive to a subordinate in a social, off-the-job setting? Why or why not?
2. Was Charlene Knox at fault for failing to understand what her boss told her at the picnic? Was Jim Cross at fault? Were both managers at fault?
3. What should Knox do? Why?

CASE 2-2
Abusive Rumors

John Jacobs is supervisor for the electronics department of Appliances Galore, a chain of large superstores specializing in appliance sales to retail and commercial customers. The company has a reputation for extensive involvement in community activities. In fact, the company strongly promotes family values and has sponsored various family-oriented activities throughout the years. In addition, the company provides financial and other incentives to employees who volunteer their time in not-for-profit and other service activities. Andy George, manager of marketing operations, has just confided to Jacobs that he had heard "through the grapevine" that Steve Shepard's wife and two children appeared last night at the local women's-and-children's shelter. George also indicated that Shepard's wife was reported to have been badly bruised and that this was not the first time the family had sought refuge. Steve Shepard is one of Jacobs's outstanding salespeople. Last year, Shepard won the company's award for the most sales. George suggested to Jacobs that he should investigate the matter and make a recommendation about what the company should do.

Questions for Discussion

1. If Steve Shepard's job performance was not affected by his personal life, should the company become involved in any way? Discuss.
2. If Steve Shepard's alleged actions off the job became public knowledge and reflected on the image and reputation of Appliances Galore, should the company take any action?
3. What would you recommend that Jacobs and George do? Consider alternatives.

CASE 2-3
The Little Things Add Up!

Lynda Heredia has worked for Economy Parcel Service (EPS), a large package delivery company, for the past 22 years. She knows that pleasing the customer is the key to operating a successful business. She is extremely proud of the "Employee of the Month" awards she has received. Several times before, Heredia has been offered various supervisory positions, but she has always turned them down because she does not want the extra duties and responsibilities that come with advancement. Management considers her the "ideal employee." She rarely needs to be told what to do and never misses work. Her work is always done the right way the first time. Operations manager Josh Simpson has been overheard to remark, "I wish we could figure out a way to clone Lynda. She's by far the best employee we've got."

Heredia works the 11:00 P.M. to 7:30 A.M. shift. Her position is vital because she sorts packages on both sides of the master conveyor belt and directs them onto assorted belts where others load them into bins and then into delivery vehicles. Due to a downturn in the economy and increased competition, EPS's business recently dropped off drastically. The company cut overhead and significantly reduced its number of employees. Business had picked up in recent months such that the number of packages handled daily approached previous levels, but those employees who remained after the cutbacks were expected to get the same amount of work done with fewer people and resources, and increase productivity, tighten delivery schedules, and accept no pay raises. The last item was especially difficult for Heredia because she is principal caregiver for her elderly mother. All of her mother's Social Security income went for medical costs and other essentials. Heredia's weekly paycheck usually covered all other expenses, but nothing was left over for recreation or investment. "The harder I work, the behinder I get," Heredia lamented.

On Wednesday, Heredia came into work early, as always, and told her immediate supervisor, Tony Lehman, that she had to leave by 6:30 A.M. because her mother had an 8:00 A.M. appointment at the hospital for some much-needed medical tests. Lehman responded, "Fine. Just remind me later." Lehman had been Heredia's immediate supervisor for the past seven months, but they had known each other for about fifteen years. Heredia's previous supervisor had been downsized, and Lehman's duties had been expanded to cover several additional areas, including the one in which Heredia worked. Unlike Heredia's previous supervisor, Lehman failed to tell his employees what he expected them to do and rarely gave them positive feedback. It might have been because he was expected to do more with less.

At 5:30 A.M., Heredia reminded Lehman about the appointment, and Lehman asked the operations manager if he had an employee to cover the hour of Heredia's shift because she had to leave. The operations manager's response was, "No, I don't have anyone. In fact, we're so short of people right now that

I don't know if we'll meet the delivery schedule. If I would have known sooner, I might have been able to find coverage for you."

When Lehman told her she would be unable to leave early, Heredia immediately began to fume. "So this is the way they treat dedicated and loyal employees. After all, I asked my supervisor at the beginning of the shift if I could leave early—just like the handbook says," Heredia lamented to anyone willing to listen. She stayed until her regular quitting time, but her full attention was not on her work. As a result, several mistakes occurred.

After punching out, Heredia rushed home, hustled her mother into the car, and left for the hospital. While waiting for her mother to finish her tests, the psychologically "down and out" Heredia, in her dirty work attire, kept playing the events over and over in her mind. "I don't ask this company for much, and I bend over backward to get the job done. I'll show them: I'll call in sick tomorrow and see how they appreciate the inconvenience."

About 15 minutes before her assigned shift the next day, Heredia called her supervisor and said, "I'm not feeling well this evening. I think it might be that new strain of flu, and I'd hate to spread it to anyone else. I'll call you tomorrow evening and let you know how I'm feeling because I'm also scheduled to work tomorrow evening." Heredia still had several sick days and personal days left, and company policy only required employees to report their sicknesses at least 15 minutes before the start of their shifts.

Of course, the employee assigned to perform Heredia's duties lacked the skill or knowledge to do the job in a correct and timely fashion. Additionally, that employee feared making mistakes, so every package was checked and double-checked to ensure that it got onto the right conveyor. Work-in-progress backed up, and many trucks did not get loaded until mid-morning. In short, many customers received their packages late.

Questions for Discussion

1. What are your initial observations about the problems that must be addressed at EPS?
2. What could Lehman have done to prevent or minimize those problems?
3. Using the ABC analysis (see Chapter 4), discuss why Lynda Heredia behaved the way she did.
4. Lynda Heredia now has a negative attitude. What suggestions would you make to Lehman to change Heredia's outlook? To what extent should Lehman involve upper management in the solution?
5. How did mistrust and lack of common courtesy add to the complexity of the situation?
6. Someone once said, "Learn from the mistakes of others. You'll never live long enough to make them all yourself." How can EPS use this situation as a case study for the entire organization?
7. What did you learn from this case?

(**ROLE PLAY**) **Role-Play Activity:** Assign one student to play the role of Lynda Heredia and another to play the role of Lehman. For role-play purposes, assume that Lynda Heredia's performance shows a steady decline and that she repeatedly calls in several minutes before her assigned shift, claiming to be "not feeling well." Heredia is working the employee handbook to the maximum and is using all her allotted personal days.

PART 2 CASES

Cynthia is the proof and auditing department supervisor for Middletown National Bank and reports directly to the vice president of Internal Services. She supervises all day-shift personnel relative to assigning work and following up to make sure work is properly completed. She also supervises the night-shift supervisor, assisting and advising as required. Typical functional responsibilities include:

CASE 2-4
The Perfectionist

- Allocates work assignments and follows up to ensure the work is completed on schedule.
- Resolves any problems referred by subordinates and/or upper management.
- Sees that equipment is properly maintained and in good working order, interfacing with the vendors for proper service as required.
- Interviews and hires all new members of the department.
- Evaluates and makes recommendations for pay increases, promotions, and transfers, for all employees on the day shift.
- Reviews all job evaluations and personnel recommendations for the night-shift personnel.
- Assists, advises, and trains night-shift supervisor in the handling of employees.
- Makes recommendations regarding improved methods of handling certain types of transactions and redesign of specific documents to increase efficiency.
- Oversees the gathering, preparation, and analysis of various Proof Department reports designed to establish standards and measure productivity.
- Performs any other duties as required or assigned for the efficient operation of the Proof Department.

Cynthia loves words, and uses her large vocabulary extensively. This morning, her boss was under stress and needed to vent. In a private meeting with Cynthia, he said, "You use big words to make yourself sound better than other people, and you try to intimidate people with your intelligence." Cynthia was shocked and (would you believe) apologetic. In her most recent performance assessment, several subordinates described her as an aggressive perfectionist. At the time, she wondered what she had done to warrant that description.

Source: Case adapted with permission from Edwin C. Leonard, Jr. and Roy A. Cook, *Human Resource Management: 21st Century Challenges* (Mason, OH: Thomson Custom Publishing, 2005), p. 118.

Questions for Discussion

1. Would you like to work for Cynthia? Why or why not?
2. Cynthia's problem is not uncommon. What are the symptoms of mismanagement?
3. (**INTERNET ACTIVITY**) Using the Internet, find at least two sources that detail techniques for dealing with someone who might be described as an aggressive perfectionist. Write a one-page paper describing how a subordinate might cope with the situation.
4. What would you do if you were Cynthia?
5. In no more than forty words, describe what you learned from this case.

Speeding through the rolling Piedmont hills on his motorcycle, Vance Patterson could barely concentrate on the road. Instead, his thoughts were on his business, Patterson Fan. Things had not been going well. Founded in 1989, the Blythewood, South Carolina–based company, which makes industrial fans and coolers, had once been fun, energized, and profitable. Now at least a third of Patterson's

CASE 2-5
Disgruntled Workers Can Drive You Crazy

sixty employees seemed to be in a state of constant disgruntlement, complaining about everything. Productivity and sales were plummeting. Patterson was getting desperate.

He thought back to the company's early days. It was exactly the kind of place where he had always wanted to work. He supplied sodas and popcorn and hosted quarterly cookouts where employees danced to mariachi and steel-drum bands. Each holiday season, he would hand out bonuses and fat profit-sharing checks. In 2000, when sales hit a record $8.5 million, those checks ranged from $7,000 to $35,000.

But after a decade of steady growth, revenue slipped to $7.2 million in 2001. Even so, Patterson had about $200,000 in profits to share, but the checks came in smaller amounts than many employees had expected, which led to grumbling. And as the business climate continued to worsen, so did morale.

Employees seemed to be gossiping more about one another and the company. Sales reps began accusing colleagues of encroaching on their turf. Soon, careless errors became alarmingly commonplace. In one case, workers reported that they had performed some routine maintenance on the spinning machine that made the housing for fans. When the device broke down, it became clear that the maintenance had never been completed.

Patterson had to contract with a manufacturer in Indiana, adding high freight costs that hammered the company's bottom line. Customers began complaining about flawed products, including fans with backward blades or missing bolts. The company's hardworking employees were affected as well. "People were going around saying, 'Slow down, don't listen to so-and-so,'" said James Ballentine, the company's capacity planner. "It was bringing the whole company down."

Patterson responded by becoming the kind of manager he'd always loathed. He demanded that salespeople begin making 45 to 60 calls a day, and managers monitored them by poring over phone records. When he noticed things like eBay pages on computer monitors as he roamed the halls, he installed computer-monitoring software. And when he saw workers arriving late and leaving early, he installed time clocks—both on the factory floor and in the business office. "We were spending all our time in meetings talking about bad employees," he says.

By August 2004, Patterson felt as if he was spending every day trying to fix his employees' bad behavior. Driving to work on his Harley one morning, he tried to clear his head. Somewhere between drinking a thermos of coffee at the Kings Mountain State Park and pulling into the parking lot of the Blythewood factory, he started to imagine what would happen if he just fired all of the grousing, underperforming employees. He had to admit, it was a pretty appealing daydream.

The next day, Patterson had his weekly meeting with his three most trusted managers. He strode in and shut the conference room door behind him. "Let's get rid of the bad employees and replace them," he said. Thomas Salisbury, the company's vice-president of operations, slammed the table with enthusiasm. The other two were more skeptical and asked for some time to think it over. But by the following week's planning meeting, the entire team was on board.

Fortunately, the high season had just ended, making it a logical time to cut back. Patterson asked his sales manager to draw up a list of reps with bad attitudes or poor performance. He came back with six names. The production supervisors came back with eleven. Patterson did a review of the business office and was shocked to discover that over the previous two years, an employee had charged some $10,000 in personal products to a corporate credit card. That employee had two supervisors, and all three were added to the list, which now totaled 20—one-third of the workforce.

Patterson planned for the firings to take place over the next two months. The first round began the first week of September. The dismissed workers were offered two weeks' severance for every year served. Then they were asked to gather their personal belongings, hand over their keys, and leave the premises. The next round of dismissals began two weeks later.

It was a tough couple of months, not only for Patterson and his managers but also for the company's forty other employees, some of whom began to fear that their jobs also were at stake. Patterson reassured people in informal individual meetings, but he never made a big speech about the effort. "I sound kind of cold, but I'd gone so long dealing with these folks, trying to make everybody happy, that I didn't care how people felt," he said. "My attitude was just 'Deal with it, we're doing it, and it's going to be better.'"

Because the layoffs took place in the off-season, they were not particularly disruptive. Surprisingly, no one threatened to sue. Patterson began filling the positions immediately although he changed his hiring policies. Now, new employees face a 45-day probation and a 90-day review; he's already fired a couple of new hires who didn't live up to expectations.

All told, Patterson estimates he paid about $100,000 in severance, but he has no regrets. Since the layoffs, he says, "Patterson Fan is a happy place." Many employees agree. "It's a different work environment now," says Robert Lane, a shop-floor supervisor. "It feels more like a team." Patterson unplugged the time clocks and started ignoring the computer-monitoring software. Productivity is up. Last year, the company had forty people on the manufacturing floor, and shipments sat for as long as four weeks before being sent. Now eighteen people are managing the same number of orders, and shipments go out the next day. He's rewarded the most productive workers by raising their wages.

But for Patterson, the real proof that he made the right call came in April 2005 when the company held its quarterly meeting. It turned into a raucous, '60s-themed party. Employees donned costumes while a 130-pound pig, replete with apple in its mouth, roasted in a pit in the courtyard. Firing a third of his employees was drastic, Patterson says, but it turned out to be the best way to encourage those who remained. "I got rid of the unhappy people," he said, "to make room for the good ones."

Source: Case reprinted here with permission. Hands on Case Study: "Disgruntled workers were driving Vance Patterson crazy," *Inc. Magazine* (July 2005), pp. 42–43.

Questions for Discussion

1. What techniques of performance management are illustrated by this case?
2. Using the concepts discussed in Chapter 3 (communication), Chapter 4 (motivation), Chapter 5 (problem solving), and Chapter 6 (discipline), how might the problems experienced at Patterson Fan have been avoided or at least minimized such that the drastic action of termination did not have to be taken?
3. What else could Vance Patterson have done prior to firing the disgruntled/underperforming employees?
4. What roles should the supervisors have played in turning around employee performance before Vance Patterson made the decision to fire?
5. How do you believe the remaining employees will perform in the months ahead? Why?
6. What did you learn from this case?

CASE 2-6
To Accept or Not to Accept

Dave Harris is a newly hired information services (IS) supervisor for Cedarville Hospitality Enterprises (CHE). He joined the firm three months ago after a ten-year stint with Washington Insurance's office of information services. In contrast with the publicly owned Washington Insurance, CHE is owned by the Wendling family and has 13 hotels and 6 upscale restaurants located throughout a six-state area.

Robert Wendling, the patriarch of the firm, has instituted a number of personnel policies, including a "no gift, no gratuity" policy. Although the owner has issued the "no gift, no gratuity" policy to all employees, it is well known throughout the organization that, over the past year, the owner has received gifts, tickets, vacation trips, and other perks from vendors, customers, government officials, and the like.

Stewart Clark, the operations vice president, asked Dave Harris to join him in a vendor-sponsored golf outing to be held at a prestigious country club. Harris likes golf, played on his college team, and won several men's amateur golf tournaments. He decided to participate in the golf event, believing it to be acceptable under company policy. However, at dinner following the golf festivities, the vendor had a door-prize giveaway. Stewart Clark was announced as the winner of a four-day golf trip to Hilton Head Island, South Carolina. The final name drawn was Dave Harris, and he was summoned to come forward and accept a new 42-inch television set. As Harris walked to the award stand, he contemplated his alternatives.

Questions for Discussion

1. (**INTERNET ACTIVITY**) Use the Internet to find two companies that have "no gift, no gratuity" policies. What are their similarities? What are their differences?
2. What are the purposes of these companies' "no gift, no gratuity" policies?
3. If you were Dave Harris, what would you do? Why?

CASE 2-7
Community Medical Center: Preferential Treatment

Georgia Mason is supervisor of the laundry at Pine Village Community Medical Center (CMC). Most of the time, she supervises eight to ten people. One of her employees is Paula Whisler, a widow with five school-age children. Whisler is a very good worker, but she is almost always late for work in the morning. Mason had spoken to Whisler numerous times about her tardiness, to no avail. Just last Wednesday, Whisler assured Mason that she tried hard to be at work on time, but she "just did not seem to be able to make it" by 6:30 A.M. because she had to get her children off to school. She argued that she worked twice as hard as anyone else and that she stayed over in the afternoon to make up for the time she lost in the mornings. There was little doubt in Mason's mind that Whisler produced as much as or more than anyone else and that she did stay later in the evening to make up the time she lost by being late in the morning.

One Monday morning, however, Paula Whisler's tardiness was holding up a job that had to be finished by noon. Regardless of how hard Whisler might work during the morning, it would be difficult to finish the job on time because the items had to dry for three hours before they could leave the department. While some other worker could have performed the operation, Georgia Mason felt that Whisler was most qualified to do it. However, should she arrive late again, the entire operation's schedule would be thrown off. All of this was going through Mason's mind when she heard one of the workers say to another worker, "Whisler is getting preferential treatment. Why should she be given any favors, like she's better than the rest of us?"

Sure enough, Paula Whisler arrived 45 minutes late. Georgia Mason realized that the situation required action on her part, but she did not know what that action should be.

Questions for Discussion

1. Explain how the principles of the "hot stove rule" discussed in Chapter 6 were applied improperly by Georgia Mason in this case.
2. Should Georgia Mason consider Paula Whisler's home situation when trying to maintain departmental standards? Why or why not?
3. Can the conflict between organizational demands and employees' personal problems be reconciled and still accomplish the objectives of the organization? If so, how?
4. What action should Mason take? What alternatives are open if the problem is not solved quickly?

Robert Brown is the plant manager for Kelmer Manufacturing, a unionized manufacturer of cement mixers. Kelmer Manufacturing works Monday through Friday with two fully operational production shifts and a third shift supervised by Richard Ellis, one of Brown's direct reports. The third shift provides maintenance, materials handling, and support for the other two shifts. Brown rarely has to worry about the efficiency of the third shift. Nevertheless, his management by wandering around (MBWA) style led him to periodically drop in on each of the shifts—not to spy or investigate but to reward and recognize the contributions of employees. The nine third-shift workers are a tightly knit, fun-loving group, who socialize frequently off the job.

Richard Ellis, a very likeable twenty-year veteran of Kelmer Manufacturing, was pleased to announce his forthcoming wedding to Susan Jones on the Friday following Thanksgiving. Jones, divorced with two grown children, worked for a local law firm. According to Ellis, it seemed like a match made in heaven. Brown, along with most of the management team and third-shift employees, attended the wedding.

In early December, President Gene Biggs received an anonymous phone call from someone claiming that one of his [the caller's] friends had taken pictures of nude women frolicking with Kelmer employees—in the plant and during work hours. Biggs initially dismissed the phone call as a prank until Carl Simmons, the vice president of marketing, reported that a customer had seen Internet photos of nude women at what appeared to be the Kelmer plant.

Not knowing the specific Internet site or having any other specifics, Biggs called his legal counsel, Loren Adams. Adams's investigation found 97 pictures on a pornographic Web site. It was clear that the photos were from the Kelmer plant.

Biggs was appalled. He relayed the results of the investigation to Robert Brown and other members of the management team, saying, "Any time there are unauthorized visitors in the plant, it is wrong. Any time we're talking about nudity in the plant, it's embarrassing. One of our supervisors allowed these photos to be taken. We have a major problem, and I need your help to get this thing resolved. In the past three years, we have overhauled our manufacturing processes, solved our quality problems, and built a solid reputation. Everything we do has been at the highest level, and this one makes me very angry. I want to fire the whole bunch."

Discussion of the Web site spread like a wildfire through the employee ranks. One member of the management team remarked, "I had several questions about this at a Rotary meeting this morning. All I could say was that we're looking into it."

CASE 2-8
How Could It
Happen Here?

In a meeting with Brown, Attorney Thomas Adams, and HR professional Jessica Salisbury, the nine employees involved in the investigation at first denied any knowledge of the photographs. Later, during videotaped interviews and with representation from their union, four of the men accused Richard Ellis and fellow employee Jay Bracey of urging them to keep silent about the photographs. Two other employees alleged that Ellis and Bracey called them repeatedly and urged them to lie if asked about the event.

About the same time that President Biggs received the anonymous phone call, Ellis stumbled upon the Web site. "We've got problems," Ellis allegedly told Bracey. "They've got pictures on the Internet. What are we going to do?"

Biggs contacted each member of the board of directors and familiarized them with the situation. The good news that the company was expected to exceed its fourth-quarter earnings estimates was clouded by the fact that he had to admit that things hadn't gone as expected. When Biggs dropped the bombshell regarding the nude Internet photos, the board members were stunned. "How could such a thing have happened?" they wondered.

Biggs instructed Brown to work with Thomas Adams and Jessica Salisbury to recommend what disciplinary action to take. He concluded by saying, "People are laughing at us, and I don't know how we can correct this public-relations problem. I can't believe that something like this could ever happen here!"

The union-management contract provisions give management the right to discipline for just cause, but Brown has never had a situation like this. (Figure 6.4 in chapter 6 is a partial listing of the Kelmer Company rules and regulations.) As Brown sat in the company parking lot, thinking about the events of the last few days, he remembered his old college instructor's words: "Management has the right to discipline employees for just cause, but there must be a clearly identifiable and justifiable reason for taking disciplinary action." As he turned the ignition key to drive home, Brown thought to himself, "I trusted those guys, and they did this. They are among the best employees we have. I feel like a failure."

Questions for Discussion

1. What would motivate employees to act the way they allegedly did? Was there behavior reasonable? Why? Why not?
2. Discuss the implications of not "disciplining" the employees for their involvement.
3. If you were assigned responsibility for conducting an investigatory interview of each of the employees alleged to have been involved in the episode:
   a. Describe the approach you would use to conduct the interview.
   b. What specific questions would you ask?
   c. How would you verify the information provided by the employees to be fact, rumor, conjecture, or a fabrication?
4. Role-Play Exercise
   a. (ROLE PLAY) Prior to participating in this exercise, each student should review the supervisory tips boxes in chapters 3, 4, 5, and 6 carefully and then, individually, prepare an action plan for dealing with the charge from President Gene Biggs to recommend disciplinary action for the employees involved in the situation.
   b. Divide the class into groups of three. Students should be assigned the roles of Robert Brown, Thomas Adams, or Jessica Salisbury. Allow the group ten minutes to develop a proposal for President Gene Biggs.

c. Select one group to present their recommendations to President Biggs. The remaining students should assume the role of President Biggs. All students can participate in the ensuing discussion.

d. In Chapter 6, we discussed progressive discipline and how to apply the "hot stove rule." To what extent did the groups consider these two concepts in determining appropriate action? What else should they have considered?

5. Some organizations, particularly in the public sector, have a five-person board that hears all charges of inappropriate behavior; investigates, if necessary; and recommends disciplinary action, if any, to be taken. If Kelmer Manufacturing has a disciplinary committee comprised of two members of management, a representative from HR, and two rank-and-file union members, what do you suppose the disciplinary board would recommend in this case? Explain your reasoning.

6. What suggestions would you give President Gene Biggs to minimize the recurrence of this or a similar problem?

7. Write a one-page paper detailing what you learned from this case.

PART 2 CASES

PART 3

GETTY IMAGES

CHAPTER 7

(Supervisory Planning)

After studying this chapter, you will be able to:

1 Define planning and explain why all management functions depend on planning.

2 Explain the concept of strategic planning and its relationship to mission statements and visioning.

3 Describe the supervisor's role in organizational planning.

4 Discuss the need for well-defined organizational goals and objectives, particularly as they relate to the supervisor.

5 Explain management by objectives (MBO).

6 Identify the major types of standing and single-use plans and explain how these plans help supervisory decision making.

7 Describe how the supervisor plans for efficient and effective resource use.

8 Explain the key concepts of quality planning.

9 Recognize the importance of planning for the unthinkable (crisis management).

YOU MAKE THE CALL!

You are Alan Knuth, junior business major at Old Ivy University. It was a beautiful spring day, April 16, 2007, as you strolled through the student center. There were Professor Vaught, Dean Johnson, and Chancellor Michaels talking over coffee. As you walked by the table, Professor Vaught asked you to sit down and, after brief introductions, the discussion revolved around your classes, the weather, and the university's volleyball team. The Chancellor fully expected the team to win the conference and qualify for the NCAA Division I tournament.

Just as you were getting up to leave to meet your study team at the library, all attention was directed to the televisions. There was a breaking news story about a shooting at Virginia Tech. Concern escalated as both Professor Vaught and Chancellor Michaels knew administrators and faculty at Tech. When you arrived at the library, most students were clustered in front of the television. The rest of the day was a blur; it was tough to concentrate on the lectures. By day's end you knew about the carnage that had occurred.

Everyone was talking about Seung Hui Cho, the 23-year-old English major, who used handguns to vent his rage at the world. He murdered 32 students and wounded dozens more before killing himself. Your grandfather always talked about "days of infamy"—where and what he was doing on December 7, 1941. Your father told stories about the day President Kennedy was assassinated and the mourning that followed. And you vividly recall 9/11. The memories of a tragedy linger on forever. Your grandfather always said, "preventing tragedies is like saying we can prevent auto accidents."

In a business and society course, you had heard incredible stories about how employees "go postal." Before you went to sleep that night, you and your suitemates talked about how something like that could never happen at Old Ivy. Your thoughts were drawn to several of the students you had seen on campus and in classes. You wondered whether they knew "right from left" and if they "were playing with a full deck." You recalled how hurt you were when your sweetheart since your junior year in high school broke off the relationship. You brooded about it and it affected your grades. Your friends and the campus minister helped you get over it. It took a while to stop nursing the hurt and count your blessings. Your feelings were normal and you appreciated the generosity of those who reached out to you in your time of need.

Mid-morning the next day, you received a text message that Professor Vaught wanted to see you as soon as possible. When you arrived at his office, he ushered you to the conference room. Dean Johnson and fellow business student Kelly Notter were already there. The short of the story was that Chancellor Michaels wanted a blue-ribbon task force of students to review the university's policies and procedures on safety and security, review what other organizations were doing, and then meet with faculty and staff committees to draft new policies and procedures to deal with potential disasters. You and Kelly Notter, along with students from nursing and health sciences, computer technology, engineering, communications, and psychological sciences, would be on the student leadership task force. Don Henderson, Associate Director of Safety and Security, would chair the task force and serve as a resource. Saying thank-you in advance, the Chancellor announced that a special honors study—a three-credit-hour course—was being established and each student would receive credit for their participation. You knew that this was quite an honor and a formidable undertaking. The first meeting was the next morning at 7 A.M. You wondered what could be done to prepare for the meeting. **YOU MAKE THE CALL!**

Management Functions Begin with Planning

Management scholars and practitioners disagree about the number and designation of managerial functions. However, the consensus is that the first, and probably the most crucial, managerial function is planning.

Planning means deciding what is to be done in the future. It includes analyzing a situation, forecasting events, establishing objectives, setting priorities, and deciding which actions are needed to achieve those objectives. Logically, planning precedes all other managerial functions because every manager must project a framework and a course of action before trying to achieve desired results. For

Planning
The process of deciding what needs to be done by whom by when

example, how can a supervisor organize a department's operations without a plan? How can a supervisor effectively staff and lead employees without knowing which avenues to follow? How can a supervisor control employee activities without standards and objectives? All managerial functions depend on planning.

Planning is a managerial function every supervisor must perform every day. It should not be a process used only occasionally or when the supervisor is not engrossed in daily chores. By planning, the supervisor realistically anticipates and analyzes problems and opportunities, anticipates the probable effects of various alternatives, and chooses the course of action that should lead to the most desirable results. Of course, plans alone do not bring about desired results, but without good planning, activities would be random, thereby producing confusion and inefficiency.

The Strategic-Planning Process

2 Explain the concept of strategic planning and its relationship to mission statements and visioning.

Turbulent and rapid changes in economic conditions and technology, coupled with increasing domestic and international competition, have forced organizations to plan more thoroughly and systematically. As the first function of management, planning must start at the top level of management and permeate all levels of the organization. For the organization as a whole, this means top management must develop an outlook and plans that guide the organization. We call this process **strategic planning**, which essentially means establishing goals and making decisions that enable an organization to achieve its long- and short-term objectives.

Strategic planning
The process of establishing goals and making decisions that enable an organization to achieve its long- and short-term objectives

For many years, noted management scholar Peter Drucker stressed that every organization must think through its reasons for being and constantly ask the question, "What is our business?" Only by asking this question can an organization set goals and objectives, develop strategies, and make decisions that lead to success. Drucker emphasized that answering this question has to be done by that part of the organization that can see the entire business, balance all current objectives and needs against tomorrow's needs, and allocate resources to achieve key results.[1]

Peter Skarzynski and Linda Yates, co-founders of Strategos, a global strategy innovation firm, have echoed Drucker's assertions with their own emphasis on innovation as the guiding principle for all companies in the future. They write:

> *Getting to the future first…requires companies and their leaders to be courageous and farsighted. The company that wins the race to the future is driven by innovation. Not an innovation, but a conscious, built-in, continuous process of innovation that keeps a company on a pathbreaking streak. Innovation must become, like the quality revolution of twenty years ago, the right and responsibility of every individual in a company, not the pet project of the executive suite. Companies that eat and breathe innovation never suffer from prosperity-induced slumbers. They are not predicting the future; they are inventing it.*[2]

In most organizations, top-level managers are primarily responsible for developing and executing strategic or long-term plans. However, once strategic goals and plans have been identified, middle managers and supervisors must be involved in the corresponding planning activities of the organization.[3] These employees must plan their work units' policies and activities to achieve the organization's overall goals. A supervisor likely becomes involved in developing and carrying out certain overall strategic plans for the corporation. Many supervisors like Alan Knuth in the chapter's "You Make the Call!" will not be a part of the organization's budget decisions, but they will certainly be involved in developing policies and procedures that impact the budget.

Strategic planning need not be a burdensome, voluminous undertaking. Strategic planning principles apply to small businesses as much as they do to major corporations. Time limitations and lack of strategic planning knowledge are often impediments for small business owners. The benefits of strategic management in directing the organization as a whole are just as important to small business. Regardless of the size or nature of the organization, managers must be involved in strategy formulation because their participation in the strategic-planning process is essential to gaining commitment for the chosen directions and strategies. Remember: "The inability to create a vision and develop plans is the sure route to failure."

MISSION STATEMENTS AND VISIONING

Effective strategic planning usually begins with the development of a **mission statement** that reflects the philosophy and purpose of the organization as defined by its top leadership. An organization's mission is usually understood to be the purpose of reason for the organization's existence. While many organizations historically had voluminous mission statements that left people scratching their heads and wondering what business they're really in, the trend is toward more precise statements.

Mission statement
A statement of the organization's basic philosophy, purpose, and reason for being

How would you account for the fact that highly unionized Southwest Airlines (SWA) has consistently been the most profitable of U.S. airlines and has not strayed from its core business strategy of flying point-to-point? Colleen Barrett, former president of Southwest Airlines, proudly pointed to the fact that SWA's mission statement added up to less than 100 words:

> 1. *"The mission of Southwest Airlines is dedication to the highest quality of Customer Service delivered with a sense of warmth, friendliness, individual pride, and Company Spirit."*
> 2. *"We are committed to providing our Employees a stable work environment with equal opportunity for learning and personal growth. Creativity and innovation are encouraged for improving the effectiveness of Southwest Airlines. Above all, Employees will be provided the same concern, respect, and caring attitude within the organization that they are expected to share with every Southwest Customer."*[4]

Historically, SWA has worked very, very hard to keep their employees informed and motivated as a means to keep their customers satisfied. SWA treats their internal customers (employees) the way they are being asked to treat their external customers (passengers).

SWA's mission statement is well-known to all employees and the customers who fly Southwest. Top management from CEO Gary Kelly to the line-supervisors is responsible for providing the leadership that sets the desired patterns for employees' behavior. As such, the mission statement serves as a springboard or basis for assessing the company's performance and results.

The concept of visioning goes beyond that of a mission statement. **Visioning** is the process of developing a mental image of what the firm or organization could become; it seeks to define what it is that distinguishes the organization and what will make it better. The vision can become the foundation for all of a firm's activities. There is, of course, some overlap in vision statements and mission

Visioning
Management's view of what the company should become; reflects the firm's core values, priorities, and goals

statements. See Figures 1.9 (page 24) and 6.2 (page 180) for other examples of vision, mission, values, and code of conduct statements.

Visioning and vision statements should not be mere "advertising slogans" that primarily laud the organization and its accomplishments. Rather, visioning should reflect the firm's core values, priorities, and goals, which can be translated into concrete plans and actions.[5]

As mentioned previously, visioning should not be thought of as solely the responsibility of top management. In fact, effective supervisors use visioning to guide their parts of the organization. For example, in the "You Make the Call!" section of this chapter, you can solicit ideas from fellow students as well as from other stakeholders who might be impacted by the policies and procedures that your group develops. Proactive supervisors will glean the "best practices of the best" and figure out how to take those to a higher level for his or her area of responsibility.

Widespread participation in visioning is crucial to realizing the vision. Using contacts and networks, the task force members should strive not only to generate ideas about what should be included in the policy and procedure documents, but also to set the stage for acceptance of the final project. The task force has an opportunity to shape the future.

Many CEOs credit their organization's recent accomplishments to clearly defining what they want to be, identifying their competitive edge, and involving employees in quality improvement efforts. It appears clear that those organizations that diligently work to eliminate ineffective processes and implement customer-first quality improvement programs are increasing their chances for success.

| 3 | Describe the supervisor's role in organizational planning. |

All Managerial Levels Perform the Planning Function

Planning is the responsibility of every manager, whether chairperson of the board, president, division manager, or supervisor of a department. However, the magnitude of a manager's plans depends on the level at which those plans are carried out. Planning at the top level is more far-reaching than it is at the supervisory level. The top-level executive is concerned with overall operation of the enterprise and long-range planning for new facilities and equipment, new products and services, new markets, and major investments. At the supervisory level, the scope is narrower and more detailed. The supervisor is usually concerned with day-to-day plans for accomplishing departmental tasks, such as meeting production quotas for a particular day.

While planning always involves looking to the future, evaluating the past should be part of managerial planning. Every manager can plan more effectively by evaluating previous plans and trying to learn from past successes and failures. While there is no recipe that guarantees success, the guidelines in the accompanying "Supervisory Tips" box are recommended for increasing the probability of reaching the intended target.

In formulating plans, a supervisor may find that certain aspects of planning call for specialized help, such as for implementing employment policies, computer and accounting procedures, or technical know-how. In such areas, the supervisor should consult with specialists in the organization to help carry out the required planning responsibilities. For example, a human resources staff specialist can offer useful advice concerning policies involving employees. A supervisor should pp. 73–78; and Gary Bielous, "How to Fire" *Supervision* (November 1996), pp. 8–10.

23. See Michael J. Phillips, "Toward a Middle Way in the Polarized Debate Over Employment at Will," *American Business Law Journal* (November 1992), pp. 441–83, or Kenneth Gilberg, "Employers Must Protect Against Employee Lawsuits," *Supervision* (November 1992), pp. 12–13.

24. See "Loss of At-Will Job is Compensable," *HR News* (February 1999), p. 8.

25. See Matt Siegel, "Yes, They Can Fire You," *Fortune* (October 26, 1998), p. 301.

26. See Diane Cadrain, "Helping Workers Fool Drug Tests Is a Big Business," *HR Magazine* (August 2005), pp. 29, 32. This article purports that Quest runs over seven million drug tests annually. Federal agencies spent $16.1 million in 2004 under the Federal Drug-Free Workplace Program. The U.S. Department of Labor says that alcohol and drug abuse costs American businesses roughly $81 billion in lost productivity. Employers also shouldered hidden costs related to tardiness, absenteeism, healthcare benefits, and turnover. The newest cost: As new drug-masking products enter the market, test labs have to develop new detection technologies, and they pass the costs along to employers.

    The American Council on Drug Education said that drug abusers are 10 times more likely to miss work, 3.6 times more likely to be involved in on-the-job accidents, and 5 times more likely to file a workers' compensation claim. They also are two-thirds as productive and are responsible for healthcare costs that are 3 times as high.

27. The author first heard the term *CYR (cover your rear)* while an ROTC student in 1958. For a recent discussion on the advantage of CYR, see Jared Sandberg, "Covering Yourself is Counterproductive But May Save Your Job," *The Wall Street Journal* (June 8, 2005), p. B1.

28. For an expanded discussion of no-fault and other employee attendance policies, see M. Michael Markowich, "When Is Excessive Absenteeism Grounds for Disciplinary Action?" *ACA News* (July/August 1998), pp. 36–39.

29. For a thorough discussion of the pros and cons and applications of discipline-without-punishment approaches, see Dick Grote, *Discipline without Punishment* (New York: American Management Association, 1995). See also Dick Grote, "Discipline without Punishment," *Across-the-Board* (September/October 2001) pp. 52–57; and Jathan Janove, *Managing to Stay out of Court* (Berrett-Kohler, 2005). Janove reaffirms that the following will likely land you in court: acting inconsistently, treating one employee differently from another; treating employees differently from what documented policies require; letting documents conflict with one another; or treating one person in different ways over time.

30. Definition of norms adapted from discussion by Don Harvey and Robert Bruce Bowin, *Human Resource Management; An Experiential Approach* (Upper Saddle River, NJ: Prentice Hall, 1996), pp. 15–21.

31. For a discussion of what fairness means to employees, see Susan E. Jackson, Randall S. Schuler and Steve Werner, *Managing Human Resources*, 10th ed. (Mason, OH: South-Western/Cengage Learning, 2009), pp. 116–120. Also See Maurice A. Ramirez, "Outrage of Enthusiasm: The Choice is Yours," *Supervision*, 69, 4 (April 2008), pp. 17–19; Bill Catlette and Richard Hadden, "Consistency Does Not Equal Fairness," *Supervision*, 69, 2 (February 2008), pp. 19–21; T. Simons and Q. Roberson, "Why Managers Should Care about Fairness: The Effects of Aggregate Justice Perceptions on Organizational Outcomes," *Journal of Applied Psychology*, 88, 3 (2006), pp. 432–443; and M. L. Williams, M. A. McDonald and N.T. Nguyen, "A Meta-Analysis of the Antecedents and Consequences of Pay Level Satisfaction," *Journal of Applied Psychology*, 91 (2006), pp. 392–413.

32. Many psychology and biology texts discuss the psychological and biological aspects of stressful situations. For an expanded discussion of the fight/flight responses see Bronston T. Mayes and Daniel C. Ganster, "Exit and Voice: A test hypotheses based on the fight/flight response to job stress," *Journal of Organizational Behavior*, 9, 3 (July 1998), pp. 199–216 (published online November 20, 2006). Also see, S. E. Taylor, et.al., "Biobehavioral responses to stress in females: Tend-and-befriend, not fight-or-flight," *Psychological Review*, 107 (2000), pp. 411–429; or H.S. Friedman and R.C. Silver, *Foundations of Health Psychology* (New York: Oxford University Press, 2007).

33. See "Employee Engagement Report 2008 (BlessingWhite, http://www.blessingwhit.com/EEE, April/May 2008). Also see Ann Pomeroy, "Senior Management Begins Regaining Employee Trust," *HR Magazine* (February 2005), p. 14.

(PART 2 CASES)

CASE 2-1
The Picnic Conversation

Barry Automotive's Glendale Plant's annual picnic was well attended, as usual. It was a well-planned, daylong family affair for all employees of the firm, giving them an opportunity to get together informally. At the picnic, Charlene Knox, one of the supervisors, had a long chat with her boss, Jim Cross, the general manager. They spoke about many things, including some work problems. Cross greatly emphasized the need to cut costs and generally tighten company finances. He told Knox that he had already received a number of written suggestions and plans from some other supervisors. He highly praised their efforts as appropriate and helpful.

Three weeks after the picnic, Charlene Knox received a memo from her boss asking her why her "report in reference to cost cutting" had not yet arrived. At first, she wondered what Jim Cross was referring to, and then she remembered their talk at the picnic. She realized that was the only time Cross had discussed with her the need to cut costs. Knox pondered what her response should be.

Questions for Discussion
1. Is it appropriate for a supervisor to give a directive to a subordinate in a social, off-the-job setting? Why or why not?
2. Was Charlene Knox at fault for failing to understand what her boss told her at the picnic? Was Jim Cross at fault? Were both managers at fault?
3. What should Knox do? Why?

CASE 2-2
Abusive Rumors

John Jacobs is supervisor for the electronics department of Appliances Galore, a chain of large superstores specializing in appliance sales to retail and commercial customers. The company has a reputation for extensive involvement in community activities. In fact, the company strongly promotes family values and has sponsored various family-oriented activities throughout the years. In addition, the company provides financial and other incentives to employees who volunteer their time in not-for-profit and other service activities. Andy George, manager of marketing operations, has just confided to Jacobs that he had heard "through the grapevine" that Steve Shepard's wife and two children appeared last night at the local women's-and-children's shelter. George also indicated that Shepard's wife was reported to have been badly bruised and that this was not the first time the family had sought refuge. Steve Shepard is one of Jacobs's outstanding salespeople. Last year, Shepard won the company's award for the most sales. George suggested to Jacobs that he should investigate the matter and make a recommendation about what the company should do.

Questions for Discussion

1. If Steve Shepard's job performance was not affected by his personal life, should the company become involved in any way? Discuss.

2. If Steve Shepard's alleged actions off the job became public knowledge and reflected on the image and reputation of Appliances Galore, should the company take any action?

3. What would you recommend that Jacobs and George do? Consider alternatives.

CASE 2-3
The Little Things Add Up!

Lynda Heredia has worked for Economy Parcel Service (EPS), a large package delivery company, for the past 22 years. She knows that pleasing the customer is the key to operating a successful business. She is extremely proud of the "Employee of the Month" awards she has received. Several times before, Heredia has been offered various supervisory positions, but she has always turned them down because she does not want the extra duties and responsibilities that come with advancement. Management considers her the "ideal employee." She rarely needs to be told what to do and never misses work. Her work is always done the right way the first time. Operations manager Josh Simpson has been overheard to remark, "I wish we could figure out a way to clone Lynda. She's by far the best employee we've got."

Heredia works the 11:00 P.M. to 7:30 A.M. shift. Her position is vital because she sorts packages on both sides of the master conveyor belt and directs them onto assorted belts where others load them into bins and then into delivery vehicles. Due to a downturn in the economy and increased competition, EPS's business recently dropped off drastically. The company cut overhead and significantly reduced its number of employees. Business had picked up in recent months such that the number of packages handled daily approached previous levels, but those employees who remained after the cutbacks were expected to get the same amount of work done with fewer people and resources, and increase productivity, tighten delivery schedules, and accept no pay raises. The last item was especially difficult for Heredia because she is principal caregiver for her elderly mother. All of her mother's Social Security income went for medical costs and other essentials. Heredia's weekly paycheck usually covered all other expenses, but nothing was left over for recreation or investment. "The harder I work, the behinder I get," Heredia lamented.

On Wednesday, Heredia came into work early, as always, and told her immediate supervisor, Tony Lehman, that she had to leave by 6:30 A.M. because her mother had an 8:00 A.M. appointment at the hospital for some much-needed medical tests. Lehman responded, "Fine. Just remind me later." Lehman had been Heredia's immediate supervisor for the past seven months, but they had known each other for about fifteen years. Heredia's previous supervisor had been downsized, and Lehman's duties had been expanded to cover several additional areas, including the one in which Heredia worked. Unlike Heredia's previous supervisor, Lehman failed to tell his employees what he expected them to do and rarely gave them positive feedback. It might have been because he was expected to do more with less.

At 5:30 A.M., Heredia reminded Lehman about the appointment, and Lehman asked the operations manager if he had an employee to cover the hour of Heredia's shift because she had to leave. The operations manager's response was, "No, I don't have anyone. In fact, we're so short of people right now that

I don't know if we'll meet the delivery schedule. If I would have known sooner, I might have been able to find coverage for you."

When Lehman told her she would be unable to leave early, Heredia immediately began to fume. "So this is the way they treat dedicated and loyal employees. After all, I asked my supervisor at the beginning of the shift if I could leave early—just like the handbook says," Heredia lamented to anyone willing to listen. She stayed until her regular quitting time, but her full attention was not on her work. As a result, several mistakes occurred.

After punching out, Heredia rushed home, hustled her mother into the car, and left for the hospital. While waiting for her mother to finish her tests, the psychologically "down and out" Heredia, in her dirty work attire, kept playing the events over and over in her mind. "I don't ask this company for much, and I bend over backward to get the job done. I'll show them: I'll call in sick tomorrow and see how they appreciate the inconvenience."

About 15 minutes before her assigned shift the next day, Heredia called her supervisor and said, "I'm not feeling well this evening. I think it might be that new strain of flu, and I'd hate to spread it to anyone else. I'll call you tomorrow evening and let you know how I'm feeling because I'm also scheduled to work tomorrow evening." Heredia still had several sick days and personal days left, and company policy only required employees to report their sicknesses at least 15 minutes before the start of their shifts.

Of course, the employee assigned to perform Heredia's duties lacked the skill or knowledge to do the job in a correct and timely fashion. Additionally, that employee feared making mistakes, so every package was checked and double-checked to ensure that it got onto the right conveyor. Work-in-progress backed up, and many trucks did not get loaded until mid-morning. In short, many customers received their packages late.

Questions for Discussion

1. What are your initial observations about the problems that must be addressed at EPS?
2. What could Lehman have done to prevent or minimize those problems?
3. Using the ABC analysis (see Chapter 4), discuss why Lynda Heredia behaved the way she did.
4. Lynda Heredia now has a negative attitude. What suggestions would you make to Lehman to change Heredia's outlook? To what extent should Lehman involve upper management in the solution?
5. How did mistrust and lack of common courtesy add to the complexity of the situation?
6. Someone once said, "Learn from the mistakes of others. You'll never live long enough to make them all yourself." How can EPS use this situation as a case study for the entire organization?
7. What did you learn from this case?

(**ROLE PLAY**) **Role-Play Activity:** Assign one student to play the role of Lynda Heredia and another to play the role of Lehman. For role-play purposes, assume that Lynda Heredia's performance shows a steady decline and that she repeatedly calls in several minutes before her assigned shift, claiming to be "not feeling well." Heredia is working the employee handbook to the maximum and is using all her allotted personal days.

Cynthia is the proof and auditing department supervisor for Middletown National Bank and reports directly to the vice president of Internal Services. She supervises all day-shift personnel relative to assigning work and following up to make sure work is properly completed. She also supervises the night-shift supervisor, assisting and advising as required. Typical functional responsibilities include:

- Allocates work assignments and follows up to ensure the work is completed on schedule.
- Resolves any problems referred by subordinates and/or upper management.
- Sees that equipment is properly maintained and in good working order, interfacing with the vendors for proper service as required.
- Interviews and hires all new members of the department.
- Evaluates and makes recommendations for pay increases, promotions, and transfers, for all employees on the day shift.
- Reviews all job evaluations and personnel recommendations for the night-shift personnel.
- Assists, advises, and trains night-shift supervisor in the handling of employees.
- Makes recommendations regarding improved methods of handling certain types of transactions and redesign of specific documents to increase efficiency.
- Oversees the gathering, preparation, and analysis of various Proof Department reports designed to establish standards and measure productivity.
- Performs any other duties as required or assigned for the efficient operation of the Proof Department.

Cynthia loves words, and uses her large vocabulary extensively. This morning, her boss was under stress and needed to vent. In a private meeting with Cynthia, he said, "You use big words to make yourself sound better than other people, and you try to intimidate people with your intelligence." Cynthia was shocked and (would you believe) apologetic. In her most recent performance assessment, several subordinates described her as an aggressive perfectionist. At the time, she wondered what she had done to warrant that description.

Source: Case adapted with permission from Edwin C. Leonard, Jr. and Roy A. Cook, *Human Resource Management: 21st Century Challenges* (Mason, OH: Thomson Custom Publishing, 2005), p. 118.

Questions for Discussion

1. Would you like to work for Cynthia? Why or why not?
2. Cynthia's problem is not uncommon. What are the symptoms of mismanagement?
3. (**INTERNET ACTIVITY**) Using the Internet, find at least two sources that detail techniques for dealing with someone who might be described as an aggressive perfectionist. Write a one-page paper describing how a subordinate might cope with the situation.
4. What would you do if you were Cynthia?
5. In no more than forty words, describe what you learned from this case.

Speeding through the rolling Piedmont hills on his motorcycle, Vance Patterson could barely concentrate on the road. Instead, his thoughts were on his business, Patterson Fan. Things had not been going well. Founded in 1989, the Blythewood, South Carolina–based company, which makes industrial fans and coolers, had once been fun, energized, and profitable. Now at least a third of Patterson's sixty employees seemed to be in a state of constant disgruntlement, complaining about everything. Productivity and sales were plummeting. Patterson was getting desperate.

He thought back to the company's early days. It was exactly the kind of place where he had always wanted to work. He supplied sodas and popcorn and hosted quarterly cookouts where employees danced to mariachi and steel-drum bands. Each holiday season, he would hand out bonuses and fat profit-sharing checks. In 2000, when sales hit a record $8.5 million, those checks ranged from $7,000 to $35,000.

But after a decade of steady growth, revenue slipped to $7.2 million in 2001. Even so, Patterson had about $200,000 in profits to share, but the checks came in smaller amounts than many employees had expected, which led to grumbling. And as the business climate continued to worsen, so did morale.

Employees seemed to be gossiping more about one another and the company. Sales reps began accusing colleagues of encroaching on their turf. Soon, careless errors became alarmingly commonplace. In one case, workers reported that they had performed some routine maintenance on the spinning machine that made the housing for fans. When the device broke down, it became clear that the maintenance had never been completed.

Patterson had to contract with a manufacturer in Indiana, adding high freight costs that hammered the company's bottom line. Customers began complaining about flawed products, including fans with backward blades or missing bolts. The company's hardworking employees were affected as well. "People were going around saying, 'Slow down, don't listen to so-and-so,'" said James Ballentine, the company's capacity planner. "It was bringing the whole company down."

Patterson responded by becoming the kind of manager he'd always loathed. He demanded that salespeople begin making 45 to 60 calls a day, and managers monitored them by poring over phone records. When he noticed things like eBay pages on computer monitors as he roamed the halls, he installed computer-monitoring software. And when he saw workers arriving late and leaving early, he installed time clocks—both on the factory floor and in the business office. "We were spending all our time in meetings talking about bad employees," he says.

By August 2004, Patterson felt as if he was spending every day trying to fix his employees' bad behavior. Driving to work on his Harley one morning, he tried to clear his head. Somewhere between drinking a thermos of coffee at the Kings Mountain State Park and pulling into the parking lot of the Blythewood factory, he started to imagine what would happen if he just fired all of the grousing, underperforming employees. He had to admit, it was a pretty appealing daydream.

The next day, Patterson had his weekly meeting with his three most trusted managers. He strode in and shut the conference room door behind him. "Let's get rid of the bad employees and replace them," he said. Thomas Salisbury, the company's vice-president of operations, slammed the table with enthusiasm. The other two were more skeptical and asked for some time to think it over. But by the following week's planning meeting, the entire team was on board.

Fortunately, the high season had just ended, making it a logical time to cut back. Patterson asked his sales manager to draw up a list of reps with bad attitudes or poor performance. He came back with six names. The production supervisors came back with eleven. Patterson did a review of the business office and was shocked to discover that over the previous two years, an employee had charged some $10,000 in personal products to a corporate credit card. That

Sure enough, Paula Whisler arrived 45 minutes late. Georgia Mason realized that the situation required action on her part, but she did not know what that action should be.

Questions for Discussion

1. Explain how the principles of the "hot stove rule" discussed in Chapter 6 were applied improperly by Georgia Mason in this case.
2. Should Georgia Mason consider Paula Whisler's home situation when trying to maintain departmental standards? Why or why not?
3. Can the conflict between organizational demands and employees' personal problems be reconciled and still accomplish the objectives of the organization? If so, how?
4. What action should Mason take? What alternatives are open if the problem is not solved quickly?

Robert Brown is the plant manager for Kelmer Manufacturing, a unionized manufacturer of cement mixers. Kelmer Manufacturing works Monday through Friday with two fully operational production shifts and a third shift supervised by Richard Ellis, one of Brown's direct reports. The third shift provides maintenance, materials handling, and support for the other two shifts. Brown rarely has to worry about the efficiency of the third shift. Nevertheless, his management by wandering around (MBWA) style led him to periodically drop in on each of the shifts—not to spy or investigate but to reward and recognize the contributions of employees. The nine third-shift workers are a tightly knit, fun-loving group, who socialize frequently off the job.

Richard Ellis, a very likeable twenty-year veteran of Kelmer Manufacturing, was pleased to announce his forthcoming wedding to Susan Jones on the Friday following Thanksgiving. Jones, divorced with two grown children, worked for a local law firm. According to Ellis, it seemed like a match made in heaven. Brown, along with most of the management team and third-shift employees, attended the wedding.

In early December, President Gene Biggs received an anonymous phone call from someone claiming that one of his [the caller's] friends had taken pictures of nude women frolicking with Kelmer employees—in the plant and during work hours. Biggs initially dismissed the phone call as a prank until Carl Simmons, the vice president of marketing, reported that a customer had seen Internet photos of nude women at what appeared to be the Kelmer plant.

Not knowing the specific Internet site or having any other specifics, Biggs called his legal counsel, Loren Adams. Adams's investigation found 97 pictures on a pornographic Web site. It was clear that the photos were from the Kelmer plant.

Biggs was appalled. He relayed the results of the investigation to Robert Brown and other members of the management team, saying, "Any time there are unauthorized visitors in the plant, it is wrong. Any time we're talking about nudity in the plant, it's embarrassing. One of our supervisors allowed these photos to be taken. We have a major problem, and I need your help to get this thing resolved. In the past three years, we have overhauled our manufacturing processes, solved our quality problems, and built a solid reputation. Everything we do has been at the highest level, and this one makes me very angry. I want to fire the whole bunch."

Discussion of the Web site spread like a wildfire through the employee ranks. One member of the management team remarked, "I had several questions about this at a Rotary meeting this morning. All I could say was that we're looking into it."

CASE 2-8
How Could It
Happen Here?

In a meeting with Brown, Attorney Thomas Adams, and HR professional Jessica Salisbury, the nine employees involved in the investigation at first denied any knowledge of the photographs. Later, during videotaped interviews and with representation from their union, four of the men accused Richard Ellis and fellow employee Jay Bracey of urging them to keep silent about the photographs. Two other employees alleged that Ellis and Bracey called them repeatedly and urged them to lie if asked about the event.

About the same time that President Biggs received the anonymous phone call, Ellis stumbled upon the Web site. "We've got problems," Ellis allegedly told Bracey. "They've got pictures on the Internet. What are we going to do?"

Biggs contacted each member of the board of directors and familiarized them with the situation. The good news that the company was expected to exceed its fourth-quarter earnings estimates was clouded by the fact that he had to admit that things hadn't gone as expected. When Biggs dropped the bombshell regarding the nude Internet photos, the board members were stunned. "How could such a thing have happened?" they wondered.

Biggs instructed Brown to work with Thomas Adams and Jessica Salisbury to recommend what disciplinary action to take. He concluded by saying, "People are laughing at us, and I don't know how we can correct this public-relations problem. I can't believe that something like this could ever happen here!"

The union-management contract provisions give management the right to discipline for just cause, but Brown has never had a situation like this. (Figure 6.4 in chapter 6 is a partial listing of the Kelmer Company rules and regulations.) As Brown sat in the company parking lot, thinking about the events of the last few days, he remembered his old college instructor's words: "Management has the right to discipline employees for just cause, but there must be a clearly identifiable and justifiable reason for taking disciplinary action." As he turned the ignition key to drive home, Brown thought to himself, "I trusted those guys, and they did this. They are among the best employees we have. I feel like a failure."

Questions for Discussion

1. What would motivate employees to act the way they allegedly did? Was there behavior reasonable? Why? Why not?
2. Discuss the implications of not "disciplining" the employees for their involvement.
3. If you were assigned responsibility for conducting an investigatory interview of each of the employees alleged to have been involved in the episode:
   a. Describe the approach you would use to conduct the interview.
   b. What specific questions would you ask?
   c. How would you verify the information provided by the employees to be fact, rumor, conjecture, or a fabrication?
4. Role-Play Exercise
   a. (**ROLE PLAY**) Prior to participating in this exercise, each student should review the supervisory tips boxes in chapters 3, 4, 5, and 6 carefully and then, individually, prepare an action plan for dealing with the charge from President Gene Biggs to recommend disciplinary action for the employees involved in the situation.
   b. Divide the class into groups of three. Students should be assigned the roles of Robert Brown, Thomas Adams, or Jessica Salisbury. Allow the group ten minutes to develop a proposal for President Gene Biggs.

   c. Select one group to present their recommendations to President Biggs. The remaining students should assume the role of President Biggs. All students can participate in the ensuing discussion.
   d. In Chapter 6, we discussed progressive discipline and how to apply the "hot stove rule." To what extent did the groups consider these two concepts in determining appropriate action? What else should they have considered?

5. Some organizations, particularly in the public sector, have a five-person board that hears all charges of inappropriate behavior; investigates, if necessary; and recommends disciplinary action, if any, to be taken. If Kelmer Manufacturing has a disciplinary committee comprised of two members of management, a representative from HR, and two rank-and-file union members, what do you suppose the disciplinary board would recommend in this case? Explain your reasoning.

6. What suggestions would you give President Gene Biggs to minimize the recurrence of this or a similar problem?

7. Write a one-page paper detailing what you learned from this case.

(Planning and Organizing)

PART 3

CHAPTER 7

(Supervisory Planning)

After studying this chapter, you will be able to:

1 Define planning and explain why all management functions depend on planning.

2 Explain the concept of strategic planning and its relationship to mission statements and visioning.

3 Describe the supervisor's role in organizational planning.

4 Discuss the need for well-defined organizational goals and objectives, particularly as they relate to the supervisor.

5 Explain management by objectives (MBO).

6 Identify the major types of standing and single-use plans and explain how these plans help supervisory decision making.

7 Describe how the supervisor plans for efficient and effective resource use.

8 Explain the key concepts of quality planning.

9 Recognize the importance of planning for the unthinkable (crisis management).

YOU MAKE THE CALL!

You are Alan Knuth, junior business major at Old Ivy University. It was a beautiful spring day, April 16, 2007, as you strolled through the student center. There were Professor Vaught, Dean Johnson, and Chancellor Michaels talking over coffee. As you walked by the table, Professor Vaught asked you to sit down and, after brief introductions, the discussion revolved around your classes, the weather, and the university's volleyball team. The Chancellor fully expected the team to win the conference and qualify for the NCAA Division I tournament.

Just as you were getting up to leave to meet your study team at the library, all attention was directed to the televisions. There was a breaking news story about a shooting at Virginia Tech. Concern escalated as both Professor Vaught and Chancellor Michaels knew administrators and faculty at Tech. When you arrived at the library, most students were clustered in front of the television. The rest of the day was a blur; it was tough to concentrate on the lectures. By day's end you knew about the carnage that had occurred.

Everyone was talking about Seung Hui Cho, the 23-year-old English major, who used handguns to vent his rage at the world. He murdered 32 students and wounded dozens more before killing himself. Your grandfather always talked about "days of infamy"—where and what he was doing on December 7, 1941. Your father told stories about the day President Kennedy was assassinated and the mourning that followed. And you vividly recall 9/11. The memories of a tragedy linger on forever. Your grandfather always said, "preventing tragedies is like saying we can prevent auto accidents."

In a business and society course, you had heard incredible stories about how employees "go postal." Before you went to sleep that night, you and your suitemates talked about how something like that could never happen at Old Ivy. Your thoughts were drawn to several of the students you had seen on campus and in classes. You wondered whether they knew "right from left" and if they "were playing with a full deck." You recalled how hurt you were when your sweetheart since your junior year in high school broke off the relationship. You brooded about it and it affected your grades. Your friends and the campus minister helped you get over it. It took a while to stop nursing the hurt and count your blessings. Your feelings were normal and you appreciated the generosity of those who reached out to you in your time of need.

Mid-morning the next day, you received a text message that Professor Vaught wanted to see you as soon as possible. When you arrived at his office, he ushered you to the conference room. Dean Johnson and fellow business student Kelly Notter were already there. The short of the story was that Chancellor Michaels wanted a blue-ribbon task force of students to review the university's policies and procedures on safety and security, review what other organizations were doing, and then meet with faculty and staff committees to draft new policies and procedures to deal with potential disasters. You and Kelly Notter, along with students from nursing and health sciences, computer technology, engineering, communications, and psychological sciences, would be on the student leadership task force. Don Henderson, Associate Director of Safety and Security, would chair the task force and serve as a resource. Saying thank-you in advance, the Chancellor announced that a special honors study—a three-credit-hour course—was being established and each student would receive credit for their participation. You knew that this was quite an honor and a formidable undertaking. The first meeting was the next morning at 7 A.M. You wondered what could be done to prepare for the meeting. **YOU MAKE THE CALL!**

Management Functions Begin with Planning

1 Define planning and explain why all management functions depend on planning.

Management scholars and practitioners disagree about the number and designation of managerial functions. However, the consensus is that the first, and probably the most crucial, managerial function is planning.

Planning means deciding what is to be done in the future. It includes analyzing a situation, forecasting events, establishing objectives, setting priorities, and deciding which actions are needed to achieve those objectives. Logically, planning precedes all other managerial functions because every manager must project a framework and a course of action before trying to achieve desired results. For

Planning
The process of deciding what needs to be done by whom by when

example, how can a supervisor organize a department's operations without a plan? How can a supervisor effectively staff and lead employees without knowing which avenues to follow? How can a supervisor control employee activities without standards and objectives? All managerial functions depend on planning.

Planning is a managerial function every supervisor must perform every day. It should not be a process used only occasionally or when the supervisor is not engrossed in daily chores. By planning, the supervisor realistically anticipates and analyzes problems and opportunities, anticipates the probable effects of various alternatives, and chooses the course of action that should lead to the most desirable results. Of course, plans alone do not bring about desired results, but without good planning, activities would be random, thereby producing confusion and inefficiency.

2 Explain the concept of strategic planning and its relationship to mission statements and visioning.

Strategic planning
The process of establishing goals and making decisions that enable an organization to achieve its long- and short-term objectives

The Strategic-Planning Process

Turbulent and rapid changes in economic conditions and technology, coupled with increasing domestic and international competition, have forced organizations to plan more thoroughly and systematically. As the first function of management, planning must start at the top level of management and permeate all levels of the organization. For the organization as a whole, this means top management must develop an outlook and plans that guide the organization. We call this process **strategic planning**, which essentially means establishing goals and making decisions that enable an organization to achieve its long- and short-term objectives.

For many years, noted management scholar Peter Drucker stressed that every organization must think through its reasons for being and constantly ask the question, "What is our business?" Only by asking this question can an organization set goals and objectives, develop strategies, and make decisions that lead to success. Drucker emphasized that answering this question has to be done by that part of the organization that can see the entire business, balance all current objectives and needs against tomorrow's needs, and allocate resources to achieve key results.[1]

Peter Skarzynski and Linda Yates, co-founders of Strategos, a global strategy innovation firm, have echoed Drucker's assertions with their own emphasis on innovation as the guiding principle for all companies in the future. They write:

> Getting to the future first...requires companies and their leaders to be courageous and farsighted. The company that wins the race to the future is driven by innovation. Not an innovation, but a conscious, built-in, continuous process of innovation that keeps a company on a pathbreaking streak. Innovation must become, like the quality revolution of twenty years ago, the right and responsibility of every individual in a company, not the pet project of the executive suite. Companies that eat and breathe innovation never suffer from prosperity-induced slumbers. They are not predicting the future; they are inventing it.[2]

In most organizations, top-level managers are primarily responsible for developing and executing strategic or long-term plans. However, once strategic goals and plans have been identified, middle managers and supervisors must be involved in the corresponding planning activities of the organization.[3] These employees must plan their work units' policies and activities to achieve the organization's overall goals. A supervisor likely becomes involved in developing and carrying out certain overall strategic plans for the corporation. Many supervisors like Alan Knuth in the chapter's "You Make the Call!" will not be a part of the organization's budget decisions, but they will certainly be involved in developing policies and procedures that impact the budget.

Strategic planning need not be a burdensome, voluminous undertaking. Strategic planning principles apply to small businesses as much as they do to major corporations. Time limitations and lack of strategic planning knowledge are often impediments for small business owners. The benefits of strategic management in directing the organization as a whole are just as important to small business. Regardless of the size or nature of the organization, managers must be involved in strategy formulation because their participation in the strategic-planning process is essential to gaining commitment for the chosen directions and strategies. Remember: "The inability to create a vision and develop plans is the sure route to failure."

MISSION STATEMENTS AND VISIONING

Effective strategic planning usually begins with the development of a **mission statement** that reflects the philosophy and purpose of the organization as defined by its top leadership. An organization's mission is usually understood to be the purpose of reason for the organization's existence. While many organizations historically had voluminous mission statements that left people scratching their heads and wondering what business they're really in, the trend is toward more precise statements.

Mission statement
A statement of the organization's basic philosophy, purpose, and reason for being

How would you account for the fact that highly unionized Southwest Airlines (SWA) has consistently been the most profitable of U.S. airlines and has not strayed from its core business strategy of flying point-to-point? Colleen Barrett, former president of Southwest Airlines, proudly pointed to the fact that SWA's mission statement added up to less than 100 words:

> 1. *"The mission of Southwest Airlines is dedication to the highest quality of Customer Service delivered with a sense of warmth, friendliness, individual pride, and Company Spirit."*
> 2. *"We are committed to providing our Employees a stable work environment with equal opportunity for learning and personal growth. Creativity and innovation are encouraged for improving the effectiveness of Southwest Airlines. Above all, Employees will be provided the same concern, respect, and caring attitude within the organization that they are expected to share with every Southwest Customer."*[4]

Historically, SWA has worked very, very hard to keep their employees informed and motivated as a means to keep their customers satisfied. SWA treats their internal customers (employees) the way they are being asked to treat their external customers (passengers).

SWA's mission statement is well-known to all employees and the customers who fly Southwest. Top management from CEO Gary Kelly to the line-supervisors is responsible for providing the leadership that sets the desired patterns for employees' behavior. As such, the mission statement serves as a springboard or basis for assessing the company's performance and results.

The concept of visioning goes beyond that of a mission statement. **Visioning** is the process of developing a mental image of what the firm or organization could become; it seeks to define what it is that distinguishes the organization and what will make it better. The vision can become the foundation for all of a firm's activities. There is, of course, some overlap in vision statements and mission

Visioning
Management's view of what the company should become; reflects the firm's core values, priorities, and goals

statements. See Figures 1.9 (page 24) and 6.2 (page 180) for other examples of vision, mission, values, and code of conduct statements.

Visioning and vision statements should not be mere "advertising slogans" that primarily laud the organization and its accomplishments. Rather, visioning should reflect the firm's core values, priorities, and goals, which can be translated into concrete plans and actions.[5]

As mentioned previously, visioning should not be thought of as solely the responsibility of top management. In fact, effective supervisors use visioning to guide their parts of the organization. For example, in the "You Make the Call!" section of this chapter, you can solicit ideas from fellow students as well as from other stakeholders who might be impacted by the policies and procedures that your group develops. Proactive supervisors will glean the "best practices of the best" and figure out how to take those to a higher level for his or her area of responsibility.

Widespread participation in visioning is crucial to realizing the vision. Using contacts and networks, the task force members should strive not only to generate ideas about what should be included in the policy and procedure documents, but also to set the stage for acceptance of the final project. The task force has an opportunity to shape the future.

Many CEOs credit their organization's recent accomplishments to clearly defining what they want to be, identifying their competitive edge, and involving employees in quality improvement efforts. It appears clear that those organizations that diligently work to eliminate ineffective processes and implement customer-first quality improvement programs are increasing their chances for success.

All Managerial Levels Perform the Planning Function

3 Describe the supervisor's role in organizational planning.

Planning is the responsibility of every manager, whether chairperson of the board, president, division manager, or supervisor of a department. However, the magnitude of a manager's plans depends on the level at which those plans are carried out. Planning at the top level is more far-reaching than it is at the supervisory level. The top-level executive is concerned with overall operation of the enterprise and long-range planning for new facilities and equipment, new products and services, new markets, and major investments. At the supervisory level, the scope is narrower and more detailed. The supervisor is usually concerned with day-to-day plans for accomplishing departmental tasks, such as meeting production quotas for a particular day.

While planning always involves looking to the future, evaluating the past should be part of managerial planning. Every manager can plan more effectively by evaluating previous plans and trying to learn from past successes and failures. While there is no recipe that guarantees success, the guidelines in the accompanying "Supervisory Tips" box are recommended for increasing the probability of reaching the intended target.

In formulating plans, a supervisor may find that certain aspects of planning call for specialized help, such as for implementing employment policies, computer and accounting procedures, or technical know-how. In such areas, the supervisor should consult with specialists in the organization to help carry out the required planning responsibilities. For example, a human resources staff specialist can offer useful advice concerning policies involving employees. A supervisor should

SUPERVISORY TIPS
How to Reach Your Goal

1. Create a vision.
2. Develop a mission statement.
3. Involve others in setting SMART[1] goals/objectives:
   Stretching, yet attainable.
   Measurable by expressing it in a quantity.
   Accountable by identifying the individual responsible for accomplishment.
   Realistic, set in light of past performance, organizational resources, states of nature, and the competitive environment.
   Time limited. This is often accomplished by expressing the objective in terms of the conditions or results to be achieved by a specific point in time. *What is to be done by when.*
4. Communicate goals/objectives to all those who must know.
5. Develop plans/strategies for reaching the goal/objective.
6. Put the plan in writing.
7. Secure commitment to the plan.
8. Put the plan into action. Assign responsibility, accountability, and authority.
9. Establish feedback controls and monitor progress.
10. Make changes, if necessary.

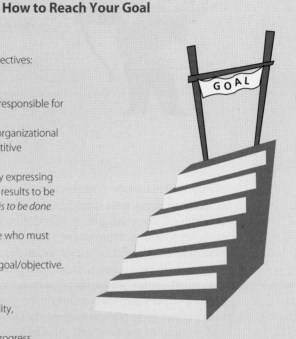

Note: (1) In early editions of this text, we advocated that objectives be specific, measurable, attainable, realistic to organization resources, and time limited. The authors would like to thank Mike Lynch and Harvey Lifton for introducing us to the notion of evaluating objectives by applying their SMART criteria. See "Training Clips: 150 Reproducible Handouts: Discussion Starters and Job Aids," *HRD Press* (1998), p. 118.

use available help in the organization to plan thoroughly and specifically. This includes consulting with employees for their suggestions on how to proceed in certain situations. Employees like to be consulted, and their advice may help the supervisor develop day-to-day plans for running the department. In small firms, expertise may not be readily available, so the supervisor may want to draw on personal contacts outside the firm. In the final analysis, each supervisor is personally responsible for planning (see Figure 7.1 for a list of questions to ask before developing plans).

PLANNING PERIODS

For how long should a manager plan? Usually, a distinction is made between long-range and short-range planning. The definitions of long-range and short-range planning depend on the manager's level in the organizational hierarchy, the type of enterprise, and the kind of industry in which the organization is operating. Most managers define *short-range planning* as that which spans less than one year. Most of the time, supervisors devote their attention to short-range

FIGURE 7.1 Planning requires answering these questions

Why must it be done?

When should it be done?

Who should do it?

Where should it be done?

How should it be done?

planning. This means a supervisor must take time to think through the nature and amount of work that is assigned to the department. Very short-range planning is involved, for example, in scheduling a production run or staffing an end-of-summer sale in a department store. Many supervisors prefer to do this type of planning at the end of a day or at the end of a week when they can evaluate what has been accomplished. There are some activities, such as preventive maintenance, for which the supervisor can plan several months in advance. The plans a supervisor makes should be integrated and coordinated with the long-range plans of upper management. These long-range plans stem from the vision and mission of the firm and are often called the **strategic plan**.

Strategic plan
Long-term plans developed by top management

Supervisors who are well-informed about an organization's long-range plans are better positioned to integrate their short-range plans with overall corporate plans. By the same token, each supervisor should bear in mind that employees are affected by plans. Whenever possible, a supervisor should explain to employees in advance what is being planned for the department. At the very best, well-informed employees appreciate that they have been kept informed and that they need not look to the grapevine for information about their future.

The "doom-and-gloom" economic forecasts during the summer of 2008 severely hampered most organizations' ability to plan. Rather than focus on a longer time-horizon, some "mom-and-pop" organizations familiar to the author developed very short planning time frames. Generating enough sales revenue to meet Friday's payroll took precedence over focusing on long-term plans. Remember: In order to develop realistic and meaningful plans, managers must make assumptions about the future and make adjustments as necessary. Economic volatility and a rapidly changing competitive environment require constant monitoring and adjustments. Regardless of such challenges, it is essential that long-range plans be developed. Ask yourself these questions:

● Where do I see myself a year from now? Five years from now?
● What will I be doing?
● Who will I be doing it with?

As illustrated in Chapter 5 (see Figure 5.1, page 157), "Before individuals can decide in which direction to go, they must determine where they want to get to," or, as author Stephen Covey says, "Always begin with the end in mind."

Organizational Goals and Objectives

A first, major step in planning is to develop a general statement of goals and objectives that identifies the overall purposes and results toward which all plans and activities are directed. Setting overall goals is a function of top-level management, which must define and communicate to all managers the primary purposes for which the business is organized. These overall goals usually reflect upper-level managers' vision for such things as the production and distribution of products or services, obligations to the customer, being a good employer and responsible corporate citizen, profit as a just reward for taking risks, research and development, and legal and ethical obligations. Figure 7.2 is a statement of corporate goals and objectives, sometimes called a mission statement.

While some firms make a distinction between the terms *goals* and *objectives*, we use these terms interchangeably. Some firms define a *goal* as any long-term target—that is, one that will take more than a year to achieve—and an *objective* as a short-term target—that is, one that will take less than a year to achieve.

The goals formulated for an organization as a whole become the general framework for operations and lead to more specific objectives for divisional and departmental managers and supervisors. Each division or department must clearly set forth its own objectives as guidelines for operations. These objectives must be within the general framework of the overall goals, and they must contribute to the achievement of the organization's overall purposes. Sometimes these objectives are established on a contingency basis—that is, some may depend on certain resources or may reflect changing priorities.

> **4** Discuss the need for well-defined organizational goals and objectives, particularly as they relate to the supervisor.

FIGURE 7.2 Statement of Corporate Objectives

Qwik Home Center and Lumber Company, Inc.

Qwik Home Center and Lumber Company, Inc. depends on the respect and support of four groups: (1) its customers, (2) employees, (3) shareholders, and (4) the public, which includes the citizens of each community in which we do business. For us to have a satisfactory future, we must continuously earn the support, respect, and approval of all four of these groups. We believe in fostering an environment that encourages superior products, service, and performance. This requires each employee to clearly understand our corporate objectives.

CORPORATE OBJECTIVES

1. We will, by September 1, 2011, become the low-cost provider of lumber products.
2. We will reduce the number of customer complaints (as measured by merchandise returns) by 10 percent this year.
3. We will reduce accounts receivable by 50 percent in the next six months.
4. We will develop plans for revitalizing one-fourth of our stores during the next two years.
5. We will institute a profit-sharing plan for our employees by the end of the year.
6. A program of Customer Retention Management (CRM) will be instituted in the next six months.
7. Our long-term same store sales growth is expected to increase by 7 percent per year for each of the next three years, while cost of goods sold are reduced to below the industry average.

This continuing long-term growth in earnings and record of financial stability is expected to attract to our organization the capital required to support its growth.

Objectives are usually stated in terms of what is to be accomplished and when. In general, a department's "what by when" statements are more specific than the broadly stated objectives of the organization. While the higher-level goal may be "to provide quality maintenance services for the entire organization," the maintenance supervisor's objective might be "to reduce machine downtime by twelve percent by year end." While the supervisory-level objectives are more specific than the broadly stated objectives of an organization, they are consistent with, and give direction to, departmental efforts to achieve organizational objectives.

Supervisors must remember two things when developing their departmental objectives: (1) department objectives must be aligned with the organization's goals and objectives, and (2) there must be a means to measure and document the department's contribution to the organization's bottom line. Not all goals are equally important. First, with the help of upper-level managers, the supervisor must prioritize the goals. Then the problem is knowing what is to be done, how it is to be done, and how to measure the results. Noted author Peter Senge said that there is a simple principle to guide you: "Measure quantitatively that which should be quantified; measure qualitatively that which should not be quantified."[6] Simply stated, **metrics** are standards of measurement.[7] For example, Charlotte Kelly ("You Make the Call!", Chapter 2) may use mortality rates as a metric while Don Davis ("You Make the Call!", Chapter 4) might use on-time delivery as one of his metrics. Regardless of the scope of one's responsibilities, supervisors must keep an eye on the financial statements and other scorecards to ensure that goals and objectives become reality.

Whenever possible, objectives should be stated in measurable or verifiable terms, such as "to reduce overtime by five percent during the month," "to increase output per employee-hour by ten percent during the next quarter," "to achieve a ten-percent increase in employee suggestions during the next year," and so on. Each of these becomes a metric. Thus, a supervisor is able to evaluate performance against specific targets. This approach is an essential part of management-by-objectives programs, which have been implemented by many organizations as ways to plan and attain results.

Metrics
A standard of measurement used to determine that performance is in line with objectives

---

5 **Explain management by objectives (MBO).**

Management by objectives (MBO)
A process in which the supervisor and employee jointly set the employee's objectives and the employee receives rewards upon achieving those objectives

Management by Objectives—A System for Participative Management

Management by objectives (MBO) is a management approach in which managers, supervisors, and employees jointly set objectives against which performance is later evaluated. It is a management system that involves participative management. MBO requires full commitment to organizational objectives, starting with top-level management and permeating throughout all levels. MBO is also called "managing by results" or "managing for performance."[8]

As Figure 7.3 shows, an effective MBO system has four major elements. The determination of specific, measurable, and verifiable objectives is the foundation of the system. The other three elements are (1) the inputs, or resources, needed for goal accomplishment; (2) the activities and processes that must be carried out to accomplish the goal; and (3) the results, which are evaluated against the objectives. While MBO emphasizes results rather than the techniques used to achieve them, an effective MBO system is constructed such that all four of the aforementioned elements are integrated and support the others.

FIGURE 7.3 Elements of the MBO Approach

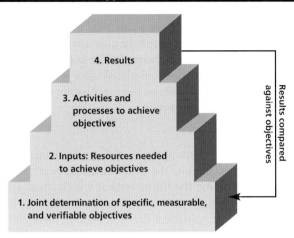

4. Results

3. Activities and processes to achieve objectives

2. Inputs: Resources needed to achieve objectives

1. Joint determination of specific, measurable, and verifiable objectives

Results compared against objectives

WHY USE MANAGEMENT BY OBJECTIVES?

There are numerous reasons many firms have adopted the MBO approach. The following are among the most important. First, MBO is results-oriented. It requires thorough planning, organization, controls, communication, and dedication on the part of an organization. Properly implemented MBO motivates and encourages commitment to results among all employees. In addition, MBO provides a sound means of appraising individuals' performances by emphasizing objective criteria rather than vague personality characteristics. Finally, MBO provides a more rational basis for sharing the rewards of an organization, particularly compensation and promotion based on merit.

With or without MBO, effective high-level managers recognize the importance of delegating authority and responsibility to managers, supervisors, and employees if goals and objectives are to be achieved. Research has shown that employees will generally be more motivated to try to meet these objectives because they are "our goals" rather than "their goals." The advantage of a formal MBO system is that it ties together many plans, establishes priorities, and coordinates activities that otherwise might be overlooked or handled loosely in day-to-day business operations. A sound MBO program encourages the contributions and commitment of people toward common goals and objectives.

Types of Plans

After setting major goals and objectives, all levels of management participate in the design and execution of additional plans for attaining desired objectives. In general, such plans can be broadly classified as (a) standing or repeat-use plans, which can be used over and over as the need arises, and (b) single-use plans, which focus on one purpose or undertaking.

6 Identify the major types of standing and single-use plans and explain how these plans help supervisory decision making.

PLANS

Many of a supervisor's day-to-day activities and decisions are guided by the use of so-called **standing plans,** or repeat-use plans. Although terminology varies, these types of plans typically are known as policies, procedures, methods, and rules. All these plans should be designed to reinforce one another and should be directed toward the achievement of both organizational and work-unit objectives.

Standing plans
Policies, procedures, methods, and rules that can be applied to recurring situations

Top-level managers formulate company-wide standing plans; supervisors formulate the necessary subsidiary standing plans for their work units.

In contrast to repeat-use plans are plans that are no longer needed or are obsolete once the objective is accomplished or the period of applicability is over. These are **single-use plans**. For example, the conversion of a section of the student-union building into a coffeehouse/bookstore would require a single-use plan. Generally, the supervisor's role in the establishment of single-use plans is one of giving thought and suggestions.

Single-use plans
Plans to accomplish a specific objective or to cover a designated time-period

POLICIES

A **policy** is a general guide to thinking when making decisions. Corporate policies are usually statements that channel the thinking of managers and supervisors in specified directions and define the limits within which those staff must stay as they make decisions.[9]

Policy
A standing plan that serves as a guide to making decisions

Effective policies promote consistent decision making throughout an enterprise. Once policies are set, managers find it easier to delegate authority, because the decisions a subordinate supervisor makes are guided by policies. Policies enable supervisors to arrive at about the same decisions their managers would, or at least to make decisions within acceptable parameters. While policies should be considered guides for thinking, they do permit supervisors to use their own judgment in making decisions, as long as those decisions fall within the parameters of policy.

For example, most companies have policies covering employee conduct and other work-related issues. Do you know of any employees surfing the Internet rather than working?[10] The average employee is using the company's computer for some activities that are not work-related, and most organizations have instituted computer use policies. Figure 7.4 is an example of one university's computer use and code of conduct policy. Note that this policy statement does not spell out the supervisor's responsibility, while other policies will more clearly specify the supervisor's role. It should be noted that many organizations have installed systems that will show who is visiting which sites and when, and track the number of keystrokes and other data.

FIGURE 7.4 Example of a Computer Use Policy and Procedure Statement

Computer Use Policy

(Code of Computer Usage Rights and Responsibilities, adopted 12.10.2001 as amended 7.1.2008)

In support of the University's mission of teaching, research, and public service, Old Ivy University provides computing, networking, and information resources to the campus community. The University Information Technology (IT) System is designed to be used in connection with legitimate, university-related purposes. The use of university computing resources to disseminate obscene, pornographic, or libelous materials, to threaten or harass others, or otherwise to engage in activities forbidden by the policy is subject to disciplinary action.

Students and employees may have rights to information about themselves contained in computer files, as specified by federal and state laws. Files may be subject to search under court order. In addition, system administrators may access or examine files that are suspected of unauthorized use or misuse, and that have been corrupted or damaged.

Intellectual Property Rights and Responsibilities. Central to an understanding of the rights and responsibilities of computer users is the notion of intellectual property. In brief, this concept holds that materials stored in electronic form are the property of one or more rightful owners. Like any other property, electronically stored information, whether data or programs, can be stolen, altered or destroyed, misappropriated, or plagiarized. Such inappropriate activities violate the Code and are subject to disciplinary action as set forth in the Code.

Access Rights and Responsibilities. The use of lab, e-mail, Web, and other computing resources should be focused on activities that facilitate student learning, faculty research, and necessary administrative tasks. Other uses—for example, using computer resources to conduct a commercial enterprise or private business—constitute theft from the university subject to disciplinary action. Similarly, the introduction of information that interferes with the access or information of others—for example, the introduction of programs of a type commonly called "viruses" or of nonacademic, networking game simulations—is subject to disciplinary action. E-mail should not be used for junk mailings.

Certain university-controlled computing resources are openly available to all students, faculty, and staff on a first-come, first-served basis. Users are also responsible for ensuring the confidentiality of access rights under their control. For example, release of a password, whether intentional or inadvertent, invites misuse by others and may be subject to disciplinary action.

Examples of Misuse. The University strives to maintain a quiet, library-like environment in its computer labs in order that users can use their time productively and with minimal distractions. Proper use of computer resources follows the same standards of common sense and courtesy that govern the use of public facilities. Improper use violates those standards by infringing upon others' ability to fulfill their responsibilities.

In addition to the illustrations outlined above, other examples of misuse include, but are not limited to, the following activities:

- Using a computer account that you are not authorized to use.
- Using the Campus Computer Network to gain unauthorized access to any computer system.
- Knowingly performing an act which interferes with the normal operations of the Information Technology System.
- Knowingly running or installing, or giving to another user, a program intended to damage or place an excessive load on the IT System.
- Attempting to circumvent data protection schemes or uncover security loopholes.
- Violating terms of applicable software licensing agreements or copyright laws.
- Posting materials on electronic bulletin boards that violate existing laws or the University's Code of Conduct.
- Attempting to monitor or tamper with another user's electronic communications, or reading, copying, changing, or deleting another user's files or software without explicit agreement of the owners.
- Using e-mail to harass others.

Enforcement. All inappropriate use of IT resources should be reported to proper authorities.

1. Minor infractions of this policy or those that appear to be accidental in nature will be handled by e-mail or in-person discussions.
2. A second infraction that appears to be minor or accidental in nature will necessitate a meeting with the IT-use committee. Account privileges may be suspended to prevent ongoing misuse until after the investigation and hearing process is completed. The IT-use committee's recommendations will be forwarded (1) for student infractions—to the Office of Student Affairs; (2) for faculty infractions—to the departmental chairperson or dean; and (3) for staff infractions—to the appropriate administrative official.
3. Repeated minor infractions or more serious infractions may result, after investigation by the IT-use committee, in a temporary or permanent restriction of IT privileges or notification of the student's academic advisor.
4. The IT-use committee shall have sole responsibility for restricting IT access.
5. Offenses which are in violations of local, state, or federal laws will result in the restriction of IT privileges, and will be reported to the appropriate University and law enforcement agencies.

Report misuse of IT resources to **abuse@oldivy.edu** or call 260.xxx.xxxx.

Origin of Policies. Major company-wide policies are originated by top-level managers because policy making is one of their important responsibilities. Top-level managers must develop and establish overall policies that guide the thinking of subordinate managers so that organizational objectives can be achieved. Broad policies become the guides for specific policies developed within divisions and departments. Departmental policies established by supervisors must complement and coincide with the broader policies of the organization. In this regard, a firm's policy manuals should not become too excessive in concept, design, and detail. One corporate executive expressed his disdain for "bloated policy manuals" by replacing a multivolume manual at his company with two pages of "clear yet flexible guidelines." In his view, this turned his supervisors into decision makers who knew their responsibilities and acted accordingly.[11]

Small firms tend to have fewer policies than their large counterparts. On the one hand, the absence of policies gives the supervisor greater flexibility in dealing with situations as they occur. For example, many small firms do not have policies for drug or alcohol use; they prefer to handle problems on an individual basis if and when such problems occur. On the other hand, the absence of policies may cause inconsistent supervisory practices and lead to charges of unfairness or discrimination. Information concerning the kinds of policies and practices that exist in an area—especially those involving employee matters—is usually available through surveys conducted by employer associations. Such survey data can be helpful if a firm's management wants to make comparisons and perhaps adjust its policies and practices to align more closely with those of most area employers.[12]

In addition to policies formulated by top-level managers, some policies are imposed on an organization by external forces, such as government, labor unions, trade groups, and accrediting associations. The word *imposed* indicates compliance with an outside force that cannot be avoided. For example, to be accredited, schools, universities, hospitals, and other institutions must comply with regulations issued by the appropriate accrediting agency. Government regulations concerning minimum wage, pay for overtime work, and hiring of people without regard to race, age, and gender automatically become part of an organization's policies. Any policy imposed on the organization in such a manner is known as an externally imposed policy, and everyone in the organization must comply with it.

Written Policy Statements Promote Consistency. Because policies are guides to decision making, they should be clearly stated and communicated to those in the organization who are affected by them. Although there is no guarantee that policies always will be completely followed or understood, they are more likely to be followed consistently if they are written. Few organizations have all their policies in written form; some have few or no written policies, either because they simply never get around to writing them or because they would rather not state their policies publicly. However, the benefits of well-stated written policies usually outweigh the disadvantages. The process of writing policies requires managers to think through issues more thoroughly and consistently. Supervisors and employees can refer to a written policy as often as they wish. The wording of a written policy cannot be changed by word of mouth; when there is doubt or disagreement, the written policy can be consulted. Additionally, written policies are available to supervisors and employees who are new to the organization so they can quickly acquaint themselves with the policies. Every policy should be reviewed periodically and revised or discarded as conditions or circumstances warrant.

The Supervisor's Role. Supervisors seldom have to issue policies. If a department is extremely large or geographically dispersed, or if several subunits exist within the department, the supervisor may find it appropriate to write departmental policies. For the most part, however, instead of writing policies, the supervisor will be called on to apply existing policies in making decisions. That is, most of the time, it is the supervisor's role to interpret, apply, and explain policies. Because policies guide supervisors in many daily decisions, supervisors must understand the policies and learn how to interpret and apply them.

A supervisor may occasionally experience a situation for which no policy exists or seems applicable. For example, suppose a group of employees asks the supervisor for permission to visit the user of their product to better understand how the product is used. To make an appropriate decision in this matter, the supervisor should be guided by a policy so that the decision will be in accord with other decisions regarding time away from work. If, upon investigation, the supervisor finds that higher-level management has never issued a formal policy to cover such a request, the supervisor needs guidance and should ask his or her manager to issue a policy—a guide for action. The supervisor can then apply the policy in this case as well as in the future so that there is consistency not only in the supervisor's particular department but also across the organization. After consulting with other supervisors who may have stakes in the issue, the supervisor may want to draft a suggested policy and present it to the manager. In large firms, it is unlikely that many such instances will happen because top-level management usually has covered the major policy areas. In small firms, where fewer policies exist, supervisors must use good judgment to determine when to make decisions themselves and when to consult their managers.

PROCEDURES

A **procedure**, like a policy, is a standing plan for achieving objectives. It derives from policies but is more specific. They define a chronological sequence of actions that carry out the terms and objectives of a policy. They promote consistency by listing the steps to be taken and the sequence to be followed. At times, procedures are combined with or incorporated into policy statements.

Procedure
A standing plan that defines the sequence of activities to be performed to achieve objectives

Another very common example is a company policy that requires supervisors to use the human resources department in the preliminary steps of hiring. This policy may contain several guidelines designed to meet nondiscriminatory hiring goals. To carry out this policy, management develops a procedure governing the selection process. For example, the procedures to be followed by a supervisor who wants to hire a word processor might include completing a requisition form, specifying the job requirements, interviewing and testing potential candidates, and other such actions. In this way, the procedure details exactly what a supervisor must do or not do to comply with the company's hiring policies. All supervisors must follow the same procedure.

At the departmental level, the supervisor must often develop procedures to determine how work is to be done. When supervisors are fortunate enough to have only highly skilled employees to lead, they depend on the employees to a great extent to select efficient paths of performance. However, this situation is uncommon. Most employees look to the supervisor for instructions on how to proceed.

One advantage of preparing a procedure is that it requires an analysis of work to be done. Another advantage is that once a procedure is established, it promotes more uniform action, reduces the need for much routine decision making, and encourages a predictable outcome. Procedures also give the supervisor standards for appraising employees' work. To realize these advantages, a supervisor should devote considerable time and effort to devising departmental procedures to cover as many phases of operations as practical, such as work operations and work flow, scheduling, and personnel assignments.

METHODS

Like a procedure, a **method** is a standing plan for action, but it is even more detailed than a procedure. A procedure shows a series of steps to be taken, whereas a method is concerned with only one operation or one step, and it indicates exactly how that step is to be performed. For example, a departmental procedure may specify the chronological routing of work in the assembly of various components of a product. At each subassembly point, there should be a method for the work to be performed in that step.

For most jobs, there are usually "best methods," that is, the most efficient ways for the jobs to be done given existing technology and circumstances. Again, when a supervisor can rely on skilled workers, the workers often know the best method without having to be told. For the most part, however, the supervisor or someone in management must design the most efficient method for getting the job done. Much time should be spent devising methods, because proper methods have all the advantages of procedures. In devising methods, the supervisor may use the know-how of a methods engineer or a motion-and-time-study specialist if such individuals are available in the organization. These are specialists who have been trained in industrial-engineering techniques to study jobs systematically to make those jobs more efficient. When such specialists are unavailable, the supervisor's experience and input from experienced employees actually doing the work should suffice to design work methods that are appropriate for the department.

In some activities, a supervisor need not be overly concerned with devising procedures and methods because employees have been trained in standard methods or procedures. For example, computer technicians are exposed to many years of education and training, during which proper procedures and methods of performing certain tasks are emphasized. Similarly, in the supervision of a department of highly skilled or professional employees, the supervisor's main concern is to ensure that generally approved procedures and methods are carried out in professionally accepted ways. However, most supervisors have employees who are not well-trained and for whom procedures and methods must be established.

RULES

A rule is different from a policy, procedure, or method, although it also is a standing plan that has been devised to attain objectives. A rule is not the same as a policy because it does not guide thinking or leave discretion to the involved parties. A rule is related to a procedure insofar as it is a guide to action and states what must or must not be done. However, a rule is not a procedure because it does not provide for a time sequence or a set of steps. A **rule** is a directive that must be applied and enforced wherever applicable. When a rule is a specific guide for the behavior of employees in a department, the supervisor must follow that rule, without deviation, wherever it applies. For example, "Safety equipment must be worn in posted areas" is a common organizational rule. It means exactly what it says, and there are no exceptions.

Occasionally, supervisors must devise their own rules or see to it that the rules defined by higher-level managers are obeyed. For example, rules concerning employee meal periods usually specify a certain amount of time employees can be away from their jobs for meals. Usually, high-level managers develop these rules, but often a supervisor must formulate departmental rules concerning the actual scheduling of meal periods. Regardless of who develops the rules, it is each supervisor's duty to apply and enforce all rules uniformly as those rules relate to each area of responsibility.

There should be no deviation from this rule!

BUDGETS

Although budgets are generally part of the managerial controlling function, a budget is first and foremost a plan. A **budget** is a plan that expresses anticipated results in numerical terms, such as dollars and cents, employee hours, sales figures, or units produced. It serves as a plan for a stated period, usually one year. All budgets are eventually translated into monetary terms, and an overall financial budget is developed for the entire firm. When the stated period is over, the budget expires; it has served its usefulness and is no longer valid. For this reason, a budget is a single-use plan.

Budget
A plan that expresses anticipated results in numerical, usually financial, terms for a stated period

As a statement of expected results, a budget is associated with control. However, the preparation of a budget is planning, and this again is part of every manager's responsibilities. Because a budget is expressed in numerical terms, it has the advantage of being specific rather than general. There is a considerable difference between just making general forecasts and attaching numerical values to specific plans. The figures that the supervisor finds in a budget are actual plans that become standards to be achieved.

The Supervisor's Role in Budgeting. Because supervisors must function within a budget, they should help prepare it. Supervisors should have the opportunity to propose detailed budgets for their departments or at least to participate in discussions with higher-level managers before departmental budgets are finalized. Supervisors must substantiate their budget proposals with their managers, and possibly with their financial managers, when budgets are being finalized.

Generally, supervisors are more concerned about the expense side of the budget and are held accountable for variations. There are numerous types of budgets in which supervisors can play a part. For example, supervisors may design budgets in which they plan the work hours to be used for jobs in their departments. Supervisors also may prepare budgets for materials and supplies, wages, utility expenses, and other departmental expenditures.

Budget Review. Most organizations have interim monthly or quarterly reviews when the budget is compared to actual results. Therefore, a budget is also a control device. If necessary, the budget is revised to adjust to results and forecasts. This topic is discussed further in Chapter 14. Supervisors should carefully study and analyze significant variations from the budget to determine where and why plans went wrong, what and where adjustments need to be made, and what the revised budget should reflect, including new factors and any changes in the department. When an annual budget is about to expire, it becomes a guide for preparing the next year's budget. Thus, the planning process continues from one budget period to the next in a closely related pattern.

PROGRAMS AND PROJECTS

Program
A major single-use plan for a large undertaking related to accomplishing the organization's goals and objectives

A **program** is a single-use set of plans for a major undertaking related to the organization's overall goals and objectives. A major program may have its own policies, procedures, and budget, and it may take several years to accomplish. Examples of major programs are the expansion of a manufacturing plant or office and the addition of new facilities in a hospital. Such expansion programs usually involve plans for architectural design, new equipment or technology, financing, employee recruitment, and publicity, all of which are part of the overall program. Once the expansion program is complete, its plans will not be used again. Therefore, a program is a single-use plan.

Project
A single-use plan for accomplishing a specific, nonrecurring activity

Supervisors are typically more involved in planning projects. While a **project** may be part of an overall program, it is an undertaking that can be planned and fulfilled as a distinct entity, usually within a relatively short period. For example, the creation of a brochure by a public-relations department to acquaint the public with the new facilities of a hospital-expansion program would be a project. Arranging construction financing for the building expansion would be another project. Although connected with a major program, these projects can be handled separately.

An example of a project at the supervisory level is the design of a new inventory-control system by a warehouse supervisor. Another example is a research project conducted by a marketing department supervisor to determine the effectiveness of a series of television commercials. Projects like these are a constant part of the ongoing activities at the departmental level. The ability to plan and carry out projects is another component of every supervisor's managerial effectiveness.

Expansion programs usually involve plans for architectural design, new equipment or technology, financing, employee recruitment, and publicity, all of which are part of the overall program

Supervisory Planning for Resource Use

Because supervisors are especially concerned with day-to-day planning, they must plan for the best use of all their resources. Making effective use of time is one of the most important supervisory activities. In addition to employees, another important resource is the supervisor's time. We all have the same amount of time. The adage "time is money" applies equally to the supervisor's and employee's time.

In the following sections, we will briefly discuss physical and human resources planning techniques.

7 Describe how the supervisor plans for efficient and effective resource use.

EFFICIENT SPACE USE

Supervisors must always plan for space allocation and use. They should determine whether too much or too little space is assigned to the department and whether that space is used efficiently. In most organizations, space demands typically far exceed the available office or plant space. Some firms have facilities managers or industrial engineers who can help the supervisor allocate space. Most supervisors, however, must assume this responsibility.

When planning space use, a floor-layout chart can be drawn and analyzed to determine whether there is sufficient space for the work to be performed and whether the space has been laid out appropriately. If the chart indicates a need for additional space, the supervisor should include with the space request a thorough analysis of how the space is currently allocated. Chances are that the supervisor must compete with other departments that also need more room. Unless the supervisor plans thoroughly, the space request has little chance of being granted. Even if the request is denied, the supervisor's plans are useful. They alert the supervisor to some of the conditions under which employees are working and where improvements might be made.

USE OF OTHER MAJOR PHYSICAL RESOURCES

Supervisors must plan for the efficient use of their departments' other major physical resources, such as tools, machinery, computers, and various types of equipment and furniture. Usually, these resources represent a substantial investment. When these items are poorly maintained or are inefficient for the jobs to be done, operating problems arise and employees' morale degrades. A supervisor does not always have the most desirable or advanced equipment, but any equipment, when adapted and properly maintained, usually suffices to do the job. Therefore, before requesting new equipment, supervisors should first determine whether employees are using their tools and equipment properly. Many times, when employees complain about poor equipment, they are operating that equipment incorrectly. Therefore, supervisors should periodically observe their employees using equipment and ask those employees whether the equipment serves their purposes or needs improvement. The supervisor is responsible for working closely with the maintenance department to plan the periodic maintenance of tools, equipment, and machinery. Poorly maintained equipment may be blamed on the maintenance department in some cases, but supervisors share in the blame if they have not planned or scheduled maintenance with the maintenance department. The maintenance department can do only as good a job as other departments allow it to do.

Properly maintained equipment can minimize breakdowns

The supervisor may sometimes decide that equipment must be replaced. In making this request, the supervisor should develop and submit to higher-level management a plan for disposing of the inefficient equipment. To determine when a major physical resource should be replaced, supervisors should review trade journals, listen to what salespeople say about new products, read literature circulated by distributors and associations, and generally keep up with field developments. When supervisors thoroughly study the alternatives and prepare to make recommendations based on several bids and models, they make stronger arguments to higher-level managers. Facts are more likely than emotions to persuade higher-level managers to support the supervisor's position.

Even when supervisors recommend equipment changes that are supported by well-documented reasons, higher-level managers may turn down those changes because they are not economically feasible. While supervisors should support those decisions, they should not hesitate to point out the decrease in productivity and morale that may result from failing to replace the equipment in question.

In the long term, a supervisor's plans for replacing or buying equipment probably will be accepted in some form. Even when they are not, the supervisor will be recognized as being on top of the job by planning for better use of the department's physical resources.

USE AND SECURITY OF MATERIALS, SUPPLIES, MERCHANDISE, AND DATA

Another supervisory responsibility is to plan for the appropriate use, conservation, and security of materials, supplies, and merchandise. In most departments, substantial quantities of materials and supplies are used and maintained in inventory.

Even if each item represents only a small value, the items together add up to sizable dollar amounts in the total budget. Many employees do not realize the magnitude of money tied up in materials and supplies, and they sometimes use these items carelessly. The supervisor should remind employees that using all resources economically is to their advantage, ultimately; whatever is wasted cannot be used to raise wages or improve working conditions.

A major problem in recent years has been the loss and theft of materials, supplies, merchandise, and other company property, sometimes by employees. To prevent such losses, supervisors must make sure that adequate security precautions are taken to discourage individuals from theft and to make it difficult for items to be lost or stolen. For example, many supplies can be kept locked up, with someone assigned the responsibility for distributing them as needed. If the firm has its own security force, the supervisor should meet with security personnel to plan and implement security devices and procedures that are suited to the department. In retail establishments, this may mean removing the opportunity for theft and training employees to pay attention to customers' bags, clothing, carts, and boxes. Increased attention can often deter a theft or a fraudulent return or exchange. A supervisor may even request such assistance from local police or a private security agency.[13]

In recent years, another major concern of many firms has been the theft of data and information, mostly associated with computer break-ins and related thefts. Supervisors may work very closely with IT specialists to plan for limited access to certain data and to protect important hardware and software.

While a supervisor's plans for the use and security of materials, supplies, merchandise, and data cannot eliminate all waste and loss, such planning usually reduces some waste and loss and promotes a more efficient and conscientious workplace.

SAFE WORK ENVIRONMENT

Most managers and supervisors recognize that a safe work environment is one of their major responsibilities because such an environment is essential for employees' welfare and productivity. Safety data have long indicated that, due to carelessness, poor attitudes, inadequate training, and many other reasons, employees cause accidents more often than do faulty tools and equipment. The supervisor shares a major responsibility, ethically and legally, to do everything possible to see that the safest possible work environment is maintained. Of course, some job categories, by their very nature, are more hazardous than others. For example, supervisors in mining, construction, and heavy manufacturing face major challenges in working to reduce the potential for serious injuries and fatalities. By contrast, supervisors in the generally comfortable surroundings of an office usually do not have to worry about major injuries. Nevertheless, the potential for accidents exists in any situation if employees are not fully trained and reminded to follow safe work habits.

According to the most recent report from the Bureau of Labor Statistics (BLS), "Over 4 million nonfatal workplace injuries occur each year in the private sector. Almost 6,000 workers suffered death in workplace accidents and some 2 million American workers are victims of workplace violence each year."[14] The BLS defines **workplace violence** as violent acts, including physical assaults and threats of assault, directed at employees at work or on duty. Workers who exchange money with the public or work alone or in small groups are most at risk. The best protection employers can offer is to establish a zero-tolerance policy toward workplace violence against or by their employees.

Workplace violence
An act or threat of assault directed at another employee

OBSERVANCE OF OSHA AND OTHER SAFETY REGULATIONS

Both before and since the passage of the Occupational Safety and Health Act (OSHA) of 1970, supervisors have been expected to devote major attention to reducing and preventing injuries and accidents on the job. OSHA has significantly impacted the scope and administration of safety programs in many organizations. It has expanded the responsibility of the supervisor in planning for and bringing about a safer work environment.

Regardless of the size of the firm, supervisors must plan to meet with managers, as well as with employees, union leaders, and even with government officials, if necessary, to do everything possible to maintain compliance with all safety regulations.

SAFETY COMMITTEES

If they are not already in place, supervisors should endeavor to establish and participate in safety committees. The purpose of a safety committee is to help the supervisor develop safer work areas and enforce safety regulations. The supervisor and the safety committee can plan for periodic meetings and projects to communicate to employees the importance of safe work habits and attitudes.

Labor unions have been quite vocal in asserting their concerns that safe work environments and safe work practices are monitored closely. Joint union/ management safety committees invariably involve supervisors, and usually there is a concerted effort to reduce accidents and injuries. The impact of proactive safety committees has been well-documented. Many safety committees have ongoing safety meetings and site walkthroughs in which safety committee representatives identify and correct various problems. To reinforce workers' awareness of proper safety practices and use of safety gear, supervisors and workers hold weekly "toolbox" safety meetings in which they discuss such subjects as storing tools and equipment to avoid tripping accidents, proper lifting techniques, the need for protective safety gear, and other areas over which employees have direct control.

The supervisor's constant attention to safety is mandatory if a safe work environment is to be maintained. Most accidents reported on the job are caused primarily by human failure (see Figure 7.5). The supervisor must emphasize safe work habits in daily instructions to employees and ensure that all equipment in the department is used properly and has ample protective devices.

FIGURE 7.5 Inattention commonly causes accidents

A common half-truth is that a safety program is the responsibility of the safety department or the safety engineers. However, without the full support of supervisors and diligent supervisory observance of employee work practices in every department, almost any safety program will fail. Safety planning and safety in practice are everyone's responsibility.

FULL USE OF HUMAN RESOURCES

Our perspective throughout this book is that employees are a firm's most important resource. Planning for their full use should always be uppermost in every supervisor's mind. Using the workforce fully means getting employees to contribute to their fullest capabilities. This requires:

- Developing plans for recruiting, selecting, and training employees
- Searching for better ways to arrange activities
- Training employees in the proper and safe use of the materials associated with their jobs
- Supervising employees with an understanding of the complexities of human needs and motivation
- Communicating effectively with employees
- Appraising employees' performances
- Recognizing achievement
- Promoting deserving employees
- Adequately compensating and rewarding employees
- Taking just and fair disciplinary actions

These actions are ongoing aspects of a supervisor's plans for the full use of human resources.

Planning to use employees fully is at the core of effective supervision. It is mentioned here again only briefly because most chapters of this text are concerned in some way with this overall primary objective of supervisory management.

In addition to employees, another important resource is the supervisor's time. The adage "time is money" applies equally to the supervisor's and the employee's time.

EMPLOYEE WORK SCHEDULES

To plan effective work schedules for employees, supervisors should operate from the premise that most employees are willing to turn in a fair day's work. Supervisors should not expect all employees to work continuously at top speed. They should establish a work schedule based on an estimate of what constitutes a fair, rather than a maximum, output. Allowances must be made for fatigue, unavoidable delays, personal needs, and a certain amount of unproductive time during the workday. Some supervisors may be able to plan employee time with the help of a specialist, such as a motion-and-time analyst. Even without such help, most supervisors have a good idea as to what they can expect, and they can plan reasonable performance requirements their employees will accept as fair. Such estimates are based on normal, rather than abnormal, conditions. In this regard, it may be unadvisable for a supervisor to schedule a department to operate at 100 percent capacity, which would leave no room for emergencies or changes in priorities and deadlines. Because some flexibility is needed to operate, only short periods of 100 percent capacity should be scheduled. Also, several rest periods are usually included in employee work schedules.

OVERTIME AND ABSENCES

Occasionally, supervisors find it necessary to plan for overtime, although overtime primarily should be considered an exception or an emergency measure. As a general rule, supervisors should anticipate a reduction of between 5 and 10 percent in productivity from employees when they work overtime. If a supervisor finds that excessive overtime is required regularly, then alternative methods of doing the work should be found or additional employees should be scheduled or hired.

Supervisors also must plan for employee absences. Of course, a supervisor cannot plan for every employee absence due to sickness, injury, or personal problems.[15] However, the supervisor can plan for holidays, vacations, temporary layoffs, and other types of leaves or predictable absenteeism. Planning for anticipated absences ensures the smooth functioning of the department.

In recent years, a growing number of firms have established "group emergency time pools." These pools are time-sharing plans by which employees can donate some of their vacation days to a company pooled account, and an employee who is on an extended sickness or disability leave can draw on this account to receive income while off work. This type of arrangement is usually cost-effective for the employer, and it is a morale and team builder for the employees.[16] However, it can complicate a supervisor's vacation-scheduling task.

ALTERNATIVE WORK SCHEDULES AND TELECOMMUTING

Many organizations have adopted various work schedules for their employees, such as flextime, part-time work, job sharing, telecommuting, and other work-at-home arrangements, as well as unconventional hours. Alternative work-schedule plans are diverse. In some organizations, employees are scheduled for or may opt to work a 4-day work week, which is usually a 4-day, 10-hour-per-day arrangement. The most common form of alternative work scheduling is flextime, in which employees can choose, within certain limits, the hours they would like to work. Flextime usually involves permitting certain employees to select different starting and ending times within a 5-day work week. Alternative work arrangements are becoming more common, particularly in situations in which an employee's work is not closely interdependent or interrelated with that of other employees or departments.[17]

While telecommuting is popular with many employees, it can pose a challenge for their supervisors

Supervisors have found that alternative work schedules create problems when trying to cover workstations and job positions, and that it may be difficult to exercise supervisory control at certain times of the workday. Nevertheless, supervisors who work with alternative work schedules learn to adapt within their departments and in their relations with other departments. Some supervisors may be in charge of different work groups on different days and at different times of the day as a result of flexible work scheduling. This situation requires supervisors on different shifts and in different departments to coordinate their activities if they are to achieve overall organizational effectiveness.

Telecommuting and other work-at-home arrangements present a number of different problems for supervisors. In general, time scheduling is not that important because work-at-home employees tend to make their own work schedules. However, supervisors must plan well in advance and communicate with these employees concerning such items as project work to be completed, deadlines, budget constraints, productivity expectations, and customer requirements. Some firms are making special efforts to train supervisors to manage "telecommuters" and other work-at-home employees.[18]

Most studies of alternative work schedule plans have concluded that employees generally appreciate the opportunity to select their work schedules. Further, flexible work schedules usually are associated with improvements in absenteeism rates, tardiness rates, retention, morale, and productivity.[19]

PART-TIME AND TEMPORARY EMPLOYMENT

The number of part-time employees is increasing. Retailers, service establishments, and healthcare centers, in particular, often have large numbers of part-time workers. Scheduling part-time employees requires considerable planning to match the needs of the department or business operation. Part-time work arrangements must be developed and monitored if they are to benefit employees and management. Some part-time employees are content to work limited schedules. Other part-time employees are eager to work as many hours as possible, and they also hope to obtain full-time employment. Supervisors must plan work schedules carefully to accommodate part-time workers' special interests and needs without creating scheduling problems with full-time employees and departmental work requirements.

Another complicating factor for supervisors in work scheduling is the growing phenomenon of temporary employment. For the most part, temporary employees fall into two basic categories. The first type includes employees who are hired by agencies and are "farmed out" for short-term work assignments with various employers. Companies typically contact agencies to obtain individuals who have certain skills, and those companies pay the agencies for each employee who works. A supervisor who uses this type of temporary employee must schedule the employees with the sponsoring agency. The second type of temporary employee, called an interim employee, is hired directly by a firm for a specific need or project. Interim employees clearly understand that there is no guarantee of employment when the company's hiring need or project ends. Typically, the interim employee is paid a wage or salary with limited or no benefits.

While temporary employees are often justified to meet short-term staffing needs and cut costs, supervisors must be prepared to address their associated problems. These problems include a lack of commitment to the firm, especially as the project or interim period of employment nears completion. Temporary employees often leave jobs prematurely for other opportunities. They take with them knowledge and training, which can demoralize permanent employees, and they can leave companies in difficult situations.[20] For the most part, supervisors should try to give temporary employees job assignments they can do without disrupting the regular workforce. The supervisor should not treat temporary employees as "second-class citizens." Instead, supervisors should view temporary employees as staff members who can help attain the department's objectives. Temporary employees can show by their performance that they are worthy of consideration for full-time positions. Therefore, temporary work situations can serve as trials that allow supervisors to determine whether temporary employees should be offered full-time status.[21]

IMPROVEMENT IN WORK PROCEDURES AND METHODS

Supervisors often are so close to the job that they may not recognize when work procedures and methods need updating. Therefore, supervisors should periodically try to look at departmental operations as strangers entering the department for the first time might view them. By looking at each operation from a detached point of view, the supervisor can answer such questions as:

- Is each operation needed?
- What is the reason for each operation?
- Can one operation be combined with another?
- Are the steps performed in the best sequence?

- Are there any avoidable delays?
- Is there unnecessary waste?

Improvement generally means any change in the way the department is doing something that will increase productivity, lower costs, or improve the quality of a product or service. Improvement in work procedures, methods, and processes usually makes the supervisor's job easier. Besides personally looking for ways to improve operations, the supervisor should solicit ideas from employees. Employees usually know their jobs better than anyone else in the organization. Alternatively, the supervisor may be able to enlist the help of a specialist, such as an industrial engineer or a systems analyst, if this type of person is available in the organization. When studying areas for improvement, a supervisor should concentrate on situations in which large numbers of employees are assigned; costs per unit are unacceptably high; or scrap figures, waste, or injury reports appear out of line. A good reason to concentrate on such areas is that it will be easier for the supervisor to convince employees and higher-level managers that recommended changes will bring about considerable improvement, savings, or other benefits.

Organizations must more proactively meet the pressures of increasing competition. Every supervisor should consider the benefits of a methods-improvement program, perhaps in conjunction with a firm's employee suggestion system if one is in place. At all times, a supervisor should urge employees to look for better ways to do their jobs.

The supervisor sometimes can apply work-sampling techniques to cut costs, save time, and increase employee efficiency. Broadly stated, work sampling involves inspecting a small amount of work from a job to determine areas for improvement. Generally, work-sampling techniques are the tools of the industrial engineer.[22] However, in small firms, supervisors usually perform this role. While work sampling is useful, every effort should be made to ensure that the sample typifies the whole.

PLANNING INVENTORY

Maintaining large inventories of component parts and finished goods is costly. It requires warehouse space that must be rented or bought, heated, and lighted. It also requires workers to store and track the materials. To reduce the costs of maintaining large inventories, many firms use inventory-control techniques that better plan the inflow of materials needed for production.

A **just-in-time (JIT) inventory-control system**, also called **kanban**, is a system for scheduling the raw materials and components of production to arrive at the firm precisely when needed. This system avoids having to stock large amounts of items. JIT requires close coordination between the firm and its suppliers. For the system to work, suppliers must be willing and able to supply parts on short notice and in small batches. Also, so that suppliers can plan their production efficiently, the firm must keep suppliers well-informed about its projected needs for their products.[23]

Just-in-time (JIT) inventory control system
A system for scheduling materials to arrive precisely when they are needed in the production process

kanban
Another name for a just-in-time (JIT) inventory-control system

SCHEDULING AND PROJECT PLANNING

Much supervisory time is spent planning projects. Supervisors must consider what must be done, which activities must be undertaken, the order in which activities must be done, who is to do each activity, and when activities are to be completed. This process of planning activities and their sequence is called scheduling. Two well-known project planning tools are Gantt charts and PERT.

A **Gantt chart** is a graphic scheduling technique that shows the relationship between work planned and necessary completion dates.[24] Gantt charts are helpful in projects in which the activities are somewhat independent. For large projects, such as a complex quality improvement program, PERT is more applicable.

Program evaluation and review technique (PERT) has been used successfully in many major production and construction undertakings. PERT is a flowchart-like diagram showing the sequence of activities needed to complete a project and the time associated with each. PERT goes beyond Gantt charts by clarifying the interrelatedness of the various activities. PERT helps a supervisor think strategically. A clear statement of goals serves as the basis for the planning process. PERT begins with the supervisor defining the project in terms of not only the desired goal but also all the intermediate goals on which the ultimate goal depends.

PERT is a helpful planning tool because it requires systematic thinking and planning for large, non-routine projects. The development of PERT flowcharts by hand is time consuming, but use of Gantt charts and PERT is likely to increase because of the proliferation of commercially available computer software packages that can assist supervisors in planning, decision making, and controlling.

Gantt chart
A graphic scheduling technique that shows the activity to be scheduled on the vertical axis and necessary completion dates on the horizontal axis

Program evaluation and review technique (PERT)
A flowchart for managing large programs and projects that shows the necessary activities with estimates of the time needed to complete each activity and the sequential relationship of activities

Planning for Quality Improvement and Knowledge Management

8 Explain the key concepts of quality planning.

In recent decades, successful firms have shown an emerging commitment to quality. Many firms have turned to total quality management (TQM) and continuous improvement. In manufacturing firms, quality traditionally meant inspecting the product at the end of the production process. Today, the notion of **total quality management** means that the total organization is committed to quality—everyone is responsible for doing the job right the first time. TQM means a total effort toward meeting customer needs and satisfaction by planning for quality, preventing defects, correcting defects, and continuously building increased quality into goods and services as far as economically and competitively feasible.[25]

Total quality management (TQM)
An organizational approach involving all employees to satisfy customers by continually improving goods and services

Total Quality Management requires input and commitment by everyone

Knowledge management
The systematic storage, retrieval, dissemination, and sharing of information

Although not as widely known as TQM, many firms have been involved in planning and carrying out short- and long-term strategies for more effective "knowledge management." The "knowledge explosion," driven by computer technology, requires more systematic storage, retrieval, dissemination, and sharing of information in ways that are conducive to desired results. **Knowledge management** has been defined as:

a. Adding actionable value to information by capturing, filtering, synthesizing, summarizing, storing, retrieving, and disseminating tangible and intangible knowledge,
b. Developing customized profiles of knowledge so individuals can get at the kind of information they need when they need it, and
c. Creating an interactive learning environment where people transfer and share what they know and apply it to create new knowledge.[26]

To this end, many firms have planned and implemented a variety of approaches, processes, and techniques that, according to a recent survey, have improved customer and employee satisfaction levels and contributed to product or service innovations.[27] Some of these approaches have been within, or similar to, other quality management efforts.

Benchmarking
The process of identifying and improving on the best practices of leaders

The increased emphasis on higher product and service quality has led many firms to follow guidelines or criteria developed by others. The process of identifying and improving on the best practices of the leaders in the industry or related fields is called **benchmarking**. Some executives even advocate benchmarking using "best-in-the-world" comparisons.[28] All of us have used benchmarking. When we evaluate the performance of our favorite sports team, we look to see how well that team is doing compared with the top team. We analyze the attributes of players of the top team, coaching styles, and so forth and conclude that our team could be just as good—if not better—if the owners/managers would change and copy the successful practices of top-team leaders.

The essence of benchmarking is to be as good as, or better than, the best in the field. Benchmarking follows these steps:

1. Determine what to benchmark (e.g., a process or procedure, quality, costs, customer service, employee development, compensation).
2. Identify comparable organizations inside and outside the industry.
3. Collect comparative performance data.
4. Identify performance gaps.
5. Determine the causes of the differences.
6. Ascertain the management practices of the best.

Once these steps are completed, management can develop plans for meeting or beating "best-in-the-industry," or even "best-in-the-world," standards.

In recent years, many firms have given serious attention to ways to achieve quality improvements. See our Web site for information on the quality standards established by ISO 9000 and the Baldrige Quality Award.[29] Firms that want to compete internationally must produce products and services that conform to quality standards only the best can meet.

9 Recognize the importance of planning for the unthinkable (crisis management).

Crisis Management: Planning Required

We all face crisis situations each and every day. For some people, things like not hearing the alarm clock go off in the morning, leaving the car lights on, or being forced to take a detour to work are the most serious crises of their lives. In retrospect, these crises are minor.

For other people, an equipment failure during an important production run, not getting a desired job, or getting laid off have been major crises. Consider the father who must tell his children that their mother has a terminal illness or that their younger sibling was killed in an auto accident. In each of these examples, the directly affected parties can often be heard to exclaim, "I can't believe it happened to me!" Others who are, at best, remotely connected to the people involved say, "Gosh, that's tough!" What one person views as a crisis is not necessarily a crisis to someone else. For those directly involved, each of the preceding events is perceived as a crisis that must be addressed.

Clearly, the definition of *crisis* varies depending on people's perspectives and perceptions. Crisis planning has become integral to every organization's long- and short-term planning. The recent past is replete with crises that can appear suddenly: a robber brandishing a gun enters a bank; a ladle of molten steel falls on workers; a bookkeeper steals from a church; a distraught worker carries a bomb into the workplace; a CEO is involved in a financial scandal; an unsafe product is designed, produced, and distributed; a class-action lawsuit arises due to racial harassment in the workplace.

It is not surprising that almost eighty percent of corporate executives report that computer security is now the single most critical attribute of corporate networks. The greatest vulnerability appears to be from internal sabotage, espionage, or accidental mistakes.[30] Such crises must be addressed in a timely fashion. Clearly, the unthinkable will continue to take place in our society. All aspects of organizational and personal life will undergo major changes. Today, more so than at any time in recent memory, supervisors must prepare for the unexpected.

The most recognizable example of how to effectively deal with a crisis is Johnson & Johnson's (J&J's) Tylenol crisis of the 1980s. The unthinkable occurred when someone injected cyanide into Extra-Strength Tylenol™ capsules. In all, eight deaths were linked directly to cyanide-laced Tylenol capsules. The company recalled more than 30 million bottles of the product, with an estimated retail value of over $100 million. This voluntary recall was the first example of a corporation voluntarily assuming responsibility for its products. Because J&J's credo taught managers to focus on the company's responsibility to the public and to the consumer, the decision to recall was easy; the corporation's values were clear. J&J survived the crisis with its reputation enhanced.[31]

Contrast J&J's handling of their crisis situation with that which occurred in New Orleans and other areas affected by Hurricane Katrina. Several days before the hurricane reached land, the National Weather Service and the National Hurricane Center provided accurate forecasts about what was likely to occur. Residents were given ample lead time to take precautions. However, like the childhood fable about "chicken little" who ran around screaming the "sky is falling, the sky is falling," the reports fell on the ears of many non-believers. On August 29, 2005, the storm that many feared made land. Over 1,800 people lost their lives and Katrina became the costliest natural disaster in U.S. history. Two days after making land, 80% of New Orleans was under water. The near total failure of the flood protection system (the levees) caused most of the damage. (See http://www.hhs.gov/disasters/emergency for an overview of how to prepare for a natural disaster.)

Years later, New Orleans is still in the process of rebuilding while local, state, and federal government agencies point fingers at others to deflect blame. There had been many warnings that the New Orleans levees would not hold back the water generated by a Class 5 hurricane but, for whatever reasons, government agencies failed to act. No one can accurately tell the future but we all have hindsight. One would think that after all of this century's hurricanes, floods, terror attacks, and economic woes, that most companies would have a crisis-management plan.

But the author expects that organizations—particularly small businesses, are less prepared than they need to be. Hindsight is a wonderful thing for government officials as well as supervisors to have. Hopefully, the impact of the catastrophic events and how various government agencies or organizations responded to them can provide insights about what to do and not to do when faced with potential dangers.

People face complicated issues all the time, some of which were considered impossible days or months ago. Ask an older person what they thought in 1961, when President John F. Kennedy gave the country a clear mandate: "Within the next ten years, we will send a man to the moon and return him home safely." At that time, most Americans viewed the task as impossible. But in July, 1969,

FIGURE 7.6 Crisis Management Planning

1. **Identify the *unthinkables*.** What are your areas of vulnerability? What has been happening to or in other organizations? Become a learning organization, and learn from the experiences of others. It must be made clear that every employee is responsible for reporting potential areas of concern and to do so promptly. "Everyone knew Hurricane Katrina was coming. So why couldn't the disaster have been avoided or at least the damage minimized?"

2. **Develop a plan for dealing with the *unthinkables*.** Ask "What if?" questions. For example, "If this happens, what should be done, and who should do it?" Learn from the mistakes of others. They are good indications of what not to do. Plans should include who will be the company's spokesperson in the event a crisis occurs. Speak with one voice to ensure consistent and uniform information.

3. **Develop contingency plans.** If Plan A does not work, then what should be done?

4. **Form crisis teams.** Have a team of qualified, well-trained individuals ready to go at a moment's notice. The events of 9/11 and the experiences with Hurricane Katrina in August 2005 pointed out the need to have several backup teams ready to go into action as soon as there is an indication that something might transpire.

5. **Simulate crisis drills.** As a child, your school probably had fire drills. Why? The school may have never experienced a fire, but the potential for one existed. The exercise was repeated so that all knew what to do if the crisis occurred.

6. **Respond immediately,** if not sooner. Create a culture in your organization that empowers employees rather than compels them to send memos or e-mails and await approval. Many organizations have retreated when unthinkable situations arose. Supervisors must share all they know as soon as they know it. Management Professor James O'Toole contends, "You can't get into trouble by admitting what you don't know or by giving people too much information."

7. **Do not be afraid to apologize.** Think about how you would like to be treated if something unthinkable happened to you. What would make it right? In many situations, nothing will make it right, but the right step is to apologize sincerely and to offer to make amends. As Professor Gerald Meyers says, "If you win public opinion, the company can move forward and get through it."

8. **Learn from the experience of others.** Learn from your own mistakes. Ask what you have learned from past crises and how you can integrate that knowledge into the planning process.

9. **Plan now!** There is no "rewind" button when a crisis occurs.

Sources: Adapted from "Special Report: Understanding Katrina," *U.S. News & World Report* (September 12, 2005), pp. 18–39; "Special Report: Lots of Blame—But It's No Game," *U.S. News & World Report* (September 19, 2005), pp. 26–38; Howard Paster, "Be Prepared," the *Wall Street Journal* (September 24, 2001), p. A24; Norman Augustine, "Managing the Crisis You Tried to Prevent," *Harvard Business Review* (November–December 1995), pp. 147–58.

Neil Armstrong took "one giant step for mankind." Look at the space shuttle crises that occurred before that could happen. As a researcher remarked to the author, "Over the years, I have learned what doesn't work. By learning from past mistakes, I now know what not to do! And knowing what not to do helps me discover options that will work!"

Every organization faces potential crisis situations. Regardless of the size or nature of the organization, supervisors must be involved in crisis-management planning. Every member of the management team, utilizing concepts as suggested in Figure 7.6, should plan for the unthinkable. Planning is primarily a mental process that enables the supervisor to anticipate what must be done as well as to adjust to changing circumstances and shifting priorities. It is not an overstatement to assert that effective planning is required for supervisors to succeed.

What can you do to ease the potential pain? Make sure you know that your organization has plans and procedures for crises. Be sure you and your employees know what to do when the unthinkable happens. Remember, too, that strategic planning is certainly one of the major tools advocated by major corporations and management theorists. However, strategic planning alone is not a panacea for natural disasters or other catastrophic events. Constant monitoring of strategic plans and learning about what is happening in the world and how others have coped must be done. Making new plans and actions to deal with the unthinkable has never been more important.

SUMMARY

1 Planning is the managerial function that determines what is to be done. It includes analyzing the situation, forecasting events, establishing objectives, setting priorities, and deciding what actions are needed to achieve objectives. Planning is a function of every manager, from the top-level executive to the supervisor. Without planning, there is no direction to organizational activities.

2 Strategic planning involves making decisions that enable the organization to achieve its short- and long-term objectives. It may involve developing a mission statement that identifies the philosophy and purpose of the enterprise. Visioning goes beyond the mission statement. Visioning is the process of developing a mental image of what the organization could become. Top-level management defines and articulates its vision so that everyone in the enterprise knows where the organization intends to be. Visioning can thereby help focus company goals and objectives. The organization develops plans based on the vision.

3 While top-level managers are responsible for developing and executing the overall strategic plan, supervisors direct their work-unit plans toward achieving parts of it. Effective supervisors create mental images of their departments in the future. Plans that complement this vision are developed. The vision, when shared with employees, gives greater meaning to employees' work.

Everyone is responsible for planning. Of course, the supervisor should consult with others to develop plans that are consistent with those of upper-level management. Supervisors devote most of their attention to short-term planning. The

supervisor's short-term plans should be integrated and coordinated with the long-term plans of upper-level management. Supervisors must communicate to employees what is being planned in a timely fashion.

4 Setting objectives is the first step in planning. Although overall goals and objectives are determined by top-level management, supervisors formulate departmental objectives, which must be consistent with organizational goals and objectives. Objectives should state what should be done and when.

5 A management by objectives (MBO) approach relies on participative setting of objectives and using those objectives as the primary basis for assessing performance. The four-step process in Figure 7.3 begins with the development of specific, measurable, and verifiable objectives. This step serves as the foundation for determining necessary resources, the activities that must be carried out, and the results that are to be worked toward. MBO ties planning activities together, establishes priorities, and provides coordination of effort. MBO-type approaches, which may be called other things, usually involve objectives being agreed upon by employees and their supervisor. Periodic reviews ensure progress is being made. At the end of the appraisal period, results are evaluated against objectives, and rewards are based on this evaluation. Objectives for the next period are then set, and the process begins again.

6 To attain objectives, standing plans and single-use plans must be devised. Top-level managers typically develop company-wide policies, procedures, methods, and rules; supervisors formulate the necessary subsidiary standing plans for their work units.

Many policies, which are guides to decision making, originate with high-level management. The supervisor's primary concern is to interpret, apply, and stay within policies when making decisions for the department. Policies are more likely to be followed consistently if they are written.

Procedures, like policies, are standing plans for achieving objectives. Procedures specify a sequence of actions that guide employees toward objectives. The supervisor often develops procedures to determine how work is to be done. The advantages of procedures are that they require analysis of what must be done, promote uniformity of action, and provide a means of appraising employees' work.

In addition, the supervisor will be called on to design and follow methods and rules, which are essentially guides for action. Methods and rules are more detailed than procedures. A rule is a directive that must be applied and enforced wherever applicable.

Supervisors should help establish budgets, which are single-use plans expressed in numerical terms. A budget serves as a control device that enables the supervisor to compare results achieved during the budget period against the budget plan. Supervisors at times play a role in organizational programs and projects, which are single-use plans designed to accomplish specific undertakings on a one-time basis.

7 Planning serves to use human and physical resources to their potential. Planning how best to use a firm's material, capital, and human resources is essential. Supervisors must plan for the efficient use of the department's space and major physical resources. Such planning may include close coordination with the maintenance department and/or other staff.

A major problem has been the loss and theft of materials, supplies, merchandise, data, and other company property. Supervisors must ensure that adequate security precautions are taken to discourage individuals from misusing or stealing items.

Supervisors should have a general understanding of all safety requirements. Safety committees and safety programs help planning initiatives and bring about safe work environments.

Planning for the full use of employees is at the core of professional supervision. Planning work schedules for employees includes establishing reasonable performance requirements and anticipating overtime requirements and absences. Many organizations are experimenting with various types of alternative, part-time, and temporary work schedules.

Time is one of the supervisor's most valued resources. Everybody has the same amount of it, so time is not the problem; the problem is how we use it. Therefore, supervisors must plan and manage their own time if they are to be effective.

Planning to improve work procedures and methods means looking for more efficient ways to achieve objectives. Encouraging employees to look for better ways to do their jobs and evaluating periodic work samples may result in substantial savings for the organization.

To reduce inventory costs and better plan for materials, just-in-time (JIT) inventory control systems attempt to ensure that materials and components arrive when needed. Gantt charts and PERT flowcharts are graphic tools to help supervisors plan, organize, and control operations.

8 Various quality-improvement concepts relate directly to planning. Total quality management (TQM) means planning for quality, preventing defects, correcting defects, and continuously improving quality and customer satisfaction. Knowledge management, which involves systematically planned approaches to storing and disseminating information, has increasingly become an important part of many organizational efforts to improve customer and employee services and satisfaction.

Benchmarking, the process of identifying and improving on the best practices of others, precedes plan development. Organizations that want to be as good as or better than the best in the world strive to attain national or international quality standards. Plans must be developed to establish, maintain, and increase product and service quality. Quality improvement does not just happen; it must be planned.

9 Crisis management has become a necessity for every organization. Being prepared for the unthinkable, especially in today's uncertain and chaotic world, requires that the supervisor identify potential crisis situations and develop plans for responding to the threats. Planning helps supervisors anticipate possible unthinkable events and their consequences. Supervisors must use their information-getting and information-giving skills to help employees prepare for and address crisis situations.

KEY TERMS

Benchmarking (p. 246)
Budget (p. 235)
Gantt chart (p. 245)
Just-in-time (JIT) inventory control
    system (p. 244)
Kanban (p. 244)
Knowledge management (p. 246)
Management by objectives (MBO)
    (p. 228)
Method (p. 234)

Metrics (p. 228)
Mission statement (p. 223)
Planning (p. 221)
Policy (p. 230)
Procedure (p. 233)
Program (p. 236)
Program evaluation and review
    technique (PERT) (p. 245)
Project (p. 236)
Rule (p. 234)

Single-use plans (p. 230)
Standing plans (p. 229)
Strategic plan (p. 226)
Strategic planning (p. 222)
Total quality management (TQM)
    (p. 245)
Visioning (p. 223)
Workplace violence (p. 239)

QUESTIONS FOR DISCUSSION

1. Define planning. Why is planning primarily a mental activity rather than a "doing" type of function?

2. Why should a first-line supervisor understand the organization's objectives? Why is this knowledge important to planning?

3. Discuss the step-by-step model for management by objectives (MBO). Explain why each step is crucial if MBO is to be successfully implemented.

4. Define and distinguish between each of the following:
   a. Policy
   b. Procedure
   c. Method
   d. Rule

5. If you were a supervisor in a small firm that had few policies and procedures and you believed that the organization needed to pursue a TQM program, how would you go about developing a plan to improve the company's production processes?

6. Some organizations have formed crisis management teams comprised of both hourly workers and supervisors to conduct risk assessments, develop action plans, and perform crisis interventions. Reports from Virginia Tech and Northern Illinois acknowledged that some students, staff, and faculty did not want to return to the buildings where the violence occurred. Consider the following scenario: *As your professor is passing back an exam paper, the person across the aisle from you crumbles her exam before she throws it at him, runs toward the door, and screams, "That was the worst exam I've ever had!" as she storms from the room.*
   a. Are you concerned that this might be a crisis situation—akin to an employee going "postal" in the workplace—waiting to happen? Is so, what would you do? Why?
   b. Should the university have a policy that would prohibit this student from returning to class? Why or why not?
   c. What do you see as the "downside" of a crisis-management policy?

SKILLS APPLICATIONS

Skills Application 7-1: Impossible Mission Made Possible!

1.  Note: Review this chapter's "You Make the Call!" Secure a copy of your school's crisis-management policy, if available. Search the Web to secure at least two examples of a crisis-management policy.

2.  Your instructor will cluster the class into groups of 8 to 12 students. Each group should determine who will play the following roles: Don Henderson, Alan Knuth, Kelly Notter, nursing/health services major (1 or 2), computer technology major (1 or 2), engineering major (1 or 2), communication major (1 or 2), and psychological sciences major (1 or 2). Working together as a task force, complete the following:

a. Make a list of all the potential crises that may occur at Old Ivy.
b. Make an outline of the topics that should be considered in the policy.
c. Develop a crisis-management policy and procedure statement.
d. Outline how the policy and procedure statement could be used to handle the crises successfully.
e. Collaboratively, write a one-page paper detailing the benefits of your policy and procedure statement.
f. Collaboratively, write a one-page paper detailing potential limitations of your policy and procedure statement.

Skills Application 7-2: Thinking Outside the Box

1. Look at the nine dots to the left. Your assignment is to connect all of them by drawing only four straight lines.
   Rule # 1: You must draw only four straight lines.
   Rule # 2: You must not retrace a line previously drawn.
   Rule # 3: Once you begin drawing, you may not remove your pencil or pen from the page as you draw.

2. Your instructor will provide you with the correct strategy for completing this skills application.

3. Given that "success requires you to think outside of the box," write a one-page paper describing what you learned from this skills application.

Skills Application 7-3: You Need to See It, Before You Can Do It!

1. Read the following quotes:

   "The best way to predict the future is to invent it!"

   "Nothing is more exciting than venturing into the unknown. There is a need to plan effectively to reach the unknown."

   "If you can't make accurate predictions, be prepared to deal with all possible outcomes."[32]

   a. Which of the statements comes closest to what you believe? Explain.

2. Close your eyes for a few seconds. Visualize what you would like to be doing five years from today.

3. Write a paragraph describing your vision. Assume that this vision is a goal you want to attain, so conclude by writing specific ("what by when") objectives and statements (e.g.,

"Five years from today, I will _____"). Make a copy of your vision and put it in your purse or wallet for safekeeping.

4. List the interim events that must be attained to reach your five-year vision.

5. What are the underlying assumptions/actions/events, etc. that might block you from realizing your vision?

6. Make a list of others from whom you will inevitably need help to realize your vision. What will you need from them?

7. Develop a road map and timetable for achieving the things that will lead you to your vision.

8. Describe how you will periodically check your progress toward your objectives, making necessary corrections and adjustments.

Skills Application 7-4: Dealing with People Who Make Your Life Difficult—"The Backstabber"

This is the fourth in a series of Skills Applications that introduces you to people who might make your life difficult.

1. Read the following statement from Joe Jordan, an employee at Barry Automotives' Jonesboro plant:

   Working with Brutus sure is frustrating. He has the uncanny ability to pull off any work assignment given to him. Not long ago, Brutus was on my project team to develop an electrical harness system for a new classic car. Paul had been given the assignment of researching other successful efforts so that we didn't spend all our time "reinventing the wheel." At the meeting when Paul presented his findings, Brutus waited until just the right moment before jumping in with his own research findings. Several of the things Brutus found flew in the face of Paul's research and made Paul appear incompetent.

   I don't trust Brutus. He is very controlling, greedy, and driven by his hunger for power. He is always behind the scenes, maneuvering and manipulating to get what he wants. Brutus knows just what to do to get the work done and always has his own agenda. He never volunteers suggestions or ideas to the group's planning meetings. If the meeting includes people from corporate,

   Brutus is really great at sabotaging the group's plan. He always seems to have a plan or two in his hip pocket to spring on the group. His surprises mean you always have to be on your guard.

   I've learned not to turn my back on Brutus. He is always spreading rumors and will try his best to ruin your career to promote his. You're always on your guard with him. His team spirit is minimal, but he steps forward to take credit for any successes. He'll double-cross teammates for personal gain and make excuses for any missed work. We work in an organization where the rewards aren't great, but Brutus is still there, trying to figure out a way to "work the system."

2. Using the Internet, find at least three sources for coping with a backstabber in the workplace. Carefully review each site for suggestions for dealing with this type of behavior.

3. Based on your findings, what suggestions would you give to Joe Jordan for coping with Brutus?

4. Write a one-page paper explaining how this Skills Application increased your working knowledge of how to cope with the behaviors of this type of difficult person.

SKILLS DEVELOPMENT

Skills Development Module 7-1: The Second City

Before you view the video clip, the author suggests that you take a virtual tour of Second City Chicago. Go to http://www.secondcity.com and launch their virtual tour (QuickTime Player required). Even if you have visited one of the Second City venues, you will find this tour interesting .

The Second City Theatre opened in Chicago on December 16, 1959 and the comic careers of John Belushi, Bill Murray, and Gilda Radner amongst others were launched on that stage. Second City evolved from the Compass Players, a 1950s cabaret style show started by a group of undergraduates at the University of Chicago.

Co-founder Bernard Sahlins owned the theatre company until 1985 when he sold it to Andrew Alexander. Alexander headed Second City of Toronto and started The Second City Entertainment Company in 1974.

Second City has since expanded to Toronto, Detroit, Los Angeles, and New York (Second City Las Vegas closed in August 2008). The Second City also has touring groups, a training center that teaches improvisation, acting, writing, and other skills, and a communications division that services corporate accounts.

After viewing the Skills Development Module video, answer the following questions:

1. A mission statement reflects the philosophy and purpose of the organization. After viewing the Second City video clip and reviewing their Web site, in less than 100 words, write what you think their mission statement should be.

2. It is said that "Kelly Leonard excels at strategic planning for The Second City." Discuss the attributes, qualities, and achievements of Kelly Leonard that would lead one to conclude the he excels in strategic planning.

3. How does the culture of The Second City support their strategic vision and planning process?

4. What metrics do you suppose Andrew Alexander uses to measure the success of The Second City? If you were to visit The Second City, what would you expect? As a consumer, what metrics would you use to measure customer satisfaction? How might the metrics used by the owners differ from those used by the consumer (the user of their products or services)?

ENDNOTES

NOTE: Scott M. Patton, "The Best of Times," *Quality Digest* (July 2008), p. 56, discussed the current economic situation. According to Patton, "We are waging a war against an unseen enemy. Gasoline prices are skyrocketing. GM, Ford and Chrysler are faltering. The airlines are in trouble, too. We've just been through a historic and exhausting presidential primary. We're hemorrhaging jobs to foreign markets. The dollar is at its lowest level in decades." Robert Schuller's book, *Tough Times Never Last, But Tough People Do!* (New York: Bantam Books, 1984) described the recession of the early 1980s and the political squabbling, job losses, foreclosures, and uncertainty that surrounded it. The two decades that follows were for the most part—forget the "dot com" bust—were a period of economic prosperity.

Will we survive this downturn? Yes, with persistence, perseverance, and sound planning principles.

1. See Peter F. Drucker, *Management: Tasks, Responsibilities, and Practices* (New York: Harper & Row, 1974), p. 611. Also see Drucker, *The Practice of Management* (New York: Harper Brothers, 1954), pp. 62–65, 126–29; Drucker, "Plan Now for the Future," *Modern Office Technology* (March 1993), pp. 8–9, and Peter F. Drucker as quoted in the article by Mike Johnson, "Drucker Speaks His Mind," *Management Review* (October 1995), pp. 11–14.

2. Linda Yates and Peter Skarzynski, "How Do Companies Get to the Future FIRST?" *Management Review* (January 1999), p. 17. For information on how CEO Skarzynski's team helps companies grow and innovate, go to www.strategos.com.

3. See Byran Feller, "Death by Assumption: Why Great Planning Strategies Fail," *Supervision,* 69, 2 (February 2008), p. 18; Audra Russell, "Strategic Objectives: Part of the Company's Strategy," (http://www.shrm.org, December 7, 2007); "Home to Improve Strategic Planning," *McKinsey Quarterly Member Edition* (December 20, 2007); Rob Cross et al., "Together We Innovate: How Companies Come Up with New Ideas—By Getting Employees Working with One Another," the *Wall Street Journal* (September 17–18, 2007), p. R6; Bryan S. Schaffer, "The Nature of Goal Congruence in Organizations," *Supervision,* 68, 8 (August 2007), pp. 13–17; and Michelle Labrosse, "Do You Know Where Your Goals Are?" *Supervision,* 68, 6 (June 2007), pp. 16–17.

Numerous books and articles discuss strategic management. For example, see Michael A. Hitt, R. Duane Ireland, and Robert E. Hoskinson, *Strategic Management: Competitiveness and Globalization*, 8th ed. (Mason, OH: Cengage Learning, 2009); John A. Parnell, *Strategic Management: Theory and Practice*, 3rd ed. (Mason, OH: Cengage Learning, 2009); J. David Hunger and Thomas Wheelen, *Essentials of Strategic Management* (Upper Saddle, NJ: Pearson Prentice Hall, 2007); Peter M. Ginter, *Strategic Management of Health Care Organizations* (New York: Blackwell Publishers, 2002).

4. The Southwest Airlines' (SWA) mission statement adds up to less than 100 words. See Colleen Barrett, president, SWA, *Spirit Magazine* (April 2008), p. 14. SWA president Barrett stepped down on July 16, 2008. In her parting column she stated, "I have so enjoyed using this column over the last several years to share, explain, and sometimes clarify Southwest Airlines—and my personal—passion for Proactive Customer Service delivery" (*Spirit Magazine* online edition, July 2008). See George Anders, "In Hard Times, Some Firms 'Go for the Jugular,'" the *Wall Street Journal* (June 25, 2008), p. B2, for illustrations of how SWA is storming into new markets and developing strategies for holding down prices in a bid to pry business away from competitors.

5. Over the years there have been many management trends and buzzwords. Some of them, like *mission statements* and *visioning*, have been around a long time. See Mark Hendricks, "Go Forth and Multiply," *Entrepreneur* (May 2002), pp. 46–47. Also see James B. Lucas, "Anatomy of a Vision Statement," *Management Review* (February 1998), pp. 22–26, and Gail Dutton, "Wanted: A Practical Visionary," *Management Review* (March 1998), pp. 33–36.

6. Peter M. Senge, et al., *The Fifth Discipline Fieldbook: Strategies and Tools for Building a Learning Organization* (New York: Currency/Doubleday, 1994), p. 46. "There are times when an organization would have been better off with no measurement than with a faulty one."

7. The author likes revenue factors that can be measured to show how a particular aspect of the organization is contributing to the organization's bottom line, which is generally referred to as metrics. In recent years, it has been commonplace for CEOs and managers to talk about their metrics. With great pride they stress that "they are meeting their metrics." Investors, for the most part, only care about the financial bottom line and whether the company meets its quarterly forecast. Human resource managers, on the other hand, may use absence rate, health care costs per employees, turnover costs, and workers' compensation incident rate as part of their metrics. I like revenue factor (revenue divided by total full-time equivalent [FTE])

as a metric. In this case, employees are viewed as an investment, i.e., capital. According to Forrest Breyfogle III, "The Balanced Scorecard and Beyond," (http://qualitydigest.com/IQedit/qdarticle, accessed July 5, 2008), "Every metric will have an owner where the measurement's performance can be part of the manager's plan and review." This is the manager's scorecard.

For an interesting commentary, see Stephen Baker, "Why 'Good Enough' is Good Enough," *BusinessWeek* (September 3, 2007), p. 48.

8. For additional information on MBO, see George S. Odiorne, "MBO Means Having a Goal and Plan—Not Just a Goal," *Manage* (September 1992), pp. 8–11, and David Halpern and Stephen Osofsky, "A Dissenting View of MBO," *Public Personnel Management* (Fall 1990), pp. 59–62. Author's note: much of what has been written about MBO in recent years discusses its application in government and not-for-profit organizations.

9. The author has found that many "mom-and-pop" operations, i.e., small firms, lack comprehensive personnel policies. The following references, though dated, report that most companies, regardless of size, had no policies for workplace romance, and more than half did not police it. See Ambi Biggs, "Many Firms Lack Policy on Office Romances," (Fredricksburg, VA: *Free-Lance Star*, February 14, 2002). Also see Betty Sosnin, "Packaging Your Policies," *HR Magazine* (July 2001), pp. 66–72.

10. Gallup research estimates that the average employee with Internet access spends more than one hour per day surfing Web sites that have nothing to do with their jobs (such as auction sites, sports sites, stock market sites, news sites, gambling sites, or sex sites); 30% to 40% of Internet use in the workplace is not related to business; 64% of employees say they use the Internet for personal interest during working hours; 70% of all Internet porn traffic occurs during the nine-to-five work day; and 37% of workers say they surf the Web constantly at work. (go to Http://www.gallup.com; click on Topics A to Z; and then clip on Computer to view findings related to employee computer and Internet abuse.) Also go to www.nlrb.gov for guidance on e-mail rules. Also see *The OneSign™ Guide to Thwarting Insider Threats*, (Lexington, MA: Imprivata, 2007) and *Vulnerability Management for Dummies* (IT Security Bulletin, July 2008) for additional guidance on how to prevent attacks and minimize network weaknesses.

11. Jerre L. Stead (chairman and CEO, Ingram Micro, Inc., Santa Ana, CA), "Whose Decision Is It, Anyway?" *Management Review* (January 1999), p. 13.

12. For example, SHRM Research periodically conducts various surveys and issues reports, which cover current human resource policies and practices covering pay, benefits, working conditions, employment, and employee relations. Some of the reports are available to both the general public and SHRM members. To ascertain what might be available for your view, visit http://www.shrm.org/surveys.

13. The 19th Annual Retail Theft Survey reports that more than 530,000 shoplifters and dishonest employees were apprehended in 2006 and more than $166 million recovered from those thieves. To access more information about retail theft, visit http://hayesinternational. com. For information and suggestions concerning various types of security and loss-prevention efforts, see Derk J. Boss and Douglas L. Florence, "The Sure Hand of Surveillance," *Security Management* (September 2001), pp. 87–91; Jill A. Fraser, "Prevent Employee Theft," *Inc.* (February 1993), p. 39; James G. Vigneau, "To Catch a Thief . . . and Other Workplace Investigations," *HR Magazine* (January 1995), pp. 90–95; and other issues of *Security Management*. Also see Don Wilcox, "Teaching Your Employees to Recognize Waste is the Smart Thing to Do," *Supervision*, 69, 2 (February 2008), pp. 10–13.

14. See Kris Maher, "Work Injuries are Undercounted," the *Wall Street Journal* (June 19, 2008), p A4. Maher contends that OSHA's system for tracking workplace safety is flawed. Nevertheless, see *OSHA*

Statement, http://www.osha.gov for current information on workplace fatality data. In 2007, there were over four million nonfatal injury workplace accidents in private industry, causing employees to lose over 1.8 million days of work. The numbers of injuries to Hispanic/Latino and foreign-born workers rose dramatically. Including workplace homicides, more than 5,000 employees were killed on the job in 2007. See Kathy Gurchiek, "Workplace Violence on the Upswing," *HR Magazine* (July 2005), pp. 27, 32.

15. Notes: In 2007, employee absenteeism or "lost work" posted its highest rate of the 21st century. Remember, these are unscheduled absences. For every employee with perfect attendance, another employee misses twelve days of work per year. Those are days that he or she is scheduled to work and, for whatever reason, chooses not to show up. The average employee is scheduled to work 250 days per year. See "Employee Absenteeism Rate Since 1999 Costing Industry Billions." *PR News* (December 19, 2007) (http://www.prnewsonline. com); see www.bna.com for additional information.

16. See Carla Shore, "Time Share: Emergency Time Pools Can Be a Costeffective Way to Give Workers Paid Time Off," *HR Magazine* (December 1998), pp. 104–8.

17. "Working 24/7 may be good for the organization, but it's bad for employee's health." See Jody Miller and Matt Miller, "Get a Life!" *Fortune* (November 28, 2005), pp. 108–124, for illustrations of how some organizations are helping employees balance work/life issues. "The emerging attitude toward work is flexibility . . ." according to "Time to Plan Your Life," *Newsweek* (January 8, 2001), pp. 54–55. See Amanda Iacone, "County Appears Ready to Try Flex Hours, 4-Day Workweek," *Fort Wayne, Indiana Journal Gazette* (July 15, 2008). Allen County, Indiana, officials will provide employees with more flexible work schedules—a staggered four-day workweek with longer hours for employees— such that employees will work nine days in a two-week period. Staff requested the changes, in part, to help them conserve fuel.

Surprisingly, a Watson Wyatt Worldwide and Rand Corporation report (July 15, 2008) report on how companies communicate a change of benefits to employees showed the following results: E-mail (67%), Face-to-face meetings (64%), Website (38%), Office meetings (33%), Webcasts (26%), Information mailed to employee's home (13%). Please note that organizations use multiple channels and means to communicate policy changes to employees.

18. From Lin Grensing-Pophal, "Training Supervisors to Manage Teleworkers," *HR Magazine* (January 1999), pp. 67–72. According to a SHRM survey, 37% of companies offer telecommuting or similar flexible work arrangements. Twenty-eight million Americans now (2007) work at least one day a month from home. (See www.legalworkplace. com, July 11, 2008—Alexander Hamilton Institute.)

19. For example, see Sue Shellenbarger, "More Companies Experiment with Workers' Schedules," the *Wall Street Journal* (January 13, 1994), pp. B1, B6, and D. Keith Denton, "Using Flextime to Create a Competitive Workplace," *Industrial Management* (January–February 1993), pp. 29–31.

20. See Douglas McLeod, "Risks from Hiring Temps May Have Long-term Effects," *Business Insurance* (April 28, 1997), p. 30; Linda Stockman Vines, "Make Long-term Temporary Employees Part of the Team," *HR Magazine* (April 1997), pp. 65–70; or Michael Mandel, "Nonstandard Jobs: A New Look," *BusinessWeek* (September 15, 1997), p. 28.

21. The *Wall Street Journal* reported that "temp agencies predict an increase in demand for temporary workers," (September 18, 2001), A1. For more in-depth analysis of temporary employment, see Raymond L. Hilgert, "Understanding and Managing Temporary Employees: Observations and Insights from a Case Study," a paper presented at the meetings of the Business/Society/Government Division of the Midwest Business Administration Association (MBAA) (March 1998).

22. For information on work-sampling techniques, see Richard B. Chase and Nicholas J. Aquilano, *Operations Management for Competitive Advantage*, 11th ed. (Boston: McGraw-Hill Irwin, 2005), pp. 181–205; or Lee J. Krajewski and Larry P. Ritzman, *Operations Management* (Upper Saddle, NJ: Pearson Prentice Hall, 2005); or Lee J. Krajewski and Larry P. Ritzman, *Operations Management; Strategy and Tactics*, 3rd ed. (Reading, MA: Addison-Wesley, 1993), pp. 268–71.

23. For information on just-in-time (JIT) inventory systems and kanban, see Art Raymond, "Is JIT Dead?" *FDM* (January 2002), pp. 30–33; Norman Bodek, "Kaizen: KaZam!" *T&D* (January 2002), pp. 60–61; A. E. Gerodimos, C. A. Glass, and C. N. Potts, "Scheduling of Customized Jobs on a Single Machine Under Item Availability," *IIE Transactions* (November 2001), pp. 975–984. Paul H. Zipkin, "Does Manufacturing Need a JIT Revolution?" *Harvard Business Review* (January–February 1991), pp. 40–50; and Satish Mehra and Anthony Inman, "Determining the Critical Elements of Just-In-Time Implementation," *Decision Sciences* (January–February 1992), pp. 160–73. For a contrary opinion on JIT, see Mary Aichlmayr, "The Future of JIT—Time Will Tell," *Transportation & Distribution* (December 2001), pp. 18–23; R. Anthony Inman and Larry D. Brandon, "An Undesirable Effect of JIT," *Production and Inventory Management Journal* (First Quarter 1992), pp. 55–58.

24. For additional information on Gantt charts, see Andrew J. DuBrin, *Essentials of Management*, 7th ed. (Mason, OH: South-Western Thomson, 2006); or search the Internet for "Gantt charts". For additional information on PERT flowcharts, see Li-Chih Wang and Wilbert E. Wilhelm, "A PERT-Based Paradigm for Modeling Assembly Operations," *IIE Transactions* (Volume 25, Number 2, March 1993), pp. 88–103, or search the Internet for "PERT".

25. For additional information on TQM and continuous improvement, see H. James Harrington, Six Sigma in Health Care: A New Prescription, *Quality Digest* (December 2007), p. 14; Kim Klesen, "Building Human Resources Strategic Planning, Process and Measurement Capability: Using Six Sigma as a Foundation," *Organizational Development Journal,* 25, 2 (Summer 2007), pp. 37–42; Laura Smith, "The Six Sigma Cure," *Quality Digest* (March 2006), pp. 22–26; George Eckes, "Making Six Sigma Last (and Work)," *Ivey Business Journal* (January/February 2002), pp. 77–81; Donald S. Miller, "Q-u-a-l-i-t-y: Realities for Supervisors," *Supervision* (May 2000), pp. 3–5; A. Blanton Godfrey, "Is Quality Dead?" *Quality Digest* (December 2000), p. 14; W. J. Duncan and J. G. Van Matre, "The Gospel According to Deming: Is It Really New?" *Business Horizons* (July–August 1990), pp. 3–9; and Richard M. Hodgetts, *Implementing TQM in Small and Medium-Sized Organizations: A Step-by-Step Guide* (New York: AMACOM Division of American Management Association, 1996). For a complete overview of Six Sigma, see "Six Sigma: Quality Sourcebook," *Quality Digest* (January 2006), pp. 65–77. To view the Global Six Sigma Award winners go to www.wcbf.com/quality/5081.

26. From Louisa Wah, "Behind the Buzz: Knowledge Management Has Become a Red-hot Buzzword in Management Circles," *Management Review* (April 1999), pp. 17–26. Also see Glenn Schulz, "Information Drives Asset Management," *Manufacturing Engineering* (September 2001), p. 200, and "Do You Know What You Know? New Study Reveals Top Knowledge Management Strategies," *Business Wire* (January 24, 2000). To view the full executive summary of this study, visit http://www.benchmarkingreports.com/knowledgemanagement.

27. Ibid., Wah.

28. Stratford Sherman, "Are You as Good as the Best in the World?" *Fortune* (December 13, 1993), p. 95. Also see Geoffrey Colvin, "Catch a Rising Star," *Fortune* (February 6, 2006), pp. 46–50. Colvin identifies twelve future leaders, analyzes their management styles, and asks you to learn from them.

29. Eighty-five organizations—the largest number of applicants since 1992—applied for the 2008 Malcolm Baldrige National Quality Award. For more information, visit http://www.nist.gov/publicaffairs/teachbest/tb2008-0610.htm#baldrige. Also see Jack West, "Need a Quality Plan? ANSI/ISO/ASQ Q10005-2005 Provides Four Templates and Guidance," *Quality Digest* (December 2007), p. 18; or William A. Stimson, *Meeting the Challenge of ISO 9000:2000* (Chico, CA: Paton Press, 2004). Also see other Paton Press and QCI International Publications: *How to Audit ISO 9001:2000; Internal Quality Auditing and How to Audit ISO 9001:2000—A Handbook for Auditors.* Also see InsideQuality.com for information on how various organizations have used quality principles to improve performance. Also see Derrell S. James, "Lessons from the Trenches: Lean and Six Sigma tools can counteract the disadvantages of a small workforce and budget," *Quality Digest* (October 2004), pp. 25–28.

30. See "Survey: Security Top Concern for Corporate Networks," AccountingWeb http://www.accountingweb.com (July 16, 2004). Also see Evan Perez, "Revised Intelligence Law Would Broaden Government Surveillance Powers," *Wall Street Journal* (July 8, 2007), p. A16; Pui-Wing Tam, Erin White, Nick Wingfield, and Kris Maher, "Snooping E-Mail by Software is Now a Workplace Norm," *Wall Street Journal Online* (June 30, 2005).

31. Due to its proactive, consumer-oriented response to the Tylenol scare, Johnson & Johnson became one of the world's most respected companies. See Robert F. Hartley, *Management Mistakes and Successes*, 7th ed. (London: Wiley, 2002), chapter 8; Ian I. Mitroff and Gus Anagnos, *Managing Crises Before They Happen* (New York: AMACOM, 2001); and Matthew Boyle, "The Shiniest Reputations in Tarnished Times," *Fortune* (March 4, 2002), pp. 70–82. Much had been written about crisis management, even before 9/11. Two *BusinessWeek* articles are at the top of our recommended reading list. See John A. Byrne, "Here's What to Do Next, Dow Corning," (February 24, 1992), p. 33, and "How Companies Are Learning to Prepare for the Worst," (December 23, 1985), pp. 74+.

   Also see "Can You Suggest Any Practices for Avoiding or Reacting to Workplace Violence," Ceridian Abstracts (March 27, 2008, http://www.hrcompliance.ceridian.com); Kathy Gurchiek, "Disaster Plans Put to the Test: We Moved Quickly," *SHRM Home* (October 29, 2007), Carol Hymowitz, "Managing in a Crisis Can Bring Better Ways to Conduct Business," *Wall Street Journal* (October 23, 2001), p. B1; Jeffrey R. Caponigro, *The Crisis Counselor: A Step-by-Step Guide to Managing a Business Crisis* (New York: Contemporary Books, 2000); and Laurence Barton, *Crisis in Organizations: Managing and Communicating in the Heat of Chaos* (Cincinnati: South-Western, 1993).

32. Susan J. Wells used the first two quotes in her article, "Managing a Downturn," *HR Magazine*, 53, 5 (May 2008), pp. 49–53.

   Also see www.thinkexist.com/quotation for a more complete listing of quotes.

CHAPTER 8

(**Supervisory Organizing at the Departmental Level**)

GETTY IMAGES

After studying this chapter, you will be able to:

1 Identify the organizing function of management.

2 Discuss the impact of the informal organization and informal group leaders and how supervisors should deal with them.

3 Explain the unity-of-command principle and its applications.

4 Define the span-of-management principle and the factors that influence its application.

5 Describe departmentalization and alternative approaches for grouping activities and assigning work.

6 Explain the advantages of the project management-type organizational structure.

7 Identify why a supervisor should plan for an "ideal" departmental structure and work toward this objective.

8 Define and discuss organizational tools that are useful in supervisory organizing efforts.

9 Define downsizing (restructuring) and its implications for organizational principles.

10 Identify the major factors contributing to organizing effective meetings, especially the supervisor's role.

11 Understand the importance of self-organization, i.e., effective use of your time.

YOU MAKE THE CALL!

David Simms is the manager of the Brunswick restaurant that is part of a nationwide chain of popular restaurants. The restaurant is open 11 A.M.–10 P.M. (Monday–Thursday); 11 A.M.–12 P.M. (Friday & Saturday); and 11 A.M.–8 P.M. (Sunday). According to company policy, all supervisors and managers are to be promoted from within the corporation. David knows of a few situations in which the company hired qualified people from outside the company for management positions, but this practice is generally frowned upon by top management because management believes in promoting their own employees. David always has prided himself on his dedication to this policy. Many of his employees attained supervisory positions, and several were afforded opportunities to manage their own restaurants. David also is proud of his abilities as manager. The restaurant he manages has a reputation for being profitable, stable, and relatively problem-free. His restaurant consistently ranked in the top ten percent of all company restaurants based on the prescribed metrics the company uses.

David's employees and supervisors get along quite well, and employee turnover is one of the lowest in the company. However, during the past week David has faced a perplexing problem.

Last week, June Teevers, the weeknight supervisor, notified David that in two weeks her husband is being promoted and transferred across the country. Teevers apologized for the short notice, and she explained that she and her husband had no choice but to accept this "once-in-a-lifetime" offer. Therefore, Teevers will be supervising her last shift in about a week. David never expected, and has done little to prepare for, such an occurrence.

In the past couple of days, he has tried to find someone who could fill Teevers's position, but he has reached only dead ends. David contacted his regional manager and explained his situation. She informed David that there was not a restaurant in the region that could spare a supervisor or a supervisory trainee. Because of the fact that his best servers make wages comparable to what a new manager would make, David expected such an answer.

The only other option he can think of is to promote an employee named Margo James, who is a great server and who has helped occasionally when supervisors were sick or on vacations. However, David has heard that while James is a well-liked server, she is a thoroughly disliked temporary supervisor. James's coworkers complained that she was belligerent, a "control freak," and extremely autocratic whenever she was a temporary supervisor. David does not think that promoting Margo is prudent, but he also knows that he is supposed to promote from within, so he has a difficult set of decisions to make.

What options does David Simms have? Can he promote Margo James and maintain employee morale and stability? How can he prevent another, similar problem? **YOU MAKE THE CALL!**

Organizing as an Essential Managerial Function

1 Identify the organizing function of management.

As one of the five major functions of management, organizing requires every manager to be concerned with building, developing, and maintaining working relationships that will help achieve the organization's objectives. Although organizations may have varied objectives and may operate in many kinds of environments, the fundamental principles of organizing are universal.

A manager's organizing function consists of designing a structure—grouping activities and assigning them to specific work units (e.g., departments, teams). Organizing includes establishing formal authority and responsibility relationships among activities and departments. To make such a structure possible, management must delegate authority throughout the organization and establish and clarify authority relationships among departments. We use the term **organization** to refer to any group structured by management to carry out designated functions and accomplish certain objectives.

Management should design the structure and establish authority relationships based on sound principles and organizational concepts, such as unity of command,

Organization
Group structured by management to carry out designated functions and accomplish certain objectives

span of supervision, division of work, and departmentalization. In Chapter 2, we briefly discussed managerial authority and the process of delegation. In Chapter 11, we expand on those concepts, which reflect how management establishes authority and responsibility relationships in organizational structures.

While organizing the overall activities of the enterprise is initially the responsibility of the chief executive, it eventually becomes the responsibility of supervisors. Therefore, supervisors must understand what it means to organize. Although the range and magnitude of problems associated with the organizing function are broader at higher managerial levels than for supervisors, the principles are the same.

ORGANIZATIONS ARE PEOPLE

Throughout this chapter's discussions of the concepts and principles of organizing, never forget that people are the substance and essence of any organization, regardless of how the enterprise is structured. Managers and supervisors may become so preoccupied with developing and monitoring the formal structure that they neglect the far more important aspects of relationships with and among their employees. For example, a major survey of a large cross-section of employees revealed that 70 percent of "core workers" said they were committed to the success of their firms, but only about half felt that their organizations really cared about their job satisfaction. Significantly, too, these workers claimed that their sense of loyalty to their firms had been threatened by their dissatisfaction with the many organizational changes they had experienced.[1] See Figure 8.1 for an illustration of how one disgruntled worker broadcasts dissatisfaction with the organization to anyone who will listen.

Organizational success is more likely to happen when employees are truly given top-priority attention by their managers and supervisors.[2] Our focus in this chapter is on building the sound organizational structures that can be the

FIGURE 8.1 Disgruntled workers can easily broadcast their unhappiness throughout their organizations

building blocks and foundations that support the mutual goals of effective work performance and high job satisfaction. Following good and accepted organizational principles does not ensure organizational success, but it usually means preventing many problems and irritations.

Informal Organization

2 Discuss the impact of the informal organization and informal group leaders and how supervisors should deal with them.

Every enterprise is affected by a social subsystem known as the **informal organization**, sometimes called the "invisible organization." The informal organization reflects the spontaneous efforts of individuals and groups to influence their environment. Whenever people work together, social relationships and informal work groups inevitably arise. Informal organization develops when people are in frequent contact, but their relationships are not necessarily a part of formal organizational arrangements. Their contacts may be part of or incidental to their jobs, or they may stem primarily from the desire to be accepted as a group member.

Informal organization
Informal gatherings of people, apart from the formal organizational structure, that satisfy members' social and other needs

At the heart of the informal organization are people and their relationships, whereas the formal organization primarily represents the organization's structure and the flow of authority. Supervisors can create and rescind formal organizations they have designed; they cannot eliminate an informal organization because they did not establish it.

Informal groups arise to satisfy the needs and desires of members that the formal organization does not satisfy. Informal organization particularly satisfies members' social needs by providing recognition, close personal contacts, status, companionship, and other aspects of emotional satisfaction. Groups also offer their members other benefits, including protection, security, and support. Further, they provide convenient access to the informal communications network, or grapevine (see Chapter 3). The grapevine provides a communication channel and satisfies members' desires to know what is going on. Informal organization also influences the behavior of individuals in the group. For example, an informal group may pressure individuals to conform to the performance standards to which most group members subscribe. This phenomenon may occur in any department or at any level in the organization.

THE INFORMAL ORGANIZATION AND THE SUPERVISOR

At different times, the informal organization makes the supervisor's job easier or more difficult. Because of their interdependence, the attitudes, behaviors, and customs of informal work groups affect the formal organization. Every organization operates in part through informal work groups, which can positively or negatively impact departmental operations and accomplishments.

Numerous research studies have demonstrated that informal groups can influence employees to strive for high work performance targets or restrict production, and to cooperate with or work against supervisors, to the point of having those supervisors removed. Supervisors must be aware that informal groups can be very strong and can even shape employee behavior to an extent that interferes with supervision. So-called organizational negativity has become a major area of concern for many organizations.[3] The negative attitudes that lead to negative behavior patterns are often traced to the work groups that influence their members to conform to the groups' norms. The pressures of informal groups can frustrate the supervisor trying to get the results that higher-level managers expect.

To influence the informal organization to play a positive role, the supervisor first must accept and understand it. The supervisor should group employees so that those most likely to compose harmonious teams work on the same assignments. Moreover, the supervisor should avoid activities that would unnecessarily disrupt those informal groups whose interests and behavior patterns support the department's overall objectives. Conversely, if an informal group is influencing employees negatively, and to the extent that the department is seriously threatened, a supervisor may have to do such things as redistribute work assignments or adjust work schedules.

SUPERVISING AND INFORMAL WORK GROUP LEADERS

Most informal work groups develop their own leadership. An informal leader may be chosen by the group or may assume leadership by being a spokesperson for the group. Work-group leaders play significant roles in both formal and informal organizations; without their cooperation, the supervisor may have difficulty controlling the performance of the department. A sensitive supervisor, therefore, will make every effort to gain the cooperation and goodwill of informal leaders of different groups and will solicit their cooperation in furthering departmental objectives. When approached properly, informal leaders can help the supervisor, especially as channels of communication. Informal leaders may even be viable candidates for supervisor understudies. However, it is questionable whether these people can function as informal leaders once they have been designated as understudies.

Instead of viewing informal leaders as "ringleaders," supervisors should consider them employees who have influence and who are "in the know," and then try to work with them. For example, to try to build good relationships with informal leaders, a supervisor may periodically give them information before anyone else or ask their advice on certain problems. However, the supervisor must be careful to avoid having informal leaders lose status in their groups because the leaders' close association with the supervisor is being observed and could be interpreted negatively by employees. Similarly, the supervisor should not extend unwarranted favors to informal leaders as this could undermine their leadership. Rather, the supervisor should look for subtle approaches to have informal groups and their leaders dovetail their special interests with the department's activities. We discuss this and other aspects of work groups in Chapter 12.

---

3 **Explain the unity-of-command principle and its applications.**

Unity of Command and Authority Relationships

The chief executive groups the activities of the organization into divisions, departments, services, teams, or units, and assigns duties accordingly. Upper-level management places managers and supervisors in charge of divisions and departments and defines their authority relationships. Supervisors must know exactly who their managers and subordinates are. To arrange authority relationships this way, management normally follows the **unity-of-command principle**, which holds that each employee should report directly to only one immediate supervisor. That is, there is only one person to whom the employee is directly accountable. While formal communication and the delegation of authority normally flow upward and downward through the chain of command, there are exceptions, such as in functional authority and the matrix organizational structure, which are discussed later in this chapter. Similarly, task forces, project groups, and special committees may blur the unity-of-command concept. Committees and problem-solving groups are discussed in later chapters.

Unity-of-command principle
Principle that holds that each employee should directly report to only one supervisor

Having more than one supervisor usually leads to unsatisfactory performance by the employee due to confusion of authority. When the unity-of-command principle is violated, conflicts or confusion usually result. Therefore, a supervisor should make certain that, unless there is a valid reason for an exception, only one supervisor should direct an employee.

The Span-of-Management Principle

4 Define the span-of-management principle and the factors that influence its application.

Departments and managerial levels are not solutions; they are the sources of numerous difficulties. Departments are expensive because they must be staffed by supervisors and employees. Moreover, as more departments and levels are created, communication and coordination problems arise. Therefore, there must be valid reasons for creating levels and departments. The reasons are associated with the **span-of-management principle**, which holds that there is an upper limit to the number of employees a supervisor can manage effectively. Often, this principle is called "span of supervision" or "span of control" (see Figure 8.2).

Because no one can manage an unlimited number of people, top-level managers must organize divisions and departments as separate operating units and place middle-level managers and supervisors in charge. Top-level managers then delegate authority to those middle-level managers, who delegate authority to supervisors, who, in turn, supervise the employees.

The principle that a manager can effectively supervise a limited number of employees is as old as recorded history.[4] However, it is impossible to state how many subordinates a manager should have. It is only correct to say that there is some upper limit to this number. In many industries, a top-level executive has from three to eight subordinate managers, and the span of management usually increases the lower a person descends in the managerial hierarchy. A span of management between 15 and 25 is not uncommon at the first level of supervision.

Span-of-management principle
Principle that there is an upper limit to the number of subordinates a supervisor can manage effectively

FIGURE 8.2 A manager can effectively supervise a limited number of employees

There has long been a question concerning the link between organizational size and organizational performance. The economic "law of diminishing returns" has been applied to suggest that organizational efficiency can be impacted by size. However, the "optimal size" for a firm has never been defined; the answer remains elusive.

FACTORS INFLUENCING THE SPAN OF MANAGEMENT

The number of employees one person can supervise effectively depends on a number of factors, such as the supervisor's abilities, the types and amounts of staff assistance, employees' capabilities, employees' locations, the kinds of activities, and the degree to which departments have objective performance standards.

SUPERVISORY COMPETENCE

Among the most significant factors influencing the span of management are the supervisor's training, experience, and know-how—in other words, the supervisor's competence. Some supervisors can handle more employees than others. Some are better acquainted with good management principles, have more experience, and are better managers overall. For example, what a supervisor does with time is important. The supervisor who must make decisions on every departmental problem takes more time than the supervisor who has established policies, procedures, and rules that simplify decision making on routine problems. Comprehensive planning can reduce the number of decisions the supervisor must make and, hence, increases the span of management. Therefore, the number of employees a supervisor can supervise effectively depends to some degree on the supervisor's managerial capabilities.

SPECIALIZED STAFF ASSISTANCE

Another factor on which the span of management depends is the availability of help from specialists in the organization. If numerous staff experts are available to provide specialized advice and service, then the span of management can be wider. For example, when a human resources department helps supervisors recruit, select, and train employees, supervisors have more time for their departments. When supervisors are obligated to do all or most of these activities, they cannot devote that time to managing their departments. Therefore, the amount and quality of staff assistance influence the span of management.

EMPLOYEE ABILITIES

The span a supervisor can handle also depends on the abilities and knowledge of employees in the department. The greater employees' capacities for self-direction, the broader the feasible span. Here, of course, the employees' training and experience are important. For example, the span of management could be greater with fully qualified mechanics than with inexperienced mechanics. However, employee competence may be offset to some degree by the locations of the employees and by the nature of the activities.

LOCATION OF EMPLOYEES

The locations and proximities of employees to a supervisor can factor into the span of management. When employees are close to each other and to the supervisor, as they are when they are in the same office, a supervisor can supervise more employees because observation and communication are relatively easy.

When employees work in close proximity to each other and to the supervisor, the supervisor can observe and communicate with them easily

Because of advances in wireless technologies, telecommuting and off-shoring is expected to grow rapidly. It is not uncommon to find that your customer service call center representative is in Thailand, India, or the Philippines, with his or her supervisor located in, say, Indiana. Regardless of location, all customer service representatives will need to be proficient in technical matters and in customer service. As companies continue to seek ways to save money by moving certain operations overseas, supervisory responsibilities will change. Simply stated, how will you know that the people you hire in Thailand, for example, are qualified? Will you bring them to the United States for training? Or will the supervisor and a cadre of trainers go to Thailand to do on-site training? Or will you use some form of online learning? Think about the differences in employee backgrounds, languages, customs, cultures, and work ethics. Regardless of where employees are located, the supervisory functions remain the same and communication skills are paramount.

Thus, when employees are widely dispersed, as they are when they work in different parts of the world, work at home, or work in outdoor crews throughout a metropolitan area, the span of management may be somewhat limited because face-to-face communication and coordination are difficult.

NATURE AND COMPLEXITY OF ACTIVITIES

The amount, nature, complexity, and predictability of activities influence the span of management. The simpler, more routine, and more uniform the work activities, the greater the number of people one supervisor can manage. When tasks are repetitious, the span may be as broad as 25 or more employees. When activities are varied or interdependent, or when errors would have serious consequences, the span may be as narrow as three to five. In departments engaged in relatively unpredictable activities, such as nurses in an intensive-care unit of a hospital, spans tend to be narrow. In departments completing fairly stable activities, such as an assembly line or a data-service center, the span can be broader.

OBJECTIVE PERFORMANCE STANDARDS

Still another factor influencing the span of management is whether a department has ample objective standards for guiding and measuring employee performance. When each employee knows exactly what standards are expected, such as a certain number of sales units each week or the production of a specific amount each day, the supervisor need not have frequent discussions with employees about performance. Therefore, good standards support a broader span of management.

WEIGHING THE FACTORS

As stated previously, there is no set number of employees a supervisor can manage effectively. The span-of-management principle indicates only that an upper limit exists. In most situations, there must be a weighing, or balancing, of the factors just discussed to arrive at an appropriate span of management for each supervisor. Such weighing is, for the most part, the responsibility of high-level management, although supervisors often will be asked to express their opinions concerning what they believe is an appropriate span of management for their departments.

HOW MANAGERIAL LEVELS AND SPAN OF MANAGEMENT ARE RELATED

Lead person
Employee in charge of other employees who performs limited managerial functions but is not considered part of management

When top-level managers conclude that the span of management for a certain activity or department is too broad, they may decide to divide the span into two or three groups and to place someone in charge of each group. By narrowing the span, the manager creates another organizational level because a supervisor or "lead person" must manage each smaller group. A **lead person**, sometimes called a "working supervisor," is not usually considered part of management, especially in unionized firms. While the authority of these individuals is somewhat limited, particularly in employee evaluation and discipline, they perform most managerial functions.

Other things being equal, the narrower the span of management is, the more managerial levels are needed in organizational design. Stated another way, organizational structures tend to be taller when spans of management are narrower, and structures tend to be flatter when spans of management are wider, especially at the supervisory level. Of course, this may vary because of other organizational considerations. Adding or reducing levels of management may or may not be desirable. For example, adding levels can be costly and can complicate communication and decision making. On the other hand, reducing levels may widen the spans of management to the extent that supervisors become overburdened and cannot maintain adequate control of employees and departmental activities. There is a tradeoff between the span and the number of levels.

Division of work (specialization)
Dividing work into components and specialized tasks to improve efficiency and output

The managerial problem is to decide which is better: a broad span with few levels or a narrow span with more levels? This important question often confronts upper management. A first-line supervisor does not normally confront this question, but supervisors should understand how it influences the design and structure of their organizations.

5 Describe departmentalization and alternative approaches for grouping activities and assigning work.

Departmentalization

Organizational structure is influenced largely by the principle of **division of work (specialization)**. This principle holds that jobs can be divided into smaller components and specialized tasks to increase efficiency and output. Technological advances and increasing complexity make it difficult for employees to keep current with their work or specialty responsibilities. Dividing work into smaller tasks allows employees to specialize in narrower areas of their fields. Employees can then master these smaller tasks and produce more efficiently. For example, as cars become more complex and diverse, it becomes more difficult for a mechanic to know how to fix everything on every type of car. As a result, specialty repair shops, such as muffler shops, oil-change services, and foreign-car specialists, have sprung up. Even in shops that do many types of repairs, mechanics often specialize. By specializing, employees can become expert enough in their areas to produce efficiently.

Departmentalization is the process of grouping activities and people into organizational units, usually known as departments. A **department** is a set of activities and people over which a manager or supervisor has responsibility and authority. The terminology organizations use for this entity varies. A department may be called a division, an office, a service, or a unit. Most organizations have departments because division of work and specialization enhance efficiency and results.

The **formal organizational structure** is based on a company's number and types of departments, positions and functions, and authority and reporting relationships. Whereas major departments of an organization are established by top-level managers, supervisors are primarily concerned with activities in their own areas. From time to time, supervisors confront the need to departmentalize their areas, so they should be familiar with the alternatives for grouping activities. These are the same options available to top-level managers when those managers define the company's major departments. Departmentalization is usually done according to function, products or services, geographic location, customer, process and equipment, time, or matrix design.

There is no one best way to organize. Organizational theorists contend that structure should follow strategy. In recent years, there has been significant change in the way business is conducted. Pick up a current copy of *Fortune*, *BusinessWeek*, or the *Wall Street Journal* and read about how one organization or another is announcing plans to modify its organizational structure. Why? Intense competition for the consumer dollar, rising resource costs, globalization, and a search for ways to restore profitability is leading many organizations to alter their strategies. As you read the article, ascertain how the organization has changed its strategy. To the consternation of this author, most top managers have forgotten a fundamental principle: "organizations tend to be more effective when they are structured to fit the strategic change and the demands of the situation."

Departmentalization
The process of grouping activities and people into distinct organizational units

Department
An organizational unit for which a supervisor has responsibility and authority

Formal organizational structure
Departments, positions, functions, authority, and reporting relationships as depicted on a firm's organizational chart

WORK ASSIGNMENTS AND ORGANIZATIONAL STABILITY

Supervisors are challenged much more frequently by the problem of how and to whom to assign work than by the problem of how to organize departments. The former always involves differences of opinion. Nevertheless, the assignment of work should be justifiable and explainable on the basis of good management rather than on personal likes and dislikes or intuition. The supervisor is subject to pressures from different directions. Some employees are willing and want to assume more work, while others believe they should not be burdened by additional duties. One of the supervisor's most important responsibilities is to assign work so that everybody has a fair share and all employees do their parts equitably and satisfactorily. (See Figure 8.3.)

As emphasized previously, a supervisor's task of assigning departmental work is easier when the supervisor consistently uses the strengths and experiences of all employees. However, supervisors are often inclined to assign heavier and more

FIGURE 8.3 Work should be assigned equitably, but supervisors sometimes rely too much on certain employees

Principle of organizational stability
Principle that holds that no organization should become overly dependent on one or several "indispensable" individuals

difficult tasks to capable employees who are most experienced. Over the long term, it is advantageous to train and develop less-experienced employees so that they, too, can perform difficult jobs. When supervisors rely too much on one employee or a few employees, a department weakens because top performers can call in sick, take promotions, or leave the enterprise. The **principle of organizational stability** advocates that no organization should become overly dependent on one or several key "indispensable" individuals whose absences or departures would disrupt the organization. Organizations need enough employees who have been trained well and have flexible skills. One way to develop such flexibility is to assign employees to different jobs in the department temporarily, such as during vacation periods or employee absences. In this way, there is usually someone to take over any job if the need arises.

At times, a supervisor may have to hire temporary employees to meet workload demands for a project or other needs. As discussed in Chapter 7, temporary employees can be helpful when given work assignments they can complete and when they do not cause disruptions or disagreements with permanent employees. Some temporary employees prove themselves so competent that supervisors want to hire them for permanent positions.[5]

AUTHORITY AND ORGANIZATIONAL STRUCTURES

Once management establishes departments, it must establish and clarify relationships among and within the departments. In Chapter 2, we briefly defined managerial authority and the process of delegation. We expand on those concepts in Chapter 11. The following discussion serves as a basis for discussing how management establishes authority and responsibility relationships in organizational structures. Every organization has a vertical, direct line of authority that can be traced from the chief executive to departmental employees. **Line authority** provides the right to direct others and requires them to conform to company decisions, policies, rules, and objectives. Supervisors directly involved in making, selling, or distributing the company's products or services have line authority. Refer to Figure 8.6, on page 273, for an example of a line organization that has a clear chain of command. Line authority establishes who can direct whom in the organization. A primary purpose of line authority is to make the organization work smoothly.

Line authority
The right to direct others and to require them to conform to decisions, policies, rules, and objectives

With organizational growth, activities tend to become more specialized and complicated. Line supervisors cannot be expected to direct subordinates adequately and expertly in all phases of operations without some assistance.

Line supervisors, to perform their managerial functions, need the assistance of specialists who have been granted staff authority. **Staff authority** is the right and duty to provide counsel, advice, support, and service regarding policies, procedures, technical issues, and problems in a person's areas of expertise. Certain specialists are granted staff authority because of their positions or specialized knowledge. Staff people assist other members of the organization whenever the need arises. For example, human resource specialists often screen candidates for line managers to interview. While human resource managers can direct the work of employees in their own departments (line authority), they can only advise managers in other departments in human resource matters (staff authority).

Most organizations use a **line-and-staff-type organizational structure**. Certain departments, such as human resources and accounting, usually are classified as staff since they mainly support other departments. For example, human resource managers are responsible for seeing that certain policies and procedures are carried out by the line departments. For the most part, staff supervisors lack the direct authority to order line employees to conform to policies and procedures. They primarily counsel and advise. Line supervisors can accept the staff person's advice, alter it, or reject it, but because the staff person is usually the expert in the field, line supervisors usually accept, and even welcome, the staff person's advice.

In most organizations, the day-to-day usefulness and effectiveness of the human resources staff depends primarily on their abilities to develop close working relationships with line managers and supervisors. The quality of these line/staff relationships, in turn, depends on how clearly top-level managers have defined the scope of activities and authority of the staff.

Staff authority
The right to provide counsel, advice, support, and service in a person's areas of expertise

Line-and-staff-type organizational structure
Structure that combines line and staff departments and incorporates line and staff authority

The Project Management-Type Organizational Structure

The need to coordinate activities across departments has contributed to the development of the **project management-type organizational structure**, also called "matrix structure." The project management-type structure, which is superimposed on the line-staff organization, adds horizontal dimensions to the normally vertical (top-down) orientation of the organizational structure. It is a hybrid in which both regular (functional) line and staff departments coexist with project teams or group assignments across departmental lines.

Many high-tech firms employ project structures to focus special talents from different departments on specific projects for certain periods. Project structure enables managers to undertake several projects simultaneously, some of which may be of relatively short duration. Each project is assigned to a project manager who manages the project from inception to completion. Employees from different functional departments are assigned to work on each project as needed, either part-time or full-time.

Although the complexity of project structure varies, a basic matrix form might resemble the chart in Figure 8.4. This chart illustrates how some managers have been given responsibility for specific projects in the firm while departmental supervisors are primarily responsible for supervising employees in their regular departments. Project managers A and B are responsible for coordinating activities on their designated projects. However, the project managers must work closely with the departmental supervisors of functions X, Y, and Z. The employees who work in these departments report directly (functionally) to the departmental supervisors, but their services are used under the authority and responsibility of the project managers to whom they are assigned for varying periods.

6 Explain the advantages of the project management-type organizational structure.

Project management-type organizational structure
A hybrid structure in which regular, functional departments coexist with project teams made up of people from different departments

FIGURE 8.4 Basic Project Management-Type Organizational Structure

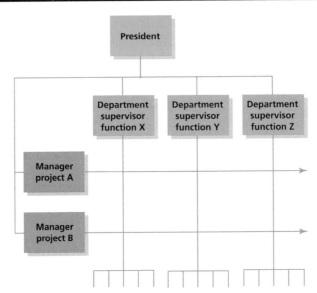

Several problems are associated with the project management-type organizational structure. The most frequent is direct accountability. The matrix structure violates the principle of unity of command because departmental employees are accountable to a departmental supervisor and project managers (see Figure 8.5). Other problems involve scheduling employees who are assigned to several projects. These problems can be avoided, or at least minimized, by planning properly and clarifying authority relationships before the project starts.

Despite such problems, this structure is increasingly common because organizations find it advantageous. Successful project teams are generally those

FIGURE 8.5 One disadvantage of the project management-type organization is that it violates the unity-of-command principle

where someone dreamed big, created a vision, aligned the project team's goals with the overall strategy, inspired and informed team members, executed, and made changes as necessary.[6] It also requires the willingness of project managers (sometimes referred to as project team leaders) and departmental supervisors and their employees to coordinate activities and responsibilities to complete projects. Such coordination is vital to work scheduling, and it is imperative to employees' performance appraisals. Consider the suggestions in the accompanying "Supervisory Tips" box when managing project teams.

SUPERVISORY TIPS
Getting Home with Project Management Teams

A good project team design enables employees to be the best they can be so they can achieve both high performance and satisfaction in their work.

1. You reach first base when you create a vision.
   - Define the project and set project objectives that can be measured.
   - Communicate the vision to everyone.
   - Know the importance of getting people to buy into and commit to the project.
2. You reach second base when you have a well-qualified, well-trained employee group committed to company objectives.
   - Use employee SKAs to their fullest when brainstorming alternative strategies.
   - Develop a plan.
   - Break the project into steps or units and set performance standards for each step or unit.
3. You reach third base when the team is working together on the project.
   - Implement the plan and control work-in-progress.
   - Share information, resolve conflicts, support and encourage teamwork.
   - Be an enabler (see Chapter 2).
4. You score when the goal is accomplished and both team and individual performers are appropriately recognized.
   - Complete and evaluate the project.
   - Learn from the experience and make suggestions for future projects.
   - Celebrate the victory.

7 Identify why a supervisor should plan for an "ideal" departmental structure and work toward this objective.

Planning the "Ideal" Departmental Structure

It has often been said that the organizational structure is not an end but the means to an end. When Hewlett-Packard (HP), the 41st-largest corporation in the world was started, the founders formulated a vision:

> *The achievements of the organization are the results of the combined efforts of each individual in the organization working toward common objectives. The objectives should be realistic, should be clearly understood by everyone in the organization, and should reflect the organization's basic character and personality.*[7]

This became known as the "HP Way." The marriage of HP and Compaq Computer Corp. in 2002 created a high-tech giant with annual sales of $82 billion and a two-pronged strategic challenge: to offer breadth of products and services to compete with IBM, while fending off such specialty and low-cost producers as Dell Computer Corp. The new, combined company faced many obstacles, starting with how to integrate the two workforces and distinctly different corporate cultures. To cut costs, the giant laid off an estimated 15,000 employees. Another 9,000 employees were bought out.[8] For a multitude of reasons, including the inability of the marriage to produce expected profits and market-share gains, CEO Carly Fiorina was shown the door three years later.

When large companies like HP are organized in traditional division structures, strategic decisions often fall to managers under intense pressure to meet earnings expectations. Shane Robison, HP's chief strategy and technology officer, in his speech, "The Next Wave: Everything is Service," stated: "To realize the full potential of the new model, . . . requires a new set of building blocks to deliver this new category of services."[9] In a previous edition, this author stated that unless HP makes a dramatic upturn, the survivors of the restructuring efforts can only wonder when they may be laid off. Under the direction of CEO Mark Hurd, HP identified and targeted services and activities that had promise of future growth and divested those that neither contributed to short-term bottom-line results nor showed promise. These were tough decisions, but had to be made.

HP's 2007 revenue grew 13.8 percent, profits rose 17.2 percent, and earnings per share rose 2.9 percent. Hurd was selected as *BusinessWeek*'s Businessperson of the Year. According to a *BW* article, Hurd focuses all of his energy on one and only one task: leading Hewlett-Packard.[10] The *BW* article had this to say about Hurd's operating style:

> *Hurd is a classic example of a no-nonsense operator hammering away at a struggling business to get it moving in the right direction again. The marching orders: squeeze out costs and improve efficiency. When Vyomesh Joshi, who leads HP's computer printer business, told his boss he was moving the entire team that works on black-and-white laser printers from Boise to China, where most of the product's sales potential lies, he got Hurd's enthusiastic approval.*
>
> *How did HP turn around its hemorrhaging PC business? It embraced a strategy known inside the company as "decommoditization",—casting PCs as more than mere boxes looking like all the others. HP redesigned its machines and infused them with new features.*
>
> *CEO Hurd does not believe in standing still. Shareholders have plenty of reasons to be optimistic. One factor behind this optimism is that the company is expected to reduce expenses in the right areas, get rid of real*

estate, consolidate data centers, and spend money in the right places. With 35,000 engineers, the company will continue to develop technology and support customers when they run into problems. At the same time, HP will place a renewed emphasis on generating revenue as it builds its sales force and distribution channels.[11]

Five years ago, this author could only imagine the burden that would fall on HP's front-line supervisors, who were charged with designing and managing the production operations. Surprisingly, HP made a dramatic upturn. Hurd reminds us, "It's easy to get motivated when you're behind, but when business is going well, that takes the pressure off. HP's growth is a journey, but it's one with a sense of urgency."[12] Designing and redesigning is not a one-and-done thing. It is a journey that requires starts, stops, and restarts. Typically, managers ask, "How should we organize this department based on the people we have?" The question should be, "What organizational structure will efficiently and effectively allow us to achieve our objectives and strategies?" In short, organizational structure decisions should follow strategy choice.

While some supervisors will have opportunities to structure new departments, most are placed in charge of existing ones. In either case, supervisors should think of an ideal departmental structure—a structure the supervisor believes can best achieve the department's objectives. The supervisor should plan the departmental structure based on sound organizational principles, not personalities. If the organization is planned primarily to accommodate current employees, shortcomings will likely persist. When a department is structured around one employee or a few, serious problems can occur when key employees are promoted or leave.[13] When departments are organized according to activities and functions, the company can seek qualified employees. For example, when a supervisor relies heavily on one or two key, versatile employees, the department will suffer if one or both of these employees leave. Conversely, if a number of weak employees do not carry their share of the load, the supervisor may assign too many employees to certain activities to compensate for the poorly performing individuals. Therefore, supervisors should design structures that best serve departmental objectives; then, employees can be best matched with tasks.

This is easier said than done, however. It frequently happens, particularly in small departments, that employees fit the "ideal" structure poorly. In most situations, the supervisor is placed in charge of a department without having had the chance to decide its structure or to choose its employees. In these circumstances, the supervisor can adjust gradually to the capacities of employees. As time goes on, the supervisor can make the personnel and other changes that will move the department toward the supervisor's concept of an "ideal" structure. In all this, of course, the supervisor's primary focus still should be finding, placing, and motivating the best employees.

While CEOs continually search for "ideal organizational structure," they often neglect a key component, that is, the concept of a **learning organization** which fosters employee collaboration and sharing of information. Author of *The Fifth Discipline*, Peter Senge describes learning organizations as places "where people continually expand their capacity (SKAs) to create the results they truly desire, where new and expansive patterns of thinking are nurtured, where collective aspiration is set free, and where people are continually learning to see the whole together."[14]

Learning organization
Employees continually strive to improve their SKAs while expanding their efforts to achieve organizational objectives

A culture is created where all employees take responsibility for identifying and resolving work-related issues. Ideally, the learning organization will more quickly be able to adapt and respond to change. The most effective organizational structure is one in which the supervisor aligns his or her department's goals with the organization's vision and engages all employees in the pursuit of being the "best of the best."

8 Define and discuss organizational tools that are useful in supervisory organizing efforts.

Organizational Tools and Their Applications

Some managers, supervisors, and employees do not understand how their positions and responsibilities relate to the positions and responsibilities of other employees. Organizational charts and manuals, job descriptions, and job specifications can reduce the confusion. These tools clarify the organization's structure and help supervisors understand their positions and the relationships among various departments of the enterprise. The obligation to prepare a firm's overall organizational chart and manual rests with top-level management. However, supervisors usually develop and maintain these tools for their departments.

DEPARTMENTAL ORGANIZATIONAL CHARTS

Organizational chart
Graphic portrayal of a company's authority and responsibility relationships

In planning their organizational structures, many firms develop organizational charts for all or parts of their operations. An **organizational chart** is a graphic portrayal of organizational authority and responsibility relationships using boxes or other depictions. The graphic elements of organizational charts are usually interconnected to show the grouping of activities that make up a department, division, or section.[15] Each box normally represents one position category, although several or more employees may be included in a position category. For example, Figure 8.6 shows a position called "nurses." This is one position, but there may be many nurses. By studying the vertical relationships of categories, anyone can readily determine who reports to whom. Although different types of organizational charts are used, most are constructed vertically and show levels of organization arranged in some type of pyramid.

A supervisor gains a number of advantages from establishing and maintaining a departmental organizational chart. First, it requires careful study and analysis of the departmental structure. When preparing the chart, the supervisor might identify duplicate efforts or inconsistencies in certain functions or activities. A chart might enable the supervisor to spot where dual-reporting relationships exist (that is, where one employee is reporting to two supervisors) or where positions overlap. The chart also may suggest whether the span of management is too wide or too narrow.

Organizational charts are convenient ways to acquaint new employees with the structure of the department and the enterprise. Most employees want to know where they stand and where their supervisor stands relative to higher-level managers. Organizational charts also show formal authority and responsibility relationships; they do not reflect the informal organization discussed earlier in this chapter. Of course, these charts are limited, especially if they are not kept up to date. All changes should be recorded promptly because failing to do so makes the chart outdated.

JOB DESCRIPTIONS AND JOB SPECIFICATIONS

Job description
Written description of the principal duties and responsibilities of a job

Job descriptions are often included in an organizational manual, or they can be obtained from the human resources department. A **job description**, sometimes called a "position description," identifies the principal elements, duties, and scope of authority and responsibility of a job. Some job descriptions are brief; others are lengthy. Job descriptions are often based on information obtained both from employees who perform the jobs and from those employees' supervisors. Some firms include certain expectations in job descriptions, such

FIGURE 8.6 **Organizational Chart for the Nursing Services Department of a Hospital**

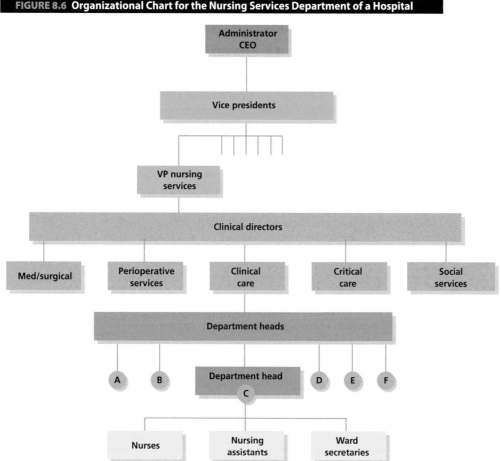

as the availability to work evenings or to travel. Some even indicate specific productivity or quality performance standards that must be attained after a training period.[16]

In practice, there is some overlap in the terms *job description* and *job specification*. Generally speaking, a job description describes the major duties of a position, whereas a **job specification** refers to the skills, capacities, and qualities—personal qualifications—that are needed to perform the job adequately. As Chapter 1 mentions, these personal qualities are sometimes called SKAs (skills, knowledge, and abilities). Many organizations include the job specification as part of each job description.

When a department lacks job descriptions or job specifications, or when jobs are created, the supervisor should ensure that such documents are produced. If help with this task is needed, the supervisor should ask the human resources department, which usually has the experience and know-how to facilitate this task. We discuss this in more detail in Chapter 9.

Supervisors should be thoroughly familiar with their own job descriptions. Often, the job description will define and describe the scope of their authority; their responsibilities; and the formal channels for obtaining information, assistance, or certain decision-making authority. Supervisors should periodically review their own job descriptions and those of their direct reports.

Job specification
Written description of the personal qualifications needed to perform a job adequately

9 **Define downsizing (restructuring) and its implications for organizational principles.**

Downsizing (restructuring, right-sizing)
Large-scale reduction and elimination of jobs in a company that usually reduces middle-level managers, removes organizational levels, and widens the span of management for remaining supervisors

Organizational Principles in an Era of Organizational Downsizings

Among the most publicized aspects of corporate business in recent years has been the large-scale reduction and permanent elimination of thousands of jobs in many major companies. Many companies have eliminated large segments of their workforces. This process, called **downsizing**, **restructuring**, or **right-sizing**, has been accomplished through such things as plant and office closings, the sales of divisions, extensive employee layoffs, attrition, and early retirements.

Typically, management restructures to reduce costs, streamline operations, and become more efficient and competitive. Noted author H. James Harrington contends that employment security is one of the most critical and complex issues facing top management. According to Harrington:

> *"Corporate America has been on a downsizing kick since the late 1980s. The answer to business pressure has been to slow down and lay off, with the hope of raising stock prices, but that doesn't work. Large layoffs produce sudden, substantial stock gains because the effects of a reduced workforce don't immediately reach the customer, and the savings from reduced wages make the organization appear more profitable than it really is. But in the long run, downsizing has a negative effect."*[17]

The companies that are repeatedly restructuring do particular damage because employee productivity declines dramatically. Even layoff survivors feel no added security or commitment.

One major organizational impact of downsizing is a reduction of middle-level managers and the removal of one or more organizational levels. For supervisors and other managers who survive downsizing, the span of management usually widens. Many supervisors are stretched because they are required to add unfamiliar departments or functions to their responsibilities.[18]

Some middle-level management and staff positions have been eliminated because information technology (IT) has made it possible for higher-level managers to acquire data and information quickly and to keep in close touch with operations. Not surprisingly, the authors are familiar with many situations where the IT function has been off-shored to India or another lower-cost country. As a result, supervisors and employees usually have to become more knowledgeable about more aspects of operations. Peter Drucker argued that the knowledge/information explosion requires restructured organizations to depend on remaining employees throughout the firm, rather than on traditional "command-and-control structures," to make decisions.[19]

The firms that have downsized most effectively appear to be those that have planned for it systematically and have tried to harmonize, as much as possible, previous and new organizational structures and operations in ways that are compatible and acceptable to those who remain. Usually, this means involving human resources staff specialists early in downsizing plans. Workforce planning, training, and skills assessment, and widespread communication of what will happen throughout the organization, are typical areas that require the human resources department's skills and major participation.[20] Additionally, ideas about authority and the use of authority must be reshaped to give supervisors and employees greater decision-making responsibility.[21] Even with a weakened organizational structure, most individuals need clear lines of accountability for their performance to be evaluated. These lines are vital if reward systems are to be meaningful and motivational.[22]

Most organizational theorists predict that downsizing will continue indefinitely and that in some firms there will be radical restructuring. In mid-2008, General Motors, Anheuser Busch, Delta Airlines, and General Electric were in the headlines every day.

- Short on cash and facing bankruptcy rumors, GM announced another round of actions including the sale of assets worth $4 billion, borrowing $3 billion, laying off salaried workers, buying out 19,000 rank-and-file workers, foregoing management bonuses, and closing plants. Defying logic, GM was considering the acquisition of Chrysler. GM Chairman and CEO Rick Wagoner said, "No one would dispute that this is a pretty challenging time for the U.S. auto industry. We will continue to take the necessary steps to align our business structure with the lower vehicle sales volume and shifts in sales mix."[23]
- InBev's acquisition of Anheuser Busch combined the second- and third-largest brewers in the world. Surely restructuring and downsizing will occur.[24]
- At the same time, Delta and Northwest airlines announced plans to merge. If the merger is approved, the merged Delta would be the largest airline in the world in traffic, employ 75,000 people, and serve 390 cities in 67 countries. Delta posted a loss of $1.04 billion in the most recent quarter. Delta executives contend that the merged company would reap substantial savings and revenue benefits. Delta says the merger would create as much as $2 billion in annual synergies by 2012.[25]
- GE's chairman Jeffrey Immelt is learning just how complicated it is to restructure the sprawling conglomerate. GE outlined plans to spin off its consumer and industrial division, home to its light-bulb and appliance units. GE was also trying to sell its $30 billion U.S. credit card business.[26]

GM's stock value has fallen 87 percent and lost over $50 billion since Wagoner took over in 2000 one has to wonder about GM's future. Remember the statement of an earlier GM CEO: "As GM goes, so goes the nation!" We had better hope that will not be the case, unless GM can make a dramatic turnaround. Is there an answer? The author believes so! It begins with creating a vision for the organization that goes outside the conventional. All organizations should develop

"Our actions are aimed at aligning the business with current market conditions" (Rick Wagoner)

proactive strategies and then design an organizational structure that helps them to achieve lofty goals.

ALTERNATIVES TO DOWNSIZING

Proponents of downsizing and restructuring have typically advocated employee empowerment and engagement. Empowerment, as identified in a number of places in this text, essentially means delegating sufficient authority to employees to allow those employees to make decisions and become more involved in achieving organizational objectives. Engagement, as discussed in Chapter 3, means that the employee is fully involved in, and enthusiastic about, his or her work. Nothing is more important than getting employees committed to the expanding opportunities that reorganization might bring. Studies show that job satisfaction increases if employees have more opportunities to use their SKAs and if career development and skills training accompany the reorganization.[27]

Self-directed (self-managed) work teams (SDWTs)
When employee groups are given wide latitude and considerable authority to make many of their own job-related decisions

When employee groups are given wide latitude and considerable authority to make job-related decisions, empowerment is associated with the creation of **self-directed (self-managed) work teams (SDWTs)**. We discuss team concepts further in Chapter 12.

Reengineering
Concept of restructuring a firm based on processes and customer needs and services rather than on departments and functions

Some firms have tried **reengineering**, whereby they restructure based more on process (e.g., meeting customer orders and requirements) than on department or function (e.g., sales and production). Reengineering requires supervisors and employees to focus on customer needs and services rather than on their own functions and specialties. Focusing on the customer may enhance a firm's efforts to be more efficient and competitive in the marketplace, but it also can mean blurring line and staff functions and roles. Some authorities have suggested that reengineering will require "process managers," who will manage key processes and whose broadened responsibilities will cut across line and staff functions and organizational levels.[28] A number of major corporations already have restructured parts of their organizations along customer-process dimensions. When carried out, reengineering could create what has been called the **horizontal corporation**, in which organizational structures flatten markedly and managerial authority relationships are minimal.[29]

Horizontal corporation
A very flat firm resulting from restructuring by customer process and organizational structure

Virtual organization
Companies linked temporarily to take advantage of marketplace opportunities

Perhaps the most extreme forecast about the corporate organization of the future is the **virtual organization**, in which companies could become temporary partners or networks that share skills, employees, and access to the other's markets to exploit various opportunities. A virtual corporation, which would have no organizational chart or hierarchy, could be considered the ultimate project-type organization. At the end of the collaboration in a project or market opportunity, virtual partners would separate and have no permanent relationship. Of course, a virtual corporation would require member companies to network with firms with whom they share a high level of trust and collaboration. In this arrangement, one concern is that firms might lose control over their own operations. Although a number of companies have moved in this direction in certain types of ventures, at this writing, the virtual organization is far more theory than reality.[30]

Although beyond the scope of this text, lean manufacturing or lean production as it would apply to service-related industries is a concept that allows employees greater authority to make decisions based on customer needs. Lean manufacturing is not about laying off people. It is about planning and organizing to use resources more efficiently. Streamlining production and cross-training employees so they can do multiple tasks is usually part of the system. All employees, from the CEO to the floor sweeper, must rethink how they work and must eliminate non-value-added time.[31]

Regardless of whether we want them, radical company restructurings will become more commonplace. It is unclear whether reengineering or the other interventions mentioned above differ significantly from what many firms try to concentrate on, with or without downsizing. What seems likely is that organizational principles will always be part of supervision and that any organizational change will require supervisors to understand how to apply and adapt certain organizational principles.

Organizing for Effective Meeting Management

10 Identify the major factors contributing to organizing effective meetings, especially the supervisor's role.

Electronic message systems are not the complete answer to effective supervision. More is needed to ensure the free flow of communication and understanding in ways that are necessary for people to carry out their jobs. Whether it is clarifying expectations, analyzing problems, or communicating policies, there is no substitute for bringing together the people who make it happen. There are other ways to supply the information people need to perform their jobs and to receive ideas and opinions, but meetings can be an effective way to achieve these objectives.

Many work teams have experimented with meeting facilitators. In this case, the group leader or the supervisor does not conduct the meeting. This role falls to the facilitator, a function that is often rotated among team members. This approach allows the supervisor, for example, to observe, listen, and ask probing questions of team members. In addition, team members gain leadership experience. A downside of this approach is that all team members must be adept at meeting management. Further, the note-taking responsibility is rotated among team members.

Meetings should be called only when necessary. When a supervisor decides a meeting is necessary, however, the topic and issues should be communicated to meeting participants, and the participants' roles should be clarified.

The accompanying "Supervisory Tips" box outlines guidelines for planning, organizing, and leading a meeting.

The meeting chairperson or facilitator must be skilled at keeping the meeting focused. Many successful work teams have adopted ground rules for their meetings. Suggested ground rules might include the items in Figure 8.7.

The meeting chairperson is ultimately responsible for the meeting's effectiveness. Figure 8.8 provides a useful list of questions to consider when planning and organizing a meeting.

The chairperson's general approach is crucial. Initially, everyone's contribution should be accepted without judgment, and everyone should feel free to participate. The chairperson may have to ask controversial questions to start the discussion and participation. This is sometimes done by asking

SUPERVISORY TIPS

Guidelines for Planning and Leading a Meeting[32]

1. Select participants who will bring knowledge and expertise to the meeting.
2. Notify participants well in advance of the meeting.
3. Have a plan and an agenda.
4. Begin the meeting on time.
5. Present the problems and issues to be discussed and the meeting's objectives.
6. Encourage all group members to participate fully in the discussion.
7. Allow sufficient time for participants to offer information and discuss alternative proposals.
8. Strive to find consensus and areas of agreement before voting on the proposal.
9. Try to stay on the subject and adjourn on time, but make adjustments as necessary.
10. Follow up, including distributing a summary of the meeting (minutes) and actions to be taken.

FIGURE 8.7   Suggested Meeting Ground Rules

- Everyone will be candid and specific.
- Everyone will have a say.
- Everyone will stop what they are doing and listen carefully to other team members' comments.
- All team members must support their opinions with facts.
- No one will be allowed to interrupt another; we will hear each other out.
- We are a TEAM—working Together Everyone will Achieve More.

provocative, open-ended questions that use words like *who, what, why, where,* and *when*. Questions that can be answered with a simple "yes" or "no" should be avoided.

As you may remember from our discussion of communication in Chapter 3, the supervisor is responsible for giving and getting information. To get information or to open discussion on a particular topic, the supervisor might want to ask the W

FIGURE 8.8   Questions to Consider When Planning a Meeting

What is the purpose (goal) of the meeting?

What are the opportunities, threats, conflicts, problems, concerns, issues, or topics that should be considered?

What information must be disseminated before the meeting?

What information must be gathered before the meeting?

What preparation is needed on the part of the participants?

What work must be completed before the meeting?

What additional resources will be needed to accomplish the purpose?

What are the ground rules for conducting the meeting?

Who is involved with the concerns, issues, or topics?

Who must do advance work or make decisions regarding the agenda?

Who should be invited because they can provide information needed for problem solving or discussing the issue?

Who will develop and distribute the agenda?

Who must attend?

Who will facilitate the meeting?

Who will be assigned as the note-taker?

How much time do we need to allot to each topic?

How should the meeting room be arranged?

How do we strive to find consensus and areas of agreement?

How do we stay focused on the subject(s)?

When and where should the meeting be scheduled?

When should the meeting end?

When and how should the meeting be evaluated?

When and what follow-up is needed to the meeting (e.g., distribute a summary of the meeting and the actions to be taken)?

questions—what, where, why, when, and who—before getting to the how. For example, the chairperson could use questions to get and keep the discussion going, such as, "What is the relationship between quality and machine setup times?" "Hank, what would be your suggestion?" "Where did the problem occur?" "Why is that important to you?" "When will we have the new machine on line?" "Who might have the experience to handle such an assignment?" "Who would like to comment on Wally's question?" and "How can we exceed the customer's expectations?"

Another technique is to start at one side of the conference table and ask members to express their thoughts on the problem in turn. While this approach forces everyone to participate, it discourages spontaneous participation and allows the rest of the group to sit back and wait until called on. This approach also may cause some individuals to take a stand on an issue before they are mentally prepared to do so.

As a general rule, the chairperson should appoint someone, for example, a scribe or note-taker, to record what happened during the meeting. Before adjourning the meeting, the chairperson may have the scribe orally summarize the key points of the meeting; the chosen action; and ascertain that participants are in agreement on the gist of the meeting. This process gives all participants a chance to review and agree on what took place.

The chairperson should see to it that the written summary, or minutes, is provided to every participant. The summary should also be distributed to all other personnel who have a need to know what took place or who and what is essential in accomplishing the necessary actions. In short, the meeting action summary lists the actions to be taken by the group, assigns accountability (who is to do what by when), and becomes a record for follow-up and feedback.

The written summary also serves as a permanent record or guideline for future situations involving similar circumstances. If some matters are left undecided, the summary can provide a review of the alternatives that were discussed and help to crystallize the thinking of participants. For permanent standing committees, such as the organization's safety committee, it is advisable to use the summary to announce when the group shall meet next.

Remember: None of us is as smart as all of us! A group of individuals exchanging information, opinions, and experiences will usually develop a better solution to a problem than could any one person who thinks through a problem alone. While meetings at the departmental level are important, supervisors often will meet with others to discuss, plan, and decide on issues and to determine what actions must be carried out. The meeting management tips and suggestions offered here should become a part of every supervisor's toolbox.

How to Use Time More Effectively

11 Understand the importance of self-organization, i.e., effective use of your time.

Author Stephen Covey suggests that we always "begin with the end in mind."[33] Effective use of time requires knowing that where we are going and why we want to go there is more important than how fast we go (see Figure 8.9). In other words, what does it matter if we accomplish many tasks if they are not in line with our goals?

Each of us has the same finite amount of time. The last time I checked, there were still 24 hours in a day and only 168 hours in a week. No one has yet found

FIGURE 8.9 Plan your work—work your plan!

a way to "save time" or store it for another day. How many times have you heard someone say, "I wish I had more time?" This author believes that the phrase "making time" is an oxymoron. Everyone has the same amount of time. Only by working smarter, i.e., effectively planning, organizing, and managing our activities, can one better use time.

Many of you have learned to balance family, school, and work. You have, with varying degrees of success, learned how to identify those tasks that are most important and urgent. President Dwight D. Eisenhower said, "What is important is seldom urgent and what is urgent is seldom important."[34] Think about how you study for this course. Do you develop blocks of regular study time, or do you pull all-nighters? Most of you probably study in blocks of time. How long before your mind turns to other things? Some of us need more frequent breaks for a variety of reasons. When studying, do you begin with your most difficult subject or task? Do you review the text and the last lecture material immediately before class? Do you review lecture material immediately after class, when it is fresh in your mind? Do you schedule time to review the more important activities? If you answered "yes" to most of these, how did you develop these habits? Most of us learn by a system of trial and error. To help you, we have offered some practical tips for making more effective use of time:

- Have a daily, weekly, and long-term planner. Use them to identify the most important items.

- Make a list of the major tasks that need to be completed. This is your to-do list. Also, make note of the reason for doing them and the timeline for getting them done. Listing some tasks wastes time. For example, every morning when I leave for the office, I kiss my wife and tell her how much I love her. There is no reason to put that on my list, even though it is important!
- Determine priorities. Focus on the most important tasks, those that support your objectives. Do not be afraid to ask your boss if a new task takes priority over other assignments.
- Clarify duties with a time-use chart. Identify which of your regular duties most directly relate to departmental objectives.
- Set up a reminder system. Use your PDA-based system or a personal planner to alert you to what needs to be done by when.
- Know your prime time. This is the time of day when you are most alert, think most clearly, and work most effectively. Schedule your most complex tasks for this period.
- Refer to your to-do list regularly. Interruptions will arise; deal with those emergencies, then go back to the high-priority task.
- Schedule routine duties at times when you have low energy.
- Schedule time at the end of the day to make tomorrow's to-do list.
- Use a pocket or desk calendar to note activities that need major attention. Write everything in a small notebook. Document what, when, who, and where.
- Use commonsense organizational and time-management techniques. For example, handle papers only once, keep your desk or workstation clear, finish one job before starting another, avoid distractions, and say "no."
- Deal with interruptions. If someone asks you for a minute on a non-life-threatening matter, tell that person you want to give the matter your undivided attention and ask to schedule a brief meeting later. It is acceptable to tell someone you will call back; wasting valuable time is not acceptable.
- Be adaptable. Don't be afraid to reschedule in the face of unexpected events.
- Enable subordinates to be the best they can be. Encourage subordinates to take responsibility and to make decisions they can make. Do not let subordinates pass these decisions to you.
- Delegate. See Chapter 11 for tips on delegating successfully.
- Get the most from meetings. See this chapter for tips on managing meetings.
- Overcome procrastination. Plan habitually and continuously, break difficult tasks into small and doable units, and work on unpleasant tasks immediately.
- Use the two-hour rule. If you have been working on a problem for more than two hours without making progress, get help. Often, by explaining a problem to someone else, you get a different perspective.
- Follow the 80/20 principle. Eighty percent of achievement comes from twenty percent of time spent.
- Remember, always begin with the end in mind.[35]

Only by developing a vision about what the end result should be, developing plans and organizing, and prioritizing activities will supervisors be able to effectively use their available time.

SUMMARY

1 The organizing function of management is to design a structural framework—to group and assign activities to work areas so as to achieve the desired objectives. Organizing includes establishing authority relationships among managers, supervisors, and departments.

2 The informal organization interacts with, yet is apart from, the formal organizational structure. It can positively or negatively influence departmental work performance. To use the informal organization positively, supervisors should become familiar with informal groups and their leaders and determine how to enlist their cooperation when promoting departmental objectives.

3 Normally, an organization should adhere to the unity-of-command principle. This principle maintains that every employee is directly accountable to only one supervisor and that formal communication flows through the chain of command.

4 The span-of-management principle should be observed when assigning employees to supervisors. Also known as the span of supervision or the span of control, this principle recognizes that there is an upper limit to the number of employees a supervisor can manage effectively. The span of management is determined by such factors as the competence of the supervisor, the training and experience of employees, employees' work locations, and the amount and nature of work to be performed. Other things being equal, the narrower the span of management is, the greater the number of levels of management that are needed; the broader the span of management is, the fewer levels that are needed.

5 Departmentalization is the process of grouping activities and people into distinct organizational units. Departmentalization is most often done according to function, but it can be done by geographic line, product or service, customer, process and equipment, or time. Rather than being able to design new departments, supervisors most often must assign activities and employees to existing departments to achieve efficiency and stability.

To perform as a manager, a supervisor must have authority. As Chapter 2 discusses, managerial authority is the legitimate or rightful power to direct and lead others. Authority is delegated from top-level managers through mid-level managers to supervisors, who, in turn, delegate to their employees. All supervisors must be delegated appropriate authority to manage their departments.

In their own departments, supervisors have line authority to direct their employees. Employees in staff-authority positions furnish counsel, guidance, advice, and service in a specialized field. Staff supervisors with specialized knowledge and skills support line managers and others throughout the organization. They often take responsibility for ensuring that certain policies and procedures are uniformly and consistently carried out. Line-and-staff-type organizational structures are the norm in large-scale enterprises.

6 A project- or matrix-type organizational structure places managers in charge of project teams whose members are drawn from different departments. Line supervisors manage the employees in regular departments. This structure uses employees on multiple projects more efficiently without disrupting regular departmental arrangements. However, a matrix structure may create problems of priority scheduling and employee accountability, both for departmental supervisors and project managers.

7 When organizing a department, the supervisor should envision the ideal arrangement based on the assumption that all required and qualified employees are available. Because there are seldom employees with all the desired qualifications, available employees must be fit to the structure. Over time, the supervisor should make changes to move the department toward its ideal structure. Supervisor that strive for superior performance should adopt the concepts instrumental in creating a "learning organization." Because structure should follow strategy, as strategy changes, structures should be reviewed and modified appropriately.

8 A departmental organization chart is a picture of authority and responsibility relationships. Supervisors must be cognizant of their own job descriptions and those of their direct reports. The job description and job specifications identify the requirements for qualifying for or performing a job.

9 Downsizing usually involves eliminating job positions and levels of management. Supervisors who survive downsizings must adapt organizational principles to the changes. This usually includes widening the span of management and giving employees more latitude in decision making. To empower employees, supervisors should structure their departments to allow for more employee participation. Various changes, such as restructuring, SDWTs, lean manufacturing, horizontal and virtual organizational structures, can help companies reduce costs and be flexible in meeting customer demands.

10 The success of any meeting depends largely on effective leadership. Supervisors usually call meetings to disseminate information or to discuss and solve problems. There is no substitute for bringing together the people who are responsible for solving a problem or discussing an issue. Numerous tips and suggestions are available to help supervisors achieve group participation and make meetings more productive and relevant.

11 "Work smarter, not harder" should become an integral part of your management vocabulary. Every supervisor needs to make effective use of time. Identifying the most important tasks is the most important step. The effective supervisor must plan, organize, prioritize, and diligently strive to complete the things that are most important. Short-range plans must dovetail with your long-term plans.

KEY TERMS

Department (p. 265)
Departmentalization (p. 265)
Division of work (specialization) (p. 264)
Downsizing (restructuring, right-sizing) (p. 274)
Formal organizational structure (p. 265)
Horizontal corporation (p. 276)
Informal organization (p. 259)
Job description (p. 272)

Job specification (p. 273)
Lead person (p. 264)
Learning organization (p. 271)
Line authority (p. 266)
Line-and-staff-type organizational structure (p. 267)
Organization (p. 257)
Organizational chart (p. 272)
Principle of organizational stability (p. 266)

Project management-type organizational structure (p. 267)
Reengineering (p. 276)
Self-directed (self-managed) work teams (SDWTs) (p. 276)
Span-of-management principle (p. 261)
Staff authority (p. 267)
Unity-of-command principle (p. 260)
Virtual organization (p. 276)

QUESTIONS FOR DISCUSSION

1. Define the organizing function, unity of command, and span-of-management principle and explain how they relate.

2. What are the advantages of the informal organization? Discuss the approaches the supervisor can take to foster cooperation with informal groups and their leaders. How can the leader(s) of the informal organization help the supervisor achieve departmental goals? . . . hinder their attainment?

3. Define and discuss the application of the following organizational tools at the supervisory level:
   a. Organizational charts
   b. Job descriptions
   c. Job specifications

4. What is meant by downsizing (restructuring)? Are downsizing and radical restructuring likely to render organizational principles obsolete? Discuss.

5. Why is the ability to conduct effective and productive meetings important for a supervisor? What steps should supervisors take to ensure that the meetings they participate in or chair succeed?

6. Go to Carnegie Mellon's Web site (http://www.cmu.edu/Randyslecture) to understand how computer scientist professor, Randy Pausch, left a prescription for life. Click on the link to watch Randy's last lecture on YouTube; his lectures on time management and his appearance at Carnegie Mellon's 2008 Commencement Ceremony. For more information, google Randy Pausch. Professor Pausch died on July 25, 2008.[36]
   a. What is the relevance of that statement for you?
   b. What else did you learn from watching his last lecture?
   c. What is its relevance to how you manage your time?
   d. Why should supervisors create "to-do" lists?
   e. What are your personal and professional goals for the next week? How can you find time to achieve them?

SKILLS APPLICATIONS

Skills Application 8-1: One of These Days We'll Get Organized!

1.  Re-read this chapter's "You Make the Call!" Search the Internet to find information about various supervisory training and development programs that David Simms might be able to use to help employees such as Margo James make the transition from server to temporary supervisor/supervisor. Then in small groups of two or three students, discuss the following:

   a. The practicality of promoting Margo James to the supervisory position. Outline the advantages and disadvantages of promoting her to the position.
   b. Why should David Simms develop a strategy to ensure that every critical function in his facility is backstopped by capable substitutes? How would you implement such a strategy?
   c. Overall, the metrics that the corporation uses shows that the Brunswick facility is in the top ten percent of

chain restaurants. David Simms has done many things very well, but he has made some mistakes. What are the three major mistakes he has made, and how can he learn from them?

2. OPTIONAL: Give yourself a break today and meet friends at a local restaurant that is part of a chain.
   a. Ask your server or the greeter the following questions:
      1. How long have you worked here?
      2. Of all the places you could possibly work, why do you work here?
      3. What do you like most about working here?
      4. Would you want to be a supervisor or manager here? Why or why not?
   b. Ask one of the managers or supervisors the following questions:
      1. How did you become a manager here?
      2. What are the rewards of being a manager?

3. What one aspect of your job would you like to "dump" or "delegate" to someone else?

4. How do members of the management team learn from the mistakes of others?

5. How did you learn to master the supervisory skills?

c. Based on your findings, what suggestions would you make to David Simms?

3. Write a one-page report answering the question: To what extent did this skills application cause you to re-think the notion that there should be a systematic and strategic plan for developing all employees within the organization for supervisory positions?

Skills Application 8-2: Thinking Outside the Box

This diagram shows one side of a chimney. Note: Only whole bricks were used, as no bricks were cut in half.

1. How many bricks were required to build all four sides? How did you arrive at that conclusion?

2. What is the relationship between this skills application and the organizing principles found in this chapter?

3. Write a one-page paper detailing what you learned from this skills application.

Source: This Skills Application was reprinted with permission from QCI International's *Timely Tips for Teams,* a monthly Internet newsletter (January 2005).

Skills Application 8-3: What Are Your Expectations?

First, think about the person who cleans the classroom. Then, make an item-by-item list of the duties and responsibilities for that position.

1. If possible, your instructor will provide you with a copy of the job description for that person.

2. You should find a current copy of a job description for the custodian/janitor/housekeeping-type position from another local organization.

3. Look at the job description for cleaner found in the Dictionary of Occupational Titles (DOT) to get a general idea of this job and the duties performed in a variety of settings.

4.  Then, go to (http://www.jobdescriptions.info/) and follow the links to gain information about this job.

You can use O*NET's resources to develop job descriptions, find job information and get information on other related HR functions. [Note: At the time of this writing, there was not cost to become an O*NET registered user.]

5. Finally, ask your instructor if you need permission to interview one or more of the custodians, janitors, or housekeepers in your building. Ask them what their job entails. What are the five or six most important things they have to do?

(Note: If it is not possible to conduct the interview, you may omit this step.)

6. Answer the following questions:

a. What is expected of a janitor in your educational setting, i.e., the job summary?

b. What SKAs are required?

c. How does the listing of what the incumbent cites as the most important duties and responsibilities align with the job description?

d. What duties and responsibilities (the essential functions) are consistently listed across all descriptions (your college's job description, those of another organization, and those cited on O*NET?)?

e. What are the major differences? How do you account for those differences?

f. Why do you think there are differences of opinion between what others expect a janitor to do and the job performed?

7. Write a one-page paper detailing what you learned from this skills application.

Source: This Skills Application was adapted with permission from Ed Leonard and Roy Cook, "Case 2-4: Conducting a Job Analysis," *Human Resource Management: 21st Century Challenges* (Mason, OH: Thomson Custom Publishing, 2005), p. 44.

Skills Application 8-4: Dealing with People Who Make Your Life Difficult—"The Boss's Favorite"

This is the fifth in a series of Skills Applications that introduces you to people who might make your life difficult.

1. Read the following statement from Steve Vincent, an employee at Harding Hardware:

Bill Allen is the model employee—or at least, upper management thinks so. His supervisors always find that he contributes significantly during customer-service meetings. Allen excels at giving his supervisors feedback. These supervisors have been overheard describing Allen as "warm and supporting." Allen always gets his work done promptly and often offers to help one of the supervisors on other sales orders.

Allen excels at flattery. He is adept at making every detail of the boss's life (e.g., clothes, house, wife, grandkids, and talents) a workplace event. Allen does not care who hears his praise, as long as they have authority. According to Allen, everything that comes from the owner's mouth is the best thing said. Allen's compliments are almost always directed toward the owner. "Oh, Mr. Harding, I'm glad you think that customer-feedback reporting system is a good idea," Allen might say. "I'll do everything possible to make it work."

To say that Allen is agreeable is an understatement. Problems arise when he does not follow through because other employees must honor his commitments. Allen, however, is first in line to take credit when things go well, and he is always willing to do special favors for Harding. Last summer, all we heard about was how Allen was building a deck on Harding's lake cottage.

However, Allen is chilly to any request from someone lower than him on the corporate ladder. This presented a problem for Bessie Colicho, one of our timid colleagues. Colicho and Allen were responsible for putting together the monthly advertising flyer. Somehow, Allen was always too busy helping with more important projects, like helping Harding orient to the new

inventory-control system. Colicho had tried to talk to Harding about the problem, but she was told that Allen was the model employee and that her perceptions of him were unrealistic. I know that when George Sutherland retires, Allen will be the first in line for his job. It's not fair! He'll get the promotion not on merit but by being the boss's favorite.

2. (**INTERNET ACTIVITY**) Using the Internet, find at least three sources for coping with a boss's favorite. Carefully review each site for suggestions for dealing with this type of behavior.

3. Based on your findings, what suggestions would you give to Vincent for working with Allen?

4. Write a one-page paper explaining how this skills application increased your working knowledge of coping with the behaviors of this type of difficult person.

Skills Application 8-5: Departmental Organizational Chart Development

To complete this project, see Figure 8.6, which is an organizational chart for a hospital department. Recognize that Figure 8.6 was simplified for demonstration purposes.

1. (**INTERNET ACTIVITY**) Develop a departmental organizational chart for a department of a firm or for any organization for which you can obtain the required information and assistance. If you are currently employed, ask your supervisor for permission and help in using your work department for this project. Keep the chart as simple as possible.
   a. Use rectangles to show an organizational unit or a position.
   b. Place the title of each position in the corresponding rectangle. The title should describe the job function (e.g.,

sales manager). Vertical lines of authority should enter at the top center of a rectangle and leave at the bottom center, except for supervisory assistants and horizontal relationships. Use solid vertical and horizontal lines for the flow of line authority and dotted lines for the flow of functional authority.

2. Review your organizational chart and answer the following questions:
   a. Identify departmentalization options in the chart.
   b. How would the chart change if the organization mandated a twenty-percent reduction in workforce?

3. Identify what you believe to be the most important concepts concerning the organizing function of management.

SKILLS DEVELOPMENT

Skills Development Module 8-1: Green Mountain Coffee Roasters (GMCR)

 *Sit down and enjoy a special cup of coffee. Green Mountain Coffee Roasters (GMCR) began in a small Waitsfield, Vermont café in 1981. From these humble beginnings, it has become a leading supplier of specialty coffee. GMCR went public in 1993 (NASDAQ) and its 2007 sales approached $350 million.*

Before you view the video clip, you might want to visit GMCR's Web site (http://greenmountaincoffee.com). The home page shows information about their products. At the bottom of this page are links to the following: About GMCR, Social and Environmental Responsibilities, The Story of Coffee, and Career Opportunities.

After viewing the Skills Development Module video, answer the following questions:

1. What makes an organization like GMCR a winner?

2. Change is a way of life in today's environment. What is it about GMCR's organizational structure that allows it to react quickly to sudden changes in its operating environment?

3. Bob Stiller set the tone for GMCR's culture, e.g., "Do the best from tree to cup," and "Engage more people to a better solution." Describe the relationship between GMCR's strategy, organizational design, and organizational culture.

4. "We have policies and procedures but employees are encouraged to adapt them to make decisions on the fly." What are the disadvantages of such an approach? The advantages?

5. Click on "Career Opportunities" on GMCR's Web site. Would you like to work for GMCR? Why or why not?

ENDNOTES

1. In the *SHRM 2008 Job Satisfaction Survey*, only 40% of U.S. workers are very satisfied with their job. Yet, three of four would change jobs if the right opportunity arose. (http://www.shrm.org, June 22, 2008). The Job Satisfaction Survey has been conducted annually since 2002. Watson Wyatt's 2005/2006 Communication ROI Study™ reported that companies that are highly effective communicators are twenty percent more likely to report lower turnover rates than their peers. Also see Jacqueline Gish, "Taking Responsibility for Your Employee's Morale," *Supervision* (May 2005), pp. 8–10; Ann Pomeroy, "Senior Management Begins Regaining Employee Trust," *HR Magazine* (February 2005), p. 16.

2. In an effort to uncover best practices, a McKinsey team surveyed over 100,000 workers from 400 companies throughout the world and concluded that (a) a compelling vision of direction, (b) an environment that encourages employees, and (c) an environment that encourages openness, trust, and challenge (culture) were the driving forces for improving organizational performance. Reported in "Management Practices that Work," *The McKinsey Quarterly* (September 2007). Also see T. Craig Williams and Juliet Rains, "Linking Structure to Strategy: The Power of Systematic Organizational Design," *Organizational Development Journal*, 25, 2 (Summer 2007), pp. 163–170; T. L. Stanley, "The Best Management Ideas are Timeless," *Supervision* (June 2004), pp. 9–11; and John R. Graham, "Seven Ways to Differentiate Your Company that Makes a Difference to the Customer," *Supervision* (August 2005), pp. 14–16.

3. P. Gregory Smith, "Attitude Counts," *Career World* (September 2003), pp. 8–12; Andrew Molinsky and Joshua Margolis, "Necessary Evils and Interpersonal Sensitivity in Organizations," *Academy of Management Review* (April 2005), pp. 245–268; and Gary S. Topchik, "Attacking the Negativity Virus," *Management Review* (September 1998), pp. 61–64.

4. See "Exodus," Chapter 18, in the Bible for the story of Moses and Jethro. Jethro has been called the "world's first management and organization consultant."

5. See J. Shapiro, P. Morrow, and I. Kesslerm "Serving Two Organizations: Exploring the Employment Relationship of Contracted Employees," *Human Resource Management*, 45, 4 (2006), pp. 561–583; J. Zapper, "Temp-to-Hire is Becoming a Full-time Practice at Firms," *Workforce Management* (June 2005), pp. 82–85; and Kent Blake, "She's Just a Temporary," *HR Magazine* (August 1998), pp. 45–51.

6. See Ryan Underwood, "OK, Everybody, Let's Do This! Managing Projects and Collaborating with Co-Workers," *Inc.* (July 2008), pp. 40–42. Also see Casimer DeCasatis, "Creating, Growing and Sustaining Efficient Innovation Teams," *Creativity & Innovation Management*, 17, 2 (June 2008), pp. 155–164; Phil Kelly, "Achieving Desirable Group-Work Outcomes through the Group Allocation Process," *Team Performance Management*, 14, 1 (2008); Rudolf Melik, "Juggling for Project Managers," *Quality Digest* (January 2007); and Wendy Bliss, Robert Austin, *et al.*, *The Essentials of Project Management* (Boston: SHRM and Harvard Business School Press, 2006).

7. David Packard and William R. Hewlett first put the statement in writing in 1957. See "David Packard: The Legacy Endures," Hewlett-Packard 1996 Annual Report (Palo Alto, CA: January 1997). 8. Cliff Edwards and Andrew Park, "HP and Compaq: It's Showtime," *BusinessWeek* (June 17, 2002), pp. 76–77; and Pui-Wing Tam and Scott Thurm, "Married at Last, HP, Compaq Face Real Test," *The Wall Street Journal* (May 8, 2002), pp. B1, B4. Visit the HP Web site to review various press releases that deal with the continual organizational restructuring. Also see Gary Bradt, "We've Merged or Reorganized. Now What?"

Supervision, 69, 2 (February 2008), pp. 16–17; and Charles Terranova, "Assessing Culture During an Acquisition," *Organizational Development Journal*, 25, 2 (2007), pp. 37–42.

9. See Richard M. Smith, "Shane Robison: Managing All the Geeks," *Newsweek* (June 2, 2008) an interview where *Newsweek* Chairman Rick Smith and Robison discuss the importance of communicating between management and engineering. You can also view the entire interview at http://www.newsweek.com/id/138370. Also Shane Robison, "The Next Wave: Everything is Service," *HP Development Company* (http://www.hp.com/hpinfo/execteam/articles/robison/08eaas.html.

10. See Louise Lee, "BW's Businessperson of the Year: Hewlett-Packard CEO Mark Hurd's single-mindedness is paying off for the tech company in profits that will be hard to beat in 2008," *BusinessWeek* (January 2008). See BusinessWeek.com's slide show of the best leaders of 2007.

11. Ibid. Also see David Kirkpatrick, "HP's Grand Vision: Measure Everything," *Fortune* online (July 18, 2008; accessed July 22, 2008) and go to Hewlett-Packard's Web site to see current new releases.

12. Ibid. Also see, Gary Bradt, "5 Simple Steps to Build a Winning Corporate Culture," *Supervision*, 69, 3 (March 2008), pp. 13–15.

13. This type of problem is inherent in the "principle of organizational stability," which advocates that no organization should become overly dependent on the talents/abilities of one individual or a few individuals. That is, no one should be indispensable to the enterprise. For an interesting viewpoint see Jan Aarum Andersen, "An Organization Called Harry," *Journal of Organizational Change Management*, 21, 2 (2008), pp. 164–187.

14. Adapted from Peter M. Senge, et.al., *The Fifth Discipline Fieldbook: Strategies and Tools for Building a Learning Organization* (New York: Doubleday, 1994). Senge said, "You can't fix things, at least permanently. You can apply theories, methods, and tools, increasing your own skills in the process. You can find and instill new guiding ideas. you can experiment with redesigning your organization's infrastructure. If you proceed in all these ways, you can gradually evolve a new type of organization." p. 4.

15. For a detailed look at the organizational charts and other organizational aspects of more than 200 major U.S. corporations, see the Organization Chart Collection, published by the Conference Board, Inc. Charts can be ordered individually and/or in any quantity. For ordering and other information, visit the Web at http://www.conference-board.org. You also may want to review Janie Kock, "Aligning the Organization: Management and Human Resource Concerns," (The Conference Board Report R-1370-05-RR. November 2005) and Brian J. Dive, "Why Organization Design is Critical To Global Leadership Development" (The Conference Board Report A-0144005-EA, April 2005). Organizations also have many informal networks. See Lowell L. Bryan, Eric Matson and Leigh M. Weiss, "Harnessing the Power of Informal Employee Networks," *The McKinsey Quarterly*, an online journal of McKinsey & Co. (November 2007) for insight on how to harness the power of the informal network.

16. For an overview of job analysis, see M.T. Brannick, E.L. Levine and F.P. Morgeson, *Job and Work Analysis* (Thousand Oaks, CA: Sage, 2007) or M.T. Brannick and E.L. Levine, *Job Analysis: Methods, Research, and Applications for Human Resource Management in the New Millennium* (Mahwah, NJ: Lawrence Erlbaum Associates, 2007). Also see C. Joinson, "Refocusing Job Descriptions," *HR Magazine* (January 2007), pp. 67–72; Danny G. Langdon and Kathleen S. Whiteside, "Redefining Jobs and Work in Organizations," *HR Magazine*

(May 1996), pp. 97–101; or J. E. Osborne, "Job Descriptions Do More Than Describe Duties," *Supervisory Management* (February 1992), p. 8. For information about developing job descriptions, google "developing job descriptions" and review examples of how to conduct a job analysis and write job descriptions.

17. See H. James Harrington, "Rightsizing, Not Downsizing: Layoffs are Costlier than You Think," *Quality Digest* (July 2005), p. 12. Visit his Web site at http://www.harrington-institute.com.

18. See John Graham, "Outsourcing a Company's Marketing: A Better Way to Meet Competitive Challenges," *Supervision*, 68, 5 (May 2007), pp. 15–17; Thomas N. Duening and Rick L. Click, *Essentials of Business Process Outsourcing* (New York: John Wiley & Sons, 2005); Amelia Kohn and David La Piana, *Strategic Restructuring for Nonprofit Organizations: Merger, Integration & Alliances* (Westport, CT: Praeger, 2003); "Organize for Efficiency," *Supervision* (October 2004), pp. 25–26; Wayne F. Cascio, "Downsizing: What Do We Know? What Have We Learned?" *Academy of Management Executive* (February 1993), pp. 95–104, or Alex Markels and Matt Murray, "Call It Dumbsizing: Why Some Companies Regret Cost-cutting," *The Wall Street Journal* (May 14, 1996), pp. A1, A6.

19. Peter F. Drucker as cited by Jennifer Reingold, "The Power of Cosmic Thinking," *BusinessWeek* (June 7, 1999), p. 17. Also see Philip Brown and Anthony Heskitt, *The Mismanagement of Talent: Employability and Jobs in the Knowledge Economy* (New York: Oxford University Press, 2004).

20. Sherry Kuczynski, "Help! I Shrunk the Company," *HR Magazine* (June 1999), pp. 40–45. See also C. K. Prahalad, "The Art of Outsourcing," *The Wall Street Journal* (June 8, 2005), p. A14; and Stephanie Crane, "Outsourcing's Newest Niche," *BusinessWeek* online (June 11, 2004).

21. See James C. Cooper and Kathleen Madigan, "Manufacturing May Already Be on the Mend," *BusinessWeek* (May 30, 2005), pp. 25–26; Lin Grensing-Pophal, "Re-Structure," *Credit Union Management* (September 2002), pp. 34–37; Jeff Higley, "La Quinta Restructures to Increase Growth Rate," *Hotel and Motel Management* (November 18, 2001), pp. 1–2; K. S. Cameron, S. J. Freemand, and A. K. Mishra, "Best Practices in White Collar Downsizing: Managing Contradictions," *Academy of Management Executive* (August 1991), pp. 57–73; and Susan Sonnesyn Brooks, "Managing a Horizontal Revolution," *HR Magazine* (June 1995), pp. 52–58.

22. See Amar Gupta, "Expanding the 24-Hour Workplace," *The Wall Street Journal* (September 15–16, 2007), p. R9; and Sandra O'Neal, "Reengineering and Compensation: An Interview with Michael Hammer," *ACA Journal* (Spring 1996), pp. 6–11.

23. See the following: "How Detroit Drove Into a Ditch," *Wall Street Journal*, October 25–26, 2008, p. W1-W2; Ken Bensinger, "Beleaguered GM Peers into Abyss," *The Los Angeles Times* as reported in *The Fort Wayne, Indiana Journal Gazette* (July 17, 2008), pp. 1A, 6A; John D. Stoll, "GM to Outline More Cost Cutting," *The Wall Street Journal* (July 15, 2008), p. B4; Bob Sechler, "Wagoner Says GM Won't File Bankruptcy or Reduce Brands," *The Wall Street Journal* (July 11, 2008), p. B10; David Gaffen, "GM, Economy Share Troubles," *The Wall Street Journal* (July 3, 2008), p. 1B; Kate Linebaugh, "In Race for Market Share, GM Tries to Hold Off Toyota," *The Wall Street Journal* (June 30, 2008), p. A2. Paul Ingrassia, "That '70s Show: Detroit," *The Wall Street Journal* (July 8, 2008), p. A21; and John D. Stoll, "GM Weighs More Layoffs, Sale of Brands," *The Wall Street Journal* (July 7, 2008), pp. A1, A9. For an uplifting sidebar see, John D. Stoll, "GM Lifts Ohio Town's Outlook," *The Wall Street Journal* (July 17, 2008), p. B12. GM's only U.S. small-car plant is adding workers. During the summer of 2008, GM CEO Rick Wagoner said, "We will continue to take steps necessary to align our business structure with the lower vehicle sales volumes and shifts in sales mix." Only time will tell whether GM's continuous reorganization efforts will be successful.

24. David Kesmodel, Dennis K. Berman and Dana Cimilluca, "Anheuser, InBev Reach a Deal for $52 Billion," *The Wall Street Journal* (July 14, 2008), p. B1. Also see David Kesmodel, Matthew Karnitschnog, and Corey Boles, "InBev Takes Bud Bid to Capital," *The Wall Street Journal* (June 18, 2008), p. B3; "InBev May Water Down Bud's Marketing," *The Wall Street Journal* (June 13, 2008), p. B6; Matt Moffett, "InBev's Chief Built Competitive Culture," the *Wall Street Journal* (June 13, 2008), p. B6; and David Kesmodel and Matthew Karnitschnig, "InBev Uncorks Anheuser Takeover Bid," the *Wall Street Journal* (June 12, 2008), pp. A1–14.

25. See Justin Bachman, "Hope Amid the Airlines' Red Ink," *BusinessWeek* online (July 22, 2008); Paulo Prada, "Higher Fares, Fees Help Stem Airline Losses," the *Wall Street Journal* (July 17, 2008), p. B1; and Bachman, "Delta and Northwest Agree to Merge," *BusinessWeek* online (April 14, 2008).

26. See Jena McGregor, "GE's Immelt: an Ever-Hotter Throne," *BusinessWeek* online (July 17, 2008) Ann Keeton and Scott Thrum, "GE to Spin Off Appliance, Bulb Units," the *Wall Street Journal* (July 11, 2008), p. B1. Also see Mark Gongloff, "GE Nears End of Ride to Nowhere," the *Wall Street Journal* (July 11, 2008), p. C1.; Dennis K. Berman, "GE's Sale: End of an Era," the *Wall Street Journal* (July 11, 2008), p. C3.

27. See Blessing White 2008 Employee Engagement Report (April/May 2008), accessed August 24, 2008 (http://www.blessingwhite.com). To see all of Blessing White's research reports, go to their Web site and click on Research and Articles. The report concluded that "Engaged employees are not just committed. They are not just passionate or proud. They have a line-of-sight on their own future and on the organization's mission and goals. They are 'enthused' and 'in gear,' using their talents and discretionary effort to make a difference in their employer's quest for sustainable business success." Also see Watson Wyatt's 2005/2006 Communication ROI Study™. Additional findings included: (1) Companies that communicate effectively have a 19.4% higher market premium. (2) Shareholder returns for organizations with the most effective communication were over 57% higher over the past five years. (3) Firms that communicate effectively are 4.5 times more likely to report high levels of employee engagement. Also see Nancy Lockwood, "Leveraging Employee Engagement for Competitive Advantage: HR's Strategic Role," *HR Magazine* (March 2007), pp. 1, 11; and Tim Rutledge, *Getting Engaged: The New Workplace Loyalty* (Mattanie Press, 2005).

28 See "Management's New Gurus," *BusinessWeek* (August 31, 1992), pp. 44–47, 50–52, and Robert B. Blaha, "Forget Functions, Manage Processes," *HR Magazine* (June 1993), pp. 109–10. Our students have found Vincent P. Barrabba, *Surviving Transformation: Lessons from GM's Surprising Turnaround* (New York: Oxford University Press, 2004) to be most interesting reading, particularly in light of GM's recent (2007–2008) problems. To contrast Barrabba's contentions, see endnote 23 above or "GM Plans to Cut 25,000 Jobs by '08 in Restructuring," *The Wall Street Journal* (June 8, 2005), pp. A1, A6. It does not appear that GM has enjoyed much success during this century. One thing is certain: GM cannot survive without a substantive change in strategy and a massive reorganization.

29. See Lizabeth Yacovone, "Organizational Design for a Supply Chain Transformation: Best Practice at Johnson & Johnson Health Care Systems Inc.," *Organizational Development Journal*, 25, 3 (Fall 2007), pp. 105–112; John A. Byrne, "The Horizontal Corporation," *BusinessWeek* (December 20, 1993), pp. 76–81, and Frank Ostroff, *The Horizontal Corporation: What the Organization of the Future Actually Looks Like and How It Delivers Value to Customers* (New York: Oxford University Press, 1999).

30. See Philip L. Hunsaker and Johanna S, Hunsaker, "Virtual Teams: A Leader's Guide," *Team Performance Management*, 14, 1 (2008),

pp. 86–101; Ronald Ashkensas, *The Boundless Organization* (San Francisco: Jossey-Bass Publishers, 1995); "The Virtual Corporation," *BusinessWeek* (February 8, 1993), pp. 98–99, 100–103; and Roger Nagel, as quoted in Challenges (published by the Council on Competitiveness, June 1993), p. 4.

31. Lean manufacturing is often identified with the "Toyota Production System," a business practice that allows workers to identify waste in operations and to focus on tasks that add value to the product. See Jerry Feingold, "Lean Roots—A Quick History Lesson," *Quality Digest* (May 2008), pp. 35–39 for a roadmap in how the Toyota Production System began and what it means today. For more information on lean manufacturing, visit the *Quality Digest* Web site (http://qualitydigest.com)

32. Someone once said, "The best way to get the most from a meeting is—don't go!" Unfortunately for most of us that is not an option. For discussions on meeting management tips and skills, see Don Schmincke, "Do Your Meetings Sabotage Profits?" *Supervision*, 68, 10 (October 2007), pp. 5–6; T. L. Stanley, "Making Meetings Count," *Supervision* (August 2004), pp. 6–8; Bryan R. Fisher, "Listen to What's Really Going On," *Supervision* (August 2004), pp. 9–11; Jann Dyer, "Meetings, Meetings, Meetings," *Chartered Accountants* (May 2004), pp. 64–65; Craig Harrison "Meeting Monsters," *Executive Excellence* (January 2004), p. 18; Jerome Finnigan, "Is This Meeting Necessary? Ten Questions to Make Meetings More Productive," *Supervision* (November 2001), pp. 6–8; and Eric Matson, "The Seven Sins of Deadly Meetings," *Fast Company* (April 1999), p. 122.

33. Hundreds of quotes from President Dwight D. Eisenhower can be found at http://www.brainyquotes.com. Two other interesting quotes are: "I have only one yardstick by which I test every major problem and that yardstick is: Is it good for America?" and "It is far more important to be able to hit the target than it is to haggle over who makes the weapon or who pulls the trigger."

34. "Begin with the end in mind," served as the basis for Stephen R. Covey's, *The Seven Habits of Highly Effective People: Restoring the Character Ethic* (New York: Simon & Schuster, 1989). For additional ideas on time management principles, see Jared Sandberg, "To Surrender All My Days," *Wall Street Journal* (September 11, 2007), p. 1B.

35. IBID. Covey. Also see, Covey, A. Roger Merrill and Rebecca R. Merrill, First Things First (New York: Simon & Schuster, 1994); and Jared Sandburg, To Surrender All My Days, The Wall Street Journal (September 11, 2007), p. 1B.

36. Carnegie Mellon computer scientist professor Randy Pausch's book and YouTube interview, *The Last Lecture*, drew tears to this professor's eyes. Pausch's questions and comments are relevant for all of us. "If you gave one last lecture before you died, what would you say? You can't change the cards you were dealt!"

The rumors about Paul's Furnishings, Gifts, and Novelties' economic problems were at an all-time high. Since the widening of State Road 57, the retail development in the store's neighborhood has abounded. In the past six months, a Wal-Mart, a Do It Best Lawn, Garden, and Home Center, and a Walgreens have been added to the already-saturated retail mix. In March, an Ace Hardware store closed, and in mid-July, the IGA grocery shuttered its doors after 47 years in business. In fact, Sally Paul's father Jerome and Don Swanson, founder of the IGA, had started their businesses about the same time.

Sally Paul, now the current owner of this general merchandise store, had decided to face the Big Boxes head on. She purchased an adjacent building, added parking spaces, lowered prices, and embarked on a customer service campaign that had employees bending over backward to give personal attention and greater service to customers.

Phil Bearman, a salaried maintenance supervisor for Paul's, is 45 years old and married, with five children ages 9 to 18. Shortly after graduating from high school, Bearman joined the Army and spent six years on several military bases in the U.S. and Korea. His military experience helped hone both his maintenance and supervisory skills. He left the military with the rank of sergeant to return home and marry his high school sweetheart. He has worked at Paul's for the past twelve years. He's a working supervisor, and until three months ago he had four direct reports. When one of the younger employees quit to follow his spouse to another position out of state, Sally Paul, the owner of the store, decided not to allow Bearman to fill the position.

Bearman has been busy supervising the renovation of the adjacent building and the construction of the new parking lot. This past weekend should have been wonderful for Bearman and his family. Labor Day Weekend had always been a day to relax, set all worries aside, and spend time at the in-laws' lakeside cottage. Historically, the store had always closed at 1:00 P.M. on Saturday and was never open on Sundays or holidays.

Basically, the store is now open from 9 A.M. to 9 P.M. Monday through Saturday and from noon to 6:00 P.M. on Sundays and all holidays except for Thanksgiving, Christmas, New Year's, Day and Easter. The additional hours have stretched the maintenance staff and led to increased stress. Bearman has not spent a day away from the business in over two months.

Bearman reflected on the events of the past two weeks: "This is not a dream or a newspaper story about someone in another part of the country. This is happening to me. I have to beg my people to do more, and I have been putting in ten- and twelve-hour days to get the work done. The past two weeks have been unreal. The temperature set record highs almost every day, and the humidity hovered near 100 percent."

Bearman knows that he is very short-handed and that if things do not improve the remaining employees will leave. One of the long-term cashiers confided to him that sales receipts were down 14 percent in the first half of the year and that

CASE 3-1
Too Much to Do—Not Enough Time to Get It Done!

last month's sales were the worst since she had worked there. Surely something can be done to improve the situation, but he is at a loss as to what to do.

Questions for Discussion

1. What are the issues in this case? List them in order of priority.
2. Evaluate Sally Paul's planning skills. Are her strategies realistic and feasible? Justify your answer.
3. Because of the extended hours and expansion activities, Bearman knows that he does not have the right number of employees with the right level of talents and skills in the right jobs at the right time performing the right activities to achieve what needs to be done—and done right the first time. What suggestions do you have for him?
4. What would you do if you were Phil Bearman? Why?

CASE 3-2

Whatever Happened to Planning and Control?

Juan Sanchez is store supervisor at Store 16 of Sanders Supermarkets. For about three months, he has been talking to his district manager, Sandy Greenberg, about a major renovation for the grocery section in the store. At last, Greenberg called Sanchez to tell him that a meeting at the corporate main office would be held to discuss the renovation project for Store 16.

The meeting was attended by supervisors from the sales and construction departments, several district managers, and the corporate operations manager. By the end of the meeting, it was generally agreed that Store 16 should be reorganized (or "reset," in the language of the company) and that several main aisles should be relocated. The supervisor of the reset crew and the construction supervisor were to submit final plans and a cost estimate at the next meeting of the group, which was scheduled for a week later.

During her next visit to Store 16, Greenberg told Sanchez about the meeting. Greenberg informed Sanchez about the plans for Store 16, adding that nothing was yet finalized. She failed to mention that part of the reset would include moving some aisles.

The next week, plans and costs were submitted and approved by the corporate operations manager. Because new shelving had to be ordered and schedules made, the supervisor of the reset crew and the construction supervisor were assigned the job of putting the necessary paperwork into motion. Greenberg then called Sanchez and said, "The reset project for your store has been approved. I'll let you know more as soon as I hear."

One month later, as Sanchez was driving to work after a day off, he made a mental note to call Greenberg to ask about the reset project. However, when Sanchez arrived at Store 16, he soon forgot his plan. He walked into the store to find three major problems: (1) the frozen food case had broken down the previous afternoon, (2) the floor scrubber had been malfunctioning for three days, and (3) the grinder in the meat department had just quit working. After some checking, Sanchez found that no maintenance calls had been made because each of his two assistant supervisors, Jane Oliver and Wally Withers, had thought the other was going to do it.

"It just doesn't pay to take a day off," Sanchez muttered to himself as he headed for the telephone. He called the maintenance department, explained what had happened, and requested immediate service. While waiting for the maintenance person, Sanchez called Oliver and Withers to talk to them about letting him and each other know about these kinds of problems and how to control them. "All it takes," he said, "is working together, communication, and follow-through to ensure that our customers get the best service available. We can't be out of merchandise, especially frozen food. And we have to make sure that when we are busy, as we will be this week, our customers aren't stepping over workers in the aisles."

At about that time, Sanchez was called to his office. When he arrived, he was greeted by five carpenters and laborers. "We just wanted to tell you we're here, and we'll get started right away," said the carpenter in charge.

"How come it takes this many people to fix a frozen food case?" asked Sanchez.

"We're not here to fix a frozen food case," said the carpenter. "We're here to move the shelving in the aisles and to reset the store."

"Today?" replied Sanchez. "Nobody told me that you guys were doing this today. I can't have you moving aisles during the day. What are my customers going to do?"

Sanchez then called Greenberg. "Sandy, did you know that they were going to start the reset project in the store today?"

"No," said Sandy, "I wasn't notified either."

"Why wasn't I consulted on this?" exclaimed Sanchez. "First of all, the first week of the month is always too busy for laborers to be working in the aisles. Second, this type of work must be done at night. Maybe other stores can handle this work in the daytime, but my customers will not tolerate that kind of inconvenience."

"Okay," Greenberg said. "It sounds like things are really out of control at your store right now. What are you going to do about it?"

"Sandy, don't you mean, 'What are we going to do about it?'"

Questions for Discussion

1. Define various places where members of management did not plan in specific terms and then failed to follow through on their responsibilities.
2. Analyze Sanchez's discussion with his two assistants, especially when he said that, "All it takes is working together, communication, and follow-through." Are these factors the essence of supervision, or does good supervision require something more? Discuss.
3. What should Greenberg and Sanchez do about the immediate problem of the carpenters in the store?
4. Develop a list of general recommendations to improve planning in Sanders Supermarkets Store 16.

   This case can also be used effectively after the students have read Chapter 14 and Chapter 15, for which the following questions are applicable:
5. What is the real problem here? Who is responsible for causing this problem?
6. How can this conflict benefit Sanders Supermarkets?
7. List the characteristics of an effective control system. Which of these characteristics should Sanchez and Greenberg use to stop the problem from worsening?
8. What is your contingency plan in case your first recommendation for Question 3 fails?

CASE 3-3

Vision? What Vision? How Do We Engage Employees?

Joan McCarthy is supervisor of the "hottest" new project design group in an original equipment manufacturing (OEM) company employing over 15,000 people. She has ten years' experience with the company at several locations, including the past seven years with the company's engineering facility. Joan's strengths are her communication and leadership skills. "Give me a direction and authority, and I'll be able to get it done!" has always been her motto. Although some people thought that Joan was not technical enough for her last job, she was always able to compensate with her interpersonal skills. In addition to her appointment as supervisor of the new group, Joan was selected as one of the "Top 100 Employees" in the company for this year.

The new project design group, or team—which was developed from Joan's interactions with her coworker Bryan Barton, her manager, Lyle Hasaka, and a consulting firm—was to have one supervisor and six employees. Joan was instrumental in gaining support for the program from senior management. Barton worked with several functional areas through all the internal systems to implement the new project team processes.

When it came time to launch the group, Joan was the obvious choice for supervisor. Barton filled the first reporting position. Others were selected as they were found. Only the best from the available workforce were taken for the project team. It was a whole new world of responsibility. This was the first time Joan had served in a supervisory position, and she looked forward to the opportunity.

The outline for operations was to rely on the expertise of the team to gather data, make decisions, and direct the flow of changes in the new ordering and design systems. Joan's role would be to provide guidance where necessary and provide the "big picture" perspective. She decided to delegate many of the supervisory functions to Barton. Barton would be able to expedite various supervisory tasks, including training new employees in the team's IT protocol and various computerized design systems used by the team. Carefully designed metrics were developed to evaluate product-change decisions. Existing team members trained new employees, and responsibilities were to be shared by team members and handed back and forth. As a result, Joan was generally free to travel and to meet with customers at their locations, which she did often. She always made sure to keep in contact with the team while away.

Todd and Stacie, who had been on the team from the outset, had grown dissatisfied as they usually ended up doing more work than the rest of the group combined. A number of unforeseen changes had caused a great deal of extra work for the team. Updates typically were not completed until the last possible moment. The newest employee, Lois Hunter, who had been hired from outside the company, still was not working up to speed and could not really contribute. Barton claimed he could not help Hunter until other team members gave her some basic orientation and training.

Team morale really began to decline when Joan instituted some changes a vice president had requested. The team had been struggling to use the decision metrics already laid out; now they were going to have to use some data and procedures that clearly violated the team's previous operating rules. The vice president's ideas were not completely without merit, but team members argued that they should be allowed to refuse the vice president's mandates.

Joan knows her team has made some strides over the first few months, but clearly she must now act to improve her team's functioning.

Questions for Discussion

1. How can the principles of planning and organizing assist Joan McCarthy in managing her team?
2. Identify the driving and restraining forces toward acceptance of the vice president's ideas. What should have been done to ensure acceptance?
3. Make a preliminary diagnosis of the problems in McCarthy's team.

4. (**INTERNET ACTIVITY**) Surf the Web to gather information on the characteristics of effective project teams.

   a. Make a list of the characteristics of effective project teams.
   b. Put a **+** next to those that are present in McCarthy's team.
   c. Put an X next to those that McCarthy needs to work on.
   d. Then briefly outline a plan of action that McCarthy could use to improve her team's performance. [Note: You may want to surf the Web to get additional information on planning devices such as Gantt charts, PERT, and MBO that could be used to help the team's project scheduling.]

5. If you were Joan McCarthy, how would you describe your management style? What two things would you do to modify your style? How would you do this?

CASE 3-4
Multi-Tasking or Asset Elimination?

[Note: This case occurred in the months following Hurricane Katrina and the events that followed that tragedy. The issues germane to the original case are still relevant today, perhaps even more so. United Parcel Service Inc. (UPS), a competitor of Global Delivery, and widely recognized as a barometer of the U.S. economy because it handles 15 million shipments per day whose value represents six percent of the U.S. gross domestic product, posted a twenty percent decline in net income in the second quarter of 2008. UPS also announced it would reduce spending for the next eighteen months and freeze hiring for all non-sales positions. UPS's new labor contract allows the company to pay new drivers less than veterans. For more information see Alex Roth, "UPS Braces for Prolonged Slowdown, Sets Hiring Freeze as Profits Falls 21%," the Wall Street Journal *(July 23, 2008), p. B3.]*

For the past ten years, Todd Bowen has been the southern district supervisor of customer relations for Global Delivery, a leading international parcel delivery service. Located in Baton Rouge, Louisiana, Bowen supervises eight account supervisors, several of whom were in their positions before his arrival. Historically, the account supervisors are responsible for the 30 largest customer accounts in a defined area. They have been intimately involved in each customer's operations, assessing and addressing needs, providing employee education and orientation, implementing and interpreting changes due to the introduction of new products and regulations, and keeping abreast of all customer-service issues. These value-added activities gave Global a competitive advantage.

For the first nine years of Bowen's tenure, his district consistently ranked first in revenue among the nine districts in the immediate four-state area. In addition to their record of regularly exceeding revenue goals, the district and the account supervisors received numerous awards and commendations at both the area and national levels for their consistently outstanding, customer-focused service. When a team of five top service and marketing professionals assembled at Global's national headquarters three years ago to define, create, and implement the standard account-management process, one of Bowen's charges was selected as the lone account supervisor representative. Customer-satisfaction ratings for the district have been stellar, and complaints or problems going unresolved beyond the district level have been virtually nonexistent.

The morale among Bowen's eight direct reports was consistently high. Bowen and the experienced supervisors made concerted efforts to mentor and support new team members, and the only members to leave the group had been promoted up the corporate ladder. The relative autonomy of the account supervisor position was a significant factor contributing to the team's success. It allowed account supervisors to direct and refine their energies, efforts, and skills as necessary to ensure continued revenue growth and customer satisfaction. Account supervisors had been lauded for their ability to identify and pursue potential customers in their areas and thereby initiate and grow revenue opportunities as they added them to their account portfolios.

The past year has been a difficult one for the organization and especially for the district. In early September 2005, the influx of hundreds of thousands of evacuees from Hurricane Katrina changed the "business as usual" mentality. Most employees expected to have relatives and/or friends staying with them for a month or two. Being without lights, and, more important, air conditioning, caused tempers to flare. Mother Nature wreaked havoc on southern Alabama, Mississippi, and Louisiana and caused Bowen and other members of his team to contemplate their future, both personally and professionally.

The business downturn further decreased revenues. In addition to rising fuel and labor costs, new security and transportation measures had to be implemented. Bowen's district had been deeply affected as well by the fact that local, state, and federal government didn't do enough before or immediately after Katrina hit. Relatives of some of Bowen's workers were without food, water, medicine, or bathroom facilities.

Several months before Hurricane Katrina, Global's management had developed a new long-term strategy of moving its internal focus to its core business. At the same time, Global announced that it was in the midst of making sure its own house was clean. An internal audit review was instituted to ensure that financial statements were accurate. This internal investigation examining accounting errors was triggered, in part, by a formal inquiry in June 2005 by the Securities and Exchange Commission.

The "Mission Redefined" strategy resulted in the displacement of a number of supervisory personnel. Rather than being eliminated, many personnel were organized into two new levels of supervision. This new class of supervisors, unfamiliar with the account-management process, had taken steps to redefine the process. A series of sequential indicators were implemented to monitor employee activities and micromanage the process. All customer-service focus was eliminated.

The account supervisor position was redefined as merely a marketing position. The account supervisors were forbidden not only to perform any customer-service functions (value-added activities) but also to seek new customers. Account supervisors were now required to file a seemingly endless series of reports to individuals and positions previously uninvolved in any marketing or customer-service capacity. The new process, constantly in flux as new restrictions and reporting requirements were added, limited the account supervisor to a thirty-account portfolio, imposed strict customer visitation requirements, and entailed a substantial increase in reporting and data entry.

Bowen faced a near-mutiny. Morale among his account supervisors, once the national model of excellence and performance, was abysmal. There was a dearth of new revenue, and established revenue streams were drying up. Customers were incensed that their account supervisors could no longer provide value-added services and that they insisted on an increased number of sales-only calls. As one of Bowen's veteran team members stated, "I used to have an intimate working relationship with my customers. They knew they could count on me to be at their disposal for any service-related issue. They trusted me to know their needs, and because of this, they welcomed my proposals and suggestions. Now they are livid when I tell them I cannot participate in solving service issues and pass them off to employees and departments they don't know. At the same time, I'm supposed to make greater demands on their time with increased sales calls and coerce them into producing new revenue. Instead of having a relationship based on trust and quality service, I'm supposed to badger them incessantly with sales calls. And when I make these calls, I have to start the conversation by telling them, 'I can't help you with that, call so-and-so. I'm not involved with that anymore, but I do need more of your business.' We're in a service industry, and there's no service."

Bowen is caught in an unenviable position. Higher management is demanding revenue growth while at the same time taking steps that are clearly counterproductive. His team of account supervisors, who were once enthusiastic, professional, and customer focused, have been handcuffed and demoralized. Bowen knows that several of his best and most experienced team members will leave the organization if an opportunity presents itself.

Questions for Discussion

This case is designed to fulfill three purposes. First, we want you to discuss why crisis planning is important and to understand why individuals as well as organizations should have a plan in place. Then you can specifically discuss how Global Delivery adapted job redesign and reengineering organizing principles when faced with an economic downturn.

Crisis Management Planning/Social Responsibility Discussion Questions
1. Discuss the impact that a crisis such as Hurricane Katrina can have on a business such as Global.
2. Hundreds of thousands of evacuees were scattered around Louisiana and other states and no one seemed to know what to do with them. Many of them did not have a home to go back to for months or even years. What social responsibility does an organization like Global's Baton Rouge facility have to provide for the evacuees and to those employees who provide them with a spare bedroom or a sofa?
3. Should Global Delivery designate a portion of sales or corporate profits for the Katrina disaster victims? Why? Why not?
4. Less than six weeks after Hurricane Katrina, thousands of people were believed dead when a 7.6-magnitude quake hit Pakistan and India. The U.N. reported that more than 2.5 million people needed shelter. What assistance, if any, should Global Delivery provide those victims? Why?

Strategy / Planning / Organizing Discussion Questions
5. List the things that could have been done differently to improve the effectiveness of the customer relations function. Search the Internet for information on customer relationship management (CRM). After reviewing the literature on CRM, what other suggestions would you add to your list?
6. Why was Bowen's work group less successful after the change? Bowen is clearly caught in a critical situation. He must take corrective action at once. Where should he begin?
7. What strategies do you recommend that Bowen use to increase the likelihood that his unit will return to the production and morale levels before the economic downturn and Hurricane Katrina?
8. If you were Bowen, how would you communicate your concerns to upper management?

Finally, this case also can be used effectively after reading Chapters 11 and 12, for which the following questions are applicable:

9. Identify the common sources of resistance to change in the Global Delivery customer-service unit.
10. What should upper management have done to effectively implement a change of this magnitude?
11. Explain how Bowen can make sure group needs are given careful attention.
12. Historically, Bowen's customer-service team was a self-managed work team. That is, they were well-trained employees who had a specific responsibility and authority to provide quality customer service. Today, that job has changed. If you were Bowen, what leadership style would you use in each of these scenarios? How would your leadership style differ? Why?

CASE 3-5
Balancing Production, Quality, and Inventory

The mission of Barry Automotive's Allisonville plant is to be the leading manufacturer of sealing system products and fluid systems while focusing on innovative, continuously improving solutions to customer problems with world-class quality, leading-edge technologies, service, and competitive pricing. General Motors (GM) accounted for over one-third of the plant's sales. Toyota, Chrysler, and Ford were also customers, but to lesser degrees. The economic downturn during the early part of the twenty-first century led to many plant closings and consolidations and reduced demand for automobiles. GM tried substantial rebates and the "Every Customer Can Buy at Employee Prices" promotion in an effort to increase sales of existing stock. GM and Ford have struggled to stabilize their market share, reduce high production costs, and reduce their excess manufacturing capacity.

During a meeting with Barry Automotive's upper management, GM representatives said, "Effective immediately, we will pay for Barry parts only when the parts are used, not when they are delivered." This policy would mean that Barry would have to let its finished parts sit in inventory, either in the Allisonville warehouse or in GM's warehouse, and get paid only when those parts were consumed in the final assembly process. Chrysler management also met with Barry management and stated, "We can get equally good parts from other suppliers at a lower cost, so to continue doing business with us, you will have to give us a four-percent cut in price." GM and Chrysler together make up more than 70 percent of the Allisonville plant's business.

Paul Allen, production control manager, was asked by upper management to cut production costs as much as possible and to order parts from suppliers only a day or two before they were needed in the manufacturing process. Allen knows that many workers on the floor have a habit of keeping a few more containers of supplier parts at their workstations than they need. Barry's IT system generates supplier-part requirements weekly, which means that Barry has to order parts a week before they are to be used.

Allen is in a dilemma. He does not want the production line to stop or slow due to unavailable supplier parts. He knows he must keep enough supplier parts on hand to meet customer needs and maintain an efficient production schedule.

Questions for Discussion

 Students should visit a Web site like http://www.qualitydigest .com or the Society of Automotive Engineers' Web site at http://www.sae.org or the *Quality Digest* Web site

(www.qualitydigest.com) to get additional information on such topics as JIT, six sigma, lean manufacturing, kaizen, and value stream. Then, students should couple this information with the material in Chapters 7 and 8 of this text to make suggestions for improving the manufacturing operations at Barry Automotive.

1. What can Paul Allen do to improve final product quality such that Barry Automotive will have a quality advantage over its competitors?
2. What can Allen do to reduce the plant's inventory costs?
3. What steps can Allen take so that Barry retains business with its customers and remains profitable?
4. How can Barry Automotive lower costs and improve product quality at the same time?
5. Will a just-in-time (JIT) inventory-control system, kaizen, six sigma, and the like work in any manufacturing firm? Why?

CASE 3-6
Who Made the Coffee?

As the production supervisor at the Denver facility for Baker Manufacturing, Tony Martin had been extremely interested in the discussion following this morning's management meeting. Sarah Lally, human resources specialist, had reported on what Martin considered to be the bizarre behavior of employees that other organizations had encountered. The problems faced in other organizations fell outside anything he had experienced during his thirty years in manufacturing.

The Denver facility employs 450 people, working on rotating ten-hour shifts, seven days a week. Under Martin's and Lally's leadership, the Denver facility has improved its production and personnel practices but still has a way to go before becoming "the employer of choice." Sure, the facility has its usual share of people who stretch the policies and rules to the limit, and sometimes, make life difficult for others. But they paled in comparison to the challenges faced by supervisors in other organizations. All of Martin's direct reports have been trained to ensure that, when a performance problem occurs, it is handled immediately. Compared with other organizations, Baker Manufacturing has few disciplinary problems beyond the typical absenteeism and tardiness issues.

Upon returning to the office, Martin stopped by the break room to get a cup of coffee before he began analyzing several new machining processes the company was considering. Baker's break room is state-of-the-industry: a modern, well-lighted, climate-controlled room with refrigerators where employees can store their lunches or snacks, microwaves where they can heat items, and a complete complement of vending machines, the proceeds from which supported the annual employee picnic and holiday party, and is the pride of all employees. The company also provides free coffee for all employees. The person emptying the pot is expected to clean the pot, add a new filter, fresh coffee, and water so that freshly brewed coffee is ready for the next person.

As he was reviewing the various machining processes, Martin was interrupted by Harold Pope and B.K. Moustpha. It was obvious that Moustpha, one of the plant engineers, and Pope, an employee in the maintenance department, were angry about something. They asked if they could close the door and talk in confidence.

Martin listened to their story. It seems as if several of the employees thought their coffee sometimes just didn't taste right, so Moustpha and Pope set up a hidden video camera in the break room to find out why. What they found was that co-worker Jones was using the coffee pot as a urinal. To support their claim, they asked Martin to watch a video.

Sure enough, Jones entered the empty break room, looked around, climbed up on a chair, removed the lid from the coffee pot and proceeded to urinate into the coffee pot. Martin gulped as he pushed his coffee cup aside. Shaking his head in frustration, he knew that immediate action was required, but what steps should he take?

Questions for Discussion

1. (**INTERNET ACTIVITY**) Organizations are required under OSHA to provide a safe and healthy work environment for employees. Review the OSHA Web site (http://www.osha.gov) to more fully understand Baker Manufacturing's responsibilities under the act. List the major responsibilities that may have been compromised by Jones's behavior.

2. In *O'Connor v. Ortega*, the U.S. Supreme Court established the parameters of the Fourth Amendment's protection of a public employee's right to privacy in the workplace. Other court cases have limited how surveillance cameras can be used to monitor employee activity in the workplace. Search the Web to find at least two cases that detail an employee's reasonable expectation of privacy in the workplace.
   a. Do the actions of Moustpha and Pope violate an employee's "zone of privacy"? Explain your answer.
   b. Should Moustpha and Pope be disciplined? Why or why not?

3. If you were Tony Martin, what would you do now? Why would you take these actions rather than alternative ones?

4. What steps need to be taken to minimize a recurrence of a similar situation?

5. (**ROLE PLAY**) Role-play Activity: Option A: Select one student to play the role of Tony Martin and another to play the role of HR specialist Sarah Lally. A review of employee Jones's file revealed that he had worked at Baker for the past three years, and other than a couple of reprimands for tardiness and absenteeism, his record is unblemished. A closer look revealed that he had recently been turned down for a higher-paying position that had gone to a more senior person. Martin and Lally are to discuss the disciplinary options available to them. A quick review of the material contained in Chapter 6 might be appropriate before assigning this task. Other class members are assigned as observers and charged with the responsibility of critiquing Martin's and Lally's actions.

CASE 3-7
Romance on the Assembly Line

Louise Nance has been working on the assembly line of Jackson Manufacturing Company for about six months. During recent weeks, Nance's supervisor, Ben Miller, has noticed that her production has gone down to such an extent that she cannot keep up, and she has caused serious delays. When Miller called this to her attention, Nance told him about the difficulties she was having at home. Her husband had recently left her without any explanation. Miller replied that her personal affairs were of no interest to him and that he was concerned only with her work. He warned her that unless her production improved she would be separated from the company.

Shortly thereafter, Miller was promoted to a high-level management position. His supervisory position was filled by Jack Armstrong, who had joined the company recently. Armstrong immediately took a liking to Nance and started dating her. Although she told Armstrong about her marital difficulties, he kept seeing her. When she remarked to him one day that her car needed some repairs, he offered to see whether he could fix it for her.

On the following Saturday, Nance's estranged husband appeared and found Armstrong repairing her car, which was parked on the street in front of her apartment. The two men got into a fight on the street, and police were called to separate them. The local newspapers carried a short report about the incident, mentioning that Nance and Armstrong were employed at Jackson Manufacturing Company.

A few days later, Armstrong was called into the office of Kay McCaslin, the human resources director, who had read the newspaper report. McCaslin advised Armstrong to stop seeing Nance or risk being fired. McCaslin reminded Armstrong that informal company policy discouraged close fraternization between supervisors and employees because it tended to weaken a supervisor's authority in dealing with employees. Moreover, publicity of this sort would undoubtedly hurt the company's image in the community. Armstrong replied that this was none of the company's business and that he could spend his time away from the plant any way he chose. He stated that a threat of discharge was totally improper because his private life was his own and not subject to company regulations. Furthermore, he pointed out that Nance's work record had improved under his supervision, and it was now at the same level as most of the other people on his line. Armstrong left McCaslin's office with the comment that he would continue to date Nance because they were very much in love.

McCaslin wondered whether she should drop the matter or discuss it with higher-level management, including Miller, who now was Armstrong's superior.

Questions for Discussion

1. Is the informal company policy that discourages close fraternization between supervisors and employees sound? Why or why not?
2. **(INTERNET ACTIVITY)** Using the Internet, find information regarding recent court decisions or other dilemmas caused by organizations having "no-fraternization" policies. What appears to be the concerns regarding such policies?
3. What alternatives are available to McCaslin, the human resources director? What should she do?
4. Should Armstrong's immediate supervisor, Miller, be called into the situation? Why or why not?
5. If you were Armstrong, what would you do?
6. If you were Nance, what would you do?
7. Put yourself in the shoes of one of the other employees on Armstrong's line. What are your feelings about the situation? How could your feelings impact your performance on the line?
8. Organizations should have a written policy to guide supervisors' actions. Organize the class into teams of three to five students. One person in each group will play the role of HR director Kay McCaslin. Others will play the role of either supervisors or employees. The team's mission is to (1) make a list of what should be included in the policy, and (2) develop a formal "no fraternization" policy and procedure for Jackson Manufacturing. Each team member should use the Internet and/or review the handbooks of several organizations to get an overview of existing policies.
9. Each team's policy statement should not be more than two pages in length. After completion of this portion, make extra copies of your policy statement and exchange with at least two other groups. After reviewing the other policy statements, answer the following questions:
   a. What is there about your team's policy that distinguishes it from the policies developed by the other groups?

b. What one thing was there in each of the other policy statements that should have been considered by your group?

c. What difficulties might there be in putting any of the policies into action?

d. If your formal "no fraternization" policy had been in effect prior to Armstrong's alleged romance with Nance, how would the situation have been handled?

e. What did you learn from this exercise?

CASE 3-8
Just Another Crisis?

Luis Siqueira had worked for Jiffy Mart for the past ten years. Jiffy Mart was a 24/7, standalone gas station located on North Anthony Boulevard. Customers prepaid for the gasoline, either at the pump or at the customer-service window. Customers also could purchase milk, sodas, snack foods, tobacco products, and other high-margin incidentals through the customer-service window. Company policies stated specifically that no one other than authorized personnel was allowed inside the building. Because of the proclivity of gasoline drive-offs and hold-ups, the parent company had installed surveillance cameras to record suspicious behavior.

As a cost-control measure, only one employee was scheduled to work at any one time. One of the three district managers visited each store every day. During these visits, the district manager collected the cash from the drop safe, reconciled credit card purchases with inventory, brought fresh supplies, and helped the employee restock the shelves. Generally, these visits occurred between 10:00 A.M. and 3:00 P.M.

One night, around 10:00 P.M., as three customers were at the customer-service window, a car stopped directly between the customer-service window and the gas pumps. Two men wearing ski masks, one with a shotgun and the other with a revolver, jumped out. The robbers demanded that Luis fill a garbage sack with money that he had on hand. Frightened, Luis pointed to the sign that said "No cash on hand except for $25. Cash transactions go immediately into the dump safe."

The robber with the shotgun then placed a garbage sack on the window ledge and demanded that Luis fill it with cartons of cigarettes. The other robber demanded that the three customers place their jewelry, purses, and wallets in another garbage sack. The robbers threatened to kill the three customers if Luis pushed the silent alarm button.

Luis and the customers chose to play it safe and complied with the robbers' requests. Unbeknownst to anyone, Luis had a permit to carry a handgun. Shortly after he began working at Jiffy Mart, he started carrying the gun to work. As the robbers retreated with their loot but before they could leave the scene, Luis burst from the building blasting away. Luis fired the gun three times at the fleeing vehicle. Simultaneously, the police and the Channel 4 camera crew arrived. The television crews routinely traveled the area looking for news as it happened. They monitored police channels, and did live reports on what was happening almost as it happened.

No one was able to provide the police with the license number of the car. A review of the surveillance tapes showed clearly the make and model number but not the license number. One of the robbed customers described Luis's actions as "John Wayne-like. The robbers were fleeing the scene, and then that employee came out blasting away. Sure I was scared, but when the bullets started flying, I really became frightened!" Another customer stated, "I'm going to start carrying a gun. I wish that employee would have shot them both! It's not safe to go anywhere!"

Within minutes of the robbery, the management of Jiffy Mart was fully aware of the happenings at the North Anthony store. An hour later, Channel 4 reported that an unidentified person had been dumped on the steps of Community General

Hospital. The person had been shot several times. Ballistics tests later confirmed the bullets were fired from Luis's gun.

The next day, Luis was summoned to the general offices of Jiffy Mart. The president and the three district managers met him and immediately informed him that he was no longer employed by Jiffy Mart. He was told that he had violated several company policies: (1) Jiffy Mart's policy for robbery was to fulfill the robber's request without trouble and report it to the authorities and company officials when the danger had passed; (2) Jiffy Mart's employee handbook stated that weapons were not permitted on company premises; (3) Luis had seriously injured someone and had created a situation where customers could have lost their lives; and (4) Luis had not used good judgment. They demanded the return of his keys, company ID, and other work-related items. Luis was handed a termination notice and was told that he would receive his final check in the mail.

Questions for Discussion

1. Survey various Internet sites to gain information to answer the following questions:
   a. What is the likelihood or probability that a store such as the Jiffy Mart North Anthony store will be robbed in any given year?
   b. What is the chance that any employee such as Luis or one of the customers would have been killed in the commission of the robbery?
   c. What are some of the common organizational policies and procedures for dealing with a robbery situation? Are they similar to or dissimilar from those of Jiffy Mart? How so?
2. How would you have handled the robbery if you had been in Luis's situation?
3. Did Jiffy Mart's management do the right thing by firing Luis? Why or why not?
4. **(ROLE PLAY)** Step 1: Divide participants into groups of six or seven. Assign students to play the following roles:

   Roles: Company president, Luis Siqueira, Luis Siqueira's district manager, two other district managers, and observers.

   Step 2: The four members of the management team meet to discuss whether the firing of Luis Siqueira is justified, particularly in light of his excellent employment record (Luis did not have any reprimands or prior occurrences during his ten years with Jiffy Mart) and the fact that it will be difficult to find someone as capable.
   a. What did the group decide? What was the rationale they used to arrive at the final decision?
   b. What are the implications of their decision?
   c. What did the group do exceptionally well in arriving at their final decision?
   d. What could the group have done to improve their problem-solving effectiveness?

   Step 3: If the management group sustains the original disciplinary action, what is the likelihood that Luis Siqueira, a member of a protected class, will file discrimination charges against Jiffy Mart for terminating him? What would you think about Luis's allegations that he was (1) only protecting himself, (2) safeguarding company property, and (3) that he was only fired because he is an Hispanic?

   Why might fellow employees and the general public be sympathetic to Luis's arguments?

   Step 4: Each observer announce final action taken by the management team.

(**Staffing**)

PART 4

CHAPTER 9

(The Supervisor and Employee Recruitment, Selection, Orientation, and Training)

After studying this chapter, you will be able to:

1 Discuss the staffing function and describe the role of the human resources department.

2 Explain how the supervisor prepares to fill job openings and why job descriptions and job specifications are essential to this task.

3 Discuss the selection process and the use of directive and nondirective interviewing techniques.

4 Describe how the supervisor should prepare for and conduct an effective selection interview.

5 Explain the hiring decision and the importance of documentation.

6 Understand how to conduct an effective onboarding program.

7 Explain approaches to training and the supervisor's role in employee development.

YOU MAKE THE CALL!

The Staffing Function and the Human Resources Department

The management of human resources is the supervisor's most important activity, and it begins with staffing. As Chapter 2 discusses, staffing is the recruitment, selection, placement, orientation, and training of employees. These activities are part of every supervisor's responsibilities, although in large organizations staff specialists provide help and support. The supervisory staffing function also includes the evaluation of employees' performance and input regarding how employees will be rewarded for their performance.

In a broad sense, **human resource management (HRM)** is the philosophy, policies, procedures, and practices related to the management of people in an organization. To perform the activities necessary to accomplish its goals, every

Human resource management (HRM)
Organizational philosophies, policies, and practices that strive for the effective use of employees

FIGURE 9.1 **An Overview of the Role of the Human Resources Department[2]**

organization must have human resources and use them effectively. To facilitate these activities, many firms have a human resources department with a director of human resources and other personnel.[1]

In most organizations, the director of human resources and the human resources department operate in a staff capacity. The **human resources (HR) department** usually exists to provide advice and service to all departments concerning such employment matters as applicant recruiting, screening, and testing; maintaining personnel records; providing for wage and salary administration; advising line managers on problems of discipline and fair employment practices; and providing other services and assistance. See Figure 9.1 for an overview of the HR functions.

Not every organization has a human resources department. Very small firms, for example, usually do not need or cannot afford to have specialized staff personnel. In these firms, supervisors, in consultation with their managers, may carry out certain employment-related tasks, or the firm may designate someone to share hiring and recordkeeping duties with other managerial personnel. At some point, however, when an organization grows, top-level managers will likely hire a human resources director and staff specialists to help carry out human resources functions. For most organizations, the role and size of the typical human resources department have expanded considerably in recent years. Because of expanded needs, many organizations have found it cost effective to contract out, or outsource, some human resource activities.[3]

HUMAN RESOURCES ADVICE AND SUPERVISORY DECISIONS

Regardless of its official name, the usefulness and effectiveness of any human resources department depends on its ability to develop close working relationships with managers and supervisors. The quality of these line-staff relationships, in turn,

Human resources (HR) department
Department that provides advice and service to other departments on human resource matters

depends on how clearly top-level managers have defined the scope of activities and the authority of the human resources department. Effective human resource professionals are responsible for developing and implementing strategies, policies, and procedures that enable the organization's employees to be the best they can be. Professors Leonard and Cook contend that human resources professionals must:

- Monitor the external environment for forces that are beyond the control of the organization but could affect long-term performance.
- Develop and initiate strategic initiatives that support the organization's mission and objectives.
- Manage the human-resource process, from recruiting and training to compensating and coordinating employee-management relations activities.
- Deal with day-to-day supervisor/employee issues that could impede organizational effectiveness.[4]

The human resources department often is given primary responsibility for certain activities, and supervisors must follow HR requirements with little or no discretion. For example, certain policies and practices regarding Equal Employment Opportunity (EEO), labor relations, and wage rates are typically formulated and directed by the human resources department, but there are many areas and situations in which supervisors must make decisions.

Because employee problems arise continually, supervisors should consult with the human resources department staff for assistance, information, and advice. Human resource staff members usually prefer to offer suggestions to line supervisors, who, in turn, must decide whether to accept, alter, or reject those suggestions or recommendations. Whenever a member of the human resources staff has expertise and knowledge directly related to a decision, the supervisor will usually follow the person's advice and recommendations.

When supervisors feel a recommendation of the human resources staff is not feasible, those supervisors should make their own decisions. For the most part, line supervisors will accept the recommendations of human resources staff members because they are supposed to be experts in employee-relation matters.

There are some situations that pit the supervisors against the HR department. Imagine how your analysis of this chapter's "You Make the Call!" would be different if Paul Sablic had said, "I know a good person when I see one, and Dean Fuller isn't one." The statement is in reference to his apparent disability. Remember that HR has ultimate responsibility to ensure that no applicant is discriminated against because of their race, gender, or other protected characteristics. Supervisors like Sablic must follow both the letter and spirit of CMC's equal employment guidelines as well as federal and state requirements.

Some supervisors readily welcome the willingness of the human resources staff to make certain decisions for them so that they will not have to solve difficult employee problems in their own departments. These supervisors reason that their own departmental tasks are more important than dealing with issues the human resources staff can handle just as well or better than they can. Other supervisors may accept the staff's advice based on the premise that if the decision later proves to be wrong or dubious (e.g., in disciplinary cases), they can say, "It wasn't my choice; human resources made the decision—not me!" For them, it is a relief to rely on the staff's advice and consider it a decision. In so doing, these supervisors defer to the human resources department in the hope they will not be held accountable for the decision. However, even when supervisors follow the advice of the human resources staff, they are still accountable for their decisions.[5]

While it is easy to understand why some supervisors are reluctant to reject the advice of a human resources staff member, those supervisors should recognize that the staff person may see only part of the picture. The director of human resources is not responsible for the performance of a supervisor's department. Usually, many unique factors are better understood by each departmental supervisor than by anyone else.

<table>
<tr><td>2 Explain how the supervisor prepares to fill job openings and why job descriptions and job specifications are essential to this task.</td></tr>
</table>

Preparing to Meet Staffing Needs

The staffing function is an ongoing process for the supervisor; it is not something that is done only when a department is first established. It is more realistic to think of staffing in the typical situation in which a supervisor is placed in charge of an existing department. Although it has a nucleus of employees, changes in the department take place due to employee separations from the workforce, changes in operations or growth, or other reasons. Because supervisors depend on employees for results, they must make certain that there are enough well-trained employees to fill all positions.

DETERMINING THE NEED FOR EMPLOYEES[6]

An ongoing aspect of the supervisory staffing function is that of determining the department's need for employees, both in number and job positions. Supervisors should become familiar with departmental jobs and functions and should consult the organization chart or manual if one is available. For example, the supervisor of a maintenance department may have direct reports who are painters, electricians, and carpenters, each with different skills. The supervisor should study each of these job categories to determine how many positions are needed to get the work done and how employees should work together. The supervisor may have to compromise by adjusting a preferred arrangement to existing realities or by combining several positions into one if there is not enough work of a particular function to keep one employee busy. By carefully studying the organization of the department, the supervisor can reasonably determine how many employees and what skills are needed to accomplish the various work assignments.

DEVELOPING JOB DESCRIPTIONS AND JOB SPECIFICATIONS

After determining the number of positions and skills that are needed, the supervisor's next step is to match jobs with individuals. This usually is done with the aid of job descriptions (as discussed in Chapter 8), which indicate the duties and responsibilities of each job. A supervisor may have access to existing job descriptions; however, when such descriptions are not available, they can be developed with the assistance of higher-level managers or the human resources staff. Similarly, when a new job is created, the supervisor should determine its duties and responsibilities and develop an appropriate job description.

The supervisor may find it helpful to ask departmental employees to write down the tasks they perform during a given period, such as a day or a week. This task list gives the supervisor considerable information from which to develop a job description. While the final job description may be written by a human resources staff person, the supervisor is responsible for determining what goes into it.[7] Figure 9.2 shows a step-by-step approach to developing a job description that would be adaptable to many other types of jobs.

FIGURE 9.2 How to develop job descriptions[8]

The following steps were taken to prepare a job description for the position of housekeeper in a hospital:

Step 1: Prepare a questionnaire to be sent to housekeeping employees and their supervisors asking them to list what they feel are the major functions and subfunctions that must be performed to do this job effectively.

Step 2: Have several higher-level managers who are interested in housekeeping list the functions they feel should and should not be performed by housekeepers.

Step 3: Find out from others in the organization what they believe should and should not be housekeeping functions.

Step 4: Tabulate the results from each of the preceding three sources.

Step 5: Reconcile the three preceding viewpoints with the objectives of your organization, and prepare a detailed list of housekeeper activities.

Step 6: Classify activities as major or minor.

Step 7: Determine what each housekeeper needs to know and what qualifications are necessary to perform designated activities, and specify why each activity is to be performed.

Step 8: Submit the results of Steps 5 through 7 to a committee of housekeepers and supervisors for discussion and recommendations. At this point, you may find that you have listed more than could reasonably be accomplished by a person holding the position. Revise and finalize the job description and job specification as needed.

Step 9: Follow the eight preceding steps when you feel changes in products, equipment, the economic climate, or service demands necessitate a change in the job. Review and update when a position opening occurs and at performance review time.

A supervisor should at least annually compare each job description with what each employee does. Outdated job descriptions that no longer fit job duties should be corrected. The supervisor may find that some of the duties assigned to a job no longer belong to it. These duties should be deleted or assigned elsewhere. Supervisors should not take the preparation of job descriptions lightly because job descriptions can be used to explain to applicants the duties and responsibilities of a job. Job descriptions that describe jobs accurately help supervisors provide realistic job previews, develop performance standards, conduct performance appraisals, and perform other staffing functions.

When the content of each job has been determined or reevaluated, a supervisor next should identify the knowledge and skills that are required of employees who are to perform the job. As discussed in Chapter 8, a written statement of required knowledge, skills, and abilities is called a job specification. The process for determining what an employee must know is found in Figure 9.2, Step 7. Typically, the job description and job specification are combined into one document.

DETERMINING HOW MANY EMPLOYEES TO HIRE

Supervisors are not frequently confronted with a situation in which large numbers of employees have to be hired at the same time. This situation occurs when a new department is created or when a major expansion takes place. The more typical pattern is to hire one or a few employees as the need arises. Of course, some supervisors constantly request additional employees because they feel pressured to get their work done on time. In many cases, however, a supervisor's problems are not solved by getting more help. In fact, the situation may become worse. Instead of reducing problems, new problems may arise due to the inefficiencies that accompany overstaffing.

Normally, a supervisor must hire a replacement when a regular employee leaves the department for reasons such as promotion, transfer, resignation, dismissal, or retirement. There is little question then that the job must be filled. However, if major technological changes or a downsizing are anticipated, a replacement may not be needed. There are other situations in which additional employees must be hired. For example, if new functions are to be added to the department and no one in the department possesses the required knowledge and skills, it may be necessary to go into the labor market and recruit new employees. Sometimes, a supervisor will ask for additional help because the workload has increased substantially and the department is under extreme pressure. Before requesting additional help, the supervisor should make certain that the employees currently in the department are being used fully and that any additional help is necessary and in the budget.

SOLICITING RECRUITMENT AND SELECTION ASSISTANCE

When supervisors have open positions in their departments, they normally ask the human resources department to recruit qualified applicants. Whether a job will be filled by someone from within the organization or someone from outside, the human resources department usually knows where to look to find qualified applicants. Most organizations try to fill job openings above entry-level positions through promotions and transfers. Promotions reward employees for accomplishments; transfers can protect employees from layoffs or broaden their job knowledge. Internal applicants already know the organization, and the costs of recruitment, orientation, and training are usually less than those for external applicants. Hiring from within sends two clear messages:

The human resources department makes reference checks of applicants' employment and other records

- There is a future for someone long-term, not just to grow within the current job but also grow within the company, and
- If you continue to learn more and more about the business and add skills to your toolbox, there are always opportunities waiting for you.[9]

Generally, internal applicants can be found through computerized skills inventories or job postings and biddings. Information on every employee's skills, educational background, work history, and other pertinent data can be stored in a database that can be reviewed to determine quickly whether any employees qualify for a particular job. This procedure helps ensure that every employee who has the necessary qualifications is identified and considered. Most organizations communicate information about job openings by posting vacancy notices on bulletin boards or in newsletters. Interested employees apply or "bid" for vacant positions by submitting applications to the human resources office and copies to the supervisors. Job posting opens the organization by making all employees aware of job opportunities. Job posting and job bidding are common where labor unions represent employees.

Outside sources for job applicants vary depending on the type of job to be filled. In all likelihood, a data-entry clerk will not be recruited from the same source as a medical technologist. Advertising, bulletin boards or other Internet posting, public or private employment agencies, educational institutions, employee referrals, walk-ins, and contract or temporary-help agencies are some of the sources companies may use.[10]

To select from among job seekers, usually the human resources department first has applicants fill out applications, and then it conducts preliminary interviews to determine whether the applicants' qualifications match the requirements of the positions. The human resources department also conducts reference checks of the applicants' employment and background. For certain positions, the department may administer one or more tests to determine whether applicants have the necessary skills and aptitudes.[11] Eventually, applicants who lack the required qualifications are screened out. Those who do have the qualifications are referred to the supervisor of the department where the job is open.

Interviewing and Choosing from Among Qualified Applicants

3 Discuss the selection process and the use of directive and nondirective interviewing techniques.

After the human resources department has screened and selected qualified applicants for a job opening, the departmental supervisor normally interviews each candidate before any decision is made. Supervisors should make, or at least should have considerable input in making, the final decisions to hire candidates for jobs in their departments. However, supervisors should not make staffing decisions without considering the legal ramifications of their decisions. It is easy to understand why supervisors are confused by the numerous laws, executive orders, regulations, and guidelines that they may have heard or read about (see Figure 1.10 on page 25 for an overview of federal legislation affecting supervisors). Title VII of the Civil Rights Act of 1964 prohibits employment discrimination. The Equal Employment Opportunity Commission (EEOC) was created to increase job opportunities for women and minorities and to enforce the law. The law prohibits employment practices that discriminate on the basis of race, gender, color, religion, and national origin. Laws protecting people who have physical and mental disabilities, Vietnam-era and other veterans, and older applicants and employees give a broader definition to the so-called protected classes. These laws are discussed extensively in Chapter 13.

Under equal employment opportunity (sometimes referred to as EEO) and affirmative-action programs, employers must make good-faith efforts to recruit, hire, and promote members of protected classes so that their percentages in the organization approximates their percentages in the labor market. While it is difficult to be current on all aspects of the law, effective supervisors acquaint themselves with the Uniform Guidelines on Employee Selection Procedures because these guidelines apply to all aspects of supervisors' staffing responsibilities.[12]

Corporate restructuring or downsizing—the temporary or indefinite removal of employees from the organization—has created serious staffing concerns. Supervisors are being asked to do more work with fewer employees. The consolidation of various job activities may not be a decision that supervisors make, but it is one those supervisors must live with. Employees may be transferred from one job to another, or additional responsibilities may be added to existing ones. Some employees may even be involuntarily demoted from supervisory or staff positions. Unfortunately, supervisors sometimes may find themselves with little or no authority in staffing decisions. In general, however, the supervisor should make the decision to hire or not.

Regardless of who makes the final hiring decision, selection criteria must be developed. **Selection criteria** are the factors used to differentiate applicants. Education, knowledge, experience, test scores, application forms, background investigations, and interpersonal skills often serve as selection criteria.

THE SELECTION PROCESS

Selection is the process of screening applicants in order to choose the best person for a job. Once job applicants have been located, the next step is to gather information that will help determine who should be hired. Usually, the human resources staff or the supervisor reviews résumés or applications to determine which applicants meet the general qualifications of the position. Then, qualified applicants may be further screened with tests, reference or background checks, and interviews to narrow down the pool of applicants.

For supervisors, the most frequently used selection criterion, and often the most important part of the selection process, is the employee-selection interview.[13] It is difficult to accurately appraise a person's strengths and potential during a brief interview. If there are several applicants for a position, the supervisor must ascertain which applicant is the most qualified, meaning which applicant is most likely to perform best on the job and to stay with the company long-term. The employment interview plays a very important role in the selection process. Depending on the type of job, the applicant may be interviewed by one person or by several members of a work team, but the applicant also is interviewing the organization (see Figure 9.3). How can one reconcile a major employer goal—to promote the organization—with a survey report that twenty percent of job applicants say they were "insulted" in job interviews?[14] The supervisor and team members must properly prepare for the interview and remember that they are "selling" the organization. Interviewing is much more than a technique; it is an art every supervisor must learn. Although our focus in this chapter is on the employee selection interview, over time, every supervisor will conduct or be involved in other types of interviews. Among these are appraisal and counseling interviews, interviews regarding complaints and grievances, interviews regarding disciplinary measures or discharge, and exit interviews when employees quit voluntarily. The basic techniques are common to all interview situations.

ADOPTING BASIC INTERVIEWING APPROACHES

There are two basic approaches to interviewing: directive and nondirective. These approaches are classified primarily according to the amount of structure imposed on the interview by the interviewer. Regardless of the approach used, it is essential that all applicants be asked the same questions and that interviewers receive training in how to conduct legally defensible interviews.[15]

CONDUCTING THE DIRECTIVE INTERVIEW

In a **directive interview**, the interviewer guides the discussion with a predetermined outline and objectives in mind. This approach is sometimes called a "patterned" or "structured" interview. An outline helps the interviewer ask specific questions to cover each topic on which information is wanted. It also allows the interviewer to question and expand on related areas. For example, if a supervisor asks about the applicant's work experience, it may lead to questions about what the applicant liked and did not like about previous jobs. The supervisor guides and

Selection criteria
Factors used to choose among applicants who apply for a job

Selection
The process of choosing the best applicants to fill positions

Directive interview
Interview approach in which the interviewer guides the discussion along a predetermined course

FIGURE 9.3 Setting the Stage of an Effective Employment Interview

Set the Stage (HR department and the Supervisor)
1. Arrange a meeting with HR, the supervisor, and other key employees before the interview to review the interview and selection process.
2. Make sure that all the interviewers know the "do's and don'ts" of interviewing, e.g., appropriate protocol and questions.
3. Remind all interviewers of the implications of EEO laws during the interview process to avoid discriminatory bias.
4. Review the "hard data," i.e., the application form, resume, references, test scores, and, if appropriate, the background check.
5. Make sure the applicant knows what to expect during the interview process.
6. Give the interview the time it takes to "sell the organization" and ascertain the applicant's suitability for the open position.

Goals of the Applicant (the Interviewee)
1. Obtain information about the job.
2. Obtain information about the organization.
3. Ascertain how the opening/vacancy occurred.
4. Determine whether the job matches my needs.
5. Determine whether I want the job.
6. Communicate important information about myself.
7. Favorably impress the employer (the interviewer).

Goals of the Employer (the Interviewer)
1. Involve those who will be working closely with the applicant to provide input into the selection process.
2. Serve as a public relations tool by promoting the organization.
3. Gather information about the applicant.
4. Assess how well the applicant's qualifications match the job requirements.
5. Determine whether the applicant will fit well with the organization and other employees.
6. Differentiate among the applications.
7. Hire the applicant with the most potential.

Note: Ideas for this Figure were adapted from those presented in Kristen Weirick, "The Perfect Interview," *HR Magazine* (April 2008), pp 85–88 and Northeastern University's Career Services "Successful Interviewing" Web site. Students may wish to visit http://careerservices.neu for tips on interviewing.

controls the interview but does not make it a rigid, impersonal experience. If all applicants are asked the same questions, it makes it easier to compare applicants fairly because all applicants respond to the same questions.

CONDUCTING THE NONDIRECTIVE INTERVIEW

The purpose of a **nondirective interview** is to encourage interviewees to talk freely and in depth. The applicant has freedom to determine the course of the discussion. Rather than asking specific questions, the supervisor may stimulate the discussion by asking broad, open-ended questions, such as "Tell me about your work in the computer field." Generally, the supervisor will develop a list of possible topics to cover and, depending on how the interview proceeds, may or may not ask related questions. This unstructured approach to interviewing allows for great flexibility, but it is generally more difficult and time-consuming to conduct than directive interviews. For this reason, the nondirective interview is seldom used in its pure form in employee selection.

Nondirective interview
Interview approach in which the interviewer asks open-ended questions that allow the applicant latitude in responding

BLENDING DIRECTIVE AND NONDIRECTIVE APPROACHES

Ultimately, the purpose of any interview is to promote mutual understanding—to help the interviewer and interviewee understand each other better through open communication. In employee selection interviews, the directive approach is used most often because supervisors find it convenient to obtain information by asking the same direct questions of all applicants. At times, however, supervisors should strive to blend directive and nondirective techniques to obtain additional information that might help them reach a decision. Often, interviewers use situational questions to assess what the applicant would do in a certain situation. All applicants are given a specific situation to which to respond. For example, the question, "How would you assign daily work when two employees are absent?" allows the applicants to organize and express their thoughts about a realistic work situation. The supervisor may gain deeper insight into applicants' abilities to think and solve problems that could make the difference in choosing which applicant to hire.

Would it surprise you that "What computer skills do you have?" is a commonly asked interview question? Regardless of the approach used, the initial questions about computer skills should lead to the development of additional, relevant, job-related questions. For example, questions such as these allow applicants to reveal their knowledge, skills, and values more clearly than could be ascertained from other sources: "What is your knowledge of Quality Companion 2 by Minitab™?"[16] or "Explain how you trained other employees in the use of a quality improvement software program," or a situational interview question such as, "Just as you are walking out the door to take your family to Disney (a scheduled vacation), you receive a phone call from me explaining that a problem has arisen with the computer system and that you are the only one who might be able to come in and take care of things. What would you do?" The supervisor should avoid using judgmental questions, such as, "I believe the IT department is a detriment to our goals. What do you think?" Also, answers to questions that require a "yes" or "no" response, such as, "Do you like to work with figures?" reveal very little about the applicant's ability to perform a job. It is better for the supervisor to ask why the applicant does or does not like to work with figures.

---

4 Describe how the supervisor should prepare for and conduct an effective selection interview.

Preparing for a Selection Interview

Because the purpose of an employee selection interview is to collect information and arrive at a decision concerning a job applicant, the supervisor should prepare carefully for the interview. The supervisor must know what information is needed from the applicant, how to get this information, and how to interpret it. Guidelines for planning and conducting the employee interview are found in the accompanying Supervisory Tips box. We elaborate on these guidelines in the following sections.

As stated earlier, the directive interview is the most common approach for selecting employees. While most supervisors develop their own questions, some organizations have forms and procedures to guide supervisors in interviewing. For example, some firms require supervisors to fill out detailed forms on all applicants who are interviewed. Others use a standard interview form that more or less limits supervisors to only the questions on the form. These interview forms are sometimes used to prevent supervisors from asking questions that might be considered discriminatory and in violation of laws and regulations. Therefore, to prepare for an employee selection interview, the supervisor must know what can be asked and what should not be asked of job applicants during the interview. A general rule is to seek information that is related to job qualifications and the candidate's ability to do the job.

UNDERSTANDING THE INFLUENCE OF EQUAL EMPLOYMENT OPPORTUNITY (EEO) LAWS

EEO legislation has restricted the questions employers may ask job applicants. The overriding principle to follow in employee selection interviews is to ask job-related questions. Questions about topics not related to a person's ability to perform the job should be avoided. For example, asking an applicant for a data-entry clerk position about keyboarding experience is valid. However, asking applicants whether they own or rent their homes is questionable. Employee selection procedures must ensure that legally protected groups, such as minorities and women, are treated fairly. Information that would adversely affect members of protected groups can be used only if it is directly related to the job. For example, the question, "Who cares for your children?" is potentially discriminatory because traditionally it has adversely affected women more than men. On the other hand, the question, "Do you speak Spanish?" is legitimate if speaking Spanish is a job requirement. It would be wrong to ask the question selectively. The same basic questions must be asked of every applicant for a job. When the questions and the selection criteria differ, the hiring decision cannot be justified if it is challenged. Figure 9.4 lists some of the most common areas of unlawful and potentially unlawful inquiry.

SUPERVISORY TIPS

Supervisory Guidelines for Conducting an Employee Interview

- Carefully review the application, the applicant's resume, and other background information about the job candidate.
- Determine the objectives and the form of interview to be conducted (i.e., directive and/or nondirective); develop specific questions to ask.
- Find a quiet, private place to hold the interview where interruptions will not occur.
- After a cordial "warm-up," explain the nature of the job and its requirements; do not attempt to oversell the job or what is needed.
- Ask directive questions to verify information and qualifications on the application and also to fill in any gaps that may be significant to the hiring decision.
- Ask the candidate to state what he or she could most contribute to the job in question; ask the applicant to provide examples of previous job situations that might be relevant.
- Encourage the candidate to speak freely and to ask as many questions as necessary.
- Take notes of the candidate's statements and comments that are most pertinent to meeting the requirements of the job.
- Avoid judging the candidate's suitability until the interview is completed; be aware of possible biases and stereotypes that could unfairly influence the hiring decision.
- Close the interview positively by thanking the candidate and indicating when a hiring decision will be made.

Applications, tests, interviews, reference checks, and physical examinations must be nondiscriminatory and must focus on job-related requirements. To determine whether a selection criterion is appropriate and complies with the law, one consulting firm has suggested the "OUCH" test.[17] OUCH is a four-letter acronym that represents the following:

Objective

Uniform in application

Consistent in effect

Has job relatedness

A selection criterion is objective if it systematically measures an attribute without being distorted by personal feelings. Examples of objective criteria include work sample test scores, number of years of education, degrees, and

FIGURE 9.4 Areas of Unlawful or Potentially Unlawful Questions in Applications and Employment Interviews

Subject of Inquiry	Unlawful or Potentially Unlawful Questions
Applicant's name	1. Maiden name 2. Original name (if legally changed)
Civil and family status	1. Marital status 2. Number and ages of applicant's children 3. Childcare arrangements 4. Is applicant pregnant or does she contemplate pregnancy?
Address	1. Foreign addresses that would indicate the applicant's national origin
Age	1. Before hiring, requests for birth certificate, baptismal certificate, or statement of age
Birthplace	1. Birthplace of applicant (national origin) 2. Birthplace of applicant's spouse, if any, and parents 3. Lineage, ancestry, or nationality
Race and color	1. Any question that would indicate the applicant's race or color
Citizenship	1. Country of citizenship, if not the United States 2. Does the applicant intend to become a U.S. citizen? 3. Citizenship of spouse, if any, and of parents
Disabilities	1. Pre-employment physical examinations or questions about an applicant's physical or mental condition
Religion	1. Religious denomination 2. Clergyperson's recommendation or references 3. Any inquiry into willingness to work a particular religious holiday
Arrests and convictions	1. Numbers and kinds of arrests
Education	1. Nationality, race, or religious affiliation of schools 2. Native tongue or how foreign-language skills were acquired
Organizations	1. Is the applicant a member of any association other than a union and/or a professional or trade organization?
Military experience	1. Type of discharge from the U.S. Armed Forces 2. Did the applicant have military experience with governments other than the U.S. government?
Relatives	1. Names and/or addresses of any relatives

The Immigration Reform and Control Act of 1986 requires that employers determine that anyone they hire is a U.S. citizen or has legal residency status. Visit the U.S. Citizenship and Immigration Services Web site (http://www.uscis.gov) for information on verification of new hires.

length of service in previous positions. Examples of subjective criteria include a supervisor's general impression about a person's interest in a job or feelings that a person is "sharp."

A selection criterion is uniform in application if it is applied consistently to all job candidates. Asking only female applicants a question such as, "Would working on weekends conflict with your childcare arrangements?" is not uniform application. However, it would be permissible to ask all applicants, "Would you be able to meet the job's requirement to work every third weekend?"

A selection criterion is consistent in effect if it has relatively the same proportional impact on protected groups as it does on others. For example, criteria such as possessing a high school diploma or living in a certain area of town may be objective and uniformly applied to all job candidates, but they could screen out proportionately more members of minority groups. When a selection criterion is not consistent in effect, the burden of proof is on the employer to demonstrate that the criterion is job-related.

A selection criterion has job relatedness if it can be demonstrated that it is necessary to perform the job. For example, in most cases it would be extremely difficult to prove that a selection criterion such as marital status is job-related. Job-related criteria should stress the skills required to perform the job.

Supervisors may not always understand the reasons for some of the restrictions imposed on them by the EEO policies of their organizations. They should not hesitate to consult with specialists in the human resources department for explanations and guidance in this regard.

REVIEWING THE APPLICANT'S BACKGROUND

Before interviewing a job applicant, the supervisor should review all background information that has been gathered by the human resources office. By studying whatever is available, the supervisor can develop in advance a mental impression of the general qualifications of the job applicant. The application will supply information concerning the applicant's schooling, experience, and other items that may be relevant.

When studying the completed application, the supervisor should always keep in mind the job for which the applicant will be interviewed. If questions come to mind, the supervisor should write them down to remember them. For example, if an applicant shows a gap of a year in employment history, the supervisor should plan to ask the applicant about this gap and why it occurred.

A supervisor should also review the results of any employment tests taken by the applicant.[18] An increasing number of organizations are administering job-performance, integrity/honesty, and drug tests before the interview stage. Tests should be validated before they are used to help make hiring decisions.

Consider all qualified candidates regardless of appearance

As part of their normal procedures to screen out unqualified applicants, human resources departments often administer job performance tests that measure skill and aptitude for a particular job. The human resources department must be able to document that these tests are valid, job-related, and nondiscriminatory. This typically involves studies and statistical analyses by staff specialists—procedures that are normally beyond the scope of a supervisor's concern. Applicants whose test scores and other credentials appear to be acceptable are referred to the departmental supervisor for further interviewing. It is essential for the supervisor to understand what a test score represents and how meaningful it is in predicting an applicant's job performance. By consulting with the human resources department, the supervisor can become more familiar with the tests that are used and can learn to interpret the test scores.

References provide additional information regarding the applicant. Generally, telephone checks are preferable because they save time and allow for greater feedback. For the most part, information obtained from personal sources, such as friends or character references, will be positively slanted because applicants tend to list only people who will give them good references. Information from previous supervisors who were in positions to evaluate the applicant's work performance is best. However, because of emerging personal privacy regulations and potential damage claims, an employment background investigation is usually conducted by the human resources department. If possible, job references should be obtained in writing, should deal with job-related areas, and should be gathered with the knowledge and permission of the applicant. After reviewing all available background information, the supervisor should be able to identify areas in which little or no information is available and areas that require expansion or clarification.

THE CONSEQUENCES OF FAILING TO CHECK ADEQUATELY

Although no one knows exactly how many people embellish their resumes, a comprehensive study by Automatic Data Processing Inc.'s Screening and Selection Services found that more than 50 percent of the people on whom it conducted employment and education background checks had submitted false information on their resumes.[19] This negligence has led applicants to omit or creatively explain the less positive aspects of their backgrounds. Even when job opportunities are plentiful, really good jobs are still in relatively scarce supply. Some people will lie, cheat, and steal to get great jobs.

Who is responsible for checking a job prospect's credentials and work history? For certain types of low-level, large-scale hiring positions, such as retail clerks, it would be economically and logistically unlikely that a firm would be willing to go beyond just a routine check of resume information. However, the employer could be found negligent and liable if, at some point, an employee engaged in serious misconduct that might have been avoided had the employer fully investigated the individual's background before making its hiring decision.

A common complaint from supervisors and HR departments is that the applicant's former employer will acknowledge only that he or she worked there from this date to this date. The company won't provide any substantive information. As of the time of this writing, more than half of the states have enacted laws granting some measure of immunity from legal liability for employers who respond to reference requests. The laws generally assume that a good-faith effort is being made by the employer and that the information is true and dispensed without malicious intent.[20]

The message in all of this seems to be, "Employers beware! Your employees and potential employees may not be what they claim to be, and there may be trouble ahead if you are negligent in taking some steps to deal with resume exaggeration and fraud." So, is background checking fruitless? No! Businesses today have many companies to turn to for conducting educational, employment, and criminal background checks on applicants. Some managers will contend that the cost of checking is too expensive. We maintain that the costs of not checking can potentially bankrupt the organization.

Consultant and author Bradford Smart recommends using threat of reference check (TORC). He suggests using the question, "If I were to ask you to arrange an interview with your last boss, and the boss were very candid with me, what's your best guess as to what he or she would say were your strengths, weaker points, and overall performance?" The interviewer then may gain insight into what makes this applicant tick and how the person is apt to function in the job.[21]

The importance of verifying reference or application form data cannot be overemphasized. Various organizations have been charged with negligently hiring employees who later commit crimes. Typically, the lawsuits charge that the organizations failed to adequately check the references, criminal records, or general background information that would have shown the employees' propensity for deviant behavior. The rulings in these cases, which range from theft to homicide, should make employers more aware of the need to check applicants' references thoroughly. Not surprisingly, you can be held liable if you knew or should have known that the person you were hiring was a potential risk to others.

As a safeguard, organizations should include on the job application a statement to be signed by the applicant stating that all information presented during the selection process is truthful and accurate. The statement should note that any falsehood is grounds for refusal to hire or for termination.[22]

PREPARING KEY QUESTIONS

In preparing for the interview, the supervisor should develop a list of key questions, which may include directive and nondirective components.[23] It is preferable that the supervisor list six to ten directive and nondirective questions that are vital to the selection decision and are job-related. It is important that all applicants be asked the same set of key questions so that responses can be compared and evaluated. For example, the supervisor may want to know technical information about an applicant's work experience, why the applicant left a previous employer, and whether the applicant can work alternative shift schedules and overtime without difficulty.

Some organizations appear to have changed their focus from fixed job descriptions and job specifications to the competencies that differentiate average performers from superior ones. Ron and Susan Zemke, nationally known HR specialists, contend that, "If you can identify the key skills, knowledge, and personal attributes that make a master performer successful at a given job, then group these things into appropriate clusters, then you have a set of **competencies**. Link each of these broad competencies to a set of behaviors that answer the question, 'How do we know it when we see it?' and they can serve as sort of a blueprint to help you hire, train, and develop people."[24] Figure 9.5 illustrates how to use one competency to develop interview questions. By planning to ask such questions in advance, the supervisor can devote more attention to listening to and observing the applicant instead of having to think about what else should

Competencies
The set of skills, knowledge, and personal attributes possessed by the superior performer

FIGURE 9.5 Using One Competency to Develop Behavioral Indicators and Interview Questions

COMPETENCY: INDEPENDENT JUDGMENT

Definition: Uses discretion in interpreting company procedures to make decisions in ambiguous situations.

Behavioral Indicators

- Performs well with minimal supervision.
- Tries to handle issues independently rather than passing them on.
- Uses the supervisor as a resource but acts independently most of the time.
- Demonstrates the ability to learn and draw inferences from difficult experiences.

Interview Questions

- Describe a situation in which you had to arrive at a quick conclusion and take action.
- Tell me about a situation in which you had to make a decision on your own under pressure.
- Describe a time when you had to rely on your own judgment to make a decision.
- Tell me about the most difficult decision you've had to make in your job. What made it difficult?

Source: This example, from Linkage Inc.'s Interviewing Skills Workshop, appeared in Ron Zemke and Susan Zemke, "Putting Competencies to Work," *Training* (January 1999), p. 72. Reproduced with permission. © 1999. Lakewood Publications, Minneapolis, MN. All rights reserved. Not for resale.

be asked. A thorough plan for the employment interview is well worth the time spent preparing it.

ESTABLISHING A CONDUCIVE PHYSICAL SETTING

Privacy and some degree of comfort are important components of a good interview setting. When a private room is not available, the supervisor should at least create an atmosphere of semi-privacy by speaking to the applicant in a place where other employees are not within hearing distance. This much privacy, at least, is necessary.

CONDUCTING THE SELECTION INTERVIEW

The employee selection interview is not just a one-way questioning process; the applicant also will want to know more about the company and the job. The interview should enable job seekers to learn enough to help them decide whether to accept the position if it is offered. The supervisor must conduct the interview professionally by opening the interview effectively, explaining the job requirements, and using good questioning and note-taking techniques.

OPENING THE INTERVIEW

The experience of applying for a job is often filled with tension for an applicant. It is to the supervisor's advantage to relieve this tension. Some supervisors try to create a feeling of informality by starting the interview with social conversation about the weather, city traffic, the World Series, or some broad-interest but noncontroversial topic. The supervisor may offer a cup of coffee or make some other appropriate social gesture. An informal opening can help reduce an applicant's tensions, but it should be brief and then the discussion should move quickly to job-related matters.

Many supervisors begin the employee selection interview with a question that is nonthreatening and easily answered by the applicant but that contains job-related information the supervisor might need. An example is, "How did you learn about this job opening?"

The supervisor should avoid excessive informal conversation because studies of employee selection interviews have revealed that frequently an interviewer makes a favorable or an unfavorable decision after the first five minutes of the interview. If the first ten minutes are spent discussing items not related to the job, the supervisor may be basing the selection decision primarily on irrelevant information.

EXPLAINING THE JOB

During the interview, the supervisor should discuss details of the job, working conditions, wages, benefits, and other relevant factors in a realistic way. A **realistic organizational preview (ROP)** includes sharing complete information about the organization: its mission, philosophy, opportunities, and other information that gives applicants a good idea of where the job fits in and why it is important. In discussing the job, a **realistic job preview (RJP)** informs applicants about the desirable and undesirable aspects of the job. Because of eagerness to make a job look as attractive as possible, the supervisor may be tempted to describe conditions in terms that make it more attractive than it is in reality. For example, a supervisor might oversell a job by describing in glowing terms the possible career progression that is available only for exceptional employees. If the applicant is hired and turns out to be an average worker, this could lead to disappointment and frustration. Applicants who are given realistic information are more likely to remain on the job because they will encounter fewer unpleasant surprises.[25]

Realistic organizational preview (ROP)
Sharing information by an interviewer with a job applicant concerning the mission, values, and direction of the organization

Realistic job preview (RJP)
Information given by an interviewer to a job applicant that provides a realistic view of both the positive and negative aspects of the job

ASKING EFFECTIVE QUESTIONS

Even though the supervisor will have some knowledge of the applicant's background from the application and from information the applicant volunteers, the need still exists to determine the applicant's specific qualifications for the job. The supervisor should not ask the applicant to repeat information on the application. Instead, the supervisor should rephrase questions to probe for additional details. For example, the question, "What was your last job?" is likely to be answered on the application. This question could be expanded as follows: "As a computer technician at Omega, what type of computer problems did you most frequently encounter?" Then a follow-up question would be, "How did you solve that problem?"

A supervisor must use judgment and tact when questioning applicants. The supervisor should avoid such leading or trick questions as, "Do you have difficulty getting along with other people?" or "Tell me about a person in your last work situation who you would describe as your least preferred co-worker." Questions like these are sometimes used by interviewers to see how applicants respond to difficult personal questions. However, these questions may antagonize the applicants. By no means should the supervisor pry into personal affairs that are irrelevant or removed from the work situation.

TAKING NOTES

In their efforts to make better selection decisions, many supervisors take notes during or immediately after the interview. Written information is especially important when a supervisor interviews a number of applicants. Trying to

Interviewing is much more than a technique; it is an art every supervisor must learn

© MIKE POWELL/TAXI

remember what several applicants said during their interviews and exactly who said what is virtually impossible.

However, the supervisor should avoid writing while an applicant is answering a question. Instead, it is more courteous and useful for the supervisor to jot down brief response summaries after the applicant has finished talking. While the supervisor is not required to take notes on everything said in the interview, key facts that might aid in choosing one applicant over the others should be noted.

AVOIDING INTERVIEWING AND EVALUATION PITFALLS

The chief problem in employee selection usually lies in interpreting the applicant's background, personal history, and other pertinent information. As human beings, supervisors are unable to eliminate their personal preferences and prejudices, but they should face their biases and make efforts to avoid or control them. Supervisors should particularly avoid making judgments too quickly during interviews with job applicants. Although it is difficult not to form an early impression, the supervisor should complete the interview before making any decision and should strive to apply the **OUCH** test to avoid the numerous pitfalls that can occur both during and after an interview.

Supervisors also should avoid generalizations. The situation in which a supervisor generalizes from one aspect of a person's behavior to all aspects of the person's behavior is known as the "halo" or "horns" effect. In practice, the halo or horns effect means that the supervisor bases the overall impression of an individual on only partial information about that individual and uses this limited impression as a primary influence in rating all other factors. This may work favorably (the **halo effect**) or unfavorably (the **horns effect**), but in either case, it is improper. For example, the halo effect occurs when supervisors assume that if applicants have superior interpersonal skills, they also will be good at

Halo effect
The tendency to allow one favorable aspect of a person's behavior to positively influence judgment on all other aspects

Horns effect
The tendency to allow one negative aspect of a person's behavior to negatively influence judgment on all other aspects

keyboarding, working with little direction, and so forth. On the other hand, when supervisors judge applicants with hearing impairments as being low on communication skills and allow this assessment to serve as a basis for low ratings on other dimensions, the horns effect prevails. The process we have suggested does not guarantee that the supervisor will not form erroneous opinions. However, objectivity minimizes the chances of making the wrong choice.

CLOSING THE INTERVIEW

At the conclusion of the employee selection interview, the supervisor will likely have a choice among several alternatives, ranging from hiring the applicant to deferring the decision to rejecting the applicant. The supervisor's decision will be guided by the policies and procedures of the organization. Some supervisors have the authority to make selection decisions independently; others are required to check with their managers or the human resources department. Still others may have the authority only to recommend which applicant should be hired. For purposes of brevity, we assume in the following discussion that the supervisor has the authority to make the final selection decision. Under these circumstances, the supervisor can decide to hire an applicant on the spot. All the supervisor has to do is tell the applicant when to report for work and provide any additional, pertinent instructions.

If the supervisor wishes to defer the decision until several other candidates for the job have been interviewed, the applicant should be informed that he or she will be notified later. The supervisor should indicate a timeframe within which the decision will be made. However, it is unfair to use this tactic to avoid the unpleasant task of telling an applicant that he or she is not acceptable. By telling the applicant that a decision is being deferred, the supervisor gives the applicant false hope. While waiting for the supervisor's decision, the applicant might not apply for other jobs, thereby letting opportunities slip by. Therefore, if a supervisor has made the decision not to hire an applicant, the supervisor should tell the applicant tactfully. Some supervisors merely say that there was not a sufficient match between the needs of the job and the qualifications of the applicant. Tony Lee, editor in chief at CareerJournal.com, said it best:

> *Although rejecting all but one applicant is part of the process, employers should be cautious in how they communicate with potential new hires. Remember that those applicants may buy your products and services and have long memories of how they're treated. Nothing can damage a company's reputation faster than bad word of mouth.*[26]

Regardless of its outcome, applicants should leave interviews feeling that they have been treated fairly and courteously. It is every supervisor's managerial duty to build as much goodwill as possible because it is in the organization's self-interest to maintain a good image.

COMPLETING THE POST-INTERVIEW EVALUATION FORM

Some organizations have the supervisor and other members of the interview team complete an evaluation form shortly after the interview while the information is still fresh in their minds. Figure 9.6 is an adaptation of a form used by one retail store. Its approach increases the likelihood that the same selection criteria are applied to each applicant. Other firms may require that supervisors submit a written evaluation that summarizes their impressions of and recommendations for each job candidate.

FIGURE 9.6 A Post-interview Evaluation Form

POST-INTERVIEW EVALUATION FORM		
Position	Major Job Requirements	
	(List major job requirements here.)	
Applicant's Name:	(Evaluate SKAs here.)	
		(Total)
Strengths:		
Weaknesses:		
Applicant's Name:	(Evaluate SKAs here.)	
		(Total)
Strengths:		
Weaknesses:		
Applicant's Name:	(Evaluate SKAs here.)	
		(Total)
Strengths:		
Weaknesses:		

Instructions to Interviewers

1. The interviewer(s) may decide that some job requirements are more important than others. Therefore, it may be appropriate to assign weights to those requirements to illustrate their relative importance.
2. Evaluate each applicant's skills, knowledge, or abilities (SKAs) for each of the major job requirements:
   - 1 = Unacceptable   2 = Moderately acceptable
   - 3 = Acceptable   4 = Strongly acceptable
3. Total the rating for each applicant. (By totaling the ratings, the interviewer[s] will have a system by which to make a more objective choice.)
4. Record each applicant's strengths and weaknesses.
5. Make a copy of the form: (a) Retain one copy for documentation. (b) Deliver one copy to HR.

Making the Hiring Decision

5 Explain the hiring decision and the importance of documentation.

The decision to hire can be challenging when the supervisor has interviewed several applicants and all appear qualified for the job. There are no definite guidelines a supervisor can use to select the best-suited individual. At times, information from the applications, tests, and interviews indicate which applicants should be hired.[27] However, there will be other times when information is unconvincing or perhaps is even conflicting. For example, an applicant's aptitude test score for a sales job may be relatively low, but the person has favorably impressed the supervisor in the interview by showing an enthusiastic interest in the job and a selling career.

At this point, supervisory judgment and experience come into play. The supervisor must select employees who are most likely to contribute to good departmental performance. The supervisor may consult with members of the human resources staff for their evaluations, but, in the final analysis, it should be the supervisor's responsibility to choose. Before the final decision is made, the supervisor should evaluate each applicant against the selection criteria. By carefully analyzing all the information and keeping in mind previous successes and failures in selecting employees, the supervisor should be able to select applicants who are most likely to succeed.

Of course, hiring decisions always involve uncertainties. There are no exact ways to predict how individuals will perform until they are placed on the job. A supervisor who approaches the hiring decision thoroughly, carefully, and professionally is likely to consistently select applicants who will become excellent employees.

INVOLVING EMPLOYEES IN THE HIRING DECISION

The degree to which employees are involved in the selection process differs among organizations. Generally, subordinates, peers, or work-team members meet with the applicant and give their impression to the ultimate decision maker. Members of employee work teams, for example, are generally most knowledgeable about job responsibilities and challenges. They can offer valuable insight into the employee selection process. Even without formal teams, some organizations allow employees to fulfill various roles, from assisting with the definition of job responsibilities to having a direct say in the final hiring decision. However, it is important to note that the downside of involving employees in the hiring decision is the possibility of favoritism and violation of EEOC regulations. Supervisors must be aware of company policies regarding **nepotism**. The practice of hiring relatives may eliminate other applicants from consideration.[28]

Nepotism
The practice of hiring relatives

DOCUMENTING THE HIRING DECISION

Documentation is necessary to ensure that a supervisor's decision to accept or reject an applicant is based on job-related factors and is not discriminatory. At times, a supervisor's hiring decision will be challenged; the supervisor must be able to justify that decision or risk it being reversed by higher-level managers. Similarly, supervisors sometimes will be strongly encouraged by higher-level managers or human resources staff members to give preferential hiring considerations to minority or female applicants, especially if the organization is actively seeking such employees. Some supervisors resent this type of pressure, but they should recognize that the organization may be obligated under various laws to meet certain hiring goals. In general, when supervisors follow the approaches suggested in this chapter, they should be able to distinguish the most qualified people from among applicants and also be prepared to justify their employment selections.

6 Understand how to conduct an effective onboarding program.

Orientation
The process of smoothing the transition of new employees into the organization

Onboarding
A continuous process of assimilation and growth within the organization for new hires

Bringing New Employees Onboard

According to author Carole Fleck, "Some organizations use the terms *orientation* and *onboarding* interchangeably, but there is a difference."[29] In large organizations, when new employees report for their first day of work, HR usually conducts an initial session that familiarizes the new hire with the organization's vision, structure, culture, handbook, policies, and procedures, and perhaps includes a quick tour of the facilities. This initial phase is called orientation.[30] **Orientation** is a process designed to help new employees become acquainted with the organization and understand the organization's expectations. In short, orientation helps the employee develop a sense of belonging to the organization.

Onboarding occurs when the new employee begins and continues indefinitely. It is about helping employees to understand their roles, effectively perform their jobs, learn new tasks, gain new SKAs, and acquire the attitudes, behaviors, and knowledge needed to be a successful member of the team. Helping new employees to feel comfortable in their new work environment is a supervisory responsibility. The supervisor sets the stage for building working relationships within the department and may want to select a couple of employees to serve as guides or resources for the new hire. A chain hardware and building supply company has hitched their new hires to several of their "stars." The stars model the desired behaviors and can serve as mentors or coaches for the new employee. Some organizations have found it beneficial to add a pre-boarding component that provides information online so that the new hire can sign up for benefits, computer passwords, and other necessities before they show up the first day.[31] As shown in Figure 9.7, there are several important aspects that the supervisor must consider to help the employee become a "star."

FIGURE 9.7 Getting new hires onboard

The manner in which the supervisor welcomes them and introduces new hires to other employees in the department may have a lasting effect on their future performance. The first days on the job for most new employees are disturbing and anxious. They typically feel like strangers in new surroundings among people whom they have just met. It is the supervisor's responsibility to make the transition as smooth as possible by leading new employees in the desired directions and helping them become productive as soon as possible.

A supervisor can use several approaches to bringing new employees onboard. The supervisor may choose to escort new employees around the department personally, showing them equipment and facilities and introducing them to other employees. However, the supervisor may prefer to assign new employees to an experienced, capable employee and have this person do all the orienting, perhaps even instructing new employees on how to perform their jobs.

USING A CHECKLIST

A useful technique to ensure that new employees are well-oriented is to use a checklist. When developing an orientation checklist, the supervisor should strive to identify all the things that a new employee ought to know. The supervisor should ask the question: "To do this job well, what does a new employee need to know?" Without some type of checklist, the supervisor is apt to skip some important items. Checklists can also be used to help new employees understand the company and its objectives, and to build a more positive attitude toward the supervisor, fellow employees, and the company.

DISCUSSING THE ORGANIZATION

In most firms, the human resources department provides booklets that give general information about the firm, including benefits, policies, and procedures. There may even be a formal class that provides this type of information to employees and includes a tour of the firm's facilities. In small firms, it may be appropriate to introduce new employees to the owner or top-level managers. In large firms, this may not be practical, so sometimes these firms videotape an interview with the CEO or other members of top-level management in which the CEO/managers present the company's vision for the future, corporate philosophy, market and product development, and the like.[32] Employees should receive an explanation of what they can expect from the organization. Realistic organization and job previews should clarify employee expectations. The key is that the information must be accurate and that all employees must receive the same information.

A common mistake supervisors make when onboarding new employees is to give them too much information on the first day. Presenting too many items in a very short time may result in information overload. New employees are unlikely to remember many details when those details are presented in the first two hours of the first day. Consequently, the supervisor should spread different aspects over a new employee's first few weeks or months. Also, the supervisor should schedule a review session several days or weeks later to discuss any problems or questions the new employee might have.

BEING SUPPORTIVE

More important than the actual techniques used to orient new employees are the attitudes and behaviors of the supervisor. When a supervisor conveys sincerity in trying to make the transition period a pleasurable experience and tells new employees that they should not hesitate to ask questions, it will smooth the early days on the job. Even when the human resources department provides formal orientation, it remains the supervisor's responsibility to help each new person quickly become an accepted member of the departmental work team and a contributing, productive employee.

SETTING THE STAGE

Supervisory responsibility goes beyond making sure that the employee has received a handbook and department work rules. The supervisor should inform the other employees that someone new is joining the group and should let them know something positive about the new person. Imagine how difficult it would be for a person to be received into the work group if the employees had been told "we had to hire this person." The supervisor needs to set the stage for the new employee's arrival so that the new employee is socialized properly into the work group.

Organizations that use work teams believe in spreading authority, responsibility, and accountability throughout the organization. For many employees, this has meant learning to work more closely with others as team members and depending on each other for the completion of assigned tasks. Over time, effective teams develop open communication and relationships. New employees need to understand the purpose and goals of the work group, why the job is important, and where the job fits in. They also need to understand the roles various team members fulfill. Supervisors must make certain that members of the work team understand that it is their responsibility to communicate and contribute to this understanding.

Part of the onboarding process is to shape positively the new employee's behavior. Because people observe and imitate others' behavior, it is not enough for a supervisor simply to state what is expected of the employee. People tend to act—productively and counterproductively—like those with whom they closely identify. Effective work-team members model positive norms for the new employee. An effective technique is to place the new employee with an outstanding performer who acts as a coach or mentor. The reason for placing the new employee with an outstanding performer is to perpetuate excellent performance. Finally, as discussed in Chapter 4, all employees need positive feedback on performance, and an effective supervisor reinforces the new employee's early successes by giving sincere praise.

MENTORING

Mentoring
An experienced employee guiding a newer employee in areas concerning job and career

Since the publication of the classic *Harvard Business Review* article "Everyone Who Makes It Has a Mentor," researchers have explored the roles that mentors or sponsors play in employee development.[33] **Mentoring** is the process of having a more-experienced person provide guidance, coaching, or counseling to a less-experienced person. Broadly defined, the mentor teaches "the tricks of the trade," gives the new employee all the responsibility he or she can handle, thrusts the new employee into new areas, directs and shapes performance, suggests how things are to be done, and provides protection.[34]

Mentoring should be looked upon as one way to smooth the transition of new employees into the organization and develop them into productive employees. New employees can build a network of people who can collectively provide the many benefits of a mentor. The ultimate question for the new employee is, "How do I attach myself to a role model who will guide my career?" Professor Kathy Kram suggests, "Putting all your eggs in one basket is a mistake. I think people ought to think in terms of multiple mentors instead of just one. Peers can be an excellent source of mentorship."[35] Increasingly, new employees are responsible for their career development. How does one go about selecting a mentor? Kram says, "Would-be mentors are most receptive to people who ask good questions, listen well to the responses, and demonstrate that they are hungry for advice and counsel. Mentoring is a chance for the mentor to revitalize their own learning."[36] Should supervisors mentor? Yes, when they feel comfortable doing so. In Chapter 11, we further discuss the delegation of authority, which the supervisor can do to add to the employee's knowledge base and which can be considered a form of mentoring.

Training and Developing Employees

> **7** Explain approaches to training and the supervisor's role in employee development.

In today's world, I like to see every person as a potential coach. While that may seem farfetched, think back over the last ten years of your life. Who provided you with an opportunity to add SKAs to your toolbox? Who encouraged you to get into situations that caused you to learn something new and unusual? Who forced you to think independently or gave you an opportunity to make a difference (contribute in ways that you never thought possible)? Was there a person who helped unlock your potential? Your success is a tribute to all of those who helped you along the way. The supervisor/coach does not have to be a solution provider, but rather one who engages employees in activities that help them to reach their potential and the organization to reach or exceed its goals.[37]

In most job situations, new employees require general and specific training. When skilled workers are hired, the primary training need may be in the area of company and departmental methods and procedures. When unskilled or semiskilled workers are hired, they (the trainees) must understand the importance of the job and why each step must be done correctly. The supervisor or another capable employee should demonstrate the proper way to do the job. It is critical to the learning process that the supervisor frequently monitor the work being performed, answer questions, make adjustments, provide additional guidance as necessary, and encourage them. We will further discuss the supervisor's coaching responsibilities in Chapter 10 (see Figure 10.9 for an overview of the supervisor's coaching responsibilities).

Formal training methods vary among organizations and depend on the unique circumstances of each situation. At the department level, helping employees improve their SKAs to perform current and future jobs is an ongoing responsibility of the supervisor.[38] Remember: If the "trainee fails, the supervisor/ coach fails."

PROVIDING ON-THE-JOB TRAINING

Most training at the departmental level takes the form of on-the-job training. The supervisor may prefer to do as much of the training as time permits. Doing on-the-job training provides the advantage of helping the supervisor get to know the new employees while they are being trained. It also ensures uniform training, because the same person is training everyone. When the supervisor lacks the time or the technical skills to do the training, the training should be done by one of the best employees. The supervisor should give the training task only to experienced employees who enjoy this additional assignment and are qualified to do it. The supervisor should follow up periodically to see how each new employee is progressing.

When supervisors do on-the-job training, they can get to know their new employees

PROVIDING OFF-THE-JOB TRAINING

Many training programs for new and existing employees are conducted outside of the immediate work area. Some of these training programs may be coordinated or taught by human resources staff or training departments. For skilled crafts involving, for example, electricians, machinists, or toolmakers, a formal apprenticeship training program may be established. Usually these programs require employees to be away from the job for formal schooling and work part of the time.

Increasingly, business firms are initiating college-campus-based programs for employee training. Generally, college representatives work together with the firm's supervisors to develop a curriculum for employees. Employees attend classes on the campus during nonworking hours. Tuition is paid by the firm, and employees receive credit for taking classes related to their jobs. A continual process of curriculum review and assessment of employees' on-the-job performance ensures that the program meets the firm's needs.

E-learning and other non-traditional instructional technologies have gained in popularity. Most of these allow the employee to work on company time and at their own speed. These approaches allow the company to bring the training directly to the employees and can be specialized to individual needs. A limitation is that employees may not retain the material as well as they would in face-to-face hands-on training.[39]

There also may be programs offered within the firm during or outside of working hours. For example, safety training meetings and seminars are commonly scheduled during working hours for supervisors and employees alike.

ENSURING ONGOING EMPLOYEE DEVELOPMENT

Supervisors should assess the skills and potential of employees and should provide opportunities for the ongoing development of employee skills so that those employees can perform better now and in the future. When supervisors believe that training is needed that cannot be provided at the departmental level, those supervisors should go to higher-level managers or to the human resources department to see whether there are courses outside the organization that can meet training needs.

Many organizations have tuition-aid programs to help employees further their education. A supervisor should be aware of course offerings at nearby educational institutions and encourage employees to take advantage of all possible educational avenues. These learning experiences can help employees develop the SKAs that improve their performance and prepare them for more demanding responsibilities.[40]

UNDERSTANDING THE SUPERVISOR'S ROLE IN EMPLOYEE DEVELOPMENT

The impetus for a training program can come from many directions, but generally, operating problems and the failure to accomplish organizational objectives may highlight the need for training. Training activities should be based on the identification of the combined needs of the organization and the employees.

Training must be viewed as an ongoing developmental process, not a simple solution to a short-term problem. Therefore, training must be relevant, informative, interesting, and applicable to the job, and it must actively involve the trainee. As Confucius put it:

I hear and I forget;
I see and I remember;
I do and I understand.

Skills that employees need to perform essential departmental tasks should be the initial training focus. However, in the current business environment, **cross-training** is becoming essential. Downsizings, outsourcing, or **RIFs** (reductions in force) have left hundreds of thousands of employees wondering what the future holds. Consolidation of job duties suggests that supervisors must identify the jobs that are important to the ongoing performance of their departments and that other employees can learn. Employees will need to learn new skills that will make them more valuable to their organizations. Cross-trained employees learn how to do a variety of jobs within the organization. An employee's ability to perform a variety of tasks makes him or her more valuable and able to assume additional responsibilities in the future.

Cross-training
Training employees to do multiple tasks and jobs

RIF
An acronym for "reduction in force"

In formulating an employee-development program, supervisors should seek answers to the following types of questions:

- Who, if anyone, needs training?
- What training do they need?
- What are the purposes of the training?
- What are the instructional objectives that need to be incorporated into the training program? (Instructional objectives are basically what the employee will know or be able to do upon completing the training.)
- Which training and development programs best meet the instructional objectives?
- What benefits are anticipated to be derived from the training?
- What will the program cost?
- When and where will the training take place?
- Who will conduct the training?
- How will the training effort be evaluated?[41]

Efficient and effective training should contribute to the achievement of organizational objectives. Instructional objectives are essential to an evaluation plan. Training and development expert Donald Kirkpatrick formulated four levels of evaluation that can be used to measure the benefits of training:

1. Employees' reactions to the training program
2. Employees' learning
3. Employees' application of learning to the job
4. The training's business results[42]

MAKING YOURSELF MORE VALUABLE

The need for training and development is not limited to departmental employees. Supervisors also need training and development to avoid obsolescence or status-quo thinking. By expanding their perspectives, supervisors are more likely to encourage employees to improve their knowledge and abilities and to keep up to date.

Most supervisors attend supervisory management training and development programs as well as courses in the technical aspects of company and departmental operations. Supervisors may want to belong to one or more professional or technical associations whose members meet periodically to discuss problems and topics of current interest and share experiences. In addition, supervisors should subscribe to technical and managerial publications and should read articles of professional interest.

We contend that today, more than at any other time, supervisors are responsible for their own destinies. To survive, supervisors must give some thought to their long-term career development. Ambitious supervisors will find it helpful to formulate career plans by writing down the goals that they would like to achieve in the next three to five years. Such plans include a preferred pattern of assignments and job positions and a listing of educational and training activities that will be needed as part of career progression.

Our former students have reported that Richard Bolles's *What Color Is Your Parachute? A Practical Manual for Job-Hunters and Career-Changers* helped them to think and rethink their career options and opportunities. In an interview, Bolles outlined his career-development strategies:

> *Sending out resumes doesn't work. Neither does answering ads. Employment agencies? No way. What does work is figuring out what you like to do and what you do well—and then finding a place that needs people like you. Contact organizations you're interested in, even if they don't have known vacancies. Pester others for leads.*[43]

SUMMARY

1 Managing human resources should be one of the supervisor's top priorities. In fulfilling staffing responsibilities, the supervisor can be substantially aided by the human resources department. Some organizations use firms that supply temporary workers to do some of the staffing work.

There should be a balance of authority between line supervisors and human resources staff in staffing policies and decisions. Usually, the human resources department aids in recruitment—advertising the opening, recruiting a pool of applicants, screening, testing, checking backgrounds, and the like. The departmental supervisor then interviews applicants and either makes or has most of the say in the final hiring decision.

The pervasive presence of equal employment opportunity (EEO) laws and regulations has resulted in the human resources staff assuming much of the responsibility to ensure that an organization's employment policies and practices comply with these laws. Sometimes, human resources departments take primary responsibility for such things as hiring, interpreting policy, determining selection criteria, writing job descriptions and specifications, and testing applicants. Supervisors should not release these staffing areas to human resources totally, although at times it might seem expedient to do so. A supervisor remains accountable for decisions, even when relying on the advice of the human resources staff.

2 One ongoing process of staffing is determining how many employees and what skills are needed to accomplish various work assignments. Job descriptions indicate the duties and responsibilities of the job and must be reviewed periodically. Job descriptions that accurately describe jobs help supervisors provide realistic job previews, develop performance standards, conduct performance appraisals, and other staffing functions.

Job specifications detail the SKAs an employee should have to perform a job adequately. Applicants are recruited and screened based on the job specifications.

Supervisors must ascertain how current employees are being used before they make requests for additional help. When new functions are added to the department or the workload increases substantially, supervisors must determine the number and types of employees needed.

3 Selection is the process of choosing the best applicant to fill a particular job. After job applicants are located, information must be gathered to help in determining who should be hired.

Supervisors are most likely to be involved in employee selection interviews. Two basic approaches are the directive interview and the nondirective interview. The directive interview is highly structured; the supervisor asks each applicant specific questions and guides the discussion. In the nondirective interview, the supervisor allows the applicant freedom to determine the course of the discussion.

Regardless of the approach, supervisors should develop job-related questions. Situational questions may be used to assess how the applicant would act in a given situation. Trick questions and questions that can be answered with a simple "yes" or "no" should be avoided.

4 It is vital for a supervisor to thoroughly prepare for the selection interview. A supervisor should be aware of EEO restrictions and should ask only job-related questions that foster nondiscriminatory treatment. Selection criteria should be objective, uniform in application, consistent in effect, and job related. Before conducting the interview, the supervisor should review the applicant's application, test scores, and other background materials. With a list of key questions, the supervisor should be able to cover the most important areas in which more information is needed.

The supervisor may open the employee selection interview by using an approach that reduces tension, such as asking a question that is easily answered. The supervisor should explain the job, use effective questioning techniques, and take appropriate notes.

When evaluating an applicant, the supervisor should avoid such common pitfalls as making hasty judgments; allowing

generalizations, such as the halo effect or the horns effect; or forming impressions based on personal biases or preferences. The OUCH test will help the supervisor minimize judgmental errors.

At the conclusion of the interview, the supervisor should remember that the applicant is entitled to a decision as soon as possible. The supervisor should strive to have the applicant leave with an impression of fair and courteous treatment.

5 The supervisor wants to select employees who will contribute to excellent departmental performance. A review of the selection criteria is critical to identifying the best applicant. Depending on the organization, subordinates, peers, or team members may have a say in determining who is hired. This involvement varies from assistance in defining job duties to having a say in the final decision.

Documentation of the selection process is critical in helping to demonstrate that the process is based on job-related factors and is nondiscriminatory.

6 Efficiently and effectively bringing employees onboard should be one of the supervisor's top priorities. Traditionally, orientation means helping new employees become acquainted with the organization and its policies and procedures. This is done with the help of the HR department. The supervisor ensures that new hires understand what is expected in the way of job duties. A checklist can ensure that each new employee receives the same information. In most large organizations, the human resources department helps the supervisor with the basic orientation process. Effective onboarding is a process that continues beyond the first day on the job. The supervisor's supportive attitude and the involvement of other employees are significant. Using other employees as mentors is an effective way to shape the new employee's behavior positively. Positive role models, coaches, or mentors should be used to perpetuate excellent performance standards.

7 The notion of the supervisor as coach and mentor is depicted in Figure 1.5 on page 12. On-the-job training is one of the supervisor's major responsibilities. When supervisors lack the time or technical skills to do the training personally, they can delegate the task to an experienced employee with excellent job performance. Off-the-job training programs also can help employees perform better. Training and development is a continual process, not just a one-time effort.

Supervisors must determine the skills employees need to do their jobs better. Factors such as failure to meet organizational objectives, operating problems, introduction of new machines and equipment, and addition of new job responsibilities to a position can help the supervisor pinpoint training needs. The supervisor should constantly monitor the training that each person needs. Instructional objectives and a procedure for evaluating the effectiveness of training are essential.

Also, supervisors must recognize the need for their own training and development, and they should explore all opportunities for career development. Supervisors should consider having career plans to help them chart and monitor their long-term career progression.

KEY TERMS

Competencies (p. 319)

Cross training (p. 331)

Directive interview (p. 312)

Halo effect (p. 322)

Horns effect (p. 322)

Human resources (HR) department
(p. 306)

Human resource management (HRM)
(p. 305)

Mentoring (p. 328)

Nepotism (p. 325)

Nondirective interview (p. 313)

Onboarding (p. 326)

Orientation (p. 326)

Realistic job preview (RJP) (p. 321)

Realistic organizational preview (ROP)
(p. 321)

RIF (p. 331)

Selection (p. 312)

Selection criteria (p. 312)

QUESTIONS FOR DISCUSSION

1. What are some of the major activities of the human resources department that can assist the line supervisor in the staffing function? What should be the primary responsibility of the human resources staff and of line supervisors for various employment and other staffing activities? Is there a clear dividing line of responsibility? Discuss.

2. Define some of the major laws and regulations governing equal employment opportunity (EEO). Why have many organizations assigned to the human resources department the primary responsibility for making sure that their employment policies and practices are in compliance?

3. Why is adequate supervisory preparation for an employee selection interview crucial to the interview's success? Discuss each of the following aspects of conducting an employee selection interview:
   a. Opening the interview
   b. Explaining the job

   c. Using effective questioning techniques
   d. Taking notes
   e. Concluding the interview

4. Do you remember your first day on a job? What were your feelings? Most of our students admit to being nervous as well as concerned about their ability to measure up.
   a. Why do many employers fail to adequately "socialize" or "orient" their new hires to the organization?
   b. How is onboarding for a new employee related to future performance? Discuss the approaches a supervisor may take in onboarding a new employee.
   c. Why is on-the-job training most likely to be the type of training used at the departmental level?
   d. Enumerate the other training and development approaches that may be available.
   e. Why should training programs be evaluated?

SKILLS APPLICATIONS

Skills Application 9-1: What Would You Do?

Fortunately for CMC and Paul Sablic, there was an ample pool of potentially qualified applicants for the purchasing department position. It was apparent that at least four applicants met the job specifications and passed the work sampling tests. Based on Sablic's numerical ranking system, Helen Hocyk clearly was the number-one choice. She was offered the job and accepted.

No one likes to be accused of bias or prejudice. Dean Fuller waved the "d-card" and Michael Connors and Paul Sablic must prepare for the worst-case scenario—a complaint filed by Fuller with the EEOC or other government agency. These series of exercises are designed to help you better understand the importance of covering all the right bases in the selection process.

   a. Identify a number of unlawful and potentially unlawful areas of inquiry.
   b. Review the BFOQs (Bona Fide Occupational Qualifications) that Paul Sablic and CMC (see this chapter's "You Make the Call!") might use to show that certain selection criteria are reasonably necessary to meet the "normal" operations of the purchasing department.

2. Why is it important for supervisors to be up-to-date on legislation that affects staffing decisions?

3. Working alone, prepare a list of things that CMC and supervisor Paul Sablic might use to demonstrate that they followed the "spirit" and "letter" of the law.

Part A

1. (**INTERNET ACTIVITY**) It is unlawful to ask certain personal questions before making an employment offer. Legislation on equal employment opportunity (EEO) has restricted the questions employers can ask job applicants. Using the Internet:

Part B

1. (**ROLE PLAY**) Divide students into groups of six or so. Assign the following roles: Michael Connors (HR director); Paul Sablic; Member A (direct report number 1); Member B

(direct report number 2); Member C (direct report number 3); observer (as many as needed).

a. HR director Michael Connors is to conduct a meeting with the key purchasing department personnel to prepare for the forthcoming EEOC investigation. CMC received a complaint regarding the decision to not hire Dean Fuller.

b. The observers should make a list of the key points that CMC will use in its defense.

2. At the conclusion, each student should write a one-page paper detailing what they learned from this Skills Application.

Skills Application 9-2: Ethical Issues

You are Paul Sablic, and you have an unexpected opening in your department. The job is very similar to the one for which Dean Fuller previously interviewed, and you have decided to call Dean in for an interview regarding this new opening.

1. Develop a list of interview questions that you will use to uncover Fuller's employment potential.

2. Identify a series of performance tests that you might use to allow Fuller to demonstrate his ability to perform the basic job functions.

3. Identify some accommodations for the disabled that CMC may need to incorporate before Fuller could work at CMC. (You may want to review the provisions for the Americans with Disabilities Act (ADA) discussed in Chapter 13.) Should these be a factor in deciding whether to hire Fuller?

4. Summarize on one page or less what you learned from this Skills Application.

Skills Application 9-3: Staffing the New Facility

Pine Village Community Medical Center (CMC) is constructing an 80-bed assisted-living facility. You are the newly hired maintenance supervisor. You will have responsibility for all of the activities associated with maintaining the facility 24/7, including the building and grounds. Initially, housekeeping will fall under nursing services and will not be part of your responsibilities. You will be working with one of CMC's HR reps to determine your staffing requirements. The facility is expected to be open in three months, and your staff should be ready to go two months from now.

1. Interview at least one maintenance supervisor or a couple of persons working in building maintenance to get an overview for their job responsibilities. See ENDNOTE #6 for some illustrative questions that you might want to consider.

2. List the major tasks that must be done before you can begin the selection process.

3. Outline your strategy for attracting a sufficient pool of applicants. Compare and contrast the various recruitment methods you might use.

4. Establish selection criteria.

5.  Develop a list of the questions that you will ask the applicants. Go to www.job-interview.net or search the Web for other sources to guide you.

6. What performance tests should the applicants be given? Cite your rationale for a particular test.

7. How will you decide which applicants will receive offers from you? Explain your rationale.

8. Compare your lists and responses with those of several classmates. Is there anything you omitted?

9. How has this skills application caused you to look differently at the recruiting and selection process?

Source: Adapted with permission from Edwin C. Leonard, Jr., and Roy A. Cook, "Case 2-1: Staffing the New Facility," *Human Resource Management: 21st Century Challenges* (Mason, OH: Thomson Custom Learning, 2005), pp. 30–40.

Skills Application 9-4: Career Development

1. Think back to a time in your life when you were exuberant because you or a group to which you belonged accomplished something that others thought was nearly impossible. List four to six things that you have accomplished that make you extremely proud.

2. Write a paragraph describing each accomplishment.

3. Carefully analyze each paragraph to identify specific SKAs that you used to accomplish those things.

4. Now look at your list of SKAs. What SKAs appear most often? These are your "proven" SKAs and no one can take them away from you. Remember: We build on strengths!

5. Take a moment to close your eyes and develop a mental picture of where you will be five years from now. What will you be doing? Where will you be doing it? Who will you be doing it with?

6. You know where you have been. You know where you are currently. You now have a vision of where you want to be five years from now. What is it going to take to get you there?

7. How can you use your "proven SKAs" to get there?

8. What forces inside you (weaknesses) will interfere with you getting there? What will you do over the next five years to shore up your weaknesses?

9. In one page or less, outline a plan (your career plan) for getting where you want to go.

SKILLS DEVELOPMENT

Skills Development Module 9-1: The Baker's Best Story

Owner and co-founder Michael Baker started in a 500 square-foot building in 1984. From its humble beginning, the company now has full-service catering, corporate catering, a café, and an evening restaurant. Baker's Best does no advertising and relies on 'word of mouth' to grow sales.

After reviewing the Baker's Best video for Skills Development Module 9-1, answer the following questions:

Questions for Discussion

1. Describe the approach used by Michael Baker to recruit, select and train employees.

2. What do you think about the recruiting and selection process used to hire Mark Venette and Ken Gasse´?

3. Go to www.bakersbestcatering.com and click on 'employment opportunities,' Look at current positions available.

Is there is a position for qualified managers or supervisors or another position that you might be interested in?

a. What are the SKAs that the company is looking for?
b. How do they match with your SKAs?
c. If there is an opening for a manager or supervisor, what would cause you to apply for that position?

ENDNOTES

1. Visit the Society for Human Resource Management (SHRM) Web site at www.shrm.org to see the types of resources available and find research reports and white papers on current HR-related topics.

2. Adapted from Edwin C. Leonard, Jr. and Roy A. Cook, *Human Resource Management: 21st Century Challenges* (Mason, OH: Thomson Custom Publishing, 2005), p. 4.

3. Outsourcing of various HR-related activities is a practice used by most large firms. A review of the July 2008 *HR Magazine* lists some the organizations that provide services such as benefits, career development, computer/HRIS, diversity, drug testing, employment and staffing, health and wellness, HR technology, pre-employment testing/screening, recruiting and hiring, staffing and temporary services, and training and development.

   Also see Stephen Miller, "Companies Continue to Selectively Outsource Benefits, Other HR Programs," (*SHRM Online—Outsourcing Focus Area*, July 2008); Leslie A. Weatherly, "HR Outsourcing: Reaping Strategic Value for Your Organization," (*SHRM Research Quarterly*, August 2005).

4. For an excellent overview of the history and future of human resources management, see Michael R. Losey and Susan R. Meisinger, *The Future of Human Resource Management*, (Alexandria, VA: SHRM, 2005); Michael Losey, "HR Comes of Age," *HR Magazine* (50th anniversary publication, 1998), pp. 40–53; Dave Ulrich, et al., *HR Competencies* (Alexandria, VA: SHRM, 2008); William J. Rothwell, Robert K. Prescott and Maria W. Taylor, *Human Resource Transformation: Demonstrating Strategic Leadership in the Face of Future Trends* (Alexandria, VA: SHRM, 2008); Jack J. Phillips and Patricia Pulliam Phillips, *Proving the Value of HR* (Alexandria, VA: SHRM, 2005); Shari Caudron, "HR is Dead—Long

Live HR," *Workforce* (January 2003), pp. 26–30; Rich Vosburgh, "The State of the Human Resource Profession: An Interview with Dave Ulrich," *Human Resource Planning Journal*, 26, 1 (2003), pp. 18–22; and Jonathan Tompkins, "Strategic Human Resources Management in Government: Unresolved Issues," *Public Personnel* (Spring 2002), pp. 95–110.

   In a controversial article, author Keith Hammonds claims that Human Resources strangles us with rules, cuts our benefits, and blocks constructive change. See "Why We Hate HR," *Fast Company* (August 2005), pp. 40–47.

5. See Diane Frisch, "Human Resources: Part of the Team," *HR Magazine* (July 2008), pp. 66–67; and Jathan Janove, "Can't Beat 'Em, So Join 'Em: In this corner—operations: in the opposite—human resources," *HR Magazine* (June 2008), pp. 153–160.

6. Leonard and Cook identified a simplistic job analysis approach. They suggest asking the incumbent employee(s) or those doing similar work the following questions:

   • What are your duties and responsibilities?
   • What is the most important thing you do during the day?
   • What is the toughest assignment you face in doing this job?
   • What are the three biggest challenges you face in doing this job?
   • What are you doing that you shouldn't be doing?
   • What should you be doing that you currently are not doing?
   • What is the most personally rewarding thing you did in the past week?

   After gathering employee inputs, ask the same questions of managers and other employees who are familiar with the job, only phrase them in such a way that you get an impression of what they believe the job is, ought to be, and is not. Then determine the qualifications necessary to perform these tasks. This can be a starting point for development and/or revision of the job description. See Edwin C. Leonard, Jr., and Roy A. Cook, *Human Resource Management: 21st Century Challenges* (Mason, OH: Thomson Custom Publishing, 2005), pp. 30–31.

7. For an extended discussion of job analysis, including job descriptions and job specifications, see M.T. Brannick, E.L. Levine and F.P. Morgeson, *Job and Work Analysis* (Thousand Oaks, CA: Sage, 2007). Visit the SHRM Web site (www.shrm.org) for tips on writing job descriptions. Visit www.hrtools.com for information on how to create effective and legally appropriate job descriptions.

8. It is not enough to have a job description. They need to be reviewed and updated on a regular basis. For example, in this chapter's "You Make the Call!", Michael Connors and Paul Sablic should have reviewed the job descriptions and job specifications, and re-analyzed the job when the position became vacant. Performance evaluation time is also a good time to review the job description.

   See Margie Mader-Clark, *The Job Description Handbook*, 2nd ed. (Berkeley, CA: Nolo, 2008); and Chris Burand, "Good Job Descriptions Can Boost Productivity," *American Agent and Broker*, 19, 3 (October 2002), p. 8.

9. See Urvaksh Karkaria, "Rising Up the Ranks," *The Fort Wayne, Indiana Journal Gazette* (June 1, 2004), p. 6B; and Susan J. Wells, "Who's Next?" *HR Magazine* (November 2003), pp. 45–50.

10. The following are recommended reading for discussions of sources for job candidates both internal and external to a firm: Jennifer C. Berkshire, "Social Network Recruiting," *HR Magazine* (April 2005), pp. 95–98; Stacy Foster, "The Best Way To . . . Recruit New Workers," *The Wall Street Journal* (September 15, 2003), p. R8; Mike Miller, "Recruiting the Best of the Best," *Credit Union Magazine* (March 2003), pp. 16–17; Phillip M. Perry, "Hiring the I've-Never-Held-a-Job-Before Worker," *Rural Telecommunications* (January/February 2001), pp. 64–67; and Shannon Peters Talbott, "How to Recruit Online," *Personnel Journal* (March 1999), pp. 14–17.

    Also see K.H. Ehrhart and J.C. Ziegert, "Why Are Individuals Attracted to Organizations?" Journal of Management, 31, 6 (2005), pp. 901–919; and D.S. Chapman, *et al.*, "Applicant Attraction to Organizations and Job Choice: A Meta-Analytic Review of the Correlates of Recruiting Outcomes," Journal of Applied Psychology, 90, 5 (2005), pp. 928–944.

11. According to John T. Neighbours, "Seventh Circuit Rejects Use of MMPI for Applicant Screening," *Indiana Employment Law Letter* (August 2005), pp. 1–2, "Preemployment testing is one technique used to screen applicants for such things as intellectual ability, physical ability, aptitude in specific skill areas, personality, and honesty. Tests are generally allowed as long as they don't have a disparate impact on a protected status or characteristic. Additional limitations apply, however, if the tests qualify as medical examination under the Americans with Disabilities Act (ADA). The Seventh Circuit Court rejected Rent-A-Centers use of MMPI for applicant screening."

    At the time of this writing, the verification of new employees is still in question. The E-Verify was scheduled to expire at the end of 2008 and Congress was still proposing ways for employers to check the eligibility status of new hires. The U.S. Citizenship and Immigration Services (USCIS) Web site has electronic versions of the I-9 handbook and forms.

12. A thorough discussion of equal employment opportunity and applications is the major substance of Chapter 12. For an overview about protected classes of people, see http://www.eeoc.gov/; *Employer EEO Responsibilities* (Washington, D.C.: Equal Employment Opportunity, U.S. Government Printing Office, 1996).

    "Employment disability is defined as a physical, mental, or emotional condition lasting six months or more that causes difficulty working at a job or business," as quoted by Susan J. Wells, "Counting on Workers with Disabilities," *HR Magazine* (April, 2008), pp. 45–49. For specific information on recruiting, hiring, and accommodating individuals with disabilities, a federal Web site (http://www.disAbility.gov) is available. See also Linda Wasmer Andrews, "Hiring People with Intellectual Disabilities," *HR Magazine* (July 2005), pp. 72–77; Jonathon A. Segal, "Hiring Days Are (Almost) Here Again," *HR Magazine* (June 2002), pp. 125–34, and Richard Dalglish, "Avoiding the Legal Pitfalls of Hiring and Firing," *JCK* (June 2000), pp. 306–12.

13. See Bob Schultz, "Recruiting, Interviewing, and Hiring: The Ultimate Game of 'Survivor,'" *Supervision*, 69, 3 (March 2008), pp. 3–4; Patricia M. Buhler, "Interviewing Basics: A Critical Competency for all Managers," *Supervision* (March 2005), pp. 20–22; "It's Not Your Grandfather's Hiring Interview," *Supervision* (April 2005), pp. 21–22; Martha Frase-Blunt, "Dialing for Candidates," *HR Magazine* (April 2005), pp. 78–82; and Clifford M. Koen, Jr., "Supervisor's Guide to Effective Employment Interviewing," *Supervision* (November 2004), pp. 3–6.

    "Any job interview can be a nerve-wracking experience. However, nothing is quite as intimidating as being interviewed by two or more people at the same time." For tips on how the job hunter can manage the interview process, see Kemba J. Dunham, "The Jungle/Career Journal," *The Wall Street Journal* (April 20, 2004), p. B8.

14. Frederic M. Biddle, "Work Week," *The Wall Street Journal* (September 28, 1999), p. A1. Will "textspeak" become the language of the workplace? For an interesting view, see "Casual Job Seekers Turn off Interviewers," *The Wall Street Journal* (July 29, 2008), pp. D1, D4.

15. Bolander and Snell, amongst others, contend that the structure of the interview and training of interviewers strongly influence the success of the hiring process. Interviews range from highly structured (supervisor controls the course of the interview) to less-structured (applicant plays a larger role in determining the direction of the interview). See George Bohlander and Scott Snell, *Managing Human Resources*, 14th ed. (Mason, OH: South-Western/Cengage Learning, 2007). Regardless of the approach used, Professor Leonard contends that each applicant must be given equal opportunity, i.e., asked the same questions and evaluated on the same criteria.

16. Minitab's Quality Companion helps managers develop, organizing and managing a quality improvement program. Go to http://www.minitab.com for an overview of their quality support programs.

17. This concept was part of a training program developed by Jagerson Associates, Inc., for the Life Office Management Association and has been presented in earlier editions of this text.

18. Work sample tests (skills tests) are a relatively inexpensive and objective way to measure whether the applicant meets minimum requirements for the job. Selection criterion of pre- and post-employment testing must be validated by the test—that is, the selection criterion bears directly on job success.

    The Bureau of National Affairs and CCH published a series of papers related to pre-employment testing: (1) "Policy Issues in Pre-Employment Testing" (2008). (2) "Developing and Administering Pre-Employment Tests" (2008). Also see Dino di Mattia, "Testing Methods and Effectiveness of Tests," *Supervision* (August 2005), pp. 4–5 or Leslie A. Weatherly, "Reliability and Validity of Selection Tests," *SHRM Research Report* (June 2005).

    A note of caution is illustrated by Allen Smith, "Tests Raise Flags," *HR Magazine* (June 2008), p. 36, "Pre-employment testing cases have become an area of emphasis for the EEOC because every test has an adverse impact against somebody."

19. See "Resume Fraud by Job Applicants on the Rise," *Employment Digest online* (May 30, 2004); "Surfeit of False CVs as Tech Job Demand is Up," *Economic Times* (December 18, 2004). Also see Joey George and Kent Marett, "The Truth About Lies," *HR Magazine* (May 2004), p. 11–14.

Federal law requires companies to inform job applicants that they intend to get credit reports, and to get the applicants' permission. The law requires companies to let applicants know they wouldn't hire them because of what they found on the reports and to give them a chance to correct the erroneous information. The law does not require companies to keep a job open while an applicant fixes the mistake.

20. See "State Reference Regulations," *Feature Report*, Alexander Hamilton Institute, Inc. (2004).

21. Bradford Smart as interviewed by Geoffrey Colvin, "How GE Topgrades: Looking to Hire the Very Best? Ask the Right Questions. Lots of Them," *Fortune* (June 21, 1999), p. 194. Also see Smart, *Topgrading: How Leading Companies Win by Hiring, Coaching, and Keeping the Best People* (Englewood Cliffs, NJ: Prentice-Hall, 1999),

22. From "Beware of Resumania," *Personnel Journal* (April 1996), p. 28. See also, Nick Saffieri, "Interviewing Techniques: Looking for That Perfect Employee," *Supervision*, 68, 5 (May 2007), pp. 3–5; "The Right Staff Survey: Resume Review, Asking Good Questions, Top Hiring Challenges," *Supervision* (August 2005), pp. 17–18; William C. Byham, "Can You Interview for Integrity? Yes, and You Don't Need a Lie Detector to Do It," *Across the Board* (March/April 2004), pp. 35–38; and Max Messmer, "A Closer Look at Résumés," *Strategic Finance* (September 2001), pp. 8–10.

23. Patricia M. Buhler identified ten keys to better hiring, "Managing in the New Millennium," *Supervision*, 68, 11 (November 2007), pp. 17–20. She argued that "If the applicant was not dressed appropriately for the interview or did not display signs of enthusiasm, chances are that they will not change once they are on the job." Buhler strongly suggests the use of behavioral or situational questions during the interview. An example of a question that could be asked a prospective hardware and building materials supervisor might be, "If you were approached by an employee who contended that another employee was stealing merchandise from the store and selling it on eBay, what would you do?"

    For lists of questions that might be asked during the employment interview, see Fred S. Steingold, *Hiring Your First Employee* (Berkeley, CA: Nolo, 2008).

24. Ron Zemke and Susan Zemke, "Putting Competencies to Work," *Training* (January 1999), pp. 70+. Visit the American Society for Training & Development Web site (http://www.astd.org) to glean information about the ASTD Competency Model. Or see Bruce Meger, "A Critical Review of Competency-Based Systems," *Human Resources Professional* (January–February 1996), pp. 22–25, and Donald J. McNerney and Angela Briggins, "Competency Assessment Gains Favor among Trainers," *HR Focus* (June 1995), p. 19.

25. John P. Wanous, "Installing a Realistic Job Preview: Ten Tough Choices," *Personal Psychology* (Spring 1989), pp. 117–33. Also see Carol Hymowitz, "How to Avoid Hiring the Prima Donnas Who Hate Teamwork," *The Wall Street Journal* (February 15, 2000), p. B1.

26. Tony Lee, "Companies Should Treat Job Seekers Well," Business Monday, *Fort Wayne, Indiana News Sentinel* (August 26, 2004), p. 1. Visit the Career Journal Web site (http://www.onlinewsj/com/career) for recruitment tips. Also see http://www.monster.com for interviewing techniques.

27. To understand how to evaluate the effectiveness of the hiring function, see Charlotte Garvey, "The Next Generation of Hiring Metrics," *HR Magazine* (April 2005), pp. 70–77. For a general discussion on making the hiring decision, see T. L. Stanley, "Hire the Right Person," *Supervision*, 68, 7 (July 2007), pp. 11–12; or Max Messmer, "Finalizing the Hiring Decision," *Strategic Finance* (November 2001), pp. 8–10. AHI's Web site (http://www.ahipubs.com) provides reports and other employment-related information.

28. For a discussion of the pros and cons of hiring relatives, see Mary S. Yamin, "Think Long and Hard Before Hiring Relatives and Friends," *Capital District Business Review* (June 1998), pp. 26–27; Kevin Steel, "Nepotism Is a Human Right," *Western Report* (June 15, 1998), pp. 17–19; Sharon Nelton, "The Bright Side of Nepotism," *Nation's Business* (May 1998), p. 72.

29. See Carole Fleck, "Now Boarding New Hires," *SHRM Tools & Techniques*, 3, 3 (July-September, 2007). Also see, "Welcome On Board: Press 1 for Training," *SHRM Online Technology Focus Area* (July 2006); or Derek Moscato, "Using Technology To Get Employees on Board," *HR Magazine* (April 2005), pp. 107–109.

30. For an expanded discussion of new-hire orientation, Kathy Gurchiek, "Orientation Programs Help New Hires Find Bearings," *SHRM Home* (May 25, 2007); D.G. Allen, "Do Organizational Socialization Tactics Influence Newcomer Embeddedness and Turnover?" *Journal of Management*, 32, 2 (2006), pp. 237–256; M.J. Wesson and C.I. Gogus, "Shaking Hands With A Computer: An Examination of Two Methods of Newcomer Orientation," *Journal of Applied Psychology*, 90, 5 (2005), pp. 1018–1026; and R.F. Morrison and T.M Brantner, "What Enhances or Inhibits Learning a New Job? A Basic Career Issue," *Journal of Applied Psychology*, 77 (1992), pp. 926–940.

31. See Belin Tai and Nancy R. Lockwood, "Organizational Entry: Onboarding, Orientation and Socialization," *SHRM Research* (November 2006).

32. In large companies, there may be other ways for top management to meet new employees. In several organizations with which the author is familiar, the CEO and other members of top management meet a group of new employees for lunch and discuss the company's history and philosophy, and answer questions they may have.

33. Franklin J. Lunding, "Everyone Who Makes It Has a Mentor," *Harvard Business Review* (July–August 1978), pp. 91–100.

34. See Nancy D. O'Reilly, "Women Helping Women: How Mentoring Can Help Your Business," *Supervision*, 69, 1 (January 2008), pp. 12–13; Pam Slater, "Careers Can Be Made or Derailed Over Choice or Absence of a Mentor," *Knight-Ridder Tribune Business News: The Sacramento Bee* (August 9, 1999).

35. From Karen Dillon, "Finding the Right Mentor for You," *Inc.* (June 1998), p. 55. Also see Edward O. Welles, "Mentors," *Inc.* (June 1998), pp. 48+; Kathy Kram, *Mentoring at Work* (Glenview, IL: Scott, Foresman, 1985); Julie Connelly, "Career Survival Guide," *Working Women* (April 1999), pp. 58–62; and Donna Brooks, *Seven Secrets of Successful Women* (New York: McGraw-Hill, 1998).

    Patricia Buhler contends that the mentoring process is changing because there are four generations working in the typical organization today and they were socialized differently. Buhler argues that the mentor-mentee alignment is crucial to the success of the arrangement. See Patricia M. Buhler, "Managing in the New Millennium, *Supervisor*, 68, 5 (May 2005), p. 18.

    Donna M. Owens contends that online mentoring can offer you better matches from a wider pool of mentors. See Owens, "Virtual Mentoring," *HR Magazine* (March 2006), pp. 105–107.

36. Dillon, ibid., p. 55.

37. For an interesting perspective on coaching, read about how Bill Campbell, a former college football coach, is coaching, mentoring, and advising at multiple levels in Jennifer Reingold, "The Secret Coach," *Fortune* (July 21, 2008), pp. 125–134. Also see, Jean Thilmany, "Passing on Know-How," *HR Magazine* (June 2008), pp. 100–104; or Mary Massad, "The Benefits of Employee Coaching," *Entrepreneur.com* (May 23, 2005).

38. See Grace M. Endres, "The Human Resource Craze: Human Performance Improvement and Employee Engagement," *Organizational Development Journal,* 26, 1 (Spring 2008), pp. 69–78; David

Clutterback, *Coaching the Team at Work* (Boston: Nicholas Brealey, Intl, 2007); David Lindbloom, "A Culture of Coaching: The Challenge of Managing Performance for Long-Term Results," *Organizational Development Journal,* 25, 2 (Summer 2007), pp. 101–106; or J. Richard Hackman and Ruth Wageman, "A Theory of Team Coaching," *Academy of Management Review* (April 2005), pp. 269–287. For discussions on training and approaches to training, see Edmond Friley, "Today's Training," *Supervision* (September 2005), pp. 18–19; and "Training Employees as Partners," *HR Magazine* (February 1999), pp. 64–70.

39. Candice G. Harp, Sandra C. Taylor, and John W. Satzinger, "Computer Training and Individual Differences: What Really Matters?" *Human Resources Development Quarterly* (Fall 1998), pp. 271–83; Allison Rossett and Lisa Schafer, "What to do About E-Dropouts?—What if it's not the e-learning but the e-learner," *Training & Development* (June 2003), pp. 40, 42–46.

40. According to the research of various learning theorists, people learn in different ways—hearing, seeing, reading, or doing. "Noted researcher Anthony F. Gregorc contends that the mind perceives in two different ways—through concrete perception and abstract perception. Concrete perception lets us register information directly through our five senses: sight, smell, touch, taste, and hearing. Abstract perception allows us to visualize, conceive ideas, and understand or believe that which we cannot see." See Cynthia Ulrich Tobias, "The Way They Learn," *Focus on the Family* (October 1994), pp. 12–14.

41. Adapted from Edwin C. Leonard, Jr., Assessment of Training *Needs* (Chicago: United States Civil Service Commission under Intergovernmental Personnel Act (P.L. 91–648), 1974), pp, 36–40.

42. See George Kimmerling, "How Is Training Regarded and Practiced in Top-Ranked U.S. Companies?" *Training & Development* (September 1993), pp. 29–36. For a detailed discussion of training program evaluation, see Donald L. Kirkpatrick, *Evaluating Training Programs* (Washington, D.C.: American Society for Training and Development, 1975), and "Four Steps to Measuring Training Effectiveness," *Personnel Administrator* (November 1983), pp. 57–62.

43. Daniel H. Pink, "Richard Bolles: What Happened to Your Parachute?" *Fast Company* (September 1999), p. 241. See Bolles latest annual edition of *"What Color is Your Parachute?"* (Berkeley, CA: Ten Speed Press, 2009); or visit his Web site at http://www.jobhuntersbible.com. For a current perspective by Boles, view the following podcast: Richard Leidner w/ Richard Boles, "What Happened to Your Parachute? The New Face of the Work World," (www.cce.umn.edu/conversations/audio/index.html).

CHAPTER 10

(Performance Management)

After studying this chapter, you will be able to:

1 Define performance management.

2 Clarify the supervisor's role in the performance appraisal process.

3 Explain how often performance feedback should be provided.

4 Discuss the advantages of a formal performance appraisal system.

5 Explain the concepts and techniques in using a written employee appraisal form.

6 Discuss the process of conducting a sound appraisal meeting.

7 Discuss coaching as a follow-up to performance appraisal.

8 Identify the benefits of a promotion-from-within policy.

9 Discuss the supervisor's role in employee compensation and outline the goals of an effective compensation program.

YOU MAKE THE CALL!

Walking home after a day's work, Simone Johnson thought back over the past three months on the job at the Adams Center branch of Citizen's National Bank. Prior to accepting the position at Citizen's, she had over fifteen years of experience in retail and food-service establishments. She was looking forward to building a new career and making new friends. When Simone interviewed for the job and was offered a customer-service position (teller), she was assured that she would be placed in the bank's supervisory training program after the completion of her sixty-day probationary period.

Simone was a 36-year-old single mother who had studied sociology at the local university. She had dropped out of school to get married and never completed her studies. The bank's generous tuition reimbursement program would allow her an opportunity to complete her degree, and their supervisory training program would provide a promising career path.

During her initial interview with HR director Jennifer Teeple, she was told about the bank's mission, vision, culture, employee benefits, and opportunities for professional and personal growth. Her first morning of the job was spent with Teeple and three other new hires. She completed forms, signed documents, and listened as Teeple explained the policies, procedures, benefits, and general expectations held by Citizen's for its employees. Simone and the other new employees were given a 54-page employee handbook to read. The morning session ended with a light lunch in the break room before the new hires retreated to their assigned branches.

Upon arriving at the branch, she met with vice-president/branch manager George Murphy. Murphy spent thirty minutes explaining the specific tasks and duties of the teller position. Then he introduced her to Sally Davies and Carl O'Connor, two of the more experienced tellers. Based on her years of experience with the bank, Davies was the unofficial supervisor of the teller line. Over the past three months, Davies has spent a great deal of time helping Simone get adjusted. Simone's adjustment to the branch has been smooth, and she has received several "great job!" comments from customers.

Since her brief encounter on that first afternoon with George Murphy, she has had no contact with him. Murphy is known to the employees as the "out of sight, out of mind manager." He appears to spend most of his time on banking issues with commercial and industrial customers. Arrianne Day, the assistant branch manager, handles the daily business issues and mortgage loans, larger CDs, and issues that are beyond teller capabilities. Each morning, Simone got the "Good morning, how are you?" routine from Day. About a month ago, near the end of her 60-day probationary period, Simone asked Day about the supervisory training program. Day told her that there would be a new class starting after the first of the year, but she wasn't aware of any plans to send Simone to the program. When Simone asked about it again two weeks ago, Day suggested that she check with Davies.

Shortly after lunch today, Simone received a text message from Murphy stating that he needed to see her at 5:30 P.M. Just a few minutes after closing the doors to the bank, Simone knocked on Murphy's door. As she came in, Murphy was talking on the phone to a customer. He motioned for her to sit down, and while still talking on the phone, pushed a form toward her and said, "Here is your appraisal form. I should have done this at the end of your probationary period but we've been busy. Look it over and sign on the line. I've given you good ratings." Simone felt frustrated because she thought this was going to be her opportunity to discuss the supervisory training program in particular, and job enlargement and enrichment opportunities in general. The puzzled look on her face caused Murphy to pause his phone call and say, "Just sign the form. We have to get it in. We'll talk about it later."

After signing the form and heading home, Simone thought about the benefits of working for the Adams Center branch of Citizen's Bank. The teller group worked well together and the bank had a high volume of traffic. School started last week and she had signed up for two classes in pursuit of her general studies degree. The bank's policy was to reimburse tuition and books upon completion of a course with a grade of 'C' or better. Additionally, the Adams Center branch was within two blocks of her home, which meant she could walk to work and save on gas and car expenses. Her two children were in the tenth and eighth grades, and she could more easily attend their school and church functions. Unlike National City and some of the other area banks, Citizen's appeared to be sheltered from the mortgage loan problems, foreclosures, declining deposits, and deteriorating stock prices.

Still, as she walked in the door, she felt as if she were knocking her head against a stone wall. "What can I do to get Day and Murphy to really tell me how I am doing?" **YOU MAKE THE CALL!**

1 **Define performance management.**

The Performance Management Process

This section reintroduces some of the key concepts in understanding what causes people to behave the way they do. As stated throughout this text, *management* is the process of getting things accomplished with and through people by guiding and motivating those people's efforts toward common objectives. Clearly, people are an organization's most important assets and as such must be managed effectively to achieve organizational objectives. In previous chapters, we addressed the importance of effective communication, the ABCs of employee behavior, a participatory approach for setting measurable objectives, and various tips for ensuring employee success. In this chapter, we focus on the process of employee appraisal, but before we begin, let us look at how the concepts are related.

Professors Kreitner and Kinicki of Arizona State University have stated, "Managers are better able to identify and correct performance problems when they recognize poor performance is not due solely to inadequate motivation. This awareness can foster better interpersonal relations in the workplace."[1] Once an employee joins the work group, the task for supervisors becomes one of maintaining and enhancing employee SKAs. Various coaching and mentoring activities are opportunities to provide information as well as feedback to employees about their job performance.

System of performance management
All those things a supervisor must do to enable an employee to achieve prescribed objectives

Our **system of performance management** (see Figure 10.1) identifies all those things a supervisor must do to enable an employee to achieve the organization's objectives. The system of performance management begins with the supervisor setting the stage for employee success.[2] While the system is presented in a detailed, straightforward form, we caution that no system survives without feedback and controls. To ensure that the necessary work is done, the supervisor must monitor performance regularly and provide support, guidance, and direction as needed.

2 **Clarify the supervisor's role in the performance appraisal process.**

The Employee Performance Appraisal

From the time employees begin their employment with a firm, the supervisor is responsible for evaluating the employees' job performances. Performance appraisal is the systematic assessment of how well employees are performing their jobs and the communication of that assessment to them. As discussed in earlier chapters, supervisors establish performance standards or targets that subordinates are expected to achieve. **Performance appraisal** includes comparing the employee's performance with the standards. Often these standards may be referred to a metrics. For example, processing customer transactions with zero-defects might be a metric for a bank teller. The metrics used should enable management to compare the employee's performance to others and how he or she contributes to the overall team success. Effective supervisors provide their subordinates with day-to-day feedback on performance. Regular feedback on performance is essential to improve employee performance and to provide the recognition that will motivate employees to sustain satisfactory performance (see Figure 10.2).

Performance appraisal
A systematic assessment of how well an employee is performing a job and the communication of that assessment

Most organizations require supervisors to evaluate their employees' performance formally. These evaluations become part of an employee's permanent record and play an important role in management's training,

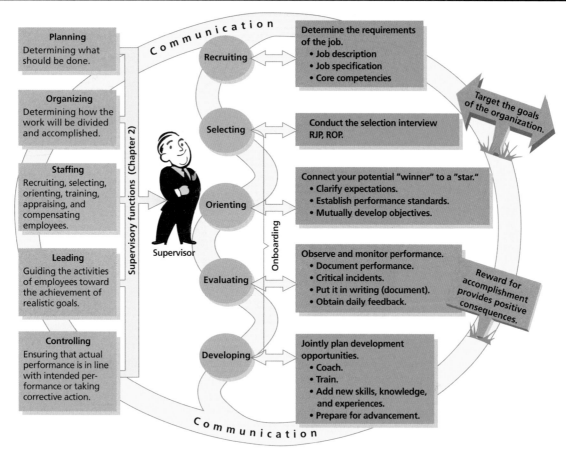

FIGURE 10.1 Performance Management

promote, retention, and compensation decisions. Figure 10.3 summarizes the reasons for evaluating performance on a regular and systematic basis.

Supervisors should approach the appraisal process from the perspective that it is an extension of the planning, organizing, leading, and controlling functions. When employees understand what is expected of them and the criteria upon which they will be evaluated, and they believe the process is administered fairly, performance appraisal serves as a powerful motivational tool. While performance appraisals are frequently used to determine compensation, supervisors also use performance appraisals to provide feedback to employees so that those employees know where they stand and what they can do to improve performance and to develop to their full potential.

The importance of documenting personnel decisions cannot be overemphasized. It is becoming increasingly important for organizations to maintain accurate records to protect themselves against possible charges of discrimination in connection with promotion, compensation, and termination.

While employee performance appraisal is a daily, ongoing aspect of the supervisor's job, the focus of this chapter is on the formal performance appraisal system. The purpose of the formal system is to evaluate, document, and communicate job achievements in understandable and objective terms, as well as secondary results of employee effort compared with job expectations. This is done by considering such factors as the job description, performance standards,

FIGURE 10.2 The effective supervisor avoids these comments by providing regular positive feedback on performance

specific objectives, and critical incidents for the evaluation period. The evaluation is based on direct observation of the employee's work over a set period.[3]

Clearly, the long-term success of an organization depends to a substantial degree on the performance of its workforce. We have learned that to get employees to work smarter, they first must know what is expected in the way of

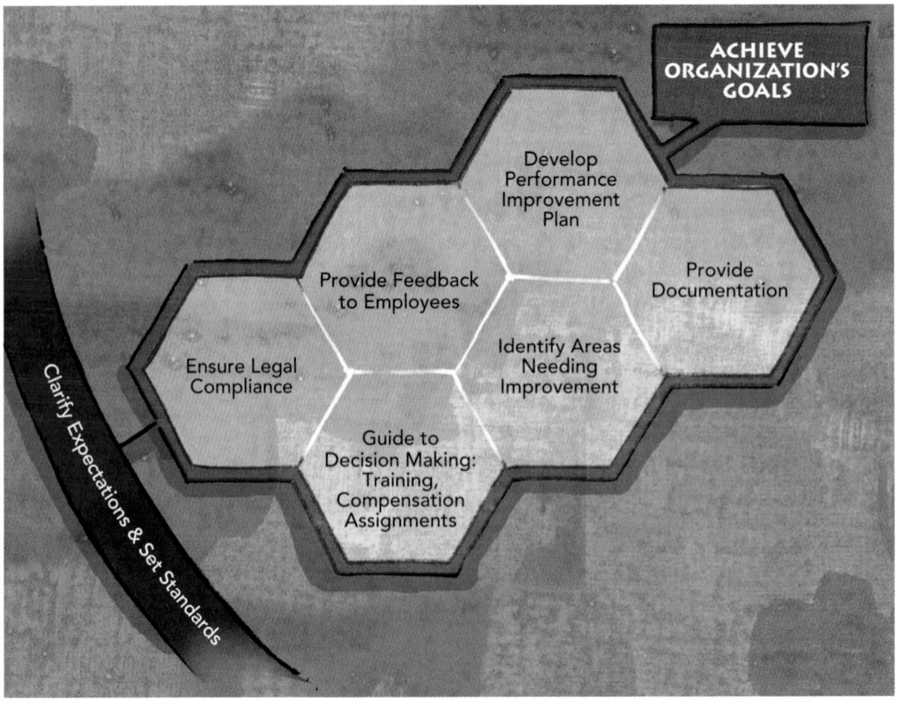

FIGURE 10.3 Reasons for Evaluating Performance on a Systematic Basis

performance, and then they must receive regular feedback on their performance. Effective supervisors should subscribe to the notion that "There is no substitute for daily feedback on performance." Unfortunately, some supervisors either fail to recognize performance problems or feel uncomfortable engaging employees in conversations about performance expectations and how to achieve those expectations. We contend that most employees want to know how well they have performed relative to the organization's expectations or performance standards. Generally, the supervisor should recognize and comment on a particular aspect of performance when that aspect occurs. The supervisor may glean this information from direct observation of the employee's work or from other sources. Because it is impossible for supervisors to observe everything employees do, those supervisors must rely on performance feedback from other sources—customers, peers, attendance records, production data, sales data, or customer feedback surveys.

Regardless of the information source, it is essential that the information is reliable. Imagine, for example, that a percentage of your course grade is determined by your class participation. The instructor sometimes records attendance and sometimes does not. At the end of the course, the instructor uses attendance data to determine your participation grade. As luck would have it, the only three days you missed class during the term were among those days the instructor took attendance. Another student was rarely in attendance but was fortunate enough to be there on the days the instructor took attendance. Even though your test scores were similar, the other student received a higher grade than you did. Obviously, from your point of view, this method is not fair. The instructor can reduce the probability of a grade appeal in several ways, including; (1) by ensuring that students understand from the start of the course that attendance will be an integral part in determining their course grades, and (2) by recording attendance regularly—that is, recording all absences. (We have observed that many problems have occurred because some supervisors record performance data selectively.)

THE SUPERVISOR'S RESPONSIBILITY TO DO PERFORMANCE APPRAISALS

A performance appraisal should be done by an employee's immediate supervisor because the immediate supervisor is usually in the best position to observe and judge how well the employee has performed on the job. In some situations, a "consensus" or "pooled" appraisal may be done by a group of supervisors. For example, if an employee works for several supervisors because of rotating work-shift schedules or because the organization has a matrix structure, a consensus appraisal may be done. Some organizations have implemented work teams that expand the supervisor's span of control, and some have become leaner and have eliminated middle-level management positions. It is impractical for a supervisor to track the performance of 20, 30, or even 50 workers and evaluate their performance objectively. Consensus or pooled appraisals could lead to inequities in the performance appraisal system. To ensure that employees feel that the appraisal process is fair, each evaluator must understand what is needed for successful job performance and apply the standards uniformly.

PEER EVALUATIONS

A **peer evaluation** is the evaluation of an employee's performance by other employees of relatively equal rank. Peers usually have close working relationships and know more than the supervisor about an individual's contributions.

Peer evaluation
The evaluation of an employee's performance by other employees of relatively equal rank

However, safeguards must be built in to ensure that peers are basing their evaluations on performance factors and not on bias, prejudice, or personality conflicts. Having an individual's performance evaluated anonymously by a team of peers is one way to encourage candid evaluation. To protect employees from prejudice or vendettas, the organization should establish an appeals mechanism to allow ratings review by upper-level managers.

Generally, employees work cooperatively to achieve common goals. Consider the situation in which members of work teams evaluate other team members' performance. On the one hand, because a peer rating system uses a number of independent judgments, peer evaluations can be more reliable than supervisory evaluations. On the other hand, when employees are forced to criticize their teammates via the performance appraisal system, their appraisals could have undesirable consequences for the cooperative culture and could defeat the purposes of teamwork. Imagine what could happen to morale and spirit among team members when one worker gets a low evaluation from an unknown coworker and wonders who was responsible. To safeguard the peer rating process, supervisors can incorporate into one composite evaluation the input from all peers. Then, ratings that may be high due to friendship or low due to bias will cancel each other out. Safeguards that ensure confidentiality and minimize bias are critical to the effective use of peer evaluations.[4]

As the concepts of total quality management (TQM) and self-directed work teams have expanded, performance appraisals may be expected to take on a different role. Some speculate that appraisals will focus more on the future than on the past and will include input from a wide variety of sources.

360-degree evaluation
Performance appraisal based on data collected from all around the employee—from customers, vendors, supervisors, peers, subordinates, and others

Increasing numbers of organizations are using a type of evaluation called a **360-degree evaluation**, which is based on evaluative feedback regarding the employee's performance collected from all around the employee—from customers, vendors, supervisors, peers, subordinates, and others. These 360-degree evaluations give employees feedback on their skills, knowledge, and abilities (SKAs), and job-related effectiveness from sources who see different aspects of their work.[5] This approach gives employees a broader perspective of what they do well and where they need to improve.

SELF-EVALUATIONS

Many effective supervisors find it appropriate to supplement their judgments with self-ratings from subordinates. About a week before the performance review, the employee is given a blank evaluation form to be used as a self-evaluation. Research has revealed that employees often rate their work less favorably than do their supervisors.[6] The supervisor compares the two evaluations to make sure to discuss all important performance specifics in the appraisal meeting. As mentioned previously, if the supervisor has provided ongoing feedback to the employee, the employee's self-ratings should be very close to the supervisor's ratings. Widely divergent ratings could mean that supervisors are giving too little feedback throughout the year for the employees to have clear pictures of how well they are doing.

Regardless of the approach, the ultimate responsibility for completing the appraisal form and conducting the appraisal meeting lies with the immediate supervisor. If peer evaluations are used, the supervisor still must reconcile the appraisals and communicate the information to the employee. The formal appraisal meeting usually takes place at a set time each year and should summarize what the supervisor has discussed with the employee throughout the year.

Timing Performance Appraisals

3 Explain how often performance feedback should be provided.

Upper-level management decides who should appraise and how often. Most organizations require supervisors to formally appraise all employees at least once a year. Traditionally, this has been considered long enough to develop a reasonably accurate record of the employee's performance and short enough to provide current, useful information. However, if an employee has just started or if the employee has been transferred to a new and perhaps more responsible position, it is advisable to conduct an appraisal within the first couple of weeks.

In an ideal world, the supervisor would meet with the new hire at the conclusion of his or her first day on the job. The purpose of this meeting is to review expectations, get input from the employee regarding "how his or her day went," provide feedback on performance, and coach and train as necessary. If the mindset of the supervisor is such that *onboarding* is a continuous process to help new hires to reach their full potential and contribute to the department's objectives, then performance appraisal meetings should be scheduled on an as-needed basis.

For an employee who is new to the organization, the supervisor should do appraisals periodically during the employee's probationary period. This will fulfill the employee's need to know how he or she is doing. Ultimately, these appraisals will determine whether the employee will be retained. The performance evaluation of the probationary employee is critical. Employees are usually on their best behavior during the probationary period, and if their performance is less than acceptable, the organization should not make a long-term commitment to them. Consider the following illustration. A supervisor tolerated a probationary employee whose attendance record was not acceptable. Extensive efforts to develop better attendance habits failed. Even so, the supervisor felt that if the employee was terminated, the position might go unfilled and be lost. The supervisor's theory of "half an employee is better than none" cost the company dearly in the long run. The employee never became a satisfactory performer, and he eventually had to be terminated after the company had a substantial investment is his training.

After the probationary period, the timing of appraisals varies. In some organizations, appraisals are done on the anniversary of the date the employee started; in other organizations, appraisals are done once or twice a year on fixed dates. If an employee exhibits a serious performance problem during the evaluation period, the supervisor should schedule an immediate meeting with the employee. This meeting should be followed by another formal evaluation within a week to review the employee's progress. If the performance deficiency is severe, the supervisor should meet daily with the employee to completely document the performance deficiency and the supervisor's efforts to help the employee.

As stated before, performance evaluation should be a normal part of the day-to-day relationship between a supervisor and employees. If an employee is given ongoing feedback, then the annual appraisal should contain no surprises. The supervisor who communicates frequently with employees concerning how they are doing will find that the annual appraisal is primarily a matter of reviewing much of what has been discussed during the year. Figure 10.4 illustrates how regular feedback, by removing uncertainty, can reduce the natural apprehension surrounding performance appraisals.

FIGURE 10.4 Regular feedback reduces the natural apprehension surrounding appraisals

Ongoing feedback throughout the year, both positive and negative, rewards good performance and fosters improvement. Over time, ongoing feedback, as well as formal appraisals, can become an important influence on employee motivation and morale. Appraisals reaffirm the supervisor's genuine interest in employees' growth and development. Most employees would rather be told how they are doing—even if it involves some criticism—than receive no feedback from their supervisors.

4 Discuss the advantages of a formal performance appraisal system.

Advantages of a Formal Appraisal System

A formal appraisal system provides a framework to help the supervisor evaluate performance systematically. It forces the supervisor to scrutinize the work of employees from the standpoint of how well those employees are meeting established standards and to identify areas that need improvement.

Most firms use some type of formal appraisal system. Management scholar Douglas McGregor identified three reasons for using performance appraisal systems:

1. Performance appraisals provide systematic judgments to support salary increases, promotions, transfers, layoffs, demotions, and terminations.
2. Performance appraisals are a means of telling subordinates how they are doing and of suggesting needed changes in behavior, attitudes, skills, or job knowledge. They let subordinates know where they stand with supervisors.
3. Performance appraisals help supervisors coach and counsel employees.[7]

Organizations that view their employees as long-term assets worthy of development adopt the philosophy that all employees can improve their performance.

Employees have the right to know how well they are doing and what they can do to improve. Most employees want to know what their supervisors think of their work. This desire can stem from different reasons. For example, some employees realize they are doing relatively poor jobs, but they hope, and want to be assured, that their supervisors are not too critical. Other employees feel that they are doing outstanding jobs and want to ensure that their supervisors recognize and appreciate their services.

Formal appraisals should become part of employees' permanent employment records. These appraisals serve as documents that are likely to be reviewed and even relied on in decisions concerning promotion, compensation, training, disciplinary action, and even termination. Performance appraisals can answer such questions as:

- Who should be promoted to department supervisor when the incumbent retires?
- Who should get merit raises this year?
- What should be the raise differential between employees?
- Who, if anyone, needs training?
- What training do employees need?
- This behavior has happened before. Does the employee need additional coaching, or is the behavior serious enough for disciplinary action?
- An employee is appealing her termination. Do we have adequate documentation to support the decision?

A formal appraisal system serves another important purpose: An employee's poor performance and failure to improve may be due in part to the supervisor's inadequate supervision. A formal appraisal system provides clues to the supervisor's own performance and may suggest where the supervisor must improve. Even when designed and implemented with the best intentions, performance appraisal systems are often sources of anxiety for employee and supervisor alike. Formal performance appraisal systems can be misused as disciplinary devices rather than as constructive feedback tools aimed at rewarding good performance and helping employees improve. As shown in Figure 10.5, not all supervisors fully understand

FIGURE 10.5 Sally and her co-workers would wholeheartedly agree: Everyone is still doing annual performance reviews—but not the right way

the importance that performance appraisals play in employee morale. Why does Ralph have to leave his employees feeling bruised, desolate, dejected, or confused about their future with the organization? We would offer the following words of advice to him: "The purpose of the annual performance review is to direct employee attention to new targets."[8]

<table>
<tr><td>5 Explain the concepts and techniques in using a written employee appraisal form.</td></tr>
</table>

The Performance Appraisal Process

Typically, a formal employee performance appraisal by a supervisor involves (a) completing a written appraisal form and (b) conducting an appraisal interview.

COMPLETING A WRITTEN APPRAISAL FORM

To facilitate the appraisal process and make it more uniform, most organizations use performance appraisal forms. There are numerous types of forms for employee evaluation. These forms are usually prepared by the human resources department with input from employees and supervisors. Once the forms are in place, the human resources department usually trains supervisors and employees in their proper use. Often, supervisors are responsible for informing new employees about the performance appraisal process as part of the onboarding process.

FACTORS IN MEASURING PERFORMANCE

Most appraisal forms include factors that serve as criteria for measuring job performance, skills, knowledge, and abilities. Following are some of the factors that are most frequently included on employee appraisal rating forms:

- Job knowledge
- Timeliness of output
- Positive and negative effects of effort
- Suggestions and ideas generated
- Dependability (absenteeism, tardiness, work done on time)
- Safety
- Amount of supervision required (initiative)
- Aptitude
- Cooperation (effectiveness in dealing with others)
- Adaptability
- Ability to work with others
- Ability to learn
- Quantity and quality of work
- Effectiveness of resource use
- Customer service orientation
- Judgment
- Appearance

Regardless of the factors, appraisal forms must relate to employees' jobs. Factors that enable the supervisor to make objective performance evaluations rather than personality judgments should be used whenever possible. For each of these factors, the supervisor may be given a "check-the-box" choice or a place to fill in the employee's achievements. Some appraisal forms offer a series of descriptive sentences, phrases, or adjectives to help the supervisor understand how to judge the rating factors. Generally, the "check-the-box" forms are somewhat easier and less time-consuming for supervisors to complete. Ideally, the supervisor should write a narrative to justify the evaluation. There should be no shortcuts to performance appraisal. Supervisors should give it as much time as it needs.

Typically, the supervisor reads each item and checks the appropriate box. The supervisor identifies the outstanding aspects of the employee's work as well as specific performance characteristics that need improvement (weaknesses) and suggests several things that might be done to improve performance. Most forms provide space for additional comments about the various aspects of an employee's performance. Many organizations continue to search for the "one best form." Unfortunately, one does not exist. We recommend that an organization have its supervisors start with a blank sheet of paper. See Figure 10.6 for how to use a blank sheet of paper to ask questions and record vital information related to an employee's performance.

If the system calls for employee self-appraisal, the employee's form is usually identical to the regular appraisal form except that it is labeled as a self-appraisal. Self-appraisals give employees an opportunity to think about their achievements and prepare for the appraisal meeting.

PERFORMANCE APPRAISAL SOFTWARE

"Point and click" has become a way of life for many people. Various vendors have developed software that allows supervisors to move effortlessly though the performance appraisal form.[9]

On some performance appraisal forms, the supervisor can choose from the list of factors for a given job (e.g., personal efficiency, job knowledge, judgment). Software can weight each factor according to its importance to the employee's job. Then, to determine whether the employee has met, exceeded, or failed to meet the performance standard, the supervisor can rate statements that appear on the screen. Programs have been developed to guide users through the process of performance appraisal, provide on-screen tutorials that answer frequently asked questions, and steer managers clear of potential problems.[10]

FIGURE 10.6 Begin with a blank sheet of paper and answer these questions

Simone Johnson (reviewee)
October 28 (date)
George Murphy (supervisor)

1. What did I expect of Simone? (i.e., duties, responsibilities, objectives, performance standards)

2. What has Simone done well?

3. What must Simone improve?

4. What have I done to help Simone improve?

5. How can I help Simone do a better job?

6. What do I need to do to help Simone grow professionally?

7. Where do we go from here? What should be the new objectives?

The author is familiar with a company that decided to implement a software appraisal package. After the first round of annual appraisals using the new system, employees were dissatisfied with the process and supervisors were more frustrated. Why? The software vendors contend that their systems should help make appraisals more consistent and better able to withstand legal tests. In this case, the human resources manager assumed that the new approach would "magically" improve the appraisal process. What was forgotten was that, for any annual appraisal to be effective, it must be built on factual information that is the culmination of the observed and reported incidents of the employee's performance over the set period. When the new computerized process was announced, some supervisors either stopped keeping paper records or failed to understand the importance of making computer entries as employees perform. It can frustrate employees to leave appraisals feeling that their supervisors ignored outstanding performance incidents or only covered performance over the preceding few weeks. Clearly, supervisors must get in the habit of logging positive and negative performance information as incidents occur. As mentioned earlier in this chapter, we want to reinforce the notion that "there is no substitute for daily feedback on performance." Supervisors should document performance as it occurs so that there will be no surprises at annual review time.

PROBLEMS WITH APPRAISAL FORMS

Despite the uncomplicated design of most performance appraisal forms, supervisors encounter a number of problems when filling them out. First, not all raters agree on the meaning of such terms as *exceptional*, *very good*, *satisfactory*, *fair*, and *unsatisfactory*. Descriptive phrases or sentences added to each of these adjectives help describe the levels that best describe the employee, but the choice of an appraisal term or level depends mostly on the rater's perceptions, which may inaccurately measure performance.

Another problem is that one supervisor may be more severe than another in the appraisal of employees. A supervisor who gives lower ratings than other supervisors for the same performance is likely to damage the morale of employees, who may feel they have been judged unfairly. One such supervisor stated that because no one is perfect, no one should ever be evaluated as above average. Another supervisor felt that if he rated his employees too high, those employees would be considered for promotions elsewhere in the organization and would be lost to his department. As a result, this supervisor rated his employees much lower than was fair. In the long run, the supervisor lost the employees' trust and respect or lost them to other firms.

Leniency error
Supervisors give employees higher ratings than they deserve

In contrast to this supervisor, some supervisors tend to be overly generous or lenient in their ratings.[11] The **leniency error** occurs when supervisors give employees higher ratings than they deserve. Some supervisors give high ratings because they believe that poor evaluations may reflect negatively on their own performance, suggesting that they have been unable to elicit good performance from their employees. Other supervisors do not give low ratings because they are afraid that they will antagonize their employees and make them less cooperative. Some supervisors are so eager to be liked by their employees that they give out only high ratings, even when such ratings are undeserved.

In addition to leniency errors, supervisors should be aware of the problems of the halo effect and the horns effect (described in Chapter 9), each of which causes a rating in one factor to inspire similar ratings in other factors. One way to avoid the halo or horns effect is for the supervisor to rate all employees on only one factor and then proceed to the next factor for all employees. This suggestion only works, however, if the supervisor is rating several employees at once. If that is not the case, the supervisor should pause and ask, "How does this employee compare on this factor with other employees?" For each factor, the supervisor must rate each employee relative to a standard or to another employee.

The supervisor should ask what conditions exist when the job is done well. These conditions, **performance standards**, are the job-related requirements by which the employee's performance will be evaluated. They should be described in terms of *how much*, *how well*, *when*, and *in what manner*. Effectiveness and efficiency measures are part of these standards. The positive and negative effects of performance also should be considered. Consider, for example, the most prolific salesperson in a store, whose product knowledge and selling ability are second to none. However, this salesperson always expects the cashiers to enter his sales first. The cashiers are frustrated, and the other salespeople are not as able to give good service. In addition, this salesperson always has the stockroom personnel running errands for him. This salesperson receives accolades on selling, but every one of his sales is a rush project, and others are expected to juggle their schedules to accommodate him. While this salesperson is proficient in the process of getting his job done, he negatively impacts the organization. His supervisor must broaden the performance standards to include more than product knowledge and selling.

To reiterate, every appraisal should be made in the context of each employee's job, and every rating should be based on the employee's total performance. It would be unfair to appraise an employee based on one assignment that had been done recently, done particularly well, or done very poorly. Random impressions should not influence a supervisor's judgment. The appraisal should be based on an employee's total record for the appraisal period. All relevant factors must be considered. Moreover, the supervisor must continuously strive to exclude personal biases for or against individuals because they can be serious appraisal pitfalls.

While performance appraisal results are by no means perfect, they can be objective and positive forces influencing employees' performance.

> **Performance standards**
> The job-related requirements by which the employee's performance is evaluated

The Appraisal Meeting

> **6** Discuss the process of conducting a sound performance appraisal meeting.

The second major part of the appraisal process is the evaluation or appraisal meeting. After supervisors complete the rating form, they arrange to meet with employees to review the employees' ratings. Because these meeting are the most vital part of the appraisal process, the supervisor should develop a general plan for carrying out appraisal discussions. When handled poorly, appraisal meetings can lead to considerable resentment and misunderstanding. The conflict that develops may be irreparable.

THE RIGHT PURPOSE

The primary purpose of appraisal meetings is to let employees know how they are doing. In the interest of maintaining employees' good behaviors, supervisors formally praise employees for their past and current good performance. Supervisors also use appraisal meetings to help employees develop good future performance. Emphasizing the strengths on which employees can build supports employees' career plans. Supervisors can explain the opportunities for growth in the organization and can encourage employees to develop needed skills. Finally, supervisors use appraisal meetings to explain behavior that needs to be corrected and the need for improvement. Even when improvement is needed, supervisors should take the approach that they believe the employee can improve and that they will do everything possible to help. It is important that supervisors conduct appraisal meetings for the right purpose.

THE RIGHT TIME AND PLACE

Appraisal meetings should be held shortly after the performance rating form has been completed, preferably in a private setting. To enable employees to prepare for their appraisal meetings and to consider what they would like to discuss, supervisors should make appointments with employees several days in advance. Privacy and confidentiality of the appraisal meeting should be ensured because this discussion could include criticisms, personal feelings, and opinions.

It is a good idea for the supervisor to complete the rating form several days before the meeting and then review it a day or two before the meeting to analyze it objectively and to ensure that it accurately reflects the employee's performance.

CONDUCTING THE APPRAISAL MEETING

Most of the interviewing discussion in Chapter 9 applies to the appraisal meeting. While appraisal meetings tend to be directive, they can take on nondirective characteristics because employees may bring up issues that supervisors did not expect or of which they were unaware. It is easy for most supervisors to communicate the positive aspects of job performance, but it is difficult to communicate major criticisms without generating resentment and defensiveness. There is a limit to how much criticism an individual can absorb in one session. If there is a lot of criticism to impart, dividing the appraisal meeting into several sessions may ease the stress.

The manner in which the supervisor conducts the appraisal meeting influences how the employee reacts. After a brief, informal opening, the supervisor should state that the purpose of the meeting is to assess the employee's performance in objective terms. During this warm-up period, the supervisor should state that the purpose of the performance appraisal is to recognize the employee for

At appraisal meetings, supervisors emphasize employees' strengths to help them improve performance

his or her achievements and to help the employee improve, if necessary. The supervisor should review the employee's achievements during the review period, compliment the employee on those accomplishments, identify the employee's strengths, and then proceed to the areas that need improvement. A secret of success is to get the employee to agree on his or her strengths first because it is easier to build on strengths than weaknesses.

Unfortunately, not every employee performs at the expected level. Limiting criticism to just a few major points, rather than to all minor transgressions, draws attention to the major areas that need improvement without being overwhelming. The supervisor must get the employee to agree on the areas that need correction or improvement. When there is agreement, the supervisor and employee can use a problem-solving approach to jointly determine how the employee can improve performance.

When dealing with an employee who is performing at substandard levels, the supervisor must clearly communicate to the employee that the deficiencies are serious and that substantial improvement must be made. Supervisors should mix in some positive observations so that the employees know they are doing some things right. The supervisor works with the employee to create an action plan for improvement with expectations and progress checkpoints along the way. It is important that the employee leaves the meeting feeling able to meet expectations.

Performance appraisals have been increasingly scrutinized by the legal system in recent years.[12] It is essential that organizations ensure that their performance appraisal systems are legally defensible. Employees often disagree with negative aspects of the performance appraisal because the ratings later affect their jobs. The supervisor must be certain that each employee fully understands the standards of performance that serve as the basis for appraisal. Also, the appraisal must accurately represent the employee's performance and must be free of bias. The employee must know that the review is fair, is based on job-performance factors, and is supported by proper documentation.

Most mature employees are able to handle deserved, fair criticism. By the same token, those who merit praise want to hear it. Figure 10.7 includes suggestions for relieving the uncertainty of the performance appraisal process through preparation.

During the appraisal meeting, the supervisor should emphasize that everybody in the same job in the same department is evaluated using the same standards. The supervisor must be prepared to support or document ratings by citing specific illustrations and instances of good or poor performance. In particular, the supervisor should indicate how the employee performed or behaved in certain situations that were especially crucial or significant to the performance of the department. This is sometimes called the **critical incident method**. To use this method, the supervisor must keep a file during the appraisal period of notes describing situations in which employees performed in an outstanding fashion or situations in which their work was clearly unsatisfactory. An example of a positive critical incident would be the following: "Shortly before closing on October 22, an employee realized that a customer had received an item of lesser value than she had paid for. The employee called the customer to verify that a mistake had been made, apologized for the error, and offered to either credit the customer's account or come to her residence to make the proper exchange. Identification and correction of the problem enabled the store to maintain customer confidence and to develop a system to prevent recurrence." When the critical incident method is used, employees know that the supervisor has a factual record upon which to assess performance.

Critical incident method
Supervisors record specific examples of outstanding and below-average performance on the part of each employee

FIGURE 10.7 Comprehensive Performance Appraisal Checklist

Supervisors are trained in the performance appraisal system:

- ❏ The forms
- ❏ Use of job standards
- ❏ Timing of appraisal
- ❏ Monitoring employee progress
- ❏ Contracting for performance improvement
- ❏ Using developmental methods and action plans

- ❏ Providing feedback
- ❏ Rating scales and dimensions
- ❏ Linkages with personnel decisions
- ❏ Objective performance assessment
- ❏ Documentation
- ❏ Interviewing techniques
- ❏ Rewarding performance

- ❏ Both the supervisor and the employee understand the purpose of the appraisal process.

The supervisor clarifies employee expectations through a job description that lists duties and responsibilities.

- ❏ An updated job description serves as the foundation for the appraisal.
- ❏ The supervisor makes the employee aware of performance standards and specific areas of accountability.
- ❏ The supervisor provides ongoing feedback on performance. Remember: *There is no substitute for daily feedback on performance!*
- ❏ Supervisor gives at least one official performance appraisal per year—within the first 30 work days for new employees or transfers and as required for problem employees.
- ❏ As soon as a performance problem is observed, the supervisor works with the employee to try to determine the cause of the problem and corrective action.
- ❏ The supervisor keeps a regular record of all unusual behavior—a critical incident file.
- ❏ The supervisor schedules the appraisal meeting several days in advance.
- ❏ The supervisor puts the employee at ease at the beginning of the appraisal meeting.
- ❏ The supervisor allows the employee to engage in self-evaluation. (The supervisor may ask the employee to complete the evaluation form.)
- ❏ The supervisor reviews the written appraisal with the employee, stating both standards and/or objectives met and not met.
- ❏ The supervisor criticizes performance, not the person, and tells the employee specifically what he or she did wrong.
- ❏ The supervisor objectively emphasizes work behaviors rather than personal traits (the O of OUCH).
- ❏ The supervisor provides positive as well as negative feedback.
- ❏ The supervisor uses specific examples to illustrate the employee's accomplishments. (The employee knows that the supervisor is using factual information that is well-documented.)
- ❏ The supervisor asks probing questions to get additional information and to seek clarification of misunderstandings or views that differ. This gives the employee an opportunity to bring forth mitigating circumstances or to discuss items of interest or concern (e.g., "What is my opportunity for advancement or specialized training?")
- ❏ The supervisor summarizes the discussion and overall rating.
- ❏ The supervisor allows the employee to summarize the interview in his or her own words.
- ❏ The employee knows that the organization has an audit procedure to review the supervisor's appraisal decisions in the event of disagreement; that is, the decision is audited to ensure that feedback is related to job performance (the H of OUCH).
- ❏ Personnel decisions are made consistent with the written results of the appraisal (the C of OUCH).
- ❏ The system is periodically reviewed to ensure that there is uniformity throughout the organization and that protected classes are not adversely impacted by the performance appraisal system (the U of OUCH).
- ❏ Performance ratings are linked to organizational objectives.

If the supervisor has chosen to use the employee self-rating approach mentioned earlier, the discussion primarily centers on the differences between the employee's self-ratings and those of the supervisor. These differences may involve considerable back-and-forth discussion, especially if there are major differences of opinion regarding various parts of the appraisal form. Typically, this is not a major difficulty unless employees have exaggerated notions of their abilities or feel that the supervisor's ratings were unjustified. The impact of downsizing and a tight job market may lead to greater disagreement over performance appraisal if there are now more people competing for fewer jobs. Conflict is particularly likely when employees perceive that the supervisor's appraisal may jeopardize their jobs.

Regardless of how supervisors approach the appraisal meeting, they must include a discussion about plans for improvement and possible opportunities for the employee's future. The supervisor should mention any educational or training plans that may be available. The supervisor should be familiar with advancement opportunities open to employees, requirements of future jobs, and each employee's personal ambitions and qualifications. When discussing the future, the supervisor should be careful to make no promises for training or promotion that are uncertain to materialize in the foreseeable future. False promises are a quick way to lose credibility.

The evaluation meeting also should give the employee an opportunity to ask questions, and the supervisor should answer those questions as fully as possible. When the supervisor is uncertain about an answer, it is better to say, "I don't know, but I'll find out and get back to you with an answer tomorrow." Employees lose trust in supervisors who evade subjects, are dishonest, and fail to return with answers in a timely fashion. In the final analysis, the value of an evaluation meeting depends on the employee's ability to recognize the need for self-improvement and the supervisor's ability to stimulate in the employee a desire to improve. It takes sensitivity and skill for a supervisor to accomplish this, and it is frequently necessary for the supervisor to adapt to each employee's reactions as they surface during the meeting.

DIFFICULT RESPONSES DURING THE APPRAISAL MEETING

Many supervisors try to avoid conducting appraisals. They believe the only thing they need to do is to fill out the form. With the increased demands placed on supervisors to do more with less, to increase productivity, and to find ways to continuously improve quality, many supervisors fail to find adequate time to properly evaluate the performance of their employees. As one manager recently stated, "We don't have time to evaluate around here. We're up to our neck in things to do." However, supervisors must evaluate their employees' performance.

People react to performance appraisals differently. Figure 10.8 lists some of the responses that have been encountered by supervisors conducting performance meetings. Difficult responses can challenge a supervisor, but they should not cause the supervisor to ignore or short-circuit the appraisal process.

CLOSING THE APPRAISAL MEETING

When closing the appraisal meeting, the supervisor should be certain that employees clearly understand their performance ratings. Where applicable, the supervisor and employee should agree on some mutual goals in areas in which the employee needs improvement. The supervisor should set a date with the

FIGURE 10.8 Difficult Responses the Supervisor May Encounter During the Appraisal Meeting

- "You hired me, so how can I be so bad?"
- "You're just out to get me!"
- "You don't like my lifestyle. This has nothing to do with my on-the-job performance."
- "This evaluation is not fair!"
- "I didn't know that was important. You never told me that."
- "Look, my job depends on getting good-quality material from others. I can't turn out quality work because I have to constantly inspect their work first."
- "You never say anything nice to me. You just make me feel so bad."
- The employee fails to comprehend what you've said.
- The employee refuses to talk, sits silently, or fails to respond to your open-ended questions.
- The employee rambles.
- The employee explodes and vents deep-seated hostilities toward you, his or her spouse, a parent, a coworker, and others.
- The employee accuses you of gender, racial, religious, age, or other bias.

employee, perhaps in a few weeks, to discuss progress toward the new goals. This reinforces the supervisor's stated intent to help the employee improve and gives the supervisor an opportunity to praise the employee for progress.

Many organizations ask that employees sign their performance appraisal forms after the meetings. If a signature is requested as proof that the supervisor held the appraisal meeting, the supervisor should so inform the employee. The supervisor should ensure that the employee understands that signing the form does not necessarily indicate agreement with the ratings on the form. Otherwise, the employee may be reluctant to sign the form, especially if the employee disagrees with some of the contents of the appraisal. Some appraisal forms have a line above or below the employee's signature stating that the signature only confirms that the appraisal meeting has taken place and that the employee does not necessarily agree or disagree with any statements made during the appraisal.

Some organizations require supervisors to discuss employee appraisals with managers or the human resources department before they place the appraisal documents in individuals' permanent employment records. A supervisor may be challenged to justify certain ratings if, for example, the supervisor has given very high or very low evaluations to most departmental employees. For the most part, if the supervisor has appraised employees carefully and conscientiously, such challenges will be infrequent.

Many organizations have an audit or a review process to review supervisors' appraisal decisions. The purposes of this audit are to ensure that evaluations are done fairly and to give employees a means of resolving conflicts arising from the appraisal process.

With or without a formal appraisal system, supervisors must provide regular feedback on performance. Most employees want to know how they are doing. We have known a few bosses who believe that "No news is good news. If I'm not yelling at you, then you're doing a good job." Supervisors are obligated to provide regular feedback on performance. See the accompanying Supervisory Tips box for some practical suggestions on appraising performance.

SUPERVISORY TIPS
Practical Suggestions for Improving Employee Performance

The Supervisory Challenge:

Good, better, best.
Never let it rest.
Until your good is better,
And your better is the very best!

- Let people know what is expected of them in the way of performance.
- Set clear and high goals and clarify performance standards.
- Find out what you can do to help the employee do the job.
- Supervise and coach employees so that they can succeed.
- Find out what people perceive as desirable consequences for good performance.
- Observe performance and record observations.

- Catch people doing something right and provide desirable consequences.
- Give timely feedback on performance and help the employee improve.
- Do not make good performance extinct by ignoring it.
- Thoroughly document employee performance; keep a list of critical incidents.
- Tie employee development to organizational goals. Be a coach.
- Encourage employee participation in the appraisal and development process.
- Take responsibility for soliciting feedback about your own performance.
- Remember: *There is no substitute for daily performance feedback.*

Managing Performance Appraisal Results: Coaching Employees

7 Discuss coaching as a follow-up to performance appraisal.

Effective supervisors use periodic performance evaluations as a way to develop their employees' competence. **Coaching**, a frequent supervisor activity, gives employees information, instructions, and suggestions relating to their job assignments and performance. In addition to being a coach, the supervisor should be a cheerleader and a facilitator who guides employees' behaviors toward desired results. If you want your people to be high performers (winners), then you need to help them get there (coach).[13] As a coach, the supervisor must identify activities that prepare employees for greater depth and breadth in their current or future jobs, reinforce employees' positive behaviors, and correct negative behaviors positively.

Coaching
The frequent activity of the supervisor to give employees information, instruction, and suggestions relating to their job assignments and performance

The supervisor's follow-up role in performance appraisal varies with the assessment. As a rule, supervisors use coaching to help superior employees prepare for greater responsibility as well as to improve the performance of all employees. In both cases, the purpose of coaching is to help employees become more productive by developing action plans. Even though a plan may be jointly determined with the employee, the supervisor is ultimately responsible for providing the plan and the instructions for carrying it out. The questions in Figure 10.9 may serve as guidelines for the supervisor's coaching effort.

Effective supervisors recognize that ongoing employee skill development is critical to the organization's success. Instruction, practice, and feedback are essential elements of development. Imagine playing golf without first receiving

FIGURE 10.9 Questions to Determine Coaching Strategies

The effective supervisor uses these questions to help the employee improve performance.

1. Have you identified specific areas of performance that need improvement?

2. Is it worth your time and effort to help the employee improve?

3. Does the employee understand that his or her performance needs improvement?

4. Does the employee know what is expected (standards of performance)?

5. Are there barriers beyond the employee's control that influence current performance?

6. Does the employee know how to do the job?

7. Could the employee do the job if his or her life depended on it? (If not, training is necessary.)

8. What happens when the employee does the job well?

9. What do you do when performance is deficient?

10. Have you considered alternative courses of action?

11. Have you and the employee mutually agreed on a course of action (e.g., set specific objectives and a timetable, developed improvement plans, and identified training programs)?

12. Have you provided information, instruction, and suggestions?

13. Does the employee fully understand the consequences if unacceptable performance continues?

14. What follow-up measures will you use and how will you measure improvements?

15. How will you reward and reinforce improvement?

16. What will you do if performance does not improve?

instruction and having a chance to practice newly learned techniques. Most golfers seek instruction because they want to improve their games. Athletes like Tiger Woods, who swiftly transitioned from amateur golf to the professional circuit and set records for wins and earnings, are gifted with fundamental ability, yet they continually seek advice from their coaches. In business, as in sports, employees benefit from coaching. The coach observes the employee's performance and communicates what went well and what specifically needs improvement. The plan for improvement usually includes defining the expected level of performance, recommending specific steps for improvement, and observing performance. After developing the plan, the coach instructs the employee and allows the employee time to practice the skills. The coach then observes the employee's performance, providing feedback about the effectiveness of the performance and offering further instruction and encouragement as needed.

Often, employees will self-select another employee—one who is perceived to be one of the best—and learn from that person. It is not surprising that Tiger Woods and Annika Sorenstam practiced together. We suspect that even the best male golfer can learn something from the best female golfer and vice versa.

© LUCY NICHOLSON/REUTERS/LANDOV

Tiger Woods's thoughts on Annika Sorenstam are reflected in the following quote:

"We have a great friendship and one I certainly treasure because to see what she's doing out there, it's a lot of fun to watch because it's precise golf. Her focus, her determination, her preparation over the winter months, people don't realize how hard she works. We worked on our short games together this fall. You can't believe how hard she works. She didn't get to this level by just hoping she could play well. She went out and worked and took it to another level. It's been great fun to be a spectator of that and to be able to watch it."[14]

Generally, the employees who benefit most from coaching are the average performers, not the superstars. The former must develop their skills and learn the fundamentals. The coach must continuously provide constructive feedback. Because improvement does not occur instantaneously, the supervisor should be patient with the employee to allow for different learning styles and speeds.

Employee performance usually improves when specific improvement goals are established during the performance appraisal. It is important that supervisors realize that they are responsible for improving the performance of deficient employees. The supervisor must remember that employees cannot improve unless they know exactly what is expected. The supervisor should maintain close contact with employees and provide instruction when needed. Supervisors also should suggest ways to improve performance and identify possible mentors. Performance improvements should be supported by positive feedback and reinforcement.

Rarely, when action plans fail to improve performance and unsatisfactory performance continues, termination may be necessary. Employee replacement is very expensive. Good coaching can avoid termination in many cases. The role of the supervisor in the positive discipline of less proficient employees was discussed in Chapter 6.

8 Identify the benefits of a promotion-from-within policy.

Managing Performance Appraisal Results: Promoting Employees

Given the proper encouragement, many employees strive to improve their performance and eventually be promoted. A promotion usually means advancement to a job with more responsibility, more privileges, higher status, greater potential, and higher pay.

Most, but not all, employees want to improve or advance. Some employees may feel that increased responsibility would demand too much of their time and energy, or they may be content with their present positions. Most employees, however, want promotions. For them, starting at the bottom and rising in status and income is a normal way of life.

PROMOTING FROM WITHIN

Most organizations have policies for promoting employees. The policy of promoting from within is widely practiced, and it is important to both an organization and its employees. For the organization, it means a steady source of trained personnel for higher positions; for employees, it is a major incentive to perform better. When employees work for organizations for a long time, more is usually known about them than even the best selection processes and interviews could reveal about outside applicants for the same job. Supervisors should know their employees well; they do not know individuals hired from outside until those individuals have worked for them a while.

Occasionally, a supervisor might want to bypass an employee for promotion because the productivity of the department would suffer until a replacement is found and trained. However, this thinking is shortsighted. It is better for the organization in the long run to have the best qualified people in positions where they can make the greatest contributions to the organization's success.

There would be little reason for employees to improve if they believed that the better and higher-paying jobs were reserved for outsiders. Additional job satisfaction results when employees know that stronger efforts on their part may lead to more interesting and challenging work, higher pay and status, and better working conditions. Most employees are more motivated when they see a link between excellent performance and a reward they covet.

When considering promotion for an employee, the supervisor should recognize that what management considers a promotion may not always be perceived as such by the employee. For example, an engineer may believe that a promotion to administrative work is a hardship, not an advancement. The engineer may feel that administrative activities are less interesting or more difficult than technical duties, and he or she may be concerned about losing or diluting professional engineering skills. Such an attitude is understandable, and the supervisor should try to suggest promotional opportunities that do not require unacceptable compromises.

Also, the supervisor should be sensitive to employees who appear to be satisfied in their present positions. They may prefer to stay with their fellow employees and to retain responsibilities with which they are familiar and comfortable. These employees should not be pressured by the supervisor to accept higher-level positions. However, if the supervisor believes that such an employee has excellent qualifications for promotion, the supervisor should offer the encouragement and counsel that may make a promotion attractive to the employee for current or future consideration.

Employee satisfaction increases when there are opportunites for advancement

MODIFYING A PROMOTION-FROM-WITHIN POLICY

Generally, it is preferable to apply a promotion-from-within policy whenever possible. However, situations will arise in which strict adherence to this policy would not be sensible and might even harm an organization. If there are no qualified internal candidates for a position, then someone from the outside must be recruited. For example, if an experienced computer programmer is needed and no existing employee has programming expertise, the departmental supervisor will have to hire one from outside the organization.

At times, bringing a new employee into a department may be desirable because this person brings different ideas and fresh perspectives to the job. Another reason for recruiting employees from the outside is that an organization may not be in a position to train its own employees in the necessary skills. A particular position may require long, specialized, or expensive training, and the organization may be unable to offer or to afford such training. To cover these contingencies, a promotion-from-within policy must be modified as appropriate. For this reason, most written policy statements concerning promotion from within include such qualifying clauses as "whenever possible" or "whenever feasible."

CRITERIA FOR PROMOTING FROM WITHIN

Typically, more employees are interested in being promoted than there are openings. Because promotions should be incentives for employees to perform better, some supervisors believe that employees who have the best records of production, quality, and cooperation are the ones who should be promoted. In some situations, however, it is difficult to measure such aspects of employee performance accurately or objectively, even when there has been a conscientious effort by supervisors in the form of merit ratings or performance appraisals.

SENIORITY

Seniority
An employee's length of service in a department or an organization

One easily measured and objective criterion that has been applied extensively in an effort to reduce favoritism and discrimination is seniority. **Seniority** is an employee's length of service in the department or organization. Labor unions have emphasized seniority as a major promotion criterion, and its use is also widespread among organizations that are not unionized and for jobs that are not covered by union agreements. Many supervisors are comfortable with the concept of seniority as a basis for promotion. Some supervisors feel that an employee's loyalty, as expressed by length of service, deserves to be rewarded. Basing promotion on seniority also assumes that an employee's abilities tend to increase with service. Although this assumption is not always accurate, it is likely that, with continued service, an employee's skills and knowledge will improve. If promotion is to be based largely on seniority, then the initial selection procedure for new employees must be careful, and each new employee should receive considerable training in various positions.

Probably the most serious drawback to using seniority as the major criterion for promotion is that it discourages young employees—those with less seniority. Younger employees may believe that they cannot advance until they too have accumulated years of service on the job. Consequently, they may lose enthusiasm and perform at only average levels. Another serious drawback is that the best performer is not always the most senior. If seniority is the only criterion, then there may be no incentive to perform well.

MERIT AND ABILITY

Although labor unions have stressed the seniority criterion in promotion, seniority alone does not guarantee that an individual either deserves promotion or is capable of advancing to a higher-level job. In fact, some employees with high seniority may lack the educational or skill levels needed for advancement. Consequently, most unions understand that length of service cannot be the only criterion for promotion. They agree that promotion should be based on seniority combined with merit and ability, and this type of provision is included in many union contracts.

Merit
The quality of an employee's job performance

Ability
An employee's potential to perform higher-level tasks

Merit usually refers to the quality of an employee's job performance. **Ability** means an employee's ability or potential to perform or to be trained to perform a higher-level job. Supervisors often are in the best position to determine the degree to which merit and ability are necessary to compensate for less seniority. However, seniority is frequently the decisive criterion when merit and ability are relatively equal among several candidates seeking a promotion.

BALANCING CRITERIA

Good supervisory practice attempts to attain a workable balance among merit, ability, and seniority. When selecting from among the most qualified candidates available, the supervisor may decide to choose essentially on the basis of seniority.

Or the supervisor may decide that in order to be promoted the employee who is most capable but who has less seniority will have to be far better than those with more seniority. This is sometimes referred to as the "head-and-shoulders" concept. Otherwise, the supervisor will promote the qualified employee with the greatest seniority, at least on a trial basis.

Because promotion decisions can have great significance, the preferred solution would be to apply all criteria equally. However, promotion decisions often involve gray areas or subjective considerations that can lead rejected employees to be dissatisfied and file grievances. Realistically, unless there are unusual circumstances, it is unlikely that a supervisor will choose to promote an employee based solely on merit and ability without some thought to seniority.

Managing Performance Appraisal Results: Compensating Employees

9 Discuss the supervisor's role in employee compensation and outline the goals of an effective compensation program.

Although it is not always recognized as such, a supervisor's staffing function includes helping to determine the relative worth of jobs. Typically, wage rates and salary schedules are formulated by higher-level management, by the human resources department, by union contract, or by government legislation or regulation. In this respect, the supervisor's authority is limited. Nevertheless, the supervisor is responsible for determining appropriate compensation for departmental employees.

The question of how much to pay employees poses a problem for many organizations. It is possible, however, to establish a compensation program that is objective, fair, and relatively easy to administer. The objectives of a compensation program should be to:

- Eliminate pay inequities to minimize dissatisfaction and complaints among employees.
- Establish and/or maintain sufficiently attractive pay rates so that qualified employees are attracted to and retained by the company.
- Conduct periodic employee merit ratings to provide the basis for comparative performance rewards.
- Control labor costs with respect to productivity gains.
- Reward employees for outstanding performance or the acquisition of additional skills or knowledge.

Generally, the HR department establishes compensation levels that will attract and retain competent employees. Too often, wage rate schedules simply follow historical patterns, or they are formulated haphazardly. At the departmental level, wage rate inequities often develop over time due to changes in jobs, changes in personnel, and different supervisors using varying standards for administering compensation. Because wage inequities and concerns arise, supervisors should immediately address them and, on balance, strive for a wage system that is uniform, consistent, and meets the aforementioned objectives.

THE SUPERVISOR'S ROLE IN COMPENSATION DECISIONS

Although a sound and equitable compensation structure should be of great concern to everyone in management, it is an area in which supervisors typically have limited direct authority. However, supervisors should try to make higher-level managers aware of serious compensation inequities at the departmental level. This often can be done when supervisors make their recommendations for wage and salary adjustments for individual employees.

It is imperative that both supervisors and employees know the "lay of the land" as it relates to the relationship between performance evaluation and salary increases. Generally, an individual employee or team of employees will be given a merit raise when they achieve some performance objective. As you recall from Chapter 4, employees are willing to put forth more effort when they perceive the following linkages: putting forth more effort will lead to achievement, which will lead to a desirable outcome: a merit raise.[15] It is imperative that supervisors be able to justify and document performance evaluations regardless of whether the employee exceeded expectations, met expectations, or did not meet expectations, and be able to explain how the performance evaluation relates to the raise an employee might receive.

RECOMMENDING WAGE ADJUSTMENTS

Unfortunately, too often supervisors automatically recommend full wage increases without seriously considering whether each employee deserves such a raise. Here is where employee performance evaluation is crucial. If an employee's work has been satisfactory, then the employee deserves the normal increase. If the employee has performed at an unsatisfactory level, the supervisor should suspend the recommendation for an increase and discuss this decision with the employee. The supervisor might outline specific targets for job improvement that the employee must meet before the supervisor will recommend a wage increase, as shown in Figure 10.10. If an employee has performed at an outstanding level,

FIGURE 10.10 A supervisor must closely monitor performance to determine who gets a merit increase

the supervisor should not hesitate to recommend a generous, above-average wage increase if this can be done within the wage structure. Such a tangible reward will encourage the outstanding employee to continue striving for excellence.

EMPLOYEE INCENTIVES

Many organizations are attempting to maximize their compensation programs. While estimates vary on the number of organizations using performance-based or incentive compensation systems in an attempt to motivate employees to perform at higher levels, many organizations are attempting to link performance to pay.[16] In this section, we review incentive systems.

PIECEWORK

In a straight **piecework** system, the employee earns a certain amount of pay for each unit or piece produced. Difficulties arise when jobs are interdependent and the employee must rely on others to complete the assigned task.

Piecework
System in which the employee earns a certain amount of pay for each piece produced

PAY FOR PERFORMANCE

In **pay for performance**, compensation is based on employee or corporate performance goals. Among these approaches are special cash awards, bonuses for meeting performance targets, team (departmental) incentive bonuses, profit sharing, and gain sharing for meeting production or cost-saving goals. **Gain-sharing plans** are group incentive plans. Group or team plans are normally used when the contribution of an individual employee is either not easily measurable or when performance depends on team cooperation. Employees share the monetary benefits (gains) of improved productivity, cost reductions, or improvements in quality or customer service. Most plans use an easy-to-understand formula to calculate productivity gains and the resulting bonus.

Pay for performance
Compensation, other than base wages, that is given for achieving employee or corporate goals

Gain-sharing plans
Group incentive plans that have employees share in the benefits from improved performance

SKILL-BASED PAY

A **skill-based pay** or *knowledge-based pay* system rewards employees for acquiring additional skills or knowledge in the same job category. It does not reward employees for the jobs they do regularly. Employees are rotated through various tasks associated with the job until they learn them all. Rewards are based on the acquisition of and proficiency in new skills, regardless of the employee's length of service.[17] Employees are rewarded according to the number of skills they have mastered.

Skill-based pay has become an attractive way to reward employees when promotional opportunities are scarce. Skill-based pay is most successful in organizations in which a participatory management philosophy prevails. The supervisor is usually the key to the success of a skill-based pay plan. Other attributes of a skill-based pay system are the:

Skill-based pay
System that rewards employees for acquiring new skills or knowledge

- Need for a deep commitment to training to achieve success.
- Use of multi-tasking or job rotation strategies.
- Choice of plan is tied to business needs.
- Supervisor support.[18]

For a skill-based pay plan to succeed, the company must require and directly benefit from the skills it pays for. A closed-ended questionnaire is used by employees to identify the activities, skills, knowledge, and abilities required by their jobs. All jobs are assigned a pay grade based on the value of their required activities, skills, and knowledge.[19] All employees now know what they must be able to do to be eligible for promotions or lateral transfers.

SUGGESTION PLANS

In earlier chapters, we discussed the fact that employees may be motivated by the sense of achievement that comes from seeing their ideas implemented. Suggestion plans are one way to solicit employee ideas; typically, employees are paid based on the value of their suggestions. Suggestion systems, however, may fail if they are evaluated on savings alone.[20]

INCENTIVE PLAN QUANDARY

No incentive plan is immune from charges of inequity. Input from primary stakeholders (e.g., employees, first-line supervisors, and customers) before implementing the program will help to identify the right things to measure. For an incentive plan to succeed, management must clearly define what they want to reward. If it is customer service, then employees must understand what is to be measured and must be able to impact those measures in their daily work.

Team-based incentive plans are not without their problems. These problems will continue to arise as team-based incentive plans grow in popularity because of the increasing use of teams.

A survey by Hewitt Associates found that only a few incentive pay plans met or exceeded their primary objectives. According to Ken Abosch, Hewitt's compensation business leader, "Unfortunately, a lot of companies don't know what they want their compensation plan to achieve; don't know how to monitor or measure plan performance; and, sometimes, don't want to know whether the plan is working because then they have to do something about it."[21] Regardless of the incentive compensation plan, supervisors must fully comprehend the plan and be able to answer employee questions.

EMPLOYEE BENEFITS

In addition to monetary compensation, most organizations provide supplementary benefits for employees, such as vacations with pay, holidays, retirement plans, insurance and health programs, tuition-aid programs, employee-assistance programs (EAPs), and numerous other services.[22] Supervisors have little involvement in establishing benefits, but they are obligated to see that departmental employees understand how their benefits operate and that each employee receives an equitable share.

When employees have questions about benefits, supervisors should consult with the human resources staff or higher-level managers. For example, a supervisor often has to make decisions involving employee benefits, such as in scheduling departmental vacations or work shifts during the holidays. In these circumstances, the supervisor must be sure that what is done at the departmental level is consistent with the organization's overall policies as well as with laws, union contract provisions, and the like.

COMPENSATION CONCERNS

Employees commonly compare their compensation to that of others. This becomes a serious motivational problem for the supervisor when the organization has wages or benefits that are considerably lower than those for similar jobs at other firms in the community.

Two-tier wage systems and contract employees are additional concerns for the supervisor in trying to maintain a perception of fairness. Depending on a firm's arrangement with a temporary agency, the temporary employee may be paid more or less than regular employees performing the same job. In organizations using a two-tier wage system, new employees are paid less than present employees performing the same or similar jobs. Unfortunately, lower-paid employees can have feelings of inequity when working under these systems. Again, supervisors should make every effort to stay informed about their organization's compensation systems and should consult the human resources or benefits office when questions arise. As easy as it might be to disregard employee concerns about compensation, supervisors must recognize that this is an important area of concern for most employees.

We cannot emphasize enough the importance of communication.[23] If the supervisor does not have the answer to the employee's question, the supervisor should say so and then should strive to find the answer. Moreover, supervisors should permit and even encourage employees to visit the human resources department or the appropriate manager for advice and assistance concerning benefits and compensation problems. This practice is particularly desirable when employees have personal problems or questions about sensitive areas, such as medical and other health benefits and retirement and insurance programs.

SUMMARY

1 Performance management consists of all those things a supervisor must do to enable an employee to achieve organizational objectives. As illustrated in Figure 10.1, the supervisor establishes goals and objectives, coaches, gives feedback, helps the employee adjust performance or take corrective action, documents performance, and rewards performance.

If the supervisor truly believes that "people are the organization's most valuable asset," two-way and frequent communication is the key to an effective performance-management system.

2 A formal performance appraisal system is the process of periodically rating an employee's performance against standards and communicating this feedback to the employee. Supervisors are responsible for appraising employee performance both informally on a day-to-day basis and formally at predetermined intervals. Supervisors must keep accurate records of employee performance.

To ensure that employees feel the appraisal process is fair, each evaluator must understand what is necessary for successful job performance. Peer evaluations and 360-degree performance evaluations are ways to provide performance feedback from perspectives other than the supervisor's, and they can contribute to a more complete performance picture. Including self-rating in the process can facilitate the open discussion of employees' perceptions of their strengths and weaknesses.

3 Ideally, the supervisor will spend time each day providing performance feedback to employees. As stressed throughout the chapter, "There is no substitute for daily feedback on performance."

Most organizations require formal performance appraisals at least once each year. Because the decision to retain a new employee is critical, the performance assessment of probationary employees should be done at the end of the probationary period. When there is a serious performance problem, the supervisor should provide immediate feedback. However,

ongoing feedback, both positive and negative, should be a regular part of the supervisor's routine. If the employee is given ongoing feedback, then the annual appraisal should contain no surprises. It should be a review of what the supervisor and employee have discussed during the year.

4 When done properly, formal performance appraisals benefit both the organization and the employee. Organizations use performance appraisals as a basis for important decisions concerning such things as promotions, raises, and terminations. Performance appraisals reward employees' good performance and tell them how they can become more productive.

The major advantage of a formal appraisal system is that it provides a framework to help the supervisor systematically evaluate performance and communicate to employees how they are doing. Formal appraisals can be employee incentives. They get positive feedback about their performance, and they know that the formal system documents their performance.

Much of the criticism of performance appraisals dwells on the fact that they often focus only on past accomplishments or deficiencies. Supervisors can overcome this criticism by emphasizing the developmental aspects of performance appraisal.

5 Appraisal forms may vary in format and approach, but they should allow supervisors to identify the outstanding aspects of the employee's work, specify performance areas that need improvement, and suggest ways to improve performance.

Supervisors should be consistent in applying the terms used to describe an employee's performance. Not all supervisors judge employees' performance accurately, and sometimes a supervisor can damage an employee's morale by giving lower ratings than the employee deserves. Additional perceptual errors include the leniency error, the halo and horns effects, and other personal biases.

When filling out the appraisal form, the supervisor should focus on the employee's accomplishments. The results should be described in terms of *how much*, *how well*, and *in what manner*. Whatever the choice of appraisal form, it is important that every appraisal be made in the context of the employee's job and be based on the employee's total performance.

6 Although the appraisal meeting may be trying, the entire employee performance appraisal system is of no use if the meeting is ignored or is carried out improperly. The supervisor should begin by stating that the overall purpose of the appraisal meeting is to let employees know how they are doing. The supervisor should give positive feedback for good performance, emphasize strengths the employee can build on, and identify performance aspects that need improvement.

The meeting should be conducted in private shortly after the form is completed. How the supervisor conducts the meeting depends to a large extent on the employee's performance. Supervisors should restrict criticism to those areas that need correction or improvement. An employee performing at a substandard level must clearly understand that the deficiencies are serious and that substantial improvement is needed. Employees are more likely to agree with the appraisal when they understand the standards of performance and recognize that the appraisal is free of bias.

The supervisor should emphasize that all employees in the same job are evaluated using the same standards. Supervisors may use a critical-incident method for documenting employee performance that is very good or unsatisfactory. Employees should be given an opportunity to ask questions, and the supervisor should answer them honestly. The supervisor should anticipate questions, potential areas of disagreement, and difficult responses that may arise during the appraisal meeting.

Employees should clearly understand their evaluations. New objectives should be set and areas for improvement identified. Generally, the employee is asked to sign the appraisal form to prove that the meeting took place. Organizations should have an audit process to resolve conflicts arising from the appraisal.

7 Supervisors should fulfill the role of coach in the conduct of their daily activities. During the performance appraisal process, supervisors should provide employees with information, instruction, and suggestions relating to their job assignments and performance.

Supervisors can use a coaching approach to prepare superior employees for greater responsibility as well as to improve the performance of all employees. Ongoing employee skill development is essential. Based on the performance appraisal, the coach develops a plan for improvement. Specific improvement goals are set. The employee receives instruction and is given an opportunity to practice. The coach provides feedback and encouragement.

8 Most employees want to improve and advance in the organization. Promotion from within is a widely practiced personnel policy that is beneficial to the organization and to the morale of employees. Supervisors know their employees' strengths and abilities; they do not know as much about individuals hired from outside. When employees know they have a good chance of advancement, they will have an incentive to improve their job performance. In short, promotion from within rewards employees for their good performance and serves notice to other employees that good performance will lead to advancement.

Although organizations should promote from within whenever possible, strict adherence to a promotion-from-within policy is not sensible. When internal employees have not received the necessary training, an external candidate may be preferred. Sometimes, an outsider may be needed to inject new and different ideas.

Because promotions should serve as an incentive for employees to perform better, it is generally believed that employees who have the best performance records should be promoted. Nevertheless, seniority still serves as a basis for many promotions. Seniority is easily understood and withstands charges of favoritism and discrimination. However, a promotional system based solely on seniority removes the incentive for junior employees who want to advance. Although it is difficult to specify exactly what should be the basis for employee promotion, there should be appropriate consideration of ability and merit on the one hand and length of service on the other.

9 The supervisor's staffing function includes making certain that employees of a department are compensated properly. Many compensation considerations are not within the direct domain of a supervisor.

Monetary rewards serve, in part, to meet the needs of employees who perform at outstanding levels. Supervisors must become aware of other compensation arrangements that may better meet their employees' needs. Pay for performance, skill-based pay, suggestion systems, and other benefit plans could be considered.

Because supervisory responsibility and authority are limited in these areas, supervisors should work closely with the human resources staff to maintain equitable compensation offerings and to ensure that departmental employees are informed and treated fairly in regard to benefits and any bonus plans that may be available.

KEY TERMS

360-degree evaluation (p. 346)
Ability (p. 364)
Coaching (p. 359)
Critical incident method (p. 355)
Gain-sharing plans (p. 367)
Leniency error (p. 352)

Merit (p. 364)
Pay for performance (p. 367)
Peer evaluation (p. 345)
Performance appraisal (p. 342)
Performance standards (p. 353)
Piecework (p. 367)

Seniority (p. 364)
Skill-based pay (p. 367)
System of performance management
    (p. 342)

QUESTIONS FOR DISCUSSION

1. What should an effective performance management system look like? How does appraising, coaching, promoting, and compensating employees fit into the system?

2. Outline the major aspects of an appraisal meeting. What are some of the major difficulties associated with this type of meeting?

3. What are the advantages and disadvantages of promotion based on seniority?

4. Explain the following statement: "Wage increases should be based solely on performance measures." How does the supervisor develop clear guidelines for determining who gets a raise and how much they should get?

SKILLS APPLICATIONS

Skills Application 10-1: Achieving Peak Performance

1.  Before beginning this Skills Application, carefully re-read this chapter's opening "You Make the Call!"

Step 1: Working individually, develop a performance management system for a bank teller at Citizen's National Bank. The job requires a great deal of personal customer attention, technology skills, and attention to details.

Step 2: Form into groups of three, one person acting as Simone, the second as HR director Jennifer Teeple, and the third as observer.

a. Read the following provision from the Citizen's employee handbook:

Team members are encouraged to first discuss the issue, concern or grievance with his or her immediate supervisor. When that is not practical or feasible, the team members should contact HR for a confidential and personal meeting.

b. Prior to the meeting, the person playing the role of Simone should prepare a list of no more than three issues that she wants to discuss with HR.

c. The person playing Jennifer Teeple should greet Simone and set the stage for the meeting.

d. The observer(s) should make notes of Simone's concerns and how Teeple addressed them.

e. All participants should answer the following questions:

1. Did Simone present her concerns in such a way that they were fully understood by the HR director? Give illustrations.

2. What might Simone have done differently to ensure that Teeple understood her concerns?

3. What else could the HR director have done to fully grasp Simone's concerns?

4. What problem-solving techniques were used to mutually arrive at the outcomes?

5. Did Simone leave the meeting feeling satisfied with the outcomes? Why? Why not?

6. What steps should HR director Teeple take to review the performance management and appraisal system at Citizen's National Bank?

Skills Application 10-2: Designing the Performance Appraisal System

1. **INTERNET ACTIVITY** Before beginning this Skills Applications, carefully re-read this chapter's opening "You Make the Call!"

2. Conduct an Internet search to gather information on 360-degree feedback; graphic rating scales; behavioral anchored rating scales (BARS); critical incident, forced-choice; employee ranking, and checklist approaches to employee appraisal.

3. Either individually or in small groups, answer the following questions:

a. What should be the purposes of a system of performance appraisal at Citizen's National Bank?

b. Why do you think that George Murphy did not take adequate time to explain Simone's appraisal ratings?

c. What should Simone have done in the meeting with Murphy to take responsibility for her own career development? Why might she have been reluctant to do so?

d. After Simone's meeting with Teeple, what steps should the HR director take to ensure a more effective feedback approach at the Adams Center branch?

e. In no more than 40 words, describe what you learned from this activity.

Skills Application 10-3: Role-play Exercise

1. **(ROLE PLAY)** Form groups of three, with one person acting as the employee, the second as the supervisor, and the third as the observer. The supervisor will evaluate the employee using the information in one of the following situations. The supervisor role will require imagination to provide feedback.

   The observer will observe the interview relationship using the "Observer Recording" form (provided by your instructor) and, at the end of each interview, the observer will provide feedback on the effectiveness of the interview.

2. Rotate roles so that each person has an opportunity to play all three roles: employee, supervisor, and observer.

   Situation A: "Nowhere to Go" Alyn Adams is a very good/above-average performer with high potential for advancement. He is the produce department team leader for Sanders Supermarkets. He has worked for Sanders for the past seven years and was promoted to his current position three years ago. Adams won a supervisory management contest sponsored by the local college last summer. His strengths lie in personal efficiency, job knowledge, and dependability. On occasion, he is "too customer service–oriented." For example, he substitutes more expensive produce for a lesser price. You approach the interview knowing the following circumstances:

   a. There are roadblocks ahead for Adams in that his opportunity for advancement is limited for the foreseeable future.
   b. There are several opportunities for advancement in the organization, but they require relocation or rotating shift work (both undesirable alternatives from Adams's perspective).

   Situation B: "The Expert" Tony Becker had been a regional supervisor for Sanders Supermarkets. When the organization consolidated operations, Becker was demoted and transferred to an assistant's position at the Pridemore location. Becker has been with Sanders for more than 30 years and is much older than his supervisor. Becker shows up for work early and stays late. Becker's knowledge of the supermarket industry is second to none. However, he is unwilling to share it with anyone. He is very angry about his demotion and is very difficult to work with in general. He is belligerent toward younger employees, resents his supervisor's authority, and insists on doing things his way. He refers to the younger female employees and to customers as "Honey." You have constantly counseled Becker on his inappropriate behaviors, and he reminds you that he started at Sanders before you were born. Some employees try to avoid him. Several have threatened to quit unless he changes. Becker has made some serious errors when scheduling deliveries. You approach the interview knowing the following circumstances:

   a. Becker's performance is unsatisfactory on most factors.
   b. You question whether Becker should be retained. Your perspective is clouded, however, because you know that your immediate supervisor trained under Becker and has said on several occasions that Becker taught him everything he knows and that if Becker had not helped him, he would not have such a great job.

   Situation C: "Miss Cue" Mary Cue has an entry-level data-processing position at Sanders Supermarkets. She has been on the job for six months and is generally performing at "less than a satisfactory level." Cue has an attendance problem. She usually misses work once every two weeks, either on a Monday or Friday. On five occasions, something happened that required Cue to leave work early to check on her elderly parents. Cue tends to rush work, thereby causing errors in payment, shipments, and the like. She is a great storyteller, and she often can be found in other parts of the building describing her "most recent late-night dates" to a very interested audience. You sent Cue to Advanced Windows, Excel, and two word-processing classes, but she continues to have trouble progressing beyond the basics of data entry. Her attention span is limited, and she does not readily grasp new concepts. You approach the interview knowing the following circumstances:

   a. Cue is a member of a protected class.
   b. Cue believes she is underpaid for the work she is expected to do.

Note: The "Observer Rating" form in the instructor's manual for this text may be reproduced for use with this Skills Application.

Skills Application 10-4: Batty the Scatterbrain

This is the next in a series of Skills Applications that will introduce another person who may make your life difficult.

1. Read the following statement from John Peters, an accounting department supervisor for the Pine Village Community Medical Center (CMC):

Wilma is a real dingbat. Everybody loves her, but she is scatterbrained. She forgets appointments all the time. We all try to help her because we know she means well, but we sometimes wonder how she got hired. I recognize *that some people have bad days, but Wilma always has trouble. When I talk about Wilma at home, my kids say she is an "airhead," and I tell them that some of the employees call her "Batty" behind her back. She is always making silly mistakes and lacks common sense. Unorganized is probably the word that best describes Wilma.*

Wilma can be truly endearing and completely frustrating. She has potential but is lost in her own world, so she can't be relied on. She's easily distracted by peripheral issues and has trouble working with the team.

She should probably be fired because she always misses deadlines, but I'm not certain that we can find anyone better to replace her.

I've tried to explain what needs to be done and how to do it and to let Wilma know that I'm available if she has any questions. I even leave her a "punch list" of what needs to be done by when and she still messes up. Just last week, she misplaced the list.

Yesterday, Wilma asked me about a patient's account that needed to be reconciled. We spent at least an hour going over the "how's" and "where's." Today, she asked me the same questions about another customer's account. I don't know if she's just dumb or just doesn't care. I don't think I can continue to be a babysitter, but what do I do?

2.  Using the Internet, find at least three sources for how to deal with people who are scatterbrained. Our students prefer to call this person the "absent-minded professor." Carefully review each site for suggestions on how to deal with this type of person.

3. Based on your findings, what suggestions would you make to John Peters on how to deal with Wilma?

4. Write a one-page paper explaining how this skill application increased your working knowledge of coping with the behaviors of this person who makes life difficult for others.

SKILLS DEVELOPMENT

Skills Development Module 10-1: Learning From Tigers

 After viewing the video clip for Skills Development Module 10-1, answer the questions provided. Hopefully, these will stimulate your analytical and thinking skills.

Most of our students recognize Accenture for their full-page ads in the Wall Street Journal. These ads generally feature Tiger Woods. Accenture began as a consulting division of Arthur Andersen, one of the nation's largest accounting firms. For many reasons, Andersen Consulting split from Arthur Andersen in the early part of century.

On January 1, 2001, Andersen Consulting changed its name to "Accenture". The word is derived from "Accent on the future".

The split and name change came at a fortuitous time. Shortly thereafter, Arthur Andersen was dissolved as a result of its role in the Enron scandal.

Accenture, with over 100,000 employees, is a global leader is consulting services.

You may want to go to http://www.accenture.com to learn more about Accenture.

Questions for Discussion

1. Many organizations contend that "people are our most important asset." What does Accenture do to reinforce this notion?

2. Accenture evaluates and rewards their employees on three criteria. For each of the criteria, develop a standard or metric, and explain how you would evaluate a typical employee's performance on each.

3. How can Accenture use a system of performance management to aid in succession planning?

ENDNOTES

Suggested readings and Web sites: (1) (online http://hrd.sagepub.com). (2) *Human Resource Development Review* (online http://hrd.sagepub.com/content/). (3) Kenneth W. Moore, "Human Resources: Adapting in the 21st Century," *SHRM White Paper* (March 2008). (4) Wayne F. Cascio and John W. Boudreau, *Investing in People: Financial Impact of Human Resources Initiatives* (Alexandria, VA: SHRM, 2008). (5) Amy Delpo, *The Performance Appraisal Handbook: Legal & Practical Rules for Managers,* 2nd ed. (Berkley, CA: Nolo, 2007). (6) Marnie E. Green, *Painless Performance Evaluation: A Practice Approach for Managing Day-to-Day Employee Performance* (Berkley, CA: Nolo, 2005). (7) "Pros and Cons of Forced Ranking and Other Relative Performance Ranking Systems," *SHRM Legal Report* (March 2003). (8) "SHRM/CNNfn Job Satisfaction Series: Job Benefits Survey," *SHRM*

Research (December 2003). (9) Society for Human Resource Management (www.shrm.org). (10) Academy of Human Resource Development (www.ahrd.org). (11) (American Society for Training and Development) www.astd.org. (12) (Learning 4 Life Resources) www.learning4LifeResources.com. (13) (Career Builder) www.careerbuilder.com.

1 Robert Kreitner and Angelo Kinicki, *Organizational Behavior* (Boston, MA: Irwin McGraw-Hill, 1998), p. 193.

2 We cannot remember when we first heard the phrase, "Managing performance to achieve organizational objectives is what supervision is all about." Peter M. Glendinning used the terms *performance management* and *performance appraisal* synonymously in his article

"Performance Management: Pariah or Messiah," *Public Personnel Management* (Summer 2002), pp. 161+. He said, "Performance management, or performance appraisal, is defined as both the process through which companies ensure that employees are working toward organizational goals."

In an interview in *Performance Management Magazine*, Aubrey C. Daniels offered this definition: "In simplest terms, performance management is a way of getting people to do what you want them to do and to like doing it." (November 13, 2000), accessed at http://www. pmezine.com/article_dtls.asp?NID=68. Also see "Performance Management," U.S. Office of Personnel Management, (http://www.opm. gov/perform/overview.asp) (Accessed September 27, 2008).

Adrienne Fox in "Prune Employees Carefully," *HR Magazine* (April 2008), pp. 66–70, says that firms need to get their performance management systems in order, engage top performers, and prepare for an economic rebound. Also see "Parallels Between Performance Management Quality and Organizational Performance," *Supervision* (August 2005), pp. 19–20.

3. Many employees dislike performance reviews. See Jared Sandberg, "Performance Reviews Often Miss the Mark," *The Wall Street Journal* (December 4, 2007), p. 6B; Jay M. Jackson and Myra H. Strober, "Fear of Feedback," *Harvard Business Review* (April 2003), pp. 101–7; "Gentler Reviews & Other Responses to Forced Rankings," *Ioma's Pay for Performance Report* (June 2002), pp. 7+ (Ioma = Institute of Management and Administration); Max Messmer, "Performance Reviews," *Strategic Finance* (December 2000), pp. 10–12; Tom Coens and Mary Jenkins, *Abolishing Performance Appraisals: Why They Backfire and What to Do Instead* (Berrett-Koehler, San Francisco: 2000).

4. A 2004 survey by Novations Group, Inc., found that 44 percent of HR professionals said that their firms' forced ranking systems damage morale and generate mistrust of leadership. See Steve Bates, "Research Finds Short-term Benefits in Forced Ranking," *SHRM Home* (March 2, 2005).

For a discussion of peer appraisals, see "Performance Appraisals: How to Handle Problems," *Ioma's Pay for Performance Report* (September 2004), pp. 1, 14–15; "Multi-Rater Feedback and Performance Evaluation Programs Do Not Mix," *Supervision* (March 1998), p. 25; Daniel Kanouse, "Why Multi-Rater Feedback Systems Fail," *HR Focus* (January 1998), p. 3; David A. Waldman, "Predictors of Employee Preferences for multi-rater and Group-Based Performance Appraisal," *Group & Organizational Management* (June 1997), pp. 264–87; Carol W. Timmreck and David W. Bracken, "MultiSource Feedback: A Study of Its Use in Decision Making," *Employment Relations Today* (Spring 1997), pp. 21–27; and Martin L. Ramsey and Howard Lehto, "The Power of Peer Review," *Training & Development* (July 1994), pp. 38–41. Also see Irene Buhalo, "You Sign My Report Card—I'll Sign Yours," *Personnel* (May 1991), p. 23, and G. M. McEvoy, P. F. Buller, and S. R. Roghaar, "A Jury of One's Peers," *Personnel Administrator* (May 1988), pp. 94–98.

5. 360-degree appraisals are controversial. Dennis Coates says, "You can use 360-degree feedback for performance management, but not for performance appraisal. Why not? Because it undermines trust." (See Coates, "Don't Tie 360 Feedback to Pay," *Training* (September 1998), pp. 58–78. Coates's sentiments are reinforced in more recent articles; see Bruce Pfau and Ira Key, "Does 360-Degree Feedback Negatively Affect Company Performance?" *HR Magazine* (June 2002), pp. 25–26; and Susan M. Heathfield, "360-Degree Feedback: The Good, the Bad, and the Ugly." (http://www.performance-appraisals.org/appraisal-library/360_Degree_Feedback/)

For an extended discussion of the pros and cons of 360-degree appraisals, see Leanne Atwater and Joan F. Brett, "Antecedents and Consequences of Reactions to 360-Degree Feedback," *SHRM Home* (2005); Nathalie Towner, "Turning Appraisals 360 Degrees," *Personnel Today* (February 17, 2004), p. 18; Tammy Galvin, "Technology Meets

360-Degree Evaluations," *Training* (February 2001), p. 24; Susan J. Wells, "A New Road: Traveling Beyond 360-Degree Evaluation," *HR Magazine* (September 1999), pp. 82–91; David A. Waldman and David E. Bowen, "The Acceptability of 360-Degree Appraisals: A Customer-Supplier Relationship Perspective," *Human Resource Management* (Summer 1998), pp. 117–29; and Scott Wimer and Kenneth M. Nowack, "13 Common Mistakes Using 360-Degree Feedback," *Training & Development* (May 1998), pp. 69+.

Forced ranking systems assess employee performance relative to peers rather than against predetermined goals. For a comprehensive overview see Dick Grote, *Forced Ranking Making Performance Management Work* (Boston: Harvard Business School Press, 2005).

6. Patricia J. Hewitt, "The Rating Game," *Incentive* (August 1993), pp. 39–41. Also see Michael Rigg, "Reasons for Removing Employee Evaluations from Management Control," *Industrial Engineering* (August 1992), p. 17.

7. Douglas McGregor, "An Uneasy Look at Performance Appraisal," *Harvard Business Review* (September–October 1972), pp. 133–4. For an expanded discussion on how supervisors can make more effective use of performance appraisals, see Charles N. Painter, "Ten Steps for Improved Appraisals," *Supervision* (June 1999), pp. 11–13.

8. A noted quality guru, the late W. Edwards Deming contended that performance appraisal is the premier American management problem. "It takes the average employee six months to recover from it." Deming, *Out of Crisis* (Cambridge, MA: MIT, 1982), p. 37. Also see Tom Peters, *Thriving on Chaos* (New York: Alfred A. Knopf, 1987), p. 495.

9. Cytiva Software Inc. has recently announced the release of SonicPerform, an employee performance management tool designed for mid-size organizations. "The system gives employers a way to align the employees SKAs and performance to organizational goals and give supervisors (HR) a method of tracking and encouraging performance year around." See "What's New," *HR Magazine* (June 2008), p. 169. Sum Total Systems has developed "Performance Now," a software product that produces worksheets for employee self-review, peer review, and supervisor use. (See HR Magazine (September 2008), p. 119.

10. Excerpted and adapted from George V. Hulme, "Using Software for Worker Reviews," *Nation's Business* (September 1998), pp. 35–36. Also see James Michael Brodie, "Optimizing HR Software Demonstration," *HR Magazine* (April 2006), pp. 99–101. Each month, *HR Magazine* provides a "Guide to HR Products & Services" section to make organizations aware of various resources available to assist with the performance management process.

11. Barbara Holmes, "The Lenient Evaluator's Hurting Your Organization," *HR Magazine* (June 1993), pp. 75–77.

12. In recent years, the courts have held that employers must have fully documented performance deficiencies in order to avoid costly lawsuits. In Reeves v. Sanderson Plumbing Products, Inc., (USS 133, No. 99–536, June 12, 2000), the court held that if an employee can provide that his or her discharge is false, i.e., the organization's record does not support the allegations, then the discrimination lawsuit can go to the jury. Also, see Timothy S. Bland, "Supreme Court Decision Makes Giving Truthful Reasons for Discharge Critical," *SHRM White Paper* (October 2002).

13. One of the supervisor's important roles is to coach; that is, to help employees learn how to become better employees. For an enlightening discussion on the supervisor's role as a coach, see Jean Thilmany, "Passing On Know-How," *HR Magazine* (June 2008), pp. 100–104; Paul Cherry, "Jump-Start Your Staff's Zest to do Their Best," *Supervision*, 68, 12 (December 2007), pp. 12–13; J. Richard Hackman and Ruth Wageman, "A Theory of Team Coaching," *Academy of Management Review* (April 2005), pp. 269–87; Chris Penttila, "To Train, No Gain?" *Entrepreneur* (October 2004), pp. 96–97; Dianne Molvig, "Yearning for Learning," *HR Magazine* (March 2002), pp. 67+; Lynda C. McDermott,

"Developing the New Young Managers," *Training & Development* (October 2001), pp. 42+.

14. Tiger Woods's quote on his relationship with Annika Sorenstam (http://www.tigerwoods.com; June 23, 2005), reprinted here with permission of IMG.

15. For a discussion of merit pay, see George Bohlander and Scott Snell, *Managing Human Resources*, 14th ed. (Mason, OH: South-Western/Cengage Learning, 2007). Also see Sarah E. Needham, "Tough Times Don't Mean Tough Luck on Salary," *The Wall Street Journal* (April 15, 2008), p. D6; and D.E. Terpstra and A.L.Honoree, "Employees' Responses to Merit Pay Inequity," *Compensation and Benefits Review* (January–February 2005), pp. 51–58.

16. The right incentive plan can motivate employees, increase productivity, and help employers differentiate rewards. The *Compensation Planning 2002* study found that 77.2 percent of companies reported having short-term incentive plans, and half had equity compensation programs. See "Seven Out of Ten Companies Now Use Variable Compensation," *Ioma's Pay for Performance* (July 2002), pp. 7+. Their findings were consistent with those reported by World at Work *2000–2009 Salary Budget Survey,* which found seven out of ten companies were using alternative pay strategies. These alternative compensation plans include skill- and competency-based pay, group and team pay incentives, gain sharing, lump-sum merit increases, and broadbanding.

For additional information on compensation concerns, see J. Newman, "Compensation Lessons from the Fast-Food Trenches," *Workspan* (March 2007), pp. 23–26; K. Mullenburg and G. Singh, "The Modern Living Wage Movement," *Compensation and Benefits Review* (January/February 2007), pp. 21–28; Lisa Orndorff, Liz Petersen, and Anne St. Martin, "Hourly Pay for Exempts, Consumer Reports, W-4s," *HR Magazine* (March 2006), pp. 45–46; Janet Sites, "Equal Pay for the Sexes," *HR Magazine* (May 2005), pp. 64–69; Betty Sosnin, "A Fresh Look at Executive Pay," *HR Magazine* (May 2005), pp. 70–75; Susan J. Wells, "No Results, No Raise," *HR Magazine* (May 2005), pp. 76–80; Michael G. Stevens, "Serve Up Cafeteria Plans," *The Practical Accountant* (May 2002), pp. 46–48; John A. Berg, "Performance Evaluation Tied to Salary Increase is Adverse Action," *SHRM Home* (March 11, 2005) and *Gillis v. Georgia Department of Corrections,* 11th Cir., No. 04-11014, Feb. 18, 2005.

Like the weather, most people complain about their pay. Their concerns are fueled by headlines reporting the disparity between CEO salaries and those of the average workers. The most recent study showed that the average CEO made more than 364 times the average pay of American workers. See Len Boselovic, "Study Slams Pay Gap Between CEOs, Workers," *Pittsburgh Post-Gazette* (September 2, 2007),

p. 3H. At the time of this writing my students have been reading about the difficulties of Fannie Mae and Freddie Mac and question why the two CEOs were being paid more than $12 million a year for grossly mismanaging their organizations.

17. For an expanded discussion of skill-based pay, see George E. Ledford, Jr., "Three Case Studies on Skill-Based Pay: An Overview," *Compensation Review* (March/April 1991), pp. 11–23; Richard L. Bunning, "Models for Skill-Based Plans," *HR Magazine* (February 1991), pp. 62–64; and Earl Ingram II, "Compensation: The Advantage of Knowledge-Based Pay," *Personnel Journal* (April 1990), p. 138.

18. Nina Gupta, Timothy P. Schweizer, and Douglas Jenkins, Jr., "Pay-for-Knowledge Compensation Plans: Hypotheses and Survey Results," *Monthly Labor Review* (October 1987), pp. 40–43.

19. R. Bradley Hill, "How to Design a Pay-For-Skills-Used Program," *Journal of Compensation and Benefits* (September/October 1993), pp. 32–38.

20. See Peggy Darragh-Jeromos, "A Suggestion System That Works for You," *Supervision* (July 2005), pp. 18–19; Pamela Bloch-Flynn and Kenneth Vlach, "Employee Awareness Paves the Way for Quality," *HR Magazine* (July 1994), p. 78; and John Allen, "Suggestion Systems and Problem-Solving: One and the Same," *Quality Circles Journal* (March 1987), pp. 2–5.

21. Joanne Summer, "The Incentive Comp Quandary," *Business Finance* (December 1998), pp. 83–86. Also see K. M. Kroll, "Let's Get Flexible," *HR Magazine* (April 2007), pp. 97–100.

22. See Dyane Holt, "Just Say 'No' to Employers Comparing Compensation Information," *SHRM Home* (August 12, 2005); "Two Approaches to a Communicative & Productive Climate," *Ioma's Pay for Performance Report* (July 2002), p. 5+, and "What Your Employees Know & Don't Know About Pay—And What You Can Do About It," *Ioma's Pay for Performance Report* (July 2002), p. 2+.

23. The SHRM *2007 Benefits Survey Report* found that organizations spend an average of 38 percent of payroll on total benefits costs. 20 percent of those costs were for mandatory benefits. Another popular benefit was to allow employees to create their own nontraditional schedule. In addition to flex-time, 56 percent of the surveyed firms offered some form of telecommuting.

The Kaiser 2007 Employer Health Benefits Survey reported that the average premium for family coverage in 2007 was $12,106, and workers on average paid $3,281 out of their paychecks to cover their share of a family policy. Individual premiums were $4,479. See the Kaiser Family Foundation and Health and Educational Trust (www.kff.org).

Also see *Metlife's Employee Benefits Trend Survey* (www.metlife.com); *Bureau of Labor Statistics' Employer Costs for Employee Compensation* or *National Compensation Survey* (www.bls.gov); *SHRM Benefits Survey* (www.shrm.org).

CASE 4-1
Up to Your Neck in Alligators?

Tanieta Gavagan owns Professional Landscape, a landscape business that provides contracted services to a variety of resorts, hotels, and other venues in southeast Georgia. She has six project crew chiefs as direct reports. These are the only employees with full-time benefits. Each project crew consists of between 6 and 11 crew members. Every January, Gavagan runs help-wanted ads to find people who are willing to spend their days mowing, trimming, edging, mulching, seeding, planting, sodding, or weeding. With wages starting at $8.35 per hour, she had no responses to her ads. Her contacts with the state unemployment office provided no worthwhile suggestions.

So, she turned to imported labor—seasonal guest workers allowed to immigrate under the federal guest-worker program. For nine months, 46 men and women from Mexico and Central America comprise her labor crews.

"I don't think it's the wage situation—it's the type of work and the nature of the work. It's hard—I've done it! I have contracts with some of the best resorts and hotels in the area, and they expect a quality job . . . and an affordable price. Any wage increase would be passed along in the form of higher prices to our customers, and that increase would be passed on to their (unhappy) consumers."

In recent years, political debate at all levels of government brought daily news coverage to the illegal immigrant situation. A study done by the Pew Hispanic Center reported that illegals accounted for one out of every 20 workers in America. During the past fifteen years, the number of illegal immigrants coming into Georgia has ranked in the top five nationally. In the coastal Georgia areas, it was estimated that as many as 40 percent of employees in the service, maintenance, and cleaning industries were illegals.

The Georgia Department of Labor recently issued employer compliance rules spelling out the details for employer compliance with the Georgia Security and Immigration Compliance Act. Section 2 of the law requires work eligibility verification of all newly hired employees through an electronic federal authorization program (E-Verify). After July 1, 2009, all public employers, their contractors, and their subcontractors have to sign affidavits agreeing to the verification requirements.[1]

"More than two-thirds of my employees are here with visas from a 'guest worker' program to fill jobs for which no American workers can be found. I'm sympathetic toward Mexican workers who come across the border illegally, not because of the poverty that drives them from their homeland but because of their willingness to take matters into their own hands. I don't care if my employees have a high school or college education," Gavagan explained, "I hire people who are willing to do the work. My crew chiefs are really good at training and helping people to do an excellent job. Ask any customer: our work is second to none!"

Under the law, all an employer has to do is to review two forms of government-issued identification to verify that a worker is a legal resident. "I keep copies of all IDs and I-9 forms on file in case I'm ever investigated," added Gavagan.

"I don't want to become an enforcer of who's legal and who's not," Gavagan said. "Sometimes, I have a gut feeling that someone may be illegal who is brought to us by one of our crew chiefs. I really don't know how to recognize a fraudulent work document or Social Security card. I heard a rumor that you could buy fake IDs at one of the Jacksonville, Florida, flea markets. I could check the Social Security numbers in the national database, but I don't see it as a priority. As long as workers show up for work every day and do a good job, the customer is happy and that makes me very happy."

Late last evening, over dinner at Ruby Tuesdays, a friend handed her a copy of the local newspaper. Georgia lawmakers approved what supporters claim would be the nation's toughest anti-immigration law, limiting state benefits such as nonemergency medical care and unemployment checks to those in the country illegally. The law would crack down on employers who knowingly hired them. Companies seeking state contracts will have to verify that their workers are not illegal immigrants. Gavagan gasped as she read about how the U.S Senate was grappling with new "get-tough" federal immigration policies. Her company had just bid on the landscaping contract for the Golden Isles State Park. The State DNR (Department of Natural Resources) was considering outsourcing various functions and had solicited bids to determine the potential benefits of outsourcing the landscaping and grounds activities. If she got that contract, it would more than double her business.

Contemplating the future, Tanieta Gavagan wondered: "What have I gotten myself into?" Then she remembered an example one of her college professors had used about facing tough situations: "Oftentimes, when you're up to your neck in the swamp with alligators all around, you must remember that your job was to drain the swamp."

Questions for Discussion

See Diane Cadrain, "Georgia: Department of Labor Issues Rules for Immigration Compliance," *SHRM Home* (November 8, 2007); Cadrain, "Georgia; Employment Agency Owners Indicted on Immigration Charges," *SHRM Home* (May 7, 2008); and Dawn Lurie, "The I-9 Form: Everything HR Professionals Need to Know About the I-9 Employment Verification Process," SHRM White Paper (March 2005).

1. Write an assessment of the situation.
2. Why are illegal immigrants so important to a business such as Professional Landscape?
3. **(INTERNET ACTIVITY)** Visit http://www.uscis.gov Web site, enter "basic pilot program" in the search box, then click on "'How Do I' Guides for Employers" to find information regarding:
   a. the current status of the I-9 Employment Verification Program and E-Verify Program.
   b. the current status of Basic Pilot Programs.
   c. an organization's responsibility to ensure that all new hires are legal.
   d. what strategies organizations are using to recruit employees for entry-level positions such as those found in the service industries.
4. What are some of the disadvantages that a small business owner like Gavagan has in complying with government regulations?
5. If Tanieta Gavagan raised her starting wage substantially, do you think that she would be able to attract native-born Americans? Why or why not?
6. Do you believe that Gavagan might lose some business because some of her competitors might be using illegals and paying them a lower wage? Why or why not?

7. Develop a recruitment and retention strategy that Tanieta Gavagan might use to assist in providing quality services to her customers while complying with the legal issues of recruitment. What are the possible advantages and disadvantages of your chosen strategy?

CASE 4-2
Someone Failed to Check!

Carrie Webster was hired a little over a year ago for an accounting analyst position in the administrative office at Sanders Supermarkets. The knowledge and skills required for the job indicated that the employee should have a college degree in accounting and at least three years of job-related experience, preferably in the supermarket/retail industry. A review of Webster's most recent performance appraisal showed that her immediate supervisor rated her as a "good" performer in relevant job categories. On Sanders' employee appraisal form, a "G" or "good" means that the employee has performed substantially all tasks assigned in a competent manner.

Sam Zehner, an eight-year veteran of Sanders who was eliminated from consideration for Webster's position because he did not possess the required degree, confronted Bill Barton, the manager of Store 11, and asked some very pointed questions. Zehner stated that Webster was enrolled in one of his undergraduate accounting courses. Zehner asked, "How could she have met the degree requirement when she is taking the same course I am?" Zehner contends that Webster is going to school at night to get the degree that she claimed to already have in order to get the job. Bill Barton, in turn, called John Morris, the vice president of financial services and told him of Zehner's concerns.

Morris, along with Stacie Stephens, the accounting department manager, and Cornell Patterson, Sanders's human resources manager, reviewed the job file and saw that the competition for the job had been keen. Stephens had interviewed six candidates—four outsiders plus one other internal candidate besides Zehner. The post-interview evaluation forms indicate that the two internal applicants were eliminated from consideration for the position because they did not possess the required degree. Further, under educational attainment, Webster cited a B.S. in business administration, with a concentration in accounting, from Midwestern State University. However, on both her application and on her resume, Webster did not mention a specific completion date.

Before Webster was offered employment, Jane Bradley, one of the HR assistants, verified Webster's employment record and found it to be very good. Apparently, no one checked Webster's educational background. Upon further investigation, it was discovered that Webster does not have a college degree and barely has enough credits to qualify as a senior. She is currently enrolled in two courses, and her degree completion is at least 18 months away. Stacie Stephens knows that if Webster is dismissed, it will take several months before a replacement can perform at Webster's level.

Questions for Discussion
1. Identify the issues in the case. Which issue needs to be addressed first?
2. Develop a list of reasons why Carrie Webster should not be terminated. Develop another list of reasons why she should be terminated.
3. **(ROLE PLAY)** Role-Play Exercise: Select students to play the roles of Stacie Stephens, John Morris, Cornell Patterson (Sanders's HR manager), and Bill Barton. Begin the role-play scenario with the four individuals seated around a conference table discussing what to do about Sam Zehner's concerns and Carrie Webster's

apparent misrepresentation on her resume and application. The group's goal is to develop a plan of action. Non-participants in the role play will be assigned the role of observers and charged with the responsibility of identifying the things that the individual participants and group, as a whole, did well and items or issues that should have been considered. They also should assess whether the outcome will stand various legal and ethical tests.

4. If you were now in Stacie Stephens's position, what would your next step be? Why?

5. Develop a policy statement that will minimize the possibility of a recurrence of the situation.

6. Write a one-page paper detailing what you learned from this case.

Harry Brown is the technical services supervisor for a regional accounting firm. The firm professes to be an equal opportunity employer. Brown coordinates and directs the job activities of six male staff members who provide technical assistance and advice to other departments in the firm and to outside clients. In a world seemingly overpopulated with consultants, the firm enjoys an excellent reputation for the quality of its advice.

CASE 4-3
Harry Brown's Delicate Choice

The six men Brown oversees are bright, white, and mostly in their thirties. They were all hired immediately upon graduation from college, and most of them have MBAs. Brown had created a fun place to work. Mutual trust and respect, coupled with a high degree of caring, sharing, and celebrating successes, marks the relationship between Brown's team members.

Shelly Klone, a 41-year-old single parent of two children, graduated in May from the local university. She was an honor student, president of the collegiate accounting society, and deemed by her fellow students as "most likely to succeed." However, because of her parental responsibilities, she was unable to engage in the school's accounting co-op or internship programs. She worked in the university bursar's office as a work-study student so that she could use the university's child-care services. Klone had many initial interviews, arranged through the campus placement office, but no second interviews. Over time, it seemed to Klone that accounting firms were unwilling to take on the challenge of hiring an older, mature graduate. Klone had talked to several professors, who confidentially told her that her chances were slim of receiving an offer comparable to offers made to classmates who were younger and who had lower grades.

Brown knew he needed to hire another accountant who would be the best possible person to join his team. However, since he became supervisor several years ago, it had bothered him that there had been an increasing number of older, single parents seeking entry-level accounting positions. He personally had no qualms about hiring a more mature person. His immediate manager, a partner of the firm, felt very strongly about the subject, however, saying, "I don't want us hiring any of those older people for entry-level accounting positions. They think they know everything. Besides, they'll never accrue the years of service to qualify for a partnership position. My theory of hiring is to bring in the best young college graduates, work them to death over the first six to ten years, and see where the cream rises to the top."

Questions for Discussion

1. What if Shelly Klone applied for a position with this firm and Harry Brown felt that Klone was the best candidate for the position? (Klone's recommendations from a reputable professor indicated that her accounting and analytical skills

were "head and shoulders" above those of other recent graduates.) What should Brown do?

2. If Brown had full and final authority for the hiring decision, what should he do?

3. Describe which factors could affect Brown's final decision. Consider the legal implications as well as the preferences of Brown's boss.

4. If you were Brown, what would you do, and why?

5. (**INTERNET ACTIVITY**) Use the Internet to find reports, articles, and areas related to the problems faced by older workers in securing entry or reentry into the workforce. Write a brief report summarizing your findings as they relate to the circumstances described in this case. In particular, address the reasons some individuals, such as Brown's manager, hold such views about older people, and explain how these views can be changed.

CASE 4-4
Orientation of a New Employee

Bob Bowen was one of the most promising young applicants Nancy Brewer had interviewed and hired in months. As the employment manager of Sanders Supermarkets, Brewer had instructed Bowen on company policies, pay periods, rate of pay, and so forth and had given him information about the union. Bowen then left with his referral slip to report to Store 21, located in a suburban shopping center.

Before Brown went to his new job, he stopped at his favorite clothing store and bought new white shirts to conform to the company dress code described by Brewer. He then went to the barber shop for a haircut, his first since graduating from high school several months ago.

Upon arriving at Store 21, Bowen introduced himself to Carl Dressel, the store supervisor. Dressel told Bowen to go over to Aisle 3 and tell Sean Kelly, the head stock clerk, that he was to work with him. Bowen walked into Aisle 3, but no one was there. Not knowing what to do next, he just waited for someone to show up. About 20 minutes later, Kelly came into the aisle with a stock truck full of cases. Bowen introduced himself and said, "Mr. Dressel told me to come and work with Sean Kelly. Is that you?" "Yeah," said Kelly, "I was just going to lunch. Here's my case cutter and stock list. You can figure it out. I'll see you in 30 minutes or so."

Kelly then left the aisle with Bowen standing there rather confused. "Some training program," he thought to himself. Brewer had said that there would be lockers in the store for his personal items, but he wondered where they were. Brewer had also told him about punching a time card, so he wondered where the time cards were. Because Kelly had an apron on to protect his clothes, Bowen tried to figure out where he could get one, too. He thought he might look in the back room to see whether the answers to some of his questions might be back there. Walking into the back room, he introduced himself to a young woman who said she was Evita Chavez, one of the store's produce department clerks. Bowen asked her whether she knew where he could hang his coat, get a time card, and find an apron. Chavez responded, "For the most part, we just throw our coats on top of the overstock; the aprons are in the office, and so are the time cards."

"At last," thought Bowen. "Now I'm getting someplace." On his way to the office, he saw several stock clerks working in Aisle 1. He had seen four stock clerks so far, and only one wore a tie. Two had on plaid shirts, and the other had hair at least 3 inches below the collar. "I don't understand why Nancy Brewer was worried about the way I looked," he thought.

Finally, Bowen found an apron and a time card. To find the time clock, he went toward the back room again and asked one of the meat cutters where the time clock was. He was given directions to go through the meat department to the other side of the store. He went through the door he was told to go through, but it had a sign on it saying, "Authorized Personnel Only." He was worried that he might not be an "authorized" person. He finally found the time clock, and, with a little difficulty, he figured out how to clock in. This done, he hurried back to Aisle 3, where Dressel stood waiting for him. "Where have you been?" asked Dressel. "And where is Kelly?"

Bowen explained that Kelly had gone to lunch and that he had been looking for an apron, the time clock, and a place to hang his coat. "You might as well learn right now that your job is putting up the loads of stock—and fast! I don't want to hear any more excuses. Now get to work," said Dressel.

As Bowen started to open the top of the first box of cases, he thought to himself, "The only thing I know for sure right now is that Nancy Brewer has never worked in this store!"

Questions for Discussion

1. Identify and discuss several places where Bob Bowen's experiences in Store 21 could have been improved by proper onboarding.
2. Although Carl Dressel's approach is certainly lacking, could some of the blame for Brown's poor orientation be attributed to Nancy Brewer? Why or why not? Discuss.
3. **(INTERNET ACTIVITY)** Using the Internet, search for information on ways to enable new employees to become effective members of the organization. Then, develop an orientation checklist and process for orienting new employees at Sanders Supermarkets. Compare your checklist with those developed by other students. How do you account for any differences?

CASE 4-5
No One Likes to Get a Report Card!

Craig Merrill, manager at the LaOtto branch of Northwest Bank, is preparing for a meeting with Shirley Campbell, one of the loan officers and a direct report.

Under the policies of Northwest's human resources department, managers are required to conduct annual performance evaluations for all employees. Although the bank has an appraisal form that may be used, the format of the performance evaluation and appraisal interview is left up to each manager, according to the manager's needs and preferences. Prior to this year, Craig's approach has been to fill out the standard appraisal form on each employee and then meet individually with each employee. Craig would show the employee the evaluation and suggest areas for improvement. However, Craig has had rather mixed results with this approach. In particular, Campbell, an eleven-year veteran of the branch, has been very defensive about the appraisals that Craig gave her on the last two occasions. In fact, Craig felt that she had become somewhat hostile and resentful of any suggestions for improvement that he had offered.

About three months ago, Craig attended a bank-sponsored supervisory training program that was mandatory for all managers and assistants. The seminar series was conducted by a university professor who had been hired by the bank to develop and present the seminar. One of the sessions dealt with performance appraisals. In that session, the professor advocated using self-appraisal and variants of a 360-degree performance evaluation. It was suggested that employees be given an opportunity to rate themselves in advance of meeting with the manager and that the manager solicit input from co-workers, peers, and others who have direct knowledge of what each employee does and/or does not do. The manager is to compile the feedback and incorporate it into his or her own evaluation. The manager and employee then meet, and the manager compares and discusses the employee's self-evaluation with the manager's evaluation. The professor stated that the research indicated that when employees are allowed to appraise themselves, they generally tend to be more critical of themselves than their managers or co-workers are. According to the professor, with this approach, employees also are usually more receptive to suggestions for improvement.

Craig decided to try this approach with Shirley Campbell. About two weeks ago, he gave her a copy of the bank's appraisal form and asked her to fill it out as she evaluated her own performance during the past year. He asked that she give it back to him at least two days before her scheduled appraisal meeting. Campbell completed the appraisal form and gave it to Craig yesterday. He was astonished to find that she had given herself a "superior" or "outstanding" rating in every category on the performance appraisal form. Further, Campbell had left the "Areas for Improvement" section entirely blank.

Craig realized that this was not the outcome he had hoped for, nor was it consistent with what the professor had said in the seminar. His appraisal of Shirley Campbell, supported by feedback from co-workers, is that her performance is "satisfactory" with several areas of serious deficiencies that need major improvement. She is scheduled to be in Craig's office tomorrow morning for the performance appraisal meeting. He now wonders if the professor's suggestions were worth the aggravation, and he is pondering how to conduct the appraisal meeting.

Questions for Discussion

1. What are the strengths of Northwest's system of performance management? What are the weaknesses?
2. (**INTERNET ACTIVITY**) Using the Internet, find information about the advantages and disadvantages of the 360-degree and self appraisals.
3. If Craig were to ask you for some suggestions for ways in which his current system of employee appraisal can be improved, how would you respond?
4. In your opinion, does Craig have the confidence and competencies to use the new 360-degree and self-appraisal rating system? If not, what does he need to do to ensure success?
5. How can Craig overcome Shirley Campbell's defensiveness during the performance feedback session?

Optional Role-Play Activity

(**ROLE PLAY**) Assume that Craig on several recent occasions had talked with Campbell about complaints from customers regarding their perceptions and accusations that she was (1) not thorough on loan applications, and (2) surly and not friendly during the loan application process. Craig had documented these events and talked with her as they occurred. The main office had to redo at least four loan applications in the past six weeks because of errors made by Campbell. Using the information contained in the case and questions for discussion, Craig is to conduct a performance appraisal meeting with Campbell with these objectives in mind:

a. As Craig, you are to develop a plan to change Campbell's behavior.
b. State short-term performance management goal for changing the behavior.
c. Determine a procedure for closely monitoring her performance.
d. What are the obstacles you are likely to face as you attempt to implement the performance management plan for Campbell?

At the conclusion of the role-play, the observers are asked to report on what Craig did well and what Craig could have done better. Observers should also be asked if the parties appeared to agree on a "win-win" performance management plan and whether Craig gained agreement from Campbell that specific aspects of her performance needed improvement.

6. If you had been Craig what would you have done to improve Campbell's performance?
7. How do you believe Shirley will perform in the future? Why?

CASE 4-6
From Part-Time to Full-Time?

Alice Toomer is supervisor of the clerical staff in the medical records department of Pine Village Community Medical Center (CMC). She has the authority to hire and fire for her department and is unaffected by a union contract because the hospital has no union. She has seven full-time employees working for her. Whenever a regular clerical employee does not show up, Toomer calls Benton Temporary Services. Normally, she requests Helen Drew, who works as a relief person on an as-needed basis. Drew expressed a preference for part-time work and likes the opportunity the hospital provides.

Toomer observed that whenever Drew came in to help out, there seemed to be friction between her and the full-time employees. Apparently, the full-time employees did not like Drew's work habits. She had the ability to turn out ten hours of work in eight hours. Drew is older, with college- and high-school-aged children. Most of the full-timers are young, unmarried people in their early twenties. Toomer did not know whose fault it was, but there were numerous complaints about Drew from the other employees. Most common among these complaints were that she did not socialize with them during breaks or lunch hour and that she did not respond in a timely manner to requests for assistance. Toomer, however, was certain of the high quality of Drew's work and knew that everything she assigned to her was done professionally and in a timely manner.

Early one afternoon, Drew told Toomer that she would like to work full time because her youngest child would be in college next year and she could use the extra income. This request came as something of a surprise and a problem to Toomer. Only the previous day, Jody Williams had announced that she would be leaving in ten days to move to Dallas with her husband. Toomer pondered whether she should offer this job to Drew. Of course, Drew would be very pleased to get this position, and it appeared that she knew it would be open, but Toomer was concerned about the reactions of the other employees in the department.

Questions for Discussion

1. (**INTERNET ACTIVITY**) Search the Web to gather information about intergenerational differences that might lead to conflict in the workplace. Identify some reasons why there may be difficulties between Drew and younger workers.

2. List reasons why it may be better to promote a "known-quantity," e.g., Helen Drew, versus hiring an "unknown" from the outside. In this situation, what might be the drawbacks for hiring Drew?
3. In considering hiring a full-time employee, which is more important: (a) the work performance of the potential employee, or (b) the way the individual will fit in with other employees in the department? Why is there seldom a clear answer to this question?
4. Did Toomer's failure to investigate the prior situation with Drew and the other employees contribute to the current problem? Discuss.
5. Toomer has to make an important decision. Should she seek the advice of employees in the department and the human resources staff, or is this a decision she must make on her own? What should she do? Consider alternatives.
6. If Toomer decides to hire Helen Drew for the full-time position, what should she do to help Drew get onboard and off to a great start? Think about specific actions in the following categories:
   a. Degree of Involvement
   b. Communication style
   c. Level of Openness and Trust
   d. Type and Amount of Direction
   e. Level of Support

CASE 4-7
I Hate Performance Appraisals!

Patrick James was distribution center supervisor for Barry Automotive's Ashton Plant. When the 12-year veteran was promoted to supervisor six years ago, there was no resentment on the part of employees because he was generally well-liked and deserving of the supervisory position. James had practiced open and honest communication with his employees and had developed a climate of mutual trust and respect. The employees would "go to the wall" to get their jobs done effectively and efficiently. However, there was little possibility for James to advance beyond his present position. A lateral move within Barry might be possible, but James did not want to uproot his family.

Barry had instituted a formal appraisal system. It consisted primarily of having each supervisor complete a rating-scale evaluation form with space for comments and then discuss the appraisal with each employee. In three weeks, James would have to conduct appraisals on all his employees. He looked forward to doing them, with one exception: Cheryl Reynolds.

The 33-year-old Reynolds was promoted to assistant supervisor about two years ago. She was regarded as an effective supervisor, was knowledgeable about the technical aspects of the job, and had shared this information with all employees. She emphasized that the success of Barry depended on how fast an employee could learn new processes and apply them to better serving the customers. A perfectionist, Reynolds demanded no less from other employees. A few employees considered her pushy and strong-willed.

Reynolds was to receive her degree from a local college at the end of this term, and James knew that she expected to advance in the organization. Reynolds would be the first person in her family to graduate from college, and she wanted a job with additional responsibility.

Generally, Reynolds's employees got the work done in an exceptional manner, but every once in a while, she overstepped her bounds. She required strict adherence to company rules in all times and circumstances. Occasionally, when Reynolds was within hearing distance, employees could be heard sharing the latest "dumb blonde" joke. Twice in the past two months, James had reprimanded employees for their behavior. He knew that Reynolds had expected him to do more to eliminate the jokes.

Barry's sales and profits had been declining over the past fifteen months. People in other area industries had been laid off. Kmart closed its northside store, and one of the telecom firms had shuttered its doors. The area's unemployment level was at a five-year high. The Ashton plant had chosen to reduce employment through retirement and normal attrition. James had five unfilled positions because replacements had not been authorized. The consolidation of duties forced managers and supervisors to find creative solutions to problems and to do more work with fewer resources.

James knew that Reynolds's performance was very good and that she very much wanted to be a full-fledged supervisor. There was little likelihood that such a position would be available at the Ashton plant. He was not looking forward to her performance appraisal.

Questions for Discussion

1. According to some experts, employee appraisals are detested by both management and employees. Outline a process that might help Patrick James feel more comfortable conducting the performance appraisal of Cheryl Reynolds.

2. Having direct reports, peers, and customers provide assessments of a manager's performance has become a new idea for some companies. Search the Web to find additional information on how various organizations have used the 360-degree performance appraisal systems to assess employee performance.
   a. List the advantages of the 360-degree performance appraisal system.
   b. List the disadvantages of the 360-degree performance appraisal system.
   c. If James decides to solicit the input of others (a modified 360-degree evaluation), how should he go about doing it?

3. What should James do to help Reynolds meet her career aspirations?

 Optional Role-Play Exercise: Your instructor may assign you to play the role of Patrick James, Cheryl Reynolds, or observer. Your mission if chosen to be Patrick James is to conduct a performance review of Reynolds. You have no more than five minutes to complete this assignment.

   a. If you played the role of Patrick James, on a sheet of paper identify the things you did well and the things you could have done better.
   b. If you were Cheryl Reynolds, make a list of the things that James did well. The things that could have been said that weren't and suggestions for how he could have left you feeling better about your job performance and the organization.
   c. Observers will share their observations on what James did well during the appraisal interview and identify areas on which he could have improved.
   d. Compare the observations. Is there substantial agreement among the participants? If there is a difference in perceptions regarding James effectiveness, how do you account for the differences?
   e. How did the role-play activity increase your awareness of the importance of preparing for the performance appraisal?

CASE 4-8
It's Not Fair!

Elaine Thornton began working at Erie Bedding and Upholstery at age 17 and, in time, became the second-shift supervisor. Although Thornton had not finished high school, her 20-plus years of hard work paid off when she was promoted three years ago. She was proud of her promotion and the work she had done to deserve the position. Thornton was known as being thorough and conscientious in her efforts to train and develop employees. Thornton had been pleased with her success as a supervisor, but she also knew there was an area that needed attention. She reflected on the events of the past 24 hours.

In recent years, it had been increasingly difficult for the firm to hire good employees. Thornton's theory was to "take people who have the potential to be winners and turn them into winners." Even as the starting wage had risen, the number of job applicants had decreased. Erie's starting wage was not quite as high as that of other area manufacturing/production firms. The shortage had been adversely impacting Erie's ability to meet customer demand.

By contacting several social service agencies, Marie Sorg, Erie's human resources manager, attracted a number of Bosnian and Asian refugees into Erie's workforce. The company offered employees ESL (English as a second language) courses and other personal-development and social-skills courses. In addition to paying the full cost of these courses, Erie paid each new employee for six hours of training per week.

Toward the end of the evening shift, Thornton was approached by Olga Stults, who expressed her concern about the unfair pay policies. Raises were given annually at the beginning of the calendar year, and wage compression had been a concern of management for some time. (Labor-market factors often drive the wages of new hires to a level near, or even above, that of long-term employees.) Stults was upset because she had learned that Hu Twong was making $0.50 per hour more than she was. According to Stults, Twong had been employed by Erie for seven months while Stults had been employed for eleven years. In addition, Twong was getting six hours of pay per week while he was taking ESL classes.

"I was under the impression that pay was a reward for doing the job and being with the organization for a long time," Stults said. "Experience doesn't seem to matter. It's not fair."

After consulting with Sorg, Thornton was really confused. Sorg explained that the human resources department determined all pay rates. Each job classification had a wide wage range, but seniority and experience differences had become nonexistent. Sorg confirmed that some of the new employees had been hired at higher rates than longer-term employees, but that it was a necessity of doing business in the new economy. Sorg reminded Thornton that management looked unfavorably on discussing wages with fellow employees, and the company handbook contained a clause that employees were not to discuss their wages with anyone else. Sorg reminded Thornton to reaffirm that the firm was very pleased with Stults's work performance and that the situation was beyond the firm's control. In conclusion, Sorg asked Thornton to try to soothe Stult's feelings about pay as much as possible and to be patient. "Things will change sooner or later, and the more senior employees will be taken care of," Sorg assured Thornton.

Questions for Discussion

1. After hearing what Marie Sorg had to say, what should Thornton do?

2.  Search the Internet to ascertain the extent of company policies prohibiting wage discussion among employees.

  a. Do you believe that you have a right to know how much everyone else in the organization is making so that you can compare your compensation with that of others? Why?

  b. In your opinion, are policies against wage discussion among employees just to protect supervisors and human resources from having to explain differences in wages? Why or why not?

  c. How do you balance "the right to free speech" and "an individual's right to privacy" in regards to a company policy prohibiting the discussion of wages and salary?

3. Discuss what you would do if you were Elaine Thornton. What can you do to soothe Stults's feelings?

4. Thornton thought that Sorg's response to her inquiries was inadequate. Do you agree? If so, how should the situation have been handled?

5. Why is communication so important in the employee pay and compensation area?

6. Has a situation like this happened to anyone you know? If so, what was the outcome?

7. If you were Olga Stults, what additional actions would you take to relieve your dissatisfaction with Erie's compensation system?

(Leading)

PART 5

CHAPTER 11

© CINDY CHARLES/PHOTOEDIT

After studying this chapter, you will be able to:

1 Define leadership and discuss its importance at the supervisory level.

2 Identify and describe the elements of contemporary leadership thought.

3 Discuss the delegation process and define its three major components.

4 Discuss why some supervisors do not delegate, and describe the benefits of delegation.

5 Compare the autocratic (authoritarian) approach to supervision with the participative approach.

6 Suggest approaches for introducing change to employees and for proposing change to higher-level managers.

7 Understand the formula for organizational renewal.

YOU MAKE THE CALL!

David Felker is the supervisor of the shipping and receiving department of the Arcola Manufacturing and Distribution Plant of Tideway Corporation. The Arcola plant produces paper products—plates, napkins, towels, and toilet tissue—for commercial, industrial, and retail accounts. Felker has supervised this department for two years after having worked as an employee in the department for about eight years. He has fourteen direct reports, all of whom are members of the plant's local union.

Shortly after he became a supervisor, two employees filed a complaint against Felker for alleged violations of the union/management contract. Felker was found to have improperly applied the work rule dealing with wash-up time. At the initial grievance meeting with Human Resources and Felker's immediate supervisor, Scott Riley, the department union steward, registered a complaint about Felker's supervisory style. After the meeting, Riley and the HR director acknowledged that perhaps they had committed an error by not sending Felker to a supervisory training program conducted by the local community college. Riley again stated that any time Felker had a question or concern about how to deal with various situations, his door was always open.

Three weeks later, Felker began attending a six-week supervisory management seminar at the college, two nights a week, at company expense. Felker learned about theories and models of supervisory leadership, especially those emphasizing a participatory approach. He read several articles and participated in group case-study discussion dealing with employee engagement. Felker heard about techniques for giving directives to employees that were less authoritative than those he had used previously.

As with much of American industry, Tideway was experiencing increased competition for the sale of its primary products. In response to the increased competition, the company was now stressing production and distribution efficiency. In collaboration with the union, it was agreed upon that the company had the right to cross-train all employees so they could perform several different duties.

In the four weeks since Felker completed the course, he had tried to implement what he had learned. On a number of occasions, he had asked employees—both individually and in groups—for their suggestions and opinions concerning what should be done and how it could be done better. Felker avoided giving direct orders and tried to suggest to employees what needed to be done rather than spelling out his own objectives and course of action in detail. However, despite his best efforts, nothing seemed to change. Work performance had not improved and the employees seemed to be going through the motions of their jobs. Even though the union had agreed to the cross-training, the employees were content to work only at their regular tasks.

This morning, the department steward told Felker that she did not think he understood how employees felt and that he had forgotten what it was like to be a worker. He wondered whether there was something wrong with this new approach. Later that evening, Felker wondered, "Was this new approach just a waste of time? Do the employees resent the fact that I was promoted to a supervisory position? Maybe I should forget about the participatory approach that we learned about and go back to being a firm and more authoritative supervisor. What should I do?" **YOU MAKE THE CALL!**

Leadership: The Core of Supervisory Management

1 Define leadership and discuss its importance at the supervisory level.

Harry S. Truman, 33rd president of the United States, once remarked that leadership is the ability to get people to do what they don't like to do and enjoy it.[1] Simple as it seems, there still is considerable misunderstanding concerning the supervisor's leadership role in influencing employee motivation and performance. This misunderstanding often stems from a misconception regarding the meaning of leadership itself. Occupying a position of responsibility and authority does not necessarily make someone a leader whom subordinates will follow.

THE TEST OF SUPERVISORY LEADERSHIP

Leadership is the ability to guide and influence the opinions, attitudes, and behavior of others. Anyone who can direct or influence others toward objectives can function as a leader, no matter what position that person holds.

Leadership
The ability to guide and influence the behavior of others

FIGURE 11.1 Supervisory leadership results in a work group's willingness to follow

In the workplace, members of the work group often assume leadership roles. The direction of informal employee leadership can be supportive of, or contrary to, the direction the supervisor desires. For example, employee resistance to changes in work arrangements, work rules, or procedures is a common phenomenon. Such resistance is usually the result of some informal leadership in the work group.

Therefore, leadership in the general sense is a process rather than just a positional relationship. Leadership includes what the followers think and do, not just what the supervisor does. The real test of supervisory leadership is how subordinates follow. Leadership resides in a supervisor's ability to obtain the work group's willingness to follow—willingness based on commonly shared goals and a mutual effort to achieve them (see Figure 11.1).

However, the willingness of others to follow is not enough by itself. We contend that there are several other tests of leadership:

- Does the leader possess a clear vision of what needs to be done (continuous pursuit of excellence and worthwhile objectives)?
- Does the leader communicate that vision and get others "on board"?
- Does the leader build a climate of mutual trust and respect?
- Does the leader create the proper infrastructure to support the vision?
- Does the leader enable the followers to be the best they can be?
- Does the leader leave the organization better than he or she found it?

Obviously, leadership effectiveness, like beauty, is in the eyes of the beholder, but the better leaders are known as great communicators and people of impeccable credibility.

LEADERSHIP CAN BE DEVELOPED

Supervisors often believe that any definition of leadership should include basic traits. That is, they believe that effective leaders have some special qualities, and they point to certain successful supervisors as representing outstanding leadership.

Does a person need to have certain natural qualities to be an effective leader? Generally, the ability to lead is something that can be learned: Many studies have shown that there is no significant relationship between one's ability to lead and such characteristics as age, height, weight, sex, race, and other physical attributes. Although there are indications that successful supervisors tend to be somewhat more intelligent than the average subordinate, they are not so

There is no significant relationship between leadership ability and such characteristics as age, height, weight, gender, race, and other physical attributes

superior in intelligence that they cannot be understood. Intelligence is partially hereditary but, for the most part, it depends on environmental factors, such as the amount of formal education and the diversity of experiences. Successful supervisors tend to be well-rounded in their interests and aptitudes. They are good communicators, are mentally and emotionally mature, and have strong inner drives. Most important, they tend to rely more on their supervisory skills than on their technical skills. These are essentially learned characteristics, not innate qualities.

Author Peter Senge objects to the notion of teaching leadership. He contends that:

> *"Teaching suggests that you have certain concepts you want to understand, and that's pretty useless in a domain like leadership. Leadership has to do with how people are. You don't teach people a different way of being, you create conditions so they can discover where their natural leadership comes from."[2]*

Putting this in perspective, supervisory leadership is something people can develop when they want to be leaders and not just people in charge of groups.

Where can the novice gain leadership experience? As noted in Chapter 1, you can volunteer in a number of service or religious organizations or seek internships through your college placement office. Imagine the dynamics that can take place among a Boy Scout or Girl Scout leader and a group of young scouts. Volunteering provides the opportunity to work on real projects and to accomplish real objectives with real people.

A few words of caution are appropriate at this point. In previous chapters we discussed the importance of finding a mentor. When you enter a volunteer experience, hitch your wagon to a star! Find an experienced, well-respected leader to work with, one who will enable you to hone the skills necessary to be an effective leader. Someone who will support, coach, protect, and give up and provide opportunities for you to be in charge of meaningful projects or programs. You should seize every opportunity to become a more effective leader and continuously strive to develop your managerial and human-relations capacities and skills.

EFFECTIVE SUPERVISORY LEADERSHIP AS A DYNAMIC PROCESS

Good communication is the foundation of effective leadership, such as getting scouts to do things they have never done before. The ability to communicate, to keep the lines of communication open at all times, and to communicate in ways that meet workers' expectations and needs is essential for any supervisor to be a leader.

Generally, the larger the work group, the more important it is for the supervisor to be an effective planner, organizer, and coordinator. The larger the work group, the more the supervisor will have to delegate authority. The smaller the work group and the closer the supervisor's location to the employees, the more the supervisor must address the individual needs of those in the group.

Understanding employee expectations is vital to effective supervision. As discussed previously, today's employees want to participate in decisions about their jobs. However, a supervisor must sometimes exercise authority and make decisions that may not be popular with the work group. The ability to assess employee expectations and the demands of the job situation and then act appropriately is a skill that can be developed with experience and practice.

2 Identify and describe the elements of leadership thought.

Contemporary Thoughts on Leadership

Contemporary writings on leadership are filled with findings—and some contradictions. One of the most noted writers on leadership, Warren Bennis, reported from his extensive research four things people want from their leaders:

1. Direction—People want leaders to have a purpose. The leader has a clear idea of what is to be done. Leaders love what they do and love doing it. Followers want passion and conviction from a strong point of view.
2. Trust—The ability to trust a leader is perhaps more important today than at any other time in recent history. Integrity, maturity, and candor are essential elements of building a relationship of mutual trust.
3. Hope—Leaders believe, and they kindle the fire of optimism in followers.
4. Results—Leaders accomplish difficult tasks. Success breeds success.[3]

We often hear employees say about management, "We don't trust them." The words "us versus them" are common in the workplace, but few managers would admit publicly that they do not trust their employees. Trust is the foundation of effective supervisory relations. Some years ago, a customer placed a special order for a child's bedroom set at a locally owned furniture store. When told the set would be delivered in three weeks, the customer asked, "Do you want me to give you some money as a deposit or sign something?" The owner said, "No problem. You told me you want it. If your word isn't any good, what good is your signature?" As Bennis and others imply, "We want to be able to trust others and to have others trust us."

Stephen R. Covey, author of *Principle-Centered Leadership*, notes that:

> *Trust bonds management to labor, employees to each other, customers to supplier, and strengthens all other stakeholder relationships. With low trust, developing performance is exhausting. With high trust, it*

is exhilarating. The principle of alignment means working together in harmony, going in the same direction, supporting each other. Alignment develops the organizational trustworthiness required for trust. And if personal trustworthiness and interpersonal trust are to mature, hiring, promoting, training, and other systems must foster character development as well as competence.[4]

Noted leadership researchers James Kouzes and Barry Posner contend, "Leadership is an observable, learnable set of practices. Given the opportunity for feedback and practice, those with desire and persistence to lead can substantially improve their abilities to do so."[5] After examining the experiences of managers who were leading others to outstanding accomplishments, Kouzes and Posner identified five practices and ten specific behaviors that can be learned and used by managers at all levels. These practices and behaviors include:

- Challenging the process (searching for opportunities, experimenting, and taking risks);
- Inspiring a shared vision (envisioning the future, enlisting the support of others);
- Enabling others to act (fostering collaboration, strengthening others);
- Modeling the way (setting an example, planning small wins); and
- Encouraging the heart (recognizing contributions, celebrating accomplishments).[6]

In short, leaders need followers who understand what is expected. Then leaders engage their followers in the pursuit of those goals. According to Gary Neilson, a Booz & Company executive, "Healthy organizations are good at execution—they get things done. Unhealthy organizations lack clear decision rights and don't share information effectively.[7]" Surprisingly, research by the author has shown that less than 40 percent of employees had a clear idea of what they were accountable for.[8] One study reported that only one in seven U.S. workers could actually identify his or her organization's top three goals while another reported that 14 percent of workers said their work team stays diligently focused on its most important goals.[9] *"If you don't know where you're supposed to go, how will you know when you get there!"*

SERVANT LEADERSHIP

In his book *Good to Great*, author Jim Collins described "Level 5" leaders as those who facilitate, coach, and empower others to find their own direction.[10] We believe that there are times when the leader must provide direction and that there are situations in which subordinates should be enabled to pursue their own direction—as long as it is consistent with the overall vision for the organization.

Former AT&T executive Robert Greenleaf defined **servant-leadership** in this way:

> *"The servant-leader is a servant first . . . It begins with the natural feeling that one wants to serve, to serve first. Then conscious choice brings one to aspire to lead. He or she is sharply different from the person who is leader first, perhaps because of the need to assuage an unusual power drive or to acquire material possessions. For such it will be a later choice to serve—after leadership is established. The difference manifests itself in the care taken by the servant-first leader to make sure that other people's highest-priority needs are being served."*[11]

Greenleaf concluded that authentic leaders are chosen by those they serve—their followers. Regardless of his or her level of competence, every employee needs

Servant-leadership
The notion that the needs of followers are looked after such that they can be the best they can be

guidance, and servant-leaders set up their employees for success. Professor Max Douglas contends that servant-leaders treat co-workers as equals, affirm their worth, and match their performance to their espoused values.[12] Larry Spears, head of the Greenleaf Center for Servant-Leadership, said, "Servant-leadership provides a strong set of values and ethics for people and organizations."[13] Figure 11.2 identifies the ten keys (characteristics) central to the concept of servant-leadership.

Earlier in this chapter, we proposed that one of the tests of leadership is whether the leader enables the followers to be the best they can be. That is not to imply that leaders solely focus on serving the needs of others. Look back at the sample values-and-belief statement for Community Medical Center (CMC) in Chapter 1 (Figure 1.9 on page 24). It clearly states that every employee is important and that employees must work together to meet or exceed the expectations of various stakeholder groups. Reflect for a moment on the following question: "If an employee is not treated as a very special person, how can you expect that employee to treat a customer as a very special person?"

LEADERSHIP STYLE DEPENDS ON MANY FACTORS

While there is general agreement among researchers and theorists that leading is not the same as managing (see Chapter 2), there is still considerable debate regarding what the leader does and how the leader does it. Most supervisors and managers recognize that no one leadership style is effective in all situations. There is no simple set of do's and don'ts a supervisor can implement to achieve high motivation and excellent performance. Although leadership skills can be learned and developed, no one formula will apply in all situations and with all people. Considerable evidence suggests that an effective approach is contingent on numerous factors in any given situation. **Contingency-style leadership** proponents advocate that these considerations include such things as the supervisor, the organization, the type of work, the skill level and motivation of employees, and time pressures.

Some approaches promote good performance better than others. The concept of leadership has been studied and discussed for decades, and the consensus from dozens of leadership theories is that there is no one best style of leadership. The lesson for practicing supervisors is that the most effective leadership depends on a multitude of factors, including the supervisor, the organization, the type of work, the

Contingency-style leadership
No one leadership style is best; the appropriate style depends on a multitude of factors

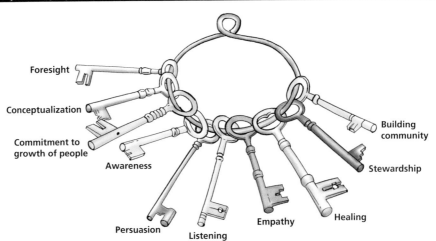

FIGURE 11.2 The essence of servant-leadership. Use these keys to unlock your employees' potential[14]

Foresight

Conceptualization

Commitment to growth of people

Awareness

Persuasion

Listening

Empathy

Healing

Stewardship

Building community

employees involved, their ability and willingness to accomplish a task, the amount of time available to complete a task, and the particular situation and its urgency. In general, we conclude that effective leaders must be able to establish standards, develop a climate in which people become self-motivated, and adapt to constant change. The effective leader provides direction, instruction, guidance, support and encouragement, feedback and positive recognition, and enthusiastic help when necessary.

The Process of Delegation

3 Discuss the delegation process and define its three major components.

A major aspect of managerial leadership styles is managers' use of the authority inherent in their positions. Just as authority is a major component of management, the delegation of authority is essential to the creation and operation of an organization. In the broadest sense, **delegation** gives employees a greater voice in how the job is to be done; the employees are empowered to make decisions.[15] Unfortunately, some managers view delegation as a means of lightening their workloads. They assign unpleasant tasks to employees and subsequently find that the employees are not motivated to complete those tasks. The manager must look at delegation as a tool to develop employees' skills and abilities rather than as a way to get rid of unpleasant tasks.

Delegation
The process of entrusting duties and related authority to subordinates

A manager receives authority from a higher-level manager through delegation, but this does not mean that the higher-level manager surrenders all accountability. **Accountability** is the obligation one has to one's boss and the expectation that employees will accept credit or blame for the results achieved in performing assigned tasks. When supervisors delegate, they are still ultimately accountable for the successful completion of work.

Accountability
The obligation one has to one's boss and the expectation that employees will accept credit or blame for the results achieved in performing assigned tasks

Delegation is a supervisor's strategy for accomplishing objectives. It consists of the following three components, all of which must be present:

1. Assigning duties to immediate subordinates
2. Granting permission (authority) to make commitments, use resources, and take all actions necessary to perform duties
3. Creating an obligation (responsibility) on the part of each employee to perform duties satisfactorily

Unless all three components are present, the delegation process is incomplete. They are inseparably related; a change in one requires change in the other two.

ASSIGNING DUTIES

Each employee must be assigned a specific job or task to perform. Job descriptions may provide a general framework through which the supervisor can examine duties in the department to decide which tasks to assign to each employee. Routine duties usually can be assigned to almost any employee, but there are other functions that the supervisor can assign only to employees who are qualified to perform them. There are also some functions that a supervisor cannot delegate—those functions that the supervisor must do. The assignment of job duties to employees is of great significance, and much of the supervisor's success depends on it.

GRANTING AUTHORITY

The granting of authority means that the supervisor confers upon employees the right and power to act, to use certain resources, and to make decisions within prescribed limits. Of course, the supervisor must determine the scope

A good manager uses delegation to develop employees' skills and abilities, not to avoid unpleasant tasks

© MICHAEL NEWMAN/PHOTOEDIT

of authority that is to be delegated. How much authority can be delegated depends in part on the amount of authority the supervisor possesses. The degree of authority also is related to the employees and the jobs to be done. For example, if a sales clerk is responsible for processing items returned to the store, that clerk must have the authority to give the customer's money back with the understanding (limit) that the clerk should alert the supervisor if the returned item was obviously abused in some way. In every instance, enough authority must be granted to the employee to enable the employee to perform assigned tasks adequately and successfully. There is no need for the amount of authority to be larger than the tasks. Authority must be sufficient to meet the employee's obligations.

DEFINING LIMITATIONS

Throughout the process of delegation, employees must be reassured that their orders and authority come from their immediate supervisor. A supervisor must be specific in telling employees what authority they have and what they can or cannot do. It is uncomfortable for employees to have to guess how far their authority extends. For example, an employee may be expected to order certain materials as a regular part of the job. This employee must know the limits within which materials can be ordered, perhaps in terms of time and costs, and when permission from the supervisor is needed before ordering additional materials. If the supervisor does not state this clearly, the employee probably will be forced to test the limits and learn by trial and error. If it becomes necessary to change an employee's job assignment, the degree of authority should be checked to ensure that the authority that is delegated is still appropriate. If it is less (or more) than needed, it should be adjusted.

CREATING RESPONSIBILITY

The third component of the process of delegation is creating obligation on the part of the employee to perform assigned duties satisfactorily. Acceptance of this obligation creates responsibility; without responsibility, delegation is incomplete.

The terms *responsibility* and *authority* are closely related. Like authority, responsibility is often misunderstood. Supervisors commonly use expressions like "holding subordinates responsible," "delegating responsibilities," and "carrying out responsibilities." Simply stated, **responsibility** is the obligation of a subordinate to perform duties as required by the supervisor. By accepting a job or accepting an obligation to perform assigned duties, the employee implies the acceptance of responsibility. Responsibility implies that the employee agrees to perform duties in return for rewards, like paychecks. The most important facet of the definition is that responsibility is something a subordinate must recognize and accept if delegation is to succeed.

Responsibility
The obligation to perform certain tasks and duties as assigned by the supervisor

SUPERVISORY ACCOUNTABILITY CANNOT BE DELEGATED

Although a supervisor must delegate authority to employees to accomplish specific jobs, the supervisor's own accountability cannot be delegated. Assigning duties to employees does not relieve the supervisor of the responsibility for those duties. Therefore, when delegating assignments to employees, the supervisor remains accountable for the actions of the employees carrying out those assignments.

To reiterate, responsibility includes (a) the subordinate's obligation to perform assigned tasks, and (b) the supervisor's obligation to his or her own manager, or accountability. For example, when a high-level manager asks a supervisor to explain declining performance in the department, the supervisor cannot plead that the responsibility was delegated to employees in the group. The supervisor remains accountable and must answer to the manager.

Regardless of the extent to which a supervisor creates an obligation on the part of employees to perform satisfactorily, the supervisor retains the ultimate responsibility, along with the authority, that is part of the supervisor's departmental position. As Figure 11.3 shows, effective delegation requires an appropriate mix of the assignment of tasks and the authority and responsibility needed to carry out those tasks.

FIGURE 11.3 Effective delegation requires an appropriate mix of task assignments and the authority and responsibility to accomplish those tasks

That accountability cannot be delegated may worry some supervisors, but responsibility for the work of others goes with the supervisory position. Delegation is necessary for jobs to be accomplished. While a supervisor may use sound managerial practices, employees will not always use the best judgment or perform in superior fashions. Therefore, allowances must be made for errors. Accountability remains with supervisors, but supervisors must be able to depend on their employees. If employees fail to carry out their assigned tasks, they are accountable to the supervisor, who must then redirect the employees as appropriate. When appraising a supervisor's performance, higher-level managers usually consider how much care the supervisor has taken in selecting, training, and supervising employees, and controlling their activities.

Implied in accountability is the notion that punishments or rewards will follow, depending on how well the duties are performed. However, the ultimate accountability to top-level managers lies with the supervisor who is doing the delegating. Supervisors are responsible and accountable not only for their own actions but also for the actions of their subordinates.

4 Discuss why some supervisors do not delegate, and describe the benefits of delegation.

Delegation by the Supervisor

Every supervisor must delegate some authority to employees, which assumes that the employees can and will accept the authority delegated to them. However, many employees complain that their supervisors make all decisions and scrutinize their work because they do not trust the employees to carry out assignments. These complaints usually describe supervisors who are unable or unwilling to delegate.

REASONS FOR LACK OF SUPERVISORY DELEGATION

A supervisor may be reluctant to delegate for several reasons. Some are valid, and some are not. Figure 11.4 shows some barriers the supervisor must overcome to achieve effective delegation.

FIGURE 11.4 Supervisors must overcome the barriers to delegation

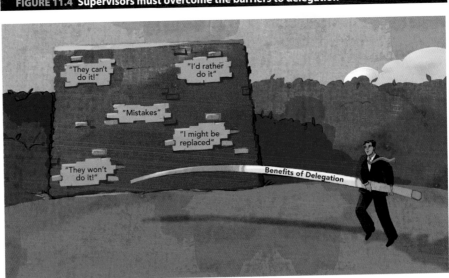

SHORTAGE OF QUALIFIED EMPLOYEES— "THEY CAN'T DO IT" MENTALITY

Some supervisors cite a lack of qualified employees as an excuse for not delegating authority. Actually, such supervisors feel that their employees cannot handle authority or are unwilling to accept it. If these supervisors refuse to delegate, employees will have little opportunity to obtain the experience they need to improve their judgment and to handle broader assignments. Supervisors must always remember that unless they begin somewhere they will probably always have too few employees who can and will accept more authority with commensurate responsibility.

FEAR OF MAKING MISTAKES

Some supervisors think it best to make most decisions themselves because, in the final analysis, they retain overall responsibility. Out of fear of mistakes, such supervisors are unwilling to delegate, and as a result, continue to overburden themselves. However, indecision and delay often are more costly than the mistakes supervisors hope to avoid by refusing to delegate. Also, these supervisors may make mistakes by not drawing on employees for assistance in decision making.

THE "I'D-RATHER-DO-IT-MYSELF" MENTALITY

The old stereotype of a good supervisor was that of one who pitched in and worked alongside employees, setting an example by personal effort. Even today, this type of supervision often occurs when a supervisor has been promoted through the ranks and the supervisory position is a reward for hard work and technical competence. The supervisors, therefore, resort to a pattern in which they feel secure by working alongside employees and doing tasks with which they are most familiar. Occasionally, the supervisor should pitch in, such as when the job is particularly difficult or when an emergency arises. With the trend toward eliminating management levels and consolidating operations, people will have to work together more closely. Under these conditions, the supervisor should be close enough to the job to offer help. Aside from emergencies and unusual situations, however, the supervisor should be supervising, and the employees should be doing their assigned tasks. Normally, it is the supervisor's job to get things done, not to do them.

"IF IT IS TO BE DONE RIGHT— I HAVE TO DO IT" MENTALITY

Supervisors sometimes complain that if they want something done right, they have to do it themselves. They believe it is easier to do the job than to correct an employee's mistakes, or they may simply prefer to correct an employee's mistakes rather than to clearly explain what should have been done. While this may be true, these attitudes interfere with a supervisor's prime responsibility, which is to supervise others to get the job done.

A good supervisor occasionally shows how a job can be done more efficiently, promptly, or courteously. However, an employee who does the job almost as well will save the supervisor time for more important jobs—for innovative thinking, planning, and more delegating. The effective supervisor strives to ensure that each employee, with each additional job, becomes more competent. Over time, the employee's performance on the job should be as good as or better than that of the supervisor.

FEAR OF BEING REPLACED

Ineffective supervisors may fear that if they share their knowledge with employees and allow them to participate in decision making, the employees will become so proficient at making good decisions that the supervisor will be unnecessary. The fear of not being needed can be partially overcome if the supervisor cannot be promoted unless he or she has prepared at least two subordinates to take the supervisor's place.

"THEY WON'T DO IT—YOU CAN KEEP IT" MENTALITY

Not everyone wants to take the responsibility for decisions. The supervisor must identify those employees who need the opportunity to grow and who want to be empowered. Employees may be reluctant to accept delegation because of their insecurity or fear of failure, or they may think the supervisor will be unavailable for guidance. Many employees are reluctant to accept delegation due to past managerial incompetence. For example, there is the "seagull manager" who, like the seagull, flies in, drops a load, and flies off. Too often, employees have had boring, mundane, and unpleasant tasks given to them from above.

Often, veterans will counsel new employees by saying, "Don't volunteer for anything, and if the boss gives you a new assignment, beg off." It is difficult for supervisors to create an environment of employee involvement and freedom to make decisions when their own managers do not allow them the same freedom. An environment for delegation and empowerment must be part of the organization's culture. Upper-level managers must advocate delegation at all levels.

BENEFITS OF DELEGATION

Can supervisors realize the benefits of delegation if they have only a small number of employees and there is no real need to create subunits in a department? Many supervisors face this situation. Is delegation in this type of working situation worth its trouble and risks? In general, the answer is a strong "yes."

The supervisor who delegates expects employees to make more decisions on their own. This does not mean that the supervisor is not available for advice. It means that the supervisor encourages the employees to make many of their own decisions and to develop self-confidence in doing so. This, in turn, should mean that the supervisor will have more time to manage. Effective delegation should cause employees to perform an increasing number of jobs and to recommend solutions that contribute to good performance. As the supervisor's confidence in employees expands, the employees' commitment to better performance also should grow. This growth may take time, and the degree of delegation may vary with each employee and with each department. However, in most situations, a supervisor's goal should be to delegate more authority to employees. This goal contributes to employee motivation and to better job performance.

Finally, it must be reiterated that there are some supervisory areas that cannot be delegated. For example, it remains the supervisor's responsibility to formulate certain policies and objectives, to give general directions for the work unit, to appraise employee performance, to take disciplinary action, and to promote employees. Aside from these types of supervisory management responsibilities, the employees should be doing most of the departmental work.

Approaches to Supervisory Leadership

Most employees accept work as a normal part of life. In their jobs, they seek satisfaction that wages alone cannot provide. Most employees probably would prefer to be their own bosses or at least to have a degree of freedom to make decisions that pertain to their work. The question arises as to whether this freedom is possible if an individual works for someone else. Can a degree of freedom be granted to employees if those employees are to contribute to organizational objectives? This is where the delegation of authority can help. The desire for freedom and being one's own boss can be enhanced by delegation, which in the daily routine essentially means giving directions in general terms. It means that instead of watching every detail of the employees' activities, the supervisor is primarily interested in the results employees achieve and is willing to give them considerable latitude in deciding how to achieve those results.

5 Compare the autocratic (authoritarian) approach to supervision with the participative approach.

CLASSIFYING SUPERVISORY LEADERSHIP STYLES

Organizational behavior and management literature are replete with research studies and models that have sought to establish which leadership styles are most consistently associated with superior levels of performance. The magnitude of these studies is beyond the scope of this text, and their findings and concepts are neither consistent nor conclusive.[16]

Rather than debate the differences and nuances of various leadership theories, we believe that they all can be classified into two styles or approaches. These styles range from essentially autocratic or authoritarian supervisory styles (based on Theory X assumptions), to variations of general supervisory styles (based on Theory Y assumptions). These two styles can be presented as the extremes of a continuum (see Figure 11.5). However, in practice, a supervisor usually blends these approaches based on a number of considerations that include the supervisor's skill and experience, the employee or employees who are involved, the situation, and other factors. No one style of supervision has ever been shown to be correct in

FIGURE 11.5 Leadership Style Continuum

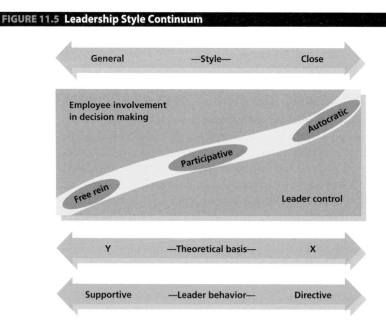

all situations. Consequently, supervisors must be sensitive to the needs and realities of each situation and to change their styles as necessary to accomplish objectives.

In Chapter 4, we discussed Theory X, Theory Y, and participative management. We expand these concepts in this chapter to relate them to a supervisor's day-to-day approaches to leading employees. While we focus primarily on supervisory leadership, recognize that not everything that influences employee behavior is in response to a supervisory approach.

AUTOCRATIC (AUTHORITARIAN) SUPERVISION

Autocratic (authoritarian) supervision
The supervisory style that relies on formal authority, threats, pressure, and close control

Many supervisors still believe that emphasizing formal authority, or **autocratic (authoritarian) supervision**, is the best way to obtain results. A supervisor of this type often uses pressure to get people to work and may even threaten disciplinary action, including discharge, if employees do not perform as ordered.[17] Employees sometimes call these managers "taskmasters." Autocratic supervision means close control of employees in which supervisors issue directives with detailed instructions and allow employees little room for initiative. Autocratic supervisors delegate very little or no authority. They believe that they know how to do the job better than their employees and that employees are not paid to think but to follow directions. Autocratic supervisors further believe that, because they have been put in charge, they should do most of the planning and decision making. Because such supervisors are quite explicit in telling employees exactly how and in what sequence things are to be done, they follow through with close supervision and are focused on the tasks to be done.

Bureaucratic style of supervision
The supervisory style that emphasizes strict compliance with organizational policies, rules, and directives

Autocratic supervision is sometimes associated with what has been called the **bureaucratic style of supervision**. This style emphasizes an organizational structure and climate that require strict compliance with managers' policies, rules, and directives throughout the firm. Because bureaucratic managers believe that their primary role is to carry out and enforce policies and directives, they usually adopt an authoritarian approach. Their favorite sayings are "It's policy," "Those are the rules," and "Shape up or ship out!"

Autocratic supervisors do not necessarily distrust their employees, but they firmly believe that without detailed instructions employees could not do their jobs. Some autocratic supervisors operate from the premise that most employees do not want to do their jobs; therefore, close supervision and threats of job or income loss are required to get employees to work (Theory X). These supervisors feel that if they are not on the scene watching their employees closely, the employees will stop working or will proceed at a leisurely pace.

WHEN AUTOCRATIC SUPERVISION IS APPROPRIATE

Under certain circumstances and with some employees, autocratic supervision is both logical and appropriate. Some employees do not want to think for themselves; they prefer to receive orders. Others lack ambition and do not wish to become very involved in their daily jobs. This can be the case when jobs are very structured, mechanized, automated, or routine. Employees in these jobs may prefer to have a supervisor who issues orders and otherwise leaves them alone. Some employees prefer an authoritarian environment and expect a supervisor to be firm and totally in charge. For example, most passengers and flight attendants would prefer that the pilot use an autocratic style when faced with an "emergency in flight." The same is true in any organization when a situation requires immediate attention.

Probably the major advantages of autocratic supervision are that it is quick and fairly easy to apply and that it usually gets rapid results in the short run. It may be appropriate when employees are new and inexperienced, especially if the supervisor is under major time pressures and cannot afford to have employees take time to figure out on their own how to get the work done.

EFFECTS OF AUTOCRATIC SUPERVISION

For the most part, the autocratic method of supervision is not conducive to developing employee talents, and it tends to frustrate employees who have ambition and potential. Such employees may lose interest and initiative and stop thinking for themselves because there is little need for independent thought. Those who believe in the sheer weight of authority and the "be strong" form of supervision tend to discount the fact that workers may react in ways that were not intended by the supervisor. Employees who strongly resent autocratic supervision may become frustrated rather than find satisfaction in their daily work. Such frustration can lead to arguments and other forms of discontent. In some cases, employees may become hostile toward an autocratic supervisor and resist the supervisor's directives. The resistance may not even be apparent to the supervisor when it takes the form of slow work, mistakes, and poor work quality. If the supervisor makes a mistake, these employees may secretly rejoice.

PARTICIPATIVE MANAGEMENT AND GENERAL SUPERVISION

Because of the potentially negative consequences associated with autocratic and close supervision, most supervisors prefer not to use it or to apply it sparingly. Is one leadership style better than another? Many research studies have suggested that effective supervisors tailor their leadership styles to situations and to the abilities and motivation of subordinates. Effective supervisors who want to guide employees to higher levels of performance recognize that they cannot rely solely on managerial authority. **General supervision** means that the supervisor sets goals, discusses those goals with employees, and fixes the limits within which the work must be done. Within this framework, employees have considerable freedom to decide how to achieve their objectives.

Participative management means that the supervisor who uses a participative approach discusses with employees the feasibility, workability, extent, and content of a problem before making a decision and issuing a **directive**. General supervision and participative management are grounded in Theory Y assumptions. Regardless of one's preference for a leadership style, the supervisor must ensure that the assigned work gets done efficiently and effectively. Whether assigning tasks to subordinates or helping subordinates decide on how to do a task, the supervisor must provide directives. The degree to which the supervisor uses directives will, in part, vary with the task to be performed; the skill level, experience, and willingness of the subordinate; and the urgency of the situation. The accompanying Supervisory Tips box offers five major characteristics for issuing good supervisory directives.

A participatory style does not lessen a supervisor's authority; the right to decide remains with the supervisor and the employees' suggestions can be rejected. Participation means that a supervisor expresses personal opinions in a manner that indicates to employees that these opinions are subject to critique. It also means sharing ideas and information between supervisor and employees and thoroughly discussing alternative solutions to a problem, regardless of who originates the solutions. A high degree of mutual trust must be evident.

As discussed previously in this text, the term *empowerment* has been used to describe an approach by which employees and work teams are given more

General supervision
The style of supervision in which the supervisor sets goals and limits but allows employees to decide how to achieve goals

Participative management
Allowing employees to influence and share in organizational decision making

Directive
The communication approach by which a supervisor conveys to employees what, how, and why something is to be accomplished

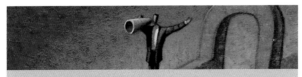

SUPERVISORY TIPS
Guidelines for Issuing Good Directives

Reasonable—The supervisor should not issue a directive if the employee receiving it does not have the ability or experience and willingness to comply.

Understandable—The supervisor should make certain that an employee understands a directive by speaking in words that are familiar to the employee and by using feedback to ensure that the employee understands.

Specific—The supervisor should state clearly what is expected in terms of quantity and quality of work performance.

Time-limited—The supervisor should specify a time limit within which the work should be completed.

Congruent—Supervisory directives must be compatible with the philosophy, mission, policies, regulations, and ethical standards of the organization.

responsibility and authority to make decisions about the jobs they do. The essence of any empowerment approach is participative management because they both stem from the same model or philosophy of how to manage and supervise. Empowerment, like participative management, is a matter of degree. It is not some form of an absolute approach that involves the same amount of participation or empowerment for every individual and every situation.

More important than approach is the supervisor's attitude. Some supervisors are inclined to use a pseudo-participatory approach simply to give employees the feeling that they have been consulted. These supervisors ask for suggestions even though they already have decided on a course of action. They use this approach to manipulate employees to do what will be required, with or without employees' consultation. However, employees can sense superficiality and will usually perceive whether a supervisor is genuinely considering their ideas. When employees believe their participation is false, the results may be worse than if the supervisor had practiced autocratic supervision.

If participative management is to succeed, the supervisor and the employees must want it. When employees believe that the supervisor knows best and that making decisions is none of their concern, an opportunity to participate is not likely to induce higher motivation and better morale. Further, employees should be consulted in those areas in which they can express valid opinions and in which they can draw on their knowledge. The problems should be consistent with employees' experiences and abilities. Asking for participation in areas that are far outside employees' scopes of competence may make employees feel inadequate and frustrated.

ADVANTAGES OF PARTICIPATIVE MANAGEMENT AND GENERAL SUPERVISION

Perhaps the greatest advantage of participative management is that a supervisor's directive can be transformed into a solution that employees have discovered or at least into a decision in which they have participated. This normally leads employees to cooperate with more enthusiasm in carrying out a directive, and their morale is apt to be higher when their ideas are valued. Active participation provides an opportunity to make worthwhile contributions. Still another advantage is that participative management permits closer communication between employees and the supervisor so that they learn to trust and respect each other better and, for the most part, the workplace can become more enjoyable with less tension and conflict.

General supervision means permitting employees, within prescribed limits, to work out the details of their daily tasks and to make many of the decisions about how tasks will be performed. In so doing, the supervisor believes that employees want to do a good job and will find greater satisfaction in making decisions themselves. The supervisor communicates the desired results, standards, and limits within which the employees can work and then delegates accordingly.

For example, a school-maintenance supervisor might assign a group of employees to paint the interior walls of the school. The supervisor tells the group where to get the paint and other materials and reminds them that they should do the painting without interfering with normal school operations. Then, the supervisor suggests a target date for completing the project and leaves the group to work on its own. The supervisor may occasionally check back with the group to see whether group members are encountering any problems or need help. The advantages of participative management/general supervision are listed in Figure 11.6.

For general supervision to work, employees should be trained and know the routine of their jobs and which results are expected, but the supervisor should avoid giving detailed instructions that specify precisely how results are to be achieved. Further, general supervision also means that the supervisor, or the supervisor and employees together, should set realistic standards or performance targets. These standards should be high enough to represent a challenge but not so high that they cannot be achieved. Such targets sometimes are known as **stretch targets**. Employees know that their efforts are being measured against these standards. If they cannot accomplish the targets, they are expected to inform the supervisor so that the standards can be discussed again and perhaps modified.[18]

Stretch targets
Targeted job objectives that present a challenge but are achievable

PARTICIPATIVE MANAGEMENT AND GENERAL SUPERVISION AS A WAY OF LIFE

When practiced simultaneously, participative management and general supervision are a way of life that must be followed over time. A supervisor cannot expect sudden results by introducing these types of supervision into an environment in which employees have been accustomed to authoritarian, close supervision. It may take considerable time and patience before positive results are evident.

The successful implementation of participative management and general supervision requires a continuous effort on a supervisor's part to develop employees beyond their present skills. Employees learn more when they can work out solutions for themselves. They learn best from their own successes and failures.

FIGURE 11.6 The Advantages of Participative Management/General Supervision

FOR SUPERVISORS

- Frees the supervisor from many details, which allows time to plan, organize, and control.
- Gives the supervisor more time to assume additional responsibility.
- Instills confidence that employees will carry out the work and develop suitable approaches to making decisions on the job when the supervisor is away from the department.
- The decisions made by employees may be better than the ones made by the supervisor because the employees are closest to the details.

FOR EMPLOYEES

- Have a chance to develop their talents and abilities by making on-the-job decisions.
- May make mistakes but are encouraged to learn from those mistakes and the mistakes of others.
- Are motivated to take pride in their decisions.
- May feel that they have a better chance to advance to higher positions.

The participative supervisor spends considerable time encouraging employees to solve their own problems and to participate in and make decisions. As employees become more competent and self-confident, there is less need for the supervisor to instruct and watch them. A valid way to gauge the effectiveness of a supervisor is to study how employees in the department function when the supervisor is away from the job. This is the essence of employee empowerment.

While supervisors may use participative management and general supervision whenever possible, from time to time they will have to demonstrate some authority with those employees who require close supervision. Supervisors who practice a participatory or general style of leadership must still be performance-conscious. However, the style they use differentiates them from their more authoritarian counterparts.

THE PROPER BALANCE OF DELEGATION

Although we have stressed the advantages of delegation that can be realized through general supervision, it is important to recognize that the process of delegation is delicate. It is not easy for a supervisor to part with some authority and still be left with the responsibility for the performance and decisions made by workers. There are numerous illustrations of how effective leadership requires sound judgment and skill. The supervisor must achieve a balance among too much, too little, and just the right amount to delegate without losing control. There are situations in which supervisors must resort to their formal authority to attain the objectives of the department. Supervisors at times have to make decisions that are distasteful to employees. Delegation does not mean a supervisor should manage a department by consensus or by taking a vote on every issue.

---

6 Suggest approaches for introducing change to employees and for proposing changes to higher-level managers.

Introducing Change

Change is expected as part of life, and the survival and growth of most enterprises depend on change and innovation. Many books and articles have been written concerning the imperatives for change faced by most organizations. Indeed, the survival of a firm may depend on the abilities of its managers to make fundamental changes in virtually all aspects of operations while facing the risks of an uncertain future. The impact of change has become so common that security and stability are often concepts and practices related to the past.[19]

We are all familiar with planned change. For example, about this time in the term, most of our students are planning their schedules for the next term. After having met with their advisors, they have a list of four courses needed to finish the degree. Two of those are required courses, and the others are electives. They, like you, browse through the course schedule to find when those two required courses are offered. They discover that one of the courses they need to complete the degree requirements is not being offered next term. They didn't plan on that! Their blood pressure rises, and their frustration level increases. Why? Because they did not anticipate this situation. **Unplanned change** comes as a result of circumstances beyond our control. For example, a hurricane hits the Gulf coast and destroys your manufacturing plant; a competitor launches a new product that makes your best seller obsolete; or a colleague or close friend dies unexpectedly. As mentioned in Chapter 7, we can have a crisis plan in place, but only minimal precautions can be taken. The students' situation presents a new challenge along with fears—the fear of not being able to graduate at the end of next term. Then they pause, collect their thoughts, and ponder a strategy for coping with the unexpected situation.

Unplanned change
An unexpected situation causes you to initiate a strategy for change

MAKING CHANGE MEANS SUPERVISORY INVOLVEMENT

Despite the emphasis on change, there still appear to be numerous problems and considerable resentment concerning both the introduction and effects of many organizational changes. There is an adage that says, "All progress is change, but not all change is progress." Too often, managers look for a quick response in their organizations when making changes, and they become frustrated when expected results are not achieved. Mediocrity is then tolerated, and the net result is that the more things have changed, the more they have stayed the same.[20]

Our focus in the remaining part of this chapter is not to discuss comprehensive strategies for total organizational change.[21] Rather, it is to discuss the introduction and management of change from the supervisory perspective, which is another challenging aspect of a supervisor's leading function of management. As with so many other areas of concern, the introduction of change, such as a new work method, a new product, a new schedule, or a new human resources policy, usually requires implementation at the departmental level. In the final analysis, whether a change has been initiated by upper management or by the supervisor personally, it is the supervisor who has the major role in affecting change. The success or failure of any change is usually related to a supervisor's ability to anticipate and deal with the causes of resistance to change.

People don't resist change—they resist being changed

REASONS FOR RESISTANCE TO CHANGE

Some supervisors are inclined to discount the existence and magnitude of human resistance to change. What may seem like a trifling change to the supervisor may bring a strong reaction from employees. Supervisors should remember that employees seldom resist change just to be stubborn. They resist because they believe a change threatens their positions socially, psychologically, or economically. Therefore, the supervisor should be familiar with the ways in which resistance to change can be minimized and handled successfully.

Most people pride themselves on being up-to-date. As consumers, they expect and welcome changes in material things such as automobiles, convenience items, electronic appliances, and computers. As employees, however, they may resist changes on the job or changes in personal relationships, even though such changes are vital for the operation of the organization. If an organization is to survive, it must be able to react to prevailing conditions by adjusting.

Change disturbs the environment in which people exist. Employees become accustomed to a work environment in which patterns of relationships and behavior have stabilized. When a change takes place, new ideas and new methods may be perceived as a threat to the security of the work group. Many employees fear change because they cannot predict what the change will mean in terms of their positions, activities, or abilities (Figure 11.7). It makes no difference whether the change actually has a negative result. What matters is that the employees believe that the change will have negative consequences. For example, the introduction of

FIGURE 11.7 Many people fear change because they cannot predict what the change will mean in terms of their future in the organization

new equipment is usually accompanied by employee fears of loss of jobs or skills. Even if the supervisor and higher-level managers announce that no employees will be laid off, rumors circulate that layoffs will occur or jobs will be downgraded. Employee fears may still be present months after the change.

Change affects individuals in different ways. Remember that a change that greatly disturbs one person may create only a small problem for another. A supervisor must learn to recognize how changes affect different employees and observe how individuals develop patterns of behavior that serve as barriers to accepting change.

OVERCOMING RESISTANCE TO CHANGE

Probably the most important factor in gaining employee acceptance of new ideas and methods is the relationship between the supervisor who is introducing the change and the employees who are affected by it. If the relationship has confidence and trust, employees are more likely to accept the change.[22]

PROVIDE ADEQUATE INFORMATION

In the final analysis, it is not the change itself that usually leads to resistance. Rather, it is the manner in which the supervisor introduces the change. Resistance to change, when it comes from fear of the unknown, can be minimized by supplying all the information employees consciously and subconsciously need to know.

Whenever possible, a supervisor should explain what will happen, why it will happen, and how the employees and the department will be affected by a change. If applicable, the supervisor should emphasize how the change will leave employees no worse off or how it may even improve their present situation. This information should be communicated as early as appropriate to all employees who are directly or indirectly involved, either individually or collectively. Only then can employees assess what a change will mean in terms of their activities. This will be facilitated if the supervisor has tried consistently to give ample background information for all directives.

Employees who are well-acquainted with the underlying factors of departmental operations usually understand the need for change. They will probably question a change, but they then can adjust to that change and go on.

When employees have been informed of the reasons for a change, what to expect, and how their jobs will be affected, they usually make reasonable adaptations. Instead of insecurity, they feel relatively confident and willing to comply.

A change that involves closing certain operations and losing jobs should be explained openly and frankly. It is especially important to discuss which employees are likely to be affected and how the job cuts will be made. If higher-level managers have decided not to identify which individuals will be terminated until it actually happens, the supervisor should explain this as a reality and not try to hide behind vague promises or to raise unrealistic expectations.[23]

ENCOURAGE PARTICIPATION IN DECISION MAKING

Another technique for reducing resistance to change is to permit the affected employees to share in making decisions about the change. If several employees are involved in a change, group decision making is an effective way to reduce their fears and objections. When employees have an opportunity to work through new ideas and methods from the beginning, usually they will consider the new directives as something of their own making and will give those changes their support. The group may even apply pressure on those who have reservations about going along with the change, and it is likely that each member of the group will carry out the change once there is agreement on how to proceed.

Group decision making is especially effective in changes in which the supervisor is indifferent about the details. In these cases, the supervisor must set limits for the group. For example, a supervisor may not care how a new departmental work schedule is divided among the group as long as the work is accomplished within a prescribed time, with a given number of employees, and without overtime.

Change affects every aspect of what the organization does and how it does it. Typically, employee responses to changes taking place in the organization have been "lukewarm" at best. Figure 11.8 provides a guide for supervisors to use to help overcome the barriers to change.

Employee involvement is the key to overcoming resistance to change

© MICHAEL NEWMAN/PHOTOEDIT

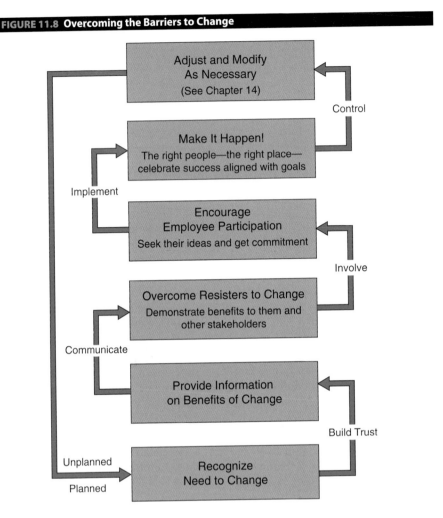

FIGURE 11.8 Overcoming the Barriers to Change

PROPOSING CHANGE TO HIGH-LEVEL MANAGERS

In many organizations, high-level managers complain that supervisors are too content with the status quo and are unwilling to suggest new and innovative ways to improve departmental performance. Supervisors, on the other hand, complain that higher-level managers are not receptive to ideas they suggest for their departments. There is probably some truth to both allegations. In Chapter 8, we discussed the concept of the "learning organization." Author Peter Senge says that for big companies to succeed, they must start acting like gardeners: "I have never seen a successful organizational-learning program rolled out from the top. Not a single one. Conversely, every change process that I've seen that was sustained and that spread has started small. Just as nothing in nature starts big, start creating change with a pilot group—a growth seed."[24]

It should be clear that top management's job is to pollinate those seeds (ideas) and help them to bear fruit. Unfortunately, that is not the way it works. If supervisors wish to propose changes, it is important that they understand how to present ideas not only to their employees, but to higher-level managers. "Selling" an idea to a manager involves the art of persuasion, much as a good salesperson uses persuasion to sell a product or service to a reluctant customer. What do I really do about my boss, if he or she is a tough sell? Cartoonist Scott Adams of *Dilbert* fame suggests that:

Whatever you do, never use the so-called direct approach: "I have an idea. Let's do this." Dilbert would take exactly that approach because he's an engineer and totally ignorant of the human condition. But the only way that a boss will respond to a reasonable suggestion is unreasonably—like with some of those great-idea-sinker questions: "If this is such a good idea, why isn't everybody doing it?" Or, "Have you asked everybody in the organization—all 1,000 of them—to buy into your idea?" The worst thing you can do is assume that your boss is a thoughtful person who will immediately recognize a good idea and take a personal risk to implement it. Instead, I suggest using the hypnosis approach. Lead your boss to your idea through subtle questioning—giving the impression that it was his idea in the first place.[25]

As unlikely as it may seem, at times the supervisor must use various strategies to convince the boss that a proposal was the boss's idea.

OBTAIN NEEDED INFORMATION

A supervisor who has a good idea or who wishes to suggest a change should first ask, "What aspects of the idea or change will be of most interest to the boss?" Higher-level managers usually are interested if a change might improve production, increase sales and profits, improve morale, or reduce overhead and other costs. It is important to do considerable homework to see whether a proposed change is feasible and adaptable to the departmental operation. By thinking through the idea carefully and getting as much information as possible, the supervisor will be better positioned to argue strong and weak points of the proposal. In addition, the supervisor should find out whether any other departments or organizations have used the proposed idea—successfully or unsuccessfully. The manager will be impressed that the supervisor has invested time and effort to investigate the best practices of other organizations.

CONSULT WITH OTHER SUPERVISORS

To get an idea or a proposal beyond the discussion stage, the supervisor should consult with other supervisors and personnel who might be affected and get their reactions to the proposed change. Checking an idea out with them gives them a chance to think the idea through, offer suggestions and criticisms, and work out some of the problems. Otherwise, some supervisors may resist or resent the change if they feel they have been ignored.

If possible, it is helpful to get the tentative commitment of other supervisors. It is not always necessary to obtain total approval, but higher-level managers will be more inclined to consider an idea if it has been discussed at least in preliminary form with knowledgeable people in the organization.

FORMAL WRITTEN PROPOSAL

At times, a manager may ask a supervisor to put a proposed idea in writing so that copies may be forwarded to higher-level managers, other supervisors, or other personnel. This requires effort. The supervisor may have to engage in considerable study outside of normal working hours to obtain all the needed information. Relevant information on costs, prices, productivity data, and the like should be included in the proposal, even if some data are only educated guesses. Highly uncertain estimates should be labeled as tentative, and exaggerated claims and opinions should be avoided. Risks, as well as potential advantages, should be acknowledged in the formal proposal.

FORMAL PRESENTATION

If a supervisor is asked to formally present the proposal, ample planning and preparation are required (see the tips presented in Chapter 3 for managing up). The presentation should be made thoroughly and unhurriedly, allowing sufficient time for questions and discussion.

A supervisor who has carefully thought through an idea should be unafraid to express it in a firm and convincing manner. The supervisor should be enthusiastic in explaining the idea, but at the same time should be patient and empathetic with those who may not agree with it. A helpful technique in a formal presentation is to use some type of chart, diagram, or visual aid.

ACCEPTANCE OR REJECTION OF CHANGE BY HIGH-LEVEL MANAGERS

A supervisor who can persuade higher-level managers and other supervisors to accept a proposed change will likely feel inner satisfaction. Of course, any good idea requires careful implementation, follow-up, and refinement. Rarely does a change follow the suggested blueprint. Following up and working out the problems with others are important aspects of making a change effective.

However, despite a supervisor's best efforts, an idea may be rejected, altered greatly, or shelved. This can be frustrating, particularly to supervisors who have worked diligently to develop ideas they believed would lead to positive results. The important thing is to avoid becoming discouraged and developing a negative outlook. There may be valid reasons an idea was rejected, or the timing may not have been right. A supervisor should resolve to try again and perhaps to further refine and polish the idea for resubmission.

A supervisor who has developed an idea for change, even if it has not been accepted, usually will find that such efforts are appreciated by higher-level managers. Moreover, the experience of having worked through a proposal for change will make the supervisor a more valuable member of the organizational team, and there will be many other opportunities to work for change.

---

7 Understand the formula for organizational renewal.

A Formula for Organizational Renewal

We must accept the reality that organizations must change or die! Many organizations, like people, wait until they are near death before they recognize the need to make changes. Harvard professors Michael Tushman and Charles O'Reilly pointed out that "leading an organization is an ongoing process."[26] This author has found that when he asks a business leader what his or her most formidable challenge is, the answer is usually, "Figuring out how to do a better job of doing what we are doing." Unfortunately, that answer is only partially right. Are they doing the right things that will position their organizations for tomorrow? Renewal requires doing the right thing today so that they are prepared to meet the challenges of tomorrow. In short, *organizational renewal* means that management must improve upon and sustain what they are doing today while creating processes for long-term success.

Think of it this way. A good friend—let's call him Alex—goes to the doctor for his annual physical. You know that Alex is carrying a few extra pounds. When the two of you dine out, you always order smaller portions, but Alex orders the king-size portions. After conducting a series of tests, the doctor tells Alex that he must shed thirty or more pounds, take blood pressure medicine, and

Organizational renewal
A continuous process for long-term success

commence a rigorous supervised exercise program. For the past several years, everyone could see that Alex was having problems, but he was either ignoring the reality or couldn't see it. The same is true for certain persons in leadership positions. Hopefully, Alex will be up to the challenge, and will successfully make the appropriate changes. It is difficult to do. Alex must be willing to accept the recommendations and implement the change strategy or suffer the consequences.

Throughout this chapter we have discussed various leadership styles and methods for overcoming the barriers to change. The following section provides a conceptual framework of initiating and implementing the process of organizational renewal and the SKAs needed to accomplish it.

RECOGNIZING THE NEED FOR RENEWAL: ONE ORGANIZATION'S QUEST FOR EXCELLENCE

Let's rewind to 1996—At the time, Jim Vickary was president of Baptist Health Care (the system) in Pensacola, Florida, and Al Stubblefield was president of Baptist Hospital (the hospital). Vickary created a new position of executive vice president (of the system) and promoted Stubblefield, leaving the administrator position for the hospital open. Stubblefield recruited Quint Studer from Holy Cross Hospital in Chicago to replace him as administrator of Baptist Hospital.[27]

When Studer arrived at Baptist Hospital in 1996, admissions were flat, and patient satisfaction, as measured by a national survey, was slightly below average. Stubblefield had hired Studer to implement many of the organizational change tools that were developed during Studer's tenure at Holy Cross. The goal was to improve both patient and employee satisfaction. Studer refined those tools and developed others while at Baptist.

Studer left Baptist Hospital, Inc. in 2000 and formed the Studer Group to take his methods of cultural change to other organizations. He now coaches other organizations on how to create a culture of excellence.[28] Jim Collins, author of *Good to Great*, wrote, "Great organizations benefiting from the Flywheel effect where the power of continued improvement and the delivery of results creates momentum."[29] The Studer Group developed the Healthcare Flywheel (see Figure 11.9) to help organizations understand their role in creating great places for employees to work, physicians to practice, and patients to receive care. Working in health care organizations for twenty-plus years and studying "the best of the best," Studer found that what motivates people is the accomplishment of desired results. By tying results back to purpose, worthwhile work, and making a difference, the organization is inspired to follow more prescriptive behaviors to achieve even greater results, thereby creating a self-perpetuating culture of excellence, fueled by the momentum of the flywheel.[30]

According to Studer, the beginning of the journey starts with a focus on the organization's core values. The five Pillar Resources (Figure 11.9) serve as a starting point for establishing organizational objectives: Service, Quality, People, Finance, and Growth. Once objectives are set for each pillar, they are cascaded throughout, from division to department to unit to individual. These pillars then lay the metrics and framework for consistent evaluations. Studer suggests that additional pillars can be added to meet the uniqueness of a particular organization.[31] Studer believes that you create movement by connecting the dots to the hub so that people truly know they can make a difference. This allows organizations to implement initial changes.[32]

Among the true tests of leadership are (1) whether anyone follows, and (2) the legacy the leader leaves. That is, what does the organization look like three years

FIGURE 11.9 A Process for Organizational Renewal[33]

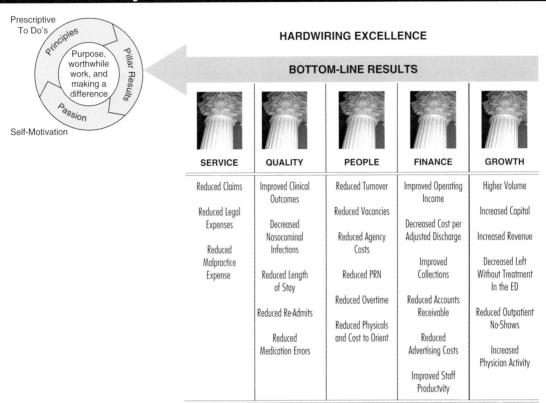

Prescriptive To Do's
Principles
Purpose, worthwhile work, and making a difference
Pillar Results
Passion
Self-Motivation

HARDWIRING EXCELLENCE

BOTTOM-LINE RESULTS

SERVICE	QUALITY	PEOPLE	FINANCE	GROWTH
Reduced Claims	Improved Clinical Outcomes	Reduced Turnover	Improved Operating Income	Higher Volume
Reduced Legal Expenses	Decreased Nosocominal Infections	Reduced Vacancies	Decreased Cost per Adjusted Discharge	Increased Capital
Reduced Malpractice Expense	Reduced Length of Stay	Reduced Agency Costs	Improved Collections	Increased Revenue
	Reduced Re-Admits	Reduced PRN	Reduced Accounts Receivable	Decreased Left Without Treatment In the ED
	Reduced Medication Errors	Reduced Overtime	Reduced Advertising Costs	Reduced Outpatient No-Shows
		Reduced Physicals and Cost to Orient	Improved Staff Productvity	Increased Physician Activity

after they leave? At this point, you are probably wondering what has happened to Baptist Hospital, Inc. Did Studer leave a legacy? You be the judge!

The rest of the story—As of late 2005, the Baptist Health Care system included two hospitals—Baptist Hospital (BHI) of Pensacola, a 492-bed tertiary-care and referral hospital; Gulf Breeze, a 60-bed medical and surgical hospital; and Baptist Medical Park, an ambulatory-care complex that delivers an array of outpatient and diagnostic services.

Since 1998, patient satisfaction has been near or above the 99th percentile every quarter. Patient surveys of staff sensitivity, attitude, concern, and overall cheerfulness of hospital staff all have been near the 99th percentile. Employee turnover rates have declined substantially since 1996 and are at the "best-in-class" levels nationally.[34] In 2005, Baptist Health Care's efforts in engaging employees received the leadership award for operational excellence from VHA, the nation's largest healthcare alliance. The connection between happy employees and outstanding customer service is most evident at Baptist Health Care.

Baptist Healthcare Corporation (the system), BHI's parent, has been ranked among the "Best Companies to Work for in America" by *Fortune* magazine's annual survey for six consecutive years.[35] Baptist Hospital (the hospital) was the 2003 Malcolm Baldrige National Quality Award Recipient.[36]

A MODEL FOR RENEWAL

Is the model for organizational change used by Stubblefield and Studer one that is applicable to other organizations? Yes, but remember that what works in one organization may not work in another. While most organizations are impacted by external forces, e.g., rising gas prices, the internal forces for change vary greatly. If we could look inside two organizations, we would find them to be very, very different. Each organization has its own culture. Managers vary in leadership styles and communication skills. Employees bring different values and SKAs to the workplace. Clearly, when the need for change is recognized, management will respond in radically different ways. Ordinarily, management may agree that change is needed but have difficulty agreeing on the process to follow. To that end, we offer the following to point you in the right direction:

- Remember that as leader of the team, you are also a member of the team.
- Identify the issues confronting the organization.
- Analyze how those issues prevent goal attainment.
- Recognize the difference between needed change and change for the sake of change.
- Identify metrics that will be used to monitor and evaluate the change process.
- Communicate to and involve all who have a stake in the change.
- Understand what needs to be changed.
- Seek consensus, but recognize when to sacrifice unanimity for decisiveness.
- Confront the "resisters" to change.
- Establish clear targets.
- Take risks, experiment, and innovate.
- Spend money to develop (train) employees so they have the competencies to implement the change.
- Focus on the outcome(s).
- Monitor progress and make adjustments as necessary.
- Provide feedback and encouragement.
- Guarantee total commitment to organizational renewal—to be the "best of the best."
- Celebrate victories!

Noted leadership theorist John Kotter said, "Behavior change happens mostly by speaking to people's feelings."[37] Clearly, Stubblefield and Studer created passionate, empowered employees who made a difference in their organization and, ultimately, in the lives of those they serve.

SUMMARY

1 Effective supervisory management means that supervisors must become leaders in the true sense of the word. Supervisory leadership primarily resides in the ability of the supervisor to influence the opinions, attitudes, and performance of employees to accomplish company goals. The test of supervisory leadership is whether subordinates follow willingly. Supervisory leadership skills can be developed.

2 Several different thoughts on leadership have been identified and discussed in this chapter. Warren Bennis categorized four things people want from their leaders: (1) direction, (2) trust, (3) hope, and (4) results. Stephen Covey believes that the principle of alignment is essential for developing trust. James Kouzes and Barry Posner believe that successful leaders exhibit a series of five practices: (1) challenging the process,

(2) inspiring a shared vision, (3) enabling others to act, (4) modeling the way, and (5) encouraging the heart.

The Servant-Leadership concept is a notion that puts people first. Robert Greenleaf and others contend that truly great leaders lead with integrity and have a strong set of values and ethics that make sure their employees' needs are served. Servant-Leadership helps develop the employee's full potential. Supervisors who embody this style have the ability to set the stage for success.

The common threads are creating a corporate vision, communicating honestly with employees, holding employees accountable, and engendering mutual trust and respect. In addition, managers must develop a culture in which subordinates buy into the organization's purpose and values. Although no one supervisory leadership style is universally acceptable, the need to establish standards and develop a climate in which people are self-motivated and adapt to constant change are key traits of effective leaders.

3 The process of delegation is made up of three components: (1) assigning a job or duties, (2) granting authority, and (3) creating responsibility. For delegation to succeed, supervisors must give employees enough authority and responsibility to carry out their assigned duties. All three components are interdependent in that a change in one requires a corresponding change in the other two. The supervisor must be specific in telling employees what authority they have and what they can and cannot do. The supervisor delegates authority to employees to accomplish specific jobs, but the supervisor's own accountability cannot be delegated.

4 Included among the many reasons supervisors are reluctant to delegate are a shortage of qualified employees, a fear of making mistakes, the "I'd-rather-do-it-myself" mentality, a fear of not being needed, reluctant employees, and lack of managerial support for decisions. "Seagull managers" have conditioned some employees to avoid receiving tasks from their immediate supervisor, who "dumps" rather than delegates.

Effective supervisors see the benefits of delegation. Employees become more involved and gain knowledge and confidence in their skills. The supervisor benefits from greater flexibility, better decisions, higher employee morale, and better job performance.

5 Participative management and general supervision promote delegation because they provide employees with considerable involvement in making decisions and doing their jobs to meet departmental objectives. They offer many advantages to supervisors as well as employees. The supervisor saves time in the long term. By giving employees practice in making decisions and using their own judgment, the supervisor

encourages employees to become more competent and more promotable.

Some supervisors believe that autocratic supervision is more likely than general supervision to get results from employees. There are occasions when supervisors have to rely on their managerial authority. For the most part, however, these should be the exceptions rather than the rule.

The extent to which a supervisor uses the autocratic or general approach requires a delicate balance. The advantages of delegation are realized through general supervision. However, at times, supervisors have to resort to their formal authority to attain departmental objectives.

6 To cope with employees' normal resistance to change, supervisors must understand why resistance surfaces and what can be done to help employees adjust to and accept changes. A supervisor also should learn the principles of selling change to higher-level managers. Sometimes, supervisors may have to subtly convince their managers that changes were the managers' ideas. Regardless of the approach, the supervisor must persuade all affected personnel that accepting proposed change will benefit them and the organization.

7 Leadership and change go hand in hand with organizational renewal. Organizational renewal should be a continuous process. Baptist Health Care serves as an example of how one organization responded to the swiftly changing health care environment and effectively managed the changes necessary to achieve success. Striving for a culture of continuous improvement where employees under their role is a critical component. The process begins with setting objectives (the Five Pillars). Then metrics are established against which to measure progress. The implications for supervisors are that they need to fix the problems of today while keeping an eye fixed on where they want to be tomorrow.

KEY TERMS

Accountability (p. 397)
Autocratic (authoritarian) supervision
   (p. 404)
Bureaucratic style of supervision (p. 404)
Contingency-style leadership (p. 396)

Delegation (p. 397)
Directive (p. 405)
General supervision (p. 405)
Leadership (p. 391)
Organizational renewal (p. 414)

Participative management (p. 405)
Responsibility (p. 399)
Servant-leadership (p. 395)
Stretch targets (p. 407)
Unplanned change (p. 408)

QUESTIONS FOR DISCUSSION

1. How would you define leadership?
   a. If there is one person (living or dead) whom you would really like to follow, who would it be? Why would you want to follow that particular person? What characteristics of servant-leadership did that person exhibit?
   b. Think of a person whom you would not have wanted to follow. Why? How would this person's knowledge of the characteristics of servant-leadership have helped the person to be a better leader?

   c. In your opinion, what perceptual factors distinguish followership from non-followership?

2. Why are the concepts of responsibility, authority, and accountability closely related? Why can't a supervisor's personal accountability be delegated? Why are many supervisors reluctant to delegate? What benefits typically accrue to a supervisor who learns to delegate?

3. Distinguish between autocratic (authoritarian) supervision, participative management, and general supervision. What theoretical differences are implied in these approaches? Relate these to concepts concerning the delegation of authority, motivation, and empowerment.

4. Why is it inappropriate to assume that a leadership style that works best in one situation will be just as effective in another? Why is trust a key ingredient in the leadership equation?

5. Consider the following statement, "People don't resist change; they resist being changed." To what extent is this statement true? Discuss strategies for overcoming resistance to change. Discuss the principles of proposing change to higher-level managers.

6. What are the major ways in which the concepts and principles of organizational renewal might be incorporated into every supervisor's job?

SKILLS APPLICATIONS

Skills Application 11-1: How Would You Make The Call?

In this skills application, you are asked to play the role of David Felker, supervisor of shipping and receiving at Tideway Corporation's Arcola plant.

1. What do you suppose the union steward meant when she said, "You have forgotten what it was like to be a worker?"
   a. If we could play it again, how should David have responded to her allegation?
   b. What actions should Dave take now? Or should he wait to see if things change? Why?

2. One size does not fit all, and that applies to leadership styles. What should be the key factors that David should

consider in determining an appropriate style for leading his subordinates?

3. Identify the restraining forces that have caused David's subordinates to reject his new approach to leadership?

4. Should David take his concerns to his immediate supervisor, Scott Riley, or should he seek guidance from the HR director? What would be the advantages and disadvantages of each approach?

5. As David, how could you apply the concepts of servant-leadership to the situation? In your opinion, would servant-leadership work in a unionized situation?

Skills Application 11-2: Look In The Mirror

(**INTERNET ACTIVITY**) Conduct an Internet search for "best leaders" to see who ranks among the best. See "Where Have All the Leaders Gone?" *U.S. News & World Report* (August 25, 2008) (http://www.usnews.com/usnews/news/leaders.); "The Best Leaders of 2007," (http://www.businessweek.com); "Top 50 Women to Watch," *Wall Street Journal* (November 10, 2008), pp. R1–R8. (http://

www.dowjones.com/womentowatch); "Meet the TIME 100," *Time* (May 12, 2008), pp. 36–52 (www.time.com) for a look at their list of those who are changing the world; or "The Power 100 – Meet the Most Influential People in the Business of Sport," *BusinessWeek* (October 8, 2007), pp. 43–74.

1. Look at the picture frame collage. Our leader list includes (from left to right) JP Morgan Chase's Jamie Dimon, American Express's Kenneth Chenault, PepsiCo's Indra K. Nooyi, and Proctor & Gamble's Alan (A.G) Lafley.

2. By searching the Internet and/or reading the Special Report, learn about the background for each of these leaders.
   a. For each leader, identify what you perceive to be their SKAs.
   b. For each leader, in fifty words or less, describe their leadership styles.

3. After reading the article by Robert J. Thomas, "Life's Hard Lessons: Recognizing and Discussing Moments in Both Your Professional and Personal Life Makes You a Better Leader," *HR Magazine* (June 2008), pp. 143–146, **picture yourself in the vacant frame**.
   a. Think about what you have accomplished.
   b. Would others call you a "leader"? Why or why not?

RESERVED FOR YOU

© CAROL T. POWERS/ BLOOMBERG NEWS/LANDOV

© NORM BETTS/BLOOMBERG NEWS/LANDOV

© STEFAN WERMUTH/ REUTERS/LANDOV

© GIUSEPPE ARESU/ BLOOMBERG NEWS/LANDOV

4. Now think for a minute about what you bring to any situation. Then answer the following questions:
   a. What are your SKAs?
   b. If a very close friend made a list of your SKAs, what would be on the list that would be different from your list? What accounts for the difference?
   c. How would you describe your leadership style?

d. What changes in SKAs and leadership style would you have to make in order to fill the vacant frame?
e. What else would you have to do to make the "America's Best Leaders" list?

5. Would you want to be on the "America's Best Leaders" list? Why or why not?

Skills Application 11-3: Practice Your Leadership Skills

There are four people on one side of a bridge. Only two can cross at a time, and it is so dark that a flashlight has to be used to light the way. There is only one flashlight. Your job as leader is to determine the best method for getting everyone across in only 17 minutes, when it takes:

Person #1 (you), one minute to cross
Person #2, two minutes to cross
Person #3, five minutes to cross
Person #4, ten minutes to cross

1. Identify and discuss some of the barriers you might face in getting everyone across safely.

2. What is your strategy for completing the task? How did you determine that?

3. How can you apply the lessons learned in this skills application to your life?

Source: (1) Adapted with permission from QCI's International's "Timely Tips for Teams," (August 2003), a monthly Internet newsletter. QCI International (http://www.qci-intl.com).

Skills Application 11-4: Becoming An Agent For Change

For the purpose of this skills application, students will be placed into groups of 4 to 8 individuals and will be assigned one of the following situations:
   a. Your mission is to renovate this classroom. There is no money to spend.
   b. Your mission is to renovate this classroom. You cannot spend more than $1,000.
   c. Your mission is to renovate this classroom. You cannot spend more than $10,000.
   d. Your mission is to renovate this classroom.

1. Working as a group, address the following:
   a. Identify reasons for resistance to any change(s) you might propose.
   b. Develop your renovation blueprint.
   c. Outline a strategy for presenting your recommended changes to whoever has final decision authority. This may be your instructor, a dean, the financial officer, the physical plant manager, or others.

2. After your group has developed a strategy for change, your instructor will have you formally present it to the class. Your instructor will designate persons to play the following

specific roles: instructor, dean of the college, chief financial officer, physical plant manager, and others as appropriate for your situation. The persons in these designated roles are encouraged to ask probing and clarifying questions, suggest alterations to the proposal, and express why they can or cannot accept the proposal. Other class members will act as observers.

3. Debriefing session: After all groups have presented their strategy for change, answer the following questions:
   a. To what extent did you personally own the recommendation that your group made?
   b. To what extent were you personally committed to seeing the recommendation "bear fruit"?
   c. Was your recommendation a success or failure? Why?
   d. What could you have done to make it easier for others to accept your group's recommendations?

4. Each group could be assigned a collaborative writing project (maximum of two pages):
   "This is what we would do differently if we had to do it over again."

Skills Application 11-5: Dealing with People that Make Your Life Difficult: Roary—the Exploder!

This is the next in a series of skills applications that introduce another of those people who might make your life difficult. Roary is very challenging because he has the potential to lose control at any time.

1. Read the following statement from B. J. Karim, an employee at Poore Brothers, a plumbing supply and distribution company:

I have a boss, Ralph Poore, who is the consummate Dr. Jekyll and Mr. Hyde. On some days, Poore can be the nicest and kindest person, but on others—that's another story. Behind his back, we call him Roary because when he's angry, he speaks at such a loud volume that anyone within miles can hear him. He shows his impatience and displeasure by exploding at the drop of a hat. He has meetings where, if someone disagrees with him or delivers bad news about what is happening at the company, he will pound his hands on the table and yell at the top of his lungs. More than once, Poore has ended the meeting with one of these tirades, either by kicking everyone else out or by leaving.

Once, Roary went into one of the salespeople's offices to ask if he had called on a contractor as asked. When the salesperson answered that the person was not there when he called but that he had sent a fax and a copy of some new fixtures the company had just gotten in, Poore stormed out of the office, shouting obscenities.

When Poore hears bad news, it doesn't matter whose fault it is—he blows up at whoever is there. Another time, Poore was speaking to another of my coworkers about a delivery she needed to arrange. She told Poore that Crane's manufacturing facility was about three months behind in its production runs. We couldn't deliver the product because Crane hadn't

produced it. Poore picked up a flower vase and threw it across the room.

Poore is always right—in his mind. If anyone disagrees with him or tells him something he doesn't want to hear, he throws a tantrum. This man is a time bomb waiting for something to set him off. I haven't felt his wrath, but it's only a matter of time. What should I do?

2.  Using the Internet, find at least three sources of information on how to deal with hostile people like Roary. Carefully review each site for suggestions on how to cope with this difficult person.

3. Based on your findings, what suggestions would you make to Karim on how to cope with Roary?

4. Write a one-page paper explaining how this skills application increased your working knowledge of coping with the behaviors of this difficult person.

SKILLS DEVELOPMENT

Skills Development Module 11-1: Hard Rock Café

 For most organizations, fear of the unknown is a major barrier to change. To see how one organization embraces change by discussing and involving employees in the changes that will affect what they do and how they do it, view the Skills Development Module 11.1 video clip.

Hard Rock Café was founded in 1971 by Isaac Tigrett and Peter Morton. From their first Hard Rock Café near Hyde Park in London in a former Rolls Royce car dealership, the venture has grown to more than 140 Hard Rock Cafés in over 43 countries. Hard Rock Café's motto "Love All, Serve All" was adopted from Tigrett's guru Santhya Sai Baba.

In 2006, the Seminole Indian Tribe of Florida bought 124 Hard Rock Cafés, four hotels, two hotels and casinos, two Hard Rock Life! Concert venues, and stakes in three unbranded hotels for $965 million. The Hard Rock Hotel and Casino in Las Vegas and several other properties were not part of the transaction. The Hard Rock Café International of Myrtle Beach,

South Carolina, opened in April 2008. The park includes more than 40 attractions.

Perhaps some of you are wearing the classic Hard Rock tee-shirt which was created when the original café sponsored a soccer team. Go to http://www.hardrock.com or http://www.hardrockhotels.com to see what is currently happening at various venues.

1. How does Hard Rock Café's philosophy of change spark a continuous process of organizational renewal?

2. Discuss several reasons cited that caused Hard Rock's leadership to recognize the need to change.

3. Hard Rock's organizational structure was described as "siloed." What were the advantages of getting out of the "silo mentality"?

4. Discuss several methods or approaches for reducing resistance to change.

ENDNOTES

Many students have found the article about Nelson Mandela to be inspirational. See. Richard Stengel, "Mandela: His 8 Lessons of Leadership," *Time* (July 21, 2008), pp. 42–48.

The text author also recommends that you add the following to your reading list: A.G. Lafley and Ram Charan, *The Game-Changer* (New York: Crown Business, 2008). Lafley is CEO of Proctor & Gamble which is noted for becoming an integrated innovative organization and having tripled profits during the past seven years.

1. Harry S. Truman's (1884–1972) other famous quotes included: "The buck stops here" and "If you can't stand the heat, get out of the

kitchen." All of these relate to the concepts introduced in this chapter. See the *Oxford Dictionary of Quotations*, 3rd Ed. (New York: Oxford University Press, 1980).

For general discussions on leadership, the following are recommended: A.G. Lafley and Ram Charan, *The Game-Changer* (New York: Crown Books, 2008); Scott M. Paton, "It's About Leadership, Stupid" *Quality Digest* (March 2008), p. 56; Noel Tichy and Warren Bennis, "Judgment: How Winning Leaders Make Great Calls," *BusinessWeek* (November 18, 2007), pp. 68–72; Alison Stein Wellner, "Leadership: Creative Control – Even Bosses Need Time to Dream," *Inc.* (July 2007), pp. 92–97;

John Wooden and Steve Jamison, *Wooden on Leadership* (New York: McGraw-Hill, 2005); Ellen Samic and Scott Campbell, *5-D Leadership* (Palo Alto, CA: Davies-Black, 2005); Phil Dourado and Phil Blackburn, *Seven Secrets of Inspired Leaders* (New York: Wiley, 2005); Trudy Jean Evans, "Entering Your New Leadership Position," *Supervision* (August 2005), pp. 12–13.

We urge you to read Alan Deutschman, "Change or Die!" *Fast Company* (May 2005), pp. 52–62. Deutschman asks, "Why is it so darn hard to change our ways?" Our students have found that the article provides some practical recommendations on how leadership has been used to change people's behavior and improve the organization's effectiveness.

Also see Bryan Schaffer, "Leadership and Motivation," *Supervision*, 69, 2 (February 2008), pp. 6–9; Martin Wood, "The Fallacy of Misplaced Leadership," *Journal of Management Studies* (September 2005), pp. 1101–22; Jane M. Howell and Boas Shamir, "The Role of Followers in the Charismatic Leadership Process: Relationships and Their Consequences," *Academy of Management Review*, 30, 1 (2005), pp. 96–112; and David D. Henningsen, Mary Lynn Miller Henningsen, and Ian Bolton, "It's Good to be a Leader: The Influence of Randomly and Systematically Selected Leaders on Decision Making Groups," *Group Dynamics: Theory, Research and Practice*, 8, 1 (2004); pp. 62–76. Remember: *"Without followers, there can be no leaders or leadership!"*

2. Stratford Sherman, "How the Best Leaders Are Learning Their Stuff," *Fortune* (November 27, 1995), pp. 90–102. Also see Peter Senge, *The Fifth Discipline: The Art and Practice of the Learning Organization* (New York: Doubleday, 1990) and Senge et al., *The Fifth Discipline Handbook: Strategies and Tools for Building a Learning Organization* (Doubleday, 1994).

Also see Richard S. Tedlow et.al., "Lessons in Leadership: The Education of Andy Grove; Follow the Leaders; 10 Top Leaders Tell Their Secrets; Advice from the Master: Peter Drucker; and Quoted Often, Followed Rarely," *Fortune* (December 12, 2005), pp. 116–152. Also see Warren Bennis and Sharon D. Parks, *Leadership Can Be Taught* (Boston: Harvard Business School Press, 2005), in which they discuss the best ways to teach the skills needed to become a leader.

3. As reported in Gerald Graham, "Results Among Four Traits Workers Want in Their Leadership," *The Fort Wayne, Indiana News Sentinel* (July 8, 1996), p. 11B. Trust is the foundation of all relationships.

In a survey by Ernst & Young, college students were asked about what they wanted from work. The top three choices were: work/life balance, to be secure and stable in their job, and to be dedicated to a cause. Supervisors must develop a climate of mutual trust and respect so that employees can develop their full potential. See "Where College Students Want to Work," *BusinessWeek* (June 9, 2008), p. 17. We agree that mutual trust and respect are the foundation of effective supervision. Also see Donna Fenn, "Sometimes Even CEOs Have to Say They're Sorry," *Inc.* (October 2007), pp. 37–38; Eric Krell, "Do They Trust You?" *HR Magazine* (June 2006), pp. 59–63. Ram Charan and Geoffrey Colvin, in "Why CEOs Fail," *Fortune* (June 21, 1999), pp. 69–78, identified eight qualities that characterize successful CEOs. Not surprisingly, integrity was at the top of their list. Kevin Cashman, author of "Leadership from the Inside Out" (*Executive Excellence*, 1998), argues that there are three core qualities to leadership: (1) authenticity, (2) self-expression, and (3) value creation. Also see the review on Kathleen M. Sutcliffe's *Ethics, the Heart of Leadership* in the *Academy of Management Review* (October 2005), pp. 869–71.

4. Stephen R. Covey, "Principle-Centered Leadership," *Quality Digest* (March 1996), p. 21. Richard L. Daft and Robert H. Lengel, authors of *Fusion Leadership* (San Francisco: Berrett-Koehler, 1998), describe a method for bringing people together to accomplish mutual goals based on shared vision and values. The principles of fusion (joining together) rather than fission (splitting apart) support individual employee growth and ingenuity.

5. A more complete discussion can be found in James M. Kouzes and Barry Z. Posner, "Exemplary Leaders," *Executive Excellence* (June 2001), pp. 5–7; *The Leadership Challenge: How to Get Extraordinary Things Done in Organizations* (San Francisco: Jossey-Bass, 1987), and *Leadership Practices Inventory (LPI): A Self-Assessment and Analysis* (available from Pfeiffer & Company, San Diego).

6. James M. Kouzes and Barry Z. Posner, *Credibility: How Leaders Gain and Lose It, Why People Demand It* (San Francisco: Jossey-Bass, 1993).

7. As quoted in Justin Bachman, "Healthy Companies," Associated Press, as reported in the *Fort Wayne, Indiana Journal Gazette* (November 11, 2005), p. 2C. Also see, Gary Neilson and Bruce Pasternick, *Results: Keep What's Good, Fix What's Wrong, and Unlock Great Performance* (New York: Crown Business, 2005). Booz & Company conducts an annual *CEO Succession Survey*. The 2008 survey found that CEOs generally have six years to design and implement their strategies. Also see Neilson's Web site (http://www.orgdna.com), which provides tips, suggestions, and results of their research to uncover the DNA of successful organizations.

8. The text author conducted the following exercise in March 2008. Thirty-nine store managers were asked to identify their MPC (most preferred co-worker) and list the three most important things for which the person was responsible. Then the MPCs were sent e-mails asking them to briefly describe the functions of their job and list the three most important things for which they were responsible. There was less than ten percent agreement between manager and subordinate as to the most important aspects of the job. We have been conducting similar research each year since 1978 and the results are strikingly similar. "If you don't know what the boss expects you to do, how can you do it well?"

9. As reported in "Lack of Direction and Too Many Goals Keep Businesses from Achieving Top Goals," *AccountingWeb* (June 9, 2004).

10. See Jim Collins, *Good to Great: Why Some Companies Make the Leap…And Others Don't*. (New York: Harper Collins, 2001). Collins wrote about great organizations benefiting from the flywheel effect where the power of continued improvement and the delivery of results create additional momentum. Also visit Collins's Web site (http://www.jimcollins.com) to look over the "good to great" tool kit and his latest findings.

11. Visit the Greenleaf Center of Servant Leadership (www.greenleaf.org) for their current research and thoughts on how to become a servant-leader. Also see; Kent M. Keith, *The Case for Servant-Leadership* (Indianapolis, IN: The Greenleaf Center, 2005); and a review of Frank Hamilton's *Practicing Servant-Leadership: Succeeding Through Trust, Bravery, and Forgiveness* in the *Academy of Management Review* (October 2005), pp. 875–77.

12. Max E. Douglas, "Service to Others," *Supervision* (March 2005), pp. 6–9. Also see Voss W. Graham, "Shared Leadership," *Supervision* (September 2007), pp. 3–4.

13. Interview with Larry C. Spears, CEO and president of the Greenleaf Center for Servant-Leadership in "Leading by Serving," *Philanthropy Matters* (Spring 2008), pp. 8–10.

14. Larry C. Spears and John C. Burkhardt listed the ten characteristics central to the development of servant-leaders in *Servant-Leadership and Philanthropic Institutions* (Indianapolis, IN: The Greenleaf Center, 2006).

15. For general discussions on delegation and the benefits of effective delegation, the following are recommended: Ken Fracaro, "Making Delegation Work," *Supervision* (September 2004), pp. 14–16; *Manager's Toolkit: The 13 Skills Managers Need to Succeed* (Boston: Harvard Business School Publishing, 2004); H. A. Richardson et al., "CEO Willingness to Delegate to the Top Management Team: The Influence of Organizational Performance," *International Journal of Organizational Analysis*, 10, 2, (2004), pp. 134–55; S. Gazda, "The Art of Delegating," *HR Magazine* (January 2002), pp. 75–78; W. H. Weiss, "The Art and Skill of Delegating," *Supervision* (September 2000), pp. 3–5.

16. Ronald E. Merrill and Henry D. Sedgwick, in their article "To Thine Own Self Be True," *Inc.* (August 1994), pp. 50–56, identified six styles of entrepreneurial management: (1) the Classic, (2) the Coordinator, (3) the Craftsman, (4) the Team Manager, (5) the Entrepreneur plus Employee Team, and (6) the Small Partnership.

   They contend that any one of them can be effective. For a discussion on seven essential leadership skills, see Kennard T. Wing, "Become a Better Leader," *Strategic Finance* (February 2001), pp. 65–68.

17. Much of this is based on my personal observations and inferences drawn from articles like that by Sue Shellenbarger, "The Care and Feeding (and the Avoiding) of Horrible Bosses," the *Wall Street Journal* (October 20, 1999), p. B1; Stanley Bing, "Hail and Farewell, Chainsaw Al! Don't Let the Door Hit You on the Way Out, Y'Hear," *Fortune* (July 20, 1998), pp. 43–44; and Brian Dumaine, "America's Toughest Bosses," *Fortune* (October 18, 1993), pp. 38–50. For a research study concerning employee creativity as it relates to managerial styles of leading, see Maria M. Clapham, "Employee Creativity: The Role of Leadership," *Academy of Management Executive* (August 2000), pp. 138–9.

18. See *Stretch! How Great Companies Grow in Good Times & Bad* (New York: John Wiley & Sons, 2004). Vice-presidents of A.T. Kearney, a global consulting firm, present in-depth illustrations of how short-term cost-cutting strategies don't work but how *stretch* creates new products, new markets, and new customer opportunities. Also see, Jeremy C. Short and G. Tyge Payne, "First Movers and Performance: Timing is Everything," *Academy of Management Review*, (January 2008), pp. 267–269.

19. See "Masters of Design," *Fast Company* (June 2004), pp. 60–75, for an overview of 20 individuals who have changed the way their organizations innovate, create, and compete. Also, Donald Chrusciel, "What Motivates the Significant/Strategic Change Champion(s)," *Journal of Organizational Change Management,* 21, 2 (2008), p. 148.

   For general discussions on change and overcoming resistance to change, the following are recommended: Jeffrey D. Ford, Laurie W. Ford, and Angelo D'Amelio, "Resistance to Change: The Rest of the Story," *Academy of Management Review*, 33, 2 (April 2008), pp. 341–361; Tom R. Tyler and David De Cremer, "Process-based Leadership: Fair Procedures and Reactions to Organizational Change," *The Leadership Quarterly* (August 2005), pp. 529–46; "Case Study: Modeling How Their Business Really Works Prepares Managers for Sudden Change," *Strategy & Leadership*, 32, 2 (2004), pp. 28–35; Peter de Jager, "Resistance to Change: A New View of an Old Problem," *Futurist* (May/June, 2001), pp. 24–28; David Foote, "The Futility of Resistance to Change," *Computerworld* (January 15, 2001), p. 36; and Devid Geisler, "Bottom-Feeders: People Who Reject Change," *Executive Excellence* (December 2001), pp. 19–20.

20. Oren Harari, "Why Don't Things Change?" *Management Review* (February 1995), pp. 30–32. Author Jim Collins presents an interesting aspect of change. He says that while many experts say "'Change or die—the reason to get better is that bad things will happen to you if you don't.' Is that kind of fear a good motivator? Not for long." See Collins, "Fear Not," *Inc.* (May 1998), pp. 30–40.

21. For overviews of strategic organizational change approaches, see A.G. Lafley and Ram Charan, "Making Inspiration Routine," *Inc.* (June 2008), pp. 98–104; Oliver Gassmann and Marco Zeschky, "Opening Up the Solution Space: The Role of Analogical Thinking for Breakthrough Product Innovation," *Creativity and Innovation Management*, 17, 2 (June 2008), pp. 97–106; Lotte S. Lushcer and Marianne W. Lewis, "Organizational Change and Managerial Sensemaking: Working Through Paradox," *Academy of Management Journal* 51, 2 (April 2008), pp. 221–240; Jean Ann Larson, "Using Conceptual Learning Maps and Structured Dialogue to Facilitate Change at a Large Hospital System," *Organizational Development Journal*, 25,

3 (Fall 2007), pp. 25–32; T. L. Stanley, "Change: A Common Sense Approach," *Supervision* (December 2002), pp. 7–9.

22. For discussions on building trust between supervisors and employees when changes are being made, see Parry Pascarella, "Fifteen Ways to Work for You," *HR Magazine* (April 1996), pp. 75–81; and Max Messmer, "Leading Your Team Through Change," *Strategic Finance* (October 2001), pp. 8–10.

23. The Worker Adjustment and Retraining Act (WARN) requires that employers must give at least 60-days notice before closing or layoffs are carried out. For an overview of the requirements go to http://www.doleta.gov/programs/factsht/warn.htm

24. Peter Senge in Alan M. Webber, "Learning for Change," *Fast Company* (May 1999), pp. 178+. Also see Senge's *The Dance of Change: The Challenges of Sustaining Momentum in Learning Organizations* (New York: Doubleday/Current, 1999).

25. Scott Adams in Anna Muoio, "Boss Management," *Fast Company* (April 1999), pp. 91+.

26. Interview with Michael Tushman and Charles O'Reilly, "Leading Change and Organizational Renewal," *Harvard Business School Working Knowledge* (November 16, 1999) (http://hbswk.hbs.edu/item/1156.html, accessed August 27, 2008). Also see Tushman and O'Reilly, *Leading Change in Organizational Renewal* (Cambridge: Harvard Business School Press, 1997).

   See Drew Stevens, "Increase Employee Productivity Without Additional Time and Resources," *Supervision* (October 2007), pp. 7–11. Note: There is an organization of professionals committed to organizational renewal: *ACCORD*—Association for Creative Change in Organizational Renewal and Development (www.accord.org).

27. Adapted from interviews with Chris Roman (Studer Group representative) and Quint Studer. (Visit their Web site at (http://www.studergroup.com). Also see Studer, *Hardwiring Excellence* (Gulf Breeze, FL: FireStarter Publishing, 2005.)

28. Nancy J. Lyons, "The 90-Day Checkup," *Inc.*, (March 1999), pp. 111–12.

29. Jim Collins, Good to Great: Why Some Companies Make the Leap . . . and Others Don't (New York: HarperCollins Publishers, 2001).

30. Adapted from Quint Studer, "Healthcare Flywheel," Studer Group; and Bill Bielanda, "Rules for Developing Effective Leader Goals," Studer Group, with permission.

31. Adapted after interviews with Chris Roman (Studer Group representative) and Quint Studer. (Visit their Web site at (http://www.studergroup.com).

32. Studer, *Hardwiring Excellence*, op. cit., with permission.

33. Studer, *Hardwiring Excellence*, op. cit., adapted with permission.

34. For comprehensive information about Baptist Health Care, Inc., visit its Web site (http://www.ebaptisthealthcare.org). Also see Al Stubblefield, *BreakOUT: Unleash the Power of Human Capital* (Pensacola, FL: Baptist Health Care Leadership Institute, 2004); Richard C. Huseman and Pamela A. Bilbrey, "BreakOUT!" http://www.LeaderExcel.com; Baptist Hospital Baldrige Application (http://www.nist.gov/public_affairs/releases/bhitrauma.htm); and "Within Reach," www.healthexecutive.com/features/sept_2005_coverstory.

35. Robert Levering and Milton Moskowitz compile a listing of the best companies to work for. See for example the 2008 list at www.cnnmoney.com or see the February 4, 2008 issue of *Fortune* magazine. BHI's parent organization's ranking has varied between 10th and 59th during the past seven years. That is among all organizations in America!

36. For a complete profile on all Malcolm Baldrige Award winners, see http://baldrige.nist.gov.

37. Kotter as quoted in Alan Deutschman, "Change or Die," *Fast Company* (May 2005), p. 55.

CHAPTER 12

(Managing Work Groups: Teamwork, Morale, and Counseling)

After studying this chapter, you will be able to:

1 Explain how work groups form and function and why they are important.

2 Classify work groups and their relevance for supervisors.

3 State some important research findings about work groups.

4 Discuss the importance of employee morale and its relationship to teamwork and productivity.

5 Identify the factors that influence employee morale.

6 Discuss techniques for assessing employee morale, including observation and employee attitude surveys.

7 Understand why counseling is an important part of the supervisor's job.

8 Identify programs that organizations use to help employees with personal and work-related problems.

YOU MAKE THE CALL!

Charlie Graham is director of operations for Belmont Manufacturing. The company's 250 non-unionized employees manufacture plastic interior parts for the auto industry.

Five years ago, employee turnover at Belmont was over 75 percent. Belmont was scraping the "bottom of the barrel" when hiring employees. Some employees could barely read or write and had difficulty following basic instructions. The productivity problems alienated customers. Belmont was scrapping more product than they were shipping. Then Charlie Graham and Elaine Knight, the new director of marketing, attended a total quality management (TQM) seminar.

When Charlie and Elaine returned from the seminar, they began calling customers and vendors; visiting manufacturing plants known for their total quality commitment; and analyzing production processes, methods, and costs. Working with Bob Watters, the newly hired personnel manager, Charlie and Elaine conducted an in-depth analysis of employee morale, followed by an identification of the costs, savings, and potential benefits of improving morale.

The three of them, along with seven other employees, formed the Belmont Excellence Team. The team's mission was to make Belmont a better place to work. After several starts and stops, and a few glitches, the team came up with several ideas.

"The real key," Charlie recalled, "was learning how to listen carefully to our people. Those people told us what they needed to be satisfied at work and in life." Additional data from the attitude surveys, exit interviews, and customer service indexes played a role in the restructuring. Watters served as the conduit for all employee concerns. The Belmont Excellence Team instituted a basic literacy program for employees and eliminated two management layers—plant superintendent and foreperson. Removing those layers showed that the team was serious about the future—front-line workers would be empowered.

"When I came in here, corporate management had directed us to bring about improvement or they would close the plant," Charlie said. "I knew from experience that there was no instant quality improvement program that would produce miraculous results overnight. Elaine, Bob, and I had a commitment from top management that they would give us 30 months to show progress before the plant would be shut down. The three of us agreed to follow Stephen Covey's 'Law of the Farm' model—we must plow and plant in the spring and tend the crops during the summer so that we can harvest in the fall."

"We instituted job skills and process training," Knight continued. "After the classroom training, all employees swung on ropes, climbed trees, and helped colleagues through a challenge course. It is common in a high-output, just-in-time production plant for workers not to communicate with others outside their work areas. The team training really helped to bring people from different departments together. As a result, new teams were formed to deal with specific projects—work processes, scrap, defects, productivity, and the like."

All the team's plans resulted in a scrap rate less than the industry average. In the most recent quarter, customer complaints decreased to just 4, from over 90 per quarter before Charlie and Elaine implemented the techniques they learned in the TQM seminar. Individual productivity jumped more than 50 percent, and rework dropped to almost zero.

Charlie recounted, "We now have a reputation as a good place to work. Cross-functional team members act like Belmont is their personal company. We've built a continuous improvement process into our culture. Increased employee wages and benefits have more than been covered by the savings generated through employee suggestions." As director of operations, Charlie knows that more changes will be needed. Where does he go from here? How can he help sustain the momentum that he has helped build over the past four years? **YOU MAKE THE CALL!**

Understanding Work Groups and Their Importance

> **1** Explain how work groups form and function and why they are important.

In Chapter 8, we presented an overview of the informal organization with particular reference to the supervisor's relationship with informal work groups and their leaders. We mentioned that informal work groups can positively or negatively influence employee motivation and performance. Throughout this book, we have emphasized that a supervisor must be concerned not only with employees as individuals but also with how those employees relate to groups both inside and outside the supervisor's department.

An individual's motivations and behavioral clues are often found in the context of the person's associates, colleagues, and peers. On the job, an employee's attitudes and morale can be shaped to a large degree by coworkers, at times even more than by the supervisor or other factors in the work environment. Therefore, a supervisor should be aware of work groups and how those groups function. Moreover, a supervisor must understand how morale influences employee performance and what can be done to maintain a high level of morale at the departmental level.

WHY WORK GROUPS FORM AND FUNCTION

Work groups form and function in work settings for many reasons.[1] Among the most common reasons are:

- *Companionship and identification.* The work group provides a peer relationship and a sense of belonging, which can help satisfy the employee's social needs.
- *Behavior guidelines.* People tend to look to others, especially their peers, for guides to acceptable workplace behavior.
- *Problem solving.* The work group may be instrumental in providing a means by which an employee may solve a personal or minor work-related problem.
- *Protection.* Employees often look to the work group for protection from outside pressures, such as those pressures placed by supervisors and higher-level managers.

Much behavioral research has focused on factors that make work groups tightly knit, cohesive, and effective. A work group is usually most cohesive when the group:

- Has members who perceive themselves as having higher status than other employees, as in job classification or pay.
- Is small.
- Shares similar personal characteristics, such as age, gender, ethnic background, and off-the-job interests.

Members of a cohesive work group enjoy their group affiliation

© MICHAEL NEWMAN/PHOTOEDIT

- Is relatively distant from other employees, as in geographically dispersed work groups and groups away from the home office.
- Has formed due to outside pressures or for self-protection, such as a layoff or disciplinary action taken by management.
- Has members who communicate relatively easily.
- Has succeeded in some group effort, which encourages members to seek new group objectives.

Of course, a supervisor will never be completely aware of the kinds of forces that are most prevalent in the group dynamics of the department. However, sensitivity to employee needs and concerns can help the supervisor address work groups more effectively.

Classifications of Work Groups

2 Classify work groups and their relevance for supervisors.

Four major types of employee work groups can be identified in most organizations:

1. Command
2. Task
3. Friendship
4. Special interest[2]

Because these classifications overlap, a supervisor should recognize that employees may be members of several such groups.

COMMAND GROUP

The **command group** is a group of employees according to the authority relationships on the formal organizational chart. Members of this group work together daily to accomplish regularly assigned work. For example, at the departmental level, a command group consists of the supervisor and the employees who report to the supervisor. Throughout the organization are interrelated departments or command-group divisions that reflect the formal authority structure.

Command group
Grouping of employees according to authority relationships on the formal organization chart

TASK GROUP OR CROSS-FUNCTIONAL TEAM

Consisting of employees from different departments, a **task group** or **cross-functional team** comes together to accomplish a particular task or project. For example, for a telephone to operate in a customer's home, the telephone company's employees and supervisors from a number of departments, such as customer service, construction, plant installation, central office equipment, accounting, and testing, may work together to accomplish the job. Another example is a hospital, in which numerous interdepartmental task relationships and communications take place among hospital personnel, from such departments as admitting, nursing, laboratory, dietary, pharmacy, physical therapy, and medical records, to care for a patient.

A specialized subset of the task group is the customer-satisfaction team. Members of this team represent many different functions and may include customer and supplier representatives. Team members come together to solve a specific problem, and they disband upon initiating a solution. In the true sense of self-directed task groups, members develop the systems and processes that help them do their jobs. For example, the Sun Microsystems team program (SunUP) is a collaboration of Sun, its customers, and its vendors to analyze, develop, implement, and manage the services, infrastructure, and products that achieve measurable improvement in end-to-end availability. According to Sun, "the knowledge gained

Task group or cross-functional team
Grouping of employees who come together to accomplish a particular task

from this collaboration drives best practices, process improvements, and cultural and organizational changes that will help reduce frequency of failure due to people, process, and product, thereby providing a reliable environment to run a mission-critical business."[3] Simply put, Sun's use of task groups or cross-functional teams brings groups of people together so they can apply their combined talents to continuously improve quality and ultimately increase customer satisfaction.

FRIENDSHIP GROUP

The **friendship group** is an informal group of people who have similar personal characteristics and social interests. Many friendship groups are related primarily to such common factors as age, gender, ethnic background, outside interests, and marital status. Command and task groups may be instrumental in bringing friendship groups together.

Friendship group
Informal grouping of employees based on similar personalities and social interests

SPECIAL-INTEREST GROUP

Special-interest group
Grouping of employees that exists to accomplish something as a group that would not likely be pursued individually

The **special-interest group** exists to accomplish in a group something that individuals feel unable or unwilling to pursue individually. A temporary special-interest group might be a committee of employees who wish to protest an action taken by a supervisor or management, promote a charitable undertaking, or organize an employee picnic.

A labor union is an example of a more permanent special-interest group because it is legally and formally organized. A labor union brings together employees from different departments and divisions as they strive to achieve economic and other objectives. A labor union official once made the comment to the author of this text: "Labor unions don't just happen, they're caused. And it's the management, not labor unions, that cause them!" This labor union official was quite candid about his opinion that labor unions were a direct response to failures of management to respond to employee needs. The sentiments (morale) of workers are usually determined more by conditions existing in their work situations and the need to fulfill unmet needs. Thus, employees may join a labor union primarily to obtain economic objectives such as higher wages and greater benefits. Or they may join a group to satisfy objectives of a psychological or sociological nature. Some employees believe that membership in a group provides them with greater security and better control over their jobs. Other employees believe that it is important for a labor union to be present in processing grievances and complaints in order to get a fairer settlement in their disputes. Still others find a greater sense of identity when they are part of a group.

As stated earlier, an employee may be a member of a number of groups in the workplace, and the supervisor who understands these different groups is more likely to influence these groups. Some research studies have suggested that a supervisor has a better chance of influencing an employee's behavior as a member of a work group than to address that employee individually without the work group's influence. Some of these concepts are discussed later in this chapter.

3 State some important research findings about work groups.

Research Insights for Managing Work Groups

Numerous behavioral studies have been done on work groups and how they function. From these studies, a number of approaches for managing work groups effectively have been suggested. While these approaches are not certain to produce desired results, they are consistent with behavioral research findings concerning work-group dynamics and group behavior.

INSIGHTS FROM THE HAWTHORNE STUDIES

The work group studies that have probably had the most lasting influence during the 20th century and beyond were conducted in the late 1920s and early 1930s at Western Electric Company's Hawthorne plant near Chicago, Illinois.[4] Known as the **Hawthorne Studies**, they remain a comprehensive and definitive source on the subject of work-group dynamics as they relate to employee attitudes and productivity. Many of the lessons of the Hawthorne Studies still apply to supervisory practice today, supporting the adage that "The more things change, the more they stay the same."

Hawthorne Studies
Comprehensive research studies that focused on work-group dynamics as they related to employee attitudes and productivity

INSIGHTS FROM TEAM RESEARCH

In a number of chapters, we have mentioned various organized participative management programs. Regardless of what these programs are called, they share certain characteristics. For the most part, these programs try to build effective work teams that foster the continual improvement of work processes, project tasks, and customer service. One of the most comprehensive surveys was conducted by Jon Katzenbach and Douglas Smith, two management consultants who interviewed hundreds of team members in dozens of organizations that had used teams to address various problems. Katzenbach and Smith identified principles that are most closely associated with effective work teams, including:

- Team members must be committed to the group and to the performance of the group.
- Teams function better when they are small, usually ten or fewer members.
- Teams should be composed of individuals who have skills that are complementary and sufficient to deal with the problem.
- Teams should be committed to objectives that are specific and realistic.[5]

Much also can be learned from the case studies reported in Steven Jones's and Michael Beyerlein's *Developing High Performance Work Teams*. One such study, which describes Eastman Chemical Company's decision to move to a team management approach at its Kingsport, Tennessee, facility, delivered the following findings:

- Because supervisors must take on more responsibility and receive less recognition, they feel threatened by transitions to teams. Therefore, supervisors must be coached, supported, and encouraged in their new roles.
- Team members must be held accountable for their actions to increase feelings of personal responsibility for the team's success.
- New team leadership roles for supervisors include coaching and facilitating.
- Communication becomes more important. Team leaders must be process-oriented and have meetings to clarify team roles.[6]

AN ILLUSTRATION OF A HIGHLY EFFECTIVE TEAM

Highly effective teams are hard to find. Think back to the 2008 Olympics and the performance of the U.S. men's volleyball team. The team beat the odds and overcame tragedy to win the Olympic gold medal. The team claimed the gold with a four-set win over the defending champion, Brazil. Coach Hugh McCutchen's father-in-law was stabbed to death in Beijing on the eve of the team's first game. He turned the reins over to his assistant for the first three matches.

Having lost the first game 25 to 20, the Americans' backs were against the wall. They came back to win the next two games and, when the Brazilian star player popped the ball out of bounds, the Brazilians crouched on the floor in disbelief. The U.S. team rushed the court and savored the moment and what they had just accomplished. McCutchen said, "When it dawned on me that we'd just won the gold, I grabbed my staff and players. They have been so instrumental in our success. They won the first three matches without me and they did a wonderful job."[7] In volleyball, every player is intensely involved in each and every play. What each one does or doesn't do is critical to the success of the team.

Beach volleyball also had its Olympic moments. The team of Misty May-Treanor and Kerri Walsh captured the gold in their sport. They are undoubtedly the most successful beach volleyball team in history. They won 112 consecutive matches before losing in August, 2008, a remarkable record set by two people who were willing to set aside their personal agendas and work together to accomplish something that no one else had ever done.

When you watch a highly effective team, they are always supporting and encouraging one another. Chris Widener, president of Made for Success, said it well: "The coach always does a pre-game talk, laying out the vision. During the game, the coach is always updating the team as to where they are and what changes need to be made. He or she coaches and communicates throughout the game. When you watch a great team, they are talking to each other all of the time, helping one another out, encouraging one another, praising one another, and telling each other how they can make changes so the same mistakes aren't made again."[8]

Regardless of the activity, good communication skills are needed to create trust and collaboration among the various players. Remember, there is no "I" in the word team.

THE IMPORTANCE OF TEAM MEMBERS

In Chapter 8, we postulated about various organizational designs, but many forces in the marketplace can rapidly change even our best guesses. Nevertheless, we expect that teamwork will be as important tomorrow as it was yesterday—perhaps even more so. A study from Development Dimensions International found

Winning teams work together to achieve their goals

that 75 percent of hiring managers surveyed want employees who are compatible in a team setting, supporting the notion that very little is accomplished without strong collaboration.[9]

When asked about effective teams, another illustration from professional and amateur sports comes to mind. Why? Few organizations, their leaders, and members are as well-documented as sports teams. Legendary basketball coach John Wooden won ten national championships at UCLA, including an unbelievable seven in a row from 1966 to 1973. Coach Wooden's team won over 80% of their games.[10] Imagine making the right choice at the right time that turns out the right way—the way it was intended—8 out of 10 times.

John Schuerholz, who took over as general manager of the Atlanta Braves in 1990, shared his tips for transforming the Braves' culture:

- Gather everyone, communicate the plan, and preach it daily.
- Constantly remind them what works.
- Don't be afraid to get rid of people who don't buy in.
- Make the lowest-level employee feel as important to success as the top-level executives.
- Show trust in everyone to do their jobs well.[11]

Schuerholz's philosophy transformed the team's mentality from "we might have a chance to win" to "we will win!" Yet with all the divisional and league success enjoyed by the Braves, they have won only one World Series in the last fifty years.

It appears to the author of this text that another factor helps to explain the difference between "winning" and "losing." Synergy! A **synergistic effect** takes place when the whole is greater than the sum of the parts. Many organizations like great sports teams lose their competitive advantage when key team members leave or the coach retires. Under legendary Coach John Wooden, the UCLA Bruins won ten NCAA basketball championships, but they have won only once since his retirement in 1975. Unfortunately, success increases the appetite for additional successes. If you don't "win it all" every year, people are clamoring for your head. The same is true for the CEO who doesn't meet Wall Street expectations.

Astute sports fans can recall some of the stars from these winning teams, but for every star, there are dozens of unheralded role players. These role players show up for work every day, clearly understand their roles, are trained so that they know how to perform and continuously improve on their jobs, and want to feel that they are contributing meaningfully to the effectiveness of their teams. As author Kenneth Turan said, "Team sports could not exist without, well, teams. Competent, superbly professional role players, the good soldiers who do what's asked of them and don't bask in anyone's attention, are the *sine qua non* of the organizations that win year after year."[12]

Several observations are pertinent here. First, a team is a group of individuals who *must work together* to meet their individual and team objectives.[13] It is important to remember that people are more motivated to achieve goals they help set. Second, strong leadership and effective communication are key ingredients for successful teams. As stated previously, the ability to trust a leader (i.e., an upper manager) is more important today than at any time in recent history. Perhaps nothing is more important to the success of a team than the leader's ability to build an environment of mutual trust and respect. Finally, not everyone is suited for team play. Throughout this text we have introduced people, who, at best, are not team players, and they make your life difficult. As one engineering vice president related, "Some people can leave their ego at the door, and some

Synergistic effect
The interaction of two or more individuals such that their combined efforts are greater than the sum of their individual efforts

can't, and you will immediately know who is on (board) and who isn't."[14] The key is to identify people who can work in teams and those who cannot.

COLLABORATIVE WORKPLACE

None of the great sports teams or business organizations could have succeeded without **teamwork**—people working cooperatively to solve problems and achieve goals important to the group. Stated succinctly, a **collaborative workplace** means that, throughout the organization, employees and management share authority for decision making. Teamwork processes promote trust, integrity, consensus, and shared ownership as team members strive to achieve common objectives. Collaboration recognizes that people want and need to be valued for their contributions and that improvements and changes are best achieved by those who are responsible for implementing changes and are committed to making those changes work.[15]

Noted quality writer H. James Harrington wrote:

The disadvantage with teams is that they are inwardly focused. They are small groups that, if functioning properly, strive to better other teams. Teams by their very nature are competitive. . . . In well-managed organizations, trust runs high and people are empowered to make decisions on their own. These organizations focus on promoting teamwork between individuals. It's an attitude of "How can I help?" "What can I do to make your job easier?" and "How can we work together to produce more value for the whole organization?"[16]

Another series of studies conducted among work teams in a large financial services company concluded that teams were most effective when (1) the focus was on managing the team as a group and having the team manage its members and (2) the work teams were designed to be effective, both in terms of improving productivity and improving the satisfaction of team members. These studies emphasized that the success of teams was largely attributable to the careful design and focus of the teams at the outset.[17]

Figure 12.1 summarizes the characteristics of effective work teams. While no one approach succeeds in all situations, a group must know where it is going. Throughout this text, we have stressed the importance of setting goals and the notion that the supervisor must provide direction. As noted in Chapters 1 and 2, if supervisors want their work groups to perform at higher levels, there must be a shared purpose and values, and the supervisor must constantly strive to balance employees' needs with the organization's needs.

VIRTUAL TEAMS

As many companies have expanded their operations domestically and internationally, they have found that virtual teams can help them focus on meeting customer requirements. A virtual team is one that has members who rarely, if ever, meet face-to-face, even though they work on a project or in an area of operations with a common goal. In a **virtual team,** also known as a **Geographically Dispersed Team** (GDT), members share a common purpose, are physically separated by time and/or space, and primarily interact electronically.[18] GDTs are a variant of work teams that present unique supervisory challenges at every stage of development and performance.

Virtual teams function primarily through technological tools that enable them to communicate. Most prominent are e-mails, shared space technologies,

---

FIGURE 12.1 Characteristics of Effective Work Teams

KEYS TO EFFECTIVE WORK TEAMS

- Top management removes the barriers, i.e., clears the roadblocks out of the way.
- Team members receive training on how to work together.
- Group members agree on team goals and objectives and commit to those goals.
- All members participate actively in team meetings and discussions.
- All team members follow team rules, guidelines, and procedures.
- All members are valued and treated with respect and dignity.
- Team members share vital information and ensure that everyone is informed on a need-to-know basis.
- Members express their ideas without fear of retribution. Team members also feel free to disagree, and the group grows with differences of opinion.
- The team uses a systematic problem-solving approach, but members are encouraged to think "outside the box" (i.e., alternative ways of thinking are encouraged).
- All members are included in solving problems, developing alternatives, and institutionalizing decisions.
- Decisions are made by consensus (i.e., all team members support decisions, even though they may not totally agree with those decisions; therefore, every team member feels ownership for the team's decisions and responsibility for the team's success).
- The team is cohesive—openness, trust, support, and encouragement are always present.
- Conflict is viewed as healthy and is brought out into the open and addressed in a timely manner.
- Group members give each other honest feedback on performance; constructive feedback is used to improve performance.
- Team training and peer helping are essential elements of the team process. Peers help team members who may need individualized attention.
- The team continually evaluates its performance and uses that information as the basis for improvement.
- Team members take pride in team accomplishments. Challenging tasks, recognition of accomplishments, and continued support from top management fuels the drive for continued success.
- Members enjoy their team affiliation.

---

video conferences, online chatting, telephone conference calls, personal digital assistants (PDAs), and other digital tools. Virtual teams require their members to receive specialized training in technology use, and they require careful planning and organization to establish regular times for group interaction as well as other communication needs. One advantage of virtual teams is that members can communicate quickly when needed to bring team members up to date on events and to keep each other informed. Scheduling becomes critical as one team member may be located, for example, in Mason, Ohio and another in Australia. Communication must cross several time zones, i.e., twelve or more hours' difference. When one employee is working, the other may be sleeping.

The requirements of virtual-team managers and supervisors are slightly different than those for conventional teams. Virtual teams require strong management support, which typically means that managers and supervisors have less direct control over team members. Nevertheless, the need for supervisory feedback and evaluation is paramount. One recommended approach is that team members be brought together initially or at some point to help them become better acquainted.

The challenge for a manager or supervisor of a virtual team is to hold team members together and keep them motivated, even though they are separated geographically. The focus must be on overall results rather than on the specific activities of team members. Managers of virtual teams have tried various techniques to help team members stay focused on their projects and to strengthen their functioning and team spirit. Among these techniques are giving the project team a name or logo, rotating the hosting of conference calls, sharing information on personal dates (e.g., birthdays and weddings), and recognizing accomplishments.

In essence, managing virtual teams, while it has some unique challenges and problems, differs slightly from managing teams that are close geographically. Regardless of the approach used, supervisors must be adept at applying their managerial skills with appropriate human relations approaches. Remember: The manager's challenge is to build commitment, cooperation, and collaboration through effective communication.

4 **Discuss the importance of employee morale and its relationship to teamwork and productivity.**

Morale
A composite of feelings and attitudes that individuals and groups have toward their work, working condition, supervisors, top-level management, and the organization

Understanding and Maintaining Employee Morale

Most definitions recognize that morale is essentially a state of mind. For example, Merriam-Webster's online dictionary defines *morale* as "the mental and emotional condition (as of enthusiasm, spirit, loyalty) of an individual or a group with regard to the function or tasks at hand." We consider **morale** the attitudes and feelings of individuals and groups toward their work, their environment, their supervisors, their top-level management, and the organization. Morale is not one single feeling or attitude but a composite. It affects employee performance and willingness to work, which in turn affects individual and organizational objectives. When employee morale is high, employees usually do what the organization wants them to do; when it is low, the opposite tends to occur.

Numerous articles have suggested that today's employees are less happy with many aspects of their jobs than were employees of earlier decades. For example, *The Work USA 2004 Survey* reports that only 51 percent of workers say they have trust and confidence in their immediate supervisor. Now surprisingly, fewer believe what top management tells them. Obviously, there is a credibility gap.[19] As discussed in Chapter 11, trust is a key ingredient for getting employees aligned with organizational goals.

Much of this lowered morale is attributed to a belief that many employers distrust and are disloyal to their employees. As a result, employees distrust and are disloyal to their employers. It has long been recognized and documented that the reasons employees stay with or leave employers are more frequently attributable to factors other than pay.[20]

MORALE SHOULD BE EVERYONE'S CONCERN

Every manager, from the chief executive down to the supervisor, should be concerned with the morale of the workforce. It should be a priority to develop and maintain employee morale at as high a level as possible without sacrificing the company's objectives.

Because of widespread concern about deteriorating employee morale and the alienation of many workers, many firms have launched programs and efforts that collectively have been called **workplace spirituality**. This term essentially covers organizational efforts that are designed to make the work environment more meaningful and creative by recognizing and tapping into people's deeply held

Workplace spirituality
Organizational efforts to make the work environment more meaningful and creative by relating work to employees' personal values and spiritual beliefs

values and spiritual beliefs. Some believe that spirituality can improve employees' personal lives and mental outlook and that this outlook might translate to a better work environment.[21]

Listen carefully to what Ben Cohen, cofounder of Ben & Jerry's homemade ice cream company, had to say: "At Ben & Jerry's, we learned that there's a spiritual life to businesses as there is in the lives of individuals. As you give, you receive. As you help others, you are helped in return."[22] When some people accused Cohen and cofounder, Jerry Greenfield, of doing "nice things" only to sell more ice cream, Cohen responded, "We did what we believed in; it just happened to sell more ice cream. Our actions are based on deeply held values. We are all interconnected, and as we help others, we cannot help but help ourselves. Creating a consonance of values with employees and customers builds loyalty and even more value."[23]

Our concern in this chapter is not to analyze these and other organization-wide efforts aimed at improving morale. Rather, we primarily discuss the role played by the first-line supervisor, who, probably more than anyone else, influences morale in day-to-day contact with employees. Bringing morale to a high level and maintaining it is a continuous process; morale cannot be achieved simply through short-run devices, such as pep talks or contests. High morale is slow to develop and difficult to maintain. The level of morale can vary considerably from day to day. Morale is contagious in both directions because both favorable and unfavorable attitudes spread rapidly among employees. Unfortunately, it seems to be human nature that employees quickly forget the good and long remember the bad when it comes to factors influencing their morale.

The supervisor is not alone in desiring high morale. Employees are just as concerned with morale because it is paramount to their work satisfaction. High morale helps to make the employee's day at work a pleasure, not a misery. High morale also is important to an organization's customers. Customers can usually sense whether employees are serving them enthusiastically or are just going through the motions.

MORALE, TEAMWORK, AND PRODUCTIVITY RELATIONSHIPS

Teamwork is often associated with morale, but the two are not the same. *Morale* refers to the attitudes and feelings of employees, whereas *teamwork* relates primarily to the degree of cooperation among people who are solving problems and accomplishing objectives. Good morale helps achieve teamwork, but teamwork can be high when morale is low. Such a situation might exist when jobs are scarce and employees tolerate bad conditions and poor supervision for fear of losing their jobs. On the other hand, teamwork may be absent when morale is high. For example, employees working on a piecework basis or salespeople being paid on straight commissions are typically rewarded for individual efforts rather than for group performance.

Many supervisors believe that high morale is usually accompanied by high productivity. Much research has been done to study this assumption. While there are some contradictions in research results, there is substantial evidence to suggest that, in the long run, employees with high morale tend to be highly productive. That is to say, well-motivated, self-disciplined groups of employees tend to do more satisfactory jobs than those from whom the supervisor tries to force performance. When supervisors are considerate of their employees and try to foster positive attitudes among them, there tends to be greater mutual trust, lower absenteeism and turnover, and fewer grievances.[24] Regardless of its other effects, there is little question that a high level of morale tends to make work more pleasant, particularly for the supervisor.

Factors Influencing Morale

Virtually any factor can influence employee morale, positively or negatively (see Figure 12.2). Some of these factors are within the supervisor's control, while others are not. Influences outside the organization are generally beyond the supervisor's control. Nevertheless, they may significantly affect employee morale. Examples of such external factors are family relationships, care of children or elderly parents, financial difficulties, problems with friends, vehicle breakdowns, and sickness or death in the family. What happens at home can change an employee's feelings very quickly. An argument before work may set the tone for the rest of the day. Even headlines in the morning newspaper may depress or uplift.

Company conditions can also influence morale. Examples of internal factors are compensation, job security, the nature of the work, relations with coworkers, working conditions, and recognition. These factors are partially or fully within the supervisor's control. For example, when compensation is adequate, other factors may be more significant, but even when wages are good, morale can sink quickly when working conditions are neglected. The critical factor is whether the supervisor tries to improve working conditions. Employees often will perform well under undesirable conditions and still maintain high morale when they believe their supervisors are seriously trying to improve work conditions.

BULLIES AT WORK

During childhood, many of us experienced the playground bully. In some instances, the playground bully has grown up and now works alongside us. The dilemma for many employees is learning to work with such a person. The findings of various studies, which report that "rude behavior is on the rise in the workplace and can undermine an organization's effectiveness," are summarized as follows:

FIGURE 12.2 Dark clouds affect on-the-job performance

- Incivility has worsened in the past ten years.
- Thirty-seven percent of U.S. workers have been bullied at work.
- Bullying is four times more prevalent than illegal forms of harassment.
- Women are targeted by bullies more frequently (in 57 percent of cases), especially by other women (in 71 percent of cases).
- Rude people are three times more likely to be in higher positions than their targets.
- Men are seven times more likely to be rude or insensitive to the feelings of their subordinates than to superiors.
- Twelve percent of people who experience rude behavior quit their jobs to avoid the perpetrators.
- Forty-five percent of bullied targets report that the actions affect their health.
- Fifty-two percent of respondents reported losing work time worrying.
- Nearly half of respondents said they are sometimes angry at work.
- Twenty-two percent of respondents deliberately decreased their work efforts as a result of rudeness.
- One out of six employees reported being so angered by coworkers that they felt like hitting those coworkers.
- Forty percent of bullied targets never complain.[25]

Almost everyone has been on the receiving end of a rude person's temper or a bully's wrath. Whether the crude or impolite behavior takes place behind closed doors or in the open, it directly affects the recipient and lowers group morale. Throughout the text, we have provided various skills applications that focus on workplace behaviors that deter teamwork. These Internet activities and experiential exercises should help you work with those people who make your life and the lives of their coworkers difficult.

ADDRESSING WORKPLACE INCIVILITY

Who determines "good behavior" in the workplace? Have you ever been confronted by a workplace bully? How did you respond? Did you try to gain an advantage by "going one up," i.e., one punch deserves two? Or did you respond in a courteous and civil manner? *Workplace incivility* occurs when one acts in a discourteous, rude, or demeaning manner. Bullying is one form of incivility. Verbal abuse, swearing, making fun of you, or giving you impossible jobs for which you either lack the SKAs or the time to get them done are all forms of psychological incivility. Physical incivility is when the employee is physically attacked, touched, or threatened.

In recent years, **workplace violence**, defined as violent acts, including physical assaults and threats of assaults directed toward employees at work or on duty, has increased dramatically both in large-scale enterprises and small businesses. The National Census of Fatal Occupational Injuries (CFOI) reported 5,488 fatal workplace deaths in 2007. Unfortunately, greater than one in ten workplace deaths was a homicide.[26] Homicides are perennially among the top three causes of workplace fatalities. "Robberies committed by total strangers—not crimes of passion committed by disgruntled coworkers or spouses—are the cause of a majority of these incidents."[27]

Workplace violence
Assaults or threats of assaults against employees in the workplace

A survey by Prince & Associates found that more than half the respondents reported that disgruntled employees have threatened senior managers in the past twelve months. Further, 82 percent of the respondents said that violence is increasing in their organization, placing the blame on an overall softening of the economy, increased outsourcing, downsizing, wage garnishments, salary reductions, and the perception that raises or bonuses are insufficient.[28]

SUPERVISORY TIPS
Strategies for Addressing Workplace Incivility

Remember, your purpose is to:
- Eliminate the problem behavior.
- Help the team accomplish its goals.
- Preserve team cohesiveness.
- Maintain the self-esteem of team members.

Pause and evaluate what was really said (content, context, tone).

Be assertive.

Stay in control when attacked; do not counterattack.

Speak clearly and calmly and choose your words carefully.

Address the person by name.

Take action—stop problem behavior when it happens.

State how you feel: "David, when you do _____, I feel _____."

State why you feel: "... because ... it may be discrimination, it may be harassment, it is inappropriate."

State your expectations: "David, I expect this behavior to stop immediately."

Ask the individual to commit to ceasing the behavior.

State the repercussions if the behavior happens again.

Document the discussion and, if appropriate, report the incident to the HR department, security, or higher management.

While experts agree that it is impossible to accurately predict violent behavior, some studies have identified certain behavioral problems that may portend serious problems on the job. Supervisors are typically best positioned to identify the warning signals, which include an individual's extreme interest in weapons or bringing weapons to the workplace; paranoid behavior, such as panicking easily or perceiving that the "whole world is against me"; reacting to or failing to take criticism, either from a supervisor or a colleague; and unexplained dramatic changes in an individual's productivity, attendance, or hygiene.[29] Often, incidents of workplace incivility escalate to violent actions. Studies of violent acts in the workplace have shown that these acts typically start as verbal disputes and involve people who know each other. Disputes may be over trivial matters, or they may be major disagreements with supervisors or employees. The supervisor should address problem behaviors immediately, before they escalate. The accompanying Supervisory Tips box presents some strategies for addressing workplace incivility.[30] A supervisor should be alert to those employees who have difficulty adjusting to their coworkers or who make the lives of others unbearable. Through private counseling sessions with such individuals, the supervisor may be able to uncover the reasons for problem behaviors and to help individuals stop those behaviors. In many instances, however, disagreements mushroom and intensify despite the supervisor's best efforts to solve the problems.[31]

THE IMPACT OF DOWNSIZING AND OUTSOURCING ON MORALE

The magnitude of downsizing is nothing compared with the impact of outsourcing. According to recent studies, 75 percent of U.S. and European multinational companies now use outsourcing to support their financial functions, and many expect to increase their use of outsourcing.[32] Outsourcing is not limited to the financial field. Information technology (IT), call center operations, and production processes have been a favorite target of the outsourcers. Consider the following scenario:

> *It was a beautiful morning, August 5, 2005, when Gary, aged 39, married with two small children, ages 7 and 4, left home for his software development job. He usually arrived at work early on Friday so that he could leave early and get home to spend some time with his children. Shortly after 8:00 A.M., Gary and 31 of his software development and IT team members were summoned into the conference room. The announcement came as a shock. Effective immediately, his job, as well as those of his colleagues, was eliminated. That day was his last day of work. The employees were escorted from the facility—told that their personal effects would be boxed up and that they could come back for them at 4:30 P.M. They were informed of the day and time for their scheduled exit meetings with human resources. Their meetings with HR would clarify what severance they might be entitled to, if any. The work would still need to be done, but not in the United States. Their work projects had been outsourced to India. The story of Gary and his colleagues has been repeated over and over during the last several years. After 13 years of service with the same company, what would he do? Where would he go?*

Clearly, these events have disturbed workers. Many downsized and/or outsourced employees feel they might never find jobs like those they had. The survivors, those who remain, worry about being laid off and are concerned about the futures of their firms. Employees have lost trust in their organizations and their leadership. As one study reported:

> *A worker's ability to form "best" friendships at work is among the most powerful of twelve indicators of a highly productive workplace. Workplaces with low turnover and high customer satisfaction, productivity, and profitability also tended to be places where employees reported having a best friend present.*[33]

Downsizings and outsourcings force employees to sever workplace friendships. Those who remain suffer from what has been termed "survivors' syndrome." Few companies are prepared to address widespread employee fears and insecurities. However, some firms have developed training programs and have provided counseling services to plan for and implement job reductions and to help surviving employees cope with the aftereffects of downsizing. A detailed discussion of these types of programs is beyond the scope of this text, but among the recommended strategies are (1) early and ample communication with clear and specific details concerning which jobs have been eliminated and, more important, why they have been eliminated, and (2) working with surviving employees to develop the new short-term objectives that will help those employees focus on activities and targets over which they have some control.[34] Here, as in many other situations, first-line supervisors play a crucial role in influencing employee morale.

6 Discuss techniques for assessing employee morale, including observation and employee attitude surveys.

Assessing Employee Morale

While most firms believe that employee morale is important in the long run if the organization is to succeed, good measures of employee morale are elusive. Some firms rely on statistical comparisons to assess their morale. They look at data that compare their employees with industry standards for employee attendance, turnover, sick leave use, and other broad indicators.[35]

These comparisons are useful, but for supervisors they may or may not relate to the department. Some supervisors pride themselves on their abilities to assess morale intuitively. However, most supervisors are better advised to approach morale measurement more systematically. It may not be possible to measure morale precisely, but there are techniques for assessing prevailing levels and trends. The two most frequently used techniques are (1) observation and study and (2) attitude surveys.

OBSERVING AND STUDYING MORALE INDICATORS

By observing, monitoring, and studying patterns of employee behavior, a supervisor often can discover clues to employee morale. The supervisor should closely monitor such key indicators as job performance levels, tardiness and absenteeism, the amount of waste or scrap, employee complaints, and accident and safety records. Any significant changes in these indicators should be analyzed because they often are related. For example, excessive tardiness and absenteeism seriously interfere with job performance. The supervisor should find out why employees are often tardy or absent. If the reasons are related to morale, the supervisor should determine if the causes are within the supervisor's control or if the employees should be referred for counseling or assistance.

It is relatively easy to observe morale extremes. However, it is quite difficult to differentiate among degrees of morale or to assess when morale is changing. For example, an employee's facial expression or shoulder shrug may or may not reflect that person's morale. Only an alert supervisor can judge whether the employee is becoming depressed or frustrated. Supervisors must sharpen their powers of observation and be careful not to brush aside indicators.

Daily working relationships offer numerous opportunities for a supervisor to observe and analyze changes in employee morale. However, many supervisors do not take time to observe; others do not analyze what they observe. It is only when morale clearly drops that some supervisors first take note. By then, the problems that lowered morale probably will have magnified to the point that major corrective actions are necessary. As is often the case in supervision, an "ounce of prevention" is worth more than a "pound of cure."

Many companies conduct exit interviews with individuals leaving their employ. **Exit interviews** are usually conducted by a human resources staff person, although sometimes, especially in small firms, the supervisor may fill this role.

Exit interviews
Interviews with individuals who leave a firm that are used to assess morale and the reasons for employee turnover

Overloading an employee with too much work can deflate his or her morale

The interviewer asks why the person is leaving and about the person's perceptions of firm conditions. Results of exit interviews are used to assess morale in the firm as a whole or in certain departments of the firm, as well as to identify reasons for employee turnover.

EMPLOYEE ATTITUDE SURVEYS

Another technique used to assess employee morale is an **attitude survey**, also called an "opinion survey" or "morale survey." All employees, or a sample of the employees, are asked to express their opinions about major aspects of organizational life, usually in the form of answers to questions printed on a survey form. The survey questionnaire elicits employee opinions about such factors as management and supervision, job conditions, job satisfaction, coworkers, pay and benefits, job security, and advancement opportunities.

Employee attitude surveys are rarely initiated by a supervisor. Usually, they are undertaken by top-level management and are prepared with the help of the human resources department or an outside consulting firm.[36] The survey questionnaire should be written in language that is appropriate for most employees.

Attitude surveys or questionnaires may be completed on the job or in the privacy of the employee's home. Some organizations prefer to have employees answer these questionnaires on the job because a high percentage of questionnaires that are taken home or mailed are never returned. On the other hand, a possible advantage of completing the questionnaire at home is that employees may give more thoughtful and truthful answers. Regardless of where they are completed, questionnaires should not be signed so that they remain anonymous. However, some surveys may ask employees to indicate their departments.

Attitude survey
Survey of employee opinions about major aspects of organizational life that is used to assess morale

Many attitude survey forms allow employees to choose answers from a list. Other forms that are not so specific give employees opportunity to answer as freely as they wish. Because some employees may find it difficult to write their opinions in sentences or to fill in answers, better results usually are obtained with survey forms on which employees simply check the responses that correspond to their answers.

FOLLOW-UP OF SURVEY RESULTS

The tabulation and analysis tasks of questionnaires usually are assigned to the human resources department or to an outside consulting firm. Survey results are first presented to top-level and middle-level managers and eventually to departmental supervisors. In some organizations, survey results are used as discussion materials during supervisory training, especially when they provide clues about ways to improve employee morale.

Attitude surveys may reveal deficiencies the supervisor can eliminate. For example, a complaint that there is a lack of soap in the washroom can be resolved easily. Frequently, however, responses are difficult to evaluate, such as a complaint that communication channels are not open to employees. Such complaints raise more questions than answers and may necessitate a careful study of existing policies and procedures to see whether corrective actions are warranted.

If the attitude survey reveals a correctable problem at the departmental level—perhaps with a supervisor—the solution should be developed and implemented by the involved supervisor. On the other hand, a broader problem that requires the attention of higher-level managers should be reported to the appropriate manager for action. When supervisors and higher-level managers do not make needed changes as a result of a survey, the survey wastes time and money. In fact, if no changes materialize, or if changes are not communicated to employees, morale may decline after the survey. Employees may feel that their problems and suggestions have been ignored. Therefore, whenever possible, dissatisfactions expressed in an attitude survey should be addressed promptly by managers and supervisors. At a minimum, employees should be informed that management is aware of the dissatisfactions and will work to change things by some future date.

ORGANIZATIONAL DEVELOPMENT

Many companies follow up their attitude surveys with feedback meetings and conference sessions with groups of employees and supervisors. Typically these meetings are conducted by outside consultants or by staff members from human resources or some other department. In these meetings, the results of attitude surveys are discussed and debated openly. The groups are expected to recommend improvements, which are forwarded anonymously to higher-level management for consideration and possible implementation.

Organizational development (OD)
Meetings with groups under the guidance of a neutral conference leader to solve problems that are hindering organizational effectiveness

This approach is often part of a broader concept that also has become widespread in large enterprises. Known as **organizational development (OD)**, or "process consultation," this concept usually involves group meetings under the guidance of a neutral conference leader. The groups may consist of just employees, employees and supervisors, only supervisors, only higher-level managers, or whatever composition is appropriate. For the most part, these meetings focus on solving problems that may be hindering work performance or causing disruption, poor coordination, inadequate communication, or strained personal relations. When there is frank discussion in a relatively open and informal atmosphere, individuals tend to open up about what really is on their minds and what might be done to solve problems and reduce conflict. Organizational development can take numerous forms that are beyond the scope of this text.[37] However, supervisors may be involved in organizational development efforts because these programs can improve morale and organizational effectiveness.

The Supervisor's Counseling Role

Counseling is not the same as coaching. In **counseling**, the supervisor tries to address on-the-job performance problems that result from an employee's personal problems.[38] As mentioned in Chapter 10, an employee's performance problems may stem from a job-related personal problem, such as the failure to get a promotion, or from an off-the-job situation, such as a financial crisis due to divorce. When unaddressed, these problems can impede morale and the quality of work. Therefore, the supervisor must help the employee return to productivity. The most effective way to get an employee back on track is to counsel—to ask, listen, reflect, and encourage. A **counseling interview** is essentially nondirective (as described in Chapter 10); the supervisor serves primarily as an empathetic listener, and the employee is encouraged to discuss the problem frankly and to develop solutions.

By being a good listener, the supervisor can find out what happened and may help the employee develop alternatives. For example, perhaps Laura, one of the employees at Belmont Manufacturing (this chapter's "You Make the Call!"), is upset because of a sudden financial crisis, and her work performance shows a marked decline. She spends more of her time thinking about how to solve her financial problems than she does thinking about her work. In short, a counseling interview might begin when the supervisor addresses a performance problem and expresses concern: "Laura, I'm concerned about your performance. You were late for work two days last week, and the Finegan report did not get done. Could you explain?" The supervisor should listen carefully and without interruption to understand Laura's perspective. In Chapter 3, we discussed the importance of paraphrasing and reflecting to improve understanding. Paraphrasing involves expressing, in different words, Laura's response, such as, "Let me see if I understand what you're saying. . . ." A follow-up question might be, "Why do you feel that way?" Through reflection, the supervisor can help Laura talk about her feelings.

The supervisor may discuss with Laura possible ways to obtain financial assistance. The supervisor should not offer specific advice because it might bring unwanted repercussions. If Laura is dissatisfied with the results of following a supervisor's advice, for example, she might blame the supervisor, which would complicate an already difficult situation. If Laura's problem is beyond the supervisor's expertise, perhaps the supervisor can arrange for Laura to get help from a professional or refer her to the human resources department where assistance may be available. For example, many employers provide assistance and referral services for employees with personal problems. Many large employers also have employee assistance programs (EAPs), which are discussed later in this chapter. Regardless, the supervisor's job is to help the employee explore alternatives and choose the course of action that is best for the particular situation.

Aside from conducting a private counseling interview or referring the employee to some source of assistance, there may be little else the supervisor can do to cope with the factors affecting an employee's morale. The supervisor's main role is to help get the employee's performance back to an acceptable level. Figure 12.3 presents a roadmap to guide your steps when dealing with employee problems.

---

7 Understand why counseling is an important part of the supervisor's job.

Counseling
An effort by the supervisor to deal with on-the-job performance problems that are the result of an employee's personal problems

Counseling interview
Nondirective interview during which the supervisor listens empathetically and encourages the employee to discuss problems openly and to develop solutions

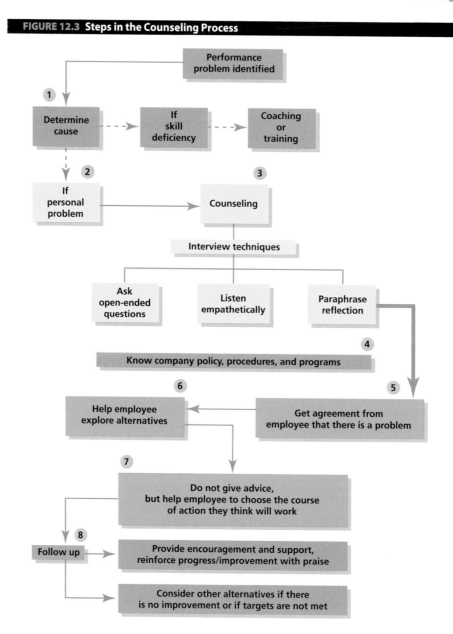

FIGURE 12.3 Steps in the Counseling Process

Performance problem identified

1. Determine cause

If skill deficiency → Coaching or training

2. If personal problem

3. Counseling

Interview techniques

Ask open-ended questions

Listen empathetically

Paraphrase reflection

4. Know company policy, procedures, and programs

5. Get agreement from employee that there is a problem

6. Help employee explore alternatives

7. Do not give advice, but help employee to choose the course of action they think will work

8. Follow up

Provide encouragement and support, reinforce progress/improvement with praise

Consider other alternatives if there is no improvement or if targets are not met

8 Identify programs that organizations use to help employees with personal and work-related problems.

Programs for Employees with Personal and Work-Related Problems

As discussed previously, the supervisor may refer an employee to the human resources department or a designated manager who will conduct the counseling interview and suggest possibilities for help.

FAMILY AND MEDICAL LEAVE PROVISIONS

If the employee's problem involves requesting a leave of absence due to sickness or such family considerations as childbirth or caring for a seriously ill member of the immediate family, the supervisor normally should refer the request to the human resources department or to higher-level managers. Many employers, in connection with the federal Family and Medical Leave Act (FMLA), have developed policies for handling such requests. Passed in 1993, the FMLA generally requires employers with 50 or greater employees to grant up to twelve weeks of unpaid leave to workers for various reasons, particularly serious medical problems experienced by employees or their families, and the births or adoptions of children. Paid sick leave or vacation time under a company policy may be substituted for the unpaid leave allowed by the FMLA.[39] Because major changes to FLMA went into effect January 16, 2009, supervisors should rely on the advice of HR or the company's legal counsel for interpretation of the regulations. Clearly, the leave policies must be applied consistently and uniformly in the organization.

EMPLOYEE ASSISTANCE PROGRAMS

Many organizations, especially large corporations and major government agencies, have adopted **employee assistance programs (EAPs)**. These programs typically involve a special department or outside resources retained by the firm to whom supervisors may refer employees with certain types of problems. Alternatively, employees may seek help on their own from the EAP, or they may be referred to the EAP by other sources, such as their union. Most EAPs provide help for alcoholism and substance abuse; marriage, child-care, and family problems; financial questions; and other personal, emotional, or psychological problems that may be interfering with job performance.

> **Employee assistance programs (EAPs)**
> Company programs to help employees with personal or work-related problems that are interfering with job performance

The supervisor's role in an EAP is essential to the program's effectiveness. The supervisor must be alert to signs that an employee may be troubled, even though the supervisor may have tried to respond to the employee's work performance using normal supervisory procedures. For example, a supervisor may be concerned about an employee's recent poor attendance and low production at work. The supervisor may even suspect that the employee is struggling with an alcohol-related problem or substance abuse. Drug and alcohol abuse costs American businesses almost $100 billion in lost productivity annually. Employers also incur hidden costs related to tardiness, absenteeism, healthcare benefits, and turnover.[40] The American Council on Drug Education reports that drug abusers are:

- 10 times more likely to miss work,
- 3.6 times more likely to be involved in on-the-job accidents,
- 5 times more likely to file a workers' compensation claim,
- Two-thirds as productive, and
- Responsible for health care costs that are 3 times as high.[41]

When talking with the employee, the supervisor should focus primarily on the person's poor or deteriorating job performance and then suggest the EAP services that might be of help. Figure 12.4 is an EAP procedural statement excerpted from a major firm's supervisory policy manual. The guidelines in this policy represent the approaches most major organizations have adopted in their EAP efforts.

Most EAPs emphasize the confidential nature of the services. Supervisors should discuss this confidentiality with employees and assure them that no stigma will be associated with their seeking EAP help. However, the supervisor should inform an employee who refuses EAP assistance and whose work performance continues to deteriorate that such a refusal might be a consideration in a termination decision.

WELLNESS PROGRAMS

Another approach used by some firms, often where EAPs are in place, is what has been called a wellness program. A **wellness program** is essentially a firm's organized effort to help employees stay healthy physically and mentally, and to

> **Wellness program**
> Organized effort by a firm to help employees get and stay healthy to remain productive

FIGURE 12.4 Procedural Guidelines for EAP Case Handling by Supervisors

SUPERVISORY PROCEDURE FOR EAP CASE HANDLING

The employee assistance program (EAP) is for all employees—management and occupational—who want help with their personal problems. The EAP is prepared to accept referrals from many sources, including supervisors and union representatives, who believe personal problems are causing an employee's job performance to deteriorate. Experience has shown that many employees will seek assistance once they realize help is readily available, but the decision to seek help must always be the employee's, and counseling should be left to professionals.

The following procedures generally apply when trying to help an employee improve job performance:

- Talk about job performance in an initial discussion with the employee. Discuss only deteriorating job performance. Opinions and judgments about possible personal problems should be avoided—leave those to the professional counselor. Specific instances of deteriorating job performance, such as unsatisfactory attendance, quality of work, or productivity, will be the basis for the initial discussion.

- Employees who initiate discussion of personal problems with supervisors or union representatives should be informed of the EAP and encouraged to participate voluntarily.

- Describe the EAP after discussing job performance. Tell the employee about the service available through the EAP. Stress that EAP contacts are confidential; no information concerning the nature of the problem or the specific treatment will be revealed without the employee's consent. Usually, the employee will not be terminated for unsatisfactory job performance until an opportunity to use EAP has been offered.

- If the employee chooses to accept help, referral will be made directly to the EAP counselor to determine the nature of the problem and to develop a course of action.

- To help the EAP counselor, any information pertaining to the employee's job performance or behavior should be provided by the supervisor or union representative at the time of referral.

- The EAP counselor may determine that outside resources are appropriate. If so, these referrals will be made as necessary.

- The employee will be allowed a reasonable period to improve job performance with the aid of counseling and supervisory support.

- If the employee rejects the offer of assistance and the job performance problems do not continue or recur, nothing further need be done.

- If the offer is rejected by the employee and job performance problems continue or recur, appropriate action may then be taken according to company policy and the union agreement for handling problems of deteriorating job performance.

Wellness programs provide exercise facilities, counseling, and other resources on company premises and elsewhere

© PHOTODISC RF/GETTY IMAGES

reduce employer health costs. Wellness programs vary, but they often focus on areas of recovery and staying free of certain problems, such as stress, substance abuse, and injury. Wellness programs can include exercise facilities, counseling, and other resources, both on company premises and elsewhere. In some firms, corporate wellness programs are viewed as an employee benefit, but for the most part, they are directed efforts by the firm to improve employee health and safety, which should positively impact morale and work performance.[42]

PAID TIME OFF (PTO)

It is well known that "all work and no play will negatively impact the best of us." We all need time to pause, relax, and recharge our batteries. Did you ever wonder why schools have a spring break? How do you spend your time off?

We suspect that you use it for personal reasons. The same is true for employees. Did you ever know an employee who used a sick day to tend to personal business? Of course; we all do. Belmont Manufacturing recently eliminated the distinction between vacation, sick, and personal days by granting employees *paid time off.*

Increasingly, companies are developing **paid time off (PTO) programs** where employees can use their accrued time off for personal reasons rather than solely for illnesses or vacations. PTO programs are in place at about one-third of the companies that responded to a SHRM Benefits Survey.[43] Under the PTO plan, employees can take time off with pay as needed without the restrictions imposed by traditional time-off policies. As seen in Figure 12.5, Belmont employees put days in their "personal leave bank," and make withdrawals as needed. At Belmont, the average employee previously received ten days of paid vacation, five sick days, and three personal days. Now employees receive eighteen days of personal time to use as they wish. It eliminates the problem of employees "calling in sick" when they want to play golf. PTO plans should be coordinated with FMLA, and employees have more control over how they use their time-off days.

Paid time off (PTO) program
PTO allows employees to establish a personal time-off bank that they can use for any reason they want

GOOD SUPERVISION IS THE FOUNDATION FOR HIGH MORALE

All aspects of good supervision impact employee morale as it relates to job conditions. However, perhaps the most significant day-to-day influence on employee morale is the supervisor's general attitude and behavior in departmental relationships. When a supervisor's behavior indicates suspicion of employees' motives and actions, low morale will likely result. When supervisors act worried or depressed, employees tend to follow suit. When supervisors lose their tempers, some employees also may lose theirs. Conversely, supervisors who show confidence in their employees' work and commend employees for good performance reinforce their positive outlook.

This does not mean that a supervisor should overlook difficulties that are present from time to time. Rather, it means that if something goes wrong, the supervisor should act as a leader who has the situation in hand. For example, supervisors often will be called on to mediate conflict among their employees. The supervisor should demonstrate the attitude that the employees will be relied on to correct the situation and to do what is necessary to prevent similar situations.

Supervisors should not relax their efforts to build and maintain high employee morale. However, they should not become discouraged if morale drops from time to time, because many factors impacting morale are beyond their control. Supervisors can be reasonably satisfied when employee morale is high most of the time. We have found that effective supervisors embrace that old saying, "If it [high morale] is to be, it is up to me!"

FIGURE 12.5 Example of PTO Policy

Paid Time Off (PTO) Policy

Effective: January 5, 2009

Policy—Belmont Manufacturing recognizes an individual's need to have time away from work to help meet personal needs and circumstances. The PTO policy has been established for all employees to tend to those needs. It is intended to provide the employee with flexibility and tangible reward for time unused at the end of the Plan Year. Employees are accountable and responsible for managing their own PTO hours to allow adequate reserves if there is a need to cover vacation, illness or disability, emergencies or other needs that require time off from work.

Procedure—PTO is accrued upon hire or transfer into a benefit-eligible position. All employees are eligible to earn PTO. The PTO program will commence with the January 5, 2009 workday.

Transition Period—All accrued sick, absence, personal, and vacation time that current employees have earned as of 11:59 P.M. on January 4, 2009 will be placed in their PTO bank.

Availability—PTO accruals are available for use in the pay period following completion of 30 days of employment. All hours are available for use in the pay period following the pay period in which they are accrued.

Accrual—PTO is earned on the following schedule:

Years of Service	Job Grades	PTO (accrual rate per hour worked)
0 to three years	1–3	.065
	4–6	.080
	7 and above	.095
4 to 10 years	1–3	.085
	4–6	.100
	7 and above	.115
11 or more years	1–3	.105
	4–6	.120
	7 and above	.135

Carry Over—A maximum of 120 hours may be carried over to the next calendar year.

Administration—PTO should be scheduled as early as possible in advance. PTO must be scheduled at least one week (seven calendar days) in advance for vacations. PTO is subject to supervisory approval, unit staffing needs, and established departmental procedures. Unscheduled absences (less than 24 hours' notice) will be monitored by the supervisor and the HR department. An employee will be counseled when the frequency of unscheduled absences adversely affects the operations of the unit.

- The supervisor may request the employee to provide a statement from his or her healthcare provider at any time concerning justification for an unscheduled absence.
- PTO may not be used for missed time because an employee reports late to work, except during inclement weather.
- PTO is paid at the employee's regular pay rate.
- Employees are required to use available PTO when taking time off from work.
- Employees may not borrow against their PTO banks.
- When PTO is used, an employee is required to request payment of PTO according to his/her regularly scheduled workday. For example, if an employee works a ten-hour day, he/she would request ten hours of PTO when taking that day off.

Cash Out—After the accumulation of 80 PTO hours, employees are eligible to cash out their PTO. An employee cashing out must leave at least 40 hours in his/her bank as a buffer for unforeseen illness or personal needs. For PTO cash out, eligible employees are required to indicate the cash-out amount on their time sheet. The benefit will be paid in the next regular pay period.

SUMMARY

1 Work groups are typically formed to provide companionship and identification, behavioral guidelines, problem-solving help, and protection. Various factors can contribute to the cohesiveness and functioning of the work group, including the group's status, size, personal characteristics, location, and previous successes. Work groups can significantly influence employee attitudes and job performance, a reality supervisors must recognize and be prepared to address.

2 At any time, an employee may be a member of a command group, a task group or cross-functional team, a friendship group, or a special-interest group. Command and task groups are primarily based on job-related factors. Friendship and special-interest groups primarily reflect personal relationships and interests. Employees who are dissatisfied with their jobs or working conditions, or fear losing their jobs due to outsourcing or economic downturn, may be attracted to form a special-interest group, e.g., a labor union. As a supervisor, you need to be aware of any hint of employee dissatisfaction that may lead to a unionizing effort. There is increasing use of customer-satisfaction teams, which may include customer and supplier representatives. Supervisors should be sensitive to all these groups and how they impact their employee members.

3 The Hawthorne Studies demonstrated that work groups can positively or negatively influence employee performance. To influence work groups positively, supervisors should review the keys to effective team building. Teams should be relatively small, and members must have the necessary skills and be committed to specific and realistic objectives. Organized participative management programs primarily involve building effective teams to work on tasks that will improve work performance and customer service.

Virtual or geographically dispersed work teams (GDTs) are a way for organizations to leverage the SKAs from workers located in all parts of the world. For such programs to be effective, top-level and other managers must give their full support and encouragement.

Members of these teams communicate electronically so they rarely or never meet face-to-face. Thus, the supervisor's ability to communicate and encourage collaboration is fundamental to the success of these teams.

4 Employee morale is a composite of feelings and attitudes of individuals and groups toward their work environment, supervision, and the organization as a whole. Morale can vary from very high to very low and can change considerably from day to day. All in the organization should be concerned about morale. Workplace spirituality is an effort to improve employees' personal lives and mental outlook. Morale and teamwork are not synonymous, but high morale usually contributes to high productivity.

5 Morale can be influenced by factors from outside the organization as well as by on-the-job factors. Workplace incivility, rudeness, and bullying negatively affect morale and can lead to turnover, dissatisfaction, and violent acts. Downsizing and corporate restructuring during the past decade have created a legacy of fear among workers. Supervisors must be aware of employee needs, feelings, and perceptions because they impact morale. In general, a supervisor's attitude and behaviors can significantly influence employee morale.

In response to increasing concerns about workplace violence, some firms have established programs and procedures that help supervisors recognize the symptoms of problem employees that could lead to violent behavior and know what to do in such circumstances.

6 Astute supervisors can sense changes in morale by observing employee behaviors and such key indicators as absenteeism and performance trends. Another means of assessing employee morale is the attitude survey. When possible, supervisors and higher-level managers should correct problems that have been brought to their attention through the survey. It is also desirable to discuss the results of an attitude survey with groups of employees and supervisors and to encourage those groups to recommend improvements.

7 Counseling is an effort by the supervisor to deal with on-the-job performance problems that are the result of the employee's personal problems. When left unattended, these problems may decrease morale and eventually erode quality and productivity. The counseling process includes identifying the performance problem, asking questions, listening empathetically to employee concerns, and perhaps referring the employee to a source of assistance. Sound interviewing and communication practices are the foundation of counseling.

8 Supervisors should be aware of the Family and Medical Leave Act (FMLA) and the company's related policies in case an employee requests a leave of absence due to personal sickness, childbirth, or other family medical concerns. To help employees with personal and work-related problems a supervisor would not be competent to handle, some organizations have employee assistance programs (EAPs) and wellness programs. EAP efforts typically help employees solve problems that detract from job performance, with the goal of restoring those employees to full capabilities that meet acceptable work standards. Wellness programs aim to promote and maintain proper physical conditioning and other personal or health habits that will tend to keep employees healthy and on the job. Paid time off (PTO) programs are increasing in popularity as employers recognize the need of employees to take time off for personal reasons rather than solely for illnesses and vacations.

KEY TERMS

Attitude survey (p. 441)
Collaborative workplace (p. 432)
Command group (p. 427)
Counseling (p. 443)
Counseling interview (p. 443)
Employee assistance programs
  (EAPs) (p. 445)
Exit interviews (p. 440)

Friendship group (p. 428)
Hawthorne Studies (p. 429)
Morale (p. 434)
Organizational development
  (OD) (p. 442)
Paid time off (PTO) program (p. 447)
Special-interest group (p. 428)
Synergistic effect (p. 431)

Task group or cross-functional
  team (p. 427)
Teamwork (p. 432)
Virtual or geographically dispersed
  team (GDT) (p. 432)
Wellness program (p. 445)
Workplace spirituality (p. 434)
Workplace violence (p. 437)

QUESTIONS FOR DISCUSSION

1. What are some of the most common reasons for forming work groups? What are some factors that make a work group cohesive? Is work group cohesiveness always desirable? Discuss.

2. Consider a team (work group) of which you are presently a member.
    a. Describe the leadership dynamics of this team.
    b. Is your team successful? Why?
    c. What are some reasons that your team might not be achieving to its full potential?
    d. What steps should you be taking to make the team more successful, i.e., a high-performance team?

3. Imagine that you are located in El Paso, Texas with responsibility for managing a customer-service call center. Your team members are located in El Paso; Calcutta, India; and Teresopolis, Brazil. What are the strengths and shortcomings of using GDTs to provide customer service? Identify the leadership and team-building skills that you will have to use to facilitate the development and performance of your team.

4. Define employee morale. Differentiate between the external factors and the internal factors influencing employee morale.
    a. What should a supervisor do to minimize the influence of external factors on an employee's work?
    b. How could you as a supervisor develop a strategy to minimize workplace bullying?
    c. Discuss the impact of downsizing on employee morale and supervisory responses to the effects of downsizing.

5. Discuss the use of employee assistance programs (EAPs) and wellness programs. What should a supervisor do when an employee requests a family or medical leave?

SKILLS APPLICATIONS

Skills Application 12-1: Is There a Way to Manage This Team?

In this Skills Application, you are assigned the role of Charlie Graham, director of operations for Belmont Manufacturing (refer to this chapter's "You Make the Call!"). As you reflect on the past few years, you are pleased with the progress that the plant has made but know that more can be done. Employees have been able to diagnose, problem-solve, and implement changes successfully.

Your mission, if you choose to take it, is to develop a strategy for sustaining the momentum that you helped build over the past four years.

1. Two criteria for measuring team effectiveness are performance and viability. As you reflect back on where you started and where you are today, what is your current assessment of Belmont Manufacturing on these two criteria?

2. What factors (internal and external) could cause Belmont Manufacturing to lose the momentum it has built up during the past four years?

3. How would you proceed with implementing a strategy for sustaining what has been built during the past four years while implementing a program for continuous improvement? In other words, you need to figure out how to get the Belmont team to go where they have never been before.
    a. What would be the driving forces toward acceptance of your strategy by team members?
    b. What would be the restraining forces that might cause team members not to get "on board"?
    c. How would you overcome or minimize the restraining forces?

4. Write a one-page paper detailing what you learned from this skills application.

Skills Application 12-2: Team Assessment

1. Describe the most effective team with which you have ever been associated.
   a. Why were you able to perform successfully on the team?
   b. Provide specific examples to illustrate how team members used feedback to help you grow, develop, and improve.
   c. Compare your responses with those of a classmate. What are the similarities? How do you account for these similarities?

2. Contact two supervisors or managers who are willing to be interviewed and ask them the following:

   a. Think of a time you experienced great pride or significant satisfaction from being associated with a team. What did you like most about being a member of that team?
   b. What did the team leader do to blend the team members into an efficient and effective group?
   c. What would have made you feel even better about your team experience?
   d. Compare the two supervisors' responses. To what degree are their responses similar? To what degree are they different? If there were major differences in the supervisors' responses, what do you feel are the reasons?

Skills Application 12-3: Thinking Outside the Box—Advantages of Teamwork

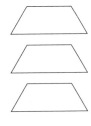

1. Your instructor will randomly organize the class into a team of four to six persons.

2. Each team should decide how it will arrange these three identical pieces into one figure that forms a triangle. Compare your team's final solution with the solution that the instructor will provide.

3. At the conclusion of the exercise, each member of the team should list the advantages and limitations of working as a team on this project as opposed to doing it as an individual.

4. Each group should select one individual to be its reporter. The reporter should take notes and report what the group decided was the major benefit of working as a team on this project and the major obstacle the team faced in completing the task. Your instructor will then develop a composite listing of the advantages and limitations of team problem solving.

5. In conclusion, analyze the dynamics of your team.
   a. Were you satisfied with the solution your team developed?
   b. How did you arrive at the solution?
   c. Did anyone just sit there and refuse to participate? If so, why?
   d. What were the patterns of communication within the group?
   e. Did the group work well together?
   f. Who was the person with the most influence?
   g. Did you feel welcome in the group?
   h. Did you personally make an effort to involve everyone in the process?
   i. Would you like to work with this group of individuals on another project? Why? Why not?

Source: The idea for this skills application was adapted with permission from QCI International's *Timely Tips for Teams*, a monthly Internet newsletter © November 2004 by QCI International, Cottonwood, CA.

Skills Application 12-4: Dealing with People who Make Your Life Difficult—"The Dead Weight"

This is another in a series of skills applications that introduce you to people who might make your life difficult.

1. Read the following statement from Chandra Morris, a pet shop employee:

I love working at the pet shop—mostly. I enjoy what I do, but I do not look forward to coming to work when I'm scheduled to work the same shift as Jay. Jay goes around as if nothing is ever wrong and nothing has to be done on time. Yesterday, I arrived at work at 8:00 A.M. to get things organized for our opening at 10:00 A.M. Jay was supposed to be here at 8:00 A.M., but he didn't show up until 9:15 A.M. We're supposed to clean cages and feed and water the animals. Every morning, I end up cleaning the cages by myself. Jay said it was too early in

the morning for him to deal with animal droppings. He says he'll get around to it later, once he wakes up. I asked him if he could start filling food and water bowls while I finished cleaning cages. To my surprise, he actually started filling the bowls. At 9:30 A.M., the phone rang, and Jay answered it. We're not supposed to answer the phone until after 10:00 A.M. as the message system clicks in to tell people our hours of operation, but it was Jay's girlfriend. After he talked for about 15 minutes, I asked Jay if he would hurry up and feed the animals as we were about ready to open the store. He said not to worry about it, that it would get done.

I should have known better. As I opened the doors at 10:00 A.M., the customers started to come in. Jay got off the phone, but he didn't finish his duties. I proceeded to answer the customers' questions and work the cash register until my shift was over at 4:00 P.M. I've asked Jay if he ever worries about losing his job because of the lack of effort, and his responses have included, "What? Me worry? No way!" and "Don't sweat the small stuff. Everything works out in the end."

I've talked with the other employees, and they have expressed the same concern. During the week, there are only two of us on duty, so we have to work as a team to get everything done. I have lots of responsibility, including opening and closing the store, but no authority. I've reported my concerns to the owner, Aaron Minnick, but he only says, "Figure out a way to work together." I'm starting to feel like the Lone Ranger. It's always the same thing: Every time I'm scheduled to work with Jay, I end up carrying the entire load.

2.  Using the Internet, find at least three sources of information for working with people who fail to carry their loads. Carefully review each site for suggestions on how to deal with these types of people.

3. Based on your findings, what suggestions would you make to Chandra Morris on how to deal with the "dead weight"?

4. If you were the owner, Aaron Minnick, what would you do to increase the levels of cooperation, trust, and cohesiveness among your employees?

5. Write a one-page paper explaining how this skills application increased your working knowledge of coping with the behaviors of this type of difficult person.

SKILLS DEVELOPMENT

Skills Development Module 12-1: Welcome to Zingerman's

 Before viewing the Skills Development Module video clip, we suggest that you read the following summary and visit Zingerman's Web site (http;//www.zingermans.com).

Each one of Zingerman's Community of Businesses (ZCoB) is operated by one or more managing partners who share ownership and day-to-day responsibility for running their business.

- *Zingerman's Delicatessen: Opened in 1982 in an historic building near the Ann Arbor, Michigan Farmers Market. The deli started with a staff of two and offered a small selection of specialty foods. Go to http://www.zingermans.com to read more about their operations.*
- *Zingerman's Bakehouse: In 1992, the company opened a bakery complete with a baking school. (www.bakewithzong.com)*
- *Zingerman's Roadhouse: A full-service, sit-down restaurant.*
- *Zingerman's Catering: Catering services offering everything from caviar to champagne to corned beef.*
- *Zingerman's Creamery: Offering hand-crafted fresh cheeses and other dairy products.*
- *Zingerman's Coffee Company: A wholesale roaster supplies other cafés, restaurants, and businesses.*

The company also has a mail-order operation that will send their products anywhere in the world and, ZingTrain, a training and consulting services operation.

After viewing the Skills Development Module video clip, answer the following questions:

1. ZCoB's mission is "to bring a great experience to all stakeholders." What has the organization done to engage employees in the process of bringing about the changes necessary to accomplish that?

2. One employee said, "The reason I wanted to work at Zingerman's was because I wanted to work for a business where I respected the people who worked there." In your own words, explain what you think was important to the person. Would you like to work in such an environment? Why or why not?

3. "Understanding people, communicating, building teamwork, and inspiring others are the essentials of organizational leadership." What is your assessment of the value of this statement as it relates to Zingerman's? Rank the four items in order of importance to you. Compare your ranking with those of two other students. Why is there a difference?

ENDNOTES

1. For an expanded discussion of group processes in organizations, see John M. Ivancevich, Robert Konopaske, and Michael T. Matteson, *Organizational Behavioral and Management* (Boston: McGraw-Hill Irwin, 2005), pp. 321–46; and Steven L. McShane and Mary Ann Von Glinow, *Organizational Behavior* (Boston: McGraw-Hill Irwin, 2005), pp. 264–288.

2. See Steven L. McShane and Mary Ann Von Glinow, *Organizational Behavior* (Boston: McGraw-Hill Irwin, 2005), pp. 294–318. Also see

Natasha Calder and P. C. Douglas, "Empowered Employee Teams: The New Key to Improving Corporate Success," *Quality Digest* (March 1999), pp. 26–30, for a discussion of empowered teams. Access the following (http://www.teambuilding.com) for information on teams.

3. Sun Microsystems Inc. employs almost 35,000 worldwide and develops the technologies that power the global marketplace. A single vision, "The Network is the Computer," guides employee efforts. Visit the company's Web site (http://www.sun.com) for information

on how employees are teaming and collaborating with customers and users. Click on "Our Values" or "People and Places."

To understand how Johnson & Johnson uses the team approach, see "What Makes Good Teams Better: Research-Based Strategies That Distinguish Top-Performing Cross-Functional Drug Development Teams," *Organizational Development Journal*, 25, 2 (Summer 2007), pp. 179–186.

4. For discussion of the Hawthorne Studies and their impact, see Ivancevich, op. cit., pp. 12–13. See Fritz J. Roethlisberger and W. J. Dickson, *Management and the Worker* (Cambridge, MA: Harvard University Press, 1939); and Elton Mayo, *The Social Problems of Industrial Civilization* (Boston: Harvard University Press, 1945) for a complete picture of the works of Mayo, Roethlisberger, and Dickson at the Hawthorne Works.

5. Jon R. Katzenbach and Douglas K. Smith, *The Wisdom of Teams: Creating the High-Performance Organization* (Boston: Harvard Business School Press, 1993). Review Chapters 4, 7, 8, and 11 of this text for useful checklists for building team performance, leading teams effectively, and overcoming team obstacles. Also see Diane McLain Smith, *Divide or Conquer—How Great Teams Turn Conflict into Strength* (New York: Portfolio, 2008); Casimer DeCusatis, "Creating, Growing and Sustaining Efficient Innovations Teams," *Creativity & Innovation Management*, 17, 2 (June 2008), pp. 155–164; Maria Isabell Delgado Pina, Ana Maria Romero Martinez, and Luis Gomez Martinez, "Teams in Organizations: A Review on Team Effectiveness," *Team Performance Management*, 14, 1–2 (2008), pp. 7–21; and Nancy R. Lockwood, "Teams—Just the Basics," *SHRM Research* (August 2004).

6. "From Supervisor to Team Manager," by Allen Ferguson, Amy Hicks, and Steven D. Jones, is one of the case studies in *Developing High-Performance Work Teams*, edited by Jones and Michael M. Beyerlein, (Washington, D.C. ASTD, Part 1, 1998, and Part 2, 1999). Also visit the *Center for the Study of Work Teams* Web site (http://www.workteams.unt.edu) for additional information. Also see, Phred Dvorak, "Munchausen at Work: Employees Advances by Fixing Problems They had Created," the *Wall Street Journal* (August 25, 2008), p. B4.

7. One of our IPFW graduates, Lloy Ball was the setter on the 2008 U.S. gold medal volleyball team. Ball had appeared in three previous Olympics without success. See Anne M. Peterson, "Ball, U.S. Strike Volleyball Gold," *Fort Wayne, Indiana Journal Gazette* (August 25, 2008), pp. 1B, 7B. Misty May-Treanor and Kerri Walsh won 112 consecutive matches and 19 titles before losing in the AVP Crocs Cup Shootout in Mason, Ohio on August 31, 2008. Also see, Nancy R. Lockwood, "High-Performance Teams," *SHRM Research* (August 2004).

8. Adapted from Chris Widener, "Secrets of Successful Teams," *IJR Business* (www.insiderreports.com, accessed September 1, 2008). Widener spent seven years working for the Seattle Supersonics.

9. See *AccountingWeb* "As Hiring Rebounds, Managers Seek a Different Labor Force," (August 20, 2004) for details of the survey conducted by Development Dimensions International (DDI).

10. At the time of this writing, Legendary Coach John Wooden still attracts a huge following. We urge you to review the following: Coach Wooden's Web site at www.coachjohnwooden.com; and his two books: John Wooden and Steve Jamison, *Wooden on Leadership* (New York: McGraw-Hill, 2005), and *My Personal Best: Life Lessons from an All-American Journeyman* (New York: McGraw-Hill, 2004).

11. Russell Adams, "The Culture of Winning," *The Wall Street Journal* (October 5, 2005), pp. B1, B4. The Braves started in Boston in 1871, resided in Milwaukee from 1953 to 1965; and moved to Atlanta in 1966. See John Schuerholz, *Built to Win* (New York: Warner Books, 2006). Schuerholz resigned as GM on October 11, 2007 and assumed the role of President. Also see, Monte Burke, "The Best Team in Sports," *Forbes* (September 19, 2005), pp. 122–28.

12. Kenneth Turan, "Tales from the Trenches: Role Players," *ESPN Sports Century* (December 12, 1999), p. 19.

13. The emphasis is on the word *must,* from the Mescon Group, Inc., *Strengthening Teamwork* (Cincinnati: Thomson Executive Press, 1995), p. 19. Also see, T. L. Stanley, "Taking on the Challenges of High-Performance Work Teams," *Supervision* (December 2004), pp. 10–12; and W. H. Weiss, "Team Management," *Supervision* (November 2004), pp. 19–21.

14. As quoted in Randi Brenowitz and Tracy Gibbons, "Workforce Collaboration: Building a Strong Team Foundation," *Information Executive* (January/February 2002), pp. 5–6.

15. See Edward M. Marshall, "The Collaborative Workplace," *Management Review* (June 1995), pp. 13–17.

16. H. James Harrington, "Beyond Teams: Teamwork," *Quality Digest* (August 1999), p. 20. Also Harrington, "Horsing Around: A Parable About Teamwork," *Quality Digest* (November 2004), p. 16; and Harvey Robbins and Michael Finley, *The New Why Teams Don't Work: What Went Wrong and How to Make It Right* (San Francisco: Berrett-Koehler Publishing, 2000).

17. From Michael A. Campion and A. Catherine Higgs, "Design Work Teams to Increase Productivity and Satisfaction," *HR Magazine* (October 1995), pp. 101–7. Also see Rob Cross and Sally Colella, "Building Vibrant Employee Networks," *HR Magazine* (December 2004), pp. 101–4.

18. See Terri L. Griffith, Elizabeth A. Mannix, and Margaret A. Neale, "Conflict & Virtual Teams" in *Virtual Teams that Work* (San Francisco: Jossey-Bass, 2003). They contend that the virtual team model can be used in any organization. Also see, Philip L. Hunsaker and Johanna S. Hunsaker, "Virtual Teams: A Leader's Guide," *Team Performance Management*, 14, 1–2 (2008), pp. 86–101; Bill Snyder, "Teams That Span Time Zones Face New Work Rules," *Stanford Business* (May 2003, accessed September 1, 2008); Nancy R. Lockwood, "Global Virtual Teams," *SHRM Research* (August 2004); Carla Johnson, "Managing Virtual Teams," *HR Magazine* (June 2003), pp. 69–73; Deborah Duarte and Nancy Snyder, *Mastering Virtual Teams* (San Francisco: Jossey-Bass, 2000); or Jessica Linack and Jeffrey Stamps, *Virtual Teams: Reaching Across Space, Time, and Organizations with Technology* (New York: John Wiley & Sons, 1997).

19. Watson Wyatt's Work USA 2004 Survey reported in Ann Pomeroy, "Senior Management Begins Regaining Employee Trust," *HR Magazine* (February 2005), p. 16. Also see, Rebecca R. Hastings, "Poll: Confidence in Leaders Might be on the Decline," *SHRM Home* (March 2008); J. Colquitt, B. Scott and J. LePine, "Trust, Trustworthiness, and Trust Propensity: A Meta-Analytic Test of Their Unique Relationships with Risk Taking and Job Performance," *Journal of Applied Psychology*, 92, 4 (2007), pp. 909–927; Eric Krell, "Do They Trust You?" *HR Magazine* (June 2006), pp. 58–63; R. Mayer and M. Gavin, "Trust in Management and Performance: Who Minds the Shop While the Employees Watch the Boss?" *Academy of Management Journal*, 48, 5 (2005), pp. 874–888; and Watson Wyatt "Weathering the Storm: A Study of Employee Attitudes and Opinions," (2002), retrieved August 2008 from www.watsonwyatt.com.

20. See "Why I Do This Job," reporting survey data developed by William M. Mercer, Inc.–Yankelovich Partners, Inc., in *BusinessWeek* (September 11, 1995), p. 8.

21. A 1999 Gallup Poll reported that 78 percent of U.S. citizens felt they needed to experience spiritual growth. See George Gallup, Jr., and Tim Jones, *The Next American Spirituality* (Gallup Organization: National Opinion Research Center, 2000); Kent Rhodes, "Six Components of a Model for Workplace Spirituality," Graziadio Business Report (http://gbr.pepperdine.edu/062/workplace.html, retrieved September 1, 2008); Michelle Conlin, "Religion in the Workplace: The Growing Presence of Spirituality in Corporate America," *BusinessWeek*

(November 1, 1999), pp. 153+; and Nancy K. Austin, "Does Spirituality at Work Work?" *Working Women* (March 1995), pp. 26–28.

22. Ben Cohen, co-founder of Ben & Jerry's Homemade Ice Cream Company with Jerry Greenfield as quoted at a Babson College symposium. See Frederica Saylor, "Businesses Benefit from a Low-Key Spirituality," May 12, 2005), accessed at www.northway.org August 2008.

23. Cohen, Ibid.

24. For a comprehensive source on how to develop and maintain a positive work environment, see Jim Harris, *Getting Employees to Fall in Love with Your Company* (New York: AMACOM, 1996).

25. In Kate N. Grossman, "Boys Behaving Badly: Men Mostly at Fault for Rising Incivility at Work," *Associated Press* (August 11, 1999). This news release summarized the work of University of North Carolina professor Christine M. Patterson et al., "Workplace Incivility: The Target's Eye View," presented at the *Academy of Management's Annual Meeting* (Tuesday, August 10, 1999). Jim Owen, "Workplace Incivility: Bullying and Rudeness on the Rise," *Career Builder, Inc.* (1999). See also Rudy M. Yankrick, "Lurking in the Shadows," *HR Magazine* (October 1999), pp. 60–68; Alice Ann Love, "Survey Finds Workplace Angst: Colleagues, Communications Equipment Sources of Anger," *Associated Press* (September 6, 1999), reports on the Gallup Organization's telephone survey of workers to assess the extent of workplace anger and stress. Also see Noa Davenport, Ruth Distler Schwartz, and Gail Pursell Elliott, *Mobbing: Emotional Abuse in the American Workplace* (Ames, IA: Civil Society Publishing, 1999); and Dyane Holt, "HR Solutions," *HR Magazine* (November 2003), p. 42. Holt discusses how to cope with bullying behavior.

The U.S. Workplace Bullying Survey (September 2007) reported that bullying is a top-down phenomenon, 55% of targets are non-supervisory employees. 45% of targets have stress-related health problems. 40% never report it, only 3% sue, and 4% complain to state or federal agencies. See complete survey report at www.bullyinginstitute.org.

A more recent study found that employees who experience bullying, incivility, or interpersonal on-the-job conflict were more likely to quit their jobs. See "Study Spotlights Workplace Bullying," SHRM Home *Business and Legal Reports, Inc.* (April 10, 2008). Also see, Robert Caldwell, "Work to Reduce Exposure to Workplace Violence Threats," *SHRM Home* (April 2008); and Pauline Wallin, *Taming Your Inner Brat: A Guide for Transforming Self-Defeating Behavior* (Dallas: Wildcat Press, 2004).

26. In August 1986, a U.S. Postal Service employee shot and killed 14 co-workers and wounded 6 others in Edmond, Oklahoma. Since that incident, the news media has created an awareness of workplace violence concerning employees killed by fellow employees as "going postal."

In 2007, there were 5,488 fatal workplace injuries and 610 of those were homicides. See the following: National Census of Fatal Occupational Injuries (CFOI) (http://www.bls.gov/iif/ochcfoil.htm), National Institute for Prevention of Workplace Violence, Crisis Prevention Institute, Inc. (www.crisisprevention.com), National Institute for Occupational Health and Safety., National Center for Analyzing Violent Crime (www.Fbi.gov/publications/violence.pdf), or (www.worktrauma.com.)

27. The study by Prince & Associates as reported in Kathy Gurchiek, "Workplace Violence is on the Upswing, say HR Leaders," *SHRM Home* (May 12, 2005). Also see Philip S. Deming, "Workplace Violence: Trend and Strategic Tools for Mitigating Risk," *SHRM White Paper* (March 2006). It is estimated that 70% percent of employers do not have a program or policy addressing workplace violence.

28. Ibid.

29. See Sandra J. Kelley, "Making Sense of Violence in the Workplace," *Risk Management* (October 1995), pp. 50–57.

30. Many authors have applied their own terms to problem behaviors. As cited in Rita Zeidner, "Problem of Workplace Bullying Demands Attention, Researchers Say," *SHRM Home* (March 2008): M. Sandy Hershcovis and Julian Barling distinguished among different forms of workplace aggression:

"Incivility included rudeness and discourteous verbal and non-verbal behaviors. Bullying included persistently criticizing employees' work; yelling; repeatedly reminding employees of mistakes; spreading gossip or lies; ignoring or excluding workers; and insulting employees' habits, attitudes or private life. Interpersonal conflict included behaviors that involved hostility, verbal aggression, and angry exchanges."

Regardless of the terms used, there is no place for inappropriate behavior in the society.

Those practicing incivility (bullying) in the workplace may be called *atomic bombs, unguided missiles, backstabbers, jabbers, ridiculers, hotheads, showoffs, tyrants, Sherman tanks, hostile aggressives,* and *snipers,* among others. When left unchecked, this behavior will destroy a team. Underlying strategies for dealing with difficult people is the notion of self-esteem, assertiveness, and trust.

Also see Linda Wasmer Andrews, "HardCore Offenders," *HR Magazine* (December 2004), pp. 43–48; Rick Brinkman and Rick Kirschner, *Dealing with People You Can't Stand: How to Bring Out the Best in People at Their Worst* (New York: McGraw-Hill, 1994); and Muriel Solomon, *Working with Difficult People* (Englewood Cliffs, NJ: Prentice-Hall, 1990).

31. See Christine McGovern, "Take Action, Heed Warnings to End Workplace Violence," *Occupational Hazards* (March 1999), pp. 61–63, and John W. Kennish, "Violence in the Workplace," *Professional Safety* (November 1995), pp. 34–36.

32. See *AccountingWeb* "Survey Says Less than Half of Companies Consider Outsourcing to be Cost Effective," (October 29, 2004) for details of the survey conducted by PricewaterhouseCoopers' Management Barometer Survey. See Evren Esen, "SHRM Human Resource Outsourcing Survey Report," *SHRM Research* (July 2004); and Jennifer C. Berkshire, "Career Move," *HR Magazine* (September 2004), pp. 42–48 for outsourcing trends in HR and what it is like to work for an outsourcing firm.

33. Sue Shellenbarger, "An Overlooked Toll of Job Upheavals: Valuable Friendships," *The Wall Street Journal* (January 12, 2000), p. B1; and Michael T. Brannick, *The Necessary Nature of Future Firms: Attributes of Survivors in a Changing World* reviewed by Walter R. Nord, *Academy of Management Review* (October 2005), pp. 873–75.

34. Jacqueline Gish, "Taking Responsibility for Your Employees' Morale," *Supervision* (May 2005), pp. 8–10; and Robert J. Grossman, "Damaged, Downsized Souls: How to Revitalize the Workplace," *HR Magazine* (May 1996), pp. 54–61.

35. For ideas on assessing employee morale, see Charlotte Garvey, "Connecting the Organizational Pulse to the Bottom Line," *HR Magazine* (June 2004), pp. 70–75.

36. See Elaine McShulkis, "Employee Survey Sins," *HR Magazine* (May 1996), pp. 12–13.

37. For a detailed explanation of OD, see Warren G. Bennis's classic, *Organizational Development: Its Nature, Origins, and Perspectives* (Reading, MA: Addison-Wesley, 1969). Also see Oleen Miranda-Stone and Michael C. Leary, "Organizational Development: Acting as One with the Business—Best Practices at Chevron Corporation," *Organizational Development Journal*, 25, 3 (Fall 2007), pp. 77–82; or Carol Pledger, "Building Manager Effectiveness by Combining Leadership Training and Organizational Development," *Organizational Development Journal*, 25, 2 (Summer 2007), pp. 77–80.

38. See Marianne Minor, *Coaching and Counseling: A Practice Guide for Managers* (Crisp Publications, Inc., 1989).

39. Eligible employees covered under the Family and Medical Leave Act (FLMA) must be granted up to a total of 12 workweeks of unpaid leave during any 12-month period for one or more of the following reasons: for the birth and care of a newborn child of the employee; for placement with the employee of a child for adoption or foster care; to care for an immediate family member (spouse, child, or parent) with a serious health condition; or to take medical leave when the employee is unable to work because of a serious health condition.

The U.S. Department of Labor (DOL) updated the FMLA effective January 16, 2009. The revisions expanded the definition of "a parent." The law affirms that a person standing in *loco parentis* (in place of a parent) assumes the obligations of the parental relationship without going through the formalities of legal adoption.

Public Law 110-181 permits a spouse, son, daughter, parent, or next of kin to take up to 26 workweeks of leave to care for a member of the Armed Forces who is undergoing medical treatment, recuperation, or therapy; is otherwise on outpatient status; or is otherwise on the temporary disability retired list for a serious injury or illness. This act also permits an employee to take FMLA leave for "any qualifying exigency."

Go to http://edocket.access.gpo.gov/2008/pdf/E8-26577.pdf to review the updated regulations. See also the FMLA NDAA Web site (http://www.dol.gov/esa/whd/fmla/ndaa_fmla.htm) or FMLA Final Rule Website (http://www.dol.gov/esa/whd/fmla).

Also see, Diane Cadrain, "Noble Headache: The Family and Medical Leave Act Achieves a High Purpose–at a Price," *HR Magazine* (July 2008), pp. 54–59.

40. As reported in Diane Cadrain, "Helping Workers Fool Drug Tests is a Big Business," *HR Magazine* (August 2005), pp. 29, 32. The Drug-Free Workplace Act of 1988 requires companies receiving $25,000 or more in federal government contracts to maintain a "drug-free workplace," which includes establishing policies and conducting awareness programs to achieve this objective. See "Best Practices: How to Establish a Workplace Substance Abuse Program," *U.S. Department of Labor Web site* (http://www.dol.gov).

Also visit the following Web sites:

American Council on Drug Education (http://www.acde.org)

Center for Substance Abuse Prevention (http://www.drugfreeworkplace.gov)

Drug-Free America Foundation (http://www.dfaf.org)

National Institute on Alcohol Abuse & Alcoholism (http://www.niaaa.nih.gov)

National Institute on Drug Abuse (http://www.nida.nih.gov)

41. Ibid.

42. One study found that 85 percent of surveyed companies offered wellness programs. See Susan J. Wells, "The Doctor Is In-House," *HR Magazine* (April 2006), pp. 38–54; Francis P. Alvarez and Michael J. Soltis, "Preventive Medicine: Employee Wellness Programs Are Prone to Legal Maladies that Require Careful Monitoring," *HR Magazine* (January 2006), pp. 105–109; "Here's to Your Health," *HR Focus* (January 1996), p. 18; and Paul L. Cerrato, "Employee Health: Not Just a Fringe Benefit," *Business and Health* (November 1995), pp. 21–26.

43. "Time Off From Work," *SHRM Home—Knowledge Center* (November 3, 2005). According to John Reh, "Sick Leave vs. PTO," *Your Guide to Management Newsletter—New York Times* (accessed November 3, 2005), "PTO invites abuse. Since a company no longer knows why an employee takes off, and officially doesn't care, employees are gone more frequently." However, Alexander Hamilton Institute's (AHI) 2008 Survey of Traditional Time Off (TTO) and PTO Program Practices stated that more than two-thirds (69%) of PTO users reported that, on average, an employee missed four workdays or fewer due to unscheduled absences each year versus only 57% for TTO users. Almost half of the PTO users indicated that the number of unscheduled absences dropped by more than 10 percent after converting to a PTO program. You should review the literature and determine whether PTO is appropriate for you and your organization.

CHAPTER 13

(**Supervising a Diverse Workforce**)

After studying this chapter, you will be able to:

1 Define the concept of workforce diversity.

2 Identify the major categories of legally protected employees and general guidelines for supervising a diverse workforce.

3 Explain the issues involved in supervising racial/ethnic minority employees.

4 Discuss factors that are particularly important when supervising female employees.

5 Identify and discuss the legal and other considerations of supervising employees with physical and mental disabilities.

6 Discuss the considerations of supervising older workers.

7 Provide examples of religious accommodation.

8 Recognize several pressures faced by supervisors who are members of protected groups.

9 Explain the issue of reverse discrimination.

10 Understand how to best supervise a diverse workforce.

YOU MAKE THE CALL!

Assira Ali is a well-respected, dependable employee at Fairfield Bank and Trust. She has moved up the corporate ladder quickly because upper-level management recognized her commitment and dedication to the bank. Assira's coworkers enjoy working with her and find her well-organized, quick-witted, and fair. Five months ago, she was promoted to a low-level supervisory position.

One of Assira's new job duties is finding high-traffic locations for automated teller machines (ATMs). She welcomed the challenge of this new assignment and enjoyed the opportunity to market the bank and its ATMs to various retail stores, shopping malls, and government facilities.

This morning, Assira's boss, Marshall H. Watson III, who is the great-grandson of the bank's founder, called her into his office and said, "Assira, I knew you could do it. Only you could have placed fourteen ATMs around town so quickly and efficiently. Your contacts with local retailers have been flawless and very lucrative for the bank. On behalf of Fairfield Bank, I want to thank you. Also, Mr. Johnston, our president, wants me to pass along his sincere thanks. How about letting me take you to lunch?"

Assira smiled and said, "Why, yes, that sounds nice. Thank you, sir. But, I must say, I was only doing my job." As she went back to her office to gather her purse, Assira thought, "I've come a long way. It is nice to be singled out for good work. I'm glad Mr. Watson and Mr. Johnston

appreciate my contributions." Her spirits were high. As she and Watson were being seated for lunch, Watson asked what she wanted. Assira took a moment to look at the menu and asked Watson what he would recommend. Watson replied, "Oh, everything here is really good, but I meant, what would you like to drink in celebration of your raise and new title of assistant vice president?" Momentarily, Assira was taken aback. Then she asked, "Really? I've been promoted and given a pay raise?"

"Yes! That's why we're here! So let's celebrate! What would you like to drink?" Watson inquired. Assira bit her tongue, organized her thoughts, and looked Watson directly in the eyes. "Sir," she said, "I do not drink alcohol, but I will have a Coke."

Watson looked up at the server and said, "That will be two rum and Cokes, please."

Assira waited until the server left, and then said, "Mr. Watson, really—I don't drink alcohol. It goes against my religious beliefs."

Watson flippantly replied, "Oh, you'll get over that. All the assistant vice presidents under my direction like to have a good time and relieve stress by having a couple of drinks when we get together. You are a team player, aren't you?"

Assira replied, "Yes, sir, I am a team player, but—"

Watson cut her off and said, "Well, good. So let's make a toast." Assira sat back in her chair, feeling trapped. She didn't want to offend her boss, but she also didn't want to violate her religious beliefs. **YOU MAKE THE CALL!**

Managing Diversity is the Bottom-Line Concern

1 Define the concept of workplace diversity.

In Chapter 1, we presented an overview of some of the principal demographic and societal trends that impact organizations in general and supervision in particular. We mentioned that the increasingly diverse characteristics of people in the workplace have become a reality in organizational life that will continue to be among the major challenges facing managers at all levels.

The reality of diversity in the workplace, sometimes called the "multicultural workforce," was summarized rather well in two management journal articles:

> *Diversity is a reality. Just look around you. The American workforce is changing—in age, gender, race, national origin, sexual orientation, and physical ability. So are customers and suppliers. Minority populations are increasing in every part of our country. Workers 55 and older are the fastest-growing segment of the workforce. Communication and information technology is enabling more and more people with disabilities to enter the workforce.[1]*

Hispanics constitute the largest and fastest-growing minority in the United States. Projections call for the Hispanic population to nearly triple in size and account for most of the nation's population growth in the near future. Assisting language-challenged and culturally challenged Hispanics is a skill that many HR leaders and supervisors have never been trained for. All HR and supervisory activities must be adjusted for language and cultural integration.[2]

Because of these and other factors, diversity management now encompasses many considerations, including legal, demographic, economic, and political. Diversity management touches virtually all aspects of a firm's operations, especially on the supervisory level. Initiatives and efforts to better manage a diverse workforce are growing significantly, not just because of legal requirements or social considerations but also because there is a recognition that this has become an area of vital importance to a firm's long-term success and bottom-line results.[3] Figure 13.1 illustrates one company's recognition of the value of diversity.

FIGURE 13.1 The value of diversity

Reproduced with permission of MetLife and Director of Licensing, Peanuts, 2000.

Protected-Group Employees and Supervising Diversity

2 Identify the major categories of legally protected employees and general guidelines for supervising a diverse workforce.

Throughout this book, we have stressed that employees are individuals shaped by various forces from within and without the organization. In Chapter 12, we discussed how employees form groups and why supervisors should be aware of group dynamics. In this chapter, we focus on the need for supervisors to develop a special awareness, sensitivity, and adaptability to *protected-group employees*, a term that we recognize in a legal sense but one that also has many human dimensions.

The identification of employees who have been afforded special legal protection comes primarily from civil rights legislation, equal employment opportunity (EEO) regulations, and numerous court decisions. Various laws and regulations that govern employment policies and practices appear in Chapter 1 (see page 25). Areas of lawful and potentially unlawful inquiry during the selection process of job applicants were presented in Chapter 9. For our purposes in this chapter, we use the term **protected-group employees** to identify classes of employees who have been afforded certain legal protections in their employment situations. The underlying legal philosophy is that many individuals in these classes have been unfairly or illegally discriminated against or should be afforded special consideration to enhance their opportunities for fair treatment in employment.

Protected-group employees
Classes of employees who have been afforded certain legal protections in their employment situations

Reports by the U.S. Justice Department indicate that alleged discrimination in the workplace has escalated rapidly during the past two decades. In 2007, the EEOC (U.S. Equal Employment Opportunity Commission) resolved 82,792 charges of employment discrimination. The largest number of claims came from allegations of racial discrimination (37 percent), sexual harassment/gender (30.1 percent), age (23.2 percent), disability (21.4 percent), and national origin (11.4 percent).[4] Often, these cases allege employer discrimination in hiring, promoting, firing, pay and benefits, and opportunities for training due to a person's race, color, religion, gender, national origin, age, disability, or exercise of legal rights.

Plaintiffs in certain job bias cases have the right to a jury trial and can win compensatory and punitive damages. A review of lawsuits filed on behalf of employees who were allegedly discriminated against, harassed, or retaliated against for filing charges under the law has found many multimillion-dollar awards. Usually, the organization agrees to pay a sum of money and provide significant remedial relief to the aggrieved employees. The EEOC has vigorously prosecuted claims of harassment, especially cases involving teenagers, many of whom are in the workplace for the first time. Since 2004, the EEOC's Youth @Work Initiative has conducted thousands of programs to inform teens about their employment rights and responsibilities and to help employers create more positive work experiences for youth.[5]

Because employment discrimination laws can at times be quite complicated, we will not attempt to become too legalistic in our discussion.[6] Supervisors normally should refer questions that are of a legal or a compliance nature to higher management or to an appropriate human resources staff person. The human resources department usually will have the expertise to answer the supervisor's questions and to give appropriate advice. At times, human resources staff will seek outside legal counsel to determine what should be done regarding certain matters and to avoid legal difficulties.

CLASSIFICATIONS OF PROTECTED-GROUP EMPLOYEES

The protected-group employees we discuss in this chapter are classified according to:

- Racial/ethnic origin
- Sex (i.e., women)
- Physical or mental disability (i.e., disabled or handicapped)
- Age (i.e., over 40)
- Religion
- Military service (e.g., Vietnam-era or other veterans)

In this chapter, we do not directly discuss the emerging issues of gender orientation, such as discrimination against homosexuals. To date, homosexuality has not been given legally protected status by federal legislation, nor is it considered a disability. However, author Diane Cadrain noted that, "It's worthwhile for employers to take the basic steps, such as worker education and company policy reviews, in trying to make their workplaces more open to gay, lesbian, bisexual and transgender (GLBT) employees."[7]

The supervision of protected-group employees is, by definition, part of a firm's efforts to manage diversity so as to benefit both the firm and the employees. Regardless of personal views, supervisors must be sensitive to possible illegal discriminatory actions and adjust their supervisory practices accordingly. More important, however, is that supervisors recognize the strengths and potential contributions of all employees and supervise in ways that do not limit employees' development for inappropriate reasons (See Figure 13.2). Stated another way, effective supervision of a diversified workforce can be viewed as an opportunity to draw on and use the differences of people in a positive, productive, and enriching manner.

As discussed in previous chapters, incivility in the workplace is on the rise. It is a sad commentary on our society when certain inappropriate behaviors continue

FIGURE 13.2 Managing diversity means being aware of differences and managing employees as individuals. To manage diversity does not mean just recognizing and tolerating differences but also supporting and using the differences to the organization's advantage

unabated. Perhaps it is an escalation of the adage, "The squeaky wheel gets the grease." Indeed, rude, obnoxious, and inappropriate behavior appears to get more attention in the popular press and on late-night television talk shows than other, more important issues.[8] Harassment in the workplace has been unlawful for a long time, but it is still pervasive.

THE OUCH TEST IN SUPERVISING EMPLOYEES

The OUCH test, which we discussed in Chapter 9 as a guideline for selecting employees, also applies to day-to-day supervision. This test should remind supervisors to make their actions:

Objective

Uniform in application

Consistent in effect

Have job relatedness

For example, assume that an organization's policy specifies a disciplinary warning for being tardy three times in one month. The supervisor should give the same warning to every employee who is late the third time in one month, regardless of whether the employee is in a protected-group category. This supervisory approach would meet the OUCH test because tardiness is an observable behavior that is measured objectively for all employees. The penalty is the same for all employees, is consistent, and is clearly job-related.

A myth occasionally voiced by some supervisors is that certain categories of employees cannot be disciplined or discharged because of government regulations (Figure 13.3). This view is unfounded. Laws and regulations do not prevent a supervisor from taking disciplinary action against protected-group employees. However, they do require that such employees be treated the same as other employees whenever disciplinary actions are taken. Therefore, it is extremely important that supervisors be careful in meeting the OUCH test and in justifying

FIGURE 13.3 **A myth occasionally voiced by some supervisors is that protected-group employees cannot be disciplined or discharged**

their actions through adequate documentation. We discussed how to take appropriate disciplinary actions in considerable detail in Chapter 6.

3 Explain the issues involved in supervising racial/ethnic minority employees.

Supervising Racial and Ethnic Minorities

The most frequently identified racial and ethnic minority populations in the United States are African Americans (blacks), Hispanics, Asian Americans, and Native Americans. With the passage of major civil rights legislation, most employers have developed nondiscrimination and/or affirmative-action policies or programs for employing people from racial and ethnic minority groups. A major thrust of these policies and programs is to ensure that minorities, as well as certain other protected-group individuals, receive special consideration in hiring and promotion decisions. The philosophy underlying affirmative-action plans is to overcome the impact of past discriminatory practices and to provide greater opportunities for under-represented groups to participate more fully throughout the workforce. The long-term goal is to have a fully diversified workforce in which all employees are hired and supervised solely on the basis of their capabilities and performance.

While most organizations recognize the importance of integrating their workplaces, minorities still face substantial barriers. A Society for Human Resource Management (SHRM) survey indicated the following barriers for minorities:

- Limited education because of higher drop-out rates
- Lack of role models
- Language difficulties
- Limited mentoring opportunities
- Exclusion from informal networks
- Stereotypes or preconceptions based on race or ethnicity
- The perception that the corporate culture favors nonminorities[9]

A review of these barriers warrants another question: Why should qualified minority applicants join an organization when they can look and see that, in the past, no other minority has succeeded? If the adage "Success begets success" holds—that is, if a company is known as a great place for women and minorities—it follows that other qualified minority applicants will be attracted to the company.

Author Pamela Paul noted that "Americans do not see eye-to-eye on whether all races should have equal opportunities in education and the workplace and whether affirmative action itself is a 'discriminatory' policy."[10] Opponents and proponents of affirmative action alike have extensively debated the direction of affirmative action, both legally and as a practicality.

UNDERSTANDING DISCRIMINATION'S EFFECTS

Minority employees who have experienced prejudicial treatment may resent supervisors of different racial/ethnic backgrounds. The most common area of tension continues to be between African-American employees and Caucasian managers. Even though nondiscrimination laws have been in place for several decades, annual data compiled by the federal Equal Employment Opportunity Commission (EEOC) show that minority group members file tens of thousands of complaints about unfair treatment because of their race. Typically, alleged discriminatory discipline and discharge have been the most frequent bases for these complaints.

Because the responsibility for initiating discipline and discharge actions usually rests with supervisors, such decisions play a significant role in discrimination charges.[11] Charge investigation requires the extensive time, effort, and involvement of supervisors, human resources and legal specialists, and others. Therefore, supervisors must be sensitive to the feelings of minority employees who may have experienced discriminatory treatment in the past or who believe that they are currently experiencing discrimination. Supervisors should not enter into racial debates with minority employees who display lingering resentment and suspicion.

Rather, supervisors always should strive to be fair and considerate when making decisions that affect these employees. By demonstrating that minority employees will be supervised in the same manner as other employees, a supervisor can reduce the negative effects of past discrimination. In the event that a minority employee's feelings of resentment interfere with job performance or department relations, the supervisor should refer the employee to the human resources department.

APPRECIATING CULTURAL DIFFERENCES

A continuing debate about human behavior concerns how much heredity, as compared to environment, shapes an individual. Obviously, heredity is a major factor in the physical and ethnic makeup of a person. Moreover, because members of various races or ethnic origins often have different environmental experiences, unique subcultures have developed for each racial/ethnic minority group. For example, the ties that Native Americans have to their heritage reflect their subculture. People of Asian descent have distinctive values and traditions that reflect their heritage and cultures.

Unfortunately, differences in ethnic/cultural backgrounds can contribute to prejudicial attitudes and treatment of minority employees. For example, a minority employee's values regarding the importance of work and punctuality may differ from those of a supervisor. If a minority employee has not grown up

Supervisors must be sensitive to past and present effects of racial discrimination

© MICHAEL NEWMAN/PHOTOEDIT

in an environment that stresses the importance of punctuality, especially in a work situation, the supervisor must be prepared to spend extra time explaining to that employee the reasons for punctual attendance and the consequences of tardiness and absenteeism. Regardless of what cultural differences exist, it is the supervisor's job to exert special efforts to reduce the effects of these differences. By so doing, the supervisor can help the minority person learn to accept the requirements of the work environment and to meet the standards expected of all employees in the department.

As a result of the tragic circumstances of September 11, 2001, and the continued threat of terrorism, many individuals of Arab/Islamic descent have been subjected to various forms of harassment and negative stereotyping. If Arab/Islamic employees are working in a department with other employees, the supervisor must endeavor to make sure that any harassing conduct is not tolerated or condoned. The supervisor may want to discuss with the employees the cultural backgrounds and customs of Arab/Islamic people and to emphasize their positive contributions in the workplace. The supervisor may need to use the services of the human resources department to do so. For example, if Arab/Islamic employees need dress, appearance, and/or scheduling accommodations, these needs must be explained to other employees so that those employees can understand and accept them.

OVERCOMING LANGUAGE DIFFICULTIES

Another consideration in supervising minority employees relates to the different languages that may be spoken in a work environment. The 2000 census reported that 18 percent of all U.S. residents spoke a language other than English at home. Another census report contended that many Mexican-born immigrants and other Hispanics do not speak English well.[12] In an effort to familiarize non-English-speaking employees with the dominant language of the United States, an increasing number of employers sponsor English improvement and business English courses for minority employees. These programs focus on the writing and speaking skills needed for job improvement and advancement.[13] Some employers have held training programs to sensitize supervisors and managers to minority language patterns and to make those staff members more knowledgeable of the cultural and language backgrounds of certain minorities.

To accommodate non-English-speaking residents, states such as Indiana provide driver's license tests in the applicant's native language. The state also provides interpreters to assist in the process. One financial institution in Fort Wayne, Indiana, provides the same type of services to accommodate Burmese immigrants. Since opening in August 2007, the Citizens Union Bank branch in Shelby County, Kentucky, is operated by bilingual employees of Hispanic heritage, all of whom were involved in the branch's design. The branch has a different name, "Nuestro Banco," which means "Our Bank" in Spanish. Does it make good business sense to go this route? Twenty-five percent of Shelby County's population are Hispanic.[14]

Yet, other employers are still attempting to institute English-only requirements in the workplace. In an effort to appeal to fans and sponsors, the Ladies Professional Golf Association (LPGA) announced that the women's tour would require players to speak English by 2009 or face suspension. All players would have to pass an English-speaking proficiency exam. The plan was widely criticized as discriminatory, particularly against Asian players. Two weeks after announcing the plan, LPGA commissioner Carolyn Bivens said that the LPGA was backing off the original plan and would have a revised plan that would not include suspensions. Among the tour's 121 foreign golfers from 26 nations, there are 45 from South Korea. Asians won three of the four major championships in 2008.[15]

However, such restrictions today are viewed by courts and enforcement agencies with skepticism unless interpersonal communication is a critical part of the job. The number of complaints regarding language discrimination has increased more than fivefold in the past ten years. Most instances of language discrimination go unreported because employees fear retaliation, such as job loss, or deportation if they are illegal immigrants.

Consider the following illustrations. A manufacturing company's refusal to hire a Spanish-speaking worker on an assembly line might be ruled prejudicial because in that job, communication skills may be much less important than manual dexterity. However, for a salesperson in a department store or for a nurse working in an emergency room, adequate interpersonal language skills are essential. Is it reasonable for a retail store to require employees to speak English to customers? Yes, unless the customer wishes otherwise or unless the store is located in an area where a significant number of customers speak a native language other than English. In many parts of the United States, the English language is the minority language, and a bilingual person is a valuable asset. We encourage you to add that skill to your toolbox.

BEING FAIR IN ALL SUPERVISORY ACTIONS AND DECISIONS

Some minority employees are clustered in entry-level or service positions in which they see little potential for advancement. Others find themselves in job situations in which competition for better-paying and more challenging positions is keen. Tensions between majority and minority employees may be particularly noticeable when a minority employee alleges discrimination or unfair treatment in a job assignment, promotional opportunity, or disciplinary matter.

For all employees, but especially when minority employees are part of the departmental work group, supervisors should develop *cultural competency*. **Cultural competency** means that the supervisor is scrupulously fair, yet can adapt to a variety of cultural communities. When assigning work, affording training opportunities, conducting performance appraisals, or taking disciplinary actions—in virtually all supervisory actions and decisions—supervisors must make choices on objective and job-related grounds.

Cultural competency
The ability to adapt to a variety of cultural communities

If a minority employee complains of harassment or discriminatory treatment by a fellow employee, supervisor, or some other person, the supervisor must treat that complaint as a priority. In most cases, the supervisor should listen carefully to the nature of the complaint and report it to a higher-level manager or the human resources department for further consideration and direction. In no way should a supervisor retaliate against the minority person, even if the supervisor believes the discrimination or harassment allegation is without merit. The law protects a minority employee's right to challenge management decisions and actions that the employee believes are discriminatory. The supervisor is responsible for making sure that this right is protected. In summary, supervising racial/ethnic minority employees requires understanding, sensitivity, and even "extra fairness" when the supervisor is not a member of that minority group.

4 Discuss factors that are particularly important when supervising female employees.

Supervising Women

Throughout the past several decades, both the number and the percentage of women in the labor force have increased dramatically. While there is consensus that opportunities for women will increase during the first decade of the twenty-first century, there are still barriers. These barriers include the lack of females at the board level, male-dominated corporate cultures, stereotypes or preconceptions about women, exclusion from informal networks, and lack of mentoring opportunities.[16] Yet there have been several significant changes during the lifetimes of the authors, and they didn't come without sacrifice and effort. See Figure 13.4 for an overview of two women who made a difference.

Both male and female supervisors should be aware of a number of important concerns regarding the supervision of women. While not all-inclusive, the areas discussed here represent a range of issues supervisors should recognize and address appropriately.

ENTRY OF WOMEN INTO MANY CAREER FIELDS

The combined effects of antidiscrimination laws and affirmative-action programs and the increasing number of women in the workforce have led women into many jobs that were traditionally dominated by men. For example, in greater numbers than ever before, women are financiers, scientists, engineers, utility repair specialists, sales and technical representatives, accountants, and managers. However, a high percentage of women still work in clerical and service jobs.

The entry of women into jobs requiring hard physical labor and craft skills has been comparatively limited, but when women do assume craft or other physically demanding jobs, changes may occur. A number of firms have found that some equipment can be modified without excessive cost outlays. For example, there have been changes to the shape of some wrenches and other tools to accommodate women's smaller hands. Telephone companies have changed the mounting position for ladders on trucks used by outside repair employees to make those ladders easier for women to reach, and those companies have bought lightweight ladders that are easier to carry. Also, special clothing and shoes were developed so that females could have the proper protective equipment.

While women have surmounted many of the barriers that previously limited their entry into male-dominated positions, problems still occur, especially at the departmental level. One common supervisory consideration when a woman takes a job traditionally held by a man is the reaction of male coworkers. Some men may resent and even openly criticize her. The supervisor should be prepared to deal with such attitudes to enable the woman to perform her job satisfactorily. The supervisor first should inform the men about the starting employment date of the woman so that her presence does not come as a surprise. Then, the supervisor should make it clear to the men that disciplinary action will be taken if this woman, or any female employee in the future, is ignored or subjected to abuse or harassment. The supervisor also should make it clear that any woman taking a previously all-male job will be afforded a realistic opportunity to succeed based on her ability to perform the job.

© JAMES SCHAFFER/PHOTOEDIT

When women assume physically demanding jobs, some equipment and procedural changes may be needed

FIGURE 13.4 Two Women Who Changed the World

"We hold these truths to be self-evident...that all men are created equal"

—Thomas Jefferson (Preamble to the U.S. Constitution 2.1)

Meet Rosie the Riveter

Betty Hunter remembers her first job interview. It was the 1940s, and women were needed to fill jobs left vacant by men who had gone to war. But despite the demand for workers, management was reluctant to put an inexperienced woman on the factory floor. Millions of other women like Hunter worked in World War II defense industries and support services.

© CORBIS

During WWII, Ford Motor Company's Richmond, California, factory was converted from automotive to tank production to support the war effort. Prior to 1940, only three women had worked at the plant—a daytime telephone operator and two typists. But as an increasing number of men headed off to war, Ford's managers quickly learned that women made excellent industrial workers. In fact, in certain tasks, they even concluded that women were superior to men. Betty Hunter, like thousands of other women, became known as Rosie the Riveter. According to Tom Butt, president of the Rosie the Riveter Historic Trust, "It was the first time in American history that women and minorities worked side by side with men for almost comparable wages." During the closing months of the war, Ford hired an increasing number of people of color and women as other workers who had migrated to California to work in wartime industries headed home.

It is no coincidence that Ford Motor Company was again named one of *Working Mother* magazine's *100 Best Companies for Working Mothers in 2008.*[1]

Meet Rosa Parks

Rosa Parks, a grown woman of 42, refused to give up her seat on a bus in Montgomery, Alabama. She defied what was known as the Jim Crow law—"white-only perquisites"—which limited blacks to segregated restrooms and drinking fountains (if any were available), entrance into stores through the rear door only, and seats in the back of the bus.

© BETTMANN/CORBIS

By refusing to move, Parks committed a deliberate act of civil disobedience. What would have happened if she had moved to the back of the bus as commanded? We will never know, but the inescapable truth is that Parks's actions brought the notion that change was needed for America to "walk the talk." If the talk says that "all men (people) are created equal and have inalienable rights," then it was time to translate the talk into action.

Rosa Parks died in October 2005. President Bush and members of Congress laid wreaths at her bier as it rested in the U.S. Capitol. Yet her legacy lives today.[2]

"Freedom is never voluntarily given by the oppressor; it must be demanded by the oppressed."

—Martin Luther King, Jr.

Sources: (1) "American Women I Have Always Understood, Advertisement," *Working Mother* (November 2003), p. 1–1. The Rosie the Riveter WWII Home Front National Historic Park commemorates and celebrates women's contributions to the war effort. Visit the Rosie the Riveter Historic Trust, a nonprofit organization in Richmond, CA; and http://www.RosieTheRiveter.org. Also go to www.workingmother.com and click on "Best Companies" to see their programs to help women to be the best they can be. (2) See Kiva Albin, "Rosa Parks: The Woman Who Changed a Nation" (1996 Interview); *Quiet Strength* (Zondervan, 1994); and http://www.grandtimes.com/rosa.html. In November 1956, the U.S. Supreme Court ruled that segregation on public transport was unconstitutional.

BALANCING WORK/LIFE ISSUES

While only one-fourth of Americans currently live in a "traditional" family composed of a married couple and their children, the well-being of family is still critically important. In reality, whether one is a greeter at Wal-Mart or a waitress at Happy Burger, the issue is still the same—how to balance work/life issues. Meet Tanya, our mythical "waitress mom."

> *Tanya is in my Wednesday night church group. She would like to attend Sunday services, but she has to work. A single parent with two children ages 8 and 14, Tanya is fighting to provide the basic needs for her family. She goes to work Tuesday through Friday at 5:30 A.M.—before her kids are off to school—and comes home at 2:30 P.M. She also works every Friday night from 4:30 P.M. to 10:00 P.M. and Sunday mornings from 5:30 A.M. to 3:00 P.M. The wages are low, but the tips are good. Of course, her employer does not provide medical or dental insurance, so she and the kids often don't go to the doctor when they are feeling sick. When 8-year-old Brittany ran a high fever last week, Tanya took her to Matthew 25—a free clinic where the waiting lines are long and you are exposed to additional germs in the waiting room. She rationalizes that it is better than nothing. Yet there is a stigma attached to the clinic.*
>
> *Tanya was thinking about going to the community college, but she doesn't have the time or the money. The issue for Tanya is not equal pay for equal work or discrimination in the workplace but one of being overwhelmed by the demands of job and family. As I looked over at Tanya during the service, I noticed that she often yawned and looked tired. I wondered what I could do to help the low-income, no-longer-married "waitress mom."*

Tanya is among 72 percent of women who place work and life balance as the most important aspect of job satisfaction. By contrast, surveyed men placed that priority last.[17] Look around any organization and see how many people face similar concerns. The problems that Tanya faces must be addressed if she is to be "the best employee she can be." Supervisors must be diligent and observant and aware of the "baggage" that employees bring to the workplace. While not a member of a "protected class" of employees, Tanya and others like her need special accommodations so they can be productive employees. To that end, many large organizations and some smaller ones have developed a family-friendly culture.

SEXUAL-HARASSMENT AND SEXUAL-STEREOTYPING ISSUES

A growing number of civil rights and court cases in the United States have addressed the problems of sexual harassment. Sexual harassment usually means a female employee is subjected to sexual language, touching, or sexual advances by a male employee, a male supervisor, or a male customer. If a female employee resists or protests such behavior by a male supervisor, for example, she may fear retribution when the supervisor is considering pay raises or promotions. It is important to note that a female supervisor or a female employee can be charged with the sexual harassment of a male employee and that harassment can occur when both parties are of the same sex.[18] However, sexual harassment of women by men has been the focus of most cases heard by federal agencies and the courts.

Guidelines issued by the Equal Employment Opportunity Commission (EEOC), which enforces the federal Civil Rights Act, define **sexual harassment** as sexual advances, requests for sexual favors, and other verbal or physical conduct of a sexual nature when:

Sexual harassment
Unwelcome sexual advances, requests, or conduct when submission to such conduct is tied to the individual's continuing employment or advancement, unreasonably interferes with job performance, or creates a hostile work environment

- Submission to such conduct is explicitly or implicitly made a condition of an individual's employment;
- Submission to or rejection of such conduct by an individual is used as the basis for employment decisions affecting that person;
- Such conduct has the purpose or effect of unreasonably interfering with an individual's work performance or creating an intimidating, hostile, or offensive working environment.[19]

Many firms have developed sexual harassment policy statements. Figure 13.5 is an example of such a statement by a printing company that defines harassment even beyond gender terms. This statement informs employees what to do if they encounter what they consider to be harassment.

Court decisions have generally held that an employer is liable if the sexual harassment of employees is condoned or overlooked or fails to lead to corrective actions by management. Reprimand and discipline of offending employees and supervisors are recommended courses of action.[20]

Supervisors should avoid and strongly discourage sexual language, innuendos, and behavior that is inappropriate in the work environment. Supervisors who use their positions improperly in this regard are engaging in conduct that is unacceptable and could cause their own dismissals.

In Chapter 11, we stressed that "the best leaders have employees who would follow them anywhere." How would you feel if your highly compensated CEO is romantically involved with one of your colleagues? Consider the following:

The board of directors of Boeing Co. concluded from an internal investigation that President and CEO Harry Stonecipher had a "consensual relationship" with a female manager. They determined that the facts reflected poorly on Stonecipher's judgment and would impair his ability to lead the company and that the relationship violated the company's code of conduct. The female employee did not report directly to Stonecipher, who is married.[21]

FIGURE 13.5 Illustration of a No-Harassment Policy Statement

NO-HARASSMENT POLICY

This company does not and will not tolerate harassment of our employees. The term *harassment* includes, but is not limited to, slurs, jokes, and other verbal, graphic, or physical conduct relating to an individual's race, color, sex, religion, national origin, citizenship, age, or handicap. Harassment also includes sexual advances; requests for sexual favors; unwelcome or offensive touching; and other verbal, graphic, or physical conduct of a sexual nature.

VIOLATION OF THIS POLICY WILL SUBJECT AN EMPLOYEE TO DISCIPLINARY ACTION, UP TO AND INCLUDING IMMEDIATE DISCHARGE.

If you feel you are being harassed in any way by another employee or by a customer or vendor, you should make your feelings known to your supervisor immediately. The matter will be thoroughly investigated, and, where appropriate, disciplinary action will be taken. If you do not feel you can discuss the matter with your supervisor, or if you are dissatisfied with the way your complaint has been handled, please contact the human resources director or the company president. Your complaint will be kept as confidential as possible, and you will not be penalized in any way for reporting such conduct. Please do not assume that the company is aware of your problem. It is your responsibility to bring your complaints and concerns to our attention so that we can help resolve them.

Unfortunately, one study found that 47 percent of workers have had an office romance and another 17 percent would like to have an office romance if given the opportunity.[22]

Consensual workplace dating does not in and of itself constitute sexual harassment, but there may be harassment if the employee feels coerced to engage in or continue a relationship. Other employees who lose out on a promotion or pay raise that goes to the more favored person may also have discrimination claims against the organization. Worse yet, the organization may lose the faith and trust of its various stakeholders when the indiscretion becomes public knowledge.

Because it is virtually impossible to monitor everything that happens in the workplace, many firms have required their managers, supervisors, and employees to attend training programs or seminars designed to prevent and address sexual harassment. These programs are typically developed and presented by human resources staff or by outside training consultants. Information and discussions focus on prohibited types of conduct, how employees can deal with offensive comments and behavior, and remedies.[23] These programs also may cover certain aspects of sexual stereotyping that can be problematic.

Sexual stereotyping
Use of demeaning language or judgments, usually by men toward women

Sexual stereotyping means the use of demeaning language or judgments, usually by men toward women. For example, a department store supervisor may find that women buyers strongly resent being called "the girls," or a supervisor may imply that women are more emotional, less rational, and less reliable than men. Many assertions about female employees are inaccurate. For example, one large firm examined the absenteeism records of their male and female employees. This firm found no significant difference in absentee rates between the two genders, and it found that its female employees with children had a lower absentee rate than single men. Therefore, the supervisor should not make supervisory decisions based on sexual stereotypes.

To avoid gender implications, many job titles have been changed. For example, the job title "fireman" is now "firefighter," a "mailman" is now a "letter carrier," and a "stewardess" is now a "flight attendant."

TRAINING AND DEVELOPMENT OPPORTUNITIES

Women employees should be offered equal access to training and development activities, and those employees with potential should be encouraged to develop their skills. This is especially important with regard to upgrading women to supervisory and other managerial positions.

Despite the entry of women into supervisory and lower-level management positions, upward mobility for women in organizations has been slow. White males still hold the large majority of upper- and senior-level management positions. As mentioned in Chapter 1, the barrier to the upward progression of women and minorities is called "the glass ceiling." Firms that seriously try to bring more women and minorities into higher levels of management usually do so because their top management has strongly committed to diversity management initiatives within strategic business plans.[24] Many firms find that well-conceived and well-implemented mentoring programs are essential. Mentoring efforts usually involve having both male and female senior-level managers serve as mentors or advisors for women and minority supervisors who have been identified as having the potential to hold higher management positions. Mentors provide assistance in various ways, including feedback on job performance; career counseling; and networking with other mentors, advisees, and others to make them better-known to people who can influence promotion and career decisions.[25]

PREGNANCY AND FAMILY CARE

The Pregnancy Discrimination Act of 1978, which amended the 1964 Civil Rights Act, requires that pregnancy be treated no differently from illnesses or health disabilities if an employer has medical benefits or a disability plan. Additionally, many states have laws that require certain pregnancy benefits for employed women. In response, most employers have policies that allow a pregnant employee to work as long as she and her physician certify that it is appropriate. These policies also grant the pregnant employee a leave of absence until she can return to work. To prevent the abuse of pregnancy leaves or other types of disability leaves, many employers require a physician's statement to verify a continuing disability.

In Chapter 12, we briefly discussed the Family and Medical Leave Act (FMLA). The FMLA requires that an eligible employee (male or female) must be granted up to a total of 12 workweeks of unpaid leave during any 12-month period for the birth and care of the newborn child or placement with the employee of a child for adoption or foster care; to care for an immediate family member (spouse, child or parent) with a serious health condition; or to take medical leave when the employee is unable to work because of a serious health condition. Health-care coverage must be continued during this period, and he or she must be returned to their former position or a comparable position when they return to work.

While supervisors must see to it that pregnant employees are treated in a nondiscriminatory manner, they are not required to give them easier job assignments. A more difficult problem for the supervisor is a pregnant employee's uncertainty about returning to work after her pregnancy leave is over. This affects supervisors in scheduling work and anticipating staffing needs. Supervisors may have to hire part-time or temporary help, schedule overtime work, or take other temporary actions until the employee definitely decides whether and when she will return to work. This is not unduly burdensome if a supervisor plans well in advance to accommodate the employee's temporary absence.

Many employers have adapted their work scheduling, leaves, and other arrangements to alleviate family/job tensions

One of the well-recognized major problems that accompanied the growth of women in the labor force has been the conflict between the job demands placed on women and their family responsibilities. Women with children often must cope with demanding responsibilities at home, which are not always shared equally by their husbands.

Moreover, many women head single-parent households in which they are the primary provider. Because of concerns like these, many employers have adopted flexible policies concerning work schedules, leaves, and other arrangements to help employees, especially women, meet their obligations.[26] The FMLA also requires employers to grant unpaid leave to cover certain types of family-care situations, such as caring for a seriously ill child, spouse, or parent. Some legislative proposals would provide grants to assist in arranging child care for employees who must work and for whom no other care would be available.

Regardless of the outcome of any future legislation, the tension between family and job responsibilities is one that employers and supervisors will have to address for many years to come. Supervisors should become familiar

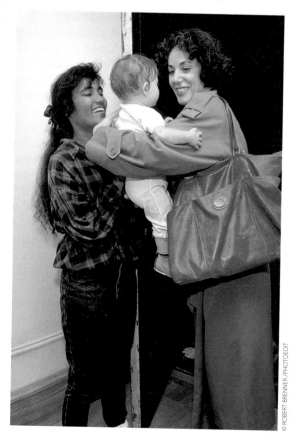

© ROBERT BRENNER /PHOTOEDIT

with their firm's policies regarding family- and child-care assistance, and, whenever possible, they should try to solve those conflicts that interfere with employees' capacities to carry out their job responsibilities.

EQUITABLE COMPENSATION

Statistically, the pay received by women employees in the U.S. workforce generally has been below that of men. According to the U.S. Bureau of Labor Statistics, the weekly earnings of women working full-time were 76.5 percent of those of men working full-time.[27] This statistical disparity exists even though the Equal Pay Act of 1963 requires that men and women performing equal work must receive equal pay. For example, a female bookkeeper and a male bookkeeper in the same firm who have approximately the same seniority and performance levels must be paid equally. Although equal pay has not always been interpreted to mean "exactly the same," a firm would probably be in violation of the Equal Pay Act if it paid the female bookkeeper $1 an hour less than her male counterpart.

Yet disparities still exist. A more complex reason for the disparity in the pay of men and women has been the issue of comparable worth. **Comparable worth** is a concept that jobs should draw approximately the same pay when they require similar skills and abilities. The issue arises when jobs that are distinctly different but require similar levels of skills and abilities have different pay scales, especially if one job is predominantly held by men and the other by women. For example, compare the job of medical technologist, which is held predominantly by women, with that of electrician, which is held mainly by men. Both jobs require licensing or certification, but medical technologists typically have more formal education. Now assume that the pay scales for medical technologists in a hospital are about one-third lower than those for electricians working in the same hospital. A comparison of these dissimilar jobs might suggest that unequal pay is being given for jobs of comparable worth.

A probable major cause for the difference in such pay scales is the labor market in the area. If unionized electricians are paid $28 per hour by other employers, the hospital would have to set its pay scale at that level to compete for electricians. Similarly, if the going rate for nonunionized medical technologists is $18 per hour, the hospital is likely to pay its medical technologists this rate. Also, the difference in pay may be attributable to numerous factors, including the supply or shortages of women in certain jobs. In the example cited, the reason the job of electrician is held predominantly by men is that, in the past, few women sought or were permitted to become electricians. Only by providing training and entry opportunities for qualified women to become electricians will the disparity in pay be eliminated. Likewise, men with the appropriate interests and abilities could be encouraged to become medical technologists.

It is important for supervisors to understand the issue of comparable worth because it may become a major issue. However, it is even more important for supervisors to identify and support qualified women to train and develop for higher-paying jobs that have been held predominantly by men. They should be willing to encourage, select, and assist these women as they progress into higher-paying positions of greater skill and responsibility.

Comparable worth
Concept that jobs should be paid at the same level when they require similar skills or abilities

5 Identify and discuss the legal and other considerations of supervising employees with physical and mental disabilities.

Supervising Employees With Disabilities

For decades, many organizations have made special efforts to provide employment opportunities for people with physical and mental disabilities. Many of these efforts were made voluntarily and from the conviction that it was the proper thing to do. However, as a result of a number of laws and government regulations, beginning with the Rehabilitation Act of 1973, people with disabilities were identified as a group that was to receive special consideration in employment and other organizational areas. The 1973 law used the term *handicapped* to define individuals with physical or mental impairments, but the preferred usage today is "individuals with disabilities." This law requires certain employers doing business with the federal government and federal agencies to develop affirmative-action programs and to reasonably accommodate the employment of such persons.

In 1990, the Americans with Disabilities Act (ADA) was passed. It is the most significant legislation dealing with legal protection for a group since the Civil Rights Act of 1964. The ADA applies to employers with fifteen or more employees and identifies coverage for people with disabilities. See Figure 13.6 for one company's ADA policy. The ADA requires employers to provide access to public spaces for people with disabilities and to make necessary alterations to public accommodations and commercial facilities for accessibility by people with disabilities.

The interpretation and application of the ADA has been the subject of a number of major court decisions. In one of its decisions, the U.S. Supreme Court took a somewhat restrictive view of what qualifies as a disability under the ADA. Generally, the court said the ADA does not protect from employment discrimination people with such physical impairments as poor eyesight or high blood pressure who can function normally when they wear glasses or take medication.[28] Nevertheless, supervisors should be familiar with major ADA provisions and, more important, ADA's implications for those supervising employees with disabilities.

FIGURE 13.6 One Company's ADA Policy

We are firmly committed to providing every employee and every applicant an equal opportunity to succeed in the workplace and during the application process. The company is committed to removing the barriers and obstacles that inhibit employees and applicants from performing to the best of their abilities, and giving them the opportunity to enjoy equal benefits and employment privileges.

It is our policy to provide reasonable accommodations to any qualified applicant or employee with a disability requesting such accommodation to complete the job application process or to perform the essential functions of his/her position. Reasonable accommodation may include, but is not limited to, making facilities accessible, restructuring jobs, modifying schedules, reassigning to a vacant position, acquiring or modifying equipment, and/or providing interpreters.

The Americans with Disabilities Act (ADA) defines a qualified individual with a disability as a person qualified to perform the essential functions of a position, with or without accommodation, who:

- Has a physical or mental impairment that substantially limits one or more of the person's major life activities;
- Has a record of such an impairment; or
- Is regarded as having such an impairment.

The company has developed, in cooperation with the Center for Independent Living, a Reasonable Accommodation Process to help management and employees handle reasonable accommodation issues. Additional information on this process can be obtained by contacting your human resources representative or the Center for Independent Living.

WHO IS A QUALIFIED DISABLED INDIVIDUAL?

**Qualified disabled
individual**
Defined by the Americans
with Disabilities Act (ADA)
as someone with a disability
who can perform the essential
components of a job with
or without reasonable
accommodation

To be protected under the ADA employment provisions, an individual with
a disability must be qualified. A **qualified disabled individual** is someone with a
disability who can perform the essential components of a job with or without
a reasonable accommodation on the part of the employer. This means that a
person with a disability must have the skills and other qualifications needed for
the job to receive employment protection under the ADA.

The definition of a disabled person is very broad. By some estimates, one in
six Americans could be considered disabled under the statute's definitions. The
law exempts a number of categories from its definition of disability. However,
the definition of disability covers most major diseases, including cancer, epilepsy,
diabetes, and HIV/AIDS.[29] The concept of reasonably accommodating individuals
with disabilities was established by the Rehabilitation Act of 1973. **Reasonable
accommodation** means altering the usual ways of doing things so that an
otherwise qualified disabled person can perform the essential duties of a job but
without creating an undue hardship for the employer. Undue hardship means an
alteration that would require a significant expense or an unreasonable change in
activities on the part of the employer to accommodate the disabled person.

Reasonable accommodation
Altering the usual ways
of doing things so that an
otherwise qualified disabled
person can perform the
essential job duties, but without
creating an undue hardship for
the employer

COMPLYING WITH THE ADA

To comply with ADA provisions, many employers conduct training programs
for supervisors who carry significant responsibility in making the necessary
adjustments. In the employment process, for example, an employer cannot require
a pre-employment medical examination to screen out applicants, with the exception
of a drug test. An employer also cannot make any type of pre-employment inquiries
about the nature of an applicant's disability. When discussing job requirements
in a pre-employment interview, supervisors must be cautious not to mention
the applicant's disability or medical record. However, after job offers have been
made, applicants may be given medical examinations to determine whether they
can physically perform the job. Most employers have reviewed their applications
to ensure that improper questions are not included. Many employers also have
revised their job descriptions to include the essential functions of each job.

Reasonable accommodation may take any number of forms. It typically
means making buildings accessible by building ramps, removing such barriers
as steps or curbs, and altering restroom facilities. Reasonable accommodation
may mean that desks and aisles are altered to allow people in wheelchairs access
to job locations. It could include modifying work schedules, acquiring certain
equipment or devices, providing readers or interpreters, and other types of
adjustments.

In some situations, job duties can be altered to accommodate people
with disabilities. The supervisor, in consultation with upper management, as
appropriate, should interact with employees to determine the accommodations
needed. The courts have generally held that an interactive process is the hallmark
of reasonable accommodation.[30] For example, in one company an employee
who assembled small component units also was expected to place the completed
units in a carton at the end of an assembly process. Several times a day, the full
carton had to be carried to the shipping area. For an employee in a wheelchair
to perform the subassembly job, the supervisor arranged for a shipping clerk to
pick up completed component units at designated times each day. This supervisor
made a reasonable accommodation so that a physically impaired employee could
handle the subassembly job. Another supervisor added a flashing warning light to
equipment that already contained a warning buzzer so that an employee with a
hearing impairment could be employed safely.

SUPERVISOR AND EMPLOYEE ATTITUDES

The ADA is aimed at changing perceptions as well as actions in the workplace. The law encourages supervisors and employees to recognize the abilities, rather than the disabilities, of coworkers and others. As much as anything else, attitudes play an important role in organizational efforts to accommodate people with disabilities.[31]

It is important that supervisors and employees recognize that the ADA is the law and that they believe it is proper to follow it. Training programs are aimed at allowing open discussion about different disabilities and opportunities to air questions and feelings of discomfort. Employees should be aware that certain words may unintentionally carry negative messages. For example, the ADA uses the term *disability* rather than *handicapped* because the former is the preference of most people with disabilities. Some training programs have used simulations in which non-disabled employees are required to experience certain types of mental, hearing, physical, or visual impairments (e.g., sitting in a wheelchair and trying to maneuver through a work area). This type of training helps employees to better understand the difficulties of coping with disabilities.

The type of disability an employee has may affect a supervisor's leadership style. For example, employees who are mentally disabled may require somewhat close and direct supervision. A physically disabled employee who uses a wheelchair and works as a proofreader probably should be supervised with a more general and participative style.

Much research has shown that individuals with disabilities make excellent employees, provided they are placed in jobs where their abilities can be adapted and used appropriately. As in so many other areas, the departmental supervisor is often the primary person to make this happen.

Supervising Older Workers

6 Discuss the considerations of supervising older workers.

There are a number of protected-group categories in addition to racial and ethnic minorities, women, and people with disabilities. A discussion of all the aspects of these categories is beyond the scope of this book. In this section, we highlight some of the supervisory considerations for older employees and employees who have different religious beliefs.

OLDER EMPLOYEES

At the dawn of the twenty-first century, those individuals who were born when John F. Kennedy was elected president turned 40 years of age. They joined the growing number of people in the U.S. labor force age 40 and older. Today, the number of workers age 40 or older comprise about half of the nation's workforce. This large segment constitutes another legally protected group. The Age Discrimination in Employment Act (ADEA), as amended, which applies to employers with twenty or more employees, prohibits discrimination in employment for most individuals over age 40. Consequently, mandatory retirement ages, such as at age 70, are illegal for most employees. Nevertheless, many workers retire at age 65 or younger, in part because of improved retirement programs and pension plans, including plans that allow early retirement. Some early retirement plans permit employees who have thirty years of service to retire before age 60. For varied reasons, many retired individuals decide to seek employment again, both part-time and full-time.

When deciding to hire, promote, or discharge, supervisors should be aware of the legal protections afforded older workers. For example, selecting a 35-year-old person for a sales position instead of a 55-year-old with more selling experience might result in an age-discrimination lawsuit. Laying off a 50-year-old engineer while keeping a 30-year-old engineer during a reduction in force might be age discrimination, unless the younger engineer has superior abilities.

Supervisory decisions to demote or terminate older employees should be documented with sound, objective performance appraisals. Terminating a 62-year-old clerical worker simply for "poor job performance" might be discriminatory if the employee's work performance was not objectively measured and compared with that of all employees in the department. Some supervisors complain that greater costs and inefficiencies are incurred when they are required to "carry" older workers who can no longer do the job. Regardless of whether this complaint is valid, the supervisor must impartially and objectively appraise the performance of all employees before making decisions that adversely affect older workers. As emphasized in Chapter 11, performance appraisal is a significant part of any supervisor's job, but it is especially important when older workers are in the department.

Proving age discrimination has been difficult as seen from the following example:

In 2000, Northbrook, Illinois-based Allstate (the "good hands" people) eliminated 6,500 agents—more than 90 percent of them over the age of 40. After the layoffs, Allstate rehired the agents as independent contractors, saving the company $600 million a year. Twenty-nine former employees considered the move as nothing more than outsourcing— Allstate outsourced the work to its former employees—and filed an age-discrimination suit. Why, they contend? "They did it because we're 'old' and because of the benefits." A federal judge in Philadelphia ruled that Allstate did not commit age discrimination because "workers of all ages were treated alike."[32]

Supervisors commonly manage employees older than themselves

© COMSTOCK RF/CORBIS

Supervisors often express concern about older workers who show declines in physical and mental abilities. While some older people do lose some of their former strengths on the job, they may be able to compensate by using their experience. Even with a decline in physical strength due to age, most firms report that older workers tend to have better quality, safety, and attendance records than do younger employees.[33]

Moreover, it may be possible, within certain limits, for supervisors to make special accommodations for some older employees. Supervisors should not disregard years of dedicated and faithful service. Adjustments in the older employee's workload, scheduling, and the like can be reasonable allowances that others in the work group can understand and accept, particularly those who are themselves advancing in years and who recognize that someday their capabilities might also diminish.

It is common for newly elevated supervisors to supervise employees old enough to be their parents, which is the proverbial "generation gap." Some older employees will reject the new supervisor and will resist changing their habits and learning new ways. In these situations, the supervisor must open the channels of communication, ask probing questions, avoid putting the older employees on the defensive, listen actively to the older employees' ideas—most older employees have a wealth of experience and information—and involve those employees in the decision-making process. Supervisors must use common sense and sound supervisory practices with older employees.[34]

Older employees who are approaching retirement present another problem that requires sensitivity from supervisors. Some employees who have worked for thirty years or more look forward to retirement as a time to enjoy leisure activities. Others, however, view retirement with anxieties about losing the security of a daily routine, steady income, and established social relationships.

Supervisors should be supportive and understanding as older employees near retirement. These employees should be encouraged to take advantage of pre-retirement planning activities that may be available in the company or through outside agencies. Some companies allow employees nearing retirement age to attend retirement-related workshops during work hours, without loss of pay. A member of the human resources department or a benefits specialist may spend considerable time with each employee nearing retirement to discuss pensions, insurance, Social Security, and other financial matters. Supervisors should encourage recent retirees to attend company social functions and to maintain contact with their former supervisors and coworkers wherever possible. Such contacts are valuable aids for those transitioning to retirement.

ACCOMMODATING DIFFERENT RELIGIOUS BELIEFS

7 Provide examples of religious accommodation.

Under the Civil Rights Act, most employers are required to afford nondiscriminatory treatment to employees who hold different religious views. Although EEOC and court decisions have not always clearly defined religious discrimination, two principles have evolved, which are:

1. Employers must make reasonable accommodations for employees with differing religious beliefs.
2. An employee may not create a hostile work environment for others by harassing them about what they do or do not believe.[35]

Employers generally may not discriminate in employment practices because of an individual's religious beliefs, and employers are obligated to prevent practices or actions that might constitute a "hostile environment" for someone based on religion.[36] There are some exclusions from the coverage of the Civil Rights Act; for example, a Methodist Church may require that only members of that faith be employed in their operations.

Relatively speaking, charges of religious discrimination have been limited. Reasonable accommodation in holiday and other work scheduling has been the most recurring area in which employers have had some compliance problems. For example, employees who follow the orthodox Jewish faith consider Saturday, not Sunday, the day of religious observance. Requiring such employees to work on Saturday would be the same as requiring employees who are members of some fundamentalist Christian sects to work on Sundays. A supervisor might be able to accommodate the religious views of such employees by scheduling their workweeks in ways that consider their religious preferences. Allowing Jewish employees to take holidays on Rosh Hashanah and Yom Kippur, instead of Christmas and Easter, is another example of accommodation, as is recognition of Ramadan for individuals of the Islamic (Muslim) faith.

Supervisors may confront situations in which it is difficult to accommodate all employees' religious preferences and still schedule the work. When this happens, supervisors should discuss the problem with their managers and with the human resources staff to determine whether scheduling alternatives that might accommodate the employees and yet not be too costly or disruptive are available.

Protected-Group Supervisors

8 Recognize several pressures faced by supervisors who are members of protected groups.

Thus far, we have discussed how the supervision of legally protected employees requires both awareness and sensitivity to various factors. Additional concerns can arise for supervisors who are themselves members of legally protected categories (e.g., minorities and women) and who may experience resistance and resentment in their supervisory positions.

For example, it is common to find a woman manager or supervisor whose subordinates primarily are men. Skepticism about the qualifications of the woman supervisor may be voiced in men's comments, such as, "She didn't deserve the job" or "She got it because she's female." A woman supervisor in such a situation may feel that she has to accomplish more than a male supervisor might be expected to achieve in a similar job. However, the experiences of many women supervisors indicate that once they have proven their competence, most initial skepticism fades.

Another example might be an African-American production supervisor in a manufacturing plant who supervises African-American employees. Because the supervisor is of the same race as the subordinates, some employees may try to take advantage of the situation, perhaps by taking more extended breaks than allowed. On the other hand, the supervisor may put greater pressure on African-American employees to perform and to obey the rules so that no charge of favoritism can be justified.

Similarly, the female supervisor who feels obliged to accomplish more than her male counterparts and who wishes to avoid charges of favoritism toward female subordinates may put greater pressure on women employees. This tendency has led some women employees to say that they would rather work for male supervisors because female supervisors are tougher on them than are men.[37]

On the other hand, it is recognized that, in general, supervisors tend to be able to communicate better with subordinates who are of the same race or the same sex. For example, an Asian-American supervisor is likely to better understand the culture, speech patterns, and attitudes of Asian-American employees.

Problems like those cited here are not unusual, and they should even be anticipated by supervisors or potential supervisors. It is helpful when such issues are discussed openly in supervisory training and development meetings. In addition, protected-group supervisors, like all other supervisors, must have performance expectations, policies, and decisions that are applied consistently and uniformly to all employees, regardless of race, gender, age, and other such considerations.

Understanding Reverse Discrimination

9 Explain the issue of reverse discrimination.

The reactions of employees who are not members of a legally protected group to hiring and promotion decisions are another challenge for supervisors. These employees may view the promotion of a protected-group employee as reverse discrimination. **Reverse discrimination** may be charged when a more senior or qualified person is denied a job opportunity or promotion because preference has been given to a protected-group individual who may be less qualified or who has less seniority.

In a Supreme Court case, the court ruled that the ADEA can't be used by younger workers when employers offer better contract terms to older employees. In 1997, a General Dynamics unit and the UAW agreed to stop providing healthcare coverage to future retirees except those current employees who were at least 50 years old, who would continue to be insured upon retirement. Younger workers sued, claiming they were being discriminated against. Writing for the majority opinion, Justice Souter said that the "notion of younger workers covered by the act bringing lawsuits was never contemplated by the Congress. We see the text, structure, purpose and history of ADEA . . . as showing that the statute does not mean to stop an employer from favoring an older employee over a younger one."[38]

EEO and affirmative-action programs most often impact white male employees. Some white males feel they lack an equal or a fair opportunity to compete for promotions or higher-paying jobs. They interpret the numerical goals of affirmative-action programs as quotas that must be met by hiring and promoting unqualified or less-qualified women and minorities.[39]

Supervisors of integrated racial groups and male and female employees may be apprehensive of their situations. For example, supervisors may be reluctant to discipline anyone so as to avoid charges of favoritism or discrimination. Another difficulty is that conflicts and distrust among these various groups may arise and stress interpersonal relationships, thereby impeding the performance of the department. Such problems are not easily overcome. Communication between the supervisor and all groups of employees is essential, and the supervisor should try to correct misperceptions about any employee's abilities and qualifications as they occur. Whether reverse discrimination exists is not really important. Rather, what is important is the supervisor's response to the feelings of all groups and individuals in an understanding, fair, and objective manner.

Reverse discrimination
Preference given to protected-group members in hiring and promotion over more qualified or more experienced workers from non-protected groups

Supervising Well: The Overriding Consideration

10 Understand how to best supervise a diverse workforce.

The issues discussed in this chapter will likely concern supervisors for years to come. Additional legislation and court decisions will specify and clarify other considerations for currently protected groups and, perhaps, for other groups to be identified in the future.

Although the diversity and complexity of the workforce varies, a supervisor can take several steps to reduce the likelihood of litigation and to deal with complaints and charges. The accompanying Supervisory Tips box presents some suggestions for how supervisors can address diversity issues positively and professionally. Supervisors must adapt their ways of managing their departments to meet the considerations afforded legally protected employees. In this effort, supervisors should always recognize that the best way to manage all employees in their departments—protected or not—is to constantly apply the principles of good supervision as presented throughout this book.

We stated at the outset of this chapter that the management of a diverse workforce is a reality that affects most aspects of organizational operations and

SUPERVISORY TIPS
Suggestions for Managing Diversity

- Make sure that the organization's policy statement on discrimination and harassment is posted in a prominent, visible place in the department or elsewhere.
- Periodically review this policy statement with employees, including procedures to be followed if an employee wishes to report a perceived violation or to lodge a complaint. Assure employees that any such complaint will initially be handled confidentially.
- Discuss diversity issues with employees at departmental meetings. Provide examples of behaviors that are unacceptable and that will not be tolerated, as well as the consequences of violations.
- Whenever an employee alleges discrimination or harassment, investigate the matter thoroughly and identify the appropriate course of action. Seek

- assistance from higher management or the director of human resources, if needed.
- If a matter cannot be resolved at the supervisory level, expeditiously report the case to the director of human resources or other such person who is designated to handle discrimination complaints at the company or corporate level.
- Do not in any way react negatively or adversely to an employee who has filed a discrimination or harassment charge.
- Always supervise on a scrupulously fair and objective basis and with equitable performance standards. Try to find ways by which all employees have the same or comparable opportunities at work assignments and training and development programs.

that impacts a firm's bottom line.[40] Because of their importance, specialized training programs in diversity management have expanded. In our view, supervision of diversity should not be viewed as something extra or separate. Supervision of diversity is, and will continue to be, an integral and significant component of good supervision that effective supervisors recognize as part of their ongoing responsibilities and challenges.

SUMMARY

1 The diverse nature of the U.S. workforce requires supervisors to manage the diverse people in the workforce who help achieve the firm's overall advantage and bottom-line results. Diversity management can impact virtually all aspects of a firm's operations and should be viewed by supervisors as both a challenge and an opportunity.

2 Protected-group employees are classified predominantly by racial/ethnic origin, sex, age, physical and mental impairment, and religion.

Supervisors must be aware of the legal protections afforded protected-group employees and understand that legislation is part of supervising a diversified workforce. All employees should be supervised in a fair and objective manner that focuses on their talents, abilities, and potential contributions.

3 When supervising racial/ethnic minority employees, supervisors should try to reduce the impact of past

discrimination. Awareness of cultural factors and recognition of language differences are important aspects of a supervisor's sensitivities to minority employees. Being scrupulously fair in all aspects of supervision and striving to prevent any type of discriminatory treatment toward minorities are essential.

4 Supervisors must try to ensure that women are provided fair opportunities as they move into a greater variety of career fields and positions. Avoidance of sexual harassment and stereotyping is mandatory. Human resources policies should stress training and development opportunities for women, nondiscriminatory treatment during pregnancy, flexibility in resolving family-care conflicts and problems, and equity in compensation.

5 The Americans with Disabilities Act (ADA) prohibits employment discrimination for individuals with physical and mental disabilities. The ADA prohibits certain pre-employment inquiries and physical examinations of job applicants. It also requires employers to reasonably accommodate otherwise qualified disabled individuals who can perform the essential components of a job. People with disabilities who are placed in jobs that are consistent with their capabilities and who are given fair opportunities to perform by their supervisors typically become excellent employees.

6 The Age Discrimination in Employment Act prohibits discrimination against most employees over age 40. Supervisors should objectively appraise the qualifications and performance of older employees. Supervisors should try to adjust to the reduced abilities of some older workers. Also, supervisors should help employees who are nearing retirement to prepare for retirement.

7 The principle of reasonable accommodation also should apply when supervising employees of different religious beliefs. Reasonable adjustments in work scheduling should be afforded individuals with certain religious requirements.

8 The supervisor who is a member of a protected group may encounter pressures from both protected-group and non-protected-group employees. These pressures typically involve questions about qualifications and fair treatment. The supervisor should act so that all employees are provided uniform and consistent/equal treatment and performance expectations.

9 Supervisors should be sensitive to the feelings of some employees—most often white males—about the issue of reverse discrimination. Employees may accuse the company of reverse discrimination if a protected-group person is hired or promoted over a more experienced or more qualified member of a non-protected group.

10 No matter how future legislation and court decisions affect the issues related to protected groups, the best way to manage will always be to apply the principles of good supervision to all employees.

KEY TERMS

Comparable worth (p. 472)
Cultural competency (p. 465)
Protected-group employees (p. 459)

Qualified disabled individual (p. 474)
Reasonable accommodation (p. 474)
Reverse discrimination (p. 479)

Sexual harassment (p. 468)
Sexual stereotyping (p. 470)

QUESTIONS FOR DISCUSSION

1. Who are classified as protected-group employees? Does "protected group" mean the same as a "special" or "privileged group," especially given affirmative-action requirements that may be present in a firm? Discuss.

2. A recent survey indicates that nearly half of the 76 million U.S. baby boomers are experiencing some degree of hearing loss. During a recent performance appraisal meeting, an employee in the call center explained that the reason for his "less than satisfactory" performance rating is due to his hearing loss. Is that a legitimate excuse? Why or why not? What accommodation might be needed?

3. Give examples of harassment that you have experienced, observed, or heard about, and describe what should have been done to address such issues.

4. How has the ADA expanded legal protections for individuals with disabilities? Discuss:
   a. The ADA's definition of a "disabled" person; and
   b. What is meant by "reasonable accommodation" for someone with a disability to perform the "essential functions" of a job.
   c. Why will these areas be difficult for supervisors to comply with in certain job situations?

5. How does the concept of reasonable accommodation apply to older workers and to employees of different religious persuasions? Are there limits to reasonable accommodation? Discuss.

SKILLS APPLICATIONS

Skills Application 13-1: You Make the Call!

Refer to the chapter's opening "You Make the Call!" As a newly promoted assistant vice president, Assira Ali's special moment has turned into a significant emotional experience. In the five months she has worked for Marshall H. Watson III, Watson has behaved appropriately.

1. Why do you think that Watson III fails to listen when Assira says, "I don't drink alcohol. It goes against my religious beliefs."?

2. In your opinion, does the behavior of Watson create a hostile work environment for Assira? Why? Why not?

3. For these questions, assume that you are Assira Ali. When Watson says, "Let's make a toast," what would you do?
   a. What are the risks associated with your response?
   b. What should you do to make certain that Watson fully understands the importance of the values you hold?

4. Based on your work experiences, what could top management or members of the management team have done to promote a cultural change, i.e., acceptance and appreciation of diversity, that would help improve the overall effectiveness of the organization.

5. In fifty words or less, highlight what you learned from this skills application.

Skills Application 13-2: Test Your Knowledge and Practice Your Skills

 You will confront many of the following situations. In reality, you will have a human resources professional or legal counsel to help guide your decision; however, for the skills application, you are the final arbiter. After reading each situation, use the Internet or library resources to research the legal implications of the question. Then answer the questions at the end of each situation. You are the manager of the housekeeping services department at Community Medical Center's (CMC's) Frankton facility. Your department is responsible for 24/7 coverage.

Situation 1: Recent staffing changes require a rotating work schedule for all shift supervisors. Jim, who was hired six years ago to supervise the early shift, has never been scheduled to work on Sundays. He informs you that he will not be able to work this Sunday as scheduled due to his religious beliefs. Can you terminate him if he fails to come to work as scheduled? Why or why not?

Situation 2: Simonette has worked for you for the past seven months. During this time, she has worked slightly less than 1,400 hours. She wants to be off each Friday and Monday for the next few months to care for an ailing cousin who is dying of cancer. She has accumulated 36 hours of PTO (paid time off). She would like to take leave under FLMA. Would you allow her to take leave under the FLMA? Why or why not?

Situation 3: Due to the closing of a wing, you have had to reassign several employees from the first shift to the second and third shifts. This reassignment was done per hospital policy and past practice. Emily Pearson told you she would not accept the transfer to second shift (3:30 P.M. to 11:30 P.M.) because she claimed to be protected under the ADA and the organization must accommodate her request. In discussions with you, she brought in a medical slip that indicated that she suffered from colitis (an intestinal disorder), tiredness, nausea, and diarrhea. Emily claimed that due to her medical impairments, you must accommodate her request to remain on the first shift. Would you grant Emily's request for reasonable accommodation. Why or why not?

Situation 4: You received a complaint from Mindy Martinez regarding one of the physicians, Dr. Daniel Johnson. Mindy claims that Dr. Johnson has been casually making suggestive remarks toward her for the past several weeks. She initially ignored his remarks, thinking he would quit and take his attention elsewhere. Mindy—a single mother of two—explained to Dr. Johnson that his attention was not welcome and that she wanted it to stop. According to Mindy, that only increased Dr. Johnson's attentiveness. Mindy is upset and wants you to do something about it. CMC views its physicians as "sacred cows," and the vice president of Medical Services is the only one who has authority over the physicians. Do you view Dr. Johnson's actions as sexual harassment? Why or why not? What do you do about Mindy's complaint?

Situation 5: John Daniel "Jackie" Phillips works in the laundry. Jackie recently "came out" and has affirmed his sexuality by becoming an activist in the local gay rights movement. Jackie worked 2,018 hours during the past twelve months. He has requested that he be granted twelve weeks of leave to care for his companion who is dying of AIDS. Would you allow Jackie to take leave under FMLA? Why or why not?

Role-Play Exercise Opportunity

 These situations make excellent role-play situations. We suggest dividing the class into five groups—one group for each situation.

Option 1: Prior to class, one person should be selected to play the role of department supervisor for each situation. Another person should be selected to play the role of CMC's human resources director for that situation. Other class members will serve as observers.

The supervisor and the director of HR should brainstorm options for handling the question posed in each situation. They should reach an agreement as to how to handle the issue.

The observers should evaluate the decision made by the HR director and the supervisor and identify the important factors used to arrive at the decision.

Option 2: Prior to class, one person should be selected to play the role of department supervisor for each situation. Another person should be selected to play the role of CMC's human resources director for that situation, and a third person should be selected to play the role of the employee raising the concern. Other class members will serve as observers.

The supervisor and the HR director should communicate their decision to the employee.

Observers will feed back their observations. If there are differences of opinion, to what could the differences be attributed, considering all participants have the same base of information?

Each participant, including the observers, should write a one-page paper critiquing the quality of the decisions made and the effectiveness of the meeting. Be sure to ascertain if the decision is legally defensible.

Source: Adapted with permission from scenarios developed by Professor Leonard for inclusion in Edwin C. Leonard, Jr., and Roy A. Cook, *Human Resource Management: 21st Century Challenges* (Mason, OH: Thomson Custom Publishing, 2005), pp. 190–1; 204–5.

Skills Application 13-3: Attitudes toward People with Disabilities and the Americans with Disabilities Act (ADA)

Following are statements that relate to attitudes toward disabled people and the ADA.

1. Mark each statement according to how much you agree or disagree with it, using the following scale:
   Strongly Agree (SA)   Agree (A)
   Disagree (D)   Strongly Disagree (SD)

   ___ 1. Individuals with severe disabilities cannot compete for jobs that require demanding physical and mental capabilities.

   ___ 2. Under the ADA, an employer can expect just as much from a disabled person as from anyone else.

   ___ 3. People with disabilities are usually more conscientious and reliable at work than other employees.

   ___ 4. Most people with severe disabilities expect others to show them sympathy and to give them extra help to hold a job.

   ___ 5. Employers will find that the ADA is impossible to comply with in many situations without extraordinary costs and efforts.

   ___ 6. The ADA will benefit attorneys far more than it will help people with disabilities.

   ___ 7. Compliance with the ADA will cause considerable resentment toward people with disabilities.

   ___ 8. The ADA is morally and ethically appropriate and helps qualified disabled individuals become more self-sufficient.

   ___ 9. People with disabilities are usually more cheerful and enthusiastic on the job than other employees.

   ___10. Reasonable accommodation under the ADA really means that people with disabilities receive preferential treatment.

2. Answer the following question: Why would awareness of attitudes toward people with disabilities and the ADA be important to supervisors?

3. Compare your responses to those of others. What common views do you have? What are your areas of difference? Discuss the bases for your differences of opinion.

Skills Application 13-4: Working with People that Make Your Life Difficult: "Bean the Bigot"

This is the latest in a series of skills applications that introduces one of those people who make life difficult for others.

1. Read the following statement from Barbara Jones, one of the employees at Sanders Supermarkets Store 17:

   I work part-time at one of the Sanders Supermarkets Stores, and I work with people of different races, religions, and ethnic backgrounds. Most of the associates and I get along very well with one another—except for a college freshman named Billy Bean. Bean is very close-minded and dislikes anyone different from him. Even though he is relatively new to the organization—he started in August just before school started—he often makes degrading comments toward coworkers who aren't like him.

   Bean loves to make fun at the expense of others. Yesterday, his target was Charlie, one of the produce clerks. Charlie does look like he is pregnant, and his shirt is always sticking out in the back. In the break room, Bean grabbed Charlie's right arm and in a loud voice said, "Do you know what this is for? It's for pushing yourself away from the

   food table, you fatty." Several people laughed, but most of us did not find it funny.

   Last week, Bean's target was Angie. Without warning, he pointed his finger at her and shouted, "U-G-L-Y. You ain't got no alibi. You're the ugliest thing I've ever seen. How can you stand to look at yourself in the mirror in the morning?" Again, several associates chortled. Angie didn't respond to Bean's baiting, but she stormed out of the break room.

   The situation is no different when Bean is around an African-American associate like me. He is known to have racial prejudices and will often spout comments like, "You wouldn't have a job if it wasn't for that affirmative-action crap," and is known to make racist "jokes."

   I know we'll encounter difficult people in life, but Bean is like a boxer. He constantly jabs at vulnerable individuals, hoping to bring them down. I'm really frustrated by his lack of sensitivity. I'd complain to management, but I don't think it would make a difference. I'm just a part-time employee, and I need this job. What should I do to make this work environment a bit more enjoyable?

2. **(INTERNET ACTIVITY)** Using the Internet, find at least three sources of information for working with people like "Bean the Bigot." Carefully review each site for suggestions on how to deal with bigotry and prejudice.

3. Based on your findings, what suggestions would you make to Barbara Jones on how to deal with Bean?

4. Write a one-page paper explaining how this skills application increased your working knowledge of coping with the behaviors of this type of difficult person.

SKILLS DEVELOPMENT

Skills Development Module 13-1: Whirlpool Promotes a Diverse Workforce

 This skills development module illustrates how Whirlpool Corporation uses its diverse workforce to an advantage. Before you view the video clip, you might want to visit Whirlpool's Web site (http://www.whirlpoolcorp.com) and click on "History," "About Whirlpool," and view the video story of Whirlpool Corporation.

Whirlpool Corporation is the world's leading manufacturer and marketer of major home appliances. With more

than 70,000 employees, Whirlpool believes that innovative thinking comes from anyone and anywhere within the company. In 1999, Whirlpool launched a worldwide effort to instill innovation as a core competency.

To understand more about Whirlpool's diversity and engagement efforts, watch the Skills Development Module 13-1 video clip.

Questions for Discussion

1. Review the following comments from the video clip: "One of the great challenges and joys of management is putting together a cohesive team of diverse individuals." "The greatest strength of our employee base today is their diversity."

   a. Most organizations have no official definition of diversity. What is your definition of workplace diversity? What do you suppose Whirlpool meant in the two statements above?

   b. Based on your work experiences, could these statements have been made in good faith by your employer? Give a couple of specific examples to support your answer.

   c. Describe how Whirlpool is using diversity as a competitive advantage.

   d. Do the benefits of diversity outweigh the costs of policies, programs, and accommodations desired by diverse employees? Why or why not?

2. Findings from a May 2008 Pew Research survey found that Hispanic women in the U.S. who work full-time earn a median weekly salary of $460, while non-Hispanic women earn $615 per week.

   a. Why might there be "glass compensation walls" for Hispanic women?

   b. Based on what you saw in the video clip or by reviewing Whirlpool's Web site, what conclusion would you draw about its treatment of employees?

3. In a workplace with a diverse workforce such as Whirlpool's, what impact would an English-only rule have on productivity?

ENDNOTES

Suggestions: The following references provide current information on the diversity of the U.S. workforce. (1) Pew Hispanic Center (http://pewresearch.org). The Pew Research Group conducts research on many workplace-related issues. (2) The Equal Employment Opportunity Commission (http://www.eeoc.gov). The EEOC issues a yearly workforce report. (3) *The Monthly Labor Review.* See Mitra Toossi, "A New Look at Long-Term Labor Force Projections to 2050," (November 2006). (4) "Selected Cross-Cultural Factors in Human Resource Management," *SHRM Research Quarterly* (Third Quarter- 2008) (www.shrm.org).

Supervisors will need to understand and comply with the ever-changing employment and labor laws. Refer to Figure 1–8 and periodically review the following: *Age Discrimination Employment Act, Americans with Disabilities Act, Civil Rights Act of 1964 (Title VII), Equal Pay Act, Fair Labor Standards Act, Family and Medical Leave Act (FMLA), Older Workers Benefit Protection Act, Worker's Compensations, Worker's Adjustment and Retraining Notification Act (WARN).*

October is National Disability Employment Awareness Month. See the U.S. Department of Labor's Office of Disability Employment Policy

(ODEP) Web site (www.dol.gov/odep) for profiles on organizations that have successfully implemented strategies to hire, support and empower employees with disabilities.

1. Adapted from Genevieve Capowksi, "Managing Diversity," *Management Review* (June 1996), pp. 13–19. For a comprehensive overview, see Rebecca R. Hastings, "SHRM 2007 State of Workplace Diversity Management Report: A Call to Action," *SHRM Workplace Diversity Library* (February 2008); Desda Moss, "Ten Changes that Rocked HR: Diversifying Demographics," *HR Magazine* (50th Anniversary 2005), p. 37; and Eva Kaplan-Leiserson, "The Changing Workforce: Findings from 'Generation and Gender in the Workplace,'" *Training & Development* (February 2005), p. 14. The demographics of the U.S. workforce have changed drastically in the past fifty years. See "Then & Now," *HR Magazine* (50th Anniversary 2005), p. 80.

   For a different perspective, see "The Conference Board Report: Middle Management: A Roadblock to Diversity Initiatives," *Supervision*, 68, 7 (July 2007), pp.8–10; and Michael Jones, "The Downside of Diversity," *The Boston Globe* (August 5, 2007, http://www.boston.com/news/globe/ideas/articles/2007/0805/the_downside_of_diversity/). Harvard researcher Robert Putnam found that the greater the diversity in a community, the fewer people vote and the less they volunteer, the less they give to charity and work on community projects. His conclusion: Diversity hurts civic life.

   The U.S. Department of Labor Bureau of Labor Statistics provides up-to-date projections and percentages in most demographic categories. Go to http://www.bls.gov for detailed information.

   Jim Giulliano, "Diversity Programs: Reap the Benefits While Avoiding Problems," (April 4, 2008, http://www.hrmorning.com/diversity) identifies three lessons of avoiding the problems: (1) Make sure everyone gets a fair shake. (2) Commit to treating all people equally and with respect. (3) Make certain that no one group is provided with an advantage or penalized with a disadvantage. His suggestions sound like common sense, but then why do we still have problems?

2. Quote adapted from information contained in the Susan J. Wells, "The Majority Minority," *HR Magazine* (September 2008), pp. 38–43.

3. Ann Pomeroy, "A Passion for Diversity," *HR Magazine* (March 2008), pp. 48–19; Bill Leonard, "Measuring Diversity's Value Remains Elusive Task," *SHRM Home* (January 18, 2006); Pamela Babcock, "Diversity—Down to the Letter," *HR Magazine* (June 2004), pp. 90–94.

   Also see Patricia M. Buhler, "Managing in the New Millennium: Interpersonal Skills," *Supervision* (July 2005), pp. 20–22.

4. Data gathered from http://www.eeoc.gov (accessed August 2008). Also see, Mitra Toossi, "A New Look at Long-Term Labor Force Projections to 2050," *Monthly Labor Review* (November 2006), pp. 19–39. According to Toossi, "Minorities, with higher population growth through immigration, higher fertility rates, and higher labor force participation rates, are projected to expand their share of the workforce considerably." Caucasians are projected to constitute less than 50% of the labor force by 2050.

5. In September 2004, EEOC vice chair Naomi C. Harp launched the agencys national Youth @Work Initiative—a comprehensive outreach and education campaign designed to inform teens about their employment rights and responsibilities and to help employers create positive first work experiences for young adults. For additional information, go to http://www.eeoc.gov/initiatives/youth/index.html or the Youth @Work Web site (http://www.youth.eeoc.gov<$>).

6. In 2007, employers paid out over $200 million in EEOC settlements. We would note that in 2004 Morgan Stanley alone paid $54 million to settle class action claims that they underpaid and failed to promote women.

   The volume of discrimination lawsuits in the workplace has been such that the EEOC has been trying different approaches to expedite and settle cases. See Jess Bravin, "Top Court Backs Workers Who Report Discrimination," the *Wall Street Journal* (May 28, 2008), p. A3.

7. Diane Cadrain, "Sexual Equity in the Workplace," *HR Magazine* (September 2008), pp. 44–50.

   Diane Cadrain, "How to Go Above and Beyond the Basic Policies," *HR Magazine* (September 2008), pp. 47.

8. There are many types of workplace aggression, but bullying is often subtle and not obvious to others. Comparing the consequences of bullying, other forms of workplace aggression, and sexual harassment, the researchers found that those who experience bullying are less satisfied with their jobs and more likely to quit than those who are sexually harassed. Regardless of who is doing what to whom, supervisors must respond and deal appropriately with these behaviors. See Rita Zeidner, "Bullying Worse Than Sexual Harassment," *HR Magazine* (May 2008), p. 28. Also see Bob Sutton, *The No Asshole Rule: Building a Civilized Workplace and Surviving One That Isn't* (New York: Warner Business Books, 2007); and Karen A. Jehn and Elizabeth D. Scott, "Ranking Rank Behaviors," *Business & Society* (September 1999), pp. 296+.

   Christopher Farrell, "Is the Workplace Getting Raunchier," *BusinessWeek* (March 17, 2008), p. 019, reports that more women are hearing sexually inappropriate comments at work.

   Carolyn Hirschman, "Giving Voice to Employee Concerns," *HR Magazine* (August 2008), pp. 50–53, says that organizations should encourage employees to speak out on workplace issues by building channels to report concerns and working toward solutions.

9. "SHRM Diversity Study Reveals Long-Term Optimism," as reported in Special Advertising Section, *Fortune* (July 1999), pp. S17–18. See Geoffrey Colvin, "The 50 Best Companies for Asians, Blacks, and Hispanics," *Fortune* (July 19, 1999), pp. 53–68; Patrick Mirza, "A Bias that's Skin Deep," *HR Magazine* (December 2003), pp. 62–67; and Robert J. Grossman, "How Will You Be Treated by the EEOC?" *HR Magazine* (December 2003), pp. 68–74. Also see Susan J. Wells, "Tips for Recruiting and Retaining Hispanic Workers," *HR Magazine* (September 2008), pp. 40–41.

10. Pamela Paul, "Attitudes toward Affirmative Action," *American Demographics* (May 2003), pp. 61–62; and the National Opinion Research Center.

11. In Fiscal Year, 2007, EEOC received 30,623 charges of racial discrimination. See http://www.eeoc.gov/types/race.html for a detailed breakdown of discrimination charges.

12. As reported by Miriam Jordan, "Testing 'English Only' Rules," the *Wall Street Journal* (November 8, 2005), pp. B1, B13. Also see, Jordan, "Employers Provide Language Aid," the *Wall Street Journal* (November 8, 2005), p. B13. Nearly one-third of Brinker International Inc.'s employees are Hispanic, and many are not proficient in English. Brinker owns Chili's, Maggiano's Little Italy, and Romano's Macaroni Grill. Many are newcomers to the U.S., work more than one job, and lack transportation. Brinker is distributing an educational kit—six books, six cartridges, and a LeapPad—so that employees can learn English as a second language.

13. As reported by Pamela Perez, "Language on the Job," *Fort Wayne, Indiana News-Sentinel* (July 16, 2001), pp. 1B, 8B–9B. Also see Kathryn Tyler, "I Say Potato, You Say Potato," *HR Magazine* (January 2004), pp. 85–87.

14. As reported in Susan J. Wells, "Say Hola to the Majority Minority," HR Magazine (September 2008), pp. 38–43.

15. See "English Only, Ladies," *Time* (September 8, 2008), p. 15; and "LPGA Backs Off on Controversial English-Only Policy," *Lafayette, Indiana Journal & Courier* (September 6, 2008), p. C6.

16. "SHRM Diversity Study," op. cit. Also see Carol Hymowitz, "Too Many Women Fall for Stereotypes of Selves, Study Says," the *Wall Street Journal* (October 24, 2005), p. B1.

17. As of 2007, less than 20% of all harassment claims are filed by men. Also see, Anthony M. Townsend and Harsh K. Luthar, "How Do Men

Feel?" *HR Magazine* (May 1993), pp. 92–96. For an extensive review of sexual harassment, including statistics where men claimed harassment discrimination, see Tamara Penix Sbraga and William O'Donohue, "Sexual Harassment," *Annual Review of Sex Research* (2000), pp. 258–86.

18. As reported in Aja Carmichael, "Professional Women Drawn to Corporations that Are Family-Friendly," *South Bend, Indiana Tribune* (July 5, 2003), p. 2L. Also see Stephen Bates, "Research Finds 'Motherhood Penalty' in Employment Process," *SHRM Home*(August 12, 2005); Neal Chalofsky, "Work-Life Programs and Organizational Culture: The Essence of Community Workplace," *Organizational Development Journal*, 26, 1 (Spring 2008), pp. 11–18; Celinda Lake, Kellyanne Conway, and Catherine Whitney, *What Women Really Want: How American Women are Quietly Erasing Political, Racial, Class and Religious Lines to Change the Way We Live* (New York: Free Press, 2005).

The SHRM 2008 Employee Benefits Survey Report found that 28% of large corporations (500 or more employees) offer full-time telecommuting, and increasingly organizations are offering telecommuting to employees as a way to help deal with high gasoline prices. See Euan Hutchinson, "'People People' Work at Home, Too," *HR Magazine* (September 2008), pp. 60–62.

19. See http://eeoc.gov and in the left hand column (Discrimination by Type: Facts and Guidance), click on "sex," "sexual harassment," and/or "retaliation" for additional information.

20. See Jonathon A. Segal, "I Did it, But . . . Employees May Be As Innocent as They Say, But Still Guilty of Harassment," *HR Magazine* (March 2008), pp. 91–95; Margaret M. Clark, "Textbook Preventive Action Avoids Liability for Sexual Harassment," *SHRM Home* (August 27, 2004) and *McPherson* v. *City of Waukegan*, 7th Cir., No. 03–2738 (August 11, 2004). Also see "Tips for Policies on Personal Relationships in the Workplace," *Public Management* (May 2000), pp. 38–43; and Tim Barnett, Amy McMillan, and Winston McVea, Jr., "Employer Liability for Harassment by Supervisors," *Journal of Employment Discrimination Law* (Fall 2000), pp. 311–16.

A hostile work environment for the purposes of an employee's harassment claim is a single event that may include conduct spanning years prior to the filing of a single charge according to the 7th U.S. Circuit Court of Appeals (*Bright* v. *Hill's Pet Nutrition Inc.*, 7th Cir., No. 06-3827, December 21, 2007).

Historically, employers were automatically liable for harassing and discriminatory actions of their supervisors. However, in the following cases the Supreme Court offered some protection for employers. In *Faragher* v. *City of Boca Raton* (U.S. Supreme Court, No. 97-282, June 26, 1998) and *Burlington Industries, Inc.* v. *Ellerth* (U.S. Supreme Court, No. 97-569, June 26, 1998), the court held that an employer may defend a harassment lawsuit not involving a tangible job detriment, i.e., termination or demotion, by showing that it (the employer) exercised a reasonable care to prevent and promptly correct any harassing behavior, and that the employee suing unreasonably failed to take advantage of such preventive or corrective measures. In *Kolstad* v. *American Dental Association* (U.S. Supreme Court, No. 98-208, June 22, 1999) the court found that while employers may be charged with punitive damages for international discrimination by supervisors, punitive damages for such unlawful conduct may be avoided if the employer has made "good-faith" efforts to prevent workplace discrimination. Clearly, supervisors must understand the organization's policies and procedures and their responsibilities to prevent workplace harassment. Policies and procedures must be clear and consistently applied. Supervisors must receive periodic training, and any action that might be considered harassment must be dealt with immediately. For additional information on legal issues, go to http://www.law.cornell.edu or http://www.findlaw.com/casecode.

21. "Boeing Ousts Top Executive Because Relationship," *HR.BLR.com* (March 7, 2005).

22. Jae Yang and Veronica Salazar, "Would You Date a Co-Worker?" *USA Today* (February 14, 2008), p. 1B, reported that 31% of men and 29% of women would not date a co-worker. Also see Sue Shellenbarger, "Getting Fired for Dating a Co-Worker: Office Romance Comes Under Attack," the *Wall Street Journal* (February 19, 2004), p. D1.

23. For prevention techniques, see Jim Milligan and Norman Foy, "Not in My Company: Preventing Sexual Harassment," *Industrial Management* (September/October 2003), pp. 26, 28–30; Anne Fisher, "Did the Bill-and-Monica Debacle Teach Us Nothing?" *Fortune* (December 30, 2002), p. 206; David Rubenstein, "Harassment Prevention Is Now a Must for U.S. Companies," *Corporate Legal Times* (August 1999), pp. 31–32; Patricia M. Buhler, "The Manager's Role in Preventing Sexual Harassment," *Supervision* (April 1999), pp. 16–18; Rebecca Ganzel, "What Sexual Harassment Training Really Prevents," *Training* (October 1998), pp. 86–94

24. See Nancy D. O'Reilly, "Women Helping Women: How Mentoring Can Help Your Business," *Supervision*, 69, 1 (January 2008), pp. 12–13; Nancy Lockwood, "The Glass Ceiling: Domestic and International Perspectives," *2004 SHRM Research Quarterly* (June 2004). Also see "Glass Ceiling Report Is No Surprise to SHRM," *Mosaics* (April 1995), p. 4; Stephenie Overman, " Mentors Without Borders," *HR Magazine* (March 2004), pp. 83–86; William B. Irvine, "Beyond Sexual Harassment," *Journal of Business Ethics* (December 2000), pp. 353–60; and John A. Pearce, II, and Samuel A. DiLullo, "A Business Policy Statement Model for Eliminating Sexual Harassment and Related Employer Liability," *S.A.M. Advanced Management Journal* (Spring 2001), pp. 12–21.

Jae Yang and Alejandro Gonzalez, "Glass Ceiling," *USA Today* (April 22, 2008), p. 1B reported responses to the question: "Has the glass ceiling (i.e., limitations that prevent qualified women from being promoted to leadership positions) for women in the workplace shifted in the past ten years? The answers: 'Yes, it is less difficult 55%.' 'Yes, no more limitations 15%' 'Yes, it is more difficult 8%' and 'No, it's the same 22%.'" What do you think?

25. See "2008 Best Companies for Multicultural Women," *Working Mother* (June/July 2008), pp. 51–90, go to www.workingmother.com to review the list and their characteristics. Also see, "The 50 Most Powerful Women in the World," "Where the Girls Aren't," and "Remodeling Martha," *Fortune* (November 14, 2005); "Meet the TIME 100," *Time* (May 12, 2008 or go to www.time.com) for a look at "the world's most influential people who are changing the world and making history." For insight into Pepsi's CEO Indra Nooyi, see "The Best Advice I Ever Got," *Fortune* (May 12, 2008), p. 74.

26. See Stephanie Armour, "Day Care's New Frontier: Your Baby at Your Desk," *USA Today* (March 31, 2008), pp. 1A, 2A; Jody Miller and Matt Miller, "Get A Life!" *Fortune* (November 28, 2005), pp. 108–124; and Sue Shellenbarger, "Baby Blues: the Dangers of the Trend Toward Shorter Maternity Leaves," the *Wall Street Journal* (May 20, 2004), p. D1.

Also see Shellenbarger, "More Women Pursue Claims of Pregnancy Discrimination," the *Wall Street Journal* (March 27, 2008), p. D1; James B. Thelen, "An Rx for FMLA Headaches," *HR Magazine* (May 2008), pp. 93–102; "Job Sharing, Flexible Work, and Managerial Performance," *Worklife Report* (March 2001), pp. 8–9; or Stephanie Armour, "Workers Put Family First Despite Slow Economy, Job Fears," *USA Today* (June 6, 2002), p. 3B. For the results of a survey of employed women's major concerns related to the workplace, see James B. Parks, "Ask a Working Woman," *America@Work* published by the AFL-CIO (June 2002), pp. 18–19.

27. From "Making Equal Pay a Reality in Your Workplace," op. cit., p. 1. Carol Hymowitz, "On Diversity, America Isn't Putting Its Money Where Its Mouth Is," the *Wall Street Journal* (February 25, 2008), pp. B1,

reported that "In 2007, full-time female employees earned 77 percent of all men's median wages; black men earned 74 percent of the wages of white men; Asian women earned 78 percent of the median annual pay of white men; and white women earned 73 percent, black women 63 percent, and Hispanic women 52 percent of what white men earned."

28. *Employment disability is defined as a physical, mental, or emotional condition lasting six months or more that causes difficulty working at a job or business.* See Susan J. Wells, "Counting on Workers with Disabilities," HR Magazine (April 2008), pp. 44–49; Allen Smith, "Supreme Court Dismisses ADA Lawsuit, Agrees to Hear Constitutional Claim," *SHRM Law* (January 14, 2008); "Supreme Court to Review Wal-Mart Policy of Hiring Only the Best," *SHRM Online Workplace Law Focus Area* (January 2, 2008); Kris Maher, "Disabled Face Scarcer Jobs, Data Show," the *Wall Street Journal* (October 5, 2005), p. D2

   See Chuck Thompson, "Standard Should Not Have Been Applied to Hearing Test," *HR Magazine* (March 2008), p. 88 suggests that "the use of pre-employment tests to screen applicants has many pitfalls under various employment laws. Employers should proceed with great caution in using any broad tests that tend to exclude persons in any protected category and should be sure any test strongly relates to an important job function." See *Bates* v. *United Parcel Service Inc.*, 9th Cir, No. 04-17295 (December 28, 2007).

   For a concise guide to compliance with the ADA and interpretations, contact the EEOC Office of Communication and Legislative Affairs, 1801 L Street N.W., Washington, DC 20507. Note: approximately 40% of those diagnosed with some form of cancer are working-age adults. For information about "Cancer in the Workplace and ADA," see http://www.eeoc.gov/facts/cancer.html.

29. For an extensive discussion, see William F. Banta, *AIDS in the Workplace* (Lexington Books, 1993). Also see Milton Bordwin, "What to Do Before AIDS Strikes Home," *Management Review* (February 1995), pp. 49–52, and Judy Greenwald, "New Threat: Complacency," *Business Insurance* (July 23, 2001), pp. 1–14.

   Attorney Tim Bland recommends "employers to educate employees about HIV and the medically recognized means by which it is transmitted; and ensure that all employees adhere to OSHA's bloodborne pathogen regulations." See "Unfounded Fear of HIV Not Compensable," *HR Magazine* (December 2003), p. 118; and *Guess* v. *Sharp Manufacturing Co. of America*, Tennessee Supreme Court, No. W2002–00818-WC-R3-CV (August 27, 2003).

30. See Allen Smith, "Reasonable ADA Accommodation Isn't One-Stop Shopping," *SHRM Home* (March 22, 2006). A disabled employee's awareness of a job's requirements before accepting a position does not override the employee's right to a reasonable job accommodation. See *Smith* v. *Henderson*, 6th Cir., No 02-6073 (July 15, 2004). Also see *Humprey* v. *Memorial Hospital Association (239 F.3rd 1128 (9th Cir. 2001)* that reinforces the notion that the reasonable accommodation is an ongoing obligation.

31. For an extensive overview of the ADA, including recommended employer responses and courses of actions, see "Questions and Answers: The Americans with Disabilities Act and Persons with HIV/AIDS," published by the *U.S. Department of Justice, Civil Rights Division-Disability Rights Section* (November 9, 2001).

32. Dave Carpenter, "Boomers Confronting Age Discrimination," *Fort Wayne, Indiana News-Sentinel* (May 24, 2004), p. 5B; and Adam Cohen, "Too Old to Work," *New York Times Magazine* (March 2, 2003), pp. 54, 56–59. Also see, James A. Johnson and John Lopes, "The Intergenerational

Workforce, Revisited," *Organizational Development Journal*, 26, 1 (Spring 2008), pp. 31–36.

   In 2007, age discrimination claims grew by 15% over the previous year. See Robert J. Grossman, "Older Workers: Running to the Courthouse?" *HR Magazine* (June 2008), pp. 63–70. Forty-six percent of claims were based on wrongful discharge or layoff charges. Also see Grossman, "Keep Pace with Older Workers," *HR Magazine* (May 2008), pp. 38–46.

   For a discussion on another issue affecting older workers, see Pamela Babcock, "Elder Care at Work: Many Employers are Making a Business Case for Helping Employees with Sudden, Short-term Elder Care Needs," *HR Magazine* (September 2008), pp. 11–12.

33. According to the U.S. Department of Labor Bureau Statistics, workers over 55 are a third less likely than their younger associates to be injured at work seriously enough to lose work time. However, when they are seriously injured, older workers typically require two weeks to recover, about twice the amount needed by younger workers. From Glenn Burkins, "Work Week," the *Wall Street Journal* (May 7, 1996), p. A1.

34. For two divergent views, see Jeffrey Zaslow, "Baby Boomers, Gen-Xers Clash in Mentoring Environment," the *Wall Street Journal* (June 9, 2003), p. 5C; and Carol Hymowitz, "Young Managers Learn How to Bridge the Gap with Older Employees," the *Wall Street Journal* (July 21, 1998), p. B1. Also see Nancy R. Lockwood, "Leadership Styles: Generational Differences," *SHRM Research* (December 2004), and Laura Landro, "Offering Help to Depressed Seniors," the *Wall Street Journal* (October 5, 2005), p. D13.

35. Judith A. Moldover, "Employers May Bar Religious Affinity Groups," *SHRM Home* (January 13, 2006); *Moranski* v. *General Motors Corp.*, 7th Cir., No. 05-1803 (December 29, 2005). Also see Michelle Conlin, "Religion in the Workplace," *BusinessWeek* (November 1, 1999), p. 158. See also Georgette F. Bennett, "Religious Diversity in the Workplace," *Diversity Factor* (Winter 2001) pp. 15–20.

36. See Deb Levine, "Religious Beliefs," *HR Magazine* (July 2008), p. 29; Rebecca R. Hastings, "Continuing Communication Helps Religious Accommodation," *SHRM Diversity* (November 2007).

37. See Barbara Brotman of the Chicago Tribune, "Women Gallup Away from Female Bosses," as reported in the *Fort Wayne, Indiana News-Sentinel* (April 17, 1996), p. 2F.

   Also see Ancella B. Livers and Keith Caver, "Dear White Boss," *Harvard Business Review* (November 2002); and *Leading in Black and White: Working Across the Racial Divide in Corporate America* (New York: Wiley, 2002).

38. Robert S. Greenberger, "Justices Limit Use of Age-Bias Laws," the *Wall Street Journal* (February 24, 2005), p. D2. Also see Margaret M. Clark, "Workers Can Sue for Unintentional Age Bias," *SHRM Home* (March 30, 2005); and *Smith* v. *City of Jackson, No. 03-1160 U.S. Supreme Court* (2005).

39. See Michele Galen and Ann Therese Palmer, "White, Male, and Worried," *BusinessWeek* (January 31, 1994), pp. 50–55.

40. The *2007 Deloitte & Touche USA LLP Ethics and Workplace Survey* reported that 91 percent of all employed adults agreed that workers are more likely to behave ethically at work when they have a good work/life balance. Sixty percent of the respondents thought that job dissatisfaction is a leading reason why people make unethical decisions at work, and more than half of the workers (55 percent) ranked a flexible work schedule among the top three factors leading to job satisfaction, second only to compensation (63 percent). (Accessed September 8, 2008 at http://www.kmsstv.com/news/trends/7066282.html.)

CASE 5-1
Micro Mike

Ann Wilson is 26 years old and a recent college graduate. She received her bachelor's degree in business with a major in human resources management. After graduation, Wilson could not find employment in her field of study. She eventually took a sales position with a computer firm and worked part-time as a server at a local restaurant called Caruso's American Cuisine. Wilson liked her restaurant job better than her sales job because she felt that the owner respected her and listened to her opinions. While the restaurant business was not exactly where Wilson thought she would end up in life, she decided to accept a full-time position as day-shift supervisor at the restaurant because it paid well and she felt that it was a good opportunity for her to develop her managerial skills.

Several months ago, the owner of the restaurant, Joe Caruso, concluded that he needed someone to be general manager. Caruso owned several other enterprises, and he usually could be at the restaurant for only a few hours each day. To fill this position, Caruso recruited a local food company sales representative who had serviced the restaurant. Michael Morton, the sales representative, had been an assistant manager of a corporate-run steakhouse in the area. Joe Caruso thought that Morton would be a good candidate because he already had some managerial experience in the restaurant business. Morton jumped at the opportunity to be general manager. His arrival at Caruso's American Cuisine restaurant was announced in a brief meeting with all employees.

Wilson initially felt that having a general manager was a good idea. Too often, she had to make supervisory decisions without clear guidance. She thought that a general manager would make her supervisory position easier. However, she was sadly disappointed in what quickly transpired.

When Morton took over, he set out to change just about everything. At an employee meeting, he stated that everyone should follow his lead without question. He instituted numerous policies and procedures and posted them along with memos that detailed additional rules. Each employee was given an employee handbook that outlined all the rules and policies. He even had all employees sign to acknowledge that they had received the handbook and agreed to abide by its provisions.

Morton caused Wilson problems by frequently assigning work directly to the servers and kitchen crews. At times, he reversed Wilson's directives and, for the most part, would fail to tell her what he had done. Additionally, Morton occasionally made decisions that appeared to contradict some of the rules he had created. In Wilson's mind, Michael Morton was a micromanager, and a very poor one at that.

Wilson was thoroughly frustrated. Other employees were heard to be grumbling about Micro Mike. Ann Wilson contemplated meeting with Caruso, the owner, but she feared that Morton would retaliate if she did. Further, Caruso might resent being accused of making a less-than-intelligent decision in hiring Morton. Even with her college major in human resources management, Wilson did not know what to do. She believed that the restaurant was doing about the same level of business as before. However, she also felt that both customers and employees would desert the restaurant in droves if the Morton situation was not corrected.

Questions for Discussion

1. Evaluate Michael Morton as a new manager. Why do you suppose he acted as he did?
2. If you had been Morton, how would you have gone about planning to manage the restaurant?
3. If you were owner Joe Caruso and Ann Wilson reported the situation to you, what would you do? Why?
4. If Morton becomes aware of Wilson's concerns, what should she do? Do you think he would retaliate against Wilson?
5. Evaluate Wilson's position and consider her career options. If you were Wilson, what would you do?

CASE 5-2
The Interfering Administrative Assistant

Christine Moreno is vice president of manufacturing at Barry Automotive's Doylestown plant. She has direct line authority over Ed McCane, plant superintendent; Charles Evans, chief engineer; Diane Purcell, purchasing and supplies supervisor; Ron Weaver, supervisor of maintenance; and Carol Shiften, supervisor of the shipping department.

Two years ago, Moreno hired Bernice Billings as a secretary. Billings was diligent, capable, and efficient. She quickly won the admiration and confidence of her boss. Moreno felt fortunate to have such a capable secretary because Billings willingly assumed numerous duties that allowed Moreno to devote more time to her broad responsibility over the five departments. Moreno, therefore, changed Billings's job title to "administrative assistant" and increased her salary. After receiving this elevation in status, Billings began to do even more than she had before. For example, Moreno's supervisors at times received memos that clearly originated with Billings but that carried Moreno's initials. Billings also took it upon herself to give oral directives to supervisors from time to time. For example, several times Billings approached the plant superintendent, McCane, and gave him instructions concerning plant scheduling problems. At other times, without seeing McCane first, Billings went directly to the production floor and asked employees to rush orders or to do other things. She often told maintenance employees to do various projects, which, she said, "Ms. Moreno would like you to do." Similar occurrences took place in the shipping department, where Billings frequently left instructions for the special treatment of some customers' orders.

In most of these situations, Moreno was unaware that Billings had taken it upon herself to communicate directly with subordinates to solve problems that had come to her attention. Some employees complained that these directives should have come from Moreno or the appropriate departmental supervisor. In most cases, however, everyone realized that Billings had the best interests of the firm in mind, and they usually complied with her requests.

However, as time went on, the supervisors began to feel that Billings was interfering more than she was helping. In several instances, some of the employees on the production floor did not check with McCane but went directly to Billings for instructions. Similar incidents took place in other departments. One day, over a cup of coffee, McCane, Shiften, and Weaver angrily shared their concerns. At the outset, they had looked upon Billings favorably, but now they considered her to be a disruptive factor that was undermining their supervisory positions.

Questions for Discussion

1. Relying on the concepts presented in Chapters 11 and 12, identify the theories and concepts of leadership and teamwork present (or not present) in this case.

2. What key mistake is Christine Moreno making?

3. Why would Bernice Billings take it upon herself to communicate directly with supervisors and employees to solve plant problems? Is this procedure to be admired or condemned? Discuss.

4. Why did various plant personnel comply with Billings's requests and orders, even though they were not sure that these requests had come from Moreno?

5. Can informal authority be just as powerful as direct line authority? Explain your response.

6. What should the supervisors do? What alternatives do they have? Make a list of their concerns. (You may want to review the Supervisory Tips for Managing Up presented in Chapter 3.)

7. You are Christine Moreno. The supervisors come to you with a list of their concerns. What should you do now? Why?

CASE 5-3
Work on What Matters the Most

Visitors to the Pine Village Community Medical Center (CMC) are wowed by the innovative approach developed to make visitors welcome. When patients and visitors pull up to the front door, they are greeted by the "hospitality committee." Free valet parking, a meditation garden, and a coffee bar in the waiting rooms are just a few of the perks that have been developed to make each patient feel as if they are at a four-star hotel.

Sixty-two year old Gordon Ostermann is the director of hospitality services. His three direct reports include Susie Jones (housekeeping and maintenance), Dick Katter (grounds and outside maintenance), and Jessica Prada (food service). During the past 21 years, Ostermann has seen many changes at CMC. Eight years ago, Sarah Anthony became CEO of CMC. Anthony had her direct reports visit innovative businesses and encouraged them to develop a collaborative team approach to engage all employees to CMC's vision (see CMC's values and mission statement on page 24 in Chapter 1).

Ostermann visited an innovative training center at Whirlpool and attended in-house training programs on team building and innovation. One presenter suggested that management target a few areas that might achieve the greatest benefit. In a recent issue of a management journal, an article began by saying that in most organizations there is a lot of untapped human potential. In excellent, renewing organizations, this potential can be released, resulting in personal growth for the individual. Personnel development and organizational renewal involves changes in attitude and behavior.

Ostermann spent a great amount of time balancing the workload and rewards between the three teams and ensuring that everyone participated. The teams were encouraged to concentrate on critical issues, set priorities, effectively manage the resources, and ensure that the effort is manageable. Unfortunately, the food service team had a fondness for working primarily on their "pet projects" rather than collaborating with the other teams. Errors became common and plenty of failed ideas emerged. Ostermann learned to recognize promising proposals that failed with the "good try" approach. The teams made presentations to the other teams about lessons learned from failures. Ostermann knew that more attention must be paid to people, innovation, process improvement strategy, and customer relationships.

As he sat back in his chair to contemplate the events of the past week, Susie Jones, leader of the housekeeping and maintenance team, stuck her head in the door and asked if he had a few minutes. Jones needed help in dealing with Tom Hoemig. She said: "One of the most difficult problems is communication. He either has a hearing problem or just doesn't want to understand. This has resulted in several errors and a slower response time. I have talked with him and even written him up on the last two instances. But he just doesn't seem to care. I don't think I am stereotyping him because he is older. In fact, Gale Dawkins is older and there is no comparison in performance."

Jones continued, "Tom has worked here for 26 years and wants to retire when he turns 65. He is only 59 years old. The other team members appear uncomfortable in providing Tom guidance, corrective action, and feedback. This prevents the free flow of communication within the team. Rather than appreciating each other, Tom's lack of effort is slowly creating a wall of indifference among the members of our team."

Ostermann got up from his chair and started pacing the room. Jones knew the routine—Ostermann often had everyone stand during meetings because he believed that people could think better on their feet. While pacing, he paused to think about Tom Hoemig. Tom was generally well liked and affectionately called "Pops" by most employees.

Jones continued, "Tom seems to be quite content with his job and the status quo. He comes to work every day on time and puts in his eight hours. He displays little interest in our team or toward the team improvement projects. He never volunteers anything during the team meetings, even when we ask him directly for his opinions. His wife died of cancer three years ago, and he spends his time away from here walking his dog, Pepper, or cruising Lake James in his boat. His children and grandchildren live out-of-state and it appears that they do not get together much since his wife's death."

Ostermann believed that through the team approach, the company and employees would both prosper. It was apparent that one employee was not with the program.

Questions for Discussion
1. What are the advantages of involving employees in a team-based system?
2. What are the challenges associated with moving from a traditional supervisor-subordinate relationship to a team-based approach?
3. Evaluate Gordon Ostermann's attempt to engage employees via the team-based approach.
4. Why would one of the team focus on their pet projects rather than look at the bigger picture? Is this inherently bad? Why?
5. What other things should Ostermann have considered before implementing the team approach?
6. "Every process can be improved." Where should Ostermann and the three team leaders go from here? What improvement opportunities remain?

Role-Play Activity

Form groups of four or five members to take the following roles:
      Gordon Ostermann, Susie Jones, Dick Katter, Jessica Prada, and others as observers.
1. Susie Jones is to give an overview of the situation with Tom Hoemig.
2. After discussing the situation, the group should develop alternatives for the following:
   a. Is Tom Hoemig worth the effort? Why or why not?

b. Where will the maintenance team be if Tom continues to be the same as always?

c. How can Susie and the team members change the problem from a negative to a positive?

d. What can the maintenance team take to get Tom to take a greater interest in his job?

e. What actions should be taken to get Tom Hoemig either on the team or out the door?

f. How did the group turn this challenge into an opportunity?

3. What did you learn from this role-play exercise?

CASE 5-4
Is He on Our Team or Isn't He?

Bob Haddad has been a team leader with Barry Automotive's Lancaster plant for the past year; he has been with the company for about five years. As team leader, Haddad has experienced new work challenges. Recently, some of Haddad's team members have complained about Angel Amin's slow pace and his failure to keep up with the rest of the team. In response, Haddad has told the complaining team members that Amin is a solid employee who always shows up for work on time. While he works a little slower than the rest of the team members, he gets the job done. That seemed to satisfy the team members temporarily, but several days later, Steve Brennan came to Haddad and said that most of the team members had indicated that they were going to slow their work pace if something was not done about Amin.

At that point, Haddad asked Brennan whether he or any of the other team members had confronted Amin about his work pace, and Brennan replied, "Yes, we have told Angel on numerous occasions to pick up speed and get the lead out, but he just continues to work at his usual, slow pace. Dorothy Kent has spent an excessive amount of time instructing Angel in some of the more efficient ways to do the job. Even that doesn't work. Maybe he's just too fat to cut the pace around here!"

Haddad decided to consult with human resources director Steven Taylor. Haddad and Taylor discussed how Haddad's team previously had been one of the most productive and how Amin had joined the team about three years ago. According to Haddad, Amin's weight had ballooned in the past two years, and he appeared to carry about 300 pounds or more on his 5'7" frame. Work records indicate that Amin has been unable to keep the pace set by other team members but that the team had been reluctant to address the issue in his most recent performance review. In fact, Amin had scored 80 points, which was an overall "good" evaluation under the company's 360-degree performance evaluation system.

Haddad said that Brennan's assessment probably reflects the views of other team members, but they had been uncomfortable or unwilling to address Amin's performance problems in the formal evaluation process. Haddad told Taylor, "I would welcome any advice you can give me."

Questions for Discussion

1. Each work team has its own personality. Discuss how a group's personality influences its ability to produce.

2. Why is it important for managers to identify the issues that detract from group cohesiveness?

3. What might be some of the issues in this case?

4. How does the work team process somewhat limit Haddad's ability to deal with the Amin situation?

5. If you were Haddad, what would you do? Why?

6. (**INTERNET ACTIVITY**) Log onto the Internet to secure information about the concern with obesity among America's workers, the *Americans with Disabilities Act (ADA),* and recent court decisions regarding accommodation of overweight workers.

   a. Define: Essential job functions, reasonable accommodation, and undue hardship.
   b. Is being overweight covered by the Americans with Disabilities Act?
   c. If Amin says his inability to keep up with the other team members is due to his health, what should Haddad do?

Curt Miller has been a supervisor for the Jefferson City water maintenance department for the past eleven years. He started out in an apprentice program about twenty years ago where his technical skills were among the best. He has attended several supervisory and leadership development courses and various motivational seminars during his tenure as supervisor.

Problems developed two months ago, when the city, in an effort to bring more diversity into its workforce, transferred Maria Chavez from the transportation garage. Immediately upon arrival, Chavez entered and won a maintenance skills contest held at the regional vocational center.

Chavez is the single parent of a six-year-old child, and her mother and father live with her. Catholic Social Services has been instrumental in helping Chavez and her parents. Her parents work as janitors at St. Paul's Catholic Church and are enrolled in an ESL (English as a second language) program.

This morning, Miller was approached by Eddie Elliott, a twice-divorced and very opinionated employee. At best, Elliott's performance is marginal, but he knows how to work the system. He has been repeatedly reprimanded for absenteeism, tardiness, violation of safety standards, and other minor infractions of work rules. Three times he has been suspended for short periods of time without pay. But his infractions have never been severe enough to warrant termination.

"Listen, Curt," Elliott began. "We've got a great work group here, but there is no place for a woman in our maintenance department. She ain't cutting it. Just yesterday she lit into Gary for that calendar he has on his tool box. He was this far (spreading his finger and thumb about three inches apart) from punching her out. She isn't a team player. We rely on cooperation to get the work done. She just does her little bit and nothing more. There's just no room for a woman in our department."

A little later in the morning, Gary Simpson asked to speak to Miller, and he echoed similar concerns. "When we need her to work on a project, what do we get? She's running around sticking her nose in stuff that doesn't concern her. The guys on the ninth floor of City Hall (the location of the Mayor's office as well as the Director of Utilities) think she's great 'cause she won some stupid skills award, but she's tearing this group apart."

"What's going on here?" Miller thought to himself, "She's ambitious and has great drive and determination. She helps fulfill the Mayor's commitment to diversity, and she has the potential to be the best maintenance person we've ever had."

Source: This case was adapted with permission from Francine Segars and Ed Leonard of IPFW, "No Place for Women in the Maintenance Department," *2004 Proceedings of the Society for Case Research,* pp. 51–59.

CASE 5-5
No Place for Women in the Maintenance Department

Questions for Discussion

1. Identify the issues in this case.
2. Evaluate the perceptions of Elliott and Simpson in terms of gender-stereotyping jobs in the maintenance department.
3. If you were Curt Miller, how would you ascertain whether the criticisms of Elliott and Simpson are representative of the entire work group?
4. What can Curt Miller do to minimize the possibility of discrimination in his department?

Role-Play Exercise

(**ROLE PLAY**) Divide the class into groups of three or four. If there is limited time, the instructor may assign one of the options.

Option 1: Assign the following roles: Curt Miller, Maria Chavez, a representative from the human resources department, and an observer. With the help of the HR representative, Curt Miller's task is to uncover Chavez's perceptions of how the job is going, respond to any concerns she has, and clarify the expectations that they have for her.

Option 2: Assign the following roles: Curt Miller, the Director of Utilities, an HR rep, and observers. Assumption: The criticisms and allegations made by Elliott and Simpson are not unique to them. Miller is to take the concerns of his employees to the Director of Utilities and the HR rep for guidance on how to cope with the situation.

Option 3: Assign the following roles: Curt Miller, the Director of Utilities, the HR rep, and Gary Simpson. Assumption: The criticisms and allegations made by Elliott and Simpson are not representative of the rest of the maintenance department workforce

Option 4: Assign the following roles: Curt Miller, Eddie Elliott, Gary Simpson, and a representative from the Human Resources Department. Curt Miller's task, with help from the HR rep, is to change the attitudes of Elliott and Simpson toward Maria Chavez.

Option 5: Assign the following roles: Curt Miller, the HR rep, Maria Chavez, and observers. Assumption: Chavez's performance is more than adequate, but there is concern that she is having a negative impact on other department members. Miller and the HR rep must address the performance concerns with Chavez.

Debriefing of the Role-Play Exercise: Share your answers to the following:

a. What did Curt Miller do well?
b. What should Curt Miller have done differently?
c. If you were Curt Miller, what would you do to get a diverse group of people to work together?

CASE 5-6
You're What?

Seaside Mortgage is a large financial services organization headquartered in Jacksonville, Florida. Seaside employs more than 3,500 individuals across all its southeastern U.S. operations. Susan Gregory, the vice president of human resources, believes that Seaside should conduct on-campus interviews on those college campuses within 100 miles of a Seaside facility.

Martina Huston interviewed with Seaside during her senior year in college. Seaside did not have any openings at the time, and company officials were open about the fact that they were building applicant files so that when the economy improved or when openings occurred, they would have an ample applicant pool.

In February, following her graduation in May, Martina received a phone call from Rex Morgan, a Seaside HR assistant, asking if she would be interested in interviewing for a potential supervisory assistant position at the Palatka office. Due to the poor job market and a reluctance to relocate beyond the Jacksonville area, Martina was still employed part-time at the Winn-Dixie Supermarket—the same store she had been working at since she was seventeen years old. However, Winn-Dixie had lost millions in the past two years, continued to lose market share, and had a revolving door among its top management personnel. The grocery chain had been struggling, to put it mildly, and as such, there appeared to be little opportunity for Martina to advance. Besides, she was ready to move on.

Martina jumped at the opportunity and scheduled the interview promptly. She was excited at the prospect of working for a company like Seaside. Several of her high school and college friends were employed there, and Martina was impressed with the picture that was painted of the company. The company provides a good salary and a competitive benefit package, flexible work schedules, and opportunity for advancement from within. Seaside is held in high regard as an "employer of choice," and several employees held key volunteer positions when Jacksonville hosted Super Bowl XXXIX.

Martina thought that there would be a good fit between their needs and her qualifications. During her seven years with Winn-Dixie, she has been a cashier and a floor supervisor and has manned the customer-service desk, where she was responsible for daily sales reconciliation along with other basic customer service duties. She holds a B.S. in business and has sung in her church choir as well as in the university co-ed choral club. The home office interview went well, and a second interview was scheduled for Martina with the key staff at the Palatka office.

Martina was offered a supervisory trainee position that began three weeks later. This gave her ample opportunity to look for housing in the Palatka area and to terminate her employment with Winn-Dixie. With the help of her parents and Ellie Corbitt—the employee assigned by Seaside to help Martina with the employment transition—she found a nice apartment close to her work at the Palatka office. Seaside's policy for newly hired exempt employees is to have them go through a two-week orientation in the Jacksonville office where they learn about the company and its policies and procedures and shadow a variety of employees. The company believes that new employees should have a chance to see exemplary performers in action. Martina was impressed with the comfort and ease of the onboarding program. On Friday afternoon, Martina said her goodbyes to the home-office folks and returned to her parents' home to prepare for the move to Palatka.

Three weeks later, Martina requested a private meeting with Ellie Corbitt, her assigned mentor at the Palatka office. Martina started to cry and proceeded to tell her, "I wasn't sure how or when to tell you this, but I'm pregnant! I thought that my upset stomach and other problems were brought on by the excitement of the new job opportunity, but the pregnancy test confirmed my suspicions. My parents will kill me! I don't know what to do."

Questions for Discussion

1. If you were Ellie Corbitt, how would you respond to Martina's announcement? Why?

2. Trust and respect are key ingredients for supervisory personnel. How might her coworkers at the Palatka office respond when they find out that Martina is pregnant and unmarried? Why might they respond this way?

3. If you were Martina, what would you do? What are the advantages and disadvantages of each alternative?

4.  Use the Internet to get information about pregnancy discrimination. What are the rules of the game for Seaside Mortgage?

5. Assume that you are Larry Fields, the Palatka Division General Manager. Consider the following: Several female employees have come to you and complained about Martina's condition—pregnant and unmarried. What can you do to keep the complaints from negatively affecting work relationships?

6. In the past, there was a greater stigma attached to one who was pregnant and unmarried. Such persons were often stereotyped as immoral! What is wrong with making such stereotypes?

7. What can Larry Fields do to get the Palatka office employees to look at Martina from the "inside out" rather than from the "outside in?"

CASE 5-7

What about The Dress Code?*

As Greg Noll, general manager for the Classic Inn, drove to work, he thought about the week ahead—the busiest week of the year. Thousands of visitors to the Auburn-Cord-Dusenburg Festival and the Kruse Auction (one of the U.S.'s largest auto auctions) would descend on Wednesday and leave the following Tuesday. It was the highlight of the year for those living in the small northeast Indiana town of Cord. Lisa Craig, the assistant general manager, had worked hard to get the staff ready for the event. Along with key staffers, Lisa and Greg had created potential crisis scenarios, and everyone was ready to handle whatever might arise.

After he arrived at work and was getting his first cup of coffee, Lisa summoned Greg to her office. "Greg, we have a problem. Sherry Smith got married last week." Greg admitted that he had heard rumors that Sherry was really serious about a university student she had met last spring and had been on vacation for the past two weeks. Lisa continued, "Sherry's back today, and we have a major problem. We have a dress code, and Sherry looks horrible. We are booked solid this week and, with sentiments regarding the Iraqi War and concerns about Islamic extremists, we cannot afford to offend anyone."

A very surprised Greg asked, "What's the problem? Sherry received our 'Most Congenial and Helpful Employee Award' last year."

"Did you know that she got married and converted to the Muslim faith? She's wearing a full-length outfit and a head covering. Check it out."

Sure enough, Sherry was working the front desk, and she was dressed in a long-sleeved dress that reached to the floor and a scarf was tied around her head. She looked neat and tidy as usual, but very different. As Greg approached the front desk, he inquired, "Sherry, I heard that congratulations might be in order."

Sherry said, with a smile, "Yes, they might be. I was married over my vacation. I need to see you today to make changes in my employee records and benefit designations. Oh, by the way, my name is not 'Sherry'; it's 'Sareya'. I'll tell you about that when I come to see you. My break time is 10:45; would that be a convenient time?"

A startled Greg responded, "Sure."

Greg shut the door to his office and poured through the Inn's HR policy manual, looking for the section on dress and appropriate behavior. The Inn's dress code is shown in Exhibit 1.

EXHIBIT 1:

Dress and Professional Appearance for the Classic Inn:

1. Employees must wear the attire as defined below:

Female Staff Members and Managers

Dresses and skirts are must be no shorter than 1" above the knee; use discretion in wearing clothing that is a respectable business length according to your height. Dress slacks must be ankle length or longer (not rolled up). Stirrup pants, stretch pants, jeans-style (for example, exterior rivets and pockets), or sweatshirt material pants are unacceptable. Stockings or pantyhose must be neutral in color or match the color of the outfit worn. Blouses and shirts with short or long sleeves are required. Sleeveless tops or tank-top blouses are not permitted. Jackets and sweaters are acceptable.

Male Staff Members and Managers

Dress slacks with a belt are required. Khakis and dress corduroys are acceptable. Jeans-style pants (for example, exterior rivets and pockets) are unacceptable. Dress shirts with short or long-sleeves are required. A tie is optional by store location. The General Manager of each location will make this decision. If a tie is worn, the top button must be buttoned. If a tie is not worn, only the top button of the shirt may be unbuttoned. Sport jackets and sweaters are acceptable. Socks are required.

Maintenance Workers

Inn-issued tee-shirt tucked into pants. Jeans or heavy duty, casual-style pants. Color must be black or blue. Plain belt must be worn if there are belt loops. Black or brown safety shoes. Inn-issued cap may be worn.

Collared polo-style shirts are acceptable. They may have the Inn's logo or brand insignia. However, they may not have insignias from local country clubs, civic groups, teams, etc. Each location also has the choice to incorporate an approved uniform program for the management team that is administered through a third party. The manager dress code is at the discretion of each individual manager.

Employees must remove all visible pierced jewelry while at work. Exception: Females are permitted to wear two small earrings in each ear.

Classic Inn reserves the right to require covering of any visible tattoo while working.

Female employees may wear clear polish and acrylic nails.

2. All employees must be in appropriate dress at the time they clock in and at all times while on duty. Employees must report to and from work in full work attire.
3. Work attire must be laundered and presentable.
4. Employees must maintain a high standard of personal hygiene and grooming when reporting to work.
5. A name tag must be worn at all times when on duty. It should be displayed on the left-hand side of the shirt.

After reviewing the requirements of Classic Inn, Greg was still concerned. There wasn't anything in the dress code concerning headscarves or hair in general. He knew from his courses in human resource management that companies could make some restrictions about dress, but he also knew that there were other requirements when a dress code was designed.

About 10:30, Greg looked for Lisa. Unfortunately, she was attending a Festival Board Meeting. Promptly at 10:45, Sherry appeared at his door. Greg invited her into his office. "I wish you much happiness in your marriage. I gathered the paperwork necessary so you could make any changes you need in your benefits and your W4."

Sherry smiled. "I've never been so happy. I met Nashwan Safwat at a party almost two years ago and we got married two weeks ago in Detroit. My parents are angry with me because I agreed to convert to the Shiite Muslim faith. I began wearing the *jilbab* (a full-length gown that covers the entire torso and legs) and the *hijab* (headscarves), and my dad won't speak to me. The dress is a part of my new religion. I know that my fellow employees here have accepted my new direction." Sherry continued, "The nature of my new religion is that it is intensely personal, and I have made a commitment to wear very modest clothing. I couldn't find anything in the handbook that would prevent me from expressing my religious views."

Greg smiled and brought out the paperwork for change of marital status. After she signed the papers, he asked, "Do you want to use Sherry at work and on your name tag? It might be easier for the staff and customers?"

Sherry looked shocked. "No. My name is now Sareya Safwat, and I would like my name tag to show the new name."

After Sherry left, Greg sat and considered what to do next. In the conservative Midwestern area of northeast Indiana, Sareya Safwat and her new dress could lose the Classic Inn many customers. With the fighting intensifying in Iraq, the name and dress certainly would cause a lot of discomfort and negative comment in the local area. However, there were a great many Amish and Mennonites in the area, and no one insisted that they change their dress. Of course, they were not often employed in areas outside of their community that required dealing with the public.

Source: This case was adapted with permission from "The Dress Code" prepared by Karen Moustafa Leonard and Ed Leonard of IPFW and Roy Cook of Fort Lewis College for presentation at the Society for Case Research Annual Meeting, Chicago, Illinois, March 2008.

Questions for Discussion
1. What are the issues in the case?
2. What is the purpose of the organization's dress code?
3. (**INTERNET ACTIVITY**) Use the Internet to find information regarding workplace dress and religious freedom in the workplace. Based on your findings, what conclusions would you draw for this situation?
4. How should Greg handle this situation? Why should he choose this course of action rather than another?
5. For diversity to work, what are some attitudes that need to be changed?

CASE 5-8
Sexual Harassment in the Accounting Office

Charlie Gillespie is office manager of a group of accountants and accounting clerks in the corporate budget office of Sanders Supermarkets. He is known as a "happy-go-lucky" supervisor who finds it difficult to confront inappropriate behavior or to take disciplinary action. Gillespie normally tries to avoid conflict by pretending he does not observe inappropriate conduct.

On a number of occasions, Gillespie observed one of his accountants, Oliver Olson, making crude and suggestive comments to a group of female accounting clerks in the department. While Gillespie did not like what he heard and had observed, he thought that most of the employees accepted Olson for what he was and did not take him seriously.

However, one day an accounting clerk named Julie Lowe entered Gillespie's office. She claimed that Olson's comments were a form of sexual harassment. Lowe stated that she understood the company had a policy prohibiting sexual harassment and that, even though Olson had not made any direct sexual overtures to any of the female employees, his vulgar language and crude questions no longer could be tolerated by the women in the office. Gillespie responded that Olson was just a "good old boy," and that if the women would just ignore him, the problem would take care of itself.

Several weeks later, Lowe resigned without explanation. One week after Lowe left, the company received a notice that she had filed charges with the Equal Employment Opportunity Commission (EEOC), claiming that she had been discriminated against because of her gender. In her complaint, Lowe stated that there was an "atmosphere of sexual harassment in the office" and that because of this continued harassment, the "hostile work environment caused her severe tension and distress," which she could no longer tolerate and which forced her to end her employment with the company.

Gillespie received a copy of Lowe's discrimination and harassment charges from Pamela Richter, the company's director of human resources. Richter asked Gillespie to come to her office to discuss the company's response to these charges.

Questions for Discussion
1. When do crude and vulgar humor and language become sexual harassment? Discuss.
2. What should Charlie Gillespie have done when he first observed Oliver Olson engaging in undesirable behavior?
3. What should Gillespie have done when Julie Lowe complained to him about Olson? Evaluate Gillespie's counsel that Olson was a "good old boy" who should be ignored.
4. What would you recommend for the company's response to the EEOC charges of discrimination and sexual harassment? Discuss.

PART 6

CHAPTER 14

(Fundamentals of Controlling)

© PATRICK MOLNAR/GETTY IMAGES

After studying this chapter, you will be able to:

1 Describe the nature and importance of the managerial controlling function.

2 Identify three types of control mechanisms based on time.

3 Explain the essential characteristics of effective controls.

4 Describe the essential steps in the control process.

5 Discuss the supervisor's role in controlling through budgets.

6 Discuss the supervisor's role in maintaining cost consciousness and in responding to higher-level managers' orders to reduce costs.

7 Identify additional control areas and explain how the controlling function is closely related to the other managerial functions.

YOU MAKE THE CALL!

In early 2009, Hugh Edwards, acting COO of Edwards Homecenter and Lumber Company, was faced with three questions: What changes should we make to increase our customer base and sales? What changes do we need to make to the store layout to improve product accessibility, improve work flow, and speed up deliveries? In addition, what other changes need to be made to restore the store to profitability?

The business began 38 years ago when Larry Edwards, Hugh's grandfather, opened the store in a medium-sized town of 18,000. Today, there are 147,000 people living within a thirty-minute drive of the store. On January 2, 2009, Larry Edwards suffered a major heart attack and the family asked Hugh to see if he could do the things necessary to make the store survive. Hugh had worked for his grandfather every summer in high school and college. Hugh had a passion for the business but knew that his passion and visions would not complement those of his grandfather's. Upon graduating from college, Hugh went to work for a regional bank and enjoyed professional and personal successes.

The past four years have not been profitable for Edwards Homecenter. When Larry started the business, he was the only game in town. Now, competition is fierce. The "Big Boxes"—Home Depot, Lowe's, Menards, Wal-Mart—are targeting many of the same customers. Edwards affiliated with Do-It-Best Corp., a member-owned cooperative (see www.doitbest.com). Hugh had taken a leave under his company's FMLA policy. That meant he had thirteen-plus weeks to make a difference. His initial plan of attack was to get the associates on board by:

(1) Encouraging their identification with the business needs of Edwards Homecenter and Lumber Company.

(2) Focusing on improving the quality of employee thinking, responding to customer needs, and creating solutions to problems.

(3) Encouraging employees to add value to relationships with customers and fellow associates.

(4) Growing sales by getting teaching associates to guide customer choices about price, quality, selection, and service, and by building add-on sales. (An illustration of add-on sales would be the customer buying a gallon of paint being shown the need for a drop-cloth, a new line of paintbrushes, and clean-up materials; the customer sets out to buy a gallon of paint and ends up with a shopping basket full of materials to help do the project better.)

Unfortunately, the store layout and floor plan have hindered the work flow, increasing costs and causing delivery backlogs. Approximately 80 percent of the business has been contractor and D-I-Y (do-it-yourselfers) sales. Hugh has charged Wilmer Bennis and two other associates with working out a program to control backlogs. Working with Brian Dietz, the Do-It-Best Corp. retail and contractor sales development specialist, they analyzed the store, the flow of inventory, work processes, and the like. Brian encouraged them to visit some of the better retailers in the area, walk their stores, and identify their best customer service practices. Brian said, "You will go nowhere if you only strive to be as good as the best. Your mission is to identify the best practices of the best and figure out a way to improve upon them for your unique store."

Wilmer and the team devised certain layout changes. Then the group identified the times and costs in critical labor steps. They developed metrics for measuring success. Brian provided them with data so they could compare themselves against the "best of the best." After discussing the ideas with all associates and other members of the Edwards family, a plan was developed. Metrics were set for each of the areas, and strategic control points were established. As was to be expected, some deliveries were delayed and orders mixed up during the implementation process, but within thirty days customer complaints were virtually non-existent.

Hugh knew that he needed to measure the store's financial performance on a daily basis. He recognized that he needed to develop a measurement system that would provide information on: (1) performance against customer requirements; (2) customer satisfaction; (3) cost performance, inventory turns, and other productivity measures; and (4) associate satisfaction. Hugh installed a computer program to track store sales. When a sale is registered, the associate code number is also entered, and Hugh is able to immediately know the average sales per hour, items and units sold, and dollars per transaction. This provides immediate information for reordering merchandise.

Every associate can go into the system to see his or her "performance metrics." The system allows Hugh to adjust hours to have the appropriate number of associates on the floor at the right time. In the beginning, some associates were resistant to having their hours changed, but no one was scheduled for fewer hours than they had worked previously. In many ways, Hugh was like an on-the-field coach. He met with each associate daily to talk about business needs, get their ideas for improvement, and encourage them to get browsers to be customers. He also made a list of the skills, abilities, and interests for all associates. His goal was to get the right people in the right place at the right time doing the right things.

Hugh knew that he and the outside salespeople needed to spend more time developing relationships with contractors, remodelers, and potential commercial accounts. He quickly became aware that government agencies and school systems could be a viable market. He found himself working sixteen-hour days to try and get the store on track. But there are only so many hours in a day and so much to do. The Edwards name was above the door, and he was an Edwards. What else needed to be done? **YOU MAKE THE CALL!**

The Supervisor's Role in Controlling

The word *control* often elicits negative reactions, but control is a normal part of daily life. At home, at work, and in the community, everyone is affected by various controls, such as alarm clocks, thermostats, fuel and electronic gauges, traffic lights, and police officers directing traffic. Controls also play an important role in organizations. Controls ensure that results match plans. Every manager, from the chief executive to the supervisor, must develop and apply controls that regulate the organization's activities to achieve desired results.

Managerial controlling
Ensuring that actual performance is in line with intended performance and taking corrective action, if necessary

As management guru Peter Drucker stated, "Checking the results of a decision against its expectations shows managers what their strengths are, where they need to improve, and where they lack knowledge or information."[1] Thus, the **managerial controlling** function consists of checking to determine whether operations adhere to established plans, ascertaining whether progress is being made toward objectives, and taking action, where necessary, to correct deviations from plans. In other words, the supervisor acts to make things happen the way they were planned. Controlling is essential whenever a supervisor assigns duties to employees because the supervisor remains responsible for assigned work. If all plans proceeded according to design and without interference, the controlling function would be obsolete. As every supervisor knows, however, this is not reality. Therefore, it is part of the supervisor's job to keep activities in line and, when necessary, to get those activities back on track. This is done by controlling.[2]

NATURE OF THE CONTROLLING FUNCTION

Controlling is one of the five primary managerial functions. It is so closely related to the other functions that the line between controlling and the other functions sometimes blurs. Controlling is most closely related to planning. In planning, the supervisor sets objectives, and these objectives become standards against which performance is appraised. When performance and standards deviate, the supervisor must carry out the controlling function by taking corrective action, which may involve establishing new plans and different standards.

Because controlling is the last managerial function discussed in this book, it might be perceived as something the supervisor performs after all other functions. This might lead to the impression that controlling is concerned with events only after they have happened. It is true that the need for controlling is evident after a mistake has been made. However, it is much better to view controlling as a function that goes on simultaneously with the other managerial functions. As we discuss later in this chapter, there are control mechanisms for before, during, and after an activity.

EMPLOYEE RESPONSES TO CONTROLS

Employees often view controls negatively because the amount of control in departments may determine how much freedom employees have to do their jobs. Yet most employees understand that a certain amount of control is essential to regulate performance. They know that a lack of control will result in confusion, inefficiency, and even chaos.

In a behavioral sense, controls and on-the-job freedom seem to conflict. However, when controls are well-designed and properly implemented, they can positively influence employee motivation and behavior. The supervisor should design and apply control systems that employees will accept without resentment but that will also monitor department performance effectively.[3] Interestingly, some firms have at times loosened certain controls and given employees more freedom, only to be disappointed by the outcome and then forced to tighten or return to discarded controls.

Rules about appropriate attire for schools and businesses provide us an example. Casual and informal dress in society certainly has grown dramatically in recent years. Look around you. Is everyone dressed appropriately? Attire such as halter tops, short shorts, T-shirts with offensive slogans, provocative blue jeans, flip-flops, and body piercing are among the types of questionable attire that have shown up in classrooms as well as in many business establishments. Should your instructor, college, or organization have the right to determine appropriate dress? Regardless of what a policy might prescribe, some people will say that it violates their "freedom of speech" or other rights. What is acceptable dress in the classroom or business world? Many years ago, a teaching colleague announced that he expected all students in his classes to be appropriately dressed, i.e., business attire, since his was a business class. Seeking clarification, one student inquired as to what exactly he expected. Without really thinking, my colleague responded, "I expect all male students to wear a tie and suit or sport coat." The next class session, he got exactly what he prescribed. Most of the male students showed up wearing flip-flops, shorts, tee-shirts, ties and suit coats. Within the bounds of decency, we cannot describe his rants at the next faculty meeting. Of course, that was thirty-some years ago, and recently he was seen at a meeting dressed very casually. We use this to illustrate the problems individuals/organizations have when they do not carefully draft policies. A couple of sidebar questions are: "Should the policy clearly specify ideas of appropriate attire?" "If so, who decides what is appropriate?" "How will students (employees) respond when they believe that the policy is not fair?"

CONTROLLING SHOULD BE FORWARD-LOOKING

A supervisor can do nothing about the past. For example, if work assigned to an employee for the day has not been accomplished, controlling cannot correct the day's results. Yet some supervisors believe that the main purpose of controlling is to assign blame for mistakes. This attitude is not sound because supervisors should primarily look forward, not backward. Of course, supervisors should study the past to learn how and why something happened, and then take steps to avoid the same mistakes.

Because supervisors should look forward while controlling, it is essential that they identify deviations from standards as quickly as possible. Controls within a process or within an activity's time frame—rather than at its end—will enable the supervisor to take prompt corrective action. For example, instead of waiting until the day is over, the supervisor could check at midday to see whether a job is progressing satisfactorily. Even though the morning is past and nothing can change what has already happened, there may be time to correct the problem before the damage becomes excessive.

CONTROLLING SHOULD BE CONSISTENT WITH STRATEGY

As you may recall from Chapter 7, strategic planning begins with establishing goals and making decisions that enable an organization to accomplish its objectives. The ultimate question becomes whether the organization achieved what it intended. The Supervisory Tips box in Chapter 7 shows that in order to reach our goal, we must establish feedback controls and monitor progress. Then changes, if necessary, must be made. In Chapter 11, we discussed how Al Stubblefield and Quint Studer developed a vision and strategy for turning around the Baptist Health Care system of Pensacola, Florida. (See Figure 11.9 on page 416.)

Managers such as Hugh Edwards must first create a vision—a picture of where he wants the store to be—and put a system in place that provides feedback and opportunity to take corrective action. See Figure 14.1.

FIGURE 14.1 You Need a Blueprint to Get from Average to Outstanding!

Someone once said that the ultimate criterion of organizational worth is whether or not the organization thrives. Today's healthcare environment is one of the most competitive, scrutinized, and regulated. You can only imagine the intense pressures—both internal and external—that hospital administrators face unless you have walked in their shoes. We believe that Pensacola, Florida-based Baptist Health Care, Inc. is an excellent example of an organization that made a decision about ten years ago to become the "best of the best" and "walk the talk!"[4]

Baptist Hospital, Inc. (BHI), one of the four Baptist Health Care hospitals, is an example of a dramatic turnaround. In the early 1990s, BHI's morale and finances were in bad shape, and in 1995, the hospital scored in the 18th percentile for patient satisfaction.[5] In 1996, Stubblefield and Studer began to redefine the culture of the organization. Studer believed that some of the lessons he learned as a special-education teacher could be applied to healthcare. "Maximizing an organization's ability is similar to maximizing a child's potential." His first step was to diagnose the situation and then set achievable goals. "The higher the goals, the closer the student—or organization—comes to reaching full potential."[6]

- **Have a Goal:** Studer believed that Baptist needed to have a measurable service goal and a means of comparison. Hiring a large patient-satisfaction-measurement company that compares Baptist to 500 other hospitals across the country was a start. Every patient gets a survey. The feedback allows the hospital to take corrective action, restate goals, and recognize those employees who have received positive comments on the survey.

- **Incorporate Training:** Training played an important role in the turnaround. All nursing managers, supervisors, and department heads go off-site for two days every 90 days for managerial training and development.

- **Seek Employee Input:** Employee forums were held every 90 days. Employees got an opportunity to make their suggestions and concerns known. Employees were encouraged to identify changes in the workplace that would make it better. Studer and the top management team acted on those suggestions. If a suggestion could not be implemented, the employee understood why.

- **Report Cards (Metrics):** Accountability was the key. All leaders got report cards every 90 days. A typical employee had four measurements: customer service (Baptist's goal was to be in the top one percent of all hospitals in the country); efficiency (how long patients are in their units per diagnosis); expense management (how well managers are controlling costs); and turnover. Everyone got a turnover goal based on his or her unit and its past history.

- **Break a few rules:** Stepping outside the box was encouraged. Studer used the following example: *"One of our nurses, Cyd Cadena, called a lady who was hospitalized to see how she was doing at home. She was in a wheelchair, and she was depressed because she didn't have a wheelchair ramp. Her family was so busy working on home healthcare and a whole bunch of other things that they didn't get a chance to put in a ramp. Cyd called Don Swartz, Baptist's plant manager, and he built a ramp. He didn't ask, 'Can I do it?' He just did it; it was the right thing to do!* We tell the story about Don Swartz all over the whole organization. We tell our people it is OK to break a few rules. Take a few risks. Don is a star. You have to celebrate your legends."[7]

Legendary college basketball coach John Wooden summed it up when he said, "You cannot live a perfect day without doing something for someone who will never be able to repay you."[8] Every organization has the potential to create many Don Swartzs but will they do it?

Within a few years, Baptist ranked number two in the country for all hospitals in patient satisfaction. Employee satisfaction had improved 30 percent, and physician satisfaction had risen from 72.4 percent to 81.3 percent. Job turnover for nurses went from 30 percent to 18 percent.[9] A short-term miracle, a one-time blip on the radar screen, or building the foundation built in the late 1990s allows BHI to sustain those accomplishments over the long haul. In his book, *Hardwiring Excellence*, Quint Studer explains that once systems and processes are in place to sustain service and operational excellence, an organization is no longer dependent upon a particular leader to ensure continued success. Results are *hardwired!*[10] In 2000, Studer moved on to form the Studer Group, which coaches hospitals on service and organizational excellence. And yet Baptist's success lives on.

The Morale of the Story: A commitment to excellence requires creating a culture that demonstrates a commitment to employees, setting high but achievable goals, holding people accountable, appraising performance on a regular basis, and taking corrective actions. Our suggestion: ***"Try it—you will like it!"***

Sources: A special thanks to Christina Roman of the Studer Group for her assistance in developing this Contemporary Issue box. Material contained in this Contemporary Issue box pertaining to Quint Studer adapted with his permission and the permission of the Studer Group (http://www.Studergroup.com). (1) Baptist Hospital, Inc. and its parent Baptist Health Care, Inc. have distinguished themselves in the healthcare field in the twenty-first century. *Inc., Fortune, HealthLeaders, Healthcare, Health Executive* and many other magazines, newspapers, and healthcare trade journals have contained articles on BHI's efforts in creating and sustaining outstanding operational and service excellence. (2) "Within Reach," *Health Executive* (September 2005 cover story—http://www. healthexecutive.com/features/sept_2005/sept05_coverstory.asp). (3) Nancy Lyons, "The 90-Day Checkup," *Inc.* (March 1999), pp. 111–12. Lyons's interview with then-president of BHI, Quint Studer, illustrates how Studer used quarterly evaluations to help BHI reach its goal of becoming an employer of choice. (4) Ibid. Also see "Quint Studer," The Studer Group (http://www.studergroup.com/$spindb.query.2quint.studview.3). (5) Quote from former UCLA coach John Wooden. We suggest that you read John Wooden and Steve Jamison, *Wooden on Leadership* (New York: McGraw-Hill, 2005); and visit Coach's Web site (http://www.coachjohnwooden.com). (6) Lyons, op. cit. (7) See Quint Studer, *Hardwiring Excellence* (Gulf Breeze, FL: Firestarter Publishing, 2003). (8) See the Malcolm Baldrige award recipient profiles (http://www.nist.gov/malcolmbaldrige and http://www.nist. gov/public_affairs/releases/bhitrauma.htm).

If you have active, hands-on, fully informed employees, who have the authority to see things that need to be done and the right to tackle any problem, ask any question of anyone, and apply their knowledge consistent with the organizational mission and culture, then the possibilities are limitless. The essence of Studer's system is the report card. Unless people know how they are doing, they won't know what to change or accelerate. Remember, in the end, the goal is to satisfy customers and other stakeholder needs.

CONTROLLING AND CLOSENESS OF SUPERVISION

Supervisors must know how closely to monitor employees' work. The closeness of supervisory follow-up is based on such factors as an employee's experience, initiative, dependability, and resourcefulness. Permitting an employee to work on an assignment without close supervision is both a challenge and a test of a supervisor's ability to delegate. This does not mean, however, that the supervisor should leave the employee alone until it is time to inspect the final results. It does mean that the supervisor should avoid watching every detail of every employee's work. By familiarizing themselves with employees' abilities, supervisors can learn how much leeway to give and how closely to follow up and control.

2 **Identify three types of control mechanisms based on time.**

Time Factor Control Mechanisms

Before we discuss the steps of the controlling process, it is important to distinguish among the following three types of control, which are classified according to time:

1. Feedforward (preliminary, preventive, anticipatory)
2. Concurrent (in-process)
3. Feedback (after-the-process)

FEEDFORWARD (PRELIMINARY, PREVENTIVE, ANTICIPATORY) CONTROLS

Feedforward control
Anticipatory action taken to ensure that problems do not occur

Because controlling has forward-looking aspects, the purpose of a **feedforward control** is to anticipate and prevent potential sources of deviation from standards by considering, in advance, the possibility of any malfunctions or undesirable outcomes. A preventive maintenance program, designed so that equipment will not break down at the height of production, is an example of a feedforward control. The produce clerk who checks samples of bananas to ensure their acceptability is another example. The clerk selects a sample from the crates before the crates are unloaded and the merchandise is placed on display. Requiring assemblers to ascertain components' quality before installation and to signify that they have done so is becoming increasingly common. Other examples of feedforward controls include such devices as safety posters; fire drills; disciplinary rules; checklists to follow before starting equipment; and the policies, procedures, and methods drawn up by managers when planning operations. Everyone uses feedforward controls at one time or another. For example, a person who checks a car's tires, oil, and gas gauge before a trip is using feedforward controls.

CONCURRENT (IN-PROCESS) CONTROLS

Concurrent control
Corrective action taken during the production or delivery process to ensure that standards are being met

A control that is applied while operations are proceeding and that spots problems as they occur is called a **concurrent control**. The traveler who notices that the fuel gauge is below half full or that the fuel warning light has just come on, and who pulls into the next gas station for a fill-up uses a concurrent control. Other examples of concurrent controls are online computer systems, numerical counters, automatic switches, gauges, and warning signals.

Practicing a concurrent control, a factory worker inspects a computer's motherboard for any deviations from company standards

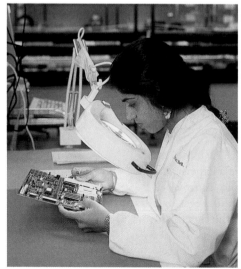

To illustrate, suppose a retail store optically scans each customer's purchases. The customers get printouts of their purchases and the prices they paid (sales receipts). At the same time, the store's inventory automatically decreases by the numbers just sold. The store's computer records the items sold. The computer has been programmed to alert the purchasing supervisor or to automatically place a purchase order when the store's inventory reaches a specified level. As a result, stock is replenished as needed, and the store risks no shortages. When these types of aids are absent, supervisors must monitor activities by observation, often with the assistance of departmental employees.

Even with feedforward controls, concurrent controls are necessary to catch the problems feedforward controls cannot anticipate. Consider the traveler who fills the fuel tank before a trip and estimates, based on experience, that she should be able to travel the 300 miles to her destination without refueling. Unexpectedly, the weather turns unseasonably warm, and the traveler experiences a lengthy delay due to a highway accident. For the convenience of her passengers, the traveler runs the air conditioner while waiting in traffic, both of which unexpectedly increase fuel consumption. Unless the driver periodically checks the fuel gauge or is alerted by the low-fuel warning light (both concurrent controls), she might run out of fuel before they reach their destination.

FEEDBACK (AFTER-THE-PROCESS) CONTROLS

The purpose of a **feedback control** is to evaluate and, when necessary, correct the results of a process or an operation and to determine ways to prevent deviations from standard. The traveler who calculates average miles per gallon and uses that feedback when planning the budget for the next trip uses a feedback control. Other examples of feedback controls include measurements of the quality and quantity of units produced, various kinds of statistical information, accounting reports, and visual inspections. Because feedback controls are applied after a task, process, service, or product is finished, they are the least desirable control mechanisms when damage or mistakes occur. When no damage or mistakes occur, feedback controls are used to further improve the process or product.

Feedback control
Actions taken after the activity, product, or service has been completed

Feedback controls are probably the most widely used category of controls at the supervisory level. Too often, however, they are used primarily to determine what went wrong and where to place blame rather than to prevent the problem from recurring.

Characteristics of Effective Controls

3 Explain the essential characteristics of effective controls.

For control mechanisms to work effectively, they should be understandable, timely, suitable and economical, indicational, and flexible. These characteristics are required of the controls used in all supervisory jobs—in manufacturing, retail, office work, healthcare, government service, restaurants, banks, and other services. Because department activities are so diverse, these characteristics are discussed here only generally. Supervisors must tailor controls to the activities, circumstances, and needs of their departments.

UNDERSTANDABLE

All control mechanisms—feedforward, concurrent, and feedback—must be understood by the managers, supervisors, and employees who use them. At higher management levels, control mechanisms may be rather sophisticated and based on management information systems, mathematical formulas, complex charts and graphs, and detailed reports. At the top levels, such controls should be understandable to all managers who use them. At the departmental level, controls should be much less complicated. For example, a supervisor might use a brief, one-page report as a control device. In a dry-cleaning store, this report might show the number of different types of clothes cleaned and the number of employee hours worked on a given day. This control is uncomplicated, straightforward, and understandable. When controls are confusing or too sophisticated for employees, the supervisor should devise new controls that meet departmental needs and are understandable to everyone who uses them.

TIMELY

Controls should indicate deviations from standards without delay, and such deviations should be reported to the supervisor promptly, even when substantiated only by approximate figures, preliminary estimates, or partial information. It is better for the supervisor to know when things are about to go wrong than to learn that they are already out of control. The sooner a supervisor knows about deviations, the more quickly the deviations can be corrected.

For example, assume that a project that requires the installation of equipment must be completed on a tight schedule. The supervisor should receive regular reports (e.g., hourly or daily) that detail project status and that compare project progress to the schedule. Roadblocks (e.g., missing parts or work absences) that might delay the project should be included in these reports. The supervisor needs this type of information early to take corrective steps—before a situation gets out of hand. This does not mean that the supervisor should jump to conclusions or hastily resort to drastic action. Generally, a supervisor's experience and familiarity with a job will help determine when a job is not progressing as it should.

SUITABLE AND ECONOMICAL

Controls must be suited to activities. For example, a complex information-system control that is necessary for a large corporation would not apply to a small department. The small department needs controls, but controls of different magnitudes. The controls the supervisor applies must also be economical for a job. There is no need to control a minor assignment as elaborately as a manager would control a major capital-investment project.

For example, the head nurse in a hospital will control narcotics more carefully and frequently than bandages. In a small company with three clerical employees, it would be inappropriate and uneconomical to assign a full-time worker to check the clerks' work for mistakes. It would be better to make employees check their own work or, possibly, to check their coworkers' work. In contrast, in a large department of several hundred employees who are mass producing a small-unit product, it makes considerable sense to employ full-time inspectors or quality-control specialists to check results. Typically, these employees sample because it is impossible to check every item in production.[11] For the many in-between situations that supervisors face, good judgment helps determine the suitability of controls.

Even though it may be difficult to determine how much controls cost and how much they are worth, controls must be worth their expense. To determine the value of controls, supervisors should consider the consequences of having no controls. For example, compare an elaborate, expensive control system in a pharmaceutical company with controls in a rubber-band manufacturer. Defective rubber bands are an inconvenience, but defective drugs can kill people. The risks to the pharmaceutical company make elaborate controls worth their expense.

INDICATIONAL

It is not enough for controls just to expose deviations as those deviations occur. A control also should indicate who is responsible for the deviation and where the deviation occurred. When several subassemblies or successive operations comprise a work process, the supervisor may need to check performance before and after each step. Otherwise, if results are below standards, the supervisor may not know where to take corrective action.

FLEXIBLE

Because work operations occur in a dynamic setting, unforeseen circumstances can wreak havoc with even the best-laid plans and systems. Therefore, controls should be flexible enough to cope with unanticipated patterns and problems. Control mechanisms must permit changes when such changes are required. For example, when an employee encounters significant condition changes early in a work assignment, such as an equipment failure or a materials shortage, the supervisor must recognize the changes and adjust plans and standards accordingly. If these difficulties are due to conditions beyond the employee's control, the supervisor also must adjust the criteria by which the employee's performance is appraised.

Steps in the Control Process

4 Describe the essential steps in the control process.

The control process involves three sequential steps. The first step, which is usually part of the planning function, is to set standards appropriate to the task. In the second step, performance is measured against these standards. If performance does not meet the standards, the third step is to take corrective action. These three steps must be followed in sequence if controlling is to achieve the desired results (see Figure 14.2). The accompanying Supervisory Tips box provides selected "do's" and "don'ts" for supervisors as they carry out control responsibilities with their employees.

SETTING STANDARDS

Standards may be defined as the units of measure or the criteria against which performance or results are judged. **Standards** are targets; they are the criteria to which performance is compared in order to exercise control. Standards must be set before a person's work, a finished product, or a service can be meaningfully evaluated. In Chapter 7, we described goals and objectives as the foundations of planning. Objectives give employees specific targets. However, the presence of

Standards
Units of measure or criteria against which results are evaluated

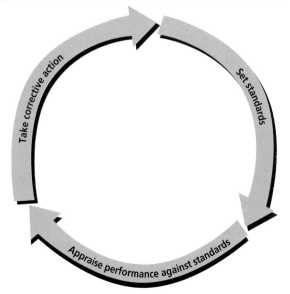

FIGURE 14.2 Steps in the Control Process

Set standards / Appraise performance against standards / Take corrective action

SUPERVISORY TIPS

Supervisory Do's and Don'ts for Controlling Employee Performance

- Be very clear when communicating the objectives and specifics of work assignments.
- Get agreement, if possible, on the standards and measures of performance assessment.
- Solicit employees' ideas for improvement; use their ideas whenever appropriate.
- Concentrate on those issues that most need attention.
- Take corrective action with improvement as the primary goal; do not just try to assign blame.
- Demonstrate consistently with all personnel that you consider budgets, standards, and controls the necessary components of effective management and supervision.
- Convey by words and deeds that in no area of your supervisory responsibilities will you compromise or accept any work performance that is unsatisfactory.

Tangible standards
Standards for performance that are identifiable and measurable

Intangible standards
Standards for performance results that are difficult to measure and often relate to human characteristics (e.g., attitude, morale)

Motion study
An analysis of work activities to determine how to make a job easier and quicker to do

Time study
A technique for analyzing jobs to determine time standards for performing each job

objectives does not mean targets will be attained. The effective supervisor must follow up to ensure that the actions that are supposed to be taken are being taken and that the objectives are being achieved.

There are many types of standards, depending on the areas of performance or results to be measured. **Tangible standards** are performance targets for results that are identifiable and measurable. Tangible standards can be set to measure such things as quantity of output, quality of output, market share, labor costs, overhead expenses, and time spent producing a unit or providing a service. (The tangible standards included on employee appraisal rating forms were identified in Chapter 10.) **Intangible standards** are targets for results that have no physical form; these standards may cover such areas as an organization's reputation, employee morale, and the quality of care in a healthcare center or nursing home. It is usually more difficult to establish intangible standards in numerical or precise terms.

The most frequent tangible standards that supervisors determine or must follow pertain to departmental operations. For example, in a production department, standards can be set for the number of units to be produced; the labor hours per unit; and product quality in terms of durability, finish, and closeness of dimensions.[12] In a sales department, standards might be set for the number of customers contacted, the sales dollars realized, and the number and types of customer complaints.[13]

In setting standards, a supervisor can use as guides experience and job knowledge. Through experience and observation, most supervisors have general ideas of how much time it takes to perform certain jobs, the resources that are required, and what constitutes good or poor quality. By studying and analyzing previous budgets, past production, and other departmental records, supervisors should be able to develop workable standards of performance for most aspects of their departments' operations.

MOTION AND TIME STUDIES

A more thorough and systematic way to establish standards for the amount of work employees should accomplish in a given time frame is to apply work measurement techniques, preferably performed by, or with the assistance of, industrial engineers.[14] The most prominent techniques are motion and time studies. In a **motion study**, engineers analyze how a job is performed to identify ways to improve, eliminate, change, or combine steps to make the job easier and faster. After thoroughly studying work motions and layout, the industrial engineers or analysts develop what they consider the best methods for doing the jobs.

Once the best current method has been identified, a **time study** is performed to determine a time standard for the job. This is accomplished in a systematic and largely quantitative manner by selecting certain employees for observation; observing the times needed to accomplish various parts of the job; applying correction factors; and making allowances for fatigue, personal needs, and unavoidable delays. When all these factors are combined properly, the result is a time standard for the job.

While the time study approach attempts to be objective, considerable judgments and approximations are part of the process. A time standard is neither wholly scientific nor beyond dispute, but it does provide a sound basis on which a supervisor can set realistic standards.[15] The standards developed through motion and time studies can help the supervisor distribute work more evenly and judge each employee's performance fairly. Such standards also help the supervisor predict the number of needed employees and the probable job cost.

Most supervisors work in organizations without industrial engineers. When a new job is to be performed in the department, the supervisor can set tentative standards based on similar operations in this or other departments. When no comparison standard is readily available, the supervisor should identify the key tasks necessary to accomplish the job and then observe employees directly or ask employees to record the time required to complete their tasks. From these data, a reasonable standard can be calculated.

To illustrate, suppose a shift supervisor in a fast-food restaurant must determine how long it takes employees to prepare a new menu item. The supervisor lists all the steps necessary to complete the job. Then, the supervisor can perform the task under several different circumstances and record the required times. The supervisor also can select several employees to perform the task under various conditions. From these several observations, the supervisor can determine the average time required to complete the task. Such an approach will not only establish realistic standards but also might uncover better ways of doing the job.

There are, of course, numerous ways to measure workers' productivity to reflect the unique nature of a department's operations and its products or services. Some worker productivity standards are expressed relative to overall sales volume, profitability, and other aggregate figures—factors over which a supervisor has limited or no control.[16]

EMPLOYEE PARTICIPATION

Some employees resent standards, especially those standards arrived at through motion and time studies. This resentment is part of a long-standing fear that so-called efficiency experts and supervisors use motion and time studies primarily to increase workers' output. However, the main purpose of performance standards should be to create realistic targets, that is, objectives that can be achieved and are considered fair by both the supervisor and the employees. Workers are more apt to accept standards as reasonable and fair when they help formulate those standards.[17] Figure 14.3 provides an interesting illustration to support the notion that those who have responsibility for achieving the targets should be involved in setting standards.

FIGURE 14.3 Whose Job Is It?

PEANUTS: © UNITED FEATURE SYNDICATE, INC.

One technique for including employees in standards establishment is to form a committee of workers to help the supervisor and/or industrial engineer carry out a work-measurement program. The employees selected for this committee should be those who, in the supervisor's judgment, consistently do a fair day's work.

When adopting this approach, the supervisor and industrial engineer should explain to all employees what is involved in motion and time studies, including areas in which judgment is involved. Employees should be allowed to challenge any standard they consider unfair and perhaps even be allowed to request that a job be restudied or retimed. Most workers accept performance standards when they feel the supervisor has tried to help them understand the basis for the standards and has been willing to reconsider and adjust standards that appear to be unreasonable. There are a number of examples where employees, or employees and their union, help set productivity standards. They jointly participate in budgeting, pricing, designing product, marketing, sourcing decisions, and appraising results.

STRATEGIC CONTROL POINTS

As mentioned previously, a metric or standard is nothing more than a measure to assess the department's performance in a particular area.[18] For example, Hugh Edwards in this chapter's opening "You Make the Call!" might want to consider developing metrics for the following:

- Customer satisfaction
- Market share
- Inventory measures
- Sales per square foot or sales of various product lines
- Income per FTE
- Associate (employee) satisfaction
- Delivery time against customer requirements
- Service quality
- Performance of suppliers against their requirements
- Revenue per full-time equivalent (FTE) employee
- Profitability
- Employee suggestions

In Chapter 7's Supervisory Tips Box, we introduced the notion of *SMART* goals. Edwards needs to develop goals in those areas where he can get "the biggest bang for his buck." It is important to remember that you have to be able to measure it. Developing strategic control points or metrics for which you cannot collect accurate or timely data is a waste of time.

For supervisors, the number of standards needed to determine performance quantity and quality may grow as a department expands. As operations become more complex and as department functions increase, it becomes time-consuming and impractical for the supervisor to constantly check against every conceivable standard. Therefore, the supervisor should concentrate on certain strategic control points against which overall performance can be monitored. **Strategic control points**, or **strategic standards**, are a limited number of key indicators that give the supervisor a good sampling of overall performance. There are no rules for selecting strategic control points. Because the nature of the department and the makeup of the supervisor and employees differ in each situation, only general guidelines can be suggested.

One major consideration that may render one standard more strategic than another is timeliness. Because time is essential to control, the sooner a deviation is discovered, the better it can be corrected. A supervisor must recognize at what critical step operations should be checked. For example, a strategic control point

Strategic control points (strategic standards)
Performance criteria chosen for assessment because they are key indicators of overall performance

might be after a subassembly operation but before the product is assembled with other parts and spray painted. A similar approach can be applied to the dry cleaning process of a soiled dress. In this example, a strategic control point can be established shortly after stain remover is applied. Imagine the cost if a stain is still present when all other dry-cleaning operations have been completed.

A supervisor should be careful to choose strategic control points that do not significantly impede other important standards. For example, excessive control to increase production quantity might erode product quality.[19] Likewise, if labor expenses are selected as a strategic control point, supervisors might try to hold down wage expenses by hiring too few workers, thereby causing both quality and quantity standards to deteriorate. Similarly, a laundry department supervisor in a nursing home must not sacrifice standards for preventing infections simply to reduce the cost of laundering linen. To some extent, decisions about strategic control points depend on the nature of the work. What serves well as a strategic control point in one department will not necessarily serve well in another.

Another example of strategic control points is the supervisor who wishes to assess departmental employee relations. The supervisor might decide to use the following indicators as strategic control standards:

- Number of employees' voluntary resignations and requests for transfer
- Levels of absenteeism, tardiness, and turnover
- Accident frequency and severity rates
- Number and types of employee grievances and complaints
- Number and types of customer complaints
- Amount of scrap and rejects and unexplained losses of materials and inventory
- Number of employee suggestions for methods or operations improvement
- Employee responses to satisfaction surveys conducted by the Human Resources Department

By closely watching trends and changes in these indicators, the supervisor should be able to spot problems requiring corrective action. If the trends of most or all of these indicators are unfavorable, major supervisory attention is needed.

Consider a wire manufacturer that used simple statistics to track the productivity of machine operators. During the preceding hour, scrap exceeded the acceptable standard by 10 percent. Using strategic control points in a timely fashion, the supervisor working with the operators and the maintenance department knew it was time to check production. A check of the diamond dies, pressure settings, and quality of the raw stock led to action so that scrap rates increased no further and could be returned to their lower levels. Strategic control points should be established so that corrective action can be taken early in production.[20]

As mentioned previously, there are also areas of an intangible nature that should be monitored closely, even though it is difficult to set precise standards for these areas. For example, employee morale is typically an important element of departmental operations that a supervisor may decide to appraise and assess as a strategic control standard. This is particularly important in an era when workplace anger and employee discontent are reportedly widespread and the potential for these feelings to erupt into violence is real. Techniques for measuring and evaluating employee morale were discussed extensively in Chapter 12.

CHECKING PERFORMANCE AGAINST STANDARDS

The second major step in the control process, an ongoing activity for every supervisor, is to check performance against standards. The primary ways for a supervisor to do this are to observe, study oral and written reports, spot check, and use statistical sampling. Figure 14.4 takes a lighthearted look at tracking performance.

FIGURE 14.4 After developing performance standards, the supervisor must be alert for any deviations from these standards

PERSONAL OBSERVATION

When monitoring employee performance, there is no substitute for a supervisor's direct observation and personal contact. The opportunity to inspect and closely observe employee performance is an advantage the supervisor has over top-level managers because the further a manager is from employees' work, the more that manager must depend on reports from others. The supervisor, however, has ample opportunity to observe directly all day long.

When supervisors find deviations from standards, they should assume a questioning, though not necessarily a fault-finding, attitude. A problem could be due to something outside the employees' control, such as a malfunctioning machine or faulty raw materials. Supervisors should question mistakes in a positive, helpful manner. For example, instead of criticizing, a supervisor should first ask what caused the problem and whether there is any way in which the supervisor can help the employees do their jobs more easily, safely, or efficiently. Supervisors also should ask employees what should be done to correct problems. When standards are stated primarily in general terms, supervisors should look for specific unsatisfactory conditions, such as inadequate output, poor quality work, or unsafe practices. It is not enough just to tell employees that their work is "unacceptable" or "unsatisfactory." When the supervisor can point to specific instances or cite recent examples, the employee is more likely to acknowledge the deficiencies that must be corrected.[21]

To identify the causes of poor performance that are not employees' fault, such as inadequate training, problems with work-flow design, or an unusual increase in workload, supervisors can use personal observation and questioning. For example, if a retail-store supervisor discovers that customers are being processed by the cashier too slowly, the reason may be that an unusually large number of customers entered the store at once. Therefore, instead of chastising employees, the proper corrective action may be to open another checkout lane. Also, the supervisor may need to hire backup cashiers or to find a better way to predict customer traffic. The supervisor may include alternative ways of doing the job in his or her plans. Employees may have valuable ideas for preventing this problem.

However, checking employee performance through personal observation has limitations. It is time-consuming, and it may require supervisors to spend hours away from other activities. Also, it may be impossible for the supervisor to observe some important activities at critical times. Some employees will perform well while being observed but will revert to poorer, less diligent habits when the supervisor is not present. Nevertheless, personal observation is still the most widely used and probably the best method of checking employee performance at the supervisory level.

ORAL AND WRITTEN REPORTS

When a department is large, operates in different locations, or works around the clock, oral and written reports are necessary. For example, when a department operates continuously and its supervisor has responsibility for more than one shift, to appraise the performance of shifts when the supervisor is not present, the supervisor must depend on reports submitted by employees. When a department operates multiple shifts and different supervisors are in charge of different shifts, each supervisor should arrive early to get a firsthand report from the supervisor who is completing the previous shift.

A supervisor watches an employee operate a laser machine and uses personal observation to assess her performance

Whenever reports are required, the supervisor should insist that those reports are clear, complete, concise, and correct. When possible, oral presentations should accompany written reports. Reports are more effective when they are substantiated with statistical or comparative data.

Most employees submit reasonably accurate reports, even when those reports contain unfavorable outcomes. Report accuracy depends largely on the supervisors' reactions to reports and their relations with employees. When supervisors handle adverse reports constructively and helpfully, appreciating honesty instead of just giving demerits, employees are encouraged to submit accurate reports, even when those reports show them unfavorably.

When checking reports, supervisors usually find that many activities have been performed according to standards and can be passed over quickly. As a result, many supervisors use the **exception principle**, which means concentrating on those areas in which performance is significantly above or below standard. Supervisors may even ask employees to forgo reporting on activities that have, for the most part, attained standards and to report only on activities that are exceptionally below or above standard. When performance is significantly below standard, the supervisor must move to the third stage of the control process—taking corrective action. When performance is significantly above standard, the supervisor should praise the employees and encourage the exceptional performance to be repeated.

Exception principle
Concept that supervisors should concentrate their investigations on activities that deviate substantially from standards

SPOT CHECKS

When the employees' work routine does not lend itself to reports, the supervisor may have to rely on periodic spot checks. For example, a data-systems supervisor who is responsible for a centralized computer department that works around the clock, six days a week, should report to work at varying times to assess the department during different shifts. Supervisors with little or no opportunity to spot check usually must depend on reports.

SAMPLING TECHNIQUES

Sampling techniques are really supplements to strategic control points and spot checks. In some firms, each part or product is inspected to determine whether it meets standards. Inspecting every item is time-consuming and costly. While a detailed discussion is beyond the scope of this book, it is becoming increasingly crucial for supervisors, particularly in production facilities, to acquaint themselves with statistical quality control (SQC). SQC is a method to help supervisors determine not only which products, product components, or services to inspect, but also how many to inspect.[22] **Sampling** is the process of inspecting some predetermined number of products from a batch to determine whether the batch is acceptable or unacceptable. To illustrate, suppose that a store manager has been concerned with the quality of produce received from a distributor. The store manager and the produce manager use SQC to determine how many items in an incoming produce shipment should be inspected. Rather than inspecting the entire lot, the store manager and produce manager compare random samples against a predetermined quality standard. If a certain number of the samples fail to meet the standard, the managers reject the entire lot. Note that if the distributor used this technique before shipping the produce, it would be feedback control. The same process used by the store manager would be feedforward control. While SQC saves time and inspection costs, the supervisor must ensure that the inspected units accurately represent all units.

Sampling
The technique of evaluating some number of items from a larger group to determine whether the group meets acceptable quality standards

TAKING CORRECTIVE ACTION

When no deviations from standards occur, the process of control is fulfilled by the first two steps of control: (1) setting standards and (2) checking performance against standards. When, however, deviations are noted through personal observation, reports, or spot checks, the supervisor must take the third step: taking corrective action to bring performance back into line.

Before taking corrective action, the supervisor should remember that deviations from standards can occur in any job for various reasons. Following are some of these reasons:

- Standards were based on faulty forecasts or assumptions;
- Unforeseen problems arose and distorted results;
- Failure occurred in some preceding job or activity;
- Employee who performed the job was unqualified or was given inadequate directions or instructions;
- Employee who performed the job was negligent or failed to follow directions or procedures.

Therefore, before taking corrective action, the supervisor should determine the causes of the deviation by analyzing the situation. Only after identifying specific causes can the supervisor decide which remedial actions will obtain better results. For example, if the reason for the deviation lies in the standards themselves, the supervisor must revise the standards. If the employee who performed the job was unqualified, additional training and closer supervision might be the answer. If the employee was given improper instructions, the supervisor should accept the blame and improve techniques for giving directives. In the case of employee negligence or insubordination, corrective action may consist of a discussion with the employee or a verbal or written reprimand. At times, more serious forms of discipline, including employee suspension or replacement, may be needed. Under such circumstances, the supervisor should follow the disciplinary procedures discussed in Chapter 6.

Budgetary Control

Among the tools for financial control, the budget is usually the one with which supervisors have the most frequent contact. A **budget** is a written plan expressed in numerical terms that projects anticipated resources and expenditures for a period, such as a month, a quarter, six months, or one year. Firms usually prepare various budgets. Supervisors are most familiar with the operating budget. The **operating budget** projects the dollar amounts of the various costs and expenses needed to run the business, given projected revenues. Operating budgets, which may be developed for every department, usually show how much is allocated for inventory, salaries, supplies, travel, rent, utilities, advertising, and other expenses.

At times, it is convenient to express budgets in terms other than dollars. Budgets pertaining to employment requirements, for example, may be expressed in the numbers of employee-hours allocated for certain activities or the numbers of workers needed for each job classification. Eventually, however, such nonfinancial budgets are converted to monetary figures—operating budgets. These statements summarize organizations' overall activities and serve as foundations on which managers can plan and control the use of financial and other resources.[23]

All managers, from the CEO to supervisors, must learn how to plan budgets, live within budgetary limits, and use budgets for control purposes. The term *budgetary control* refers to the use of budgets by supervisors, accountants, and higher-level managers to control operations so that they comply with organizational standards for making budgets.

SUPERVISORY PARTICIPATION IN BUDGET MAKING

Budget making falls under the managerial function of planning, but carrying out the budget, or living within the budget, is part of the controlling function. As is true in so many other areas of management, the planning and controlling aspects of the budget process are interrelated. Preparing a budget, whether it is expressed in monetary or other terms, requires the budget-maker to quantify estimates by attaching numerical values to each budgetary item. The numerical figures in the final budget become the desired financial standards of the organization. Similarly, the numerical figures in the final departmental budgets become the standards to be met by each department and departmental supervisors.

Most annual budgets are projections for the following year based on the previous year's budget. This approach for making a budget is known as **incremental budgeting**. Another approach, which has gained some acceptance in recent years, is zero-base budgeting. When an organization practices **zero-base budgeting**, all budgets must begin "from scratch," and each budget item must be justified and substantiated. In zero-base budgeting, the previous budget does not constitute a valid basis for a future budget. The advantage of zero-base budgeting, sometimes called zero-base review, is that all ongoing programs, activities, projects, products, and the like are reassessed by management in terms of their benefits and costs to the organization. This avoids the tendency of simply continuing expenditures from a previous budget period without much consideration. The disadvantage of zero-base budgeting is that it involves a large amount of paperwork and is very time-consuming. Moreover, in practice it is difficult to apply the concept to some departments and types of operations.[24]

The budget that most concerns supervisors is usually the departmental expense budget, which covers the expenditures incurred by the department. In the discussion that follows, we presume that a firm uses incremental budgeting practices. To many supervisors, budgets have a negative connotation

5 Discuss the supervisor's role in controlling through budgets.

Budget
A financial plan that projects expected revenues and expenditures during a set period

Operating budget
The assignment of dollar allocations to the costs and expenses needed to run the business, based on expected revenues

Incremental budgeting
A technique for projecting revenues and expenses based on history

Zero-base budgeting
The process of assessing, on a benefit-and-cost basis, all activities to justify their existence

of arbitrariness, inflexibility, conflicts, and problems. When the budget is perceived this way, it tends to breed resentment. To facilitate acceptance, expense budgets should be prepared with the participation and cooperation of those responsible for executing them. Preferably, supervisors should help make their departmental budgets. When they are allowed to do this, supervisors must be familiar with both general and detailed aspects of budget preparation. Even when a budget is just handed down to supervisors by higher-level management, supervisors should understand the budget and the reasoning behind each budget figure.

To participate successfully in budget making, supervisors must demonstrate the need for each amount they request and document their requests with historical data whenever possible. The final budget frequently contains lower figures than those that are submitted. A supervisor should not consider this as a personal rejection because other supervisors also make budget requests and have them cut. It is rarely possible for higher-level management to grant all budget requests. Much depends on how realistic the supervisors have been and how well their budgetary needs are documented or substantiated. Supervisors can only hope that the final budget will be close to what they requested and will give them sufficient resources to operate their departments efficiently.

SUPERVISING WITHIN THE BUDGET

Supervisors must manage their departments within budget limits and refer to their budgets to monitor their expenditures during the operating period. When a budget is approved by higher-level management, the supervisor is allocated specific amounts for each item in the budget. Expenditures in the supervisor's department must be charged against various budget accounts. At regular intervals (e.g., weekly), the supervisor must review budgetary figures and compare them with expenses. Cost and revenue data are usually reported to the supervisor by the accounting department. Many, if not most, firms use computer-based cost and financial control systems. Income and cost projections and reports are produced in the form of computer printouts, which may be prepared and distributed by the information technology (IT) department.

If the expenditures for an item greatly exceed the item's budgeted amount, the supervisor must find out what happened. Investigation could reveal a logical explanation for the discrepancy. For example, if the amount spent on labor in a manufacturing department exceeded the budgeted amount, it could be due to an unanticipated demand for the firm's product, which required overtime. When the deviation from the budgeted amount cannot be justified, the supervisor must take whatever actions are necessary to bring the out-of-control expenditures back to where they should be, at least from that point on. Usually, the supervisor must explain excessive deviations to higher-level managers or to the accounting department. To avoid this unpleasant task, a supervisor is well-advised to regularly compare expenditures with budgeted amounts and to keep expenses close to the budget.

A supervisor's budget should not be so detailed and rigidly applied that it becomes a burden. The budget should allow the supervisor some freedom to accomplish departmental objectives. Flexibility does not mean that the supervisor can change budget figures unilaterally or take them lightly. Rather, it means that the supervisor should not be led to believe that budget figures are rigid (see Figure 14.5). Budgets are guides for management decisions, not substitutes for good judgment.[25]

FIGURE 14.5 Budgetary flexibility means that budget figures are not rigid

To prevent budgets from becoming a burden, most organizations have budgets regularly reviewed by supervisors and higher-level managers or the accounting department. These reviews should take place about every week, or at least every month, to ensure a proper degree of flexibility. When operating conditions change appreciably once a budget is established, or when there are valid indications that the budget cannot be followed, a revision is in order. For example, unexpected price increases or major fluctuations in the general economic climate might be reasons to revise a budget. Usually, there is enough flexibility in a budget to permit the common-sense departures that accomplish the objectives of the department and the organization.

Cost Control and the Supervisor

6 Discuss the supervisor's role in maintaining cost consciousness and in responding to a higher-level manager's orders to reduce costs.

Competition from domestic companies and from abroad, and the changing economic environment, require most organizations to strive continuously to control their costs. Sooner or later, most supervisors become involved in some way with cost control because higher-level managers expect supervisors to control costs at the departmental level to help meet organizational cost goals. Therefore, cost consciousness should be an ongoing supervisory concern. Sporadic efforts to reduce costs and eliminate various processes seldom have lasting benefits. While many large organizations employ consultants trained in work efficiency and cost control, in the final analysis, it remains the supervisor's duty to look at cost consciousness as a permanent part of the managerial job.

SHARING INFORMATION AND RESPONSIBILITY WITH EMPLOYEES

While many companies practice management excellence, author Robert Levering, who examined twenty top U.S. firms, concluded that managers can turn a bad workplace into a good one by granting employees more responsibility for their jobs. According to Levering, this means "establishing a partnership with employees rather than acting as adversaries."[26] In forging a partnership with its employees, a firm should be willing to share financial information with them. However, it is not enough for a firm just to share financial information with employees. Employees must understand financial data and have a basis for comparing their firms' financial information with that of previous years and competitors.

As mentioned earlier, many organizations practice a form of open-book management where all financial information is shared with employees. Employees receive timely information on all aspects of the business, from revenues and purchasing costs to labor and management expenses. Every employee learns to understand the information; that part of their job is to move those numbers in the right directions; and how their day-to-day decisions and actions impact revenues, costs, and the bottom line.

When they have relevant financial data, employees may act more conscientiously when making decisions with cost consequences. Similarly, employees with responsibility to make choices about certain expenditures can promote a sense of cost awareness that otherwise might not occur. For example, some firms are using rather simplified approaches for controlling business expenses, approaches that rely on the prudence and integrity of their personnel. Numerous firms are now using online systems to file travel expenses. Such systems reimburse employees quickly rather than impose extended delays in processing expense voucher checks.[27] Other firms are using *per diem* allowances for business meals that tell employees, in advance, their expenditure limits when traveling or entertaining business clients.[28]

MAINTAINING COST AWARENESS

Because cost consciousness is of ongoing concern to the supervisor, plans should be made to achieve cost awareness throughout the department. Here is where planning and controlling again become closely interrelated. By setting objectives and specific results for a certain time frame, costs can be prioritized.

When setting cost objectives, the supervisor should involve the employees who will be most affected. Employees often can make valuable contributions. The supervisor should fully communicate cost-reducing objectives to employees and get as much input from them as possible. The more employees contribute to a cost-control program, the more committed they will be to meeting objectives. It also may be advisable to point out to employees that eventually everyone benefits from continuous cost awareness. Supervisors should help employees see cost containment as part of their jobs and as being in their long-term interest. Firms that do not control costs cannot remain competitive, which could mean job loss. When their supervisors approach them positively, most employees will try to do the right thing and to reduce waste and costs.

RESPONDING TO A COST-CUTTING ORDER

Reducing costs, a natural objective of most organizations, is frequently brought on by competition. It is likely that within an enterprise at one time or another, an order will come from top-level managers to cut all costs across the board by a certain percentage. At first glance, such a blanket order could be considered fair and just. However, this may not be so, because such an order could affect some supervisors more severely than others. Some supervisors are constantly aware of costs and operate their departments efficiently; others are lax and perhaps even wasteful. How should a supervisor react to such a blanket order?

Some supervisors will read a blanket order to mean that everything possible should be done immediately to bring about the desired cost reduction. They might hold "pep rallies" with employees or, at the other extreme, harshly criticize employees and others. Some supervisors might stop buying supplies, eventually leading to work delays. Others might eliminate preventive maintenance work, even though doing so could lead to equipment breakdowns and work-flow interruptions. While these actions may reduce some costs, they could be more expensive in the long run.

Other supervisors will follow cost-cutting directives halfheartedly. They will make minimal efforts here and there to give the appearance that they are doing something about costs. Such efforts are unlikely to impress employees, who also may make only halfhearted efforts. This type of supervisory response contributes inadequately to cost control.

An across-the-board cost-reduction order may present a hardship to the diligent, cost-conscious supervisor whose department is working efficiently. Nevertheless, this supervisor may strive to take some action by looking again at areas where there is still room to reduce expenses. This supervisor will call for employee suggestions because employees can bring about results. For example, some paperwork may be able to be postponed indefinitely, or certain operations may be unnecessary, even when performed efficiently. The supervisor should point out to employees which operations are most expensive and let them know what those operations actually cost. An employee might suggest a less expensive way of doing a job. If so, the supervisor should welcome the suggestion. The supervisor should commit to the cost-reduction campaign and should set a good example whenever possible. While it may be difficult to come up with large savings, at least the supervisor will have made a diligent effort to support the organization's cost-cutting drive. While supervisors play a key role in cost reduction, they cannot succeed without employee involvement and commitment.

Effective supervisors constantly seek ways to eliminate costs by questioning the necessity of everything done in their departments. It has been our experience

The greater the number of employees who contribute to a cost-control program, the more committed they will be to meeting objectives

that in times of economic downturns, organizations focus on cutting costs. Costs are associated with internal process activities and inventory. Hugh Edwards, in this chapter's opening "You Make the Call!" can focus on ways to reduce costs, but we offer another alternative. Get ideas from employees on how to increase sales revenue, expand the sales effort, and increase margins on certain products and services. Hugh and his key personnel, including outside sales personnel, could go to where their customers are, meet with them, ascertain their needs, and demonstrate to them how Edwards can fulfill those needs and make it easy for them to do business with Edwards Homecenter and Lumber.

Even when an organization lacks a formal suggestion program, supervisors can establish a climate of mutual trust and respect that encourages employee suggestions. The supervisor can formally and informally encourage employees during departmental meetings to emphasize the value of suggestions. For example, when an employee or a group of employees complains about a policy or practice, the supervisor might turn the complaint into a challenge by saying, "You may be right. Why don't you do something about it? Perhaps we need a change. Think of a better way, and we'll take it to top management. Any credit for the idea will be yours."

Whether for changing policies or controlling costs, employee suggestions can be a valuable source of ideas. Employees like to see their ideas put into effect and are more committed to goals they help set.

7 Identify additional control areas and explain how the controlling function is closely related to the other managerial functions.

Other Control Areas

In addition to accounting and budgetary controls, there are other areas of management control in many organizations. Typically, these control areas are supervised by specialized departments and are outside the realm of most supervisors' direct authority and responsibility. Nevertheless, supervisors should be aware of these control areas and, when necessary, should familiarize themselves with the methods of the specialists performing these control activities. Often, such specialists are the supervisor's fellow staff members.

SPECIALIZED CONTROLS

Inventory control means keeping watch over raw materials, supplies, work-in-process, finished goods, and the like. Maintaining sufficient, though not excessive, inventory; keeping status records of all inventory; ordering economic lot sizes; and many other tasks are part of inventory control.[29]

Quality control means maintaining the quality standards a firm sets for its products or services. Products and services must be monitored and improved continually to ensure that quality is maintained. As discussed earlier in this chapter, the quality control of products is often accomplished by testing randomly selected samples to determine whether quality standards are being met. A commitment to total quality management, or TQM, as described in Chapter 7, means making an overall effort to respond to customer needs by preventing defects/errors, correcting errors when they occur, and continuously building better overall quality into goods and services as dictated by market and other conditions.[30]

Production control usually consists of a number of activities that are designed to keep overall operations on schedule. It involves routing operations, scheduling, and, when necessary, expediting work flow. Elaborate charts and network analyses may be used. For example, the production-control department may start with a Gantt chart, which is a diagram or pictorial representation of the progress and status of various jobs in production. When practical, this can lead to a computerized network analysis. Two of the most widely used analyses, program evaluation review technique (PERT) and Gantt charts were discussed in Chapter 7.[31]

CONTROLLING AND THE OTHER MANAGERIAL FUNCTIONS

Throughout this book, we have discussed, from different perspectives, numerous aspects of effective managerial controls. At this point, we review several of those aspects as they relate to the controlling function.

In Chapter 7, we discussed management by objectives (MBO) in connection with motivation and planning. MBO provides another mechanism for providing feedback. It involves a "co-partnership" approach and calls for high involvement and accountability.

In Chapters 4 and 11, we discussed the positive aspects of participative management. In general, this management style means that employees share the objectives and plans of top managers guiding the organization. Often, this is accomplished through programs and systems that involve employees in many phases of planning how best to meet customer needs. Employees are urged to search for new ways to help customers, and employees are given timely information about their performance accomplishments and any problems that require correction.[32] Such approaches, sometimes called "commitment-to-excellence programs," are consistent with the principles of control discussed in this chapter and with the principles of motivation discussed in Chapter 4.

In Chapter 7, we discussed standing (repeat-use) plans, such as policies, procedures, methods, and rules, primarily in regard to managerial planning. When standing plans do not work or are not followed, the supervisor must take the necessary corrective actions to bring the department's operations back in line. Therefore, these types of standing plans may be seen as forward-looking control devices. Performance appraisal, which we discussed under the staffing function in Chapter 10, also has a place as a control mechanism. During a performance appraisal meeting, the supervisor evaluates an employee's performance against predetermined objectives and standards. At the same time, the supervisor and the employee may agree on steps for corrective action, as well as on new objectives and standards. The element of supervisory control can be detected throughout a performance-appraisal cycle. In Chapter 6, we discussed employee discipline. When a supervisor takes disciplinary measures because employees do not follow established rules, such measures serve as control techniques.

These managerial activities show how intrinsically related the controlling function is to all the other managerial functions. As stated previously, controlling is typically performed simultaneously with the other managerial functions. The better supervisors plan, organize, staff, and lead, the better their ability to control activities and employees. Controlling takes a forward-looking view, even though it has been discussed as the final managerial function in this book.

SUMMARY

1 Controlling is the managerial function that determines whether plans are being followed and whether performance conforms to standards. Every manager must develop and apply controls that monitor the organization's activities to achieve desired results. The controlling function is most closely related to the planning function. Supervisors set the objectives that become the standards against which performance is checked. Well-designed controls can positively influence employee motivation. Controls should be forward-looking, because nothing can be done about the past. The closeness of supervisory control depends, in part, on employees' experience, initiative, dependability, and resourcefulness.

2 Control mechanisms can be categorized as feedforward, concurrent, or feedback based on when they are implemented in the control process. Feedforward, or preliminary, controls are used to anticipate and prevent undesirable outcomes. The person who checks the tires, oil, gas gauge, and the like before a trip uses a feedforward control. The traveler who notices that the fuel gauge is below half full or that the fuel warning light has just come on and pulls into the next gas station for a fill-up uses concurrent control. Feedback controls are employed after the fact; they are the basis for correction and improvement. The traveler who calculates average miles per gallon and uses that information when planning the budget for a next trip uses feedback control. Generally, effective supervisors rely on all three types of controls to improve the control process or to prevent problems.

3 To be effective, controls should be understandable to everyone who uses them and should yield timely information so that problems can be corrected before situations get out of hand. Also, controls should be suitable to, and economical for, situations. The more serious the consequences of mistakes, the tighter the controls should be, despite the expense. Further, controls should indicate where trouble lies in the process and should be flexible enough to adjust to changing conditions.

4 When performing the controlling function, a supervisor should follow three basic steps:

1. Set standards.
2. Check performance against standards.
3. Take corrective action when necessary.

The age-old question: "How's it going?" can only be answered if you know where you want to go and how you will know if you got there. In recent years, there has been a greater emphasis on metrics. A metric or standard is a measure to assess how you are doing in a particular area. Standards may be set for tangible and intangible areas. A supervisor's experience and knowledge can help that supervisor develop performance

standards. More precise work standards can be set through motion and time studies and workflow charts. Employee participation in setting standards is crucial to employee acceptance of those standards. Many supervisors focus their control efforts on selected strategic control points, or strategic standards, which are major performance indicators.

The supervisor should continuously check performance against standards. In some instances, the supervisor must depend on reports, but in most cases, personal observation and inspection are appropriate for checking employee performance. At times, the supervisor may apply the exception principle, which means concentrating on areas in which performance is significantly below or above standards. Sampling can help the supervisor determine whether products meet standards. When discrepancies arise, the supervisor must take the necessary corrective actions to bring performance back in line and to prevent other deviations.

5 The most widely used financial control is the budget. Budget preparation is primarily a planning function. However, applying, supervising, and living within a budget are part of the controlling function. Supervisors should help prepare their departmental budgets, regardless of whether the enterprise practices traditional or zero-base budgeting. Virtually all budgets need some built-in flexibility to allow for adjustments, when necessary. When significant deviations from the budget occur, the supervisor must investigate and take whatever actions are appropriate to bring expenditures back in line.

6 Cost control and cost consciousness should be continuing concerns of all supervisors. When top-level managers issue cost-cutting orders, supervisors should avoid extreme measures that may in the long run be more costly than the reductions themselves.

Involving employees in cost-reduction efforts is one way the effective supervisor creates cost awareness. Suggestion programs can be used to solicit employee ideas for potential cost-reduction areas. The supervisor should constantly seek ways to eliminate costs. Periodically, the supervisor should look at the department "through the eyes of a stranger" and question the necessity of everything done in the department.

7 Many organizations have specialists who concentrate on inventory control, quality control, and production control. These types of control systems are not usually under the direct authority of most departmental supervisors but are handled by staff specialists. Other managerial concepts, techniques, and approaches used by departmental supervisors contain aspects of the controlling function. Among these are MBO, standing plans, discipline maintenance, and the employee performance appraisal. Thus, controlling is intimately interrelated with all other managerial functions.

KEY TERMS

Budget (p. 519)
Concurrent control (p. 508)
Exception principle (p. 517)
Feedback control (p. 509)
Feedforward control (p. 508)
Incremental budgeting (p. 519)

Intangible standards (p. 512)
Managerial controlling (p. 504)
Motion study (p. 512)
Operating budget (p. 519)
Sampling (p. 518)
Standards (p. 511)

Strategic control points (strategic
  standards) (p. 514)
Tangible standards (p. 512)
Time study (p. 512)
Zero-base budgeting (p. 519)

QUESTIONS FOR DISCUSSION

1. Define the managerial controlling function, and discuss its relationship to the other managerial functions. Why do many people view controls negatively?

2. After reviewing Figure 14.1, ponder the following statements:
   a. "It's OK to break the rules."
   b. "If in doubt, check with your boss."
   c. "Rules exist to make things work consistently, but when rules get in the way of meeting customer needs, it is appropriate to question the rule."
   Do you agree with the statements? Why or why not? Recall an instance where you followed each of these statements. Did the situation turn out OK? If not, why not?

3. Define and give examples of each of the following controls:
   a. Feedforward
   b. Concurrent
   c. Feedback

4. Define and discuss each of the following primary steps in the control process:
   a. Setting standards
   b. Checking performance against standards
   c. Taking corrective action

5. Discuss the supervisor's duty to take appropriate action when accounting reports indicate that expenditures are significantly above or below budget allocations. How do effective supervisors reduce costs?

6. "A work activity that does not add value is a candidate for elimination." Do you agree? Why or why not?

SKILLS APPLICATIONS

Skills Application 14-1: What Should Hugh Do?

Refer to this chapter's opening "You Make the Call!" Assume that you are Hugh Edwards. You are encouraged to read Dirk Dusharme, "2007 Retailer Customer Satisfaction Survey," *Quality Digest* (May 2007), pp. 48–53 (www.qualitydigest.com) and Laurie Brown, "When Good Customer Service Rules Go Bad," *SuperVision* (September 2007), pp. 8–9 before answering the following questions.

1. What do you think of the job Hugh has done so far?

2. The pressure to increase sales and control costs is not unique to Edwards Homecenter. Identify and discuss other key dimensions of organizational change and control that Hugh has overlooked.

3. Identify specific metrics (standards) that Hugh should use to determine organizational productivity, efficiency, and effectiveness of Edwards Homecenter and Lumber.

4. What are some ways to manage the metrics you established in the previous question?

5. Why might some of the associates at Edwards Homecenter and Lumber Company be resistant to some of the changes that Hugh has implemented?

   a. What else can you do to minimize resistance to change?
   b. When Hugh was talking about the need to be more innovative in a meeting with associates, Charlie Jones laughs and says, "Why would we want to do that? We're not concerned with innovation around here." How should Hugh handle this challenge?

OPTIONAL ROLE-PLAY EXERCISE: Divide the class into groups of five or six students. One is to play the role of Hugh Edwards with the other playing the role of associates.

Task 1: Hugh wants the group to develop strategies for increasing sales revenue. You and the team are to brainstorm specific strategies that might be implemented to increase sales revenue. You have ten minutes to develop a list of the target markets (customer segments) that Edwards should go after.

Task 2: You have ten minutes to develop the specific standards (metrics) that will be used to determine your progress.

Task 3: You have ten minutes to develop specific strategies (actions) for achieving your objectives.

Task 4: Your instructor will ask each group to briefly summarize their number-one strategy for increasing sales revenue.

Skills Application 14-2: Thinking Outside the Box—Systematic Sampling

You have eight golf balls, seven of which weigh exactly the same. The eighth golf ball weighs slightly less than the others. With only two opportunities to use a balance scale, your assignment is to determine which ball weighs less than the others.

1. What is your strategy for determining which of the balls weighs less than the others?

2. How does this skills application relate to the concepts presented in this chapter?

3. In forty words or less, what did you learn from this skills application?

Source: This skills application was adapted with permission from QCI International's "Timely Tips for Teams," a monthly Internet newsletter. ©2004. (http://www.qci-intl.com/home.htm)

Skills Application 14-3: Burger Control

You have been hired as a management efficiency consultant to advise the owner of Sycamore Hamburger and Shake Palace. At certain times during the day, there are varying backlogs in the burger prep area. As a result, work flow slows, waste increases, and customers complain about the wait or that their orders are not warmed evenly. Your assignment is to design a control system to address these problems.

1. List the steps you would take to complete this assignment. (Suggestion: If possible, visit a fast-food restaurant that features hamburgers, and solicit a supervisor's ideas and suggestions.)

2. What recommendations would you make for Sycamore?

3. Compare your recommendations with those of another student. Is there one recommendation the two of you could make to Sycamore? If so, what would it be?

4. Summarize, in under twenty-five words, what you learned from this skills application.

Skills Application 14-4: Wise the "Know-It-All"

This is the latest skills application that introduces you to another person who has the potential to make your life difficult.

1. Read the following statement from Dick Warfield, the operations supervisor at the New America facility of Barry Automotive:

Every time we have a quality meeting, Brenda Wise, our plant manager, constantly interrupts the discussion. She hears a portion of the discussion and quickly puts in her two cents. Here's an example: Michael, who's from the design engineering department, and I were discussing the high percentage of product returns on Part 35A1206 from Ford's assembly plant in Lorain. Wise jumped into the middle of the conversation with the statement that the assembly workers weren't following instructions. She then stated that she had looked at the blueprints and knew that if they followed directions there would be no problem. When we tried to explain other possible causes for the returns, Wise emphatically stated that inaccurate measurement was the problem and that we were both wrong.

Wise is very opinionated and demands that you follow her directions. One-way communication is her style—top-down. In her defense, Wise is very intelligent and organized. She throws facts and figures out so quickly that we are buried by her arguments. When she can't sway us with her interpretation of the facts, she tries to "bulldoze" her ideas and solutions through the entire organization. It's clear that

Wise's management style is "my way or the highway." If we were unionized, the union reps would be filing grievances left and right.

Wise even butts in where she has no business. Last week, several of us were discussing my daughter's upcoming wedding. Wouldn't you know it? Wise was passing by the break-room table, heard the discussion, and proceeded to tell me everything that ought to be done—the "Wise Way" is the only way, according to her.

I know that Wise is very knowledgeable in some aspects of work, but she hasn't realized that "none of us is as smart as all of us!" Her sarcasm and know-it-all attitude are driving me crazy. I'd like to look for another job, but I feel I'm trapped here. What do I do?

2.  Using the Internet, find at least three sources of information on how to deal with Brenda Wise. Carefully review each site for suggestions on how to deal with the "know-it-all."

3. Based on your findings, what suggestions would you make to Dick Warfield on how to cope with Wise?

4. Write a one-page paper explaining how this skills application increased your working knowledge of coping with the behaviors of this type of difficult person.

SKILLS DEVELOPMENT

Skills Development Module 14-1: Honda—A Finely Tuned Control Process

This video clip focuses on Honda. Go to http://www.honda.com for current information about the company. We suggest that you click on "The Power to Dream" and "See what we see."

In 1959, Honda American Motor Car Company opened its first showroom in Los Angeles. Honda's growth from humble beginnings is amazing. Honda opened its first U.S. auto plant in 1979 and now employs over 25,000 Americans. Another 100,000 are employed at authorized Honda automobile, motorcycle, and power-equipment dealerships in the U.S.

In 2008, when the Big Three U.S. automakers are begging government for "bailout help," Honda opened a

$550-million production facility near Greensburg, Indiana. Two thousand associates will produce the Honda Civic Sedan at that facility. Also in 2008, Honda Aircraft Company opened a plant in Greensboro, North Carolina, to produce an advanced and efficient light jet.

As a manufacturer offering consumer goods for sale, Honda strives to be in full compliance with Consumer Products Safety Laws, gathering information from their own systems, which were established to help ensure the safety of their customers, and submitting reports to the designated authorities in a timely and precise manner as required.

Now view the Skills Development Module 14-1 video clip.

Questions for Discussion

1. In this chapter, we identified three types of control mechanisms based on time. Identify and discuss the types of control that Honda uses in its design and manufacturing processes.

2. Diagnostic metrics are measures that ascertain why a process is not performing up to expectations. Cite examples from the video clip to demonstrate how Honda is using this approach to improve product quality.

3. The video clip emphasizes how Honda uses a continuous improvement process. One example was the "A-zone." Describe the process of control used by Honda and the end results.

4. Give examples of how technology, innovation, and feedback are used to improve Honda's product.

5. Go to http://world.honda.com/CSR/ to see "Insisting on Quality." What does Honda do to instill pride in production and a quality-first orientation for its employees?

ENDNOTES

Suggested Reading: Many experts predict that a disease of epic (pandemic) proportions is coming. Every employer would be at risk. The Centers for Disease Control (CDC) estimates there were 500,000 U.S. deaths in 1918 due to flu. The CDC estimates that in the United States, a 1957–58 pandemic killed 70,000, while a 1968 pandemic killed 34,000. Crisis management discussed in Chapter 7, along with other planning techniques and the principles of control discussed in this chapter, should be reviewed so that you will know how to prepare for the worst-case scenario. See Nancy Hatch Woodward, "Pandemic," *HR Magazine* (May 2006), pp. 46–52; and John M. Barry, *The Great Influenza* (New York: Penguin Books, 2005).

Also see Stephen Baker, *The Numerati* (New York: Houghton-Mifflin Company, 2008) or Book Excerpt "Management By The Numbers," *BusinessWeek* (September 8, 2008), pp. 032–044. The *BusinessWeek* article chronicles "The Science of Management" from the works of Frederick W. Taylor (scientific management), to operations research, to the work of W. Edwards Deming (statistical quality control), to Six Sigma (Motorola's management strategy), to modeling workers. The article and book describes how IBM is building mathematical models of their 50,000 employees. The goal is to optimize them, using operations research, so that they can be deployed with more efficiency.

Interestingly, job dissatisfaction is one of the system's constraints. We encourage you to read the *BusinessWeek* article.

1. Adapted from Peter F. Drucker, American Businessman Quotes, "Brainy Quotes." [We substituted the word *manager* for Drucker's *executive*.]

2. For expanded discussions on the controlling function, see Richard L. Daft, *Management*, 8th ed. (Mason, OH: Southwestern/Thomson, 2008), Chapters 19 and 20; or John R. Schermerhorn, Jr., *Management*, 8th ed. (New York: Wiley, 2005), pp. 180–99. Also see Ananya Rajagopal, "Team Performance and Control Processes in Sales Organizations," *Team Performance Management*, 14. 1/2 (2008), pp. 70–85; or Gary Bradt, "We've Merged or Reorganized, Now What?" *SuperVision* (February 2008), pp. 16–17.

3. See Allison Stein Wellner, "You Know What Your Company Does. Can You Explain It in 30 Seconds?" *Inc.* (July 2007), pp. 92–97; David K. Lindo, "Tell Them What You Expect," *SuperVision* (June 2005), pp. 16–18; Lindo, "Keeping Track of Your Promises," *SuperVision* (April 2005), pp. 111–13; William Cottringer, "Setting the Standards," *SuperVision* (April 2005), pp. 6–7; and W. H. Weiss, "Organizing for Quality, Productivity, and Job Satisfaction," *SuperVision* (February 2002), pp. 13–15.

4. "Survey Finds Generation Gap Toward Workplace Attire," *SHRM Home* www.SHRM.org (September 28, 2005). Also see, Joan Oleck, "Casual Dress: Dot-Com Casualty," *BusinessWeek* (March 19, 2001), p. 8.

5. A special thanks to Christina Roman of the Studer Group for her assistance in developing Figure 14.1 for this edition. Material contained in Figure 14.1 pertaining to Quint Studer was adapted with his permission and the permission of the Studer Group (http://www.studergroup.com). Baptist Hospital, Inc. and its parent Baptist Health Care, Inc. have distinguished themselves in the healthcare field in the twenty-first century. *Inc.*, *Fortune*, *HealthLeaders*, *Healthcare*, *Health Executive* and many other magazines, newspapers, and healthcare trade journals have contained articles on BHI's efforts in creating and sustaining outstanding operational and service excellence.

6. "Within Reach," *Health Executive* (September 2005 cover story—http://www.healthexecutive.com/features/sept_2005/sept05_coverstory.asp).

7. Nancy Lyons, "The 90-Day Checkup," *Inc.* (March 1999), pp. 111–12. Lyons's interview with then-president of BHI, Quint Studer, illustrates how Studer used quarterly evaluations to help BHI reach its goal of becoming an employer of choice.

8. Quote from former UCLA coach John Wooden. We suggest that you read John Wooden and Steve Jamison, *Wooden on Leadership* (New York: McGraw-Hill, 2005); and visit Coach's Web site (http://www.coachjohnwooden.com).

9. Lyons, op. cit.

10. See Quint Studer, *Hardwiring Excellence* (Gulf Breeze, FL: Firestarter Publishing, 2003). Also see the Malcolm Baldrige award recipient profiles (http://www.nist.gov/malcolmbaldrige and http://www.nist.gov/public_affairs/releases/bhitrauma.htm).

11. Often this is accomplished through some form of statistical quality control (SQC), which is discussed later in this chapter. See Lloyd S. Nelson, "Test on Quality Control Statistics and Concepts," *Journal of Quality Technology* (January 2001), pp. 115–7.

12. A major survey of over 700 manufacturing firms revealed that, among the identified "leading" firms, the following areas of performance measurement were used by over 90 percent of firms: manufactured/delivered costs per unit, inventory levels, worker productivity, manufacturing cycle time, and cost efficiencies in operations. See "Survey in Manufacturing," *Management Review* (September 1999), pp. 18–19.

13. See Erin White, "Quest of Innovation: Motivation Inspires Gurus," the *Wall Street Journal* (May 6, 2008), p. B6; John R. Graham, "Seven Ways to Differentiate Your Company That Make a Difference to the Customer," *Supervision* (August 2005), pp. 17–18; Carol Hymowitz, "Use Technology to Gather Information, Build Customer Loyalty," the *Wall Street Journal* (October 26, 2004), p. B1; and Dara Mirsky, "Good, Bad, and Close Customer Service as 2001 Ends," *Customer Interaction Solutions* (February 2002), pp. 44–45. Go to www.sap.com/bestrun for information on what it means to be a Best-Run Business.

14. For expanded descriptions of job-design and work-measurement techniques, see Richard B. Chase and Nicholas J. Aquilano, *Operations Management for Competitive Advantage*, 11th ed. (Boston: McGraw-Hill Irwin, 2005), pp. 181–205; or Fred E. Meyers, *Motion & Time Study* (Boston: Pearson Education, 2002).

15. See Rick Rutter, "Work Sampling: As a Win/Win Management Tool," *Industrial Engineering* (February 1994), pp. 30–31.

16. For a discussion of worker productivity measurement, see "A Company's Most Challenging Asset: Its People," *Quality Digest* (December 2002), p. 6; "Value at Work: The Risks and Opportunities of Human Capital Measurement and Reporting" (http://www.conference-board.org). Also see Edwin R. Dean, "The Accuracy of Bureau of Labor Statistics (BLS) Productivity Measures," *Monthly Labor Review* (February 1999), pp. 24–34, and Jim Carbone, "It Takes a Lot of Hard Work to Reach Top Plus Quality," *Purchasing* (November 15, 2001), pp. 244–5.

17. Employee and management co-participation is a key ingredient in any improvement effort. See H. James Harrington, "Management Participation," *Quality Digest* (July 2008), p. 12; Robert J. Grossman, "Steering a Business Turnaround," *HR Magazine* (April 2008), pp. 73–80; and Alberto Bayo-Moriones and Javier Marino-Diaz de Cerio, "Quality Management and High Performance Work Practices: Do They Coexist?" *International Journal of Production Economics* (October 13, 2001), p. 251. Also see Thomas R. Cutler, "Bored by Lean: Apathy is a Cancer that Affects Lean Continued Process Improvement," *Quality Digest* (May 2008), pp. 46–48.

18. See Karen M. Kroll, "Repurposing Metrics for HR," *HR Magazine* (July 2006), pp.64–69.

19. For additional information on productivity measurement, see Robert O. Brinkerhoff and Dennis E. Dressler, *Productivity Measurement: A Guide for Managers and Evaluators* (Newbury Park, CA: Sage Publications, Applied Social Research Methods Series, Volume 19, 1990). Also see Peter Dickin, "Find Mistakes Where They Can Be Corrected," *Quality Digest* (May 2008), pp. 31–34; Otis Port, "How to Tally Productivity on the Shop Floor," *BusinessWeek* (November 23, 1998), p. 137, and Kostas N. Dervitsiotis, "Looking at the Whole Picture in Performance Improvement Programmers," *Total Quality Management* (September 2001), pp. 687–700.

20. In the major manufacturing survey cited in Endnote 12, manufacturers were asked to identify the "critical practices" they used to compare their operations with those of competitors. The five most often cited were (1) cost efficiencies in operations, (2) speed time-to-market, (3) research and development, (4) rapid supply from suppliers, and (5) delivery logistics. See *Management Review*, op. cit., p. 18. For interesting discussions of matching production levels to the rapidly changing automotive industry, see Katherine Hobson, "The Good, the Fad, and the Ugly," *U.S. News & World Report* (April 1, 2002), p. 31; Thomas K. Grose, "License to Thrill," *U.S. News & World Report* (April 1, 2002), p. 30; and Darren Fonda, "Going Topless," *Time* (April 1, 2002), pp. 50–52. For a different perspective, see Paul Differding, "In Pursuit of Mediocrity: Fast Cycle Times and Globalization Discourage Higher Quality," *Quality Digest* (March 2008), p. 18.

21. See Susan Oakland and John S. Oakland, "Current People Management Activities in World-Class Organizations," *Total Quality Management* (September 2001), pp. 773–88. Also see, Leander Kahney, *Inside Steve's Brain* (New York: Portfolio, 2008). Kahney describes how Steve Jobs, co-founder of Apple, learned from his mistakes and applied solid management skills.

22. For expanded discussions on statistical quality control, see Chase, Jacobs and Aquilano, op. cit., pp. 318–371; or on statistical process control, see Lee J. Krajewski and Larry P. Ritzman, *Operations Management Strategy and Tactics*, 3rd ed. (Upper Saddle, NJ: Pearson Prentice Hall, 2005), pp. 202–221.

23. For an expanded discussion of short-term financial analysis, including budgets and budgetary control, see Thomas P. Edmonds, et al., *Fundamentals of Financial Accounting* (Boston: McGraw-Hill Irwin, 2006), pp. 314–35; or Chase, op.cit., pp. 750–66.

When the Sarbanes-Oxley Act (SOX) was enacted in 2002, we surmised that the new law would have little, if any, impact on supervisors. While Congress's intent was to make it harder for publicly traded companies to "cook the books," Section 404 mandates financial reporting accuracy, and the largest budget line for most organizations is payroll. See Allen Smith, "SOX Audits of Small Companies' Internal Controls Delayed," *SHRM Law* (January 14, 2008); or Robert J. Grossman, "Demystifying Section 404—Sarbanes–Oxley Compliance," *HR Magazine* (October 2005), p. 48 for a partial list of controls companies are implementing to ensure the accuracy of HR financials.

24. For a discussion comparing incremental versus zero-based budgeting and other budgeting approaches, see Richard L. Daft, *Management*,

8th ed. (Mason, OH: South-Western Thomson, 2008), Chapter 19; or O. C. Ferrell and Geoffrey Hirt, *Business: A Changing World*, 5th ed. (Boston: McGraw-Hill Irwin, 2006), Chapter 14.

The notion of *open-book management* is by opening financial records to employees and getting them to think and act as business owners by setting financial and operating targets in sales, production, and revenues, greater profits, greater efficiency, better morale, and a more engaged workforce can result. The open-book concept requires education to understand the financial data and other relevant business information and then actively engage them in setting goals, establishing metrics and encouraging them to strive for improvement. For a discussion of open-book management, see John Case, "The Open-Book Revolution," *Inc.* (June 1995), pp. 44–50; and *The Coming Business Revolution* (New York: Harper-Business, 1995).

25. While Figure 14.5 shows a manager changing the figures, we contend there is a huge difference between making budget adjustment and "cooking the books." Andy Fastow, former Enron CFO, said, "What I did was reprehensible, and it is not easy to look at yourself and to admit it. . . . All I can do is ask for forgiveness..." As quoted in Bethany McLean and Peter Elking, "Guilty Conscience," *Fortune* (April 3, 2006), pp. 34–36.

We contend that organizations need to have a confidential, anonymous reporting mechanism in place to serve as an early warning system operated by an independent, third party who can quickly investigate allegations of fraud and other charges. The foundation of the control system is that employees need to believe that someone will respond quickly to charges of malfeasance or other unethical behavior.

26. From Beth Brophy, "Nice Guys (and Workshops) Finish First," *U.S. News & World Report* (August 22, 1988), p. 44. Also see Robert Levering and Milton Moskowitz, "The 100 Best Companies to Work For," *Fortune* (February 4, 2002), pp. 72–80; or visit the Web site (http://100best @greatplacestowork.com); and "Special Report: The Best (& Worst) Managers of the Year," *BusinessWeek* (January 13, 2003), pp. 58–92.

27. See Michael Conlon, "Firm Offers Advance Pay for Travel Expense Accounts," Reuters News Service as published in the *St. Louis Post-Dispatch* (August 30, 1999), p. BP15. For a discussion of how firms are monitoring the quality of their e-mail and Internet systems, see Michelle Conlin, "Watch What You Put in That Office E-mail," *Business-Week* (September 20, 2002), pp. 114–5; and Kathleen Melymuka, "Ensuring e-Quality," *Computerworld* (January 29, 2001), pp. 44–45.

28. See Tom Belden, "Suggestions for Controlling Costs of Meals on the Road," Knight Ridder Newspapers as published in the *St. Louis Post-Dispatch* (August 30, 1999), p. BP15.

29. For expanded information on inventory control, see Krajewski and Ritzman, op. cit., pp. 667–689.

30. For expanded information concerning quality control and TQM, see Nicole Torka, Marianne Van Woerkon and Jan-Kees Looise, "Direct Employment Involvement Quality (DEIQ)." Creativity & Innovation Management, 17, 2 (June 2008), pp. 147–154; J. R. Evans and W. M. Lindsay, *The Management and Control of Quality*, 6th ed. (Mason, OH: South-Western, 2005); Bill Creech, *The Five Pillars of TQM: How to Make Total Quality Management Work for You* (New York: Truman Tally Books/Dutton, 1994); and Joseph F. Noferi and Daniel E. Worden, "Where Has Quality Gone?" *Risk Management* (May 2001), pp. 35–39; Mike Williams, Mitch Griffin, and Jill Attaway, "Observations on Quality: The Principles of Quality," *Risk Management* (October 2001), pp. 50–52; John Addey, "Quality Management System Design: A Visionary Approach," *Total Quality Management* (December 2001), pp. 849–54; and Joseph Taiwo, "Systems Approaches to Total Quality Management," *Total Quality Management* (December 2001), pp. 967–73.

31. For expanded information on production control and service quality, see Craig Cochran, "Measuring Service Quality: Even If You Can't Heft or Gauge It, You Can Still Assess It," *Quality Digest* (March 2008), pp. 30–33; Jack West, "Controlling Production and Service Provision," *Quality Digest* (September 2007), p. 20; Laurie Brown, "What Your Customers Really Want: Seven Goals of Customer Care," *SuperVision* (June 2007), pp. 20–21; Krajewski and Ritzman, op. cit., pp. 194–227; Thomas E. Vollmann, William L. Berry, David C. Whybark, and F. Robert Jacobs, *Manufacturing Planning & Control for Supply Chain Management* (Boston: McGraw-Hill Irwin, 2005); E. M. Goldratt and J. Cox, *The Goal: A Process of Ongoing Improvement* (Great Barrington, MA: North River Press, 1992). For information on total performance and measurement model systems, see Jiju Antony, Graeme Knowles, and Tolga Taner, "10 Steps to Optimal Production," *Quality* (September 2001), pp. 45–49, and Gopal K. Kanji and Patricia Moura e Sa, "Kanji's Business Scorecard," *Total Quality Management* (December 2001), pp. 898–905.

If you have a healthcare orientation, you might want to read Jeffrey C. Bauer and Mark Hagland, Paradox and Imperatives in Health Care: How Efficiency, Effectiveness, and E-Transformation Can Conquer Waste and Optimize Quality (New York: Taylor & Francis, Inc. 2007).

32. For illustrations of outstanding customer service, see Stanley A. March, "Understanding Change Management," *Quality Digest* (December 2002), p. 18; John Guaspari, *Switched-on-Quality* (Chico, CA: Paton Press, 2002); Susan Greco, "Real-World Customer Service," *Inc.* (October 1994), pp. 36–45; and Torben Hansen, "Quality in the Marketplace: A Theoretical and Empirical Investigation," *European Management Journal* (April 2001), pp. 203–11. Also see Thomas Pyzdek, "What Does Your Customer Expect?" *Quality Digest* (July 2008), pp. 14–15.

Southwest Airlines led the industry in passenger satisfaction for the fifteenth consecutive year. CEO Kelly acknowledged that the airline still had room to improve. It should be noted that SWA is one of the most unionized airlines. See "Airlines Face More Gripes about Service," the *Wall Street Journal* (May 20, 2008), p. D6. For more information about unhappy fliers, visit www.jdpower.com/corporate/news/releases/pressrelease.aspx?ID=2008050.

CHAPTER 15

(**Resolving Conflicts in the Workplace**)

After studying this chapter, you will be able to:

1 Recognize that handling disagreements and conflicts in the workplace is a component of supervision.

2 Identify and contrast five styles that are inherent in conflict-resolution approaches.

3 Distinguish between supervisory handling of employee complaints in any work setting and grievances in a unionized situation.

4 Explain the major distinctions between grievance procedures, complaint procedures, and alternative dispute resolution (ADR) procedures.

5 Describe the supervisor's role at the initial step in resolving a complaint or grievance.

6 Identify supervisory guidelines for resolving complaints and grievances effectively.

YOU MAKE THE CALL!

Disagreements and Conflicts Are Part of the Workplace

Most of us grew up in a world full of conflict situations. Perhaps as children we fought with our siblings or with others over whose turn it was to play with a certain toy, or we argued with our parents over bedtime hours. These disagreements over what should be done or what should occur, are called **substantive conflict**.[1]

However, many of us grew up disliking disagreements unless we won. Often, because we saw the dispute from only one point of view—our own—and were unwilling to compromise or to accommodate the other party, the dispute escalated and the relationship between the two parties deteriorated. Growing up, we played games in which there could be only one winner. Sometimes, the winners arrogantly touted their success. Other times, the losers pouted, ranted and raved, or cried. Someone may have countered, "You're a sore loser."

Substantive conflict
Conflict between individuals because of what should be done or what should occur

The competitive nature of our society, which tends to reward and revere winners, carries over into the workplace.

How did the preceding actions impact the people they involved? The winners wanted to win, sometimes at any cost. Some of the losers lost interest in playing the game. Still others learned to intensely dislike the arrogance of the winners or the childlike behavior of the losers. The parties may have argued for any reason, or no reason, just because they did not like each other. **Personalized conflict** is laden with emotions. According to author Robert Bacal:

Personalized conflict
Conflict between individuals that occurs because the two parties do not like one another

> When conflict is personalized, each party acts as if the other person is suspect as a person. Problem solving rarely works because neither party is really interested in solving a problem. In fact, in extreme cases, the parties go out of their way to create new problems, imagined or real. Personalized conflict almost always gets worse over time, if [it] cannot be converted to substantive conflict.[2]

As you recall from earlier chapters, personalized conflict including bullying and other forms of incivility appears to be on the rise. Personalized conflict that cannot be resolved leads to "dysfunctional conflict." The end result is that communications between the individuals break down. The workplace may become politicized as other team members either choose sides or withdraw. Energy and effort that should be devoted to accomplishment of objectives is diverted as a result of the conflict. Thus, **dysfunctional conflict** prevents the team from accomplishing its goals because communication breaks down and individual pride becomes more important than team pride.

Dysfunctional conflict
Communication between individuals breaks down and the lack of teamwork causes the team to stray from its chosen path

Sometimes, through experience, we learned that conflict was good because we learned a great deal by talking out our differences and settling on a course of action that met the needs of both parties. Good conflict, often called **constructive conflict** or "functional conflict," is healthy for the organization and helps improve performance. Various researchers have contended that "Team leaders (supervisors) need to encourage team members to express disagreement, keep the disagreement constructive, find points of agreement, and build a commitment to the team decision."[3] When the needs of the employees and the organization are met, constructive conflict results in a win-win situation for all concerned.

Constructive or functional conflict
The end result of conflict is a win-win situation for all concerned

If you think that you can go through a day without conflict, you're wrong. Conflict is inevitable, and you will need to develop conflict-resolution strategies. In this chapter, we will discuss some of the most important conflict, grievance, and complaint considerations.

WORKPLACE CONFLICT MUST BE RESOLVED

In the workplace, many supervisors become irritated and confused when employee complaints or grievances challenge their authority. Some supervisors find it difficult to function because they feel that disagreements with employees reflect on supervisory performance or perhaps that there is something wrong with their supervisory abilities. At times, supervisors must act like referees to resolve employee conflicts. Most supervisors do not like conflict because they may be drawn into the fray and they must guard against losing their tempers. When conflicts are handled improperly, employee disputes can turn into further anger and conflict that is directed toward the supervisor.

Many workplace events can trigger complaints and conflicts. Communication breakdowns, competition over scarce resources, unclear job boundaries ("That isn't my responsibility!"), inconsistent policy application ("You didn't punish

Joe when he was late, and now you're picking on me!"), unrealized expectations ("I didn't know you expected me to do that!"), and time pressures ("You didn't give us enough notice!") are workplace events that commonly lead to irritations, disagreements, and complaints.

For these and other reasons, many supervisors view workplace conflict as dysfunctional because it distracts and detracts from the completion of objectives. However, employee conflicts, complaints, and grievances should be viewed as expected parts of workplace relationships. Of course, it is undesirable for supervisors to confront a constant flood of employee disagreements because this would probably indicate severe departmental problems. Yet supervisors should understand that, as they carry out their managerial responsibilities, it is normal that supervisory perspectives and decisions will at times conflict with those of employees and/or the labor union. Further, employees are human beings who are prone to the irritations and frustrations that can lead to conflict. Therefore, a supervisor should recognize that handling conflicts and resolving employee complaints and grievances are natural components of departmental relationships and the supervisory position.

Remember: Passivity, silence, or wishful thinking will not cause the conflict to go away. There are times when the supervisor must respond to the situation on the spot. Here are some thoughts on how that can be done (see Figure 15.1). First, pause and survey the situation. Often, conflict is caused by misunderstanding. Ask yourself these questions: What is your approach to resolving conflict? Are you the person who "shoots from the hip," or do you take another approach (such as: "Angie, I want to run something by you. I could be wrong, so I need your input.")? Do you look at each situation with an open mind? Do you want to discuss this right now? If not, do you set a specific time for dialogue and discussion? Who should be involved in the discussion? Are you willing to show them the harm or potential harm that the conflict is causing? To what extent are you willing to work with them on developing alternatives and a solution? As motivational speaker and author Dale Carnegie said, "If you want to gather honey, don't kick the beehive."[4]

FIGURE 15.1 When it comes to resolving conflict, the ball is in your court!

2 **Identify and contrast five styles that are inherent in conflict-resolution approaches.**

Resolving Conflicts Successfully Requires Effective Communication

Our primary focus in this chapter is the effective handling of complaints and grievances that usually result from workplace disagreements or conflicts. However, before discussing the handling of complaints and grievances, it is appropriate to identify, in general terms, some approaches, and to discuss why communication is crucial to effective conflict resolution.

While supervisors may approach conflict resolution differently, they should understand the five basic conflict-resolution or negotiation styles (see Figure 15.2).

The horizontal axis on Figure 15.2 indicates the degree of cooperativeness, ranging from low to high. A high degree of cooperativeness implies that one desires a long-term, harmonious relationship with the other party. A customer tells a sales supervisor that a competitor can provide the same services for a substantially lower price. The price is just slightly above the supervisor's break-even point. A conflict arises between what the supervisor is willing to sell the product for and what the customer is willing to pay. If the customer is a long-time purchaser of large quantities of the product, the supervisor would be high on the cooperativeness scale. On the other hand, if the customer purchased very little and only purchased when other suppliers could not fill the orders, the supervisor might rate a moderate to low score on the scale. An important question can serve as a guide when you have a conflict with someone else: "Is this relationship worth saving?" If the answer is *yes*, then you are higher on the horizontal axis than if the answer is *no*.

Low to high concern for self, or degree of assertiveness, is found on the vertical axis of Figure 15.2. To determine location on this scale, the supervisor must ask: "What is really important to me?" For example, many supervisors have stated that employee safety and product quality are their top priorities. In other words, they will not compromise their high standards of quality and safety. Various combinations of these concerns yield five **conflict-resolution styles**:

Conflict-resolution styles
Approaches to resolving conflict based on weighing desired degrees of cooperativeness and assertiveness

1. *Withdraw/avoid:* The withdraw/avoid approach may be appropriate when the issue is perceived to be minor and the costs of solving the problem are greater than the benefits. For example, a student leaves class and sees an altercation in the parking lot. Two students unknown to her are arguing. Withdrawal is probably the best strategy because the student's potential costs outweigh the potential benefits.

   However, workplace conflict between two employees must be addressed when noticed by a supervisor. When left alone, conflict tends to fester.

FIGURE 15.2 Conflict-resolution or negotiation styles

We have all known the person who believes if you ignore the problem, it will go away. That may be true for the thunderstorm that occurred the other day—the day you forgot your umbrella. You got soaked on your way from the parking lot to class. What did you learn from that situation? Whose fault was it that you got wet? Our point here is simple: One needs to assess each situation or potential situation and accept personal responsibility for withdrawing, avoiding, going with the flow, or taking proactive action to deal with the situation (or at least putting a plan in place for dealing with future situations). Supervisors must assess each situation and decide whether to address the conflict or avoid it. Ask this question: "If I do nothing, what is likely to happen?" If there is risk that avoidance might result in declining performance or create long-term fear, resentment, or dissatisfaction in the work group, then you must take action.

2. *Accommodate/oblige:* The primary strength of the accommodate/oblige style is that it encourages cooperation. For example, Sam goes home one evening and is greeted by his wife, Mary, who says, "I thought we'd go out for dinner tonight. I'd really like to go to the seafood restaurant." Sam had his mind set on having a quick dinner at home and watching football on television. Sam decides to oblige Mary to preserve the relationship over the long term. This style is thought of as "I lose, you win." Sam wins by losing because his wife may love him more or reciprocate the next time. Because no one wants to lose all the time, this style implies the rule of reciprocity, or the **reciprocity reflex**—that is, you give up something now to eventually get something of value in return.

> **Reciprocity reflex**
> One good turn deserves another in return

No one wants to give in all the time. Some use this style because it is easy. You do not have to communicate your preferences or provide data to support your "real stance" on a situation. Supervisors who rely on this style may be well-liked but not respected.

3. *Compromise:* The compromise style is called "win some, lose some." What is wrong with splitting the difference? Consider the story of King Solomon in the Bible.[5] "Two women argued that the living child was theirs and that the dead one belonged to the other. After listening to their arguments, the King said to his aides, 'Bring me a sword.' They brought the king a sword. Then he said, 'Cut the living baby in two—give half to one and half to the other.'"

In that case, who would be the winner? Clearly, it would have been an illustration of "everyone loses." In the long term, this approach is not in the best interests of either party since neither gets what she really wants.

But the real mother said, "On no! Give her the whole baby alive; don't kill him." The other one said, "If I can't have him, you can't have him–cut away!" The wise King said, "Give the whole baby to the first woman. No one is going to kill this baby. She is the real mother." We could all use the wisdom of King Solomon.

Unfortunately, labor-management negotiations often use compromise. Unfortunately, when one party knows that the other always compromises, that party brings inflated demands to the bargaining table. As a result, valuable time is wasted trying to identify the real issues.

Remember: There are certain items for which there should be no compromise. What would be the long-term results if a company used a lesser quality component in the braking systems of the automobiles they produced? What if a supervisor bent company policies to accommodate an employee's request? The policies were written for a purpose. In every organization there are certain things for which there is no compromise.

4. *Compete/force/dominate:* The compete/force/dominate style is characterized as "I win, you lose." This style may be appropriate to resolve the following type of conflict: Employees have not been wearing their safety glasses because they are uncomfortable in humid weather. The supervisor could force a decision on the employees because the potential safety factor is deemed more important than employees' feelings. However, the question that arises is why the supervisor had to force the solution on the employees. When supervisors foster open and participative climates, they can use good communication skills to gain understanding rather than decide by edict. The forcing style may foster resentment and cause long-term problems.

There is nothing wrong with competition as long as it is healthy. As one manager was heard to say, "Now, we all know that competition between work groups is healthy. But remember, the goal is to get the work done. I want competition to be fun and a learning experience for all. If we all work to become better, the plant becomes better."

However, think back to that playground bully. He or she wants to be in control of each and every situation. Power is important to this person. Some of you have experienced the boss whose style was "my way or the highway!" What was the impact of such a style of leadership?

5. *Collaborate/integrate/problem solve:* The collaborate/integrate/problem solve style is usually characterized as "I win, you win." In essence, collaborative problem solving or **interest-based negotiating** means that you first must seek to determine what the other person really wants and then find a way or show that person how to get the desired result. At the same time, you can get what you want. This style gives the supervisor an opportunity to question the other parties to ascertain their interests and needs. Joint problem solving leads all parties to understand the issues and constraints and to consider options. Solutions are developed collaboratively, and mutual trust and respect can be primary gains of this style.

According to Louis Manchise, director of mediation services-Midwest for the Federal Mediation and Conciliation Service (FMCS), "Interest-based negotiating is about the process to find a solution, and not as much about the substance of the negotiations, like wages or which restaurant to go to for dinner.

Interest-based negotiating
Understanding why the other party wants what he or she wants, and then working toward a solution that satisfies those needs as well as your own

Collaborative problem solving means finding out what other people want, showing them how to get it, and getting what you want

One side doesn't use its power to force an agreement. It's an option that satisfies both interests."[6] Although this style of conflict resolution is ideally best, it tends to be the most time-consuming. Also, not every issue can be resolved with a "win-win" solution; some conflict resolutions clearly have winners and losers.

COMMUNICATION IN RESOLVING CONFLICTS

One of the first lessons students learn is that one need not shout to get attention. Suppose, however, that a production worker approaches a supervisor and is really angry that a material handler has let some inferior-quality material get through quality checks. The angry production employee is shouting. To defuse the employee's anger and to gain control of the situation, some communication experts advocate the following: Get the employee's attention by shouting back, "You have every right to be angry, and I'm as angry as you are." Then continue in a normal tone of voice: "Now that we both agree that this is a serious problem, what can we do about it, and how can we prevent it from happening again?" This approach puts the employee back on track by focusing on the issues. The objectives of the organization and the needs of the employee may then be met through collaborative problem solving. See Figure 15.3 for suggestions for resolving conflict.[7]

FIGURE 15.3 Suggestions for resolving conflicts

- Take responsibility for resolving the conflict—do not let it escalate.
- Identify the issue(s).
    Explore all sides of the issue(s).
    Become aware of each party's position, needs, and feelings.
    Ask open questions—probe.
    Use paraphrasing and reflective questioning to ensure understanding (see Chapter 3).
    Establish ground rules for the meeting management (see Chapter 8) (e.g., everyone will have a chance to be heard, there will be no interruptions, and feelings will be supported with facts).
- Do not be quick to use your authority or position power.
- Help parties to agree on the issue/problems.
- Ask all parties to commit to working with you to solve the problem.
- Create a climate of open communication so that you can help the parties explore "win-win" alternatives.
- Develop fallback alternatives if the parties cannot reach consensus; you may have to use your authority or position of power to force a solution if the participative approach does not work.
- Follow up to make certain the conflict has been resolved or, at the very least, minimized.

FIGURE 15.4 Want a Better World?

Mort Walker, "Beetle Bailey," *King Features Syndicate, Inc.* (July 18, 2005). Reprinted with permission.

In all this, it should be apparent that the most effective communication and problem solving take place when people try to share perspectives. When employees are on the same team and want to do a good job—and when supervisors are clear in their objectives and work to improve human relations—there is a better chance of making the organizational climate conducive to the effective resolution of most complaints, grievances, and conflicts that will inevitably occur. Remember: Employees need to know where they stand and what is expected. A sincere, genuine compliment from the other party (or boss) may go a long way toward resolving conflict. See Figure 15.4 for a lighthearted approach to dealing with conflict.

Complaints and Grievances in Supervision

3 Distinguish between supervisory handling of employee complaints in any work setting and grievances in a unionized situation.

For supervisors at the departmental level, resolving conflicts for the most part involves handling and settling employee complaints and grievances. The terms *complaint* and *grievance* are not synonyms. As commonly understood, a **complaint** is any individual or group problem or dissatisfaction that employees can channel upward to management. A complaint can normally be lodged in any work environment, and the term can be used to include legal issues, such as a complaint of racial or sexual discrimination. Typically, a **grievance** is defined more specifically as a formal complaint involving the interpretation or application of the labor agreement in a unionized setting. This usually means that it has been presented to a supervisor or another management representative by a steward or some other union official.

In earlier chapters, we discussed at some length the terminology used in union/management situations and the important relationship between the supervisor and the union steward at the departmental level. The number and types of grievances that arise in a department can reflect the state of union/management relations. Of course, grievances also can be related to internal union politics, which are usually beyond a supervisor's control.

In this chapter, we use the terms *complaint* and *grievance* somewhat interchangeably. Whether employees are unionized, every supervisor should handle employee complaints and grievances systematically and professionally. Doing so requires skills and efforts that are major indicators of a supervisor's overall managerial capabilities. The underlying principles for handling complaints and grievances are basically the same, even though the procedures for processing them may differ. The supervisory approaches suggested here should generally be followed, regardless of the issue or whether the work environment is unionized.

Complaint
Any individual or group problem or dissatisfaction employees can channel upward to management, including discrimination

Grievance
A formal complaint presented by the union to management that alleges a violation of the labor agreement

Procedures for Resolving Grievances and Complaints

While the procedures for resolving grievances and complaints are similar, there are some important distinctions supervisors should understand. This section discusses these distinctions.

4 Explain the major distinctions between grievance procedures, complaint procedures, and alternative dispute resolution (ADR) procedures.

GRIEVANCE PROCEDURES

Grievances usually result from a misunderstanding, a different interpretation of the labor agreement, or an alleged violation of a provision of the labor agreement. Virtually all labor agreements contain a **grievance procedure**, which is a negotiated series of steps for processing grievances, usually beginning at the departmental level. If a grievance is not settled at the first step, it may be appealed to higher levels of management or to the human resources department. The last step typically involves having a neutral arbitrator render a final and binding decision in the matter.

Grievance procedure
Negotiated series of steps in a labor agreement for processing grievances, beginning at the supervisory level and ending with arbitration

COMPLAINT PROCEDURES

Many nonunion organizations have adopted formal problem-solving or complaint procedures to resolve the complaints employees bring to their supervisors. A **complaint procedure**, which may be called a "problem-solving procedure," is a management-designed procedure for handling employee complaints that usually provides for a number of appeal steps before a final decision is reached. A complaint procedure is usually explained in an employee handbook or a policies and procedures manual. Even when no formal system is spelled out, it is usually understood that employees have the right to register a complaint with the possibility of appealing to higher-level management. A procedure for handling complaints differs from a union grievance procedure in two primary

Complaint procedure
A management-designed series of steps for handling employee complaints that usually provides for a number of appeals before a final decision

---

FIGURE 15.5 A problem-solving procedure for complaints

PROBLEM-SOLVING PROCEDURE

Objective

Our purpose is to give employees an effective means of bringing problems to the attention of management and getting those problems solved. A problem may be any condition of employment an employee feels is unjust or inequitable. Employees are encouraged to air any concern about their treatment or conditions of work over which the company might be expected to exercise some control.

Normal Procedure

Step 1—*Supervisor*. Problems are best solved by the people closest to them. Employees are therefore asked to first discuss their concerns with their immediate supervisors. Supervisors should, of course, seek satisfactory resolutions. If the employee feels the supervisor is not the right person to solve the problem, the employee can ignore this step.

Step 2—*District Manager*. If the problem is not resolved after discussion with the supervisor, the employee should be referred to the district manager or assistant district manager.

Step 3—*Division Manager*. If the problem has not been settled by the supervisor or the district manager, the employee should be referred to higher-level divisional management.

Step 3—*Alternate—The Human Resources Staff*. As an alternative, the employee can discuss the problem with a member of the human resources staff rather than higher-level divisional management.

Step 4—*The President*. If the matter is not adjusted satisfactorily by any of the foregoing, the employee may request an appointment with the president or executive vice president, who will see that a decision is finalized.

Policies

1. *Freedom from Retaliation*—Employees should not be discriminated against for exercising their right to discuss problems. Obviously, any retaliation would seriously distort the climate in which our problem-solving procedure is intended to operate.
2. *Prompt Handling*—A problem can become magnified if it is not addressed promptly. Supervisors are expected to set aside time to discuss an employee's concerns within one working day of an employee's request. Supervisors should seek to solve a problem within three working days of a discussion.
3. *Fair Hearing*—Supervisors should concentrate on listening. Often, hearing an employee out can solve a problem. Supervisors should objectively determine whether the employee has been wronged and, when so, seek a satisfactory remedy.

President's Gripe Box

The president's "Gripe Box" is on each floor of our home office buildings. Employees should feel free to use the "Gripe Box" to get problems to the president's attention expeditiously. Employees may or may not sign gripes. Written responses will be sent for all signed gripes.

---

respects. First, the employee normally must make the complaint without assistance in presenting or arguing the case. Second, the final decision is usually made by the chief executive or the human resources director rather than by an outside arbitrator.

Figure 15.5 is an edited excerpt of one firm's problem-solving procedure. Note that it involves a series of steps that begins at the supervisory level and ends with the company president or executive vice president. It is important to note the *Freedom from Retaliation* statement in Figure 15.5. Increasingly, the courts have taken a dim view of employer actions that hint of retaliation against employees who exercised their rights under company handbook policy and/or state and federal legislation.[8]

ALTERNATIVE DISPUTE RESOLUTION PROCEDURES

In recent years, some companies have offered their employees assistance in processing complaints by providing a neutral person or counselor to serve as an intermediary. Other companies offer the services of a mediator—usually a third party who facilitates communication but who has no direct authority to decide outcomes.

Numerous companies have adopted "juries" or "panels" of employees and managers who serve as arbitration boards in the final step of complaint procedures. This approach, often called peer review, can be adapted as an alternative to litigation to resolve various disputes.

Still other firms are using, or experimenting with, outside arbitrators as the final step to resolve complaints, mostly in discharge and discrimination cases. When outside arbitrators are used, all parties agree to abide by the arbitrator's decisions. The arbitrator is a neutral third party, and policies for the arbitrator's selection, fee, and hearing procedure are specified and agreed on before the case is heard. A number of firms have combined mediation and arbitration, called "med-arb." Under med-arb procedures, parties first attempt to resolve a dispute through some form of mediation. If mediation fails to achieve a satisfactory solution, then there is recourse to an outside arbitrator.[9]

Collectively, these approaches have been labeled **alternative dispute resolution (ADR),** which generally means processing and deciding employee complaints internally as an alternative to lawsuits, usually in discharge and/or employment discrimination cases. ADR approaches are becoming more common, driven primarily by the desire of employers to expedite dispute resolution and avoid the high costs of litigation.[10]

> **Alternative dispute resolution (ADR)**
> Approaches to processing and deciding employee complaints internally as an alternative to lawsuits, usually for disputes involving discharge and/or employment discrimination

There may eventually be legislation to expand ADR to millions of workers with no union or legal protection. Already, some organizations are experimenting with **ODR (online dispute resolution)** techniques. ODR is purported to be more cost-effective and results in quicker adjudication of disputes.[11] Only time will tell the extent to which it will be used.

> **ODR (online dispute resolution)**
> An alternative approach similar to ADR, but the dispute process is handled online

In a major organizational policy statement, the Society for Human Resource Management (SHRM), a national organization of human resources professionals, has strongly endorsed ADR procedures that "provide employees a process that is accessible, prompt, and impartial, and that results in reduced dispute resolution costs and more timely resolution of complaints as an alternative to costly litigation." In the same policy statement, SHRM has recognized that for ADR to be effective, certain standards of fairness and due process must be met. Included among these standards are:

- The opportunity for a hearing before one or more neutral, impartial decision makers
- The opportunity to participate in the selection of decision makers
- Participation by the employee in assuming some portion of the costs of the dispute resolution
- The opportunity to recover the same remedies available to the employee through litigation and confidentiality of proceedings[12]

A national legal commission, the National Conference of Commissioners on Uniform State Laws, has proposed a new uniform employment statute that would permit terminated employees to take their cases before neutral arbitrators. A number of states are seriously considering adopting this type of arbitration system; whether such a proposal will be adopted widely is conjecture. Most employers prefer that ADR be voluntary, not compulsory by law. Regardless, a major question remains: Does ADR work? One government report cautioned that "no comprehensive evaluative data" exist on the effectiveness of ADR.[13]

A review of management literature, particularly arbitration decisions, indicates that many disputes could be prevented if supervisors practiced good communication skills and displayed genuine concern for employee problems.[14] Time and time again, workers complain that they did not know their employers'

FIGURE 15.6 The dispute resolution program for employees that includes mandatory, binding arbitration as a final step

THE DISPUTE RESOLUTION PROGRAM SUMMARY

The dispute resolution process (DRP) is a structured process unintended to replace or infringe on a supervisor's communication responsibilities in the resolution of work-related issues. The three levels of DRP are in logical sequence, and employees must complete each level of the process before proceeding to the next.

Level 1—Local Management Review
At Level 1, an employee and the management team attempt to resolve the employee's dispute or complaint to a satisfactory conclusion.
1. An employee initiates Level 1 by completing a written complaint on the DRP Level 1 Form, Part 1—Notice of Dispute.
2. On the form, the employee details the dispute, complaint, or issue, as well as the desired resolution.
3. The employee identifies all individuals who may have information regarding the dispute. The employee should provide copies of other pertinent information relating to the dispute.
4. The employee should give the completed form and copies of relevant information to the employee's supervisor, the department head, or corporate human resources, and retain a copy.

The company's management will ensure that an appropriate investigation is conducted, that all information is evaluated carefully, and that a decision is made promptly. All information presented during the review process and the final determination is handled on a need-to-know basis. Human resources representatives will be involved in each claim to discuss disputes with employees, supervisors, and/or management personnel.

When a final determination is made, the Level 1 Form, Part II, will be completed and a copy will be given to the employee, the DRP administrator, and corporate human resources.

When the complaint is a covered claim and an employee wishes to appeal the decision made at Level 1, the employee may request mediation (Level 2) and binding arbitration (Level 3).

Level 2—Nonbinding Mediation
When the dispute cannot be resolved at Level 1, and the complaint is a covered claim, an employee can request Level 2—Nonbinding Meditation by submitting the appropriate form to the DRP administrator within applicable time limits. Level 2 is described fully in the DRP Policy Statement and the DRP Guide.

Level 3—Binding Arbitration
When the employee's dispute cannot be resolved at Level 2, the employee may request Level 3—Binding Arbitration by submitting the appropriate form to the DRP administrator within applicable time limits. Level 3 is described fully in the DRP Policy Statement and the DRP Guide.

Employees Covered under the DRP
The DRP applies to all salaried and nonunion hourly employees. Effective January 1, 2009 all employees agree, as a condition of employment, that all covered claims are subject to the DRP.

expectations, lack the materials to do their jobs, and cannot get timely responses from their supervisors.[15]

In summary, if ADR is to succeed, companies must train supervisors to respond positively to employee requests, concerns, and complaints, and to address conflict and resolve complaints to ensure that fairness prevails.

MANDATORY ARBITRATION MAY INCREASE

Buoyed by several recent court decisions, some large companies have instituted mandatory complaint-resolution procedures whose final step is private arbitration.[16] Figure 15.6 summarizes a dispute-resolution procedure put into effect by a major corporation for its salaried and nonunion hourly employees. The primary objectives of such a procedure are to handle complaints—including discrimination charges—internally and to avoid costly litigation. It is expected that more organizations will adopt such procedures. However, a number a legal issues remain to be clarified by statues or the courts, principally standards for fairness and other elements of basis due-process protection when private arbitration is mandatory.[17]

The Supervisor and the Significant First Step in Resolving Complaints and Grievances

5 Describe the supervisor's role at the initial step in resolving a complaint or grievance.

In the following discussions, we focus primarily on the resolution of employee complaints and grievances, with the role of the supervisor uppermost. As in so many other areas, the supervisor's role in the handling of employee complaints and grievances is often the most crucial part of the outcome. Supervisors also become involved in ADR procedures and in the resolution of other types of conflict at the departmental level. The principles of complaint and grievance handling apply to most workplace conflicts.

As the first step in a unionized firm, the departmental steward usually will present a grievance to the supervisor, and the aggrieved employee or employees may be present.[18] The supervisor should listen to these parties very carefully. The supervisor may speak with the employee directly in front of the steward. There should be frank and open communication among the parties. If the steward does not bring the employee, the supervisor should listen to the shop steward.

It is unusual for an aggrieved employee to present a grievance to a supervisor in the absence of the steward. However, if this should happen, it is appropriate for the supervisor to listen to the employee's problem and to determine whether the problem involves the labor agreement or the steward, or whether the union should be involved at all. Under no circumstances should supervisors give the impression that they are trying to undermine the steward's authority or relationship with the employee. When the labor agreement or union interests are involved, the supervisor should notify the steward concerning the employee's presentation of the problem.

When a grievance is not settled at the first step and when the steward believes the grievance is justified, the grievance proceeds to the next step. The steward may carry the grievance further with some other objective in mind. The steward is usually an elected representative of the employees, is familiar with the labor agreement, and is knowledgeable in submitting grievances. The steward may be eager to receive credit for filing a grievance. By making a good showing or by winning as much as possible for the employees, stewards enhance their chances of reelection.

When a firm is not unionized, some employees may be afraid to bring their complaints to their supervisors, even when the complaints are legitimate. They may fear that complaining may be held against them and that there may be retaliation if they dare to challenge a supervisor's decision. At the other extreme are employees who resent supervisory authority and who take every opportunity to complain about departmental matters. They may relish making the supervisor uncomfortable by lodging complaints. Because they lack union representation, these employees may approach the supervisor as a group, believing that doing so gives them strength and protection.

The importance of the supervisor's handling of employee complaints at the first step cannot be overemphasized. Open and frank communication between all parties is usually the key element in amicable resolution of a problem. When such communication does not occur, disagreement, resentment, and possibly an appeal to higher levels of management are likely.

Supervisory Guidelines for Resolving Complaints and Grievances

6 Identify supervisory guidelines for resolving complaints and grievances effectively.

For the most part, the supervisor should handle grievances and complaints with the same general considerations and skills. Regardless of the nature of an employee complaint or grievance, a supervisor should fully investigate the problem and determine whether the problem can be solved quickly. It is always better to settle minor issues before they grow into major ones. While some cases will have to be referred to higher-level managers or to the human resources staff (e.g., complaints involving charges of discrimination prohibited by law), the supervisor should endeavor to settle or resolve the issues at the first step. When many complaints go beyond the first step, supervisors probably are failing to carry out their duties appropriately. Unless circumstances are beyond the supervisor's control, complaints and grievances should be handled within reasonable time limits and brought to fair conclusions within the pattern of supervisory guidelines as discussed in the following sections. The accompanying Supervisory Tips box lists major guidelines for resolving complaints and grievances, which are expanded on in the following discussion.

MAKE TIME AVAILABLE

The supervisor should find time to hear a complaint or grievance as soon as possible. This does not mean the supervisor must drop everything to meet with the employee or steward immediately. Rather, it means making every effort to set a time for an initial hearing. When the supervisor makes it difficult for an employee to have a hearing as expeditiously as possible, the employee could become frustrated and resentful. A long delay could be interpreted to mean that the supervisor does not consider the problem important. It could even be interpreted as stalling and indifference.

LISTEN PATIENTLY AND WITH AN OPEN MIND

Often, supervisors become preoccupied with defending themselves and trying to justify their positions. As a result, they fail to give stewards and/or employees ample time to present their cases. Supervisors should bear in mind that all the principles discussed in the chapters on communication and interviewing apply to complaints and grievances. All people involved should be encouraged to say whatever they have on their minds. When employees believe the supervisor is willing to listen to them and wants to provide fair treatment, problems may seem less serious. Also, the more a person talks, the more likely that person is to make contradictory remarks that weaken the argument.[19] Employees may even uncover solutions as they talk out problems. Sometimes, employees simply want to vent frustrations. After allowing them to do so, attention can be focused on the real problem. Therefore, by listening empathetically, the supervisor can minimize tensions and even solve some problems in the initial hearing.

DISTINGUISH FACTS FROM OPINIONS

Distinguishing facts from opinions means weighing hearsay and opinions cautiously. In this process, the supervisor should avoid confusing the employee or shop steward. The supervisor should ask factual, pointed questions regarding who or what is involved; when, where, and why the alleged problem took place; and whether there is any connection between this situation and some other problem. Frequently, it is impossible to gather all relevant information at once, which makes it difficult to settle a complaint or grievance immediately. Under such conditions, supervisors should tell the employees or the stewards that they will gather the necessary information within a reasonable time and by a definite date. The supervisor should not postpone a decision with the excuse of needing more facts when the relevant information can be obtained without delay.

DETERMINE THE REAL ISSUE

In both union and nonunion work settings, employee complaints are sometimes symptoms of deeper problems. For example, a complaint of unfair work assignments may really reflect personality clashes among several employees. A complaint that newly installed machinery prevents employees from maintaining their incentive rates may indicate that employees actually are having a difficult time adjusting to the operation of the new equipment after years of operating old machines. Unless the real issue is clearly defined and settled, complaints of a similar nature are likely to be raised again.

CHECK AND CONSULT

Checking and consulting are among the most important aspects of a supervisor's role in handling employee complaints and grievances. We cannot emphasize too strongly that the labor agreement, as well as company policies and procedures, must be administered fairly and uniformly. In a unionized setting, the supervisor may be unsure whether a grievance is valid under a labor agreement, or the provisions of a labor agreement that relate to the alleged violation might be

SUPERVISORY TIPS

Guidelines for Resolving Complaints and Grievances

- Do it as soon as possible; make time available.
- Do it privately, not publicly.
- Listen patiently and with an open mind.
- Distinguish facts from opinions.
- Determine the real issue(s).
- Focus on one issue at a time.
- Deal with the behaviors the person can change.
- Check and consult.
- Avoid setting precedents.
- Exercise self-control.
- Minimize delays in reaching a decision.
- Explain decisions clearly and sensitively.
- Keep records and documents.
- Do not fear a challenge.
- Don't forget the compliments. End on a positive note. And remember: When it is over, it is over!

unclear. In all cases, the supervisor should make decisions only after carefully reviewing the company's policies and procedures and labor agreement.

As stated previously, grievances revolve around interpretation of the labor agreement, and complaints in nonunion settings may include questions of employment policies. Complaints that involve allegations of discrimination and other aspects of equal employment opportunity (EEO) have legal implications. Therefore, whenever a grievance or complaint requires contractual, policy, or legal interpretation, the supervisor should tell the complaining individuals that it will be necessary to look into the matter and that an answer will be given by a definite date. Subsequently, the supervisor should consult with the human resources department and higher-level managers for advice and guidance. Seeking assistance from human resources staff or higher-level managers is not passing the buck or revealing ignorance, nor should it be considered showing weakness, because the supervisor is usually not authorized or qualified to make the policy or legal interpretations necessary to respond to certain employee complaints and grievances.

AVOID SETTING PRECEDENTS

The supervisor should consult settlement records and ensure that any proposed decision is consistent with established practices. If an issue has not been encountered before, the supervisor should seek guidance from other supervisors or staff personnel who may have experienced similar, though not necessarily identical, problems. When circumstances require a departure from previous decisions, the supervisor should explain to the employee or steward why, as well as whether any exception will create a new precedent.

Unless there is a valid reason, or unless there has been prior approval from higher-level management or the human resources department, the supervisor should avoid making exceptions to policies. Exceptions set precedents, and precedents often haunt supervisors and the organization. In labor-arbitration issues, most arbitrators believe that precedents can become almost as binding on an organization as if they were negotiated in the labor agreement. Therefore, a supervisor should be very careful about making an exception in a union grievance because a grievance settlement may become part of a labor agreement.

EXERCISE SELF-CONTROL

Emotions, arguments, and personality clashes sometimes distort communication between the supervisor and complaining employees. The worst thing the supervisor can do in these situations is to engage in a shouting match or to "talk down" to the employees. Emotional outbursts usually impede constructive thinking. Arguing and shouting may escalate a problem to far more serious proportions. Of course, a supervisor's patience is limited. When an employee or a steward persists in loud arguments, profanity, or the like, the supervisor should terminate the meeting and schedule another, hoping that the problem can be discussed later in a calm and less emotional manner.

When a complaint or grievance is trivial or invalid, the supervisor must be careful to show no animosity toward the steward or the complaining employee. Instead, the supervisor should explain why a grievance has no merit. The supervisor cannot expect the steward to explain because the steward is the employee's official representative.

Sometimes, an employee or a steward may deliberately provoke an argument to put the supervisor on the defensive. Even this tactic should arouse no hostility on the supervisor's part. When supervisors do not know how to handle these types of situations, they should consult higher-level managers or the human resources department for assistance.

MINIMIZE DELAYS IN REACHING A DECISION

Many labor agreements require grievances to be answered within set periods. The same principle should hold true in nonunion work situations. When an employee raises a complaint, that employee should be entitled to know, within a reasonable time, exactly when management will make a decision concerning that complaint. When the complaint can be handled immediately, and when the supervisor is authorized to do so, this should be done immediately. When, however, the complaint requires consultation with higher-level managers or human resources staff, the supervisor should close the hearing with a definite commitment as to when an answer or a decision will be given.

While postponing a decision in the hope that a grievance will disappear can invite trouble and more grievances, speedy settlements should not outweigh sound decisions. When delay is necessary, the supervisor should tell the parties the reason for the delay and not leave them thinking that they are being ignored. Because delayed decisions can frustrate all parties, prompt handling is crucial.

EXPLAIN DECISIONS CLEARLY AND SENSITIVELY

The supervisor should make every effort to give a straightforward, clear answer to a complaint or grievance. The supervisor also should communicate, as specifically as possible, the reasons for the decision, especially when the decision is not in the employee's favor. It is frustrating for an employee to get just a "no" with no explanation other than that management feels it does not have to comply with the employee's request.

Even when a complaint is not justified, the supervisor should in no way convey to the employee that the problem is trivial or unnecessary. The employee likely has good reasons for raising the complaint. Therefore, the supervisor should be sensitive to the employee's perspective.

When a labor agreement requires a written reply to a grievance, the supervisor should restrict the reply to the grievance and ensure that the response relates to the case. References to labor-agreement provisions or plant rules should be confined to those in question. So that the reply is worded appropriately, the supervisor is well advised to first discuss the written reply with higher-level managers or the human resources department.

KEEP RECORDS AND DOCUMENTS

Despite the good-faith efforts of supervisors or higher-level managers to settle complaints or grievances, an employee may choose to appeal a decision. When a complaint involves discrimination, the employee may file a formal complaint with a government agency. When there is a union grievance, it may go all the way to arbitration. In a non-unionized firm, the firm's complaint procedures may provide several steps for appeal, which is why it is important for a supervisor to document all evidence, discussions, and meetings. In any appeal process, written evidence is generally superior to oral testimony and hearsay.

Many firms have policies for the confidential handling of certain employee records and documents. Supervisors must be careful to adhere to any such policies, especially when documents involve issues of employee job performance and company disciplinary actions.

The supervisor should answer complaints and grievances in a straightforward, reasonable manner

© KEN REID/GETTY IMAGES

Keeping good records is especially important when a complaint or a grievance is not settled at the supervisory level. The burden of proof is usually on management. Therefore, a supervisor should be ready to explain actions without having to depend solely on memory. Documentation can be very supportive in this regard.

DO NOT FEAR A CHALLENGE

A supervisor should make every effort to resolve a complaint or grievance at the first step without sacrificing a fair decision. Unfortunately, supervisors are at times tempted to grant questionable complaints or grievances because they fear challenges or want to avoid hassles. By giving in to an employee or the union just to avoid an argument, the supervisor may invite others to adopt the "squeaky wheel-gets-the-grease" theory. That is, other employees or stewards will be encouraged to submit minor complaints because they feel that by complaining often and loudly they have a better chance of gaining concessions. In this way, a supervisor can establish a perception that may lead to even greater problems.

In efforts to settle a complaint or grievance, there will always be gray areas in which a supervisor must use judgment. The supervisor should be willing to admit and rectify mistakes. However, when supervisors believe decisions are fair and objective, they should have the courage to hold firm, even when employees threaten to appeal. That an employee appeals a decision does not mean that the supervisor is wrong. Even if higher-level managers or arbitrators reverse a supervisor's decision, poor handling on the supervisor's part is not implied. Some decisions will be modified or reversed during appeal for reasons that may go beyond the supervisor's responsibility.

For example, upper management, perhaps on the advice of the human resources staff or legal counsel, may decide to settle a case on terms more favorable to the employee than the supervisor believes is appropriate. This occurs because management is concerned about possibly losing the case in arbitration or litigation and incurring excessive extra costs in the process. Reversal of a supervisor's decision by higher management is usually not desirable because doing so can weaken a supervisor's position with departmental employees and cause resentment. It occasionally happens, however, sometimes for political reasons, and a supervisor should avoid becoming too frustrated or distressed as a result.

Supervisors who generally follow the guidelines in this chapter and who do their best to reach equitable solutions will enjoy the support of higher-level management in most cases. At the very least, a supervisor should be able to handle a complaint or grievance professionally and to prevent minor issues from escalating into major ones.

In summary, handling employee complaints and grievances is another of the many skills of effective supervision. It requires sensitivity, objectivity, and sound analytical judgment, the same qualities required in most other areas of supervisory management.

SUMMARY

1 As supervisors manage their departments, it is natural that their perspectives and decisions at times conflict with those of employees and/or the union. Resolving employee conflicts and handling employees' complaints and grievances is part of each supervisor's job, and the supervisor's effectiveness in doing so is another indicator of a supervisor's overall managerial capabilities.

2 An understanding of the five conflict-resolution or negotiation styles can help supervisors address conflicts. The five styles are (1) withdraw/avoid, (2) compromise, (3) accommodate/oblige, (4) compete/force/dominate, and (5) collaborate/integrate/problem solve. Different issues and individuals in the workplace may require supervisors to use all these styles. The collaborative style is preferred in that it develops a "win-win" mentality, i.e., the needs and wants of all parties are fulfilled. This style also is referred to as interest-based negotiations, the process which helps to develop a climate of mutual trust and respect that is essential to attaining long-term departmental objectives.

3 An employee complaint can occur in any work environment. Complaints may involve individual or group dissatisfactions that can be initiated with a supervisor and possibly appealed further. A grievance is normally identified as a complaint involving the interpretation and application of a labor agreement where employees are represented by a union.

4 Conflict-resolution procedures have a number of steps that begin at the supervisory level. A grievance procedure in a unionized setting and a complaint procedure in a non-unionized setting differ in two major ways. In the non-unionized setting, the employee normally must make a complaint without assistance; an employee who files a union grievance has the assistance of a steward or some other union representative. Second, the final decision is usually made by the chief executive or the human resources director in a non-unionized firm, and some firms use other ways to resolve complaints. In a union grievance matter, an outside neutral arbitrator may make the decision at the final step.

Alternative dispute resolution (ADR) procedures take various forms, including mediation, arbitration, and panel or peer review. ADR is especially used to expedite and resolve discharge and discrimination cases to avoid high litigation costs. Online dispute resolution (ODR) has become a viable option for some dispute adjudication. Some organizations are mandating procedures for processing employee complaints, especially for non-union personnel and salaried staff. These types of procedures may include mandatory arbitration of disputes when preliminary steps do not resolve the issues.

5 During the initial step in handling grievances, there should be open, frank communication between the supervisor and the complaining employee and the steward. When the grievance is not settled at this step, the steward probably will carry the grievance further, and it may eventually be submitted to an outside arbitrator. The same need for open and frank communication exists in hearing and resolving employee complaints at the supervisory level. Employee complaints should be settled amicably by the supervisor whenever possible rather than having them appealed and decided at higher levels.

6 Whether employees are represented by labor unions, the supervisor should follow the same general guidelines to resolve complaints or grievances. Among the most important supervisory considerations are to make time available, listen patiently and with an open mind, distinguish facts from opinions, determine the real issue, check and consult, avoid setting precedents, exercise self-control, minimize delay in reaching a decision, explain the decision clearly and sensitively, keep records and documents, and do not fear a challenge.

KEY TERMS

Alternative dispute resolution (ADR) (p. 543)
Complaint (p. 541)
Complaint procedure (p. 541)
Conflict-resolution styles (p. 536)

Constructive or functional conflict (p. 534)
Dysfunctional conflict (p. 534)
Grievance (p. 541)
Grievance procedure (p. 541)

Interest-based negotiating (p. 538)
Online dispute resolution (ODR) (p. 543)
Personalized conflict (p. 534)
Reciprocity reflex (p. 537)
Substantive conflict (p. 533)

QUESTIONS FOR DISCUSSION

1. Why should employee conflicts, complaints, and grievances be considered natural components of supervision? Define and discuss the five conflict-resolution styles.

2. How is a grievance defined in unionized firms? What are the major distinctions between a union grievance and an employee complaint in a non-unionized firm?

3. Distinguish between a union grievance procedure and a complaint or problem-solving procedure.

4. What is meant by alternative dispute resolution (ADR)?

5. Why should most complaints and grievances be settled by the supervisor at the departmental level? Which complaints and grievances should be referred to higher-level managers or the human resources staff? Discuss.

6. Review and discuss each of the guidelines in this chapter for resolving complaints and grievances. Analyze their interrelationships. Why is the satisfactory handling of complaints or grievances a major component of effective supervisory management?

SKILLS APPLICATIONS

Skills Application 15-1: You Make the Call!

Refer to this chapter's opening "You Make the Call!"

1. (*INTERNET ACTIVITY*) Using the Internet, find information relating to the following:
   a. Several organizations have stated they will not hire smokers. Some have attempted to institute policies demanding that employees not smoke either on or off the job. Are these policies legal? Why or why not?
   b. During her pregnancy, is Angie entitled to the workplace accommodations that her physician prescribed? Why or why not?
   c. Were you able to find any specific court-decided cases that dealt with the issues of reasonable accommodation during pregnancy? What were those decisions, and what is the relevance for this case?

2. What approach should Patrick Gavin and Hermaine Garza take to find out how Angie is using her breaks?

3. The concern of Gavin and Garza escalates when they find that Angie is using every break period and part of her lunch break to go across the alley for a quick smoke. What should they do?

4. What safeguards should Gavin and Garza implement to minimize employee complaints of an action being unfair?

5. (ROLE PLAY) Role-play Activity: We have suggested two formats for this role-play exercise. Regardless of the option used, role-play participants should be encouraged to adopt the attitudes and values associated with their assigned roles.
   Option A: Students will be assigned to play the roles of Angie, Garza, and Gavin. Other class members will act as observers. During the role play, the observers should look for things that are done well—accentuate the positive. Garza and Gavin should be given a few minutes to plan their strategy for dealing with the conflict. Then Garza and Gavin should initiate a discussion with Angie to resolve the apparent conflicts—taking excess break time.
   Option B: The class will be divided into groups of three with one student in each group assigned the role of Angie, Garza, or Gavin. The same format should be followed, i.e., Gavin and Garza take a few minutes to plot strategy and then address their concerns with Angie.

6. At the end of the role play, the instructor will review Figure 15.3 and then solicit input from the observers and the participants as to what could have been done better to resolve the apparent conflict.

7. Write a paragraph describing what you learned from this skills application.

Skills Application 15-2: Your Complaint

Everyone who has held a job has had work-related problems. However, many employees do not register complaints in non-union situations. For this project, remember a situation in which you could have made a complaint to your supervisor but did not. Now is your opportunity.

1. State your complaint in one or two sentences and provide relevant background information.

2. What do you believe should have been done, assuming that you followed the firm's complaint procedure in filing the complaint?

3. What justification could the supervisor or higher-level managers cite for refusing to make any adjustments because of your complaint?

4. If a union had represented you, would you have filed a grievance in this situation? Why or why not?

5. How could a neutral arbitrator have helped resolve your complaint?

Skills Application 15-3: Does Conflict Cause You Stress?

1.  Use the Internet to find information about stress (stressors) and suggestions for coping with stress (coping strategies).

2. Think back over the last two weeks. Identify three situations that have caused you stress. Now make a chart of three columns and three rows.
   a. In the first column of the first row, write a brief paragraph describing the who, what, when, where, and why of the first situation that caused you stress.
   b. In the middle column, briefly describe the consequences (outcomes) of the first stressful situation.
   c. In the far right hand column, write down the actions you took to alleviate the stress in that situation, such as your coping behaviors.
   d. Then complete the procedure for each of the other two stressful situations, using the second and third rows to write your answers.

3. Now carefully analyze the three stressors: Think of the things, situations, characteristics of the people involved, your own personal baggage that you brought to the situation, time pressures, etc.
   a. What items or issues are common to all three situations?
   b. Were you pleased with the outcomes of each situation? Why? Why not?
   c. Were the coping strategies you used the most effective that could have been used?
   d. In retrospect, how could you have handled each of the situations to get a better outcome?
   e. Is there a way you could have avoided the situation?

4. Write a one-page paper detailing what you learned from this skills application. In the last paragraph, describe specifically how you can use one of the coping strategies the next time you are in a conflict situation.

Skills Application 15-4: The Stinky Employee

The scenario: Several employees in your patient-billing section of CMC Health Center have complained about the hygiene problems of a fellow employee. To state it bluntly, this is not just some hot summer body odor; this is from not bathing. To address their earlier complaints, you had put up a general notice, asking people to be more considerate of their fellow employees and patients and (1) to shower more regularly, and (2) to refrain from bathing in perfume and cologne. But apparently this notice has not solved the problem(s).

Today, a group of four employees, including your very best, told you that the smell from two employees is overwhelming and that they will no longer work in the same area. Transfer or relocation is not an option. You must now sit down and have a conversation with each employee and resolve this conflict.

ROLE PLAY **Role-play # 1: Meet Molly**. Molly is a good worker but of the "new age"—a throwback to the "Hippie Era" of the 1960s. To her, cleanliness is not important. She does not appear to bathe, brush her teeth, or wash her hair. She often wears the same clothes for several days in a row, and on a couple of occasions you were able to smell her from a couple of cubicles away.

Role-play Format: After reading the scenario, assign the roles of supervisor, employee, human resources manager, and observers. The person playing the role of the employee with the body odor should be excused from the room while the other participants prepare for the role play. The person playing the role of the human resources manager should discuss the legal and practical implications confronting them in the conflict-resolution (counseling) session. After a plan of action has been developed, the "stinky" employee should be invited back into the room to complete the role-play exercise.

At the conclusion of the activity, each participant should prepare a critique of how effectively this situation was handled. Suggestions for improvement should be offered.

Role-play # 2: Meet Wai. Wai is a relatively new employee. According to his fellow employees, he appears to douse himself in cologne. The smell is unpleasant; early in the day, it smells like disinfectant.

Role-play Format: After reading the scenario, assign the roles of supervisor, employee, human resources manager, and observer. The person playing the role of the employee with the excessive cologne should be excused from the room while the other participants prepare for the role play. The person playing the role of the human resources manager should discuss the legal and practical implications confronting them in the conflict-resolution (counseling) session. After a plan of action has been developed, the "stinky" employee should be invited back into the room to complete the role-play exercise.

At the conclusion, of the second role play, observers should prepare a critique of the exercise indicating what the participants did well and what could have been done better.

Write a one-page paper indicating what you learned from this skills application.

Source: Adapted with permission from Edwin C. Leonard, Jr., and Roy A. Cook, *Human Resource Management: 21st Century Challenges* (Mason, OH: Thomson Custom Publishing, 2005), pp. 23–24 (Case 1-12: The Stinky Employee).

Skills Application 15-5: Nedra "the Negativist"

This is the last skills application to introduce you to another of those folks who will make your life difficult. As you read Fred's story, you will find that Nedra is somewhat similar to a couple of previous characters who were introduced to you. We hope you have enjoyed exploring ways to cope with these people who have the potential to make your life difficult.

1. Read the following statement from Fred Roberts, operations supervisor at Barry Automotive's Dublin plant:

    The most challenging person I work with is Nedra. She has so many redeeming features. For one, she is a workaholic and has a passion for quality work. But she is a pessimist and sees only the worst in every situation. Recently, there was a quality discrepancy reported by a customer, and we were asked to solve the problem. As a member of the quality-improvement team, instead of working with us to figure out ways to improve the production process, Nedra claimed the production operators do not know how to use their brains to do the work right. In a whining and complaining tone, I can still hear her say, "It's such a simple procedure, and we have to deal with their inability to read the spec sheets. It's just not right! Those people in personnel can never find us any good employees."

    Everyone is fair game for Nedra's complaints. About a month ago, the company experienced a major machine downtime due to a mechanical failure. I can hear Nedra now: "It's either the lousy people, the old equipment, or the incompetent maintenance supervisor." She stores mistakes from the past and can't let go of them. For example, two years ago, Lee Kim, a good employee in the maintenance department, made a serious setup error that resulted in over $50,000 of product being run with the wrong specs. We ended up with two bins of scrap. Lots of people could have caught the mistake in a timely fashion, but no one did. Kim was suspended without pay for two weeks, and we used the mistake to illustrate why we need to follow our in-process controls. But

    Nedra won't let up. It's been over two years, and she is still obsessed with "Kim's mistake."

    I've tried to deal with Nedra by developing a positive attitude and smiling. But that doesn't seem to work. Nedra's negativity is destroying the team's spirit.

    Yesterday was the last straw. Three months ago I was chosen to head a project team to develop a new database to improve our customer tracking. Initially, Nedra suggested that we strive for the "optimal" solution rather than a "satisficing" one.

    The team worked diligently despite Nedra's negativity. I did everything I knew to try to get her off the bench and into the game. She was not open to any of our ideas and was unwilling to make any suggestions of her own. Her only contribution was to develop the worst-case scenarios of every suggestion we came up with. I made some notes on the words Nedra used during the past week in team meetings: "We can't do it!" "Our people aren't intelligent enough to do anything that sophisticated." "The machines will break down." "It's not possible." "We don't have enough money to do the job right." I came very close to losing it.

    I've never known anyone with such a bad outlook on life. Nowhere in my college or professional training did I have anything to prepare me for this. What should I do?

2.  Using the Internet, find at least three sources for how to work with negative people. Carefully review each site for suggestions on how to cope with this type of behavior.

3. Based on your findings, what suggestions would you make to Fred Roberts for how to work with Nedra?

4. Write a one-page paper explaining how this skills application increased your working knowledge of coping with the behaviors of this difficult person.

SKILLS DEVELOPMENT

Skills Development Module 15-1: American Flatbread—Welcome to American Flatbread

 When George Schenk arrived in the Mad River Valley in 1979 to ski-bum, his dishwashing job led him to a

cooking apprenticeship to discover the "the nature of food, the art of food, the beauty of food." American Flatbread's wood-fired, earthen oven products now anchor licensed *affiliates in California and Virginia as well as three Vermont restaurants. Schenk proclaimed: "It wasn't about slinging food on a plate. Food is fundamental to our health and well-being. Food is important enough to be careful."[1]*

The restaurant menu is simple: organic mesclun salads tossed in a raspberry-ginger vinaigrette, handmade flatbreads with their homemade organic tomato sauce fresh from the

wood-fired cauldron, organic and locally grown in-season produce, and a variety of fresh seafoods, locally raised chicken, or house-made sausage. Add a couple of desserts, micro-beer, exceptional wines, and local sodas—the feast is complete.[2]

Watch the Skills Development Module 15-1 video clip, and then answer the following questions.

Questions for Discussion

1. What is the "fun factor?"

2. Would you like to work for American Flatbread? What would attract you to such an organization?

3. What does the philosophy "We're all in this together"[3] have to do with a strategy for resolving conflicts?

4. What did you learn about conflict and conflict resolution by viewing the video clip?

Notes: (1) As quoted in Melissa Pasanen, "The Believers: For Some, Good Food is a Life's Calling," *Vermont Life* (Summer 2008), p. 47. (2) Adapted from American Flatbread's Web site (http://www.americanflatbread.com, accessed September 2008). (3) For other quotes by Henry Ford go to http://www.brainyquote.com.

ENDNOTES

For an overview of conflict-resolution techniques, the following are suggested (1) *International Journal of Conflict Management.* (2) James A. Schellenberg, *Conflict Resolution: Theory, Research, and Practice* (New York: The State University of New York Press, http://www.sunypress.edu, 2006). (3) Morton Deutsch, Peter T. Coleman and Eric C. Marcus, *The Handbook of Conflict Resolution: Theory and Practice,* 2nd ed. (San Francisco: Wiley/Jossy-Bass, 2006). (4) David J. Lieberman, *Making Peace With Anyone: Breakthrough Strategies to Quickly End Any Conflict, Feud, or Estrangement* (New York: St. Martin's Press, 2002). (5) Daniel Dana, *Conflict Resoluton* (New York: McGraw-Hill, 2001). (6) Bernard S. Mayer, *The Dynamics of Conflict Resolution: A Practitioners Guide* (San Francisco: Jossey-Bass, 2000).

1. Adapted from Robert Bacal, "Conflict & Cooperation in the Workplace," *Institute for Conflict Prevention* (http://www.conflict911.com/conflictarticles/in-communication1.htm). Robert Bacal has written many books and articles on conflict resolution. Visit Bacal & Associates Web site (http://www.work911.com/conflict/index.htm) to access some of his suggestions on conflict resolution.

2. See Robert Bacal, "The Essential Conflict Management," *Resolution and Prevention Bookshelf* (Institute for Conflict Prevention, 1998); *Conflict Prevention in the Workplace* (Winnipeg, AL: Institute for Cooperative Communication, 1998); *Defusing Hostile Customers Workbook for the Public Section* (Winnipeg: Institute for Cooperative Communication, 1998).

3. See Nancy R. Lockwood, "Workplace Conflict: Reasons, Reactions and Resolution," *SHRM Research* (November 2007); T. R. Harrison and M. L. Doerfel, "Competitive and Cooperative Conflict Communication Climates," *International Journal of Conflict Resolution,* 17, 2 (2006), pp. 129–153; G. R. Massey and P. L. Dawes, "The Antecedents and Consequences of Functional and Dysfunctional Conflict between Marketing Managers and Sales Managers," (Elsevier, Inc. 2006, accessed September 2008 at http://www.sciencedirect.com; F. J. Medina, L. Nunduate, M. A. Dorato, L. Martinez and J. M. Guerra, "Types of Intragroup Conflict and Affective Reactions," *Journal of Management Psychology,* 20, 3/4 (2005), pp. 219–230; F. McGrane, J. Wilson and T. Cammock, "Leading Employees in One-to-One Dispute Resolution," *Leadership & Organizational Development Journal,* 26, 3/4 (2005), pp. 263–279. Also see an article from *Harvard Business School's Working*

Knowledge, "Don't Listen to 'Yes'" (June 6, 2005), where Martha Lagrace, talks with Professor Michael Roberto on why it's essential for leaders to spark conflict in their organizations, as long as it is constructive. (Accessed September 2008, http://www.thepracticeofleadership.net or http://hbswk.hbs.edu/item/4833.html). Also see, Michael A. Roberto, *Why Great Leaders Don't Take Yes for an Answer* (Upper Saddle River, N.J.: Pearson Education, 2005).

4. Dale Carnegie quote accessed from http://www.brainyquote.com, September 2008). Carnegie (1888–1955), a pioneer in public speaking and seminar development, wrote *How to Win Friends and Influence People* (New York: Simon & Schuster, Inc, 1934, revised 1981) and *How to Stop Worrying and Start Living* (New York: Pocket Books, 1944, revised 1984).

5. See 1 Kings, Chapter 3, verses 16–28 for the story of King Solomon's approach for deciding which woman was the mother of the living child.

6. As quoted in Jeff Segal, "Mutual Satisfaction: Interest-Based Negotiation Means Getting What You Want By Knowing What They Want," *Southwest Airlines Spirit* (September 2004), pp. 54–57.

7. For extensive discussions of various approaches to conflict resolution and dealing with disgruntled employees, see Kathy Gurchiek, "Don't Let Conflict Go Unchecked," *SHRM Home* (accessed August 2008 at www.shrm.org); Mark A. Hyde, "5 Keys to Resolving Employee Conflict," *SuperVision,* 69, 4 (April 2008), pp. 3–6; Ronnie Moore, "Communicating Through Conflict," *SuperVision,* 68, 10 (October 2007), pp. 12–13; Rob Walker, "Take It or Leave It: The Only Guide to Negotiating You Will Ever Need," *Inc.* (August 2007), pp. 75–82; Tina Nabatchi, Lisa B. Bingham, and David H. Good, "Organizational Justice and Workplace Mediation: A Six Factor Model," *International Journal of Conflict Management* 18, 2 (2007), pp. 148–174; S. Parayitam and R. S. Dooley, "The Relationship Between Conflict and Decision Outcomes: Moderating Effects of Cognitive- and Affect-based Trust in Strategic Decision-Making Teams," *International Journal of Conflict Management,* 18, 1 (2007), pp. 42–73; Jonathon A. Segal, "Resolve or Report: Give Supervisors Detailed Directions To Help Them Avoid Making Wrong Turns," *HR Magazine* (October 2005), pp. 125–30; Cindy Fizzi, "Conflict Resolution in a Dysfunctional Team Environment," (book review) *Dispute Resolution Journal* (August–October 2005);

Mable H. Smith, "Grievance Procedures Resolve Conflict," *Nursing Management* (April 2002), p. 13; Mike Frost, "Resolving Conflicts at Work," *HR Magazine* (November 2001), pp. 136–7.

8. The California Supreme Court has upheld a ruling in favor of a woman who accused L'Oreal USA Inc. of retaliating against her because she refused to carry out an order to fire a female sales associate who a supervisor said was not "hot" enough. See *Yankowitz* v. *L'Oreal USA, Inc.* as reported in *BLR Business and Legal Reports* (August 12, 2005).

9. "Complaints through Alternatives to Litigation," *Employee Relations Weekly* (November 25, 1991), pp. 1–2.

10. For expanded discussions of ADR approaches, see Nancy R. Lockwood, "Alternative Dispute Resolution," *SHRM Briefly Stated* (February 2004); Michael Netzley, "Alternative Dispute Resolution: A Business and Communication Strategy," *Business Communication Quarterly* (December 2001), pp. 83–89; Lee A. Rosengard, "Appreciating Client Constituencies in Fashioning an ADR Solution," *Dispute Resolution Journal* (August–October 2001), pp. 56–60; and Bennett G. Picker, "ADR: New Challenges, New Roles, and New Opportunities," *Dispute Resolution Journal* (February–April 2001), pp. 20–23.

11. For a discussion of ODR and other conflict-resolution techniques, see Gabrielle Kaufman-Kohler and Thomas Schultz, *Conflict Resolution in the Age of Internet Online Dispute Resolution (ODR): Challenge for Contemporary Justice* (The Hague, Netherlands: Kluwer Law Institute, 2004).

12. See Douglas M. McCabe and Jennifer M. Rabil, "Administering the Employment Relationship: the Ethics of Conflict Resolution in Relation to Justice in the Workplace," *Journal of Business Ethics* (March 2002), pp. 33–48; and Dominic Bencivenga, "Fair Play in the ADR Arena," *HR Magazine* (January 1996), pp. 51–56.

13. Reported in Michael Barrier, "A Working Alternative for Settling Disputes," *Nation's Business* (July 1998), pp. 43–46.

14. The are many differences reported in the research literature. For example, the *2007–2008 Towers Perrin Global Workforce Study* reported that only 21% of respondents worldwide are engaged in their work (accessed October 2008, *Ceridian Abstracts: Best Practices*). The Blessing-White "2008 Employee Engagement Report" (accessed September 2008 at http://www.blessingwhite.com) reported that only 29% of employees are fully engaged in their work; 19% were actually disengaged; 75% trust their immediate supervisors; and only 53% trust top management.

The *2005 Watson Wyatt WorkUSA Study* found that 77% of employees say that their company boasts a clearly communicated ethics code but 52% believed they would be labeled as "troublemakers" if they reported unethical behavior. (See Eric Krell, "Do They Trust You?" *HR Magazine* (June 2006), pp. 58–65.

15. See Rebecca R. Hastings, "Loyalty Built on Communication, Not Compensation," *SHRM Home* (April 2008); "Perceptions of Organizational Fairness," *SHRM Home* (January 2008); S. Rama Iyer, "Driving Engagement Through Targeted HR Communication," *SHRM White Paper* (2008); Kathy Gurchiek, "Research Shows Five Ways to Gain Worker Trust," *SHRM Home* (April 11, 2007); and Carlos Tejada, "Disengaged at Work?" the *Wall Street Journal* (March 13, 2001), p. A1. Also see *2008 Quarterly CEO Survey*, (Management Action Programs, Inc. [MAP]) which stressed that open communication, employee recognition, and involvement in decision making are the prime drivers of employee loyalty and retention.

16. See Barry M. Rubin and Richard S. Rubin, "Creeping Legalism in Public Sector Grievance Arbitration: A National Perspective," *Journal of Collective Negotiations in the Public Sector*, 30, 1 (2003), p. 3; Tony Mauro, "A Victory for Mandatory Arbitration," *The Record* (American Lawyer Media) (March 22, 2001) p. 1, or Maria Coyle, "Arbitration Heaven Ahead," *The National Law Journal* (April 2, 2001), p. B1.

17. See Charles H. Smith, "When Is Arbitration Not an Arbitration?" *Dispute Resolution Journal* (August–October 2005); Mark A. Hofmann, "Court Upholds Binding Arbitration," *Business Insurance* (March 26, 2001), p. 1; Carlos Tejada, "Supreme Court Ruling Doesn't Answer Vexing Questions about Arbitration," the *Wall Street Journal* (March 27, 2001), p. A1; or Carolyn Hirschman, "Order in the Hearing," *HR Magazine* (July 2001), pp. 58–62.

18. For extensive discussions of grievance–arbitration procedures under a labor agreement, see *Grievance Guide* (Washington, DC: BNA, 1995), and Fred Whitney and Benjamin J. Taylor, *Labor Relations Law* (Englewood Cliffs, NJ: Prentice-Hall, 1998). For a condensed discussion of the grievance–arbitration process, see David A. Dilts, *Cases in Collective Bargaining and Industrial Relations: A Decisional Approach*, 11th ed. (New York: McGraw-Hill Irwin, 2007), pp. 165–183.

Note: Since 2000, unions have won slightly over half of the union-representation elections held in the U.S. The rate is remarkably low since unions usually pick the time and place for elections and typically hold them only if they think they can win. In mid-2008, Congress and the NLRB are debating the use of card checks rather than elections (The Employee Free Choice Act). Nevertheless, organizations address worker needs on a daily basis and work to engage employees in the affairs of the business. Open, honest, forthright communication is the key.

19. See Alison Stein Wellner, "Making Amends: Apologizing Is Part of Doing Business. Do It Wrong and You'll Be Sorry," *Fast Company* (June 2006), pp. 41–42; and Aaron Lazare, *On Apology* (New York: Oxford University Press, 2004). The authors look at why some apologies work, others fail, and why they are important at opening the door for conflict resolution.

Debbie Quarter, a new staff engineer at Barry Automotive's Glendale plant, had been assigned the responsibility of administering the plant's work-sampling program. This was the first assignment of this nature in Quarter's career. Her only knowledge of the program until this time came from friends working as team leaders or supervisors. Quarter heard that these people call the work-sampling program "bird dogging." They seemed universally to regard the program as unfair, a waste of time, and a personal affront. She realized that only the line superintendents and upper management supported the program, and some of them regarded it as a necessary evil.

CASE 6-1
Resistance to a Work-sampling Program

Details of the Program

The work-sampling program, or "ratio-delay" as it is sometimes called, involves the statistical sampling of the activities of hourly production and maintenance department employees, which includes approximately two-thirds of the plant's 2,000 employees. The sampling is conducted continuously by a full-time observer who walks the plant via a series of randomly selected, predetermined routes. The observer's job is to record the activity of each worker as the worker is first observed. An activity could fall into one of seven categories, which are subclasses of "working," "traveling," or "nonworking." The data are compiled monthly, and results are charted for each group and sent to the various supervisors and top management.

The program has been in effect for about five years at the plant. At the time it was initiated, management stated that the program's purpose was threefold:

1. Indicate supervisory effectiveness.
2. Help identify problems interfering with work performance.
3. Serve as a control measure of the effect of changes in work methods, equipment, facilities, or supervision.

Meetings on the Program

Realizing that the program had widespread resistance, Quarter immediately began to conduct informational meetings for all team leaders and supervisors. In these sessions, she discussed the purpose of the program and its mechanics. She also attempted to answer any questions. The team leaders and supervisors were most vocal in their negative opinions about the program, and after a few meetings, Quarter noted that certain comments were being repeated in some form by almost every group.

Most supervisory groups identified aspects of the sampling program they thought biased results against them. The most common complaint of this type was that the sampling was too often conducted when work was normally lightest, such as during coffee breaks and early or late in the day. Because the method of scheduling visits was complex, efforts to explain the program's randomness and means of ensuring fairness had never been accepted. Some basic statistical training had been attempted, but with little success—especially among the team leaders and supervisors who had traditionally risen through the ranks and had little technical background.

Another frequent complaint was that activities normally considered work (e.g., going for tools or carrying materials) were not recorded as such. It was explained to the team leaders that these activities were factors not directly accomplishing work, given that in these areas improvements could be made.

Several maintenance team leaders complained that results were repeatedly used to pressure them to, in turn, pressure their workers. When they would bear down, the supervisors said, the workers would resist, and less work was accomplished than before. One team leader quoted his boss as saying, "These figures [work-sampling results] better be up next month, or I'm going to have three new supervisors in here!" It was general knowledge that the superintendents greatly emphasized these results when appraising supervisors and team leaders.

Virtually no one at any level of supervision had a good understanding of how sample size could affect results. Small groups with few samples said they had experienced wide fluctuations in results that "just couldn't happen." This, of course, reinforced their distrust of sampling methods.

There had been few, if any, changes initiated by first-line supervisors as a result of work-sampling results. Several staff projects had been generated—some, like motorized personnel carriers, were quite popular with the workers—but these were not generally associated with work-sampling results.

After the first few sessions, Quarter wondered whether her meetings with the team leaders and supervisors were doing more harm than good. The meetings seemed to upset everyone, and anything that was learned was probably lost in the emotional discussions. Quarter pondered what she should do next.

Questions for Discussion
1. Evaluate the work-sampling program described in this case.
2. Evaluate the work-sampling program in view of the principles of a sound control system as outlined in Chapter 14.
3. Outline a course of action for Debbie Quarter. Consider the risks that are attendant to each alternative.
4. Search the Internet to secure information on quality interventions, e.g., http://qualitydigest.com, http://www.processmodel.com, http://www.minitab.com, or http://www3.best-in-class.com. Write a paper answering the following questions:
   a. **INTERNET ACTIVITY** What are the most common blunders organizations make when designing and implementing improvement programs?
   b. What are the common threads among successful implementations of improvement programs?
   c. Identify three alternatives Debbie Quarter might consider now.

CASE 6-2
Control? What Control?

Gil Pietro is the accounting department supervisor for a manufacturing plant that employs approximately 600 people. Reporting to Gil are two accountants and four data-entry clerks. All of his staff, except one accountant, are women. They work in an office area that is separate from other departments. Gil's department is involved in virtually all aspects of internal and external accounting responsibilities although some work has been outsourced to local consulting firms.

Upper management had challenged members of the management team to find solutions to some of the problems facing the organization. They were convinced that most processes and procedures would be more efficient and effective if the company would embrace some of the systems-engineering principles. Initially, two questions were asked of Gil: "How do you get rid of some of the paperwork with a more automated system, and how can your department help reduce errors?"

Several new software packages have been successfully implemented in the accounting department. A new streamlined software system for processing accounts payable and receivable was a project recently given top priority. It was so important that Gil decided to develop and carry out the project himself. His boss, the controller, specified a deadline for completion that was very tight. In developing the software package, Gil met with the data processing manager, the controller, and outside consultants that he hired to write the software package.

Gil's staff, who will be the software's primary users, were only recently told about the project, its implementation date, and scheduled training sessions.

This morning, a day after the second training session, several members of Gil's staff walked into his office quite upset. They claimed that the project's proposed implementation date was "totally unrealistic" and could not be met due to "serious flaws" in the new software package. They asserted that the new package would create more work than the old system, would confuse some customers, and would require extra time that simply was not available with existing staff. Ellen Bond, a data-entry clerk in the group, summed up the group's feelings by stating, "All this could have been avoided if we had been part of the project planning from the start!"

The group has just left Gil's office, and he is now rather distressed. The project's scheduled implementation date is two weeks away, only one training session remains, and it would be impossible to rewrite the package in time.

Questions for Discussion

1. What are some of the main causes of conflict in this case? What types of conflict are present?
2. If you were one of the other employees, would you feel the same way as Ellen Bond? Why? Why not?
3. People handle conflict in different ways. As the employee in question # 2 above, how will you behave? Why?
4. How should Gil Pietro respond to his staff?
5. What should he do to rectify the situation?
6. How could this type of issue be avoided in the future?

When Michele Stanley became front-end manager at Qwik Lumber and Homecenter's Brunswick facility, her boss gave her a mission—slow down turnover. Turnover had become a chronic and costly headache for the regional lumber and hardware chain. Front-end manager positions paid approximately $35,000 with an opportunity to earn more via Qwik's performance-based incentive system. The front-end manager oversees three levels of employees: department or section heads (who earn about $10 to $15 an hour); cashiers (starting at $7.50 with step advancement to $10.00 per hour); and stockers, most of whom make a little more than minimum wage. The stockers assist customers, cashiers, or section heads as needed.

CASE 6-3
Michele's First Job

Stanley reports directly to the store manager Paul Sullivan. In addition to Stanley, Sullivan's direct reports include the three outside salespersons (who call on current and potential contractor, commercial, and institutional customers) and the "Pro" sales staff. Since most of the store's profit is generated from outside sales and pro sales, those are the areas where Sullivan spends most of his time.

Stanley began working at Qwik as a stocker at the Camby store eleven years ago when she was in high school. After getting her associate's degree in Organizational Leadership from the local community college, she spent six months in Qwik's management training program. During this time, Stanley shadowed four different managers. She got to experience the "ins and outs" of several Qwik stores. In her own words, she got to learn from some of the best and some of the worst. The latter gave her insight into "what not to do."

According to store manager Sullivan, the turnover rate among front-end workers was 80 percent last year, with the rate for stockers being 150 percent. After doing the math, Stanley realized that her predecessor had spent a lot of time recruiting, hiring, and training people for the six stocker positions. Sullivan had been clear in his charge to Stanley: "The company is willing to let you try all sorts of things to retain hourly employees—short of paying them more money!"

Stanley's first challenge began at the end of her first week on the job. Donte Jones, a stocker, failed to report for work on Sunday morning. No one had heard from Jones, who had last worked the previous Thursday. A call to his home revealed that he wasn't coming in—he had quit. He had begun working at a fast food restaurant on Friday for slightly higher pay than he was making at Qwik. Stanley spent most of Sunday completing some of the work that Jones normally would have done or orchestrating the tasks of other employees.

Stanley thought about one thing she had learned—"good employees want to work with good employees"—therefore, ask those good employees if they would recommend someone for the opening. One employee suggested that Michele contact Susan Whitlock, placement director at the regional developmental workforce office. Whitlock was always searching for employment opportunities for some of their handicapped trainees. Knowing that Qwik promoted itself as an equal opportunity employer, Stanley made contact with Susan Whitlock. Whitlock recommended Jerry Garcia for the stocker job. Garcia had a learning disability—he could only read at the sixth grade level—and walked with a noticeable limp. After reviewing Garcia's file, conducting an interview, and checking with Qwik's HR director, Stanley decided that there was no reason that Garcia was not capable of performing the stocker duties.

During the first week on the job, Stanley noticed that Garcia seemed to have a difficult time catching on. It seemed that the busier the store was or the better the weather outside, the harder it was to get Garcia to focus on the job at hand. Time after time, Garcia would be found walking around the greenhouse or the loading yard. When a customer would approach him with a question, he would walk away. No matter how many times Stanley stressed the importance of remaining near the front of the store, it seemed to go in one of Garcia's ears and out the other.

Almost immediately, other employees started to complain that Garcia was not doing his part and that he was receiving special treatment because of his "handicap status." Comments like "I'm tired of doing his work while he wanders around the store" and "He's getting paid for loafing" were becoming common.

Just before Stanley was getting ready to call Susan Whitlock to discuss the problem, Katie, a part-time cashier, asked to discuss some concerns in private. "I don't know how to say this," she began. "I know that you're hearing lots of complaints about Jerry's work performance but I wanted to let you know that a few of the employees have been very mean towards him. I don't want to mention any names but there are a few of the guys who make fun of him and refer to him as the 'retard' or 'crip.' I just wanted to let you know that perhaps part of his problem is some of the people he works with."

Stanley wondered whether the problem was Garcia, the other employees, or her inability to adequately monitor what was going on. At the risk of losing her very first hire, she needed to decide on a course of action and quickly.

Questions for Discussion

1. What are the issues in the case? Which issues, if any, are beyond the scope of Stanley's authority and expertise? Why?
2. What factors should Stanley have taken into consideration before hiring someone with physical and learning disabilities such as those possessed by Garcia?
3. (**INTERNET ACTIVITY**) Survey various Internet sites for the purpose of answering the following questions:
   a. How pervasive is turnover among retail organizations?
   b. How does turnover impact the organization's bottom line?
   c. What tactics are being used by organizations to successfully lower turnover rates among entry-level positions?
4. Michele Stanley is faced with a dilemma. Her boss expects her to reduce turnover and her first hire is underperforming. What should Stanley do? What are some steps she can take to correct the work performance problem?

Role-Play Opportunity

(**ROLE PLAY**) Select students to play the following roles: Michele Stanley, Susan Whitlock, Paul Sullivan, and Gerald Wallace (one of Qwik's human resources reps). The remainder of the class shall act as observers. Depending on the time available, the group should role play the following scenarios:
   a. Develop several alternative courses of action to enable Jerry Garcia to succeed in Qwik's workplace.
   b. Design a control system to reduce the turnover level among entry-level Qwik employees. Observers should provide feedback on what the group did well and also be asked to identify additional alternatives that address the issues in this case.

CASE 6-4
Locker-Room Theft

For a number of months, Charlie Blair, the supervisor of the dry goods (nonperishable items) warehouse servicing for all Sanders Supermarkets stores, had been concerned about reports of valuables missing from employees' lockers in the warehouse's employee dressing room. The company gave employees metal lockers to use, but the lockers had no locks. Employees shared these lockers on a rotating shift basis; the company never considered it necessary to assign lockers. The lockers were provided mainly so that employees could store their jackets and other items while working in the warehouse.

Blair had reminded employees on a number of occasions not to leave valuables in the lockers. He told the employees that, according to company rules posted in the warehouse, the company assumed no responsibility for any loss, and he also told them that anyone found guilty of stealing a valuable would be terminated immediately for theft.

However, for the past several months Blair had received reports of numerous items missing from employees' lockers. These items included a sweater, a lunchbox, food from several lunchboxes, and a baseball glove.

For a number of reasons, including several rumors that had been circulated to Blair, Blair was suspicious of a fairly new warehouse employee named Eric Raleigh. Raleigh was a young warehouse worker who operated a tow truck. He was about 22 years old, and he had been employed by the company for about six months. Coincidentally, the reports of missing items from the locker room seemed to have become more frequent during the past several months.

On a Tuesday morning, Blair received a report from a warehouse employee named Willie Jeffries that a small transistor radio was missing from his locker. Jeffries stated that he had placed the radio in his locker when he reported to work at 7:30 A.M. and that he noticed it missing when he returned to his locker during his morning coffee break.

Upon receiving this report, Blair decided to search various lockers while all the employees were working in the warehouse. At about 11:00 A.M., Blair entered the locker room and searched the locker where Raleigh had stored his clothing and lunchbox. At the bottom of the locker, underneath a number of magazines, Blair found a transistor radio. Blair returned to the office and summoned Jeffries to identify the radio. Jeffries identified the radio as his own, but Blair did not disclose to Jeffries where he had found it.

Shortly thereafter, Blair asked Raleigh to come to his office. Blair explained to Raleigh the report he had received, what he had done, and how he had found the missing radio in Raleigh's locker. Blair did not directly accuse Raleigh of theft, but he suggested that Raleigh might want to consider resigning from the firm because of the suspicions that had been circulating about his connection to the other items missing from lockers.

At this point, Raleigh became very angry. He stated that he would not resign because he was innocent. He felt that someone else had been stealing items from employee lockers and that whoever it was had planted the radio in his locker to blame him. Raleigh even said he would be willing to take a lie detector test to prove his innocence. He told Blair, "If the company decides to fire me for this, I'll get the union and a lawyer to sue the company for everything it has for false accusation and unjust termination." With that, Raleigh left Blair's office and returned to his job.

Blair, taken aback by Raleigh's adamant denial of any involvement in the locker-room thefts, was unsure what to do in this situation. He recognized that the union contract for employees in the warehouse required that any disciplinary action must be for "just cause." Blair decided he would discuss the situation with Elaine Haas, the company's director of human resources.

Questions for Discussion

1. **INTERNET ACTIVITY** Use the Internet to find current information on the shrinkage or loss that organizations incur from internal theft.
   a. How prevalent is internal theft? External theft?
   b. What precautions are other organizations taking to minimize the likelihood of internal theft?
   c. What precautions are organizations taking to minimize the likelihood of theft from shoplifters?

2. As part of the controlling function, what safeguards should Sanders Supermarkets have in place to minimize theft?

3. Evaluate the locker search by Charlie Blair. Was this search advisable?
4. Rather than confront Eric Raleigh in his office, what alternatives might Blair have explored? Discuss.
5. Should Blair have suggested that Raleigh consider resigning? Why or why not?
6. If you were Elaine Haas, what would you say to Blair? How could you use this situation as a learning opportunity for the organization?
7. At the end of the case, what should the company do?

It was almost seven o'clock. Judy Burkett drew a deep breath as she was anxious for her shift to end. It had been a long day since her regularly scheduled day shift had begun almost eleven hours ago. Judy had worked as a packer for Christoff Packing, an Iowa meat packing plant, for the past eleven years. Shortly after her divorce, she applied for work at the soon-to-be-opened plant. She was hired, trained, and started work the first day the plant opened. The job provided a steady source of income to support her and her two children.

It was not long after the plant opened that the oppressive, authoritarian management style led the employees to support the unionization effort of the Amalgamated Meat Packers Union, Local 181. Judy supported the union and the benefits it gained for her. She rarely attended a union meeting except to cast her vote for or against contract proposals. This past March, after working under a ten-month extension of the previous contract, the workers approved a new contract by the barest of margins. The contract called for a $400 signing bonus, no wage increase for the first year, mandatory overtime with four hours' notice, and a ceiling on what the company would pay for health insurance coverage. The employees now would have to pay substantially more for medical insurance premiums. Christoff Packing was only the latest in a long list of employers that had taken a hard-line approach in dealing with wage and health-care costs.

It had been a typical August day in Iowa. There were times when you couldn't see from one end of the plant to the other because of the heat and humidity. The workers had complained that the air handling systems were not functioning properly, and they had threatened to call OSHA to complain. The plant manager, Oscar Grimes, constantly reminded complaining workers that they were lucky to have such good jobs. Times were tough in the meat-packing industry, and workers knew that if they lost their jobs at Christoff Packing, they might never find a job that paid as well as the one they currently had. Yet Christoff's business had been good, and production was at an all-time high. Rather than hire new employees, management applied the mandatory overtime provision, i.e., four hours or more before a worker's scheduled shift was to end, management had the contractual right to require the employee to work up to four hours of overtime that day. As such, many employees had been working at least ten hours a day for the past two months.

Like most workers, Judy Burkett welcomed all the extra hours she could get. She needed the money, and with her two children, she knew that she needed to start saving for their college education and to put some money aside for a rainy day. However, the overtime had its drawbacks. Burkett missed being with the kids, ages 14 and 12. They were on summer vacation, and she had difficulty balancing the uncertainty of her work hours with her child care needs.

Fred Rossiter was supervisor of the "B" line—the packing line that Judy worked on. Rossiter was the proverbial "man in the middle"—squeezed between

CASE 6-5
Could You Have Prevented the Crisis?

a rock and a hard place. Top management was demanding that he seek ways to increase quantity without sacrificing quality, but the increased production had put a strain on everyone and everything. The increased production also put a strain on the machinery, and delays often occurred while employees waited for maintenance. Rossiter was constantly fielding questions from his subordinates about when they could expect a let-up in overtime demands.

Rossiter also was being bombarded with questions from his wife. Until March of this year, all supervisors had been paid on an hourly basis, just like the people they supervised. If they worked overtime, they were paid at the rate of one-and-a-half times their base pay. In March, top management decided to elevate the status of the plant supervisors. They were put on salary, and their jobs were reclassified to "exempt status." At that time, the new arrangement seemed to be more than fair as their new salary base was equal to fifty hours of pay per week. However, during the past two months, most supervisors had been averaging sixty hours or more per week. Because of the mandatory overtime provision, Rossiter never knew when he left for work whether he would be home at the regular time or whether he would have to work overtime. Rossiter's wife was tired of not knowing when he would be home, and she constantly reminded him that if he were still on the hourly rate he would be bringing home more money.

On his way to another production meeting called by top management, Rossiter passed by Burkett's work area. Feeling very frustrated with the uncertainty, Rossiter knew that regardless of the production, quality, safety, and maintenance results he reported, the plant manager would not be satisfied. Nothing was ever good enough for Oscar Grimes.

"Judy, before you go home this evening, make sure you clean up around your machine," Rossiter remarked as he hurried to the meeting.

She thought, "What is the matter with you? I work hard for this company, and no one seems to care." The heat of the day and the long work day caused Judy to respond in an uncommon way. She moved away from her machine, placed both hands on her hips, and shouted after the rapidly moving Rossiter. "Hey, Freddie, wait a minute!" As Rossiter turned, Judy continued, "I choose not to do that at this time!"

Rossiter moved quickly toward her and gestured by pointing the finger of authority at her. "You're insubordinate. Punch out, and take three days off without pay!"

Judy was struck with pain. She thought, "He's lost it. I've given the company the best years of my life, and no one seems to appreciate what I've done." She gave him a sharp glance, then threw her apron on the floor, and responded over her shoulder, "I think I'll take five!" And out the door she went.

Questions for Discussion

1. What are the issues in this case?
2. Evaluate the major elements of Christoff Packing's policies and practices. What controls should have been in effect to minimize the issues in this case?
3. How could problems of this nature be avoided in the future?
4. What strategies do you recommend for resolving the conflict between Burkett and Rossiter?
5. What can Rossiter do to resolve the conflict between himself and plant manager Oscar Grimes?
6. If you were Fred Rossiter, what would you do now? Why?

CASE 6-6
Losing Your
Cool!

Debra Allen was the branch manager at First South's Northwood branch. She was in charge of approximately twenty people, including two assistant managers. All but two of the tellers were women. Several were employees who had difficult lives outside the workplace. Often, their personal lives influenced the work environment in a negative way. Allen regularly met with the employees, both individually and in small groups. She constantly reminded them of the need to work together to serve the customers. The bank's motto was, "Two centuries of giving customers outstanding service."

Janet Taylor was the head teller at the Northwood branch. She had started working at the bank shortly after her high school graduation three years ago. Taylor had been a model employee, coming in early for work, investigating every opportunity to learn, and seemingly enthusiastic about her job at the branch. Her work ethic was a positive influence on the other tellers. Unlike many of the tellers, Taylor still lived at home with her parents and had never experienced the personal problems or financial woes that many of her peers were experiencing.

Yesterday, Bonnie Boyce, a single parent, showed up for work late without calling in. As head teller, Taylor had the responsibility of addressing the issue with Boyce and putting documentation in her file. Subsequent attendance issues within a two-week period were referred to Allen or one of the assistant managers. As one of the youngest people in the branch, Taylor found her responsibilities stressful. She was not comfortable dealing with performance or personal problems.

Today was another matter. It was the very busy first Friday of the month. Many senior citizens came in to deposit their retirement or Social Security checks, and most businesses paid their employees on Friday. The bank also handled utility payments for its customers. The customers appreciated the convenience, and it saved them postage. Rhonda Ayers was the oldest teller. She was in her sixties, and her disposition was annoying at times. She often tried to boss or "mother" most of the other tellers.

Shortly before noon, the teller lines were long, and Bonnie Boyce strolled in—two hours after she was scheduled. Because of the workload, Taylor immediately assigned her one of the vacant windows with the comment that she would talk with her at break time.

Taylor was having lunch in the break room when Ayers came in. Two other employees were having lunch at the time. They also could tell that Ayers was upset, and Taylor made an effort to cheer her up.

TAYLOR: Rhonda, what's the matter? Is something wrong?
AYERS: (Tries to ignore Taylor.)
TAYLOR: Well, go ahead and ignore me. I was just trying to help.
AYERS: You'd help if you'd get that problem out of here. I'm tired of always having to work harder because of that woman.
TAYLOR: What do you mean?
AYERS: You know exactly who I mean—Bonnie Boyce. She's lazy, inconsiderate, and a slob.
TAYLOR: What exactly has she done?
AYERS: Yesterday, she was late, and you did nothing. Today, she showed up mid-morning on our busiest day of the month, and you welcomed her like she was the long-lost prodigal son. You never should have been promoted to head teller. (Getting louder) Your good looks might have dazzled some of the guys downtown, but I've never been impressed with you.

TAYLOR: Stop that right now. I'm just doing my job. If you'd do yours without being so rigid and motherly, things might be a lot better around here.

AYERS: You are nothing but a naïve little pipsqueak!

TAYLOR: Why don't you just back off!" (She stormed out of the break room.)

Questions for Discussion

1. Identify and discuss the stressors that appear to be present amongst the employees at the Northwood branch.
2. To what extent did Taylor handle Friday's events well? What could she have done better?
3. Given the situation, list what might have been done by either party (Taylor or Ayers) to have prevented or at least minimized the situation.
4. (**INTERNET ACTIVITY**) Taylor had been a model employee, and then she lost it. How do you explain her behavior? Search the Web for information on emotional intelligence and controlling anger. You might want to review the *Emotional Intelligence Special Issue of the Journal of Organizational Behavior*, Vol. 26, Is. 4 (June 2005) to understand different perspectives.
5. What strategies have you learned for keeping your emotions under control?
6. How do you think Debra Allen should deal with this situation?

(**ROLE PLAY**) **Optional Role-Play Activity 1**: Select one student to play the role of Janet Taylor and another the role of Bonnie Boyce. Other students are to be observers. It is break time and Taylor is to discuss the lateness, attendance, and other performance issues with Boyce.

Optional Role-Play Activity 2: Select students to play the role of Janet Taylor and Rhonda Ayers. Other students are to be observes. In this scenario, Taylor is to try to repair the damage done in the break room discussion.

a. What did you learn about techniques for resolving conflict from the role-play activities?
b. In your opinion, did Taylor resolve or diffuse the conflict? Cite examples to support your argument.
c. How might the conflict at the Northwood branch turn into dysfunctional conflict?
d. If you were Janet Taylor, what would you have done differently? Why?

CASE 6-7
Resentment toward the African-American Supervisor

"What's the matter with you, coming down so hard on me about my work? Why don't you get off my back and deal with the white employees in this department who are getting away with murder? You're worse than a white boss!" These words, uttered by Sarah Washington, one of his African-American subordinates, worried the department supervisor, Antonio Key. The thought that other minority employees might resent his supervisory management position had disturbed him ever since he took over the department. Although no one had called him an "Uncle Tom" to his face, Key knew that some of the employees thought this of him.

Key had graduated from a small, church-related college. He received a special fellowship for minority students that enabled him to complete an MBA degree at a Midwestern university. Upon receiving his MBA, Key accepted a position with a major department store chain in its accounting-services division. After a year and a half in several staff positions, he was promoted to supervisor of the customer-accounts department. Of the twenty-four employees in this department, all were women except for two male computer programmers. Eight of the employees were minorities.

Since Key had become department supervisor about a year ago, the human resources department had received several complaints from African-American employees about Key's tendency to set higher standards for black employees under his supervision than for white employees. These complaints were passed on to Key by Mark Bonham, the director of human resources. Key had responded that the charges were invalid. He told Bonham, "I let everyone set their own pace. Some employees are going to come out ahead of others. I reward the ones who come out in front. That's my job." The manager of accounting services, Phillip Freeman, believed that Key treated all employees fairly. Freeman evaluated Key's overall performance as very good.

This most recent comment was not the only occasion on which certain employees had suggested to Key that the black employees in the department felt they did not receive the same treatment as whites. However, the previous comments had involved the grapevine rather than a direct verbal confrontation.

Sarah Washington had joined the customer-accounts department in an entry-level clerical position. Over five years, she had advanced through a series of promotions to one of the highest-level clerical positions in the department. Her job was complex, involving maintaining and adjusting billing records. The billing system had undergone a major transition to a state-of-the-art computerized system. During this transition, a number of intermediate systems had been used. Washington was one of the few people in the department who understood the intermediate systems and methods of adjusting records under each system. She would occasionally try to impress Key with her knowledge of the billing system by asking him questions for which she knew he had no answers. She once asked Key in front of several employees, "How do you expect to know in a few months what took me five years to learn?"

Washington was an extremely ambitious young woman. On several occasions, she had complained to the human resources department about being passed over for promotion to a supervisory position. Freeman had passed her over for promotion to supervisor because he said she lacked the tact and interpersonal skills needed in a supervisory position.

Key decided it was time to respond to these issues, and he pondered what his response should be. At least, he knew he must be prepared to respond to Washington's next insinuation.

Questions for Discussion
1. Why is a problem like this extremely sensitive for all individuals involved?
2. To what degree, if any, should Phillip Freeman become involved in this situation? Should the director of human resources become involved?
3. Should Antonio Key approach this problem as a disciplinary matter, a racial matter, a performance question, or a work-group situation? Discuss.
4. What would you recommend Key do?
5. Review the Chapter 16 guidelines for resolving complaints and grievances. Why is the satisfactory handling of complaints or grievances a major component of effective supervisory management?

Role-Play Exercise

 Philip Freeman concludes that there is a conflict between Antonio Key and Sarah Washington. Select students to play the roles of Freeman, Key, and Washington. Using the principles

of conflict resolution, Freeman should attempt to get Washington and Key to "play on the same team." (Participants can make the following assumptions: Sarah Washington's overall performance is "good." She has not missed a day of work in the past year, and she completes routine work assignments in less time than other employees.) Upon completion of the role-play exercise, the observers should report on the causes of the conflict and the appropriateness of Philip Freeman's approach for resolving the conflict.

6. Write a one-page paper detailing what you learned from this case.

CASE 6-8
AIDS Phobia

Mid-States Financial Services Company has a strict confidentiality policy regarding employee performance appraisals, salary levels, and other personnel matters. Morgan Dennis, a 45-year-old employee, had open heart surgery about six years ago, and he has had several health-related problems during the past year. Even so, his work performance has been exemplary. Three months ago, Dennis had a complete physical examination. The health-care provider filed claims directly with the insurance carrier with copies to the Mid-States human resources department. An oversight in the provider's office allowed a copy of the health diagnosis and findings to accompany the copy of the medical claim to the human resources department. The report indicated that Dennis was infected with HIV but lacked acute AIDS symptoms.

Lena Ables, a benefits clerk in the human resources department, noted the medical evaluation report and filed it appropriately. She later shared "in confidence" her knowledge of Dennis's medical condition with two of her closest friends. They proceeded to tell others.

Upon return from a weekly progress and problem meeting, Mike Smith, information technology (IT) team leader, found five of his team members waiting for him in his office. They proceeded to inform him that they would refuse to work with Dennis on any future project. They reminded him of the company's responsibility to provide a safe workplace for all employees. They wanted to have their work stations located in other areas and to have all work reallocated so that they had no contact with Dennis.

Smith was highly regarded as a team leader, and this information hit him hard. He asked the employees to have patience while he investigated the situation. As the employees reluctantly returned to work, one stated, "AIDS kills you, you know."

Questions for Discussion
Note: Before beginning this case, you should review the discussion concerning ADA in Chapter 13 for general information about this law. In addition, we suggest searching the Internet for additional information, i.e., AIDS awareness education, company policies, court decisions concerning employee privacy, and conflict resolution techniques.

1. (*INTERNET ACTIVITY*) Use the Internet to find current information on HIV/AIDS and the ADA. Then, write a brief report that summarizes your findings and citations of recent cases and rulings that are relevant and interesting.
2. Do you believe the employees' concern is valid? Why or why not?
3. How should Mike Smith educate his team members regarding HIV/AIDS and the Americans with Disabilities Act (ADA)?

4. Assume that the employees refuse to work with Morgan Dennis on an important project. How should Smith handle the conflict?
5. Assume that Dennis became aware that several team members were reluctant to work with him. How should Smith deal with this situation to maintain an effective team?
6. What should the organization do with Lena Ables?

Role-play Exercise

(ROLE PLAY) Students should form into groups of three, four, or five. Because of the nature of this role-play exercise, it is desirable that the groups remain small so that all can actively participate. Within each group, one student should be chosen to play the role of IT supervisor, Mike Smith. The other students will play the role of IT department employees. Remember: These are the same employees that want a "safe work environment" and want to have their work activities "isolated" from Morgan Dennis. Smith's charge is to present evidence and arguments to minimize the conflict and get the IT department employees to work together as a team.

At the conclusion of the role play, each group should report on "the one thing that Smith did well to resolve the conflict," and also identify "one thing that Smith could have done better." Students should be asked to consider how their personal biases, prejudices, or stereotypes influenced the role-play exercise.

GLOSSARY

A

Ability An employee's potential to perform higher-level tasks.

Acceptance theory of authority Theory that holds that the manager only possesses authority when the employee accepts it.

Accountability The obligation one has to one's boss and the expectation that employees will accept credit or blame for the results achieved in performing assigned tasks.

Administrative skills The ability to plan, organize, and coordinate activities.

Alternative dispute resolution (ADR) Approaches to processing and deciding employee complaints internally as an alternative to lawsuits, usually for disputes involving discharge and/or employment discrimination.

Appreciative Inquiry (AI) The cooperative search for the best in people, organizations, and the world around them.

Arbitrator Person selected by the union and management to render a final and binding decision concerning a grievance.

Attitude survey Survey of employee opinions about major aspects of organizational life that is used to assess morale.

Authority The legitimate right to direct and lead others.

Autocratic (authoritarian) supervision The supervisory style that relies on formal authority, threats, pressure, and close control.

B

Benchmarking The process of identifying and improving the practices of leaders.

Body language All observable actions of the sender or receiver.

Brainstorming A free flow of ideas in a group, while suspending judgment, aimed at developing many alternative solutions to a problem.

Budget A financial plan that expresses anticipated results in numerical or financial terms for a stated period.

Bureaucratic style of supervision The supervisory style that emphasizes strict compliance with organizational policies, rules, and directives.

C

Coaching The frequent activity of the supervisor to give employees information, instruction, and suggestions relating to their job assignments and performance.

Collaborative workplace Work environment characterized by joint decision making, shared accountability and authority, and high trust levels between employees and managers.

Command group Grouping of employees according to authority relationships on the formal organization chart.

Communication The process of transmitting information and understanding.

Communication skills The ability to give—and get—information.

Comparable worth Concept that jobs should be paid at the same level when they require similar skills or abilities.

Competencies The set of skills, knowledge, and personal attributes possessed by the superior performer.

Competitive advantage The ability to outperform competitors by increasing efficiency, quality, creativity, and responsiveness to customers and effectively using employee talents.

Complaint Any individual or group problem or dissatisfaction employees can channel upward to management, including discrimination.

Complaint procedure A management-designed series of steps for handling employee complaints that usually provides for a number of appeals before a final decision.

Conceptual skills The ability to obtain, interpret, and apply information.

Concurrent control Corrective action taken during the production or delivery process to ensure that standards are being met.

Conflict-resolution styles Approaches to resolving conflict based on weighing desired degrees of cooperativeness and assertiveness.

Constructive or functional conflict The end result of conflict is a win-win situation for all concerned.

Contingency-style leadership No one leadership style is best; the appropriate style depends on a multitude of factors.

Contingent workforce Part-time, temporary, or contract employees who work schedules dependent primarily on employer needs.

Controlling Ensuring that actual performance is in line with intended performance and taking corrective action, if necessary.

Cooperation The willingness of individuals to work with and help one another.

Coordination The synchronization of employees' efforts and the organization's resources toward achieving goals.

Corporate culture Set of shared purposes, values, and beliefs that employees hold about their organization.

Corporate social responsibility (CSR) A notion that organizations consider the interests of all stakeholders.

Counseling An effort by the supervisor to deal with on-the-job performance problems that are the result of an employee's personal problems.

Counseling interview Nondirective interview during which the supervisor listens empathetically and encourages the employee to discuss problems openly and to develop solutions.

Critical incident method Supervisors record specific examples of outstanding and below-average performance on the part of each employee.

Cross-training Training employees to do multiple tasks and jobs.

Cultural competency The ability to adapt to a variety of cultural communities.

D

Decision criteria Standards or measures to use in evaluating alternatives.

Decision making Defining problems and choosing a course of action from among alternatives.

Decision-making process A systematic, step-by-step process to aid in choosing the best alternative.

Delegation The process of entrusting duties and related authority to subordinates.

Department An organizational unit for which a supervisor has responsibility and authority.

Departmentalization The process of grouping activities and people into distinct organizational units.

Directive The communication approach by which a supervisor conveys to employees what, how, and why something is to be accomplished.

Directive interview Interview approach in which the interviewer guides the discussion along a predetermined course.

Discipline State of orderliness; the degree to which employees act according to expected standards of behavior.

Discipline without punishment Disciplinary approach that uses coaching and counseling as preliminary steps and a paid decision-making leave that allows employees to decide whether to improve and stay or to quit.

Diversity The cultural, ethnic, gender, age, educational level, racial, and lifestyle differences of employees.

Division of work (specialization) Dividing work into components and specialized tasks to improve efficiency and output.

Documentation Records of memoranda, documents, and meetings that relate to a disciplinary action.

Downsizing (restructuring, right-sizing) Large-scale reduction and elimination of jobs in a company that usually reduces middle-level managers, removes organizational levels, and widens the span of management for remaining supervisors.

Dysfunctional conflict Communication between individuals breaks down and the lack of teamwork causes the team to stray from its chosen path.

E

Emotional intelligence skills The ability to intelligently use your emotions.

Employee assistance programs (EAPs) Company programs to help employees with personal or work-related problems that are interfering with job performance.

Employee entitlement The belief that the organization "owes" them.

Employment-at-will Legal concept that employers can dismiss employees at any time and for any reasons, except unlawful discrimination and contractual or other restrictions.

Empowerment Giving employees the authority and responsibility to accomplish their individual and the organization's objectives.

Enabler The person who does the things necessary to enable employees to do the best possible job.

Engaged employee One who has a strong emotional bond to his/her organization and is committed to its objectives.

Equity theory Explains how people strive for fairness in the workplace.

Ethical "tests" Considerations or guidelines to be addressed in developing and evaluating ethical aspects of decision alternatives.

Exception principle Concept that supervisors should concentrate their investigations on activities that deviate substantially from standards.

Exit interviews Interviews with individuals who leave a firm that are used to assess morale and the reasons for employee turnover.

Expectancy theory Theory of motivation that holds that employees perform better when they believe such efforts lead to desired rewards.

Extinction Good behavior occurs less frequently or disappears because it is not recognized.

F

Fair treatment Impartial and appropriate actions taken that are free of favoritism and bias.

Feedback The receiver's verbal or nonverbal response to a message.

Feedback control Actions taken after the activity, product, or service has been completed.

Feedforward control Anticipatory action taken to ensure that problems do not occur.

Filtering The process of omitting or softening unpleasant details.

Fishbone technique (cause-and-effect diagram) Cause-and-effect approach to consider the potential interrelatedness of problem causes in decision making.

Flextime Policy that allows employees to choose their work hours within stated limits.

Formal organizational structure Departments, positions, functions, authority, and reporting relationships as depicted on a firm's organizational chart.

Friendship group Informal grouping of employees based on similar personalities and social interests.

Functional approach School of management thought that asserts that all managers perform various functions in doing their jobs, such as planning, organizing, staffing, leading, and controlling.

G

Gain-sharing plans Group incentive plans that have employees share in the benefits from improved performance.

Gantt chart A graphic scheduling technique that shows the activity to be scheduled on the vertical axis and necessary completion dates on the horizontal axis.

General supervision The style of supervision in which the supervisor sets goals and limits but allows employees to decide how to achieve goals.

Glass ceiling Invisible barrier that limits the advancement of women and minorities.

Glass walls Invisible barriers that compartmentalize women and minorities into certain occupational classes.

Going green Individuals and organizations voluntarily take steps to conserve energy and behave in environmentally friendly ways.

Grapevine The informal, unofficial communication channel.

Grievance A formal complaint presented by the union to management that alleges a violation of the labor agreement.

Grievance procedure Negotiated series of steps in a labor agreement for processing grievances, beginning at the supervisory level and ending with arbitration.

H

Halo effect The tendency to allow one favorable aspect of a person's behavior to positively influence judgment on all other aspects.

Hawthorne effect The fact that special interest shown in people may cause those people to behave differently.

Hawthorne Studies Comprehensive research studies that focused on work-group dynamics as they related to employee attitudes and productivity.

Hierarchy of needs Maslow's theory of motivation, which suggests that employee needs are arranged in priority order such that lower-order needs must be satisfied before higher-order needs become motivating.

Horizontal corporation A very flat firm resulting from restructuring by customer process and organizational structure.

Horns effect The tendency to allow one negative aspect of a person's behavior to negatively influence judgment on all other aspects.

Hot stove rule Guideline for applying discipline analogous to touching a hot stove; advance warning and consequences that are immediate, consistent, and applied with impersonality.

Human relations movement /behavioral science approach Approach to management that focuses on the behavior of people in the work environment.

Human relations skills The ability to work with and through people.

Human resources (HR) department Department that provides advice and service to other departments on human resource matters.

Human resources management (HRM) Organizational philosophies, policies, and practices that strive for the effective use of employees.

Hygiene factors Elements in the work environment that, if positive, reduce dissatisfaction but do not tend to motivate.

I

Incremental budgeting A technique for projecting revenues and expenses based on history.

Informal organization Informal gatherings of people, apart from the formal organizational structure, that satisfy members' social and other needs.

Intangible standards Standards for performance results that are difficult to measure and often relate to human characteristics (e.g., attitude, morale).

Interest-based negotiating Understanding why the other party wants what he or she wants, and then working toward a solution that satisfies those needs as well as your own.

J

Jargon Words that are specific to an occupation or a specialty.

Job description Written description of the principal duties and responsibilities of a job.

Job enrichment Job design that helps fulfill employees' higher-level needs by giving those employees more challenging tasks and more decision-making responsibility for their jobs.

Job redesign The belief that well-designed jobs lead to increased motivation.

Job rotation The process of switching job tasks among employees in a work group.

Job sharing Policy that allows two or more employees to perform a job normally done by one full-time employee.

Job specification Written description of the personal qualifications needed to perform a job adequately.

Just or proper cause Standard for disciplinary action requiring tests of fairness and elements of normal due process, such as proper notification, investigation, sufficient evidence, and a penalty commensurate with the nature of the infraction.

Just-in-time (JIT) Inventory control system for scheduling materials to arrive precisely when they are needed in the production process.

K

Kanban Another name for a just-in-time (JIT) inventory-control system.

KISS technique An acronym that stand for keep it short and simple.

Knowledge management The systematic storage, retrieval, dissemination, and sharing of information.

L

Labor agreement negotiations Discussions and compromises among representatives from labor and management leading to an agreement governing wages, hours, and working conditions for union employees.

Labor agreement Negotiated document between union and employer that covers the terms and conditions of employment for represented employees.

Labor union/labor organization Legally recognized organization that represents employees and negotiates and administers a labor agreement with an employer.

Law of effect Behavior with favorable consequences is repeated; behavior with unfavorable consequences tends to disappear.

Lead person Employee in charge of other employees who performs limited managerial functions but is not considered part of management.

Leadership The ability to guide and influence the behavior of others.

Leadership skills The ability to engage followers in all aspects of the organization.

Leading The managerial function of guiding employees toward accomplishing organizational objectives.

Learning organization Employees continually strive to improve their SKAs while expanding their efforts to achieve organizational objectives.

Leniency error Supervisors give employees higher ratings than they deserve.

Line authority The right to direct others and to require them to conform to decisions, policies, rules, and objectives.

Line-and-staff-type organizational structure Structure that combines line and staff departments and incorporates line and staff authority.

M

Management Getting objectives accomplished with and through people.

Management by objectives (MBO) A process in which the supervisor and employee jointly set the employee's objectives and the employee receives rewards upon achieving those objectives.

Managerial controlling Ensuring that actual performance is in line with intended performance and taking corrective action, if necessary.

Mentoring An experienced employee guiding a newer employee in areas concerning job and career.

Merit The quality of an employee's job performance.

Method A standing plan that details exactly how an operation is to be performed.

Metrics A standard of measurement used to determine that performance is in line with objectives.

Mission statement A statement of the organization's basic philosophy, purpose, and reason for being.

Morale A composite of feelings and attitudes that individuals and groups have toward their work, working conditions, supervisors, top-level management, and the organization.

Motion study An analysis of work activities to determine how to make a job easier and quicker to do.

Motivation A willingness to exert effort toward achieving a goal, stimulated by the effort's ability to fulfill an individual need.

Motivation factors Elements intrinsic in the job that promote job performance.

Motivation-hygiene theory Herzberg's theory that factors in the work environment primarily influence the degree of job dissatisfaction while intrinsic job content factors influence the amount of employee motivation.

Multitasking When an employee performs several tasks simultaneously.

N

Negative reinforcement Making behavior occur more frequently by removing an undesirable consequence.

Nepotism The practice of hiring relatives.

Networking Individuals or groups linked by a commitment to shared purpose.

No-fault attendance policy Policy under which unscheduled absences and tardiness are counted as occurrences and their accumulation is used in progressive discipline.

Noise Obstacles that distort messages between people.

Nominal group technique (NGT) A group brainstorming and decision-making process by which individual members first identify alternative solutions privately and then share, evaluate, and decide on an approach as a group.

Nondirective interview Interview approach in which the interviewer asks open-ended questions that allow the applicant latitude in responding.

Nonprogrammed decisions Solutions to unique problems that require judgment, intuition, and creativity.

Norms Standards shared by most employees for how one should act and be treated in the organization.

ODR (Online Dispute Resolution) An alternative approach similar to ADR, but the dispute process is handled on online.

Onboarding A continuous process of assimilation and growth within the organization for new hires.

Operating budget The assignment of dollar allocations to the costs and expenses needed to run the business, based on expected revenues.

Optimizing Selecting the best alternative.

Organization Group structured by management to carry out designated functions and accomplish certain objectives.

Organizational chart Graphic portrayal of a company's authority and responsibility relationships.

Organizational development (OD) Meetings with groups under the guidance of a neutral conference leader to solve problems that are hindering organizational effectiveness.

Organizational renewal A continuous process for long-term success.

Organizing Arranging and distributing work among members of the work group to accomplish the organization's goals.

Orientation The process of smoothing the transition of new employees into the organization.

P

Paid time off (PTO) program PTO allows employees to establish a personal time-off bank that they can use for any reason they want.

Participative management Allowing employees to influence and share in organizational decision making.

Pay for performance Compensation, other than base wages, that is given for achieving employee or corporate goals.

Peer evaluation The evaluation of an employee's performance by other employees of relatively equal rank.

Performance appraisal A systematic assessment of how well an employee is performing a job and the communication of that assessment.

Performance standards The job-related requirements by which the employee's performance is evaluated.

Personal power Power derived from a person's SKAs and how others perceive that person.

Personality The knowledge, attitudes, and attributes that make up the unique human being.

Personalized conflict Conflict between individuals that occurs because the two parties do not like one another.

Physiological needs Basic physical needs (e.g., food, rest, shelter, and recreation).

Piecework System in which the employee earns a certain amount of pay for each piece produced.

Planning Determining what should be done.

Policy A standing plan that serves as a guide to making decisions.

Political skills The ability to understand how things get done outside of formal channels.

Position power Power derived from the formal rank a person holds in the chain of command.

Positive discipline Condition that exists when employees generally follow the organization's rules and meet the organization's standards.

Positive Mental Attitude (PMA) A person with a PMA usually responds favorably to the job, other people, and most situations.

Positive reinforcement Making behavior occur more often because it is linked to a positive consequence.

Positive self-discipline Employees regulating their behavior out of self-interest and their normal desire to meet reasonable standards.

Principle of organizational stability Principle that holds that no organization should become overly dependent on one or several "indispensable" individuals.

Procedure A standing plan that defines the sequence of activities to be performed to achieve objectives.

Program A major single-use plan for a large undertaking related to accomplishing the organization's goals and objectives.

Program evaluation and review technique (PERT) A flowchart for managing large programs and projects that shows the necessary activities with estimates of the time needed to complete each activity and the sequential relationship of activities.

Programmed decisions Solutions to repetitive and routine problems provided by policies, procedures, or rules.

Progressive discipline System of disciplinary action that increases the severity of the penalty with each offense.

Project A single-use plan for accomplishing a specific, nonrecurring activity.

Project management-type organizational structure A hybrid structure in which regular, functional departments coexist with project teams made up of people from different departments.

Protected-group employees Classes of employees who have been afforded certain legal protections in their employment situations.

Punishment Making behavior occur less frequently because it is linked to an undesirable consequence.

Q

Qualified disabled individual Defined by the Americans with Disabilities Act (ADA) as someone with a disability who can perform the essential components of a job with or without reasonable accommodation.

Quantitative /systems approaches Field of management study that uses mathematical modeling as a foundation.

R

Realistic job preview (RJP) Information given by an interviewer to a job applicant that provides a realistic view of both the positive and negative aspects of the job.

Realistic organizational preview (ROP) Sharing information by an interviewer with a job applicant concerning the mission, values, and direction of the organization.

Reasonable accommodation Altering the usual ways of doing things so that an otherwise qualified disabled person can perform the essential job duties, but without creating an undue hardship for the employer.

Reciprocity reflex One good turn deserves another in return.

Reengineering Concept of restructuring a firm based on processes and customer needs and services rather than on departments and functions.

Responsibility The obligation to perform certain tasks and duties as assigned by the supervisor.

Reverse discrimination Preference given to protected-group members in hiring and promotion over more qualified or more experienced workers from non-protected groups.

RIF An acronym for reduction in force.

Right to appeal Procedures by which an employee may request higher-level management to review a supervisor's disciplinary action.

Rule A directive that must be applied and enforced wherever applicable.

S

Sampling The technique of evaluating some number of items from a larger group to determine whether the group meets acceptable quality standards.

Satisficing Selecting the alternative that meets the minimal decision criteria.

Scientific management approach School of management thought that focuses on determining the most efficient ways to increase output and productivity.

Security needs Desire for protection against danger and life's uncertainties.

Selection The process of choosing the best applicants to fill positions.

Selection criteria Factors used to choose among applicants who apply for a job.

Self-directed (self-managed) work teams (SDWTs) When employee groups are given wide latitude and considerable authority to make many of their own job-related decisions.

Self-fulfillment needs Desire to use one's abilities to the fullest extent.

Self-respect needs Desire for recognition, achievement, status, and a sense of accomplishment.

Semantics The multiple meanings of words.

Seniority An employee's length of service in a department or an organization.

Servant-leadership The notion that the needs of followers are looked after such that they can be the best they can be.

Sexual harassment Unwelcome sexual advances, requests, or conduct when submission to such conduct is tied to the individual's continuing employment or advancement, unreasonably interferes with job performance, or creates a hostile work environment.

Sexual stereotyping Use of demeaning language or judgments, usually by men toward women.

Single-use plans Plans to accomplish a specific objective or to cover only a designated period.

SKAs A person's skills, knowledge, and abilities.

Skill-based pay System that rewards employees for acquiring new skills or knowledge.

Social needs Desire for love and affection, affiliation with something worthwhile.

Society for Human Resource Management (SHRM) A professional organization for HR professionals.

Span-of-management principle Principle that there is an upper limit to the number of subordinates a supervisor can manage effectively.

Special-interest group Grouping of employees that exists to accomplish something in a group individuals do not choose to pursue individually.

Staff authority The right to provide counsel, advice, support, and service in a person's areas of expertise.

Staffing The tasks of recruiting, selecting, orienting, training, appraising, promoting, and compensating employees.

Standards Units of measure or criteria against which results are evaluated.

Standing plans Policies, procedures, methods, and rules that can be applied to recurring situations.

Status Attitudes toward a person based on the person's position.

Stereotyping The perception that all people in a group share attitudes, values, and beliefs.

Strategic control points (strategic standards) Performance criteria chosen for assessment because they are key indicators of overall performance.

Strategic plan Long-term plans developed by top management.

Strategic planning The process of establishing goals and making decisions that enable an organization to achieve its long- and short-term objectives.

Stretch targets Targeted job objectives that present a challenge but are achievable.

Substantive conflict Conflict between individuals because of what should be done or what should occur.

Supervisors First-level managers in charge of entry level and other departmental employees.

Synergistic effect The interaction of two or more individuals such that their combined efforts are greater than the sum of their individual efforts.

System of performance management All those things a supervisor must do to enable an employee to achieve prescribed objectives.

T

Tangible standards Standards for performance that are identifiable and measurable.

Task group or cross-functional team Grouping of employees who come together to accomplish a particular task.

Teamwork People working cooperatively to solve problems and achieve goals important to the group.

Technical skills The ability to do the job.

Telecommuting Receiving work from and sending work to the office from home via a computer and modem.

Theory X Assumption that most employees dislike work, avoid responsibility, and must be coerced to do their jobs.

Theory Y Assumption that most employees enjoy work, seek responsibility, and can self-direct.

360-degree evaluation Performance appraisal based on data collected from all around the employee—from customers, vendors, supervisors, peers, subordinates, and others.

Time study A technique for analyzing jobs to determine time standards for performing each job.

Total quality management (TQM) An organizational approach involving all employees to satisfy customers by continually improving goods and services.

U

Underemployment Situations in which people are in jobs that do not use their SKAs.

Unity-of-command principle Principle that holds that each employee should directly report to only one supervisor.

Unplanned change An unexpected situation causes you to initiate a strategy for change.

V

Virtual organization Companies linked temporarily to take advantage of marketplace opportunities.

Virtual or geographically dispersed team (GDT) Geographically separated people who are working on a common project and linked by communication technologies.

Visioning Management's view of what the company should become; reflects the firm's core values, priorities, and goals.

W

Wellness program Organized effort by a firm to help employees get and stay healthy to remain productive.

Working supervisors First-level individuals who perform supervisory functions but who may not legally or officially be part of management.

Workplace spirituality Organizational efforts to make the work environment more meaningful and creative by relating work to employees' personal values and spiritual beliefs.

Workplace violence Assaults or threats of assault against employees in the workplace.

Z

Zero-base budgeting The process of assessing, on a benefit-and-cost basis, all activities to justify their existence.

INDEX

ROB COLVIN